ANNA KOMNENE was born in 1083, the eldest child of the Byzantine Emperor Alexios I Komnenos (reigned 1081–1118). She was engaged while a young girl to Constantine Doukas, son of the deposed Emperor Michael VII Doukas (1071–8), but for reasons which are unclear, the marriage did not take place, and she instead married Nikephoros Bryennios, a member of a prominent aristocratic family from the western part of the empire. Both Anna and her husband became increasingly visible at Alexios' court in the latter part of his reign, and on his death, actively considered taking the throne at the expense of her younger brother, John II Komnenos (1118–43). Anna suffered internal exile as a result in a lavishly endowed convent. She died in or around 1153.

Anna Komnene is the author of the *Alexiad*, one of the most famous medieval texts. Written between 1143 and 1153, it is the first major history written by a woman. Composed in elegant and sometimes elaborate Greek, the text models itself on the histories of classical antiquity, referring regularly to a wide range of ancient sources. The *Alexiad* concerns the life of Anna's father, whose reign coincided with the First Crusade, military confrontation between Byzantium and the Latin West, the deepening of the schism between the Catholic and Orthodox churches, as well as a series of fundamental reforms within the empire. The *Alexiad* covers this period in great detail, though not evenly. Its author proves to be a fascinating, intelligent and compelling guide, often intervening in the text to offer forthright opinions and commentary. The result is an outstanding historical account, and a literary work of high importance.

E. R. A. SEWTER was a well-known Byzantine scholar and editor of *Greece and Rome*. His translation of *Michael Psellus: Fourteen Byzantine Rulers* is also published in Penguin Classics. He died in 1976.

PETER FRANKOPAN read History at Cambridge, where he took a first-class degree and was Schiff Foundation scholar at Jesus College. He did a doctorate in Byzantine History at Corpus Christi

College, Oxford, where he was Senior Scholar, and at Worcester College, where he was elected to a Junior Research Fellowship. Since 2000, he has been Senior Research Fellow at Worcester College, Oxford and Faculty Fellow in Medieval and Modern Greek at Oxford University, and has written extensively on the reign of Alexios I Komnenos and on the *Alexiad*.

ANNA KOMNENE

The Alexiad

Translated by E. R. A. SEWTER
Revised with Introduction and Notes by
PETER FRANKOPAN

PENGUIN BOOKS

PENGUIN CLASSICS

Published by the Penguin Group
Penguin Books Ltd, 80 Strand, London WC2R 0RL, England
Penguin Group (USA) Inc., 375 Hudson Street, New York, New York 10014, USA
Penguin Group (Canada), 90 Eglinton Avenue East, Suite 700, Toronto, Ontario, Canada M4P 2Y3
(a division of Pearson Penguin Canada Inc.)
Penguin Ireland, 25 St Stephen's Green, Dublin 2, Ireland
(a division of Penguin Books Ltd)
Penguin Group (Australia), 250 Camberwell Road, Camberwell, Victoria 3124, Australia
(a division of Pearson Australia Group Pty Ltd)
Penguin Books India Pvt Ltd, 11 Community Centre, Panchsheel Park, New Delhi – 110 017, India
Penguin Group (NZ), 67 Apollo Drive, Rosedale, North Shore 0632, New Zealand
(a division of Pearson New Zealand Ltd)
Penguin Books (South Africa) (Pty) Ltd, 24 Sturdee Avenue, Rosebank, Johannesburg 2196, South Africa

Penguin Books Ltd, Registered Offices: 80 Strand, London WC2R 0RL, England

www.penguin.com

This translation first published in 1969
Reprinted in Penguin Classics 2003
This revised edition first published in Penguin Classics 2009

018

Translation © The Estate of E. R. A. Sewter, 1969
Revisions to the translation and editorial material © Peter Frankopan, 2009
All rights reserved

The moral right of the translator and editor has been asserted

Set in 10.25/12.25pt PostScript Adobe Sabon
Typeset by Rowland Phototypesetting Ltd, Bury St Edmunds, Suffolk
Printed in England by Clays Ltd, Elcograf S.p.A.

ISBN: 978-0-140-45527-4

www.greenpenguin.co.uk

Contents

Acknowledgements

E. R. A. Sewter's edition of the *Alexiad* has served readers well for four decades, and I am honoured to have the opportunity to revise and update it for a new generation. I am enormously grateful to those who have encouraged me to work on this translation of the *Alexiad*. My colleagues and students at Oxford University have been a constant source of inspiration and kindness. I owe James Howard-Johnston a particular debt of gratitude for steering me towards the reign of Alexios Komnenos and to Anna Komnene's history many years ago; his conviction that there was much to be said about both has proved both prescient and generous. Peter Carson in the first instance, Mariateresa Boffo and Elizabeth Merriman at Penguin, and above all Lindeth Vasey, lie firmly behind this edition. Their collective powers of persuasion, patience and eye for detail saved me from some of the pitfalls in producing a revision of a classical work. My wife and children have endured countless hours of distraction, and to them I offer my sincere thanks.

Introduction

The value of the *Alexiad*

The *Alexiad* is perhaps the most famous of all the vast range of Byzantine texts. Written in the mid-twelfth century by a princess, the beautiful and fiercely intelligent Anna Komnene, daughter of the Emperor Alexios I Komnenos (reigned 1081–1118), it is a stylish and colourful account of the defining period in the formation of modern Europe. The text covers the time of the First Crusade, the establishment of a Turkish state in Asia Minor, the decisive schism of the eastern and western churches, and ultimately, the separation of the east and west Mediterranean.

Anna Komnene's work is the first history written by a woman, not only in the literature of Byzantium, but of western Europe too. It is in many ways entirely unrepresentative of the medieval Greek canon of historical narrative, for it is an epic history in style, scope and intention; its title is a reference to that of Homer's *Iliad*. The focus is on one man, Alexios Komnenos, whose characteristics, qualities and achievements are both frequently and explicitly compared to those of the heroes of classical Greece. The allusions to Greek mythology, the close attention to the deeds of a single protagonist and the epic framework as a context for the emperor's life and achievements are the outstanding features of this book.

In this sense, the *Alexiad* is a highly unusual text, because unlike most other Byzantine narrative accounts, it does not cover a broad sweep of history, but is restricted to the coverage of a defined, narrow period and a defined, narrow subject-matter. Anna is not concerned with Byzantium, but with the

life and achievements of Alexios I Komnenos. This biographical
approach is out of the ordinary, and means that this book finds
a better parallel with Byzantine hagiography, that is, the writing
of saints' lives, than with contemporary works of historical
literature.

If the focus of the *Alexiad* is remarkable, then so too is its
scope and ambition. The account of Alexios' reign is extraordinarily rich; it is a vast survey, going into great detail about five
issues in particular: first, the attacks on Byzantium of 1081–5
which were led by Robert Guiscard, perhaps the most formidable figure of the early medieval world. Together with his
brother, Roger of Sicily, Robert established Norman authority
over Apulia, Calabria and Sicily in the middle part of the
eleventh century, transforming southern Italy in the process.
He became much sought after as an ally by the papacy as well
as by the German and Byzantine emperors, who had their own
interests in Italy to advance. Following the failure of an alliance
made with the Emperor Michael VII Doukas, Robert had
launched a major attack on Byzantium in 1081, taking advantage of unstable circumstances in Constantinople to target the
western flank of the empire, with the prospect of further and
more ambitious goals should the opportunities present themselves. Robert's assaults over the next five years presented
Alexios, the new emperor, with a major threat to his position
and to the survival of the empire.

Second, the text provides detailed coverage of the raids on
the empire in the 1080s and 1090s by Patzinak (or Pecheneg)
steppe nomads, one of the constellation of nomadic tribes
around the northern shores of the Black Sea. A notoriously
violent and fearsome people, these nomads had established
themselves on Byzantium's Danube frontier, and by the late
1070s had begun to raid imperial territory with increasing
regularity and ferocity. The efforts to negotiate truces with
them and prolonged and sustained military operations formed
a central part of Alexios' military and foreign policies in the
first decade of his reign.

Third, the *Alexiad* reports the First Crusade. In 1095, Pope
Urban II appealed at the Council of Clermont as well as else-

where for the knights of western Europe to march east and restore the Holy Places to Christian hands. The result was a massive expedition, which succeeded in recovering Nicaea, Antioch, Edessa and, in 1099, Jerusalem itself, and laid the basis for the Latin Kingdom of Outremer, which would last for two centuries against the odds. The Crusaders had extensive dealings with the emperor in Constantinople then, and later, as both came to terms with the ramifications of the commitments and oaths that were exchanged in 1097. Anna Komnene gives deliberate and careful coverage to the Crusade, picking out those points and themes which were most relevant to her presentation of Byzantium and of her father.

Fourth, the *Alexiad* devotes considerable attention to relations with the Turks throughout Alexios' reign. In 1071, ten years before he took the throne, the Turks had humiliated the imperial army at Manzikert, where the Emperor Romanos IV Diogenes was captured on the battlefield. The following years saw a steady erosion of imperial authority and power in Asia Minor and the loss of control of large parts of the subcontinent, a process which certainly deepened and perhaps even accelerated after Alexios became emperor. Anna Komnene is the principal source for the turn in fortunes in this region, and her coverage is central to our understanding of the problems of and responses by Byzantium.

Fifth and finally, the account dwells on the assault by Bohemond on the empire's western flank. The son of Robert Guiscard, Bohemond had enjoyed an outstanding Crusade: although he had failed to reach Jerusalem, he had been instrumental in taking the extraordinarily difficult target of Antioch, and what is more, securing control of it for himself afterwards. A celebrated and popular figure among the western knighthood, he had returned to the west after being captured and imprisoned by the Turks, married a daughter of the king of France and then launched an expedition against Byzantium itself in 1107. His attack and, more importantly, the terms which he was forced to agree to in a settlement once his position became desperate are reported in detail: the author includes the full text of this treaty and presents this as the culmination and justification of the foreign policy of Alexios I Komnenos.

Anna Komnene's text is distinctive too because of its geographical focus. Byzantine commentators from late antiquity onwards, like their imperial Roman predecessors, were interested in reporting what was happening close to the emperor and in the corridors of power, with the resultant focus on the imperial palace and certainly on the imperial capital, Constantinople (modern Istanbul). But the centre of gravity that Anna provides runs contrary to this rule: she tells us little about the capital, is essentially silent on the internal developments within the Byzantine Empire and reveals little – and indeed barely mentions – crucial reforms of society, economy and power undertaken by the emperor in this period. Instead, Anna Komnene writes about military campaigning in the provinces, and about Alexios' dealings with Byzantium's neighbours. In place of the normal introverted histories then, the *Alexiad* provides an exceptional view looking outwards towards the peoples who surrounded the empire and recording the various and not always successful attempts by Alexios either to neutralize the threats they posed or to harness their burgeoning potential for his own ends.

The *Alexiad* is characterized finally by the visibility of the author and by her regular interventions in the narrative, which provide strident views about events and above all about individuals – opinions invariably colourful and usually scathing. For example, Anna refuses to try to record the names of the Crusaders, saying they are too grotesque to utter (X.10); she says her modesty prevents her from going into detail about exactly what Pope Gregory VII did to envoys sent by the German Emperor, Henry IV – which leaves just about enough to the imagination (I.13); and she says that the ferocious Patzinak nomads remind her of dogs who return to eat their own vomit (VII.6). Lively statements and comments such as these make Anna a colourful and sympathetic guide, even if purists like Gibbon find her style jarring.[1]

The character and contribution of the author

Anna Komnene was born in 1083, two years after her father, Alexios Komnenos, had deposed the Emperor Nikephoros III Botaneiates and seized the throne for himself. Anna was brought up in the imperial palace in Constantinople, and took her studies seriously. A thoughtful and diligent student of rhetoric, Anna had grammar lessons in spite of the acid disapproval of her parents, for whom reading the Bible was enough to satisfy intellectual needs. She was deeply interested in medicine and even more in philosophy, later in life gathering around her a salon of scholars whom she commissioned to write tracts on metaphysics. Indeed, it was she who oversaw the first commentaries on the *Nicomachean Ethics*, which were to have such an important impact on the development of western scholarship on Aristotle and on philosophy as a whole.[2] Her personal interests can be detected in the *Alexiad* through the diversions to discuss the state of philosophy in contemporary Byzantium, and to provide her own diagnosis of ailments and illnesses suffered by her father. Anna was an astute political observer too, charting the rise and fall of key individuals in the empire, and developing a consistent theme setting Alexios' achievements against a backdrop of massive external pressure on Byzantium.

Soon after she was born, Anna was betrothed to Constantine Doukas, the son of the Emperor Michael VII Doukas (reigned 1071–8). The engagement was a political one, designed to cement the position of the Doukas family after their support had proved crucial in Alexios' seizure of power. The proposed alliance did not take place, however, as Constantine disappeared from view in the 1090s, perhaps suffering from ill-health and dying early, or perhaps because of implication in a plot against the emperor. Nevertheless, Anna expresses great tenderness towards Constantine, referring to him as a blond Menelaus and worthy of comparison to Eros (III.1). By 1097, Anna was married to Nikephoros Bryennios, who rose to become a trusted member of Alexios' inner circle, enjoying the backing not only of the emperor, but also of his wife, Eirene Doukaina.

It is widely thought that Anna made an attempt to succeed her father on his death in 1118, seeking to install her husband, Nikephoros Bryennios, in the place of her own brother and Alexios' heir, John II Komnenos. The author herself says nothing about such aspirations, although she does stress that she had been excluded from Constantinople – literally as well as figuratively – and from her family and friends, living in isolation away from the imperial palace, not receiving a visitor for thirty years if we are to believe her (XIV.7). It is two other Byzantine historians, John Zonaras and Niketas Khoniates, who write of Anna's aspirations and fate.[3]

The stigma of the plot does not appear to have extended fully to Bryennios, who campaigned alongside John II Komnenos shortly before his death in 1138. Anna's husband, himself a gifted writer, composed an account of the turbulent history of Byzantium in the decade or so before Alexios' usurpation in 1081, which has some obvious parallels with the *Alexiad*. His work, *Hyle Historias*, or *Materials for Writing History*, is an apparently incomplete account of Byzantium in the eleventh century, and was commissioned by the Empress Eirene.

The strength of Anna's relationship with Bryennios is readily identifiable in the *Alexiad*, where his appearances (a very senior figure in the empire by the second half of Alexios' reign) are accompanied with pangs of longing and regret because of his death (Prologue.4; VII.2; X.9; XIV.7, etc.). (No analogous expressions of love are extended to the couple's children, to Anna's many siblings nor to her wider family, which is striking given the cliché accepted and recycled by modern scholars that Komnenian power was based on a concentration of authority in the hands of the imperial family.) The references to Bryennios throughout the text are significant for together with other clues, including allusions and direct references to Manuel I Komnenos, Alexios' grandson, they allow us to conclude that the text was written between *c.* 1143 and Anna's death in about 1153.[4]

To judge from the text itself and the many quotations from Hellenistic literature and philosophy and from the Scriptures, Anna was highly educated and well-read, even if her use of such works is sometimes erratic and inaccurate. The *Alexiad* bears testimony to an elegant if elaborate writer, with the prose written in a classicizing literary style. The language is florid and showy, even convoluted. Anna has a strong command of rhetoric and also of her subject-matter, in spite of the obvious difficulties presented by writing about events which took place several decades earlier, sixty years before for the start of Alexios' reign. Anna proves to be an engaging and entertaining commentator. Her intellect and literary ability were well-known in contemporary Byzantium, and must have been uncommon, for they are commented on specifically by her peers and also in a funeral oration delivered in 1155. The implication which we can draw here is that it is not just the *Alexiad* which is exceptional, but that the author was too.

The significance of the reign of Alexios I Komnenos

The period which the *Alexiad* covers was pivotal in the formation and development of early medieval Europe and Asia Minor. It was in Alexios' reign that Byzantium was attacked for the first time by western knights, with major assaults in 1081–3, 1084–5, 1107–8 and later in the twelfth century, which ultimately laid the foundations for the attack on and sack of Constantinople in 1204. While Alexios was emperor, many of the major towns of Asia Minor were lost to the Turks, whose activity moved from long- and medium-distance raiding to permanent settlement.[5] This period saw the emergence of Venice from a local Adriatic power to an entity with wider horizons and more extensive ambitions – and a platform for these was provided by a series of unprecedented concessions awarded by Alexios I Komnenos and reconfirmed by his successors in 1126, 1148 and 1187. The city-state of Pisa, another maritime power, was also so favoured by the emperor, being allowed to trade with sharply reduced tariffs after a grant in 1111. Alexios' reign was a time which saw what we know as Hungary, Serbia and Croatia slip decisively out of Byzantine orbit, and when Kiev and its satellite principalities north of the Black Sea looked in other directions for alliances and opportunities.

Above all, though, it was in Alexios' reign that the First Crusade took place. This extraordinary phenomenon, resulting in the establishment of Latin states in the Levant and in Christian control of important cities and towns in the Holy Land, shaped the modern world. It marked a massive expansion of papal power, built in the first instance on the ability of the Church in Rome to dominate the knighthood. The church had long sought to intervene in the secular world, and did so with increasing effect, as penances, movements such as the Truce of God, and expeditions in Spain testify. However, it was the huge response to the appeals of Pope Urban II for military intervention which laid the basis for the papacy to seek and expect to direct the knighthood and, in due course, royal power as well – a competition for authority that ultimately broke down with the Reformation.

The Crusade also served as an accelerator of social movement and of intellectual exchange as a direct result of exposure to different cultures, languages and ideas. It served too to develop and evolve concepts of Holy War in the Christian and Muslim worlds, again with long-term implications. But certainly, the antagonisms which emerged between Alexios and the Crusade leaders at Constantinople in 1096–7 and widened over the fate of Antioch, during the protracted siege of the town and afterwards, cleaved Christian world in two – in spite of the efforts of the Emperor Alexios and some of his successors to mend this rift.

And finally, Alexios' reign is a period of profound importance because it marked a series of dramatic changes within Byzantium itself, with major upheavals taking place as the empire came under pressure from without. It saw the emergence of what has been widely seen as a specifically 'Komnenian' form of government, where power was devolved carefully and exclusively into the hands of the imperial family and its wider kinship group to the exclusion of all others. Although this is an overstatement, Alexios did orchestrate a dramatic transformation in the fortunes and make-up of the Byzantine aristocracy. This can be clearly seen from the large number of acts of resistance and opposition to the emperor, many of them recorded in the *Alexiad*: the revolts, plots and insurrections which were launched against Alexios provide a clear indication of the unpopularity of his social-economic, political and military policies. A radical recalibration of the economy, through an overhaul of the coinage, and then fifteen years later, the way in which taxation and landownership was calculated and recorded, provided statements of intent, but also fundamental revisions of systems which had been essentially unchanged for many centuries.[6]

The literary context for the *Alexiad*

The *Alexiad*'s value lies not only in the fact that it provides a specifically Byzantine vantage point on the late eleventh and early twelfth centuries, but also because although there is a plentiful corpus of material on this period, Anna's history is one of only two narrative sources that cover Alexios' reign. John Zonaras' account is brief, derivative and, while offering a sharply differing perspective on Alexios' reign, is on a different scale entirely. If the *Alexiad* had not survived, our knowledge, understanding and interpretation of Alexios' rule would have been very limited and often would have led us to conclusions diametrically opposed to what Anna actually tells us. For example, we would not have been able to establish the scale of the focus, time and resources that the emperor spent dealing with the nomads. Nor could we have guessed the levels of antagonism which Alexios generated within Byzantium. The lack of visibility of the emperor on campaign in Asia Minor – a sharp contrast to his personal involvement in military expeditions in the western part of the empire – is striking and can only be discovered from the *Alexiad*.

That the *Alexiad* fills a vacuum is itself not without significance. The later eleventh and the twelfth centuries witnessed a flourishing literature in Byzantium, with experimentation with literary forms at a peak during the reign of Manuel I Komnenos. Historical narrative as a genre in particular blossomed throughout the Komnenian period. Yet the many histories which were produced, from the 1080s onwards – including those of

Skyliztes, Attaleiates, Psellos, Nikephoros Bryennios, Constantine Manasses, John Kinnamos and Niketas Khoniates – either end with Alexios' accession or start with his death. The reluctance of historians to cover Alexios and his reign is not related to the composition of the *Alexiad* itself, nor is it a reaction to it, for no one wrote a history of this period for the three decades before Anna began writing.

The unpopularity of Alexios on the one hand, and careful control of the imperial image by the Komnenoi in the twelfth century on the other, both go some way to explaining the remarkable silence. As Anna Komnene stresses in her prologue, she has recorded her father's achievements so that they would not be forgotten (2–3). This may be a simple statement of fact: Alexios' life and deeds had not been commemorated elsewhere, whether in suitably glorious form or otherwise. Indeed, the only meaningful surviving record is in two anonymous poems, known as the *Mousai*, or *Muses*, which were broadly contemporaneous with the emperor's death, and which record his life and achievements. These two poems, however, are general records of Alexios' reign, and principally set out not so much to commemorate the period 1081–1118, but to give prescriptive advice to John II.[7]

The author's privileged status as an imperial princess and daughter of her hero, her witnessing of some of the events she describes (though not as many as she claims), and the fact of being personally familiar with and indeed related by blood or marriage to many of the people who appear serve to magnify the importance of the text. So too does the realization that Anna Komnene dedicated a great deal of time, energy and resources to gathering her information.

Problems of interpretation

In spite of the significance of Anna's account, the *Alexiad* remains a source which is under-exploited and poorly used. Perhaps because of its length and range, it is regularly mined in a piecemeal way, with single comments, individual passages or sections being extracted and utilized, but with scant attention paid to the account as a whole. It is only recently that some basic questions about the composition of the *Alexiad* have even been raised. For example, the issue of where Anna derived material was only brought up in earnest in print in 1996, and even then, its hypothesis – that the bulk of the text was assembled by her husband – was given short shrift.[8] The identification of Anna's sources has a critical bearing on the evaluation of the whole *Alexiad*. Do the silences, such as the limited coverage of relations with the papacy, the lack of discussion of Rus' and the reduced commentary on the second half of Alexios' reign, reflect the shortcomings of Anna's material? Was her focus guided by what she had available and what she was able to find out (and if so, how should we explain this)? Or should we interpret the author's failure to discuss such issues as positivist, that is, as intentional omissions, because she thought them unimportant to Alexios' achievement, or because they were disappointing? Should we read the *Alexiad* as a work of literature or as history – or as both?

The twin questions of the provenance of Anna's information and of her selections are very important. It is clear, for example, that Anna must have had access to a substantial military archive – which explains how she was able to provide detailed information about campaigns, battle formations, troop movements and communication between individual commanders, usually centred on the emperor himself. But in addition we must also consider why Anna chose to include particular expeditions and to exclude others. There are, for example, major Byzantine victories, such as that achieved by Gregory Pakourianos between 1081 and 1083, which are not even mentioned in passing.[9]

Anna was able to use official documents, for some are included verbatim: the executive powers granted to Anna Dalassene, Alexios' mother, in 1081 while the emperor absented himself from Constantinople (III.6); a letter to Henry IV of Germany at the start of the 1080s in order to solicit support for Byzantium (III.10); and the Treaty of Devol of 1108 (XIII.12). A series of sweeping trade privileges granted to Venice by the emperor are summarized in such detail that we can suppose that Anna saw the original or a faithful copy of it (VI.5).

It is not hard to show how questions about the provenance, nature and make-up of Anna's sources and her use of them are fundamental to shaping the way in which we should use the *Alexiad*. For example, Anna's history is curiously lopsided: the first half of Alexios' reign takes up nearly three-quarters of the text; indeed, the coverage of the attacks of Robert Guiscard on the western flank of Byzantium 1081–5 take up more than a third. Conversely, although she opens her account with an expression of her father's desire to let his sword drip red with Turkish blood (I.1), the Turks and Asia Minor generally receive a treatment not only limited but at times so obscure and convoluted as to be almost incoherent. Thus, what Anna says about the situation in the east before the First Crusade is brief, scattered throughout the text and riddled with errors and anomalies. Perhaps the material for the east at Anna's disposal was thinner and less detailed than for other regions. However, it may also be that she was reluctant to cover Asia Minor because her father's policies proved less successful in the long run.

Anna Komnene does tell us something by the weighting she gives to events, peoples and regions. She saw her father's principal achievement as subduing the Normans and getting the better of the westerners who showed increasing interest in Byzantium and in the east, seeking to find their fortune at the expense of the empire. Alexios was able to repel Robert Guiscard and Bohemond, and to prove himself a better tactician and a better general than these two great leaders – even if he did have terrain on his side. Indeed, the *Alexiad* builds up all of the emperor's rivals, so that Roussel Balliol, Nikephoros Bryennios (the elder), Nikephoros Basilakios, Nikephoros Diogenes and Tancred have their positive qualities outlined (alongside their faults), for comparison to Alexios' own abilities in overcoming them.

Nevertheless, a compelling case can be made that the book is not so much a eulogy or a panegyric seeking to praise the emperor, but rather is a defensive work, perhaps not an apologia, but certainly an account which sets out to provide a context for the emperor's (and empire's) setbacks, such as at Dyrrakhion in 1081 and at Dristra a few years later, where

Alexios' recklessness turned promising positions into humiliating routs of his army. We know that the emperor was roundly
criticized during his lifetime, because Anna tells us so, and also
because we can infer this from the attempts to depose him.

There are other issues which have not been properly explored
by modern scholars. Authorial bias is one; Anna's position as
a commentator is another. But most important of all is the
question of the sequence of events, for on many occasions
the chronology of the *Alexiad* is not only suspect but highly
misleading. The long-held assumption that the sequence of
events in the text is broadly reliable is refuted by a catalogue
of misplaced episodes, duplications and errors. Whether such
errors were deliberate or the result of working with extensive
and unfamiliar materials is a key question when considering
how we should interpret the *Alexiad*.

Major themes in the text

The fact that it is possible to identify consistencies running
through the text show clearly the extent to which Anna Komnene was in control of her material – or at the very least that
she sought to shape a coherent account. The themes, linguistic
devices, allusions and literary references which recur are all
signs that the *Alexiad* is intended to be a rounded account.
Leitmotifs are introduced and developed. For example, Alexios
is presented throughout as a specifically Christian emperor,
respectful and modest in his dealings with the synod and the
clergy. Likewise, he is portrayed as a bane of heretics and a
firm opponent of all heresies in their various forms – from
Bogomilism to his suspicion of astrology. Alexios' personal
valour, his restlessness, his concern for the weak, his cunning
and resourcefulness, his skill as a military leader and his dedication to Byzantium are all worked into the text with care and
consistency.

Conversely, negative themes can also be detected. Anna's
nephew, Manuel I Komnenos, is one target, decried for his
stupidity (XIV.3)[10] and no doubt partly because of the overbearing image of this emperor presented at court at the time of

the *Alexiad*'s composition. Alexios' rivals are similarly scorned
for their ambition, lust for power and intransigence.

Another important strand to stress is the lack of any meaningful commentary on the reign and achievements of Alexios'
successor (and brother of the author), John II. It is not impossible that he is ignored because of Anna's own thwarted
ambitions to take the throne; more likely, however, is that for
all the point-scoring, her main theme in the *Alexiad* is one man:
her father.

Byzantium in the *Alexiad* and in the reign of Alexios I Komnenos

The *Alexiad* is invaluable for its clear articulation of what it
meant to be Byzantine, and of what Byzantium was. This is
expressed through the habits, customs and behaviour of non-
Byzantines and by describing them in invariably unflattering
and unfavourable terms, with foreigners being routinely portrayed as venal, unpredictable and ruled solely by their passions.
In contrast the qualities and character of Alexios are presented
as ideal: he is the model emperor and the model Byzantine.
Anna's account resembles a hagiography, with the life and
deeds of the protagonist serving as much as a morality tale as
a history lesson.

The detail is hugely important for our understanding of
Byzantium in the reign of Alexios I Komnenos: there are mini-
biographies of many leading figures; insights into the working
of the imperial army through the precise accounts of a number
of expeditions and how the Normans of southern Italy were
repulsed three times; unique revelations of the Byzantine perspective on the First Crusade, including the context for Alexios'
decision not to advance on Antioch to help the beleaguered
Crusaders – which came to dominate contemporary Crusade
histories and to haunt Alexios (XI.6); and Alexios' dealings
with the many problems confronting Byzantium both from
within and from without. The topics missing from the *Alexiad*
should prompt us to handle the text with some caution.

The *Alexiad* then yields a number of surprises. Although

Anna's account is often embellished with an outstanding and impressive amount of detail, it also contains chronological corruptions, flaws and mistakes. While Anna takes Alexios as the reference point for her history and focuses her attention squarely on him, she also allows her own views and interpretations to interrupt and detract from the flow of the narrative with matters of secondary importance.

The aim of this new edition of the *Alexiad* is to encourage more readers to engage with this primary source for the reign of the Emperor Alexios I Komnenos. Anna's account is more complex and difficult than it first appears, and is also rich, diverse and rewarding, providing a unique view of a key period in the history of Byzantium and of Europe.

NOTES

1. For Gibbon, 'the elaborate affectation of rhetoric and science betrays in every page the vanity of a female author', Edward Gibbon, *The History of the Decline and Fall of the Roman Empire*, ed. J. B. Bury, 7 vols. (London, 1897–1901), vol. 5, p. 226. The significance of his comment lies as much in its notoriety as in its perception.

2. Anna was a patron of a circle of scholars whom she commissioned primarily to investigate the works of Aristotle. The resultant commentaries found their way to the Latin West, where they formed the basis of medieval intellectual thought on Hellenistic philosophy and its relevance to Christian thought.

3. Zonaras and Khoniates, writing in the mid-twelfth and early thirteenth centuries respectively, offer assessments of the Komnenoi which are negative and highly critical. Both authors report Anna's thwarted ambitions and suggest she paid a price for them.

4. Anna is explicit that her account was written in the reign of Alexios' grandson, i.e. after 1143. This is consistent with her regrets at her husband's death, which took place in 1137/8. 1153 is widely accepted as the date of Anna's death, which certainly took place before 1155 when a memorial address was given in her honour.

5. The precise profile of the extension of Turkish authority is still a matter of debate. Although much of the coastline either remained

in Byzantine hands or was recovered in this period, it is clear that Alexios' reign saw the loss of a great many of the towns in the interior of Asia Minor, and the establishment of a sultanate based on Ikonion.

6. The reform of the coinage in 1092 was the first major overhaul of the Byzantine currency system since the reforms of the Emperor Anastasios in 498. The shift in 1107 from a cadaster-based record of land ownership to a system where the property of individuals was recorded (and used as the basis for tax calculations) was no less dramatic a departure in the social and economic history of Byzantium.

7. The poems have not yet been translated: Paul Maas, 'Die Musen des Kaisers Alexios I', *Byzantinische Zeitschrift*, 22 (1913), pp. 349–60. The date and context for their composition has been much debated. They were almost certainly written after Alexios' death, and celebrate his achievements while also purporting to offer counsel to his son about how to rule Byzantium and how to manage relations with the empire's neighbours.

8. James Howard-Johnston, 'Anna Komnene and the *Alexiad*', in M. Mullett and D. Smythe (eds), *Alexios I Komnenos – Papers* (Belfast, 1996), pp. 260–302.

9. Peter Frankopan, 'A Victory of Gregory Pakourianos against the Pechenegs', *Byzantinoslavica*, 57 (1996), pp. 278–81.

10. Paul Magdalino, 'The Pen of the Aunt: Echoes of the Mid-Twelfth Century in the *Alexiad*', in T. Gouma-Peterson (ed.), *Anna Komnene and Her Times* (New York, 2000), pp. 15–43. See also Further Reading.

Further Reading

Although modern scholarship on the reign of Alexios I Komnenos is vibrant and exciting, there are few surveys of this period as a whole. The standard work is still Ferdinand Chalandon's *Essai sur le règne d'Alexis I Comnène* (Paris, 1900). Jean-Claude Cheynet's *Pouvoir et contestations à Byzance 963–1210* (Paris, 1990) provides an invaluable primer to Byzantium before, during and after the Komnenoi. The new *Cambridge History of the Byzantine Empire*, ed. Jonathan Shepard (Cambridge, 2009), offers good coverage of Alexios, as it does about so many other topics. The *Oxford History of Byzantium*, ed. Cyril Mango (Oxford, 2002), likewise provides a compelling and provocative entry point to Byzantium. Judith Herrin's *Byzantium: The Surprising Life of a Medieval Empire* (London, 2008) serves as a useful introduction to the subject too. Secondary material is available in a very wide range of languages. Only works in English appear below.

For Anna Komnene, see T. Gouma-Peterson (ed.), *Anna Komnene and Her Times* (New York, 2000) for an excellent collection of essays about the author and her work. Barbara Hill's *Imperial Women in Byzantium (1025–1204)* (London, 1999) and Lynda Garland's *Byzantine Empresses: Women and Power and Byzantium AD 527–1204* (London, 1999) say much about Anna, even if they do not focus on her writing directly. Also see Liz James, *Women, Men and Eunuchs: Gender in Byzantium* (London, 1997). Barbara Hill's 'A Vindication of the Rights of Women to Power by Anna Komnene', *Byzantinische Forschungen*, 23 (1996), pp. 45–54 provides a clear outline of the author's life and aspirations.

For the *Alexiad* as a primary source, Georgina Buckler, *Anna Comnena* (Oxford, 1929) is a solid, if dense, starting point. On the composition of the text and above all its authorship, James Howard-Johnston, 'Anna Komnene and the *Alexiad*', in M. Mullett and D. Smythe (eds), *Alexios I Komnenos – Papers* (Belfast, 1996), pp. 260–302, and Ruth Macrides, 'The Pen and the Sword: Who Wrote the *Alexiad*', in T. Gouma-Peterson (ed.), *Anna Komnene and Her Times* (New York, 2000), pp. 63–81.

The twelfth-century resonances of the text are explored by R. D. Thomas, 'Anna Comnena's Account of the First Crusade, History and Politics in the Reign of the Emperors Alexius I and Manuel I Comnenus', *Byzantine and Modern Greek Studies*, 15 (1991), pp. 269–312; Paul Magdalino, 'The Pen of the Aunt: Echoes of the Mid-Twelfth Century in the *Alexiad*', in Gouma-Peterson, *Anna Komnene*, pp. 15–43; and Paul Stephenson, 'Anna Comnena's *Alexiad* as a Source for the Second Crusade?', *Journal of Medieval History*, 29 (2003), pp. 41–54.

On the wider interpretation of the *Alexiad*, see John France, 'Anna Comnena, the *Alexiad* and the First Crusade', *Reading Medieval Studies*, 10 (1984), pp. 20–38; Peter Frankopan, 'Perception and Projection of Prejudice: Anna Comnena, the *Alexiad* and the First Crusade', in S. Edgington and S. Lambert (eds), *Gendering the Crusades* (Cardiff and New York, 2001), pp. 59–76; and Iakov Liubarski, 'Why is the *Alexiad* a Masterpiece of Byzantine Literature?', in J. Rosenqvist (ed.), *LEIMON: Studies Presented to Lennart Rydén on his Sixty-Fifth Birthday* (Uppsala, 1996), pp. 127–41.

Paul Magdalino's *The Empire of Manuel I Komnenos 1143–1180* (Cambridge, 1993) and Catherine Holmes's *Basil II and the Governance of Empire (976–1025)* (Cambridge, 2005), both provide important insights into Alexios' reign and into Alexian literature. Also Margaret Mullett, *Theophylact of Ochrid – Reading the Letters of a Byzantine Archbishop* (Aldershot, 1997), above all pp. 69–78; Michael Angold, 'Alexios I Komnenos: An Afterword', in Mullett and Smythe, *Alexios*, pp. 398–417, and Paul Magdalino, 'Aspects of

Twelfth-Century Byzantine *Kaiserkritik*', *Speculum*, 58 (1983), pp. 326–46.

For interpreting specific aspects of Byzantium in the reign of Alexios I Komnenos, Alan Harvey, *Economic Expansion in the Byzantine Empire (900–1200)* (Cambridge, 1989); Rosemary Morris, *Monks and Laymen in Byzantium 843–1118* (Cambridge, 1995); Jonathan Shepard, ' "Father" or "Scorpion"? Style and Substance in Alexios' Diplomacy', in Mullett and Smythe, *Alexios*, pp. 68–132; Dion Smythe, 'Alexios and the Heretics: The Account of Anna Komnene's *Alexiad*', in Mullett and Smythe, *Alexios*, pp. 232–59; Paul Magdalino, 'Innovations in Government', in Mullett and Smythe, *Alexios*, pp. 146–66; Ruth Macrides, 'Dynastic Marriages and Political Kinship', in J. Shepard and S. Franklin (eds), *Byzantine Diplomacy* (Aldershot, 1992), pp. 263–80; and Peter Frankopan, 'Kinship and the Distribution of Power in Komnenian Byzantium', *English Historical Review*, 122 (2007), pp. 1–34.

There is a rich and excellent corpus of secondary material for Byzantium's relations with its neighbours during this period. See, for example, K. Ciggaar, *Western Travellers to Constantinople: The West & Byzantium, 962–1204* (Leiden, 1996), for a survey of contact between east and west. William McQueen, 'Relations between the Normans and Byzantium 1071–1112', *Byzantion*, 56 (1986), pp. 427–76, and Graham Loud, *The Age of Robert Guiscard: Southern Italy and the Norman Conquest* (Singapore, 2000), provide valuable overviews of Byzantium and the Normans of southern Italy in this period.

The First Crusade has received much attention from modern scholars. Thomas Asbridge, *The First Crusade: A New History* (London, 2004) and John France, *Victory in the East* (Cambridge, 1993) provide compelling narratives. For a closer focus on Byzantium, see R.-J. Lilie, *Byzantium and the Crusader States*, tr. J. Morris and J. Ridings (Oxford, 1993), and more recently, Jonathan Harris, *Byzantium and the Crusades* (London, 2003). Jonathan Shepard's 'When Greek meets Greek: Alexius Comnenus and Bohemund in 1097–8', *Byzantine and Modern Greek Studies*, 12 (1988), pp. 185–277, and 'Cross-purposes: Alexius Comnenus and the First Crusade', in J. Phillips (ed.), *The First Crusade: Origins and Impact* (Manchester, 1997), pp. 107–29, are essential reading.

For Byzantium and the east, see Clive Foss, 'The Defences of Asia Minor against the Turks', *Greek Orthodox Theological Review*, 27 (1982), pp. 145–205, which is an important corollary to much French scholarship on this subject. For Venice, see Thomas Madden, 'The Chrysobull of Alexius I Comnenus to the Venetians: The Date and the Debate', *Journal of Medieval History*, 28 (2002), pp. 23–41, and Peter Frankopan, 'Byzantine Trade Privileges to Venice in the Eleventh Century: The Chrysobull of 1092', *Journal of Medieval History*, 30 (2004), pp. 135–60. The Balkans in the middle Byzantine period are the focus of Paul Stephenson's *Byzantium's Balkan Frontier* (Cambridge, 2000).

A complete bibliography for the reign of the Emperor Alexios I Komnenos is available at www.peterfrankopan.com

Note on Translation
and Transliteration

This translation is based on the excellent edition *Alexias*, ed. Diether Reinsch and Athanasios Kambylis (Berlin, 2001), part of the Corpus Fontium Historiae Byzantinae, which utilizes the three oldest manuscripts of Anna Komnene's history: Florentinus Laurentianus 70.2, Parisinus Coislinianus 311 and Vaticanus Graecus 981. The latter two date from the end of the thirteenth century, the former from the mid/late twelfth. Between them, it is possible to get close to the original text, as the three manuscripts are not dependent on each other.

The *Alexiad* has been translated into English twice, by Elizabeth Dawes in the 1920s and by E. R. A. Sewter in 1969, in very different styles, with the former providing a rather heavy and literal redaction, the latter a more pleasing and graceful version of what is an idiosyncratic, florid and convoluted text, written in high Attic style. This new edition of the *Alexiad* is a major reworking of Sewter's translation, retaining much but making substantial revisions. Apart from bringing the language up to date, three further tasks have been undertaken.

First, the text is closer to the original by following more faithfully Anna Komnene's language, style and form. In addition, the integrity of the text has been restored where Sewter extracted comments, some lengthy, from the main body of the text, and put them into footnotes. This gave the impression that Anna Komnene had intended these matters as asides, and was both confusing and misleading. Chapter and section breaks are now included in the main text.

Secondly, there is more comprehensive annotation. Anna's history is rich in references to her sources, primarily those of classical antiquity and classical Greece. There is an extensive and often confusing cast of characters who are identified briefly, and family trees are also provided. Anna's account has further problems, ranging from errors with the sequence of events, duplication of episodes to startling inconsistencies. Dates are cited where these are fixed and useful to understanding the text, and when Anna's chronology is corrupt there is a brief note to indicate the difficulties. Direct quotes from classical authors are identified, though allusions and indirect references are limited.

Finally, the question of transliteration is always difficult to deal with when translating a text. This affects place names, personal names, peoples, and titles and ranks. Since many of the places identified by Anna Komnene are not known from elsewhere, all toponyms (with the exception of Constantinople, Nicaea, Antioch and Chalcedon) have been transliterated from their Greek form. Inevitably, this produces some awkward cases – Kilikia and Kappadokia, for example, rather than the familiar Cilicia and Cappadocia. For the sake of consistency, however, the same rule is followed throughout the text.

Following the same principle, personal names have been transliterated, with exceptions made for obvious and everyday first names – George, Nicholas, Alexander, etc., but Alexios, Andronikos, Euthymios. And the author is Anna Komnene rather than Anna Comnena and her male relatives Komnenos, not Comnenus. Turkish names are transliterated from the Greek forms used in the text. Anna Komnene's naming of Turkish leaders is often wrong, misleading or obscure, so Greek versions are used throughout, with identifications in the Notes, following the *Encyclopaedia of Islam*. Thus, Apelkhasem rather than Abul-Kasim, Tzakhas rather than Çaka, Klitziasthlan rather than Kilidj Arslan: this allows for consistency when Anna gives names that are otherwise unknown – e.g. Poukheas and Saisan – or are clearly generic – Elkhanes. There are several instances where Anna provides the wrong name for important Muslim leaders; such errors now appear in this translation since they are often revealing about the author's attitudes to and knowledge of the people she is writing about.

Anna's terminology has been retained for the western

peoples, e.g. Kelt, Latin and Frank, and the others, Scythian, Sarmatian and Patzinak. Like her peers, Anna always refers to the Byzantines as Romans, and uses Byzantion, the old name for Constantinople, for emphasis.

Byzantine titles, ranks and positions do not translate easily or simply into English, so they have been transliterated and italicized, except on occasions that Anna uses a generic word or expression to convey a command position, and appear in the Glossary. Titles including *kaisar*, *doux* and *megas droungarios* take some getting used to; however, they do not mean the same as caesar, duke and great admiral. My practice is at times by necessity unsatisfactory, but, I hope, not distracting.

MAPS

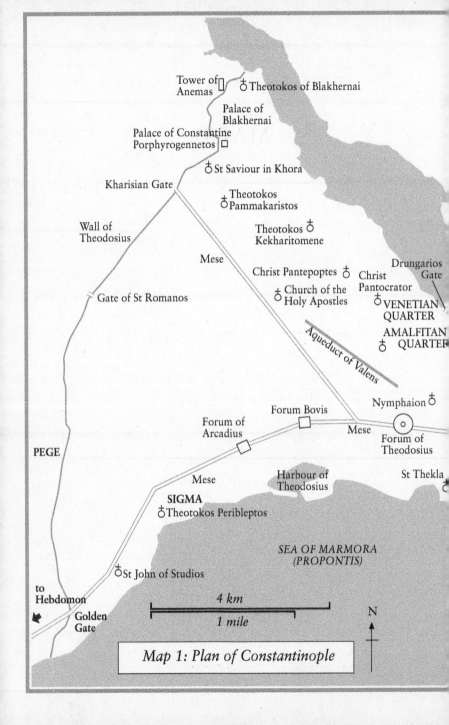

Tower of Anemas

Theotokos of Blakhernai

Palace of Blakhernai

Palace of Constantine Porphyrogennetos

St Saviour in Khora

Kharisian Gate

Theotokos Pammakaristos

Wall of Theodosius

Theotokos Kekharitomene

Mese

Christ Pantepoptes

Drungarios Gate

Christ Pantocrator

Gate of St Romanos

Church of the Holy Apostles

VENETIAN QUARTER

AMALFITAN QUARTER

Aqueduct of Valens

Nymphaion

Forum Bovis

Forum of Arcadius

PEGE

Mese

Forum of Theodosius

Mese

Harbour of Theodosius

St Thekla

SIGMA

Theotokos Peribleptos

SEA OF MARMORA (PROPONTIS)

St John of Studios

to Hebdomon

4 km

1 mile

Golden Gate

N

Map 1: Plan of Constantinople

EUROPE

BOSPHORUS

GALATA

DAMALIS

KHRISTOUPOLIS

Hebraike
Gate

GOLDEN HORN

ASIA

PISAN
QUARTER

Ophanotropheion

GENOESE
QUARTER

St Demetrios

Palace of
Botaneiates

AKROPOLIS

KHALKOPRATIA

Forum &
column of
Constantine

Hagia Eirene

Monastery of St George of Mangana

St Saviour

Mangana Palace

Basilica

Augusteion

Hagia Sophia

Forty
Martyrs

Milion

CHALCEDON

Pharos

Hippodrome

Boukoleon
Palace

Boukoleon
Harbour

Map 2: Roman Empire in the west
at the end of Alexios' reign

SCYTHIANS

Peristhlaba

Dristra
Betrinos

Danube R.

Nikopolis

BLACK
SEA

PARISTRION   Great Peristhlaba

Haimos Mtns   Bitzina

Lardeas   Mesembria

Berroia   Goloe   Ankhialos

Beliatoba   Diampolis

Philippopolis   Sozopolis

Blisnos   Agathopolis

R. Euros

Adrianopolis

Little Nicaea   Boulgarophygon   Bosphorus

Tzouroulos   Selymbria

Mosynopolis   Raidestos   Constantinople

Pamphilon   Herakleia

Kypsella   Aspron   SEA OF MARMORA

Koule

Ainos   Rousion

Kallipolis

KHERRONESOS

Hellespont

AEGEAN   LESBOS
SEA

KHIOS

RHODES

BLACK SEA

Mesembria
Ankhialos
Sozopolis
Philippopolis
Amastris

R. Euros
Adrianopolis
Heirakleia

Heiron
Constantinople *Bosphorus*
Tzouroulos Selymbria Khristoupolis
Mosynopolis Raidestos Herakleia Chalcedon
Rousion Pelekanum Nikomedia
Ainos *SEA OF MARMORA* Kibotos
Kallipolis Nicaea
Kyzikos Apollonias
Abydos Lopadion Brusa **BITHYNIA**
Hellespont Poimanenon Malagina
Mt Olympos *R. Sangaris*
PHRYGIA Dorylaion
Methymna Atramytion Akrokos
Pergamon
LESBOS Khliara Polybotos Philomelion
AEGEAN SEA Mytilene Antioch-in-Pisidia

KHIOS Smyrna Sardeis Apameia
Ephesos Philadelphia Khoma
Laodikeia
SAMOS *R. Maiandros*
Khonai **PAMPHYLIA**
Attaleia

KOS
PAMPHYLIAN GULF

250 km
150 miles

RHODES
MEDITERRANEAN SEA

KARPATHOS

N

Map 3: Roman Empire in the east
at the end of Alexios' reign

Sinope

Kastamouni

Trapezous

Paipert

PAPHLAGONIA

Koloneia **KHOROSAN** ➡

ARMENIAKON

Amaseia

Manzikert

R. Halys

Sebasteia

ARMENIA

Ankyra

**SULTANATE
OF IKONION**

R. Euphrates

Melitene

Kaisereia

Komana

Augoustopolis

R. Saron

Samosata

KAPPADOKIA

Marash

Ikonion

Tyana

Anazarbos

Edessa

Herakleia

Kilikian Gates)(

Mamistra

Lampron

Harran

Tauros Mtns

Tarsos

Adana

KILIKIA

Seleukeia

St Symeon

Antioch

Aleppo

R. Orontes

Kyrenia

Laodikeia

Nicosia

LEBANON

CYPRUS

SYRIA

Tripolis

KOILE-SYRIA

Beirut

Jerusalem

Damascus

**KINGDOM
OF JERUSALEM**

Sidon

The Alexiad

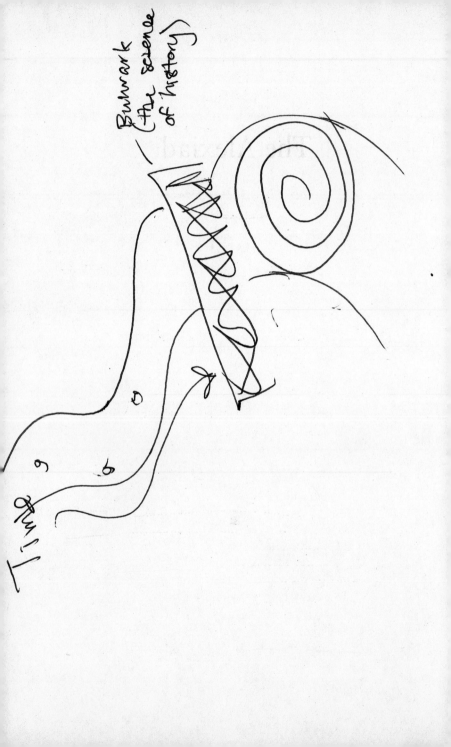

Time

Bulwark
(the science
of history)

PROLOGUE

1. Time, which flies irresistibly and perpetually, sweeps up and carries away with it everything that has seen the light of day and plunges it into utter darkness, whether deeds of no significance or those that are mighty and worthy of commemoration; as the playwright says,[1] it brings to light that which had been obscure and shrouds from us what had been visible. Nevertheless, the science of History is a great bulwark against this stream of Time; in a way it checks this irresistible flood, it holds in a tight grasp whatever it can seize floating on the surface and will not allow it to slip away into the depths of oblivion.

I, Anna, daughter of the Emperor Alexios and the Empress Eirene, born and bred in the purple,[2] not without some acquaintance with literature – having devoted the most earnest study to the Greek language, in fact, and being not unpractised in rhetoric and having read thoroughly the works of Aristotle and the dialogues of Plato, and having fortified my mind with the *tetrakus* of sciences (these things must be divulged, and it is not boasting to recall what Nature and my own zeal for knowledge have given me, nor what God has apportioned to me from above and what has been contributed by circumstance): I desire now by means of my writings to give an account of my father's deeds, which do not deserve to be consigned to silence nor to be swept away on the flood of Time into an ocean of obscurity; I wish to recall everything, the achievements before his elevation to the throne and his actions in the service of others before his coronation.

2. I approach the task with no intention of flaunting my skill as a writer; my concern is rather that a subject so significant

[Handwritten annotations:]
First ex. of Ekphrasis (how to experience Anna)
Intelligent, has authority
Interesting no more water references
Three agents: herself, God, Nature
study
all one sentence
palace born princess
royality associated with divinity (high position of Power - Less human - closer to God)

should not go unrecorded in the future, since even the greatest exploits, unless by some chance their memory is preserved and guarded in history, vanish in silent darkness. As events clearly demonstrate, my father proved able to rule as well as to obey rules, at least in so far as was reasonable.

Now that I have decided to write the story of his life, I am fearful of wagging and suspicious tongues: someone might conclude that in composing the history of my father I am glorifying myself; the history, wherever I express admiration for any act of his, may seem wholly false and mere panegyric. On the other hand, if my father should ever lead me, under the compulsion of events, to criticize some action taken by him, not because of what he decided but because of the circumstances, here again I fear the jokers: in their all-embracing jealousy and refusal to accept what is right, because they are malicious and full of envy, they may cast me in the story of Noah's son Ham and, as Homer says, blame the blameless.[3]

Whenever one assumes the role of historian, friendship and enmities have to be forgotten; often one has to bestow on adversaries the highest commendation, where their deeds merit it; often, too, one's nearest relatives have to be censured, as and when their behaviour deserves it. The historian, therefore, must shirk neither from remonstrating with their friends, nor from praising their enemies. For my part, I hope to satisfy both parties, both those who are offended by us and those who accept us, by appealing to the evidence of the actual events and of eyewitnesses. The fathers and grandfathers of some men alive today saw these things.

3. The main reason why I have to write the account of my father's deeds is this: I was the lawful wife of the *Kaisar* Nikephoros,[4] a scion of the Bryennioi, an extremely handsome man, very intelligent, and in the precise use of words far superior to his contemporaries. To see and hear him was indeed an extraordinary experience. For the moment, however, let us concentrate on what happened afterwards, lest the story should digress.

My husband, the most outstanding man of the time, went on campaign with my brother, the Emperor John,[5] when the latter led an army against other barbarians and also when he set out against the Syrians and once more restored imperial authority to the city of Antioch. Even in the midst of these wearing exertions the *kaisar* could not neglect his writing, and, among other compositions worthy of honourable mention, he chose in particular to write the history of Alexios, the Emperor of the Romans and my father, on the orders of the empress,[6] and to record the events of his reign in several books, when a brief lull in the warfare gave him the chance to turn his attention to historical and literary research. He did indeed begin the history – and in this, too, he yielded to the wishes of our empress – with references to the period before Alexios, starting with Diogenes, the Emperor of the Romans, and carrying it down to the times of his original subject. At the time of Diogenes' reign my father was only a youth; he had done nothing worthy of note, unless childhood exploits are also to be made the object of record.

The *kaisar*'s plan was such as I have described; his writings make that clear. However, he did not manage to complete what he had set out to do, and the history was not completed. After carrying on the account to the times of the Emperor Nikephoros Botaneiates, he stopped writing because circumstances prevented any further progress, to the detriment of the history itself and the sorrow of its readers. That is why I have chosen to record the full story of my father's deeds myself, so that future generations may not be deprived of knowledge about them. Everyone who has encountered his literary work knows with what symmetry and grace the *kaisar* wrote . . .

Having reached the point I have mentioned, he brought back his work to us from foreign parts half-finished and hastily put together, and also, I am sorry to say, carrying an illness which was to prove fatal, caused by too much soldiering, excessive fatigue and inordinate concern for ourselves. He was by nature a worrier and a worker; he could not relax. The unpleasant changes of climate, too, contributed to his death. He was a very sick man, then, when he set out on campaign to Syria and Kilikia; his health continued to fail in Syria; after Syria came Kilikia, Pamphylia, Lydia and Bithynia before he returned to

us in the Queen of Cities.[7] He was ill in all these regions, already
suffering from a tumour, the result of so much fatigue. In this
weak condition, although he wanted to give a graphic account
of his adventures, he could not because of his illness; besides,
we would not let him do it – the strain of talking might aggrav-
ate things further.

4. At this point my spirit becomes overwhelmed; floods of
tears fill my eyes when I think of Rome's great loss. His wisdom,
his vast practical experience, gained over so wide a field, his
knowledge of literature, the diverse learning acquired at home
and abroad. Grace suffused all his body as did a majesty befitting not, as some say, a human throne, but something higher
and more divine. My own lot has been far from fortunate in
other ways, ever since I was wrapped in swaddling clothes in
the purple chamber, and I have not enjoyed good luck –
although one would not deny that fortune did smile on me
when I had as parents an emperor and an empress, and when I
was born in the purple. The rest was full of troubles, full of
revolution. Orpheus moved rocks and forests, even inanimate
nature, with his singing; Timotheos the flute-player by his
Orthian strains once stirred Alexander to take up the sword and
for the Macedonian to arm himself without delay for battle;[8] the
story of my afflictions would move no one physically to arms
or battle, though it would stir the reader to weep with me and
wring sympathy from nature, animate and inanimate alike.

The *kaisar*'s untimely death and the suffering it brought
about touched my heart deeply and the pain of it affected the
innermost part of my being. The calamities of the past, in the
face of this infinite disaster, I regard as a mere drop of rain
compared with the whole Atlantic Ocean or the swell of the
Adriatic Sea. They were, it seems, the prelude of these later
woes, the warning smoke of this furnace flame; the fierce heat
was a herald of this unspeakable conflagration, the daily signal-
fires of this awful funeral pyre – a fire that lights up with torches
the secret places and burns, but does not consume with burning;
parching my heart imperceptibly, although its flames pierce to
the bones and marrow and heart's centre.

But I see that I have been led astray by these thoughts from my subject; the *kaisar* stood over me and his sorrow provoked heavy sorrow in me too. I will wipe away the tears from my eyes, recover from my grief and continue my story, earning thereby a double share of tears, as the playwright says, for one disaster recalls another.[9] To put before the public the life history of such an emperor reminds me of his supreme virtue, his marvellous qualities – and the hot tears fall again as I weep with all the world. When I remember him and make known the events of his reign, it is for me a theme of lamentation; others will be reminded of their loss. However, this is where I must begin the history of my father, at the point where it is better to begin, where the narrative will become at once clearer and more accurate.

Flood of Time
Flood of tears

Charon
Lethe - river
(forgetfulness)

- breaking the rules of subjectivity as a historian but fulfilling subjective role as wife

☆ structural reading- critical theory

BOOK I

1. The Emperor Alexios, my father, even before he seized the throne had been of great service to the Roman Empire.[1] In fact, his military career began in the time of Romanos Diogenes. He already seemed remarkable among his contemporaries, and exceptionally adventurous. On that occasion, although he was only fourteen years old, he wanted to serve on campaign under Diogenes, who was leading an expedition against the Persians[2] – a most important task – and the ambition of the young Alexios threatened the barbarians: he made it clear that one day he would come to grips with them, and when that happened his sword would have its fill of blood. Despite the youth's warlike fervour the emperor did not let him go on this campaign, because his mother had suffered a grievous loss. She was mourning the recent death of her eldest son Manuel,[3] whose great and heroic deeds had made him famous throughout the empire. In order that she might not be left comfortless, the young man was compelled to return to her. It was hard enough that the burial place of one son was still undecided; if another were sent off to the wars, she feared that he too might die before his time on some unknown battlefield. So he was left behind by his comrades against his will, but the future gradually opened up to him a fine opportunity for brave exploits. In the reign of Michael Doukas,[4] after the downfall of the Emperor Diogenes, the Roussel episode proved how valiant he was.

Roussel was a Kelt who had previously joined the Roman army. His good fortune made him conceited, and he gathered an army of his own, a considerable force made up partly of his own countrymen and partly of other nationalities. He was a formidable rebel. His attack on the Roman Empire was launched at a moment when its leadership had received many setbacks and the Turks had established their superiority. Roman prestige had fallen; the ground was giving way, as it were, beneath their feet. Roussel was in any case an extremely ambitious man, but at this crisis, when the condition of the empire was so desperate, he was even more tempted to rebel openly.[5] He plundered almost all the eastern provinces. The operations against him were entrusted to many generals renowned for bravery, men who had vast experience in battle as army commanders, but he was clearly master of these veterans. Sometimes he attacked in person, defeating his adversaries and falling upon them like a hurricane; at other times, when he sought aid from the Turks, it became so impossible to withstand his onslaughts that he even took prisoner some of the greatest generals and routed their armies.

My father Alexios was then serving under his brother[6] who had been put in command of the army in both East and West; Alexios was in fact second-in-command. It was at this crucial moment in Roman affairs, when the barbarian was everywhere on the move, attacking with lightning speed, that the admirable Alexios was promoted commander-in-chief by the Emperor Michael.[7] He was a worthy opponent for Roussel. He called on all his guile and experience as a general and a soldier, accumulated over a short period of time. (Despite his youth – he had only recently shown evidence of the proverbial 'first beard' – he was even then considered by Roman experts to have attained the summit of the general's art, through devotion to sheer hard work and constant vigilance; to them he was another Aemilius, the famous Roman, or a new Scipio, or a second Carthaginian Hannibal.[8]) As Roussel was descending on our people like a flood in full spate, he was captured and within a few days the affairs of the East were settled. Alexios was quick to see the right course of action to take, and even quicker to take it. As to the manner in which Roussel was caught, that is described by the *kaisar* in his second book,[9] but I will also give my account, as it concerns my own history too.

2. Not long before, the barbarian Toutakh[10] had come down

from the remoter parts of Anatolia to plunder Roman territory
with a powerful army. Roussel, meanwhile, was being repeatedly hard-pressed by the Roman general and one after another
his strongholds were falling. (Even though he had a substantial
army at his disposal which was thoroughly equipped with fine
and impressive weapons, my father Alexios completely outwitted him. To save himself Roussel decided to adopt a new
policy.) He was now at the end of his resources. So having
met with Toutakh, he made a friend of him and asked for an
alliance.   *Alexios vs "my*
                                                           father"
His scheme was thwarted by the *Stratopedarkhes* Alexios,
who by cordial offers, backed persistently by arguments, gifts,
and every device and stratagem, won the barbarian over to our
side. Nobody surpassed my father in ingenuity; he could find his
way out of the most impossible situations. The most convincing
point in the persuading of Toutakh can be summarized as
follows: 'Your sultan[11] and my emperor are friends. This barbarian Roussel prepares to attack both of them, and is indeed
a fearful enemy of both. His incursions against the emperor are
continually whittling away some part of his Roman domain,
bit by bit. At the same time Persia is being deprived of all that
she herself might win. His whole plan of campaign is carefully
thought out: for the moment he is pursuing me with your help;
later, when the time is propitious, he will leave me, thinking he
is now free from danger, alter his tactics again and make war
on you. My advice to you is this: when he returns to you, seize
him, for which we will pay you well, and send him to us in
chains. You will profit from this in three ways: first, you will
have more money than anyone else has ever received before;
secondly, you will win the friendship of the emperor, thereby
quickly attaining great prosperity; and thirdly, the sultan will
also be delighted to see so formidable an enemy out of the way,
an enemy who trained his men to fight both of us, Romans and
Turks.'[12]
Such was the message sent to Toutakh by my father, as
commander-in-chief of the Roman army. At the same time he
sent as hostages certain distinguished persons and persuaded
Toutakh's barbarians to seize Roussel at an agreed time and

for a set sum of money. Roussel was at once taken and sent to
Amaseia to the Roman general.

After that there was trouble. The money promised was slow
in arriving and Alexios himself was unable to pay the full
amount. The emperor took no interest in the affair. Far from
coming with measured tread, as the tragic playwright says,[13]
the money was nowhere to be seen at all. Toutakh's men pressed
for payment in full or the return of the captive who had been
bought; he should be allowed to go back to the place where he
had been seized. The agreed sum could not be paid, but, after
spending the whole night in deep perplexity, Alexios decided
to collect the money by contributions from the inhabitants of
Amaseia.

However, on the next morning he summoned the people,
especially those who were most influential and the wealthiest
in the town. Fixing his eyes on the latter in particular, he made
a speech. 'You all know,' he said, 'how this barbarian has
treated all the towns of Armeniakon,[14] how many villages he
has ravaged, how many people he has cruelly subjected to
intolerable persecution, how much money he has extorted from
you. But now you have a chance to free yourselves from his evil
deeds – if you wish. It is essential that he should not be allowed
to get away. As you see, he is our prisoner, thanks entirely to
the Will of God and our zeal. But Toutakh captured him and
demands the reward from us. We are quite incapable of paying
the money, being on foreign soil and having already exhausted
our capital on a long war against the barbarians. Of course, if
the emperor were not so far away and if the Turk granted some
respite, I would make haste to get the money from Constantinople. As that is altogether out of the question, as you yourselves know, it falls on you to contribute the money, which the
emperor will repay in full on my promise.'

Hardly had he ended this speech when the Amaseians broke
into loud uproar. Openly defiant, they hissed at him. There
were malevolent troublemakers who made the uproar worse
still by agitating the crowd. At any rate there was a tremendous
hubbub, some wanting Roussel to be kept and urging the mob
to lay hands on him, while others, in utter confusion (as is the

way with a rabble of a crowd), wanted to grab him and strike off his chains. Seeing the people in such a volatile mood, Alexios realized that his own position was extremely precarious. Nevertheless, he did not lose heart and bracing himself made a sign with his hand to enforce silence.

After a long time and with much difficulty he stopped the uproar and addressed them. 'Men of Amaseia,' he said, 'I am amazed that you have so completely misunderstood the intrigues of these men who deceive you, buying their own safety at the cost of your blood and continually plotting your absolute ruin. What will you get out of Roussel's revolt? Massacres, blindings and mutilations? Yet the men who engineer such things for you, by courting the favour of the barbarian, made sure that their own welfare would not be affected. At the same time they were enjoying a glut of gifts from the emperor and humoured him with assurances that they had neither surrendered you nor the town of Amaseia to the barbarian. So far they have never given a thought to you. The reason why they want to help Roussel in his revolt, flattering him with high hopes, is that they may keep their own fortunes intact, and continue to beg for honours and gifts from the emperor. If their luck should somehow alter, they will withdraw from the business and stir up the emperor's anger against you. Take my advice. Tell the troublemakers to go to blazes. Now go home, every one of you, and consider what I have said. You will know whose advice is most appropriate for you.'

3. On hearing these words, as unaccountably as the way a potsherd falls this or that side up, they changed their minds and went home. Alexios was aware how on the slightest pretext a crowd will reverse a decision, especially when influenced by scoundrels, and he was afraid that agitators would harangue them during the night, attack him, lead Roussel from his prison and set him free. Resistance against such overwhelming numbers would be impossible. However, he devised a plan worthy of Palamedes himself.[15] He pretended to blind Roussel. The man was laid flat on the ground, the executioner brought the branding iron near to his face, and Roussel howled and groaned; he was like a roaring lion. To all appearances he was

being blinded. But in fact the apparent victim had been ordered to shout and bawl; the executioner who seemed to be gouging out his eyes was told to glare horribly at the prostrate Roussel and act like a raving madman – in other words, to simulate the punishment. So he was blinded, but not in reality, and the people clapped their hands and noisily spread the news all over the town that Roussel had lost his eyes.

This bit of play-acting persuaded the whole mob, inhabitants of the town as well as those from outside, to give money to the fund. They were busy as bees. The whole point of my father's stratagem was that those who were disinclined to contribute and were plotting to steal Roussel away from him might give up in despair when they were foiled; they might abandon their original plan for his and quickly become his allies. Thus the emperor's displeasure would be averted. With this in view he seized Roussel and kept him like a lion in a cage, still wearing bandages over his eyes as evidence of the supposed blinding.[16]

Despite the glory already won, he was far from satisfied; other tasks still remained to be done. Many other towns and strongholds were subdued; those areas which had suffered under Roussel were incorporated back into the empire. After that he turned his horse straight for the imperial city. However, when he reached his grandfather's town[17] there was a short rest from labour for himself and all his soldiers. It was here that he afterwards performed a feat worthy of the famous Herakles when he rescued Alkestis, the wife of Admetos.[18]

A certain Dokeianos,[19] nephew of the former emperor Isaac Komnenos[19] and cousin of Alexios (and a man of distinction not only because of his lineage but also in his own right), saw Roussel wearing the bandages, apparently blinded, and being led by the hand. He sighed deeply, shed tears and accused my father of cruelty. He even went so far as to rebuke him personally for having deprived a man so noble and a true hero of his sight; he shouted that Roussel should have been saved from punishment altogether. For the moment Alexios merely remarked, 'My dear fellow, you will soon hear the reasons for his blinding.' But not long afterwards he took him to a little room and there uncovered Roussel's head and disclosed his eyes, fiercely blazing. Dokeianos was astonished at the sight; the miracle filled him with wonder and amazement. Again and again he put his hands on Roussel's eyes, to convince himself that it was not a dream or a magic trick or some other newly invented manifestation of that sort. When he did learn of his cousin's humane treatment of the man, of his humanity and artifice, he was overcome with joy. He embraced and kissed his kinsman repeatedly and his wonder turned to happiness. The reactions of all those close to the Emperor Michael, as well as those of the emperor himself, echoed these feelings.

4. Later Alexios was sent back to the West by the Emperor Nikephoros, who was now at the head of affairs, to deal with Nikephoros Bryennios.[20] The latter was throwing the whole of the West into confusion. He had assumed the imperial crown and was proclaiming himself Emperor of the Romans, even though Botaneiates had established himself on the throne immediately after the deposition of Michael Doukas, who had exchanged the diadem and cloak of an emperor for the alb and tunic of a high priest, and having married the Empress Maria[21] was now governing the empire. (The story of this marriage will be told in greater detail as my history proceeds.)

During Michael's reign Nikephoros Bryennios had been appointed *doux* of Dyrrakhion, and even before the accession of Botaneiates he had begun to play the part of an emperor and planned a revolt against Michael. Why and how this came about it is unnecessary for us to go into here. The *kaisar's* history has set out the reason for the rebellion. But I must briefly explain – this is most important – how he overran and subdued the whole of the western provinces, using Dyrrakhion as his operational base, and how he was captured. Those who wish to learn the details of the revolt can refer to the *kaisar's* account.

Bryennios was a mighty warrior, one of the most extraordinary men – tall, of noble lineage, very handsome, dignified and thoughtful, physically strong – an outstanding candidate for the imperial throne in that generation. So persuasive were his arguments and so great his ability to influence all men, even at first sight and the beginning of their acquaintance, that everyone, both soldiers and civilians, united in giving him precedence and judging him worthy to rule over the whole empire, east and west. Whenever towns received him, they did so with hands raised in supplication, but sent him on his way from town to town with applause. This worried Botaneiates, threw his army into extreme confusion and caused anxiety throughout the empire.

It was my father, therefore, Alexios Komnenos, whom they decided to pit against Bryennios. Alexios had recently been promoted *domestikos* of the Schools and he had with him the military forces which were available. The truth is that in this area the empire was reduced to its last men. Turkish infiltration had scattered the eastern armies in all directions and the Turks were in complete control of almost all the districts between the Black Sea and the Hellespont, the Syrian and Aegean seas, the Saros and the other rivers, in particular those which flow along the borders of Pamphylia and Kilikia and empty themselves into the Egyptian Sea.[22] So much for the eastern armies; those in the west joined Bryennios and left the Roman Empire with quite small and insignificant forces. Some Immortals[23] were left to fight for it, but they had only picked up sword and spear for the first time a short while earlier. There were also a few soldiers from Khoma and a Keltic regiment which was far below strength. At any rate, these were the men whom they gave to my father; at the same time the emperor's advisers called on the Turks to supply help. He was then ordered to set out for a campaign against Bryennios. They had less confidence in the army than in the general's own intelligence and his strategic and tactical skill.

Alexios did not await the arrival of reinforcements, but hearing that the enemy was advancing rapidly at once armed himself and his followers, left the capital and pitched camp in Thrace near the River Halmyros without ditches or rampart. He discovered that Bryennios was bivouacking on the plains of Kedoktos and he wanted to keep the two armies, his own and the enemy's, a considerable distance apart, for to attack Bryennios head-on was impossible: the state of his own forces and their inferiority in numbers might become known. He would have to fight with a handful of inexperienced soldiers against a large force of seasoned veterans. Thus he gave up the idea of a bold, open attack and planned a victory by stealth.

5. Now that the history has brought these men, Bryennios and my father Alexios Komnenos, both heroic men, to the point of battle, it is worthwhile to arrange them in their opposing battle lines and then to examine the fortunes of the war. (Neither was inferior to the other in bravery, nor was one surpassed by the other in experience.) Certainly they were both handsome and brave, in skill and physical strength equally balanced as on a scale. The task at hand is to see how fortune favoured one side. Bryennios, confident in his soldiers, relied on his own knowledge and the good discipline of his army, whereas on the other side Alexios had modest hopes, so far as his own forces were concerned, but in reply put his trust in the strength of his own ingenuity and in his art as a general.

When they had taken stock of each other and determined that now was the time for battle, Bryennios, who had learnt that Alexios, encamped near Kalaura, was intercepting his own line of march, moved to the attack with the following formation. His army was drawn up on right and left: his brother John[24] was in command of the right, where there were 5,000 men in all, Italians and members of the detachment of the famous Maniakes,[25] as well as horsemen from Thessaly and a contingent, by no means ignoble, from the *Hetaireia*. On the other wing, the left, Tarkhaneiotes Katakalon was in command of Macedonians and Thracians, well armed and numbering altogether 3,000. Bryennios personally commanded the centre of the line, where Macedonians and Thracians were posted with the elite of all the nobles. All the Thessalians were mounted on horseback; with their breastplates of iron and the helmets on their heads, they flashed like lightning. Their horses alert with pricked-up ears, their shields clashing one on another, the brilliant gleam of their armour and their helmets struck terror into the enemy. Bryennios, circling round in their midst like some Ares or a Giant standing out head and shoulders above all others, taller by a cubit, was in truth an object of wonder and dread to those who saw him.[26] Apart from the main body, about two stades distant, were some Scythian allies[27] equipped with barbaric weapons. They had been ordered to fall upon the rear as soon as the enemy appeared and the trumpet sounded the charge; they were to shoot at them and harass them ceaselessly with showers of arrows, while the others in close order, shield to shield, were to attack with all their might.

So much for Bryennios' formation. My father Alexios Komnenos, on the other hand, first inspected the lie of the land, then stationed one part of his army in some ravines with the rest facing Bryennios' line. When both the contingents, concealed and visible, had been duly arranged, Alexios addressed his soldiers, individually inciting them to deeds of bravery. The detachment already lying in ambush he ordered to fall upon the unsuspecting enemy as soon as they found themselves in their rear; they were to dash against their right wing with the greatest possible force and violence. He kept for himself the so-called Immortals and some of the Kelts; these he commanded in person. Katakalon was put in charge of the men from Khoma and the Turks; he was to be responsible for the general surveillance of the Scythians and the repulse of their forays.

So much for that. When Bryennios' men reached the ravines, my father immediately gave the signal and the party in ambush leapt upon the enemy with loud war cries, each man striking and killing any who happened to come in his path. The suddenness of this attack terrified the others and they were thrown into flight. John Bryennios, the general's brother, however, mindful of his furious might[28] and still courageous, turned his horse's bridle and with one blow struck down the Immortal who came at him. Thereupon the breaking line was restored and discipline returned: the ambushers were driven off. The Immortals began to flee headlong in some disorder, losing men at the hands of their relentless pursuers.

My father hurled himself into the midst of the enemy and fighting bravely spread havoc wherever he went, striking and at once cutting down all who opposed him. He hoped that some of his men were following and protecting him, and he continued to fight with unrestrained fury. But when he saw that his army was by now utterly defeated and scattered in many directions, he gathered together the more courageous men (of whom there were six altogether) and told them to draw sword and when they got near Bryennios to make a violent assault on him; if necessary they should be prepared to die. This plan was thwarted by a common soldier, Theodotos, who had served my father from boyhood; he said that the enterprise was foolhardy. Alexios was persuaded, and adopted the contrary plan: he decided to retire a little way from the enemy, collect some men who were known to him from the scattered army, reorganize them and again plunge into the fray.

However, before my father could disengage from the enemy, the Scythians spread panic through the ranks of the Khomatenian detachment commanded by Katakalon with their terrifying war cries. They drove them back and put them to flight without any difficulty, and then turned to plunder, following the custom of the Scythians: before they are absolutely sure of the enemy's defeat and before consolidating their advantage, they ruin their victory by carrying off the loot. Now all the camp followers, fearing they might suffer some damage from these Scythians, caught up with the rear of Bryennios' army and swelled the corps, and as others constantly joined them, having escaped the Scythian bands, they caused no little confusion in the ranks and the standards were thrown into chaos.

Meanwhile, my father Alexios was cut off, as we have said above, and as he darted here and there in Bryennios' ranks he saw one of the latter's grooms dragging away a horse from the imperial stables. It was decked out with the purple-dyed saddlecloth and had discs plated with gold; the men running beside it, too, had in their hands the great iron swords which normally accompany the emperor. Seeing all this Alexios covered his face, drawing down the visor fastened to the rim of his helmet, and with the six men I spoke of before rushed violently against them. He knocked down the groom, caught the emperor's horse and took it away together with the great swords. Then he slipped away unnoticed from the enemy. Once he reached a safe place he sent off the horse with its gold-plated bosses, and the swords which are usually carried on either side of the emperor. He also sent a herald, who was to run through all the army and in a booming voice proclaim that Bryennios had fallen.

The announcement brought together crowds of hitherto scattered men, soldiers of the *megas domestikos* of the Schools, and thus of my father. They came from all directions and marched back to their general. The news also encouraged those who had not fled to stand their ground. Wherever they happened to be they stood motionless, looking back to the rear and amazed beyond all belief by what they saw. It was indeed an extraordinary sight: the horses on which they rode were gazing to the front, but the faces of the riders turned backwards; they neither advanced nor had they any intention of wheeling about, but just stopped, dumbfounded and utterly unable to understand what had happened.

The Scythians thought of home and were already on their way; they had no further interest in pursuit, but far off from both armies wandered around with their booty. The proclamation of Bryennios' capture and downfall put courage into the hearts of those who only a little while before had been cowards and fugitives; moreover, the display of the royal horse with its insignia and the sight of the great swords, which all but spoke for themselves, convinced them that the news was true: Bryennios, who was guarded by these swords, had fallen into the hands of his enemies.

6. Chance then took a hand in the proceedings. A detachment of Turkish allies found Alexios, the *megas domestikos* of the Schools, and having learnt how the battle stood, they asked the location of the enemy. Then with Alexios Komnenos, my father, they climbed a little hill, and when he pointed it out to them they saw Bryennios' army. They looked down on it as if from a watchtower and the situation below seemed to be as follows: his men had not yet re-formed rank; they were disordered, apparently believing the victory was already won, and so, contemptuous of their adversaries, they thought the danger was past. The fact that my father's contingent of Franks had gone over to them after the first rout was the main reason for this attitude. The Franks had dismounted from their horses and given them their right hands, as is their way of pledging allegi-

ance. Thereupon a crowd gathered from all directions to see
what was going on, for a rumour spread through the army that
the Franks had abandoned their supreme commander Alexios
and actually joined their side.

My father and his men saw them in this state of confusion;
they also took into consideration the Turks who had recently
come up to them and decided to split up their combined forces
into three groups: two were to stay in ambush somewhere near
the hill, the third was ordered to advance against the enemy.
Alexios, my father, was responsible for the whole idea.

The Turks attacked not in one body drawn up in regular
formation, but in separate units at some distance from each
other. The signal was then given for each unit to attack on
horseback and fire thick volleys of arrows. My father Alexios,
who had devised the plan, followed immediately behind them
with as many soldiers collected from his scattered forces as
circumstances permitted. At this point one of Alexios' Immortals, a hot-headed, reckless fellow, spurred on his horse in front
of the rest and slackening rein charged straight for Bryennios.
He thrust his spear very hard at Bryennios' chest, but he, drawing his sword quickly before it could strike home, hitting his
attacker in the collarbone, and hacking down with all his might,
severed his whole arm, tearing straight through the breastplate.

Meanwhile the Turks riding up one after the other covered
the enemy with showers of arrows. Bryennios' men were overwhelmed by the unexpectedness of this onslaught; nevertheless
they recovered and re-formed ranks. Calling upon one another
to endure like men they bore the shock of the attack. The Turks,
however, and my father, after holding their ground for a little
while against the enemy, pretended to make an orderly withdrawal, gradually luring them and cunningly drawing them into
the ambush. When they reached the first place where their men
were hidden, they wheeled about and faced them. At a given
signal, the ambushers suddenly rode out from all sides, like
swarms of wasps, attacking with loud war cries and yelling and
with ceaseless volleys of arrows. The ears of Bryennios' men
were deafened, their eyes blinded by the streams of darts falling
upon them from everywhere.

Then, as they could not withstand them, Bryennios' army (for by now all had been wounded, horses and men) turned their standard back and retreated, allowing their opponents to strike them from the rear. Even then Bryennios showed his bravery and high spirit, exhausted though he was from the battle. At one moment he would turn about and strike some assailant, at the next he would be supervising the retreat with courage and presence of mind. On either side of him were his brother and his son, helping in the battle and in the crisis provoking the admiration of their enemy by their heroic resistance.

But when his horse grew weary, unable either to flee or even pursue (it was almost at its last gasp through constant chargings), Bryennios reined it in, and like some courageous athlete stood ready for combat, challenging two brave Turks to fight. One struck at him with his spear, but was not fast enough to give a heavy blow; instead he received a heavier one from Bryennios' right arm, which, too quick for him, cut off his hand with his sword, and hand and spear rolled to the ground. The other Turk leapt down from his horse and like a panther jumped on to Bryennios' mount, gripping tight into its side, and there he clung desperately, trying to climb on its back. Like a wild beast Bryennios kept twisting round and tried to stab him off with his sword, but without success, for the Turk behind him kept swaying to avoid the blows. Eventually his right arm tired of striking at thin air and himself worn out with fighting, Bryennios surrendered to the main body of the enemy. They seized him and like men who have won great glory took him off to Alexios Komnenos. The latter was standing not far away from the place where Bryennios was taken and was at the time marshalling the barbarian troops in his force as well as his own men, encouraging them to fight.

News of the capture had arrived earlier through messengers; now Bryennios was set before the general in person, a really formidable sight, whether fighting or in captivity. And so, having taken Bryennios into custody in this way, Alexios Komnenos sent him as a prize of war to the Emperor Botaneiates, and without any attempt to injure his eyes. It was contrary to

humane
capturing...

Komnenos' nature to inflict injury on those who had fought
against him, once they had been captured; he thought capture
was punishment enough for an enemy. He treated them
humanely, with kindness, with generosity. This was certainly
the case with Bryennios.

After his capture Alexios accompanied him for a fair distance and when he reached the place called . . .,[29] wishing to
comfort the man in his sorrow and inspire him with hopes for
the future, he said to him, 'Let us dismount and sit down for a
little rest.' Bryennios feared for his life; he seemed to be out of
his mind and certainly in no need of resting. How could he be
when he had all but given up the ghost? However, he fell in
with the general's suggestion without delay – a slave readily
yields to every command, even more so if he happens to be a
prisoner of war.

Well, the two leaders dismounted. Alexios immediately lay

how do we know
what's true

down on some green grass as though it were a couch, but
Bryennios kept apart, propping his head against the root of a
high-leafed oak. The former fell asleep but heavenly sleep, as
sweet poetry would put it,[30] did not visit Bryennios. Lifting his
eyes, however, and noticing Alexios' sword hanging from the
branches, as he spied no one anywhere present, he recovered
from his despondency and became more composed; he would
kill my father. And maybe the plan would have come off, had
not some divine power from above prevented it, calming the
man's savage wrath and compelling him to turn a benevolent
eye on the general. I have heard this story many times. Anyone
who likes can indeed learn from it how God was protecting
Komnenos like some precious object for a greater destiny, wishing through him to revive Roman power. Whatever unpleasing
fate befell Bryennios after that must be attributed to certain
people at court; my father was blameless.[31]

7. Thus ended the revolt of Bryennios. But the *megas domestikos*, Alexios, my father, was not to rest, for one struggle
followed another. Borilos, a barbarian and a confidant of
Botaneiates, arrived from the city and meeting Alexios, took
over Bryennios from him and did what he did. He also brought
an order from the emperor to proceed against Basilakios, who

had already crowned himself emperor and was triumphantly stirring up trouble in the west, like Bryennios before him. Now this Basilakios was much admired for his courageous and daring spirit as well as for his great physical strength. The man was, besides, a masterful person, arrogating to himself the high offices of state; some titles he coveted, others he usurped. When Bryennios was removed he became leader of the whole revolutionary movement as Bryennios' successor.

He started from Epidamnos[32] (the capital of Illyrikon) and came as far as the chief town of Thessaly, crushing all opposition on the way and having himself elected and proclaimed emperor. Bryennios' wandering forces he transported wherever he wished. The man's other fine qualities were supplemented by an impressive physique, great strength and a majestic presence – all of which exercise an unusual fascination on country folk and the military class. They do not see beyond them to a man's soul, nor do they regard his virtue, but stand in awe only of his physical excellence, his daring, his virility, his speed of running, his size, and these they judge to be worthy of the purple robe and the crown. Well, he had these qualities in abundance, and he had a brave and invincible spirit; in short, there was a regal aura about this man Basilakios, and he certainly looked the part. With a voice like thunder he could strike terror into a whole army, and his shout was enough to humble the boldest heart. His eloquence was irresistible whether he sought to encourage his men in battle or in flight. Such were the natural advantages with which he took the field and with an invincible army occupied the town of the Thessalians,[33] as we have said.

As for my father, Alexios Komnenos, he had made counter-preparations as if for a contest against a huge Typhon[34] or a hundred-handed Giant, summoning to his aid all his general's art and courageous spirit; he was ready to fight a worthy opponent. The dust of his previous endeavours had not yet been shaken off, his hands and sword not yet wiped clean of blood, when like a terrible lion he went forth with high hopes to do battle with this long-tusked boar, Basilakios. He arrived then at the River Bardarios,[35] as the locals call it, which flows down from the mountains near Mysia, and after passing by many places on its way divides the districts round Berroia and Thessaloniki in two, the eastern and western, and finally empties itself into our Southern Sea. It is the case with all the greatest rivers that when substantial levels of deposits have been built up, they flow on to low-lying ground as if deserting their first beds and leave the old channel empty of water and dry; the new bed they fill with abundant streams.

Between the two channels of this river, the old ravine and the newly formed course, my father Alexios, that master of strategy, saw suitable ground and pitched his camp there. He thought that the channel would protect him on one side, since he could use the natural trench which had formed as a result of the water's build-up – given it was only two or three stades away. The whole army was at once ordered to rest by day, to refresh themselves with sleep and to make sure the horses were fully fed. They were told that when evening came they would have to be awake and ready for a surprise attack from the enemy.

These arrangements were made, I suppose, because my father suspected danger that evening; he thought that they would attack, either forewarned by long experience, or guessing for some other reason. The presentiment came to him and no time was wasted in taking the necessary action. He led his army from the camp, fully armed, with horses and all supplies required for battle. In the camp lights were left burning everywhere, and a former monk, now one of his household, was put in charge of his tent with all his mess equipment and other baggage. His name was Ioannikios.[36] Alexios withdrew to a good distance with his soldiers ready-armed, and then sat down to await what would happen next. His idea was that Basilakios, finding campfires lit everywhere and my father's tent bright with lamps, would think he was there resting, and as a result, would be easily captured.

8. Alexios' premonition outlined above was not unjustified. Basilakios duly made his assault on the camp, as expected. It came suddenly, with cavalry and infantry to the number of 10,000 in all. He found the soldiers' living quarters all lit up,

but when he saw the general's tent blazing with light, he hurled himself into it with blood-curdling, terrible cries. But when the man he expected to see was nowhere to be found, and no soldier, no general at all started up from it, nobody in fact except a few disreputable servants who had been left behind, he shouted and bawled even louder, 'Where the hell is the lisper?' That was his way of mocking the *megas domestikos*, for although my father Alexios was in other respects a fine speaker and natural orator who surpassed all rivals in the setting out of proofs and arguments, yet in the matter of the 'r' sound only, there was a slight stammer and his tongue would lisp almost imperceptibly; and yet he pronounced all the other letters without hesitation.

So Basilakios roared his abuse and began a meticulous search turning everything upside down, chests, camp beds, furniture, and even my father's own couch, lest perchance the general might be hiding in any of them. From time to time he fixed his gaze on the monk called Ioannikios; Alexios' mother had taken pains to insist that on all his expeditions he should have one of the more highly esteemed monks as tent-companion, and her dutiful son submitted to her wishes, not merely while he was a boy, but when he joined the ranks of the young men – and indeed until he married. Basilakios made a complete search in the tent and never relaxed his fumbling about in darkness,[37] as Aristophanes says. At the same time he questioned Ioannikios about the *domestikos*. The monk maintained his story: Alexios had left the camp with all his army some time before. Basilakios realized that he had been much deceived. In his utter wretchedness, he changed the tone of his language, shouting, 'Comrades, we've been cheated. The enemy is outside.'

The words were not yet out of his mouth before Alexios Komnenos, my father, came upon them as they were leaving the camp. He had ridden on ahead of his army at full gallop with a few companions. He saw someone restoring order to the ranks (the majority of Basilakios' men had given themselves up to looting and pillage, which was what my father had planned long before, and while the line was still unready and the men not marshalled for battle, the *megas domestikos* came upon them suddenly, a terrible threat). He thought that the man arranging their regiments must be Basilakios himself, either because of his size or because of the brightness of his armour (which reflected the light of the stars), and with a quick onset struck at his hand. The hand, together with the sword which held it, was at once hurled to the ground – an incident which greatly dismayed the enemy. However, the person concerned was not Basilakios, but one of his retinue, a very brave man and as far as courage goes in no way inferior to him.

After that Alexios continued his whirling onslaught, shooting at them with arrows, wounding them with his spear, roaring out his battle cries, confusing them in the darkness, summoning to his aid everything – time, place, weapon – to achieve victory, and good use he made of them, with undaunted spirit and indomitable resolve. Never did he fail to distinguish friend or foe as he came across men flying in all directions. There was a man from Kappadokia, one Goules, a faithful servant of my father, a tough intrepid fighter, who saw Basilakios and, making sure it was he, aimed a blow at his helmet. Unfortunately his sword, 'thrice and four times shattered', fell from his hand and only the hilt remained – like Menelaus' when he fought Alexander.[38] The general saw him and straightway mocked him because he had no sword; he called him a coward, but was somewhat mollified when Goules showed him the hilt left in his hand.

Another man, a Macedonian called Peter, with the surname Tornikios, fell upon the enemy's centre and slaughtered many. The army in fact was following its leader blindly, not knowing what was going on, for the battle started in darkness and not all were able to see its progress. Komnenos made for that part of the line which was not yet in disorder and struck at his opponents; then back he would come to his own men, urging them to break up the still coherent remnants of Basilakios' army. He sent messages to the rear, ordering them not to delay, but to follow him and catch up more quickly.

While this was going on, a Kelt, one of the *domestikos'* guards, a brave soldier full of the spirit of Ares, saw my father just emerging from the enemy's centre with drawn sword still reeking with hot blood, and thought he was one of them. He attacked at once, striking his chest with his spear, and if the general had not seated himself more firmly in his saddle and called him by name, threatening to cut off his head with his sword there and then, he might have been thrown from his horse. Anyway the Kelt made some sort of excuse – that he had not been able to identify anyone properly in the darkness and in the heat of battle – well, he emerged as one of the survivors.

9. Such were the exploits of the *megas domestikos* of the Schools with a handful of soldiers during that night. Just after smiling dawn broke and the sun peeped over the horizon, Basilakios' officers turned their whole attention to rounding up the men who had left the battle and were busy collecting booty. The *megas domestikos* put his own army in order and then renewed his attack on Basilakios. Seeing some of the enemy from afar his soldiers charged out violently against them. They routed them and returned with some live prisoners.

Basilakios' brother Manuel meanwhile climbed a small hill and encouraged his army, crying loudly that 'Today is Basilakios' victory day!' Whereupon a certain Basil, surnamed Kourtikios, an acquaintance and confidant of the Nikephoros Bryennios who has already been mentioned in my history, and an indomitable fighter, ran forward from Komnenos' battle line and up to the hillock. Manuel drew his sword and at full gallop rushed at him furiously. Kourtikios, instead of using his sword, snatched at the club suspended from his saddlecloth and hit him on the head with it, knocked him down from his horse and dragged him back to my father a prisoner, as if he were part of the booty. While this was happening what remained of Basilakios' army saw that Komnenos had appeared with his own regiments, and after brief resistance took to their heels in flight. Basilakios fled with the rest; Alexios pursued him.

When they reached Thessaloniki the townspeople immediately received Basilakios but barred the gates to the general. But even then my father did not relax: far from taking off his breastplate, or removing his helmet, or undoing the buckler from his shoulders, or laying aside his sword, he actually pitched camp and warned them that he would attack their walls and completely ravage the town. Nevertheless he was anxious to spare Basilakios and to ensure this made proposals for peace through his companion, the monk Ioannikios (who had a good reputation for integrity). He promised him that if Basilakios surrendered himself and the town, he would suffer no ill-treatment. Basilakios was having none of it. However, the inhabitants of Thessaloniki were afraid that the town would be taken and something terrible would happen, and so they allowed Komnenos to enter.

But Basilakios, seeing what they were doing, went off to the citadel – from the frying pan into the fire. Although the *domestikos* gave his word that he would suffer no irremediable ill, Basilakios still refused to forget fighting and war; despite the dangers, hard-pressed though he was, he showed himself to be a true hero. Unflinching, always courageous, he would not yield an inch, until the inhabitants of the citadel and the guards drove him out by force and handed him over to the *megas domestikos*.

Without delay the emperor was informed of the capture. Alexios himself stayed on in Thessaloniki for a while and settled affairs there before he returned to the capital in triumph. Between Philippi and Amphipolis messengers from the emperor met him with written orders about Basilakios, which they put in his hands. They took Basilakios as their charge, led him away to some village called Khlempina and near the spring of water there put out his eyes. Ever since then to this day it has been called 'the spring of Basilakios'.

Such was the third labour borne by Alexios before he became emperor, like a second Herakles; for if you equated this Basilakios with the Erymanthian Boar, and my father Alexios with a modern and most noble Herakles,[39] you would not be wrong. So much then for his successes and achievements; as reward for them all he received from the emperor the honourable title *sebastos* and was proclaimed as such by the Senate in full assembly.

10. The infirmities of the body, it seems to me, are sometimes aggravated by external causes, but there are also

occasions when the reasons for sickness emanate from the organs themselves; often we blame the vagaries of climate and certain qualities of food for the onset of fevers, even sometimes putrid humours. In the same way the bad condition of the Roman state at that time produced mortal plagues – the afore-mentioned men, I mean, the like of Roussel and Basilakios and all who filled the ranks of pretenders. Sometimes, though, it was Fate which introduced certain foreign pretenders from outside – an evil hard to combat, an incurable disease. One such was that braggart Robert, notorious for his lust for power,[40] born in Normandy, but nursed and nourished by manifold wickedness.

This was the man whose enmity the Roman Empire drew upon itself when it gave a pretext to our foes for the wars he waged – a marriage with a foreigner and a barbarian, from our point of view quite inexpedient. To be more accurate, one should blame the imprudence of Michael, the emperor who was then on the throne, who linked our family with that of Doukas. Now if I should find fault with any one of my own blood relations (for I too am related to that family on my mother's side)[41] let nobody be surprised. I have chosen to write the truth above all and as far as this man is concerned all I have done is to note down the universal condemnation of him. This particular emperor, Michael Doukas, betrothed his own son Constantine in marriage to the daughter of this barbarian Robert, and from that sprang the hostilities which followed.[42] About Constantine, the terms of his marriage contract and the foreign alliance in general, his handsome appearance and stature, his physical and moral qualities, we shall speak in due course, when I relate the sorry tale of my own misfortunes. Before that I will give an account of this proposed wedding, the defeat of the whole barbarian force and the destruction of these pretenders from Normandy – pretenders whom Michael in his folly raised up against the Roman Empire.

But first I must carry my story back somewhat and describe this man Robert, his lineage and fortune; I must show to what heights of power the force of circumstances raised him, or rather, to speak more reverently, how far Providence allowed him to advance, indulging his ill-natured ambitions and schemings.

This Robert was a Norman by birth, of obscure origin, with an overbearing character and a thoroughly villainous mind; he was a brave fighter, very cunning in his assaults on the wealth and power of great men; in achieving his aims absolutely inexorable, diverting criticism by incontrovertible argument. He was a man of immense stature, surpassing even the most powerful of men; he had a ruddy complexion, fair hair, broad shoulders, eyes that all but shot out sparks of fire. In a well-built man one looks for breadth here and slimness there; in him all was admirably well-proportioned and elegant. Thus from head to foot the man was a fine specimen, and I have often heard from many witnesses that this was so. Homer remarked of Akhilles that when he shouted those in earshot had the impression of a multitude in uproar,[43] but Robert's bellow, so they say, put tens of thousands to flight. With such endowments of fortune and nature and soul, he was, as you would expect, no man's slave, owing obedience to nobody in all the world. Such are men of powerful character, people say, even if they are of modest background.

11. Robert then, being a man of such character, wholly incapable of being led, set out from Normandy with some knights – there were five of them and thirty foot soldiers in all. After leaving his native land, he spent his time living in the mountain peaks and caves and hills of Lombardy, at the head of a band of robbers, attacking wayfarers. Sometimes he acquired horses, sometimes other kinds of possessions and arms. The start of his career was marked by bloodshed and many murders.

While he was living in the regions of Lombardy, he did not escape the notice of William Maskabeles, who at that time happened to be ruler of most of the territory adjacent to Lombardy. From it he derived a rich income every year, and as he also recruited adequate forces from the same area he was a powerful ruler. Having learnt what kind of man Robert was, from a moral as well as a physical point of view, he unwisely attached the man to himself and betrothed one of his daughters to him. The marriage was celebrated and William admired his son-in-law for his strength and military prowess, but things did not prosper for him as he had hoped.

He had already given him a town as something of a wedding present and had shown certain other signs of friendship. Robert, however, grew disaffected and plotted rebellion. At first he pretended to be well-disposed while he built up his strength, trebling his cavalry and increasing his infantry twofold. From then on the acts of kindness gradually died away and little by little his malice was laid bare.

He never ceased his daily attempts to make or seize opportunities for wrangling, continually inventing situations which usually give birth to quarrels and battles and wars. Since William Maskabeles far excelled him in wealth and power, Robert gave up thought of any direct confrontation and instead devised a wicked plot. While feigning goodwill and simulating repentance, he was secretly preparing a terrible but well-concealed trap for him, so as to seize his towns and make himself master of all Maskabeles' possessions.

First he requested peace negotiations and sent an embassy asking William to come in person to discuss them. The latter welcomed the chance of peace, because he loved his daughter dearly, and the meeting was fixed for the morrow. Robert suggested a place to him in which they might conveniently come together to discuss and arrange terms mutually agreeable. There were two hilltops rising from the level plain to an equal height and exactly opposite one another; the space in between was marshy and overgrown by all sorts of trees and plants. The cunning Robert laid an ambush of four fully armed, brave men right there, and told them to keep a sharp lookout in all directions. As soon as they saw him coming to grips with Maskabeles, they were to run towards him without a moment's delay. Having made these preliminary arrangements the scoundrel left the hill which he had before pointed out to William as suitable for their meeting and took possession, as it were, of the other. He collected fifteen knights and about fifty-six foot soldiers; with them he climbed the hill and posted them on it. The whole scheme was explained to the more reliable among them and one of these was commanded to carry Robert's

armour, shield, helmet and short sword, so that he might easily
arm himself; the four lying in ambush were instructed, when
they saw him wrestling with Maskabeles, to run up quickly to
his aid.

On the agreed day William was on his way to the hilltop, to
the place Robert had formerly designated, with the intention of
agreeing a truce. Robert saw him not far off, met him on
horseback, welcomed him warmly and greeted him in the most
cordial manner. So, gradually moving to the slope just below
the top of the hill, they both halted, talking of what they
intended to do. Robert craftily wasted time, chatting about one
thing after another, and then said to him, 'Why should we tire
ourselves out seated on horseback? Shall we dismount and sit
on the ground? Then we can consider what we have to in
comfort.' Maskabeles, poor fool, unaware of Robert's treachery
and his own perilous situation, agreed. When he perceived that
Robert had dismounted, he at once did likewise; he renewed
the discussion, leaning with his elbow on the ground. Robert
confessed that in future he would be the servant of Maskabeles,
and to prove it called him his Benefactor and Lord. Maskabeles'
men had seen these two dismount from their horses and
apparently begin fresh negotiations. They were tired because of
the heat and the want of food and drink (it was the height of
the summer, at the hour when the sun casts its rays from directly
overhead, and the temperature becomes unbearable). Some of
them, therefore, also dismounted, tied their reins to the
branches of trees and lay down on the ground, cooling themselves off in the shade cast by horses and trees; others went
off home.

So much for them. Robert, wily as ever, now that all was
ready, suddenly grabbed Maskabeles. His gentle expression
changed to one of fury, and he attacked him murderously. The
other struggled, pulling and being pulled; both began to roll
down the slope. The four ambushers watched them, rose up
from the marsh and charged at William. They bound him well
and truly, and then ran back as if to join Robert's horsemen
who were stationed on the other hill and already galloping
down towards them. Behind them came William's men. For his

part, Robert mounted, took helmet and spear, quickly tucking the latter under his arm, and protected himself with his shield. Then he wheeled round and struck at one of William's soldiers with the spear. The blow killed him.

This had a double effect: the onrush of his father-in-law's cavalrymen was checked and their rescue attempt was foiled. (The rest, in fact, when they saw Robert's knights coming down on them from above with the advantage of higher ground, immediately fled.) In this way Robert put an end to their charge, and as for Maskabeles, he was at once led off as a prisoner of war in bonds to the very fortress which he had given to Robert as a wedding present when he betrothed his daughter to him. So it came about that the town then had its own master as a prisoner, and naturally was thereafter called 'The Fort'. The details of Robert's cruelty are horrifying in the extreme, for when he had Maskabeles completely in his power, he first had all his teeth pulled out, demanding for each one of them an enormous sum of money and each time asking him where he had hidden his fortune. As he did not cease pulling out the teeth till all had gone, and as teeth and money were exhausted at the same time, he then turned to William's eyes. Grudging him the power of sight, he blinded him.[44]

12. He was now master of all and from that time his power increased day by day. As his ambitions grew he kept adding town to town and piling up his wealth. In a short period of time, he attained high rank and was named duke of the whole of Lombardy,[45] which provoked the jealousy of everyone. However, being a wary fellow, he mitigated the popular movements against himself, flattering some of his adversaries and bribing others; by his cleverness he moderated the envy of the nobles. Occasionally he had recourse to arms. By these means he brought the whole of Lombardy and the surrounding areas under his personal control.

He was always thinking out some more ambitious project. He dreamed of ascending the throne of the Roman Empire himself, and so he seized on the pretext of his connection by marriage with the Emperor Michael. The war against the Romans was kindled anew. We have mentioned before that

Michael, for some inexplicable reason, had agreed to unite his own son Constantine in marriage with Robert's daughter (her name was Helena).

When I recall this young man again, my soul is sorely troubled and my thoughts become confused. I will defer giving a full account of his life until the appropriate time. But this at least I cannot refrain from saying, even if I speak out of place: Constantine was Nature's masterpiece, a triumph, as it were, of God's handiwork. One look at him would convince anyone that here was a descendant of the mythical Golden Age of the Greeks, so infinite was his charm. As for me, when I remember this young man after so many years, I am overcome by tears. Yet I hold back my sorrow; it shall be reserved for pride of place, lest by mingling my own lamentations[46] with the historical narrative I confuse the history.

This youth, mentioned by me here and elsewhere, was born before I saw the light of day and had become a suitor of Helena. He was a chaste and undefiled boy. The marriage settlement had been committed to writing, though it was not executed and consisted merely of promises, because he was still immature, and as soon as Nikephoros Botaneiates became emperor the contract was torn up. But I have wandered from the point; I will go back to the place where I went astray.

Robert, who from a most undignified condition had attained great distinction, having gathered about him powerful forces, was aiming to become Roman emperor. Consequently he was devising plausible excuses for his hatred and warlike attitude to the Romans.

At this point there are two different versions of the story. According to one, which is widespread and reached our ears too, a monk called Raiktor impersonated the Emperor Michael and fled to Robert, the father of his (supposed) daughter-in-law. He told him a pitiable tale of his own misfortunes. This Michael, you see, had seized the Roman sceptre after Diogenes and for a brief moment graced the throne, but was deprived of power by the rebel Botaneiates; he submitted to the life of a monk[47] and later took on an episcopal robe and the mitre; you may even add the humeral. It was the *Kaisar* John, his paternal uncle,[48] who counselled him to do this, for he knew the flippant nature of the new emperor and feared that some more dreadful fate might befall him.

The aforementioned monk, Raiktor, pretended that he was Michael, but maybe I had better call him Rektes,[49] for he was the most brazen so-and-so there has ever been. Well, he approached Robert, on the basis that he was related to him by marriage, and he acted out his tale of injustice, how he had been deprived of the imperial throne and reduced to his present state, which Robert could see for himself. For all these reasons he challenged the barbarian to help him. Helena, the lovely young girl, he said, had been left defenceless, entirely cut off from her bridegroom, for his son Constantine and the Empress Maria, he proclaimed loudly, had been forced against their will to join the party of Botaneiates. With these words he stirred the anger of the barbarian and drove him to arms in a war against the Romans. Such is the story which came to my ears and I do not find it surprising that some persons of completely obscure origin impersonate others of noble birth and glorious reputation.

But my ears are also assailed by another version of the affair and this is more convincing. According to the second authority there was no monk who impersonated Michael, nor were there any such actions which prompted Robert to make war on the Romans; rather the barbarian himself with great versatility willingly invented the whole story. The subsequent events apparently came about as follows. Robert, they say, was a thoroughly unscrupulous rascal and working hard for a conflict with the Romans; he had for a long time been making preparations for the war; but he was prevented by men of the highest rank of his entourage and by his own wife Gaita, on the grounds that he would be starting an unjust war and one directed against Christians. Several times his attempts to begin such an enterprise were put off. However, as he was determined to invent an excuse for war that would be plausible, he sent some men to Cotrone with certain instructions, having informed them first of his secret designs. If they met any monk who was willing to cross from there to Italy in order to worship at the shrine of the great apostles, the patron saints of Rome, and if his outward appearance did not manifest too lowly an origin, they were to embrace him gladly, make a friend of him and bring him to Robert. When they discovered the aforementioned Raiktor, who was a clever fellow, a criminal beyond compare, they contacted Robert, who was at Salerno at the time, via a letter. It read: 'Your kinsman Michael, deposed from his throne, has arrived and asks for your assistance.' This was the secret code which Robert had asked them to use.

With this letter in his hand Robert at once went to his wife and read it aloud to her privately. Then he gathered together all the counts and, again privately, showed them the letter. He thought no doubt that he had seized on a fine excuse and they would no longer oppose his schemes. Since they all supported his plan without hesitation, he brought Raiktor over and made his acquaintance. After that he dramatized the whole business, with the monk at the centre of the stage. It was said that he was the Emperor Michael; that he had been deprived of his throne; that his wife and son and all his possessions had been taken from him by the pretender Botaneiates; that contrary to justice and all right dealing he had been invested not with the crown and emperor's headband, but with the garb of a monk. 'Now,' said Robert, 'he has come as a suppliant to us.'

These remarks were made publicly by Robert, and he said it was of prime importance that he should be restored because of their kinship. The monk was every day honoured by him as if he were indeed the Emperor Michael; he was allotted a better seat at table, a more elevated throne and exceptional respect. Robert's public speeches were suited to the occasion: sometimes he spoke in self-pity, bewailing the fate of his daughter; at other times he would spare the feelings of his 'kinsman' by not referring to the troubles which had fallen on him; and then again he would rouse the barbarians about him and incite them to war by cleverly promising heaps of gold which he guaranteed to get for them from the Roman Empire.[50]

Thus he led them all by the nose, and when he set out he drew after him rich and poor alike – it might be more accurate to say that he drew away the whole of Lombardy when he occupied Salerno, the capital city of Amalfi. There he made excellent arrangements for his other daughters and then prepared for the campaign. Two of the daughters were with him. (The third, of course, who had been unfortunate from the day of her betrothal, was held in Constantinople. Her young betrothed, being still a young boy, shrank from the union from the outset, just as children are scared by Mormo.[51]) One daughter he pledged to Raymond, son of the Count Barcelona; the other he married off to Ebles, who was himself a count of great distinction. Nor did these alliances[52] prove unprofitable for Robert; in fact, from all sources he had consolidated and amassed power for himself – from his family, from his rule, from his inheritance rights, from all manner of ways which another man would not even consider.

13. Meanwhile there occurred an event which it is worthwhile to record (for this too promoted his good fortune). Indeed, I consider that the inability of all the western rulers to attack him contributed very much to the smooth course of Robert's affairs. In everything Fortune worked for him, raised him to power and brought about whatever was to his advantage. For example, the Pope of Rome (this is a noble office, protected by soldiers of many nationalities) had a quarrel with Henry, the king of Germany,[53] and wanted to draw Robert into an alliance with himself, since Robert had already become very famous and attained great power.

The reasons for this quarrel between pope and king were as follows: the pope accused King Henry of accepting money for church livings instead of appointing incumbents freely; he also blamed him for entrusting the office of archbishop on certain occasions to unworthy men, and he brought other charges of this nature. The German king, on the other hand, accused the pope of usurpation, saying that he had taken the apostolic chair without his consent. What is more, he had used the most insulting and reckless language, threatening that if he did not resign his self-appointed office, he would be expelled from it ignominiously.

When the pope heard these words, he immediately expended his wrath on the envoys sent by Henry. He began by treating them cruelly before cutting their hair and beards, the one with

scissors, the other with a razor, and finally he did something else
to them which was quite improper, going beyond the insolent
behaviour one expects from barbarians, and then sent them
away. I would have given a name to the outrage, but as a
woman and a princess, modesty forbade me. What was done
on his orders was not only unworthy of a high priest, but of
any man at all who bears the name of a Christian. Even the
barbarian's intention, let alone the act itself, filled me with
disgust; if I had described it in detail, pen and paper would
have been defiled. The very fact that we cannot endure to
disclose or describe even a small fraction of what was done will
be sufficient evidence of this barbaric outrage and the character
of men ready to commit any crime, any deed of daring.[54] It will
be proof enough that Time in its flow does produce such men.

And this, in the name of Justice!, was the work of a high
priest. More, it was the doing of the supreme high priest, who
presides over the whole inhabited world, according to the
claims and belief of the Latins – another example of their
arrogance. The truth is that when power was transferred from
Rome to our country and the Queen of Cities, not to mention
the senate and the whole administration, the senior arch-
bishopric was also transferred here. From the beginning the
emperors have acknowledged the primacy of the Constanti-
nopolitan bishop, and the Council of Chalcedon[55] notably
raised that bishop to the place of highest honour and subordi-
nated to him all dioceses throughout the world.

There should be no doubt then that this outrage inflicted on
the ambassadors was aimed at the man who had sent them, not
only because they were punished, but because the particular
form of chastisement was novel, the invention of the pope
himself. By his actions he hinted that the state of the king was
utterly despicable, as if some demi-god was dealing with a
demi-ass. Such, I think, was the purpose of these shameful acts.

The pope, having used the envoys as I have described and
having sent them back to the king, provoked a terrible war. To
prevent Henry becoming more unbearable by an alliance with
Robert, the pope anticipated him by making his own proposals
for peace, though previously he was not on friendly terms with

Robert. Learning that the latter had occupied Salerno, he set
out himself from Rome and arrived at Benevento. After some
communication through ambassadors they met face to face in
the following manner. The pope came from Benevento with his
own guard, and Robert from Salerno with his army, and when
the two forces were at a reasonable distance from each other,
the leaders left their ranks and met. Pledges and oaths were
exchanged and the two then returned. The pope swore on oath
that he would invest Robert with the rank of king and give
him assistance against the Romans if need arose; the duke that
he would bring help wherever the pope summoned it.[56] In
practice, however, the oaths were worthless, for Pope Gregory
was violently angry with the German king and preparations
against him were being hurried on, whereas Robert had his eye
on the Roman Empire. Like some wild boar he gnashed his
teeth and whetted his wrath against the Romans. So the oaths
amounted to no more than words, and mutual pledges given
by these barbarians one day were as quickly disregarded
the next.

Duke Robert turned his horse about and hastened to Salerno,
while the abominable pope (when I think of his inhuman acts
towards the ambassadors, there is no other word I could possibly apply to him), this despot with his spiritual grace and
evangelic peace, then marched to make war on his own flock
with all his energy and all his might – the man of peace, too,
and disciple of the Man of Peace! He at once sent for the Saxons
and their chieftains Rudolf and Welf. Among many other entic-
ing promises, he announced that he would make them kings of
all the west and so won them to his side. It seems that he paid
no attention to the advice of St Paul to 'Lay hands hastily on no
man',[57] for his right hand was only too ready for the laying-on of
hands where kings were concerned: he bound with the kingly
ribbon the Duke of Lombardy's head and crowned these
Saxons.

Each party, that is to say, King Henry of Germany and the
pope, assembled their forces, put their battle lines in order, and
as soon as the horn sounded the attack the two armies at once
clashed. The battle erupted, to be fought on either side with

ferocity and dogged resolution. Both displayed such courage and bore up so well though wounded by spear or arrow that in a short time all the plain beneath their feet was swamped in the blood of the dead, and the survivors were fighting on like ships on a sea of gore. In places they became entangled in masses of corpses and falling down were drowned in the torrent of blood. If, as they say, more than 30,000 men fell in that battle, how great the river of blood that flowed, how vast the area of earth stained by their gore!

Each side held its head high, so to speak, in this struggle as long as Rudolf, the Saxon chief, directed the battle. But when he received a mortal wound and died instantaneously, the pope's line wavered and broke. Its flight was bloody and murderous. Henry drove them on wildly in pursuit, much heartened at the news that Rudolf had fallen and become the prize of his enemies.[58] However, he gave up the chase and ordered his soldiers to rest. Later on, he armed himself again and hastened to Rome eager to submit it to a siege.

The pope thereupon recalled the agreements made with Robert and his oaths. An embassy was dispatched to him asking for help. Just at this moment Henry also, as he started for the ancient city of Rome, requested an alliance with Robert through ambassadors. To Robert it seemed that each of them on this occasion was a fool to ask. He made some sort of verbal reply to the king, but wrote a letter to the pope. The gist of it was as follows: 'To the great High Priest and my lord, from Duke Robert, by the grace of God. Although I heard of the assault made upon you by your enemies, I did not pay undue attention to the story, knowing that no one would dare to raise his hand against you. For who would attack so great a father, unless he were mad? Be sure that I am arming myself for a most important war against a people hard to conquer. My campaign is against the Romans, enemies who have filled every land and sea with their trophies. As far as you are concerned I owe fidelity from the bottom of my heart and will prove it when necessity demands it.' Thus he evaded the envoys of both sides when they called for his assistance – the former by this letter, the latter by certain plausible excuses; and he sent them away.

14. But let us not neglect to record what he did in Lombardy before coming to Avlona with his army. Certainly Robert was an overbearing and cruel man, but at this point he emulated even Herod in his madness. Not being satisfied with the men who had served in his army from the beginning and had experience in battle, he formed a new army, made up of recruits without any consideration of age. From all quarters of Lombardy and Apulia he gathered them, overage and underage, pitiable specimens who had never seen armour even in their dreams, but then clad in breastplates and carrying shields, awkwardly drawing bows to which they were completely unused and falling flat on the ground when they were allowed to march.

Naturally these things provided an excuse for incessant trouble in Lombardy. Everywhere one could hear the lamentation of men and the wailing of women who shared in the bad fortune of their menfolk, for one mourned a husband unfit for military service, another a son who knew nothing of war, and a third a brother who was just a farmer or occupied in some other job. As I said, this idea of Robert's was just as crazed as the behaviour of Herod, or even worse, for Herod raved only against newborns, but Robert against boys and older men as well.[59] Yet, however unused to soldiering they were, as it might be said, he trained them daily and hammered his recruits into a disciplined force.

This was his business in Salerno before he arrived in Otranto. He had sent on ahead a very efficient army to await him there, when he had settled all the affairs of Lombard territory and given suitable replies to the envoys. He did, however, send an additional note to the pope, saying that he had instructed his son Roger (whom he had appointed ruler of all Apulia together with his brother Boritylas[60]) to go with the utmost zeal to the aid of the pope, whenever he called for it; he was to attack King Henry with a strong force.

His younger son, Bohemond, resembled his father in all respects, in daring, strength, bravery and indomitable spirit. In short, he was the exact replica and living image of his father. Bohemond was sent with a powerful force to our country, with the aim of ravaging the areas around Avlona. He at once attacked Kanina, Hierikho and Avlona like a streaking thunder-bolt, with threats and irrepressible fury. He seized them, and fighting on ravaged the surrounding areas and set them to fire. Bohemond was in fact like the acrid smoke which precedes a fire, the preliminary skirmish which comes before the great assault. Father and son you might liken to caterpillars and locusts, for what was left by Robert, his son fed on and devoured. But we must not get him across to Avlona yet. Let us examine what he did on the opposite mainland.

15. Robert set out from Salerno and arrived at Otranto. There he stayed for a few days waiting for his wife Gaita (she went on campaign with her husband and when she donned armour was indeed a formidable sight). He embraced her when she arrived and then set off with all the army again for Brindisi, the seaport with the finest harbour in the whole of Iapygia. He swooped down on the town and stopped there, watching eagerly the assembling of all his forces and all his ships, trans-ports and longships and fighting vessels, because it was from Brindisi that he expected to sail to these shores.

While he was at Salerno, he had sent an ambassador called Raoul, a noble and one of his retinue, to the Emperor Botanei-ates, who had by now seized power in succession to the Emperor Doukas. Robert was keenly awaiting the reply. Raoul was charged to make certain complaints and to put forward some apparently reasonable excuses for the impending war: Botaneiates had separated Robert's daughter from her future husband the Emperor Constantine as this history has already made clear and had deprived him of the imperial crown. Robert, therefore, because of this injustice, was preparing vengeance. He had sent presents and letters promising friendship to the current *megas domestikos* and commander of the western forces (that is to say, my father Alexios). He was now waiting at Brindisi for his answer.

Before all the contingents had been collected or most of the ships launched, Raoul came back from Byzantion, bringing no reply to Robert's communications – which enraged the bar-barian more than ever. What made matters worse was the fact that Raoul pleaded vigorously against undertaking war with

the Romans. First, he argued that the monk in Robert's army
was an impostor and a cheat, impersonating the Emperor
Michael, and the whole story about him was an invention.
He said that he had seen Michael, after his dethronement in
Constantinople, wearing a miserable garment of some dark
colour and living in a monastery. He had taken special care to
see with his own eyes the deposed emperor. Secondly, he
reported also the event which he had heard of on his way back.
My father, you see, had seized power as I shall describe in detail
later, and had driven Botaneiates from his throne, had sent for
Constantine, Doukas' son, who of all men under the sun was
the most illustrious, and had given him for a second time a
share in the government.[61]

This news Raoul had heard on his journey and now, in an
attempt to persuade Robert to abandon his preparations for
war, he informed him of it. 'How shall we be able to make war
on Alexios with any justice,' he said, 'when it was Botaneiates
who started the wrong and deprived your daughter Helena of
the Roman throne? What happens to us at the hands of others
should not bring war on those who have done no wrong; and
if the war has no just pretext, then all is lost – ships, arms, men,
the whole of our military preparation.'

These words irritated Robert even more. He raved madly
and almost attacked the ambassador with his bare hands. For
his part, the fictitious Doukas, the Pseudo-Emperor Michael,
whom we have called Raiktor, was indignant and angry. He
did not know how to contain his wrath when it was so clearly
proved that he was not the emperor, but a sham. Robert was
filled with rage against Raoul in any case, but when Raoul's
brother Roger deserted to the Romans and gave intimate details
of all his preparations for the war, in his desire to commit some
dreadful harm against him, he threatened the man with death
on the spot. Raoul, however, wasted no time at all in fleeing to
Bohemond. Finding in him the nearest place of refuge, as it
were, he became a fugitive.

In tragic fashion Raiktor, too, uttered the most blood-
curdling threats against Raoul's brother, the deserter; with loud
cries and slapping his thigh with his right hand, he begged

Robert: 'I ask of you only one thing: if I get my hands on the crown and sit again on the throne, Roger is handed to me. If I don't consign him to the most horrible death and crucify him in the middle of the city, then let me suffer such and such at the hands of God.' In the midst of this story I cannot help laughing at the silly and farcical behaviour of these men, or rather at their mutual bragging. For Robert, of course, this rogue was a mere bait, a sort of projection of his kinsman the emperor, so he constantly exhibited him in the towns he visited and stirred to rebellion all whom he could reach and persuade. When the war and his luck went well for him, he intended to see to his neck and dispatch him with a laugh. After all, when the hunt is over the bait is no use to anyone. The monk, for his part, was being fed on false hopes: it might somehow come true, that he might end up with some share in power – such things often do happen, contrary to expectation. He would certainly grasp power with a tight fist, feeling sure that the Roman people and army would never call the barbarian Robert to the throne. In the meantime he would make use of him as a tool to achieve all his wicked designs. When I think of it I cannot but smile, and a wry smile rises to my lips as I slowly move my pen in the lamplight.

16. Robert concentrated his whole force at Brindisi, ships and men. The ships numbered 150, and the soldiers, all told, came to 30,000, each ship carrying 200 men with armour and horses. The expedition was equipped in this manner because they would probably meet the enemy in full armour and mounted when they landed. He intended to disembark at the town of Epidamnos, which in accordance with modern tradition we will call Dyrrakhion. He had thought of crossing from Otranto to Nikopolis and of capturing Naupaktos and all the country and forts round it, but as the distance by sea between these two towns was far greater than the voyage from Brindisi to Dyrrakhion, he chose the latter; it was not only the fastest route, but he was looking to the comfort of his men, for it was the winter season and the sun being on its way to the southern hemisphere and approaching the Tropic of Capricorn, the daylight hours were shortened. Rather than leave Otranto

at daybreak and voyage by night with possible heavy weather, he preferred to cross from Brindisi under full sail. The Adriatic is not so wide at this point, so the distance by sea is correspondingly shorter. He did not leave his son Roger behind, as he had originally intended, having assigned to him the lordship of Apulia; for some unknown reason, he changed his mind and included him in his retinue after all.

On the voyage to Dyrrakhion a side expedition made him master of the strongly fortified town of Corfu and some other of our forts. He received hostages from Lombardy and Apulia, raised money and exacted tribute from the whole country and looked forward to a landing at Dyrrakhion. The *doux* of all Illyrikon at that time happened to be George Monomakhatos, who had been appointed by the Emperor Botaneiates. Yet in the first place he had refused the mission, and it was by no means easy to persuade him to undertake this duty, but something compelled him to go. There were two barbarian servants of the emperor, Scythians called Borilos and Germanos, who were annoyed with Monomakhatos and were always inventing some more terrible charge against him, which they then reported to the emperor. They strung together stories to their hearts' content and so inflamed the latter's wrath against Monomakhatos that one day he turned to the Empress Maria and said, 'I suspect this Monomakhatos of being an enemy of the Roman Empire.'

John, an Alanian, heard this remark; being a friend of Monomakhatos and knowing that the Scythians in their venom brought continual accusations against him, he told him in full what had been said. He advised him to consult his own interests. However, Monomakhatos kept his head and approached the emperor and soothed him with considerable flattery. Then he quickly grasped the opportunity of service at Dyrrakhion. Arrangements were made for him to go to Epidamnos, and he received written instructions with regard to his office as *doux*. On the next day he left Constantinople for Epidamnos and Illyrikon, the Scythians Germanos and Borilos most gladly hastening his departure.

Somewhere near the so-called Pege, where a church has been built in honour of my mistress, the Virgin and Mother of Our

Lord, and which is celebrated among Byzantion's churches,[62] he met my father, Alexios. When they saw one another, Monomakhatos was the first to speak, telling Alexios with considerable emotion how he was being exiled because of his friendship for him, how the Scythians Borilos and Germanos, who envied the whole world, had set in motion against him the full force of their jealousy and were actually banishing him on a hollow pretext from his friends and beloved city. When he had ended his dramatic and detailed account of the calumnies whispered in the emperor's ear and the sufferings he had endured at the hands of these slaves, the *domestikos* of the West thought it right to comfort him to the best of his ability. Alexios was well fitted to raise up a soul weighed down by misfortune. Finally he told him that God would in truth avenge such wrongs and assured him that he remembered his friendship. Thus the one set out for Dyrrakhion, the other, left behind, went back to the imperial city.

When Monomakhatos reached Dyrrakhion he learnt of the military preparations of the tyrant Robert and also the revolt of Alexios.[63] He carefully weighed his own situation in the balance. To all appearances he was hostile to both, but in fact he was planning something more subtle than open warfare. The *megas domestikos* had written to him about what had occurred. He said he had been threatened with blinding; because of this and the cruel exercise of power he was resisting the tyrants; for his friend's sake Monomakhatos must rise in rebellion and send him money, collected from any source that was possible. 'We need money,' he wrote, 'and without it none of the things can be done which need to be done.'

Well, Monomakhatos did not send money, but he treated the envoys with kindness and put in their hands a letter instead. The gist of it was as follows: he still respected his old friendship and promised to do so in the future. But with regard to the money he requested, Monomakhatos stated that he would very much like to send him as much as he wanted. 'But,' he added, 'I cannot; it's a matter of principle. I was sent here by the Emperor Botaneiates. I gave him a pledge of loyalty. Even you would not look upon me as an honourable man, devoted to his rulers, if I yielded to your demands at once. However, if Divine Providence should judge you worthy of the throne, as I was in the first place a faithful friend, so in the future I shall be a most faithful servant.'

Monomakhatos dashed off this letter to my father. He was trying to win over both at once – my father, I mean, and Botaneiates. In addition he made more overt proposals to the barbarian Robert and broke out into open revolt. He is in my opinion much to be condemned for this. But somehow it seems that men of such character are naturally inconstant, changing their colours again and again according to the changes of government. All such men contribute nothing to the common good, but when it comes to themselves they are most circumspect, arranging what suits their convenience and theirs alone. Yet, even so, they generally fail. But these speculations have carried me off the main road of my history; we must get my horse back on the right path again – he got out of hand.

Well, even before these events, Robert had been madly impatient to cross over to our country and dreamed of Dyrrakhion; now he was all the more inflamed with a quite uncontrollable desire to make the naval expedition. He hurried on his soldiers and encouraged them with buoyant speeches. Monomakhatos' scheme had worked in that direction; he proceeded to build up another place of refuge elsewhere. By his letters he won the friendship of Bodin and Michael, commanders of Dalmatia,[64] and influenced their judgement with gifts, thereby opening up for himself by underhand means all kinds of doors. For if he failed with Robert and Alexios, if both rejected him, he would at once ride to Dalmatia and side with Bodin and Michael. If, in fact, the former pair should prove openly hostile, he could still place his hopes with Michael and Bodin to whom he might flee should Alexios' or Robert's men attack him.

So much for them. Now is the right moment for me to turn to the reign of my father and explain how and with what resources he came to rule. The events of his life before then I do not intend to speak of, but rather to give a full account of his successes or failures as emperor – if on the journey we are about to make we do find some temporary lapses, so be it. For if I should discover some action of his not commendable, I will not spare him because he is my father, nor shall I course lightly over his triumphs because of an undercurrent of suspicion that a daughter, writing of her father, may be biased. In both cases we would be doing injustice to the truth. As I have remarked on several occasions before, my object is to tell the truth, and the subject of my history is my father, the emperor. Let us then leave Robert at the point where the history has brought him in, and now consider the acts of Alexios. His battles and wars against Robert we shall reserve for a later book.

BOOK II

1. If the reader wishes to know the birthplace and family background of the Emperor Alexios, we would refer him to the writings of my husband the *kaisar*. From the same source they will also be able to find information about the Emperor Nikephoros Botaneiates. Isaac and Alexios had an elder brother, Manuel, the firstborn of all the children descended from John Komnenos, my grandfather on my father's side. He was appointed commander-in-chief of the whole of Asia by the previous ruler Romanos Diogenes, while Isaac became *doux* of Antioch after being elected by lot.[1] The two brothers fought many wars and battles, and many also were the trophies they set up over their enemies. In succession to them my father Alexios was promoted commander-in-chief by the then emperor Michael Doukas and sent out to fight Roussel.

The Emperor Nikephoros too saw in him a most capable strategist, and when he heard how while serving in the east with his brother Isaac he had proved himself valiant beyond his years in different campaigns, and how he had routed Roussel, he came to treat him with marked affection, no less in fact than Isaac. Both had a special place in his heart, as he looked on them with pleasure and occasionally invited them to share his table.

This inflamed jealousy, particularly in the case of the aforementioned Slavonic barbarians, Borilos and Germanos. These men saw that the emperor was kindly disposed towards the young brothers – and yet, despite the darts of envy to which they were so often exposed, they still remained unharmed. Borilos and Germanos were consumed by envy, for the

emperor, recognizing the fine reputation he enjoyed among
all, appointed Alexios commander-in-chief in the west and
honoured him with the rank of *proedros* – and this even though
he was barely past adolescence. We have already recorded the
number of his victories in the west and spoken of rebels subdued
and brought alive to the emperor as prisoners of war; enough
has been said on that subject. But these events, far from giving
pleasure to the barbarian slaves, fired their burning jealousy
even more. They murmured a lot and plotted evil against
Alexios and Isaac. They assiduously briefed against them, telling the emperor many things in private, but also slandering
them in public, and even having others do the same; in their
eagerness to rid themselves of the brothers they used any and
every device they could.

In such difficult circumstances the Komnenoi decided that
they must conciliate the officers in charge of the women's
quarters and through them gain the goodwill of the empress
even more than before. They were charming men and had wit
enough to soften a heart of stone. Isaac indeed had already
achieved success, for he had been chosen by the empress to
marry her own cousin;[2] he was in word and deed a true aristo-
crat, in very many ways recalling my own father. Now that his
own affairs prospered, he was greatly concerned for his brother:
as Alexios had supported him in the matter of this marriage, so
he was zealous that Alexios should not be less in favour with
the empress. According to legend Orestes and Pylades were
friends,[3] and so much affection did they have for one another
that in the crisis of battle each ignored the enemies attacking
himself and bore aid to his friend, shielding him with his own
breast from the volleys of arrows. One could see a similar
affection in the case of Isaac and Alexios, for each was willing
to face dangers for the other, and they shared prizes of valour
and honours, and in general the good fortune of each other, so
great was their mutual attachment.

In this way, thanks to the Providence of God, the interests of
Isaac were assured. Not long afterwards the officers of the
women's quarters were persuaded by Isaac to cajole the empress
to adopt Alexios as her son. She listened to their words and

when the two brothers on the appointed day came to the palace, she adopted him in the ceremony long established for such cases. Thus the future *megas domestikos* of the western armies was relieved of much anxiety from then onwards, and subsequently they both visited the palace often. After performing the act of adoration due to the ruling couple and waiting for a short time, they would go to the empress. Thereupon the envy flared up against them even more fiercely – as many persons made clear to them.

Being afraid therefore that both might be caught in the snares of their enemies, with no one to protect them, the Komnenoi sought with God's help some means of ensuring their safety. Together with their mother they turned over many ideas; multiple plans were thoroughly examined on many occasions. In the end they found one hope, man-made that is, of salvation – to approach the empress when some plausible excuse presented itself, and confide in her their secret. The plan, however, was concealed and divulged to nobody at all; like fishermen they were careful not to frighten away the catch before they were ready. What they intended to do, in fact, was to run away, but they were afraid to tell her that, in case she disclosed their plan to the emperor, being concerned both for him and for themselves. The original scheme was abandoned and a new idea took its place; they were adept at seizing any opportunity that might present itself.

2. By now the emperor was too old to have a son and fearing the moment when death would inevitably cut him off, he was looking for a successor. There was a certain Synadenos, of Anatolian origin, of illustrious descent and fine appearance, thoughtful and of strong physique, on the verge of manhood, who apart from other considerations was a family relative of Nikephoros.[4] It was to him, in preference to all others, that the emperor planned to bequeath the imperial throne as a family heritage. It was a poor decision. He might have left the crown to Constantine, the empress's son, and in a way it was his right, because of his grandfather and father. Had Nikephoros done so, he would have ensured his own safety to the end; at the same time it would have been a just settlement. The empress,

moreover, would have had more confidence in him and have been better disposed. The old man did not realize the unfairness and inexpediency of his plans, and was unaware that he was sowing trouble for himself.

The empress knew of these rumours and was much grieved at the thought of the danger which threatened her son. Although she was downhearted, she betrayed her sorrow to no one, but it did not escape the notice of the Komnenoi. Here was the opportunity for which they had been waiting. They decided to approach her. Their mother gave Isaac a pretext for an interview. His brother Alexios was to go with him. When they appeared before her, Isaac spoke: 'In the last few days, Your Majesty, you have changed. It seems to us that you are worried by private cares and because you have no one to whom you can confide your secret you have lost heart.' She, unwilling as yet to reveal anything but sighing deeply, replied, 'There is no need to question someone living far from home like that; being in a foreign land is reason enough for sorrow. Heaven knows the troubles I have had, one after another – and soon, apparently, there will be more in store for me.'[5] The brothers kept their distance and said nothing. With eyes fixed on the ground and both hands covered, they stood there for a moment in deep thought, and then after making the usual obeisance went home much distressed.

On the next day they came again to talk with her, but seeing that she was in a more cheerful mood they both approached her. 'You are our empress,' they said, 'and we, your most faithful servants, are prepared to suffer absolutely anything on Your Majesty's behalf. We beg you not to let any worry confuse or perplex you.' At this, they swore an oath to her and relieved her of all suspicion. Already they had guessed her secret, for they were quick-witted and shrewd, skilled at ascertaining from the briefest of remarks the hidden thoughts that lie deep in the hearts of men. Immediately they offered their help, and having given clear proof in many ways of their loyalty they promised to answer bravely her every call for aid. With great enthusiasm they agreed, following the apostle's bidding, to rejoice with her when she rejoiced, to feel pain with her when she was grieved.

They asked her to regard them as fellow-countrymen, as friends and relatives, adding this one request, that if any information was laid against them by their jealous rivals, in her hearing or the emperor's, they might be told at once; otherwise they might fall unawares into the traps set by their enemies. They asked for this favour, bade her to be of good courage and said that with God's help they would zealously give all possible assistance; so far at least as they were concerned her son Constantine would not lose his throne. What is more, they were willing to confirm their assurances by oaths. There was no time to lose, they said, because of their detractors.

The whole thing was a great relief to them. They recovered their spirits and in future spoke to the emperor looking much happier. Both of them, and Alexios in particular, had the art of concealing their secret thoughts and private designs behind assumed expressions. The burning jealousy of the two powerful slaves flared up into a really great conflagration, but from now on, because of the newly made pact with the empress, nothing that was said about them to the emperor escaped their notice. They knew that their enemies were plotting to do away with them. As a result, then, they no longer went together to the palace in their normal way, but each on alternate days. It was a wise provision, worthy of Palamedes. If by chance one was caught through the furtive machinations of the Scythians, the other would survive; they would not both fall into the snare together. Such were the precautions they took, but things did not turn out for them as they suspected, for they proved too strong for the schemers, as the narrative will now make abundantly clear.

3. The town of Kyzikos was captured by the Turks[6] and when the emperor heard the news he immediately sent for Alexios Komnenos. On that particular day it happened that Isaac was present at the palace. When he saw his brother enter contrary to the agreement they had made, he went up to him, asking why he was there. Alexios at once told him the reason. 'The emperor summoned me.' Both therefore went in and made the customary obeisance. As it was time for a meal, the emperor invited them to stay for a while and required them to share his

table. They were separated, one sitting on the right, the other on the left, opposite one another. After a short pause they began to assess the others there and noticed that they were whispering to each other, looking sullen. The young men feared a sudden attack: the slaves must have devised some imminent danger for them. In desperation they cast furtive glances at one another.

For a long time they had been winning the friendship of the emperor's retinue, by kindly words, by courtesies and all kinds of polite attentions; their affability had even persuaded the cook to regard them with a friendly eye. One of Isaac's servants approached this man and said: 'Tell my master that Kyzikos has fallen. A letter has come from there with this news.' He at once served the food on the table and at the same time in a low voice told Isaac what his servant had said. Isaac passed on the message to his brother by slight movements of his lips. Alexios easily grasped what he meant, as quick as lightning reading his lips. The burden of anxiety was lifted; both breathed easily again. When they had regrouped, they considered what reply they should have ready, if someone questioned them about Kyzikos; they also thought what advice they should offer if the emperor asked their opinion.

In the midst of these calculations, he did look towards them and taking it for granted that they knew nothing about it told them that Kyzikos had been taken. Ready now to comfort the emperor's soul, troubled as it was by the ravaging of his towns, they raised his fallen spirits and revived him with fine hopes, assuring him that Kyzikos would be recovered easily. 'All that matters,' they said, 'is that Your Majesty should be well. The besiegers of the town will surely pay sevenfold for what they have done.' At the time the emperor was delighted with their reply. He allowed them to take their leave from the banquet and passed the rest of the day freed of his worries.

After that the Komnenoi made it their business to attend the palace regularly, to befriend the emperor's retinue even more, to give no chance whatever to their adversaries of plotting against them, no excuse at all for hating them; on the contrary they set out to win the affection, sympathy and outspoken support of all. They were especially determined to win over the

Empress Maria and convince her that they were wholly devoted
to her in mind and soul. Isaac could speak freely to her because
he was a relative, having married her cousin, and my father
had no less access to her because of his close relationship.
His adoption, in particular, furnished an excellent reason for
visiting her and doing so without arousing suspicion. This way
a veil was thrown over the envy of evil-doers – not that he
was unaware of their blind fury and the feeble character of
Nikephoros. Naturally the brothers were anxious not to lose
Maria's goodwill; if they did, they would fall victim to their
enemies, for weak-minded folk are quite unstable, moving with
the current, first one way, then another, like Euripos.[7]

4. The slaves,[8] seeing all this and realizing that their own
scheme was making no progress – men like Isaac and Alexios
could not easily be destroyed and the emperor's kindly concern
for them grew daily stronger – formed another plan altogether,
after much debate and having decided on one thing and then
changing their minds. And what was that plan? Their idea was
to summon the young men one night, without the knowledge
of the emperor, and get rid of them by gouging out their eyes
on a trumped-up charge.

The Komnenoi got to hear of it. They knew they were in
imminent danger. With great reluctance they decided their one
hope of safety lay in rebellion; hard necessity had driven them
to it. Why should they wait for the iron rod to take out their
eyes and extinguish the light in them? Nevertheless, they kept
their plan strictly to themselves. Not long after, though, Alexios
received instructions to bring in a party of troops; they were to
be equipped for war against the Agarenes[9] who had sacked
Kyzikos. At the time he was *domestikos* of the West. Seizing
this opportunity, he sent a letter to those officers who were well
disposed to him and their men. Thus alerted they all hurried to
the capital.

Meanwhile, prompted by Borilos, one of the two Scythians,
someone went to the emperor and asked him if it was his desire
that the *megas domestikos* should bring all the forces into the
capital. Alexios was at once sent for and was interrogated as to
whether this was true. He answered without hesitation: he did

not deny that an army was being brought in at his command, but he argued convincingly against the story that the whole army was being concentrated in the city from all parts of the empire. 'The army is in fact dispersed,' he said, 'and individual men have come here from all provinces on receipt of my order. Those who see them arriving here in groups from different parts of the empire imagine that all the army is gathering; they are deceived by appearances, nothing more.' Borilos protested vigorously, but Alexios' explanation proved more convincing, and he won the emperor's unqualified approval. Germanos, who was a more sincere man, did not attack Alexios at all. However, since even these accusations failed to stir the emperor to take action against the *domestikos*, the slaves, grasping an opportunity (it was evening time), set an ambush for the Komnenoi.

It is a fact that slaves are in any case by nature hostile to their masters, but if they cannot strike at them, they seize the chance to become intolerable to one another. Such at least was Alexios' experience of the character and spirit of these men. They were certainly not filled with animosity against the Komnenoi for the emperor's sake. Borilos, according to some people, coveted the throne; and as for Germanos, he was Borilos' accomplice in the plot and carefully helped him to lay the ambush. They talked among themselves about their plans and discussed how the affair would go their way. By now they were even speaking openly of things hitherto whispered in private.

Somebody, an Alanian by birth, heard what they said. He had the rank of *magistros*, had long been attached to the emperor and was counted among his friends. In the middle watch of the night, therefore, he left home, ran off to the Komnenoi and told the *megas domestikos* everything. Some say that the empress too was not altogether ignorant of his visit to the Komnenoi. Alexios took the man to his mother and Isaac. When they learnt this frightful news, they decided that the time had come to put into practice their secret plan; with God's aid they had to ensure their own safety.

Two days later the *domestikos* heard that the army was at Tzouroulos (a small place somewhere near the Thracian

frontier) and about the first watch of the night he went to visit
Pakourianos. (The latter was tiny of body, as the poet says, but
a mighty warrior, born of a noble family in Armenia.)[10] Alexios
told him the whole story – the anger of the slaves, their jealousy,
their long-continued feud against himself and his brother, their
sudden plot to blind them; it was not right, he said, to suffer
like slaves – better to do some noble deed and perish, if it should
come to that; a man of spirit should die thus.

Pakourianos listened to all that he said, and knowing that
in such matters there was no time to lose and they must act
bravely at once, he said, 'If you leave here at daybreak
tomorrow, I will follow you and I will fight willingly at your
side; but if you defer your plan to the next day, I must warn
you that I shall go to the emperor without delay and denounce
both you and your men without hesitation.' 'Since I see that
you are concerned for my safety – and that is truly the work of
God – I will not refuse your advice,' said Alexios. 'But we
must do one thing more – take oaths to give assurance to our
agreement.' So they exchanged pledges under oath. Alexios
swore that if God elevated him to the imperial throne he would
promote Pakourianos to the rank of *domestikos*, which he
himself then held. After that Alexios Komnenos took his leave
of Pakourianos and went off to another fine soldier, Houmpertopoulos.[11] He told him of his object, explained the reason for
it and called on him for help. He agreed at once. 'You will have
my wholehearted support,' he said. 'I too am ready to risk my
life for you.'

There were other factors that inclined these men to serve
Alexios, but his exceptional courage and wisdom above all won
their loyalty. They had an extraordinary affection for him,
because he was a very liberal man, with hands unusually ready
to dispense gifts, even though he was not by any means seriously
rich. He was certainly not a man who coveted or pursued riches
for their own sake. It is not customary to judge a man's liberality
by the amount of money he distributes, but rather by the character of the giver. One could define a person of few resources
who gives within his means as liberal; on the other hand, the
very rich man who buries his wealth underground, or provides

for the needy less than he could afford, might not improperly be described as a second Croesus or a gold-crazed Midas, a greedy niggardly skinflint. These men I have mentioned had known for a long time that Alexios was endowed with all the virtues, so that they both desired and prayed for his accession to the throne.

After exchanging oaths with Houmpertopoulos too, Alexios set off home at speed and told his friends all that had happened. It was during the night of Sunday in Cheese week[12] that my father made these arrangements. On the next day, just as the sun was rising, he left the city with his friends. It was because of this that the people, who admired Alexios for his dash and wit, made up a little song in his honour. It was composed in the common idiom, but caught in a neat way the general drift of the matter, emphasizing his prescience about the plot and the measures he took to combat it. The actual words of the ditty were as follows: 'On Saturday in Cheese week their plan went phut! Alexis, hurrah!, had used his nut. Alexis, he's your boy. On Monday at dawn the hawk was off and out of sight.' The meaning of this popular ditty was roughly this: 'On the Saturday of Cheese week, Alexios, you did wonderfully well because of your wit; but on the Monday off you flew, like some falcon soaring on high, away from the scheming barbarians.'

5. Anna Dalassene,[13] the mother of the Komnenoi, had arranged a marriage between the grandson of Botaneiates and the daughter of Manuel, her eldest son. She was afraid now that the youth's tutor might tell the emperor if he found out about the plot. To avoid this, she devised an excellent plan. She ordered all her household to gather in the evening for a visit to the holy churches for worship; it was her custom to attend the sanctuaries regularly. The instruction was carried out. When all were present, in the usual way, the horses were led out of the stables and a show was made of carefully arranging saddlecloths appropriate for the women. Botaneiates' grandson, with his tutor, was asleep – a special apartment had been set aside for them.

About first watch the Komnenoi, who were about to arm and ride away from the capital, closed the gates and handed the

keys to their mother. They also closed the doors of the room in
which the young Botaneiates was sleeping, without making any
noise; in fact the double doors were not absolutely fast-closed
in case the sound should wake him. Most of the night had gone
by while these things were happening. Before first cockcrow
they opened the gates and taking with them their mother, sisters, wives and children went off to the Forum of Constantine
on foot. They took leave of them there and ran in great haste
to the Palace of Blakhernai, while the women hurried to the
church of Hagia Sophia.

Botaneiates' tutor meanwhile had been roused and realizing
what had happened went out to look for them with a torch in
his hand. He soon found them, before they had quite reached
the Church of the Forty Saints.[14] Dalassene, the mother of those
excellent sons, saw him. 'Some people have denounced us to
the emperor, I'm sure,' she said. 'I will go to the holy churches
and get what help I can from them, and when day breaks, I will
come back to the palace. So go now and when the porters open
the gates, tell them of our coming.' He at once hurried off to
do what he had been told.

The women proceeded on to the sanctuary of Bishop Nicholas, which is still called 'The Refuge' to this day. It is near the
Great Church and was built long ago as a sanctuary for people
being sought on criminal charges; in fact it is an annexe of
Hagia Sophia and was, I believe, purposely constructed by
our ancestors for all accused persons, for if they entered its
doors they were freed from the penalty of the laws. The
emperors and *kaisars* of old, you see, were much concerned for
the welfare of their subjects. The verger, who lived in the place,
was in no hurry to open the doors to them; he asked who
they were and from where they came. Someone of their party
answered: 'Women from the east. They've spent all their money
on necessary purchases and want to worship quickly before
going home.' Without more ado he opened the doors and let
them in.

On the next morning the emperor called a meeting of the
senate, having learnt what the Komnenoi had been up to, and
naturally in his speech launched a stinging attack on the *domes-*

tikos. At the same time he sent Straboromanos and a certain
Euphemianos to the women, summoning them to the palace.
Dalassene gave her reply: 'Tell the emperor this: my sons are
faithful servants of Your Majesty, and gladly bearing allegiance
to you in all things they have not spared soul or body, being
always the first to expose themselves to danger in fighting
bravely for your empire. But jealousy, which cannot bear Your
Majesty's goodwill and kindness to them, has brought them
into great and hourly peril. And when their enemies planned to
gouge out their eyes, my sons, who had discovered the plot,
found the danger intolerable, as well as unfair, and left the
city, not as rebels but as faithful servants with three objects in
view: to escape imminent peril, to convince Your Majesty of
the conspiracy against them and to implore Your Majesty's
protection.'

The envoys pressed them hard to return, but Dalassene grew
angry. 'Allow me,' she said, 'to enter the church of God for
worship. It's absurd that when I have reached its gates I should
be prevented from going in and praying to Our Lady, the
Immaculate Mother of God, to intercede for me with God and
the emperor's soul.' It was a reasonable request and they
granted it. She was allowed to enter. As if she were weighed
down with old age and worn out by grief, she walked slowly,
through in reality she was pretending to be weary, and when
she approached the actual entrance to the sanctuary made two
genuflexions; on the third she sank to the floor and taking firm
hold of the sacred doors, cried in a loud voice: 'Unless my hands
are cut off, I will not leave this holy place, except on one
condition: that I receive the emperor's cross as guarantee of
safety.'

Straboromanos took off the cross which he wore on his
breast and gave it to her. 'It is not from you,' she said, 'that I am
asking for a guarantee; I want the safeguard from the emperor
himself. I will not be satisfied with just any little cross offered
to me; it must be a cross of reasonable size.' She demanded this,
so that when the oath was taken on it all might see; if the
promise were made over a small cross, the confirmation of the
oath would probably be invisible to most spectators. 'It is to

the emperor that I appeal for judgement and mercy. Go away and tell him so.'

Her daughter-in-law, Isaac's wife (she had come into the church when the gates opened for the morning hymn), removed the veil that covered her face and said to them: 'Let her go, if she wishes, but we are not leaving this church without a guarantee, even if we have to die.' The envoys therefore went away and told the emperor everything. They saw how determined the women were and how their behaviour grew more reckless; moreover, they feared a commotion. Nikephoros was a good man and touched by the woman's words sent her the required cross and with it his guarantee, as she had requested. She then left God's holy church. The emperor ordered that she be confined, with her daughters and daughters-in-law, in the convent of Petrion near the Sidera.[15] Her kinswoman, the daughter-in-law of the *Kaisar* John, was also sent for (she had the rank of *protovestiaria*) from the sanctuary in Blakhernai, built in honour of Our Lady the Mother of God,[16] and she too was committed on the emperor's orders to the Petrion convent. Their cellars, granaries and all their storehouses were to be kept free of all interference.

Every morning both women approached the guards and asked if any news had arrived from their sons, and the guards, who behaved towards them in a very straightforward manner, told them all they had heard. The *protovestiaria*, being generous of hand and heart, and wishing to conciliate the warders, instructed them to take from the food supplies whatever they wanted for their own use, since the women were after all allowed to bring in everything they needed without opposition. After that the guards became more eager to supply information and as a result not a single detail of what was going on escaped the women.

6. So much for them. The rebels[17] reached the gate near the 'bracelet' by Blakhernai and having forced the locks gained free access to the imperial stables. Some of the horses they left there, after slitting their hind legs with their swords; all those which seemed more useful they took. From there they rode fast to the monastery called the Kosmidion on the outskirts of the city.[18]

At this point I will interrupt the narrative to make the story clearer. There they found the *protovestiaria*, whom I have mentioned above, before she had been summoned by the emperor, as already described. They took their leave of her as they were riding off and managed to persuade George Palaiologos[19] to accompany them; actually they compelled him to do so.

They had not yet revealed their plan to him, because they suspected him – for a good reason: George's father was extremely devoted to the emperor and to tell him of the revolt would not be without its dangers. At first Palaiologos was not amenable; he produced many objections and rebuked them for disloyalty; and he told them that, when they reflected on it, they would, as the proverb has it, regret their behaviour. However, when the *protovestiaria*, who was Palaiologos' mother-in-law, insisted vehemently that he must go with them and even added the most awful threats, he agreed to do so.

From then on he began to concern himself with the women, his own wife Anna and his mother-in-law Maria. The latter was of Bulgarian descent, endowed with such effortless beauty and perfect symmetry of face and form that no woman, it seems, was more lovely than she in that particular generation. It was natural then that Palaiologos and Alexios should be concerned about her. The men of Alexios' retinue were all of the opinion that the women should be taken away; some wanted to take them to a fortress, but Palaiologos felt they should go to the Church of the Theometor in Blakhernai. His advice prevailed. Without delay they took them away and entrusted them to the care of the Holy Mother of the Word who encompasses all. The men themselves went back to the place from which they had set out and considered what to do. 'You must go,' said Palaiologos, 'but I will soon catch you up, bringing my money with me.' It happened that all his movable wealth was deposited there. The others therefore lost no time in setting out on their agreed route, while he loaded his money on the monks' baggage animals and followed after them. He arrived safely with the beasts at Tzouroulos (a Thracian village), and by good fortune they all joined the army which had concentrated there on the orders of the *domestikos*.

Thinking that they ought to inform the *Kaisar* John Doukas of their adventures, they sent a messenger to tell him about the rebellion. John was living on his estate at Moroboundos. The messenger reached it in the early hours of the morning and stood outside the doors of the house asking for the *kaisar*. His grandson John, who was only a young boy and for that reason constantly with the *kaisar*, saw him and ran inside to rouse his grandfather who was asleep. He announced that a rebellion had broken out. Astonished to hear these words John boxed his ears and, telling him not to talk such nonsense, pushed him away. After a short interval the boy came back again with the same news; he also brought the message addressed to John by the Komnenoi.

At one point in the letter there was a very clever veiled reference to the revolt: 'We have prepared a very fine dish, not without rich savoury sauce. If you would like to share the feast, come as soon as you can to sit with us at the perfect banquet.' John thereupon gave orders to bring in the messenger, having first seated himself, leaning on his right elbow. The man described the whole affair. The *kaisar*'s first reaction was to cover his eyes with his hands, exclaiming, 'Oh dear me!' But after stroking his beard for a little while, like a man in deep thought, he came to a firm decision – to join in the uprising with them. At once he called his grooms, mounted his horse and took the road to the Komnenoi.

On the way he met a certain Byzantios who was carrying a large sum of gold and returning to the capital. In the usual Homeric way John asked him, 'Who are you? Where do you come from?' And when he learnt that the man had with him a considerable quantity of gold collected in taxes and that he was taking it to the treasury, he urged him to stay there with himself, promising that at daybreak he could go wherever he wished. The man protested angrily at this, but John pressed him more urgently and in the end persuaded him to agree. It was typical of John: he had a way with words, had a ready wit and a quick tongue, like a second Aiskhines or Demosthenes.[20] So he took the man along with him and spent that night in an inn of some kind. With every mark of friendship he invited Byzantios to share his table. After allowing him to have a good rest, he kept him there.

About dawn, when the sun was rising fast on the eastern horizon, Byzantios saddled his horses, impatient to ride straight to the capital, but the *kaisar* saw him. 'Wait,' he said, 'and go along with us.' Byzantios neither knew where John was going nor had he the least idea why he had been treated in such a friendly way, and he again became angry. He began to have suspicions about the *kaisar* and the *kaisar*'s friendly gestures. John advanced on him and held him back. As Byzantios would not listen, he changed his tactics and spoke in a harsher tone, with threats of what would happen if he did not obey. When he still refused, John commanded all his baggage to be loaded on his own animals; he then gave the order to set out along the road, but Byzantios, he said, could go wherever he wanted without interference. Byzantios had completely abandoned any intention of returning to the palace; he was afraid that when the treasury officials saw him empty-handed he would be thrown into prison. On the other hand he was unwilling to retrace his steps, because of the unsettled conditions and confusion which had affected everything since the revolt of the Komnenoi had come into the open. So he followed the *kaisar*, but did so reluctantly.

John was rather fortunate at this stage, for as he set out he met some Turks who had recently crossed the River Euros. He reined in his horse and asked where they had come from and what was their destination. He promised to give them much money and grant them all sorts of favours if they would come with him to join Komnenos. The Turks agreed there and then, and John, wishing to confirm the arrangement, required their leaders to take an oath. At once they swore on oath, after their own fashion, to fight with great enthusiasm on the side of Komnenos.

Thus John went on his way accompanied by these Turks to join the Komnenoi. These in turn sighted him a long way off and were more than delighted by the fresh booty. My father Alexios most of all could not contain himself for joy. He came on ahead of the others, threw his arms round the *kaisar* and embraced him repeatedly. And what happened next? Later, at the instigation of the *kaisar*, who was in a hurry, they set forth on the road to the capital.

All the inhabitants of the small towns met them spontaneously and acclaimed Alexios as emperor, except for the people of Orestias,[21] who remained loyal to the party of Botaneiates; they had long been angry with Alexios because of the capture of Bryennios. When they arrived at Athyras they rested; on the next day the march was resumed and they reached Skhitza (a village in Thrace), setting up camp there.

7. Everyone was excited, anxiously awaiting the outcome and hoping to see his own favourite proclaimed emperor. The majority prayed that the throne would fall to Alexios, but Isaac's supporters had not given up hope; they did their best to win the support of everyone for their man. To all appearances the division was irreconcilable, some keen for Isaac to become ruler of the empire, some for Alexios. Among those present then were Alexios' closest relatives: the above-mentioned *Kaisar* John Doukas, a man who gave good counsel and in the most competent fashion put it into practice, as I myself occasionally experienced; Michael and John,[22] his grandsons, were present too; as was of course George Palaiologos, the husband of their sister. All these were present, working hard to canvass votes for their own choice, pulling all the strings, as they say, and cleverly making use of every device to have Alexios proclaimed emperor. Thus they converted everyone to their way of thinking and Isaac's support gradually ebbed away.

For the *Kaisar* John simply proved irresistible; no one could rival his fine intellect, his tremendous stature, his majestic presence. What did the Doukai not do? What did they not say? What benefits did they not promise to the officers and to the rank and file of the army if Alexios was raised to the imperial throne? 'He will reward you,' they declared, 'with most magnificent gifts and honours, each according to his deserts – not haphazardly, like ignorant generals of no experience. Alexios has been your army commander for a long time, and the *megas domestikos* of the West; he has shared salt with you, fought bravely at your side in ambush and set battle, sparing neither body nor limb nor even life itself for your safety's sake, again and again crossing with you over mountain and plain, knowing the miseries of war and understanding you well, both as individuals and as a unit. He is dear to Ares, and more than anything, appreciates brave warriors.'

So much for the Doukai. Meanwhile Alexios himself treated Isaac with every respect, allowing him precedence at all times, whether through brotherly love or rather, it should be said, for the reason that the whole army was rallying to his side and was eager that he should win, but entirely ignored the claims of Isaac. Alexios therefore had the power and strength, as he saw that things would ultimately resolve in his favour. He nevertheless encouraged his brother to seek the throne. It involved no unpleasant risk, since the army to a man was determined to promote himself to the highest office; he could afford to flatter Isaac and make a pretence of yielding authority to him.

Time was being wasted then in these manoeuvres when one day the whole army was collected round the headquarters. There was intense excitement, every man praying that his own hopes would be fulfilled. Isaac stood up and taking the purple-dyed sandal[23] tried to put it on his brother's foot. Alexios objected again and again. 'Come,' said Isaac, 'it is through you that God wishes to recall our family to power.' And he reminded him of the prophecy made to him once by a man who appeared somewhere near Karpianos, as the two brothers were on their way home from the palace.

For at that place a man met them – or maybe he was a superior being; at all events, someone who really had exceptional clairvoyant powers. As he approached them bareheaded he had the appearance of a priest, white-haired, rough-bearded. He grasped Alexios by the leg and drew him down to his own level, as he was on foot and Alexios on horseback, and whispered in his ear this verse from the Psalms of David: 'Be earnest and prosper and govern with an eye to truth and mercy and justice.'[24] Then he added, 'Emperor Alexios.' Having said this in the manner of an oracle, he vanished. Alexios could not find him, although he looked everywhere in case he might catch

sight of him, and galloped at full speed in pursuit of him in case
he might lay hands on the man, to find out who he was and
whence he came. But the apparition had completely vanished.

When Alexios returned, his brother Isaac made many inquiries about the vision and begged him to tell his secret. He
persisted in his questions and although Alexios at first seemed
reluctant, he afterwards revealed the secret prophecy to him. In
speaking of it openly to his brother he explained the thing as
an hallucination and said it was humbug, but in his own heart,
when he recollected that priestly vision, he likened the old man
to the Theologian, the son of Thunder.[25]

Now when Isaac saw the prophecy being fulfilled, with words
being translated into action, he followed a more energetic
course and forcibly put on the purple sandal, especially when
he recognized the burning zeal of the whole army for Alexios.[26]
At that point the Doukai led the acclamations. Their support
derived from various reasons: one was that their kinswoman
Eirene, my mother, was the wife of my father by law. Their
blood relatives willingly followed their example and the rest of
the army took up the cry – their shouts almost reached the
heavens. It was indeed an extraordinary sight: here were men
who before had divided loyalties, prepared to face death rather
than disappointment of their hopes; now in one swift moment
they were so united in purpose that all traces of faction were
obliterated. One would have thought there never had been a
difference of opinion.

8. While these events occurred, a rumour spread that Melissenos was near Damalis[27] with a strong force, already proclaimed
emperor and clothed in the purple. At the time the Komnenoi
were not inclined to believe it, but Melissenos who had heard
of their activities quickly sent ambassadors to them with letters.
The envoys arrived and handed them over. They read something
like this:

'God has brought me safe and unharmed with my army as
far as Damalis. I have learnt about your adventures: how you
looked to your own safety after being rescued by the Providence
of God from the evil designs of those slaves and from their
fearful attempts on your lives. I myself am naturally disposed

to make an alliance with you because by the will of God we are related; sentiment too plays its part, and in my lasting friendship for you I yield to none of your blood relations, as God, who judges all, well knows. If we are to achieve a position of strength and absolute security, it is essential that we should decide on a common policy. Otherwise, instead of laying a firm foundation for the good government of the empire, we shall be at the mercy of every wind of change. Good government can without any doubt be achieved if, when you by God's will have captured the city, you administer the affairs of the west, once one or other of you has been proclaimed emperor, while I am permitted to govern Asia as my province; moreover I will wear the diadem and purple robes and receive the acclamation in the way that emperors normally do, with one of you. Thus, although we shall rule over different territories with separate administrations, we shall still pursue an identical policy. In these circumstances the empire, directed by both of us, will be free from party strife.'

The envoys did not receive a definite reply to this message, but on the next day the Komnenoi summoned them and after a long discussion pointed out the impossibility of Melissenos' proposal. Nevertheless they promised to make known to them their decision on the following day through George Manganes, who was responsible for their welfare. Meanwhile the siege operations were by no means relaxed; as far as possible skirmishing attacks continued to be made on the city walls. However, on the appointed day the envoys were informed of their decision: Melissenos was to be honoured with the rank of *kaisar*; he was to have the diadem, the acclamation and the other privileges due to his rank; he was also to be given the largest town in Thessaly – a great town in which a very beautiful church had been built dedicated to the famous martyr Demetrios; his tomb, much venerated, exudes an oil which is always effecting the most wonderful cures for those who approach it with faith.

The envoys were disappointed with these offers, but as their own terms were ignored and they saw the rebel's great preparations for the capture of the city, not to mention the enormous army under his command and the growing pressure

on themselves, they feared that once Constantinople had fallen
the Komnenoi in their confidence might refuse to fulfil even
their present promises. As a result, they asked for confirmation
in a chrysobull written with purple ink. Alexios, the newly
acclaimed emperor, immediately commissioned his secretary
George Manganes to write the chrysobull. For three days Manganes put off the task, using one excuse after another; on one
occasion he said that being overworked all day long he could
not finish the writing at night; on another that a spark had
fallen on the document in the night and burnt it to ashes; with
such excuses and others like them Manganes, true to the real
meaning of his name 'Cheater',[28] managed to keep putting
things off.

The Komnenoi now left Skhitza and soon reached Aretai,
near Constantinople and overlooking the plain.[29] If you view
it from below, it has the appearance of a hill with one side
facing the sea, a second facing Byzantion, while on the north
and west it is exposed to every wind. The water there is clear
and drinkable at all times, but the place is utterly devoid of
plants and trees; you would imagine that woodcutters had
completely stripped the hill. The Emperor Romanos Diogenes
had put up some fine buildings there, worthy of an emperor,
for brief holidays, because of its delightful situation and mild
climate. It was to this spot that the Komnenoi now came.
Attempts were made on the walls of the capital from there, not
with siege-engines or machines or catapults, because time did
not allow it, but by lightly-armed soldiers, archers, spearmen
and cavalry.

9. Botaneiates realized that the rebel army of the Komnenoi
was very numerous, extremely diverse, and was already closing
in on the gates of the city; he was also aware that Nikephoros
Melissenos was near Damalis with an army no less powerful
and with equal pretensions to the throne. His position was
desperate. It was impossible to resist on two fronts. Botaneiates'
spirit had been chilled by old age; however brave he had been
in his youth, he only breathed freely now as long as the walls
protected him, and he was becoming more and more frightened,
thinking seriously about abdicating. This terrified all his sup-

porters and threw them into a state of confusion. Everything pointed to a total collapse.

The Komnenoi however were of the opinion that Constantinople would not easily be captured: their own forces were composed of different elements, native and foreign, and where there is any heterogeneous group, discordant voices will surely be raised. Alexios, now newly shod, recognized the difficulty of his task. He also suspected the reliability of his men. So he adopted a new plan: he would tempt some of the defenders by flattery, and having stolen their allegiance, so take the city.

All night long he considered this scheme. At dawn he entered the *kaisar*'s tent and told him what he had decided, asking him to accompany him as he examined the walls and reviewed the battlements and their defenders (for they too were of different nationalities); thus he would determine how the capital could be taken. John was annoyed at this command, for he had only recently adopted monastic garb and he knew he would be laughed at by the soldiers on the walls and ramparts if he came near them in such a dress. And that is just what did happen, for when he followed Alexios against his will, they immediately spotted him from the walls and sneered at 'The Abbot' with certain ribald epithets. John scowled, and although inwardly he felt the insults, he made light of it and devoted all his attention to the task in hand. That is the way with men of strong character: they stand by their decisions, heedless of outside circumstances.

He asked the men on guard at the various towers who they were. He learnt that at one point the defenders were the so-called Immortals (a regiment unique to the Roman army); at another the Varangians from Thule (by these I mean the axe-bearing barbarians); at another the Nemitzoi[30] (these also belonged to a barbarian race which has for a long time served in the armed forces of the empire). He advised Alexios not to attack the Varangians, nor the Immortals, for the latter, being indigenous, are of necessity most loyal to the emperor and would rather lose their lives than be persuaded to plan any evil against him; and as for the Varangians, who bear on their shoulders the heavy iron sword, they regard loyalty to the

emperors and the protection of their persons as a family tradition, a kind of sacred trust and inheritance handed down
from generation to generation; this allegiance they preserve
inviolate and will never brook the slightest hint of betrayal. But
if Alexios put the Nemitzoi to the test he would not be far short
of the mark; he might have a chance of gaining entry to the city
through the tower that they guarded.

Alexios listened to the *kaisar*'s advice and accepted it like an
oracle from God. A man was sent therefore to the base of the
wall. He was to sound the leader of the Nemitzoi cautiously.
The latter, leaning over the battlements, after a lengthy exchange of words agreed to betray the city in the near future.
The soldier came back with this news. Alexios and his companions were overjoyed at this unexpected announcement and
with great enthusiasm made ready to mount their horses.

10. At this very moment the envoys from Melissenos were
most insistent as they demanded the chrysobull which they had
been promised. Manganes was at once sent for and told to
produce it. He said that the chrysobull had been written, but
protested strongly that the instruments essential for the
emperor's signature, including the pen, had been lost. Manganes was a dissembler, with a remarkable flair for discerning
the future and extracting some profit from the past; he was good
at estimating accurately the situation of the present, cunningly
altering it to suit his own purposes and obscuring certain
things to his own advantage. It was in order to keep Melissenos'
hopes in suspense that he deferred the writing of the chrysobull, for he feared that if it were sent to him before the proper
time, conferring on him the rank of *kaisar*, Melissenos might
reject that honour and insist without reservation on the title
of emperor, as indeed he had told the Komnenoi already;
Melissenos might plan some bolder action. Such was the explanation of Manganes' crafty deceit when it came to writing the
chrysobull.

While this was going on, it was becoming imperative to
force an entrance into the city. The ambassadors, who were
suspicious of this play-acting, pressed their demands more vigorously. The Komnenoi answered, 'Now that we have the city

in our power, we are with God's help going to take full possession of it. Go away and tell your Lord and Master that, and
add that if all goes according to our hopes, with him at our
side, everything will be arranged to suit his and our convenience
without any difficulty.' After this reply to the envoys, they sent
George Palaiologos to the leader of the Nemitzoi, Gilpraktos,
to find out how he stood and whether he was prepared to
admit them after giving a signal, as he had promised. The plan
was as follows: when they saw the signal, they were to hurry
inside the city the moment he had gone quickly up the tower
and opened the gates. Palaiologos undertook this mission to
Gilpraktos eagerly – he was never reluctant to engage in warlike activities and the sacking of cities. Homer called Ares
'smiter of walls'[31] and the name fitted George exactly. Meanwhile the Komnenoi armed themselves and after marshalling
the whole army with great skill advanced slowly towards the
city en masse.

In the evening George Palaiologos approached the wall,
received the signal from Gilpraktos and climbed the tower with
his men. Alexios' soldiers, during this time, had arrived at a
short distance from the walls. They threw up a palisade and
obviously made camp. For a brief part of the night they bivouacked there, but the Komnenoi later took up position in the
centre of the line, with the elite of the cavalry and the better
infantry; the light-armed forces were drawn up separately. As
day broke they went forward at a walking pace and concentrated before the walls. In order to strike terror into the
defenders every man was armed and all were at battle stations.
When Palaiologos gave the signal from the tower and opened
the gates, the rebels rushed in pell-mell, no longer in military
discipline, but each as he could, armed with shields, bows and
spears.

It was Holy Thursday, the day on which we sacrifice our
mystic paschal lamb and feast, in the fourth indiction in the
month of April 6589.[32] Thus the whole army, composed of
foreign and native troops collected from the countryside round
Constantinople and the neighbouring districts, rapidly poured
into the city through the Kharsian Gate. They knew the capital

had been stocking up with all kinds of provisions for a long time, constantly being replenished by land and sea. Once inside they scattered in all directions, in the main streets, at crossroads and in alleyways, in their cruelty sparing neither houses nor churches nor even the most sacred sanctuaries; in fact they gathered from them heaps of booty. They did refrain from murder, but all the other crimes were committed with complete and reckless disregard for decency. What was worse was the fact that even the native-born soldiers did not abstain from such excesses; they seemed to forget themselves, debasing their normal habits and shamelessly following the example of the barbarians.[33]

11. Under the circumstances the Emperor Nikephoros was now in a really serious position, for the city was besieged from the west, while on the east Nikephoros Melissenos was already in camp near Damalis. The emperor had no alternative plan but reflected that he should abdicate in favour of Melissenos. As the Komnenoi were already inside the city, he sent for one of his most trustworthy servants and ordered him to bring Melissenos to the palace with the help of the fleet. One of the guardsmen, a fine fighting soldier, accompanied this messenger.

But before the order could be carried out the city fell. Palaiologos walked down to the sea with one of his men and finding a boat there immediately boarded it and told the oarsmen to row to the place where the fleet was normally anchored. He was nearly across when he saw Botaneiates' messenger preparing the fleet; the guardsman was on one of the warships. Palaiologos recognized him a long way off, since he was an old acquaintance, and as he went by, spoke to him. He asked the usual questions, where he came from, where he was going, and then asked to be taken on board. The guardsman, with an eye on Palaiologos' sword and buckler, was frightened, and replied, 'If I hadn't seen you armed like that, I would have taken you on board very gladly.' Palaiologos agreed to lay aside his shield, sword and helmet, provided he was allowed to join him.

When the guardsman saw that he had done so, he at once took him aboard, put his arms round him and embraced him with every sign of pleasure. Palaiologos, however, being a man of action wasted little time on this; he proceeded with the task. Leaping to the prow he questioned the rowers: 'What are you up to? Where are you going? You're bringing the most terrible trouble on your own heads. You can see the city is taken. The man who was once *megas domestikos* has now been proclaimed emperor. You see his soldiers; you hear the acclamations. There will be no room for anyone else in the palace. Botaneiates is a fine man, but the Komnenoi are far too strong for him; his army is numerous, but ours easily outnumbers it. It's wrong then to throw away your lives and betray your wives and children. Come and look round the city – see for yourselves that the whole army is inside the walls. See the standards. Hear the loud cries of acclamation. See Alexios on his way to the palace, already invested with the authority of an emperor. Turn the prow and in doing so, assure him of complete victory – then join him in person.'

To a man they yielded at once to these arguments, except for the guardsman; he was disgusted. Palaiologos threatened to chain him down on the ship's deck there and then, or throw him overboard, and immediately led the acclamation. The rowers followed suit, but the guardsman still angrily refused. He was put in chains below deck.

Palaiologos, after a brief voyage, resumed his sword and buckler and moored the ship in the fleet's anchorage. There he made a public acclamation of Alexios. Meeting the messenger whom Botaneiates had sent to seize the fleet and transport Melissenos to the palace, he arrested him without delay and ordered the sailors to loose the stern cables. Thus he sailed with the fleet and arrived at the Akropolis, with loud cheers greeting the new emperor. The rowers were told to heave to and wait quietly to intercept anyone who tried to cross from the east.

Soon afterwards he saw a ship bearing down on the Great Palace and made haste to cut it off. He spied his own father on board. At once he stood up and gave the bow one usually gives to fathers, but there was no happy response; unlike the Ithacan Odysseus when he saw Telemakhos, he certainly did not call Palaiologos 'his sweet light'.[34] In Homer of course there was a banquet, suitors, games, a bow and arrows, as well as a prize for the winner – the prudent Penelope. Moreover, Telemakhos was not an enemy, but a son who came to help his father. Here it was different: battle and war, father and son on opposite sides. Each was aware of the other's loyalties, though intentions had not yet been translated into action. Looking askance at George and calling him a fool, the father asked him, 'What have you come to do here?' 'Since it is you who ask me – nothing.' 'Hold on a little then, and if the emperor listens to my advice, you will soon know what's to be done.'

Thereupon Nikephoros Palaiologos went off to the palace, but when he saw the general dispersal of the army and the widespread preoccupation with loot, implored Botaneiates to give him the barbarians from the island of Thule, thinking it would be easy to overcome the Komnenoi and drive them from the city. But Botaneiates, who had given up all hope, pretended that he wished to avoid civil war. 'If you take my advice, Nikephoros,' he said, 'now that the Komnenoi are already in the capital, you will go away and negotiate terms of peace with them.' Nikephoros left him, but most unwillingly.

12. The Komnenoi, having entered the city, waited confidently in the square of the great martyr George Sykeotes.[35] They were undecided whether to visit their mothers first and pay them the usual courtesies, according to custom, and then proceed to the palace, but the *kaisar* heard of this and sent one of his servants to threaten and reproach them severely for dawdling. They set out at once. Near the house of Iberitzes, Nikephoros Palaiologos caught them up, and said to them:

'The emperor sends you this message: I am a lonely old man, with neither son nor brother nor relative. If it is agreeable to you (and here he addressed himself to the new emperor), you can become my adopted son. For my part, I will take away none of the privileges granted by you to each of your comrades-in-arms, nor will I share in any way your authority as emperor, but will merely enjoy with you the title, the acclamation, the right to wear the purple sandals and to live quietly in the palace. The government of the empire will rest entirely on your shoulders.'

To this message the Komnenoi offered a few words which

expressed approval. When the *kaisar* heard of this, he soon hastened to the palace, full of indignation. As he came in on the right of the courtyard on foot, the Komnenoi, who were going out, met him. He rebuked them soundly. Just as he entered, his eye fell on Nikephoros Palaiologos coming back again from the left. 'What are you doing here?' he said. 'What do you want, kinsman?' 'Apparently I shall accomplish nothing here,' replied Nikephoros, 'but I have come with the same message as before from the emperor to the Komnenoi. The emperor is determined to keep his promise and treat Alexios as his son. Alexios will be invested with imperial authority and administer the empire according to his own wishes, while Botaneiates will share the title of emperor only, together with the purple sandals and the purple robe; he will also live quietly in the palace, for he is now an old man and in need of rest.' The *kaisar* glared fiercely at Nikephoros and with a scowl replied, 'Go away and tell the emperor that these offers would have been most expedient before the city was captured. From now onwards there is no place whatever for further negotiations. As he is an old man now, let him vacate the throne and look to his own safety.'

That is what the *kaisar* had to say. Borilos, meanwhile, decided to attack, having heard that the Komnenoi had entered the city and that their army was scattered in all directions in the search for booty and was entirely occupied in fact in the collection of spoils. He thought it would be a very easy matter to subdue them dispersed as they were (for the Komnenoi had been left alone with their relatives, by blood and by marriage, and a mere handful of foreign soldiers). Accordingly he concentrated all those who bore their arms on their shoulders and the soldiers who had arrived from Khoma. With perfect discipline they were drawn up in line from the Forum of Constantine as far as the Milion and beyond. They stood in close order, ready for battle but for the time staying where they were.

The patriarch[36] at the time was a saintly man, who in very truth had no possessions and had practised every form of asceticism known to the early Fathers who dwelt in deserts and mountains. He was also endowed with the divine gift of prophecy and had made many predictions on several occasions which never proved to be wrong. He was indeed a model and example of virtue to future generations. It was clear that Botaneiates' misfortunes were by no means unknown to him. Maybe he was inspired by God, or perhaps he acted on the advice of the *kaisar* (for that too was alleged), as the *kaisar* had long been a friend of his because of the patriarch's exceptional virtue. At all events, he counselled Botaneiates to abdicate.[37] 'Do not engage in civil wars,' he said, 'nor transgress the will of God. Do not allow the city to be defiled with the blood of Christians, but yield to God's will. Renounce the world.'

The emperor heeded these words. Fearful of the army's insolent behaviour, he wrapped his robes round him and went down to the Great Church with downcast eyes. In the general confusion he had not noticed that he was still wearing the costume of an emperor, but Borilos, turning on him and touching the embroidered work fastened round his arm with pearls, wrenched it off, sarcastically remarking in his mocking way, 'This sort of thing really suits us now.' Botaneiates entered the Great Church of God, the Church of the Wisdom of God, and for a time he remained there.

BOOK III

1. Having seized the palace, the Komnenoi at once sent Michael, their niece's husband,[1] to Botaneiates. He later became *logothetes* of the *sekreta*. He was accompanied by the *eparkhos* (who was an individual named Rhadenos). Michael put the emperor on a small boat and went with him to the famous monastery of the Peribleptos.[2] There he and Rhadenos urged him to adopt the habit of a monk, but he put off the decision to the next day. As they were afraid that, in the confusion and disorder which still prevailed, some new attempt at revolution might be made by the two slaves and the men from Khoma, they pressed him urgently to accept the tonsure. He obeyed and was honoured with the robes of angels.[3] Such is the way of Fortune: when she wishes to smile on a man she exalts him on high, crowns him with a royal diadem, and gives him sandals of purple; but when she frowns, instead of the purple and the crown, she clothes him in ragged garments of black. And this was the fate of Botaneiates now. When he was asked by one of his friends if he found the change tolerable, he replied: 'Abstinence from meat is the only thing that worries me; the other matters cause little concern.'

In the meantime the Empress Maria still remained in the palace with her son Constantine, whom she bore to the previous emperor Michael Doukas. She feared for her blond Menelaus, in the words of the poet;[4] and she had a perfectly respectable excuse for staying on – the ties of kinship, although some people, prompted by jealousy, speculated that there were other reasons why she had remained there. They argued that one of the Komnenoi was related to her by marriage and another was her adopted son. In fact though, the real cause which determined her actions was not the one for which she was roundly condemned, nor was it the attractive and friendly nature of the Komnenoi, but the fact that she was in a foreign country, without relatives, without friends and without a single compatriot around her. Naturally she did not wish to leave the palace hurriedly; she feared some evil might befall the child,[5] if she went before receiving some guarantee of safety. When emperors fall, that kind of thing usually happens.

Ekphrasis

The little boy, apart from other considerations, was a gorgeous child, still quite young – and not yet seven years old; no one should blame me if I praise my own when the nature of the case compels me to do so. It was delightful enough to hear him speak, but that was not all: his extraordinary agility and suppleness made him unrivalled at games, if one is to believe what his companions in those days said later. He was blond, with a skin as white as milk, his cheeks suffused with red like some dazzling rose that has just left its calyx. His eyes were not light-coloured, but hawk-like, shone from beneath the brows, like a precious stone set in a golden ring. Thus, seemingly endowed with a heavenly beauty not of this world, his manifold charms captivated the beholder; in short, anyone who saw him would say that he was like a picture of Eros.

That was the true reason for the empress's continued presence in the palace. For my own part, I am in any case naturally averse to making things up or to inventing stories about history, although I know the custom is widespread, especially among the jealous and spiteful. I am not quickly impressed by the slanders of the mob. As a matter of fact, I have other reasons to believe I know the truth in this affair: from my early childhood, before I was eight years old, I was brought up by the empress.[6] She was very fond of me and shared all her secrets with me. I have heard many others speak of these things with differing accounts, as some interpreted the events of that time in one way, and others in another; each followed their own inclination, influenced by sympathy or hatred, and I saw that they did not all share the same opinion. Moreover, I have on several occasions heard the empress herself describe in detail all that happened to her and how frightened she was, in particular for her son, when the Emperor Nikephoros abdicated. Indeed, in my opinion and in the opinion of most people who care for the truth and are best qualified to judge, it was love for her child that kept her then for a little while in the palace.

That is enough now about the Empress Maria. As for Alexios, my father, who had by then seized power, he came to live in the palace. His wife, fifteen years old at the time, he left in the lower palace, so-called because of its location, together with her sisters and mother and the *kaisar*, her grandfather on the paternal side. He himself, with his brothers, his mother and his close relatives, went up to the upper palace, also called Boukoleon.[7] It was called Boukoleon for the following reason. Near its walls a harbour had been constructed in the old days of marble and concrete, where the stone lion catches its prey, an ox; it clings to the bull's horn and having broken its neck has its teeth embedded, so to speak, in the animal's throat. The whole place, that is to say, the buildings on land and the harbour itself, has been named Boukoleon as a result.

2. As I have said, many people were suspicious when the empress stayed on there, and they suggested maliciously that the new emperor intended to marry her. The Doukas family believed no such thing (they were not carried away by idle gossip), but they knew that the mother of the Komnenoi had for a long time been undisguisedly hostile to themselves. Their suspicions made them fearful, as I myself have often heard them say. Thus when George Palaiologos arrived with the fleet and began the acclamation, the party of the Komnenoi leaned over the ramparts, trying to silence him from above, bidding him not to link the names of Eirene and Alexios in a common acclamation. He was extremely angry.[8] 'It was not for your sakes,' he cried, 'that I won so great a victory, but because of the Eirene you speak of.' And at the same time he ordered his sailors to acclaim both together, Eirene and Alexios. All this thoroughly disturbed the Doukas faction; but it also, of course, provided the spiteful with a pretext to attack the Empress Maria.

The Emperor Alexios had in fact no such thought in his mind

(how could he?). Once he had taken over the leadership of
the Romans, being always the man of action, he immediately
became immersed in matters of state. He became, one might
say, the centre of supreme power. At sunrise he entered the
palace, and before shaking off the dust of battle and resting his
body, applied himself immediately and totally to the consideration of the military position. In everything he had his brother
Isaac as his partner, whom he looked up to like a father, and
he shared his plans too with his mother. They supported him
in the running of the empire, although his own fine intelligence
and vigour were more than equal to ruling over a single realm;
he could have managed several empires of more than one type.
However, he turned his attention to a matter of urgency: the
rest of the day and all that night he spent in devising ways of
ending the indiscipline and licence of the soldiers who were
scattered over Byzantion in great number, without causing a
mutiny; he also wanted to relieve the population of the city
from anxiety for the future. Under any circumstances he feared
their wildness and all the more because of their mixed origin;
there was a danger that they might even plan a coup against
himself.

The *Kaisar* John Doukas had his own ideas. He wanted to
expedite the Empress Maria's departure and drive her from
the palace, in order to free the public from their unjustified
suspicions. He proceeded therefore to win over the Patriarch
Kosmas by all means, demanding that he should support their
cause and absolutely refuse to listen to the suggestion of the
Komnenoi's mother; next he sensibly advised the Empress
Maria to ask the emperor for a written guarantee of safety
on her own behalf and for the sake of the child, and then
withdraw. It was a Patroklos-like scheme,[9] for he had already
influenced her when the Emperor Michael Doukas had resigned
the throne: he had advised Michael's successor, Nikephoros
Botaneiates, to take the lady in marriage, because she was of
foreign birth and had no crowd of relatives to embarrass the
emperor. He spoke to him at length of her noble birth and
physical attractions; again and again he praised her.

She was in fact very tall, like a cypress tree; her skin was snow white; her face was oval, her complexion wholly reminiscent of a spring flower or a rose. As for the flash of her eyes, what mortal could describe it? Eyebrows, flame-coloured, arched above eyes of light blue. A painter's hand has many times reproduced the colours of all the flowers brought to birth each in its own season, but the beauty of the empress, the grace that shone about her, the charming attractiveness of her ways, these seemed to baffle description, to be beyond the artist's skill. Neither Apelles, nor Pheidias, nor any of the sculptors ever created such a work. The Gorgon's head,[10] so they say, turned men who saw it to stone, but a man who saw the empress walking, or who suddenly met her, would be stupefied, rooted to the spot and rendered speechless, apparently deprived in that one moment of all feeling and reason. Such was the proportion and perfect symmetry of her body, each part in harmony, that no one till then had ever seen its like among humankind – a living work of art, an object of desire to lovers of beauty. She was indeed Love incarnate, visiting as it were this earthly world.

With such praises then the *kaisar* softened the emperor's heart and won him over, although many were counselling him to marry the Empress Eudokia.[11] Some people whispered that Eudokia in her desire to become empress a second time had tried to woo Botaneiates by letters when he arrived at Damalis, during his own attempt to take the throne. Others said that she wrote, not for her own sake, but on behalf of her daughter, the *Porphyrogennetos* Zoe.[12] And maybe she would have had her way, had not one of the servants cut short her attempt, Leo Kydoniates the eunuch, who gave her much timely advice. I am not at liberty to report in detail what he said, because I have a natural abhorrence of slander, but the chroniclers of such matters will surely make it their business to write about it.

The *Kaisar* John, however, after using every form of persuasion finally achieved his purpose: Botaneiates married the Empress Maria, as I have explained previously in more detail. Thereafter John enjoyed great freedom of speech in his dealings with her. These events took place over the course of several days, for the Komnenoi absolutely refused to drive her from the palace, both because they had received many kindnesses

from her throughout the whole of her reign, and no less importantly because they were on friendly terms with her as a result
of the double relationship that bound them. At the time many
rumours were put about, emanating from many sources and
following one after the other in a constant stream. They plainly
reflected the different policies. The interpretation given to
events depended on the attitude of the individual: some were
sympathetic to her, others were filled with hate; both parties
were prejudiced, unwilling to judge the case on its merits. Meanwhile Alexios was crowned alone by the Patriarch Kosmas, a
most venerable and virtuous man, who had been elected patriarch in the fourth year of the reign of Michael Doukas, following the death of the most holy Patriarch John Xiphilinos on
2nd August of the thirteenth indiction.

The fact that the empress was still not considered worthy of
the imperial crown frightened the Doukas family more than
ever; however, they insisted that the Empress Eirene should
be crowned. It happened that a monk called Eustratios and
surnamed Garidas[13] had his dwelling near the Great Church of
God, and it seems, as a result of this, had gained a reputation
for virtue. This man in times past had frequently visited the
mother of the Komnenoi and made prophecies about power. In
any case she was well disposed towards monks, but such words
flattered her, and she made it clear that her faith in him was
increasing every day. Eventually she became eager to establish
him on the patriarchal throne of the metropolis. The reigning
high priest, she alleged, was simple, weak too, and she persuaded certain persons to put in his mind the idea of retirement,
stressing that this was in his own best interests. But the holy
man was not deceived by this pretext. 'By Kosmas,' he said, for
he went so far as to take an oath in his own name; 'By Kosmas,
if Eirene is not crowned by my own hands, I will never resign
the patriarchal throne.' They returned to their sovereign and
told her what had been said (by now they all called her by that
name, because the emperor, who loved his mother, wished her
to be addressed in this way). So, seven days after[14] the public
proclamation of Alexios' accession, his wife Eirene was
crowned by the Patriarch Kosmas.

3. The physical appearance of the two rulers, Alexios and Eirene, was remarkable, indeed quite incomparable. A painter could never reproduce the beauty of such an archetype, nor a sculptor mould his lifeless stone into such harmony. Even the celebrated work of Polyklitos[15] would have seemed to lack the principles of art, if one looked first at these living statues, by which I mean the newly crowned rulers, and then at Polyklitos' masterpieces.

Alexios was not a very tall man, but he was broad shouldered and well proportioned. When standing he did not seem particularly striking to onlookers, but when one saw the grim flash of his eyes as he sat on the imperial throne, he reminded one of a fiery whirlwind, so overwhelming was the radiance that emanated from his bearing and from his very presence. His dark eyebrows were curved, and beneath them the gaze of his eyes was both terrible and kind. A quick glance, the brightness of his face, the noble cheeks suffused with ruddy colour combined to inspire in the beholder both dread and confidence. His broad shoulders, muscular arms and deep chest, all on a heroic scale, invariably commanded the wonder and delight of the people. The man's person indeed radiated beauty and grace and dignity and an unapproachable majesty. When he came into a gathering and began to speak, you were conscious from the moment he opened his mouth of the fiery eloquence of his tongue, for a torrent of argument won universal attention and captivated every heart; hand and tongue alike were unsurpassed and invincible, the one in hurling the spear, the other in devising fresh enchantments.

The Empress Eirene, my mother, was at that time only a young girl, not yet fifteen years old. She was a daughter of Andronikos, the eldest son of the *kaisar*, and of illustrious descent, for her family derived from the famous houses of Andronikos and Constantine Doukas.[16] She stood upright like some young, proud, always blossoming shoot, each limb and her whole body in perfect symmetry and in complete harmony. With her lovely appearance and charming voice she never ceased to fascinate all who saw and heard her. Her face shone with the soft light of the moon; it was not the completely round face of an Assyrian woman, nor long, like the face of a Scythian, but just slightly oval in shape. There were rose blossoms on her cheeks, visible a long way off. Her light-blue eyes were both gay and stern: their charm and beauty attracted, but the fear they caused so dazzled the bystander that he could neither look nor turn away.

Whether there really was an Athene in ancient times, the Athene celebrated by poets and writers, I do not know, but I often hear the myth repeated and satirized. However, if someone in those times had said of this empress that she was Athene in mortal form, or that she had descended suddenly from the sky in some heavenly glory and unapproachable splendour, his description would not have been so very inappropriate. What was rather surprising – and in this she differed from all other women – was the way she humbled the proud, and restored to the subdued and fearful their courage just by a single glance. For the most part her lips were closed and when thus silent she resembled a veritable statue of beauty, a breathing monument of grace. Generally she accompanied her words with graceful gestures, her hands bare to the wrists, like ivory turned by some craftsman into the form of fingers and hands, one might say. The pupils of her eyes, with the brilliant blue of deep waves, recalled a calm, still sea, while the white surrounding them shone by contrast, giving them a dazzling and unique quality – and an indescribable beauty. So much for the physical characteristics of Eirene and Alexios.

As for my uncle Isaac, he was about the same height as his brother and indeed was not very different from him in other respects, but he was rather pale and his beard was not particularly thick; round the jaws it was thinner than that of his brother. Both brothers indulged often in hunting, when there was no great pressure of work, but they found military affairs more exhilarating than hunting. On the battlefield no one outpaced Isaac even when he commanded regiments in person: the moment he saw the enemy's line, disregarding all else, he hurled himself into their midst like a thunderbolt and quickly threw their ranks into confusion – a habit that led to his capture in battle on more than one occasion against the Agarenes in Asia.

This characteristic, that he would not control himself in battle, is the only one for which my uncle could be criticized.

4. The emperor had promised Nikephoros Melissenos (his brother-in-law) the title of *kaisar*. Isaac, the eldest of his brothers,[17] therefore had to be honoured with some higher dignity, and as there was no such rank in existence, a new name was invented, a compound of *sebastos* and *autokrator*. Isaac was created *sebastokrator*, a kind of second emperor and senior to the *kaisar*, who received the acclamation in third place. In addition, Alexios decreed that both *sebastokrator* and *kaisar* should wear crowns at public festivals, although they were much inferior to his own. The imperial diadem, decked all over with pearls and stones, some encrusted, some pendent, was shaped like a half-sphere, fitting the head closely; on either side of the temples clusters of pearls and precious stones hung down, lightly touching the cheeks. This diadem constitutes a unique ornament of the emperor's dress. The crowns of the *sebastokrator* and the *kaisar*, on the other hand, are embellished with few pearls and stones and are not cap-shaped.

At the same time Taronites,[18] who had married the emperor's sister Maria, was also honoured with the titles of *protosebastos* and *protovestiarios*, and not long afterwards he was promoted to the rank of *panhypersebastos* with the right to sit with the *kaisar*. Alexios' brother Adrian, too, was granted the title of *protosebastos periphanestatos* and Nikephoros, his youngest brother, who had been made *megas droungarios* of the fleet, was also raised to the rank of *sebastos*.

My father was responsible for inventing these honours. Some were compound names, like the example given above, others were titles put to a new use. For names like *panhypersebastos* and *sebastokrator* and so on were made up, but the dignity of *sebastos* took on a new meaning. In the old days the epithet *sebastos* had been applied to emperors only, a distinctive title, but Alexios for the first time allowed it to be more widely used. If one regards the art of ruling as a science, a kind of supreme philosophy, the art of all arts, so to speak, and the highest science of all, then one would have to admire him as a scientist in a way and a leading thinker for having invented these imperial titles and functions. Of course there was a difference: the great logicians invented names for the sake of lucidity, whereas Alexios, the master of the science of government, directed all his innovations towards the good of the empire itself, whether changes were effected in the allotment of duties or in the granting of titles.[19]

However, let us return to the saintly Kosmas, the patriarch. He presided over the sacred ceremony in honour of the blessed John the Theologian, in the church named after him in the Hebdomon,[20] and a few days later resigned his high office, which he had held with distinction for five years and nine months; he then retired to the monastery of Kallias.[21] The eunuch Eustratios Garidas, who has been mentioned previously, succeeded to the patriarch's throne.

After the deposition of his father Michael Doukas, Constantine *porphyrogennetos*, the son of the Empress Maria, had voluntarily set aside the purple sandals and adopted ordinary black ones. However, the new emperor, Nikephoros Botaneiates, who had deposed Doukas the father of Constantine, ordered him to throw them away and wear silk shoes of various colours. He felt sorry for the young man and admired him no less for his handsome appearance than for his aristocratic origin. He would not countenance the wearing of footwear resplendent with scarlet throughout but granted him the privilege of a few strands of red in the material.

Later, when Alexios Komnenos was proclaimed emperor, Maria on the advice of the *kaisar* asked for a written pledge, guaranteed in letters of purple and a golden seal, not only that she should be allowed to live in security with her son, but that he should be co-ruler with Alexios, with the right to wear the purple sandals and a crown, and the right to be acclaimed as emperor with him. Her request was granted in a chrysobull confirming all her demands. Constantine's woven silk shoes were removed and sandals wholly of purple substituted for them. In the matter of donations or chrysobulls his signature now appeared immediately after that of Alexios, and in the processions he followed him wearing an imperial diadem. Some people declared that even before the revolt the empress had made an agreement with the Komnenoi that her son should be treated in this way.

Whether that was true or not, she now left the palace with an escort worthy of her rank and withdrew to the house built by the late Emperor Constantine Monomakhos near the monastery of the great martyr George (still commonly known as Mangana[22]). The *Sebastokrator* Isaac accompanied her.

5. Such were the arrangements made by the Komnenoi in respect of the Empress Maria. As for Alexios, who had enjoyed a good formation from his earliest years and, obedient to the instructions of his mother, had the fear of the Lord deeply implanted in his soul, he grieved and was deeply ashamed at the plundering of the capital which had taken place when he had occupied it, and which had affected the whole population. Unbroken success can sometimes lead a man who has never met with any reverse to commit an act of madness; if he is of a cautious, sensible disposition, his error will promptly be followed by absolute remorse and alarm as he becomes aware in his heart of the fearfulness of God, especially if he is engaged on projects of great importance and has himself attained exalted rank. An underlying dread will affect him lest by some act of ignorance or foolhardiness or pride he should call down on himself the wrath of God and be cast down from his position of authority and lose all his present possessions. Such was once the fate of Saul, for God, because of the ruler's foolish pride, smashed and destroyed his realm.

Distraught with these reflections and deeply perturbed, Alexios feared that somehow he might be the scapegoat, the object of God's vengeance. He regarded the evil which had befallen the whole city as his responsibility, even if it was really the work of individual soldiers, all that rabble that descended in a mighty flood on all parts of Constantinople. He was sick at heart, filled with shame, as if he, personally, had committed these frightful atrocities. Majesty and power, the royal purple and the stone-encrusted diadem, the robe adorned with gold and jewels, all these he quite rightly looked upon as worthless compared with the indescribable disaster that had then afflicted the Queen of Cities; for no writer, however earnest, could possibly do justice to the terrors by which it was enveloped in those days. Churches, sanctuaries, property both public and private, all were the victims of universal pillage, while the ears of all its citizens were deafened by cries and shouts raised on every side. An onlooker might well have thought an earthquake was taking place.

Reflecting on this, Alexios suffered pangs of remorse and a grief beyond endurance. He was extremely sensitive at all times to wrongdoing, and though he was aware that these crimes against the city were the work of other hands, engineered by other men, his conscience told him in categorical terms that it was he himself who had afforded the pretext for such a calamity and had given it the original impetus. The true responsibility for the revolt, of course, lay with the slaves I have referred to before.

But even so he assumed the whole burden of guilt and was anxious and willing to heal the wound, for only thus, after healing and cleansing, could he approach the task of governing the empire or satisfactorily direct and bring to a proper conclusion his plans for the army and its wars. So he went to his mother, informed her of his anxiety, a state which did him credit, and asked how he could find relief and freedom from the cares that gnawed at his conscience. She embraced her son and gladly listened to his words. Being of one accord, therefore, they summoned the Patriarch Kosmas (he had not yet resigned his throne) and certain leading members of the Holy Synod and the monastic order.

The emperor came before them as a man on trial, a person of no account, one of those set under authority,[23] condemned and tensely awaiting at any moment the verdict of the court. He confessed everything, passing over neither the temptation, nor the yielding to it, nor the commission of evil, nor even the responsibility for what was done. He admitted all in fear and faith, passionately demanding from them a remedy for his misdeeds and offering to undergo penance. They condemned not only Alexios but his blood relations, as well as those who shared with him in the rebellion; all were to submit to the same punishment – fasting, sleeping on the ground and the performing of the appropriate rites to appease the anger of

God. The penalties were accepted and paid with enthusiasm; in fact, their wives could not bear to stand aloof (how could they, when they loved their husbands?), and of their own free will they too submitted to the yoke of penance.

The palace became a scene of tearful lamentation – not insincere nor a sign of any faint-heartedness, but rather praiseworthy and the precursor of a higher, everlasting joy. It was typical of the emperor's own piety that he should inflict on himself a further penalty: for forty days and nights[24] he wore sackcloth beneath the royal purple and next to his skin. At night he slept on bare ground, and his head was supported on nothing more than a stone while he bewailed his sins, as was only right. Thereafter, when the penance was complete, he turned his attention to the administration of the empire with clean hands.

6. It was his desire that his mother should govern rather than himself, but so far had concealed the plan from her for fear that she might leave the palace if she knew about it, since he knew after all that she was aiming for a more rewarding spiritual life. Nevertheless, in all matters however ordinary he did nothing without her advice: she became his confidante and co-partner in government. Gradually and surreptitiously he involved her more and more in state affairs; on occasions he even declared openly that without her brains and good judgement the empire would not survive. By these means he bound her more closely to himself, but prevented her from attaining her own goal and frustrated it.

She had in mind the last stage of life and dreamed of monasteries in which she would drag out her remaining years in the contemplation of wisdom. Such was her intention, the constant aim of her prayers. Despite this longing in her heart, despite the total preoccupation with a higher life, she also loved her son to a quite exceptional degree and wished somehow to bear with him the storms that buffeted the empire. She desired to guide the ship of state on the best possible course, in fair weather or in tempest when waves crashed on to it from all sides, especially since the young man had only just taken his seat in the stern and put his hand to the tiller, with no previous experience of storms, winds and waves of such violence. She was constrained, therefore, by a mother's affection for her son, and governed with him, sometimes even grasping the reins and driving the chariot of power alone – and without accident or mishap. The truth is that Anna Dalassene was blessed with a fine intellect and possessed besides a fine aptitude for governing. On the other hand, she was distracted from it by her love for God.

When in the month of August[25] in the same indiction, Robert's crossing compelled Alexios to leave the capital, the latter brought to light and put into operation his cherished plan: the whole executive power was entrusted to his mother alone and the decision was confirmed publicly in a chrysobull. As it is the historian's duty not merely to summarize the deeds and decrees of good men, but as far as possible to give some details of the former and transmit the latter in full, I myself will set out the terms of this document,[26] omitting only the subtle refinements of the scribe.

It ran thus: 'When danger is foreseen or some other dreadful occurrence is expected, there is no safeguard stronger than a mother who is understanding and loves her son, for if she gives counsel, her advice will be reliable; if she offers prayers, they will confer strength and certain protection. Such at any rate has been the experience of myself, your emperor, in the case of my own revered mother, who has taught and guided and sustained me throughout, from my earliest years. She had a place in the Senate in her own right after all, but her first concern was for her son and his faith in her was preserved intact. It was well known that one soul animated us, physically separated though we were, and by the grace of Christ that happy state has persisted to this day. Never were those cold words "mine" and "yours" uttered between us, and what was even more important, the prayers she poured out during all that time reached the ears of the Lord and have raised me now to the imperial throne.

'After I took in my hand the imperial sceptre, she found it intolerable that she was not bearing an equal share in my labours, to the interests both of your emperor and of the whole people. But now I am preparing with God's help to do battle with Rome's enemies; an army is being recruited carefully and thoroughly equipped. Nevertheless, I do not fail to recognize the importance of civil and political affairs. Fortunately, an impregnable bulwark for good government has been found – in the appointment of my revered mother, of all women most honoured, as controller of the entire administration.

'I, your emperor, therefore decree explicitly in this present chrysobull the following: because of her vast experience of secular affairs and notwithstanding the very low value she sets upon such matters, whatever she decrees in writing – whether the case be referred to her by the *logothetes* of the *sekreta*, by his subordinate officers or by any other person who prepares memoranda or requests or judgements concerning remissions of public debts – shall have permanent validity as if I myself, your Serene Emperor, had issued them or after dictating them had had them committed to writing. Whatever decisions or orders are made by her, written or unwritten, reasonable or unreasonable, provided that they bear her seal, the Transfiguration and the Assumption, shall be regarded as coming from myself, by the fact that they carry the dating of day and month in the correct form of the current head of the *sekreta*.

'Moreover, with regard to promotions and appointments to the tribunals and themes, and in the matter of honours, offices and donations of property, my saintly mother shall have full power to take whatever action shall seem appropriate to her. Further, whoever is promoted to the tribunals or to the themes and is honoured with dignities, whether higher or lower, they shall thereafter retain these positions on a permanent basis. Again, increases of salary, additional gifts, reductions of tax, economies and diminution of payments shall be settled by her without question. In brief, nothing shall be reckoned invalid that she commands either in writing or by word of mouth, for her words and her decisions shall be reckoned as my own and none of them shall be annulled. In years to come they shall have the force of law permanently.

'Neither now nor in the future shall such decisions be subjected to inquiry or undergo any examination whatsoever at the hands of anybody, whoever he may be. The same provision shall also hold good for ministers and the *logothetes* of the *sekreta* of the time, whether their actions seem to be reasonable or otherwise. It shall be absolutely impossible in the future to demand account of any action taken by them under the terms of this present chrysobull.'

7. That was the chrysobull therefore. The reader may be surprised by the honour conferred on his mother by the emperor in this matter, since he yielded her precedence in everything, relinquishing the reins of government. It was as though she drove the imperial chariot while he ran alongside, sharing only the title of emperor with her. And this despite the fact that he had already passed his boyhood years and was of an age which in the case of men like him is particularly susceptible to the lust for power. Wars against the barbarians, with all their attendant trials and tribulations, he was prepared to face himself, but the entire administration of affairs, the choice of civil magistrates, the accounts of the imperial revenues and expenditure he left to his mother.

At this point the reader may well censure my father for transferring the government of the empire to the women's quarters, but if one knew this woman's spirit, her surpassing virtue, intelligence and energy, one's reproaches would soon turn to admiration. For my grandmother had an exceptional grasp of public affairs, with a genius for organization and government; she was capable, in fact, of managing not only the Roman Empire, but every other empire under the sun as well. She had vast experience and knew the nature of things, aware of how each thing starts and how it ends, which things destroy others and which contradict and complement the other. She was intuitive about what needed doing, and clever at getting it done.

Her intellectual ability, moreover, was paralleled by her command of language. She was indeed a most persuasive orator, without being verbose or long-winded. Nor did the inspiration of the argument readily desert her, for just as she would begin by hitting the right note, she would also end up by saying the appropriate thing too. She was already a woman of mature years when she was called upon to exercise imperial authority, at a time of life when one's mental powers are at their best,

when one's judgement is fully developed and knowledge of
affairs is widest – all qualities that lend force to good administration and government. It is natural that persons of this age
should not merely speak with greater wisdom than the young,
as the tragic playwright[27] says, but also act in a more expedient
way. In the past, when she was still looked upon as a younger
woman, she had impressed everyone as having an old head on
young shoulders; to the observant her face alone revealed
Anna's inherent virtue and gravity.

But, as I was saying, once my father had seized power, he
reserved for himself the struggles and hard labour of war, while
she looked on as a spectator. However, he made her his own
sovereign and like a slave said and did whatever she commanded. He loved her exceedingly and depended on her for
advice (such was his affection for her). His right hand he
devoted to her service; his ears listened for her bidding. In all
things he was entirely subservient, in fact, to her wishes.

I can sum up the whole situation thus: he was in theory the
emperor, but she had real power. She was the legislator, the
complete organizer and governor, while he confirmed her
arrangements, written and unwritten, the former by his signature, the latter by his spoken approval. One might say that he
was indeed the instrument of her power – he was not emperor,
for all the decisions and ordinances of his mother satisfied him,
not merely as an obedient son, but as an attentive listener to
her instruction in the art of ruling. He was convinced that she
had attained perfection in everything and easily excelled all men
of that generation in prudence and understanding of affairs.

8. Such were the events that marked the beginning of the
reign. One could barely at that stage call Alexios emperor given
that he had entrusted supreme authority to his mother. Another
person might yield here to the claims of panegyric and extol
the native land of this remarkable woman; he might trace her
descent from the Adrianoi, the Dalassenoi and the Kharonoi,[28]
while embarking on the ocean of their achievements. But I am
writing history and my fitting task is not to describe her through
the family and kinsmen, but by reference to her character, her
virtue and the events that form the proper subject of history.

To return once more to my grandmother, I must add this: not only was she a very great credit to her own gender, but to men as well; indeed, she contributed to the glory of the whole human race. The women's quarters in the palace had been the scene of utter depravity ever since the infamous Constantine Monomakhos[29] had ascended the throne, and right up to the time when my father became emperor had been noted for foolish love intrigues, but Anna effected a reformation; a commendable decorum was restored and the palace now enjoyed a discipline that merited praise. She instituted set times for the singing of sacred hymns, stated hours for meals; there was now a special period in which magistrates were chosen. She herself set a firm example to everybody else, with the result that the palace assumed the appearance rather of a monastery under her influence.

She was truly an extraordinary woman and a saintly one too; for in self-control she surpassed the famous women of old, heroines of many a legend, just as the sun outshines all stars. As for her compassion for the poor and her generosity to the needy, how could one do them justice? Her house was a refuge for penniless relatives, but no less for strangers. Priests and monks she honoured in particular: they shared her meals and no one ever saw her at table without some of them as guests. Her outward serenity, a true reflection of her character, was revered by angels but dreaded by demons; pleasure-loving fools, victims of their own passions, found a single glance from her more than they could bear; yet to the chaste she seemed gentle and gay. She knew exactly how to temper reserve and dignity; her own reserve never gave the impression of harshness or cruelty, nor did her tenderness seem too soft or unrestrained – and this, I fancy, is the true definition of propriety: the due proportion of warm humanity and strict moral principle.

She was by nature thoughtful and was always evolving new ideas, not, as some folk whispered, to the detriment of the state; on the contrary, they were wholesome schemes which restored to full vigour the already corrupted empire and revived, as far as one could, the ruined fortunes of the people. In spite of her preoccupation with matters of government, she by no means neglected the duties incumbent on a religious woman, for the greater part of the night was spent by her in the chanting of sacred hymns and she wore herself out with continual prayers and vigils. Nevertheless, at dawn or even at second cockcrow, she was applying herself once again to state business, attending to the choice of officials and answering the petitions of suppliants with the help of her secretary Gregory Genesios.

Now if some orator had decided to make this the subject of a panegyric, they would no doubt have exalted her and praised her to the skies, as is the way of encomiasts, for her deeds and thoughts and superiority above all others; who among the famous ones of old, both men and women, who were renowned for their virtue would not have been thrown into the shade? But such licence is not for the writer of history. Those who know her virtue, therefore, her dignified character, her never-failing wisdom and the loftiness and sublimity of her spirit, must not blame my history, if I have done less than justice to her great qualities. But we must return now to the point where we digressed briefly to talk about her. As I said, she guided the empire's destinies, but not all day was spent on secular matters: she still attended the prescribed services in the church dedicated to the martyr Thekla. I will now tell how this church came to be built by the Emperor Isaac Komnenos,[30] her brother-in-law.

When the Dacian leaders refused to observe any longer the ancient treaty with the Romans and deliberately broke it, the Sarmatians, who used to be called Mysians[31] in the old days, heard of their actions and became restive themselves. They were not satisfied to remain in their own territory which was separated from the empire by the Ister, and when a general uprising took place they crossed the river to our lands. The reason for the migration was the deadly hostility of the Getai, who were neighbours of the Dacians and plundered Sarmatian settlements. They waited for the right moment and when the Ister was frozen, the whole tribe crossed over dry-footed and dumped themselves down on our territory. Then they proceeded to spread havoc in the towns and districts of that area.

At this news the Emperor Isaac decided that Triaditza must be occupied, and since he had already checked the ambitions of the eastern barbarians, this task presented no great difficulty. With the intention of driving them from Roman territory, he assembled the whole army and set out in their direction. The enemy, seeing the Romans in battle order, with Isaac leading the attack in person, immediately quarrelled among themselves. Isaac, who had good reason to distrust them in any case, launched a violent assault on the strongest and bravest part of their army. As he and his men drew near, the Sarmatians were filled with dismay; the sight of this man wielding a thunderbolt and the serried ranks of his army was too much for them. They lost heart. So they withdrew a little and after challenging him to do battle with them in three days' time, abandoned their tents there and then, and fled. When Isaac reached their camp, he destroyed the tents, took away the booty found there and came back in triumph.

However, when he reached the foot of Mount Lobitzos, a tremendous and unseasonable snowstorm overtook him; it was 24 September, the day on which the great martyr Thekla is honoured. The water level in the rivers rose and they overflowed their banks; the whole plain, on which the emperor and his army were encamped, became a sea. All the supplies disappeared, swept away in the river currents, while the men and baggage animals were numbed with cold. In the sky there were constant rumbles of thunder, with frequent lightning flashes which followed one another in quick succession and threatened to set the whole countryside on fire.

The emperor did not know what to do. However, during a brief lull in the storm and after losing a great number of his men who were caught up in the whirling waters of the river, he escaped with some picked soldiers and took refuge with them under an oak tree. He could hear a tremendous roaring noise apparently coming from the tree, and as the winds at that moment were becoming even more violent, he was afraid the oak might be blown down. So he moved away, just far enough to avoid being struck, and stood there speechless. At once, as though at a given signal, the tree was torn up by the roots and crashed to the ground in full view.

Isaac stood before it marvelling at God's care for him. Later,

news arrived that the east was in revolt. He returned to the
palace. It was at this time that Isaac had a lovely church built
in honour of Thekla, at considerable expense, with magnificent
decorations and works of art; there he made his thank-offering
in a manner fitting to a Christian and worshipped God in it for
the rest of his life. Such was the origin of this church. As I
have already remarked, the empress, Alexios' mother, regularly
prayed there.

I myself knew her for a short time and admired her. Any
unprejudiced witness to the truth knows and, if he cares to, will
admit that what I have said about her was not mere empty
boasting. Indeed, if I had preferred to compose a panegyric
rather than a history, I would have written at greater length,
adding more stories about her. But I must now return to the
main narrative.

9. The Emperor Alexios knew that the empire was almost at
its last gasp. (The east was being horribly ravaged by the Turks;
the west was in a bad condition, while Robert strained every
nerve to put on the throne the pseudo-Michael who had taken
refuge with him. In my opinion this was rather in the nature of
a pretext: it was love of power that inspired Robert and never
let him rest. Having found Michael he had a Patroklos-like
excuse, and that spark of ambition, hitherto lying hidden
beneath the ashes, blazed up into a mighty conflagration. In a
terrifying fashion he armed himself to do battle with the Roman
Empire. Warships, triremes, biremes, *sermones* and other transport vessels in great numbers were made ready. They were
equipped in the coastal areas, while from the mainland strong
contingents were being assembled to aid him in the coming
struggle.) The brave young emperor was in serious trouble. He
did not know which way to turn, for both enemies demanded
the right to challenge first. He was worried and vexed. The
Romans had no worthwhile forces. (In fact there were no more
than 300 soldiers in the capital, and these were from Khoma,
quite unfit for war and with no combat experience; there were
also a few mercenaries, barbarians whose custom it was to
dangle swords from their shoulders.[32]) In the imperial treasury
there were no reserves of money with which he could summon

allies from foreign countries. The emperors before him, having little knowledge of war and military affairs, had reduced Roman prestige to a minimum. Indeed, I have heard it said by men who were soldiers themselves, and by some of the older men, that no other state in living memory had reached such depths of misery.[33]

Conditions were desperate then for the emperor, distracted as he was by anxieties of all sorts. However, being not only a courageous man and undaunted, but having excellent experience in war, he wanted to restore his empire, to bring it again to a safe anchorage after its terrible buffeting and by God's aid to break up, like waves spent on the rocks, the enemies who in their madness had risen up against him.

He realized that he must quickly recall all the *toparkhes* in the east, men who as governors of forts or towns were bravely resisting the Turks.[34] At once, therefore, he dashed off important dispatches to all of them: to Dabatenos, who was serving at that time as *topoteretes* of Pontic Herakleia and Paphlagonia; to Bourtzes, the *toparkhes* of Kappadokia and Khoma; and to the other officers. He explained to them all what had happened to him and how by the Providence of God he had been promoted to the supreme rank of emperor, after being rescued beyond all expectations from imminent peril. He ordered them to ensure the safety of their own provinces, leaving for that purpose enough soldiers, but with the rest they were to come to Constantinople, bringing along with them as many able-bodied recruits as they could.

He decided, too, that he must seize the initiative in protecting himself against Robert; the leaders and counts who were joining Robert must be diverted from their plans. A messenger had been sent to Monomakhatos[35] before Alexios had become master of the capital, calling for help and asking him to supply the emperor with money. But the envoy returned with nothing more than a letter in which Monomakhatos made excuses, as I have written earlier in the history. He said that as long as Botaneiates was in control of the empire, help was out of the question. Alexios read this reply and feared that once the fall of Botaneiates became known to him Monomakhatos might go over to Robert. He was filled with despair. George Palaiologos, the husband of his wife's sister, was sent off to Dyrrakhion (an Illyrian town) with instructions to drive Monomakhatos from the place without bloodshed, because he had no force powerful enough to eject him involuntarily, and to counteract the machinations of Robert as best he could.

George was also instructed that the ramparts should be constructed in a new way: the majority of the wooden planks were to be left unnailed, so that if the Latins[36] did climb up on ladders, as soon as they set foot on the planks they would upset them and crash down to the ground, planks and all. Moreover, the commanders of the coastal towns and the islanders themselves were earnestly exhorted in letters not to lose heart, nor to relax their efforts in any way, but to be watchful and sober, providing all-round protection for themselves and keeping a wary eye open for Robert. A sudden attack, leading to the capture of all the towns by the sea and even of the islands, would cause trouble later to the Roman Empire.

10. Such were the emperor's precautions with regard to Illyrikon. It was obvious that the districts lying in the direct path of the enemy and nearest to him were now well fortified. At the same time he had not been slow to stir up trouble in Robert's rear, for letters were sent first to Hermann, the ruler of Lombardy, then to the Pope of Rome,[37] and again to the Archbishop Hervé of Capua, to the princes, and besides that to all the military leaders of the Keltic lands, courting their favour by appropriate gifts, with promises of much largess and many honours in the future. Thus he incited them to enmity against Robert. Some of them at once renounced their friendship with him; others agreed to do so, if more money was forthcoming.

Alexios knew that the German king[38] was more powerful than all the others; whatever policy he adopted, it would be successful no matter how Robert opposed it. On more than one occasion, therefore, letters full of conciliatory phrases and all kinds of pledges were dispatched to him, and when he was certain that the king acquiesced and was prepared to yield to his wishes, Khoirosphaktes once more departed with another message for him. It read as follows:

'Most noble and truly Christian brother, I pray that your mighty realm may flourish and enjoy even greater prosperity. For is it not right that a pious and imperial majesty such as ourselves should not wish you all that is good and profitable, now that we have learnt of your own piety? Your fraternal inclination and affection towards our empire, and the tasks which you have promised to undertake against that rogue so that the wickedness of this enemy both of God and of Christians will be punished – murderer and criminal – show clearly to us the righteousness of your soul and bear witness to the sincerity of your zealous respect of God.

'Although in other respects my affairs go well, to a very small degree they are in disarray and confusion because of the actions of Robert. Nevertheless, if there is any point in trusting God and His righteous judgements, then the downfall of that most iniquitous of men cannot be long delayed. For it is impossible that God should suffer the rod of evil to lie for ever upon His heritage. As for the presents that we agreed should be dispatched to you, they are now delivered through the *Protoproedros* Constantine, the *katepano* of Dignities; namely, 144,000 pieces of gold and the hundred purple cloths of silk. This is according to the arrangement concluded with your most noble and trustworthy Count Burchard. The aforementioned sum, sent to you, has been made up of pieces of silver of the old quality stamped with the bust of Romanos.[39] When you take the oath, the remaining 216,000 pieces of gold will be forwarded and the salaries of the twenty dignities conferred; your most faithful Abelard will hand them over when you come down to Lombardy.

'As to the manner of the oath-taking, that has been previously explained to you in detail, but the *Protoproedros* and *Katepano* Constantine will make it even clearer; he has been given my instructions on each of the points which will be required of you and which will be confirmed by you on oath. When the agreement was made between me and the envoys you sent, certain articles of greater importance were mentioned, but because your men said they had no mandate on these matters, I deferred the oath in the circumstances. Please take the oaths, then, as the faithful Abelard promised me and as I require of you in respect of the more important addendum.

'It is my fault that your most faithful and noble Count Burchard has been delayed: I wished him to see my beloved nephew, the son of the most fortunate *sebastokrator*, my own well-loved brother, so that when he returned he could tell you of the boy's intelligence, despite his tender years. The outward appearance and physical characteristics count less, as far as I am concerned, although in these too he is abundantly blest. Your envoy will tell you how during his visit to the capital he saw the little boy and had the usual conversation one has with a child. Since God has not blessed me with a son, this beloved nephew takes for me the place of a true heir. If it is the will of God, there is nothing to prevent an alliance between us through ties of kinship. You and I can be mutual friends as Christians, brought more closely together as kinsmen; thus deriving strength from one another, we shall be formidable to our enemies and with God's help invincible.

'I have now sent to you, as a pledge of my goodwill, a gold pectoral cross set with pearls; a reliquary inlaid with gold containing fragments of various saints, identified in each case by a small label; a cup of sardonyx and a crystal goblet; an *astropelekin*[40] attached to a chain of gold; and some wood of the balsam tree.

'May God prolong your years. May He widen the bounds of your realm and put all your adversaries beneath your feet and bring them to shame. May your kingdom enjoy peace and may the sun shed its calm light on all your people. May your foes be destroyed by the mighty Power from on High which preserves you invincible against all attacks, because you love so dearly His true name and arm yourself against His enemies.'

11. After these arrangements had been made in the west, Alexios made preparations to cope with the immediate and pressing danger which threatened him from the east. Meanwhile he remained in the capital, examining every means of dealing with the enemies before his very eyes. As my account has already explained, the godless Turks were in sight, living in the Propontis area, and Solymas,[41] who commanded all the

east, was actually encamped in the vicinity of Nicaea. (His sultanate was located there, though we would call it his palace.) The whole countryside of Bithynia and Thynia was unceasingly exposed to Solymas' foragers; marauding parties on horseback and on foot were raiding as far as the town now called Damalis on the Bosphorus itself; they carried off much booty and all but tried to leap over the very sea. The Byzantines saw them living absolutely unafraid and unmolested in the little villages on the coast and in sacred buildings. The sight filled them with horror. They had no idea what to do.

The emperor, aware of this, found it hard to decide what plan to adopt. However, after considering many schemes, with frequent changes and experiments, he chose the best and as far as he could, put it into practice. He appointed commanders of units of ten men from the men who had been hurriedly con-scripted – Romans and some recruits who came originally from Khoma – and made them embark on small ships, the lightly armed holding bows and shields only, the others who were able-bodied equipped with helmets, shields and spears. They were ordered to make their way secretly at night round the headlands offshore and then, if they were sure the enemy did not greatly outnumber them, to leap from their ships and raid the Turks; they were then to re-embark and return to base at once. These men, he knew, were absolutely ignorant of warfare, so he warned them to instruct their rowers to make no noise with their oars; they were told, too, to beware of barbarians lurking in rocky inlets.

After these tactics had been repeated for some days, the barbarians withdrew from the coast, little by little; when the emperor saw what was happening, he ordered his men to seize the villages and buildings the enemy had formerly occupied and stay there during the night; about sunrise, when the others normally went out to forage or for some other necessary reason, they were to make a sudden attack on them and if they met with any success, however small, to be content with it, for if they ran risks, looking for some greater advantage, the Turks would take heart; our men were to return at once to the strongpoints.

Not long after the barbarians withdrew a second time and this encouraged Alexios. Those who up till then had been infantrymen were ordered to ride on horseback, use a lance and make cavalry excursions against the enemy, no longer in the dark and in secret, but in broad daylight. Those who had been commanding ten men found themselves commanders of units of fifty men; and instead of fighting on foot at night, with considerable apprehension, they began to make their assaults in the morning and confidently engaged in some glorious battles when the sun was at its zenith. So it came about that while things went badly for the Turks, the hidden spark of Roman prestige began gradually to burst into flame. Komnenos not only drove the enemy far away from the Bosphorus and the places by the sea, but chased them from the districts of Bithynia and Thynia altogether, not to mention the borders of Nikomedia, and the sultan was compelled to make the most urgent pleas for a truce.

Alexios gladly accepted the offer of negotiations. He had reliable information from many sources about Robert's unlimited ambitions and he knew that enormous forces had been gathered; Robert was already hurrying to the Lombardy coast. After all, if Herakles could not fight two opponents at once, as the proverb says, how much more was it true of a young general who had but recently acquired a corrupted empire, slowly perishing over a long period and now at its last gasp, without armies and without money? For all its wealth, squandered to no good purpose, had now been exhausted. By various means he had driven the Turks from Damalis and the coastal districts near it; at the same time he had won their friendship with gifts; he had forced them to accept a treaty of peace.[42] He set the frontier with them at the River Drakon, and made them promise never to cross over it and to stop with immediate effect any incursion into Bithynia.

12. In this way the east was pacified. However, Palaiologos' arrival at Dyrrakhion was swiftly followed by Monomakhatos' defection to Bodin and Michael. Palaiologos sent a fast courier to give the news to the emperor. The truth was that Monomakhatos was afraid: he had refused to obey, and had sent the

Emperor Alexios' envoy away empty-handed before the planned rebellion had come into the open. In fact, the emperor did not intend to take any reprisal, except to deprive him of his command for the reasons already stated. Hearing what he had done, the emperor now dispatched a chrysobull guaranteeing his complete safety. Monomakhatos, with the letter in his hand, came back to the palace.

Meanwhile Robert arrived at Otranto and after handing over all his own authority to his son Roger, including the government of Lombardy itself, he went on from there to the harbour of Brindisi. In that town he learnt that Palaiologos had reached Dyrrakhion. Without delay wooden towers were constructed in the larger vessels and covered with leather hides; everything essential for a siege was hastily put on board the ships; horses and armed knights embarked on warships; and when military supplies from all quarters had been made ready with extraordinary rapidity, Robert was anxious to make the crossing at once. His plan was to surround Dyrrakhion the moment he got there with siege-engines by land and sea – for two reasons: first, he would terrify the inhabitants; secondly, having isolated them completely, he would take the town at the first assault. News of these preparations filled the islanders with dread; people living on the coast by Dyrrakhion were equally dismayed.

When he was satisfied that all was ready, the stern cables were loosed and the whole fleet of warships, triremes and monoremes, drawn up in order of battle according to naval tradition, began the voyage in disciplined fashion. Robert had a favourable wind, made Avlona on the other side, and coasted along as far as Butrint. There he was joined by his son Bohemond, who had crossed before him and had captured Avlona without difficulty. The whole army was now divided in two: one half, under Robert himself, was to make the sea passage to Dyrrakhion; the other, entrusted to Bohemond, was to march on the town by land.

Robert had actually passed Corfu and was within striking distance of Dyrrakhion when he was suddenly struck by a tremendous storm[43] off a promontory named Glossa. There was a heavy fall of snow, and winds blowing furiously from the mountains lashed up the sea. There was a howling noise as the waves built up; oars snapped off as the rowers plunged them into the water, the sails were torn to shreds by the blasts, yardarms were crushed and fell on the decks; and now ships were being swallowed up, crew and all. And yet it was the summer season; the sun had already passed the Tropic of Cancer and was on its way to the Lion – the season when the Dog Star rises, so they say. Everybody was confused and dismayed, not knowing what to do, unable to resist such enemies. A terrible cry arose as they groaned and lamented, calling on God, imploring His aid and praying that they might see the mainland.

But the tempest did not die down, as if God was venting His wrath on Robert for the unyielding, presumptuous arrogance of the man; as if He were showing by a sign at the very outset that the end would be disastrous. Anyway, some of the ships sank and their crews drowned with them; others were dashed against the headlands and broke up. The hides that covered the towers were slackened by the rain, so that the nails fell out and the hides naturally became heavier; their weight caused the wooden towers to collapse. They fell in ruins and sank the ships. Robert's own vessel, although half-shattered, barely made its way to safety, and some transport ships also escaped, unbelievably without losing their crews.

Many corpses were thrown up by the waves, and not a few treasures and other objects brought by the sailors of Robert's fleet were strewn on the sand. The survivors buried their dead with due ceremony, but because it was no easy matter to inter so many, they suffered horribly from the stench. They would soon have perished of hunger too, for all their supplies had been lost, if all the crops had not been ripe and the fields and gardens bursting with fruit. What had happened was significant to all men of sound judgement, but not to Robert. None of it frightened him, or affected his iron nerve. If he did pray that his life might be spared, it was only, I suppose, for as long as he could wage war on his chosen enemies.

The disaster by no means deterred him from his immediate aim and with the survivors (for a few had been rescued from danger by the invincible might of God) he remained for a week in Glabinitza to recover his own strength and rest his ship-wrecked mariners, but also to give time to the soldiers left behind in Brindisi, and indeed to those whom he was expecting from another quarter, to arrive by sea. He was also waiting for the heavily-armed knights and infantry, together with his light-armed forces, to cross by the overland route, for these had started a little before himself. When all the contingents, coming by land and sea, had joined up, he occupied the plain of Illyrikon in full force.

The Latin who gave me this information was with him, an envoy, so he told me, from the bishop of Bari,[44] who had been sent to Robert. He assured me that he had accompanied him on this campaign. They set up camp inside the ruined walls of the town formerly called Epidamnos. It was in this place that Pyrros, king of Epiros, once lived. He joined with the men of Taranto against the Romans and fought a fierce campaign in Apulia. As a result there was so much carnage that the whole population was put to the sword without exception and the town was left entirely without inhabitants. In later times, how-ever, according to Greek tradition and indeed according to the evidence of carved inscriptions there, Amphion and Zethos restored it to its present condition and the name was changed to Dyrrakhion. So much then for my digression[45] about this town; with it I end my third book. The fourth will relate what happened thereafter.

BOOK IV

1. Robert was already encamped on the mainland by 17 June[1] of the fourth indiction. He had with him a countless host of cavalry and infantry, for the whole force had regrouped from all directions and had assembled in one place. Its arrival and military demeanour alike inspired fear. On the sea cruised his fleet, comprising every type of vessel, manned by other soldiers with long experience of naval warfare. No wonder then that the inhabitants of Dyrrakhion, hemmed in on either side, that is to say, by land and sea, and in view of Robert's forces, which were innumerable and indescribable, were seized with the greatest dread. Nevertheless, George Palaiologos was a brave man, thoroughly trained in the art of leadership; he had fought on a thousand battlefields in the east and proved victorious; now, without alarm, he proceeded to fortify the town. The battlements were constructed according to the emperor's advice, catapults were set up everywhere on the walls, the demoralized soldiers were encouraged and scouts posted all along the ramparts. George himself moreover visited them at all hours of day and night, exhorting the sentinels to be extra watchful. At the same time he informed the emperor by letters of Robert's offensive, his presence near Dyrrakhion and preparations for the siege.

Siege-engines were outside the town and an enormous wooden tower was built, much higher than the walls even, protected at all points by hides of leather; on top of it stood rock-hurling machines; the whole circuit of walls was invested. Allies flocked to Robert from all quarters, while the towns in the vicinity were ravaged by sudden raids, and every day the

number of tents multiplied. All this terrified the people of
Dyrrakhion, for by now they knew the real aim of Duke Robert:
it was not, as his general proclamations said, to plunder towns
and the countryside, collect much booty in this way, and then
return to Apulia. It was not for that he had occupied the plain
of Illyrikon, but because he coveted the throne of the Roman
Empire; the hasty siege of Dyrrakhion was merely the first
round, so to speak.

Anyway, Palaiologos ordered the question to be put from the
top of the walls of why he had come. 'To restore Michael, my
kinsman, back to the throne from which he was deposed, to his
correct office; to punish the outrages inflicted on him; in a
word, to avenge him.' Palaiologos' men gave their reply: 'If we
see Michael and recognize him, we will without hesitation make
obeisance before him and surrender the town.' Hearing this
Robert at once gave orders that 'Michael' should be dressed in
magnificent robes and displayed to the citizens. He was led out
with an imposing escort, loudly acclaimed with all kinds of
musical instruments and cymbals, and shown to them. As soon
as they saw him, a thousand insults rained down on him from
above; he was a complete stranger, they yelled. Robert made
nothing of it and applied himself to the business in hand. However, while the conversation was going on, some men made a
quick sortie without warning, joined battle with the Latins and,
after doing them some slight damage, re-entered the town.

With regard to the monk who accompanied Robert, most
people had different views. Some announced that he was the
cup-bearer[2] of the Emperor Michael Doukas; others were certain that he was in fact the Emperor Michael, Robert's father-in-
law, for whose sake, they said, the latter had chosen to make
this terrible war; others again insisted that they knew for sure
that the whole affair had been invented by Robert, for the monk
had not appeared through his own initiative. Through his own
natural vigour and proud spirit, Robert had risen from the
direst poverty and an obscure origin to become master of all
the towns and lands of Lombardy, as well as Apulia itself; he
had confirmed his position as master of these regions, in the
way described earlier in the history. It was not long before his

ambitions grew – the normal reaction of the greedy – and he decided that he must make a tentative assault on the towns of Illyrikon; if the attempt succeeded, he would extend his operations further. Once a man has seized power, his love of money displays exactly the same characteristics as gangrene; for gangrene, once established in a body, never rests until it has invaded and corrupted the whole of it.

2. All this was reported by Palaiologos. The emperor learnt how Robert had crossed in the month of June; how he had been thwarted by storm and shipwreck (as has already been described), had been exposed to the wrath of God but had remained undismayed; how with his men he had taken Avlona at the first attack; how furthermore countless forces as thick as winter snowflakes were rallying around him from all directions, and that the more frivolous folk, believing that the pretender Michael was in truth the emperor, were joining him. Alexios saw the magnitude of the task ahead of him and was afraid. He knew that his own forces were vastly outnumbered by the Latins and therefore decided that he must call on the Turks from the east. There and then he made his views known to the sultan.

He also asked the Venetians for help, with promises and bribes (for there is a tradition that the 'Blues' in the Roman horse-racing contests got their name from Venice).[3] Some rewards were pledged, others granted at once, if only the Venetians would be willing to equip all their fleet and sail at speed to Dyrrakhion, first to protect the town and secondly to engage in sustained combat with Robert's navy. If, following his own clear instructions, they undertook to do this, either they would win a victory with God's help, or they would be defeated (as of course might happen); in either case they would have their promised reward, just as if the war had been completely successful. All their desires would be satisfied and confirmed by chrysobulls, provided that they were not in conflict with the interests of the Roman Empire.

The Venetians listened, made known all their requirements through the envoys and received formal pledges. Without delay a fleet was fitted out, comprising all types of ships, and sailed in good order towards Dyrrakhion. After a long voyage the Venetians put in near the sanctuary of the Immaculate Mother of God at a place called Pallia,[4] about eighteen stades from Robert's camp, which was pitched outside Dyrrakhion. When they saw the barbarian's fleet on the far side of the town, protected with every sort of warlike machine, they shrank from battle. Robert, who had heard of their arrival, sent his own son Bohemond to them with a squadron and orders to acclaim the Emperor Michael, and himself. They deferred the acclamation to the next day. Meanwhile, at nightfall, since they could not get close inshore and the wind had fallen, they lashed the bigger vessels together with cables and formed a so-called sea harbour.[5] Wooden towers were then constructed at their mastheads and with the help of cables the little skiffs towed by each ship were hoisted up between them. Armed men were put in these skiffs, and very thick pieces of wood cut up into lengths of not more than a cubit, into which they hammered sharp iron nails. They then waited for the coming of the Frankish fleet.

Day was already breaking when Bohemond arrived and demanded that they should acclaim the emperor and his father, but they made fun of his beard. Unable to bear the insult Bohemond led the attack on them in person, making for the biggest ships; others followed him. The battle was fiercely contested. However, when Bohemond was fighting with even greater ferocity, they hurled down one of these great blocks of wood, which I mentioned, from aloft and holed the ship on which he happened to be. The water was sucking the Franks down and as they were in danger of being engulfed, some jumped overboard but found themselves in exactly the same trouble and were drowned; others went on fighting the Venetians and were killed. Bohemond himself, with his own life at stake, leapt into another of his ships and took refuge there.

The Venetians, taking fresh heart and pressing their attack with more confidence, routed the enemy completely and pursued them as far as Robert's camp. Reaching dry land, they jumped overboard and started another battle with them. When he saw what was going on, Palaiologos made a sortie from Dyrrakhion and joined them in the fighting. After a violent

struggle which raged right up to Robert's entrenchment, many
Franks were chased away from it and many were put to the
sword.[6]

The Venetians returned to their ships loaded with booty,
while Palaiologos went back his base. After a few days of
regrouping the victors dispatched envoys to the emperor with
a full report of these events. Naturally they were received with
friendly greetings and rewarded with a thousand kindnesses;
finally he allowed them to go, taking with them large sums of
money for the Doge of Venice[7] and his officers.

3. Robert's warlike instinct told him that the war must go
on; he would have to fight hard. But there were difficulties:
because of the winter he was unable to launch his ships; the
Roman and Venetian fleets, tirelessly patrolling the straits, prevented reinforcements crossing from Lombardy; and the deliv-
ery of necessary supplies to him from that area was impeded.
But when the spring came and winter storms died down, the
Venetians made the first move. They weighed anchor and took
the offensive. Behind them came Maurix[8] with the Roman
fleet. Very heavy fighting ensued and Robert's men were routed
again. This convinced him that all his ships would have to be
dragged up on land.

The islanders, the inhabitants of the settlements along the
coast of the mainland, and all the others who were paying
tribute to Robert, were emboldened at his misfortunes and,
hearing about his defeat on the sea, were not so ready to meet
the heavy obligations he laid on them. Obviously he would
have to plan the war with greater care; a new campaign by sea
and land was inevitable. He had ideas but it was impossible to
carry them out: strong winds were blowing at that time and
through dread of shipwreck he lingered for two months in
the port of Hierikho. Nevertheless he was making ready and
organizing his forces for battle, intending to fight by sea and
land. To the best of their ability the Venetians and Romans
kept up their naval blockade, and when there was a little
improvement in the weather – enough to encourage would-be
sailors – they thwarted all efforts at a crossing from the west.
Robert's men, bivouacking by the River Glykys, meanwhile

found it no easy matter to get supplies from the mainland, for
when they left their entrenchments to forage or bring in other
necessities there was interference from the inhabitants of Dyrrakhion. They began to starve. There was other trouble: the
strangeness of the climate distressed them much, so that in the
course of three months, it is said, up to 10,000 men perished.
This disease attacked Robert's cavalry too and many died; in
fact, of the knights as many as 500 counts and elite fighting
men became victims of disease and famine, while in the lower
ranks of the cavalry the number of dead was unquantifiable.

His ships, as I have said, were drawn up on land by the River
Glykys, but when after the winter and the coming of spring the
weather became hotter and rainless, the water level dropped,
and there was not the normal flow from the mountain streams.
Consequently he was in an awkward situation; the ships could
not now be launched in the sea again. Despite his troubles,
Robert, being a man of great intelligence and versatility,
ordered piles to be driven in on either side of the river; these
were then tightly bound together with osiers; very tall trees
were felled at the roots and laid behind these piles, and sand
was spread on them, in order to direct the flow into one course,
concentrated so to speak into one canal formed by the stakes.
Gradually pools formed and the water filled the whole of the
artificial channel until it became deep enough to raise the ships,
which had rested on the land and were now afloat. After that,
when there was a good flow of water, the vessels were easily
launched in the sea.[9]

4. In view of Robert's activities, the emperor wrote at once
to Pakourianos. He explained how the man's unrestrained
ambition had led to the capture of Avlona and how he had
utter contempt for the misfortunes suffered on land and sea,
not to mention the defeat inflicted on him at the very outset of
the campaign. There must be no delay, he wrote; Pakourianos
was to assemble his forces and join the emperor with the greatest urgency. This is what Pakourianos was told. Accordingly in
the month of August[10] in the fourth indiction, the emperor
himself quickly left Constantinople. Isaac remained in the capital to maintain order and quash the sort of nonsense which

poorly disposed people are prone to indulge in. He was also to guard the palace and city, and at the same time to comfort the women inclined to be tearful. As far as his mother was concerned, help was, I suppose, uncalled for – she was herself a tower of strength and in any case a highly skilled administrator. Having read the letter Pakourianos at once appointed Nicholas Branas, a man of courage with considerable experience in war, as *hypostrategos*. He himself with all the heavily-armed infantry and the nobles hastily departed from Orestias and hurried to meet the emperor.

The emperor meanwhile had already drawn up his entire army in battle order. The commanders, appointed from the bravest of his officers, were told to march in this formation where the terrain permitted, so that every man becoming well acquainted with the general arrangement of the troops and recognizing his own place in the line would not panic in the hour of battle, nor readily change position under different circumstances.

The corps of *Exkouvitoi* was led by Constantine Opos, the Macedonians by Antiokhos, the Thessalians by Alexander Kabasilas, while Tatikios, who was at the time *megas primikerios*, commanded the Turks from the district of Akhrido. The latter was a valiant fighter, a man who kept his head under combat conditions, but his family was not freeborn. His father was in fact a Saracen who fell into the hands of my paternal grandfather John Komnenos while on a marauding raid. The leaders of the Manichaeans,[11] who numbered 2,800, were Xantas and Kouleon, themselves heretics of the same persuasion. All these men were excellent fighters, more than ready to draw the blood of their enemies when the opportunity arose; they were headstrong and devoid of shame. The soldiers of the emperor's household (commonly called *vestiarites*) and the regiments of Franks were commanded by Panoukomites and Constantine Houmpertopoulos, so-called because of his origin.[12]

When the disposition of the troops was complete, Alexios set out against Robert in full force. On the way he met a man who came from those parts and after questioning him had a clearer picture of what was happening there: Robert had moved all the

machines required for the siege near to the walls, but Palaiologos, after working night and day to oppose his siege-engines
and frustrate his schemes, had at last grown weary of this; he
had thrown open the gates, gone out and fought a determined
battle with the enemy. He had suffered serious wounds in
different parts of his body; the worst was when an arrow penetrated near his temple. He tried to draw it out forcibly, but was
unable to do it. An expert was summoned and he cut away the
end – the butt where the feathers are attached – but the rest of
it remained in the wound. Palaiologos bound up his head as
best he could, and hurled himself again into the midst of the
foe, fighting on till late evening without flinching.

The emperor realized when he heard this report just how
desperately in need of help Palaiologos must be. He quickened
his march. On his arrival at Thessaloniki, many informants
confirmed the news about Robert, and in greater detail. Robert
had finished his preparations, and having gathered a large
amount of wood on the plain of Dyrrakhion, had set up camp
there with his brave and well-trained troops, barely an arrow's
shot distance from the town walls. He had also positioned in
the meantime many troops in the mountains, in the valleys and
in neighbouring hills. The emperor heard about the careful
preparations of Palaiologos from several sources.

Palaiologos had already made up his mind to burn the
wooden tower built by Robert, and on the walls there were
catapults, naphtha, pitch and small pieces of dry wood. He
waited for the enemy's attack. As he expected it to take place
on the next day, he set up a wooden tower of his own, inside
the town and directly opposite the other. It was ready in good
time; in fact, all through the night he experimented with a beam
placed on top of it. The intention was to thrust forward this
beam against the doors of Robert's tower when it was brought
to the wall. He was testing it, to find out whether it could be
moved without difficulty and would fall right in the path of the
enemy's doors and stop them from being opened in the usual
way. Being assured that the beam did thrust forward easily and
could successfully perform its function, he had no more worries
about the coming battle.

On the next day, Robert ordered all his men to take up arms; some 500, infantry and fully equipped horsemen, were led into the tower and it was brought near to the wall. They hurried to open the door on the top, intending to use it as a drawbridge to cross over into the citadel, but Palaiologos at that very moment thrust forward his own huge beam by means of the mechanical devices prepared in advance and with the help of many brave men. As the beam made it absolutely impossible to open the door, Robert's stratagem was frustrated.

Then a never-ending shower of arrows was directed at the Kelts at the top of the tower, who were forced to take cover, being unable to bear it any longer. Palaiologos now gave orders to set the tower alight; no sooner had he given this command than the tower was on fire. The Kelts at the top threw themselves off, while those below opened up the door at the bottom and fled. Seeing this Palaiologos immediately led out some fully armed soldiers by the postern gate and others with axes, with which to smash up the tower. Here too he was successful, for with the top on fire and the lower parts broken up with stone-cutters' tools, it was completely destroyed.

5. According to the person who told me, Robert was hastening to build a second tower, similar to the first, and was making ready siege-engines against the town. Aware of the need for speedy help, Alexios pressed on. When he arrived at Dyrrakhion, he made an entrenchment for his army by the banks of the River Kharzanes. Without delay messengers were sent to ask Robert why he had come and what his intentions were.

Alexios meanwhile went off to the sanctuary dedicated to Nicholas, the great pontiff, which was four stades from the town. He reconnoitred the ground, in order to pick the most favourable site for a battle line before Robert could do so. It was then 15 October. A neck of land extended from Dalmatia to the sea, ending in a promontory which was almost surrounded by water; on this the sanctuary was built. On the side facing Dyrrakhion there was a gentle slope down to the plain, with the sea on the left and a high, overhanging mountain on the right. At this point the Roman army was concentrated and camp pitched. Then George Palaiologos was summoned. But he, with long experience of such matters, refused to come, explaining to the emperor that he reckoned it unwise to leave the town. Alexios again sent for him, more urgently this time, but in vain. Palaiologos replied, 'It seems to me absolutely fatal to leave the citadel while it is under siege. Unless I see Your Majesty's seal-ring, I will not come out.' The ring was duly sent and he at once joined the emperor with some warships.

Alexios asked him about Robert's actions and when he had received a full and accurate account, he asked whether he should risk a battle with him. Palaiologos categorically stated that he should not. Certain others too who had many years of experience in war earnestly opposed the idea and advised him to adopt a waiting policy; he should try to reduce Robert by skirmishing and by preventing his men from leaving camp to forage or plunder; the same plan should be taken up by Bodin and the Dalmatians and the rest of the officers in the neighbouring districts. They were sure that Robert could be easily defeated if he took these measures. The majority of the younger officers preferred to fight, especially Constantine *porphyrogennetos*, Nikephoros Synadenos, Nampites, the commander of the Varangians, and even the sons of the former emperor Romanos Diogenes, Leo and Nikephoros themselves.

While these arguments were going on the envoys returned from Robert and delivered his answer: 'I have not come to fight Your Majesty – that was not my intention at all – but rather to avenge the wrong done to my father-in-law. If you wish to make peace with me, I too welcome it, provided that you are ready to fulfil the conditions stated by my ambassadors to you.' He was demanding quite impossible terms, which were also harmful to the empire, although he did promise at the same time that, if he got what he wanted, he would regard Lombardy itself as his by permission of the emperor, and he would help us when the need arose. It was a mere pretext: by demanding terms he would give the appearance of desiring peace himself; by proposing the impossible and failing to obtain it he would have an excuse to make war, and then hold the Roman emperor responsible for the fighting.

Anyway his proposals were out of the question and he failed.

So, having called together all the counts, he addressed them:
'You know the wrong done by the Emperor Nikephoros Botaneiates to my father-in-law, and the disgrace suffered by my
daughter Helena when she was thrown out of the palace with
him. Finding this intolerable, we have left our country to avenge
the insult and punish Botaneiates. But he has been deprived of
his throne and now we have to deal with a young emperor and
a brave soldier, who has acquired an experience of the military
art beyond his years; we must not take up his challenge in a
light-hearted manner. Where there are many masters, there will
be confusion, brought about by the diverse strategies of the
many. In future, therefore, one man among us should command
the rest; he should consult all, not adopting his own schemes
in an autocratic way and according to his own caprice; the
others will openly express to him their own opinions, but at
the same time accept the counsel of the elected leader. And
behold, I myself am ready, first among you all, to obey whom-
ever you choose as leader.'

Everyone praised this plan and complimented Robert on his
speech. There and then, without any dissension, they offered
him the leadership. For a while he dissembled, as though indifferent, and refused to accept, but they pressed him all the more
and begged him. In the end he yielded, seeming to do so in
response to their pleas, although in fact he had been plotting
this for a long time. After an involved series of arguments and
a catalogue of reasons cleverly linked together, he made it
appear, to those who did not understand his mentality, that he
was doing this against his will, while it was actually what he
really desired with all his heart.

He ended his speech thus: 'Listen to my advice, you counts
and the rest of the army. We have left our own native lands
and come here to fight against an emperor of great courage,
one who has only recently seized the helm of power, but has
won many wars in the reigns of his predecessors and brought
to them most powerful rebels as prisoners of war. All our
energies therefore must be devoted to this struggle. If God
grants us the victory, we shall no longer be in want of money.
That is why we must burn all our baggage, hole our transport

ships and send them to the bottom of the sea, and take up this challenge from him as if today is the supreme decider of life and death.' They all agreed with him.

6. Such were the thoughts and plans of Robert; the emperor's schemes were different, but more complicated and subtle. Both generals kept their armies together while they planned their tactics and movements, so that operations might be directed in a sensible way. The emperor decided to launch a sudden night attack on Robert's camp from two sides and the whole of the allied army was ordered to surprise him from the rear. They were to go through the salt marshes, a longer route – but Alexios did not object to that, for the sake of catching the enemy unawares. He himself intended to attack from the front when he knew the others were in position. Robert left his tents empty and crossed the bridge that night. It was on 18 October in the fifth indiction. With all his forces he arrived at the sanctuary built long ago by the sea in honour of the martyr Theodore. All night they celebrated the holy and divine mysteries, trying to win the support of the heavens. Then Robert arranged his battle line: he himself commanded the centre; the wing nearer to the sea was entrusted to Amiketas, a distinguished count, physically and morally courageous; the other wing was given to his son Bohemond, surnamed Saniskos.[13]

The emperor, realizing what had happened, adapted his own plans to meet the new circumstances – in moments of crisis he was expert at choosing the right course of action – and drew up his line somewhere along the slope by the sea. His army was divided, but the barbarians already on their way to attack Robert's camp were not recalled; the others, who carry on their shoulders the two-edged swords, together with their commander Nampites, were kept back. He ordered them to dismount from their horses and march forward in their ranks a short distance in front of the line. They were carrying shields, like all men of their race. The rest of the force was split up into companies. The emperor led the centre in person; on right and left respectively he stationed the *Kaisar* Nikephoros Melissenos and the one called Pakourianos who was *megas domestikos*. Between himself and the barbarians on foot was a strong contin-

gent of skilled archers. These he intended to send first against
Robert, having instructed Nampites to open his ranks quickly
for them, by moving to right and left, whenever they wanted to
charge out against the Kelts; and to close ranks again and march
in tight order, when they had withdrawn.

When all his arrangements of the army were ready, he himself
moved to attack the Keltic front, following the coastline. As for
the barbarians who had gone through the salt marshes, they
made an assault on the enemy camp just at the moment when
the inhabitants of Dyrrakhion threw open the town gates in
accordance with the emperor's instructions. As the two leaders
approached one another, Robert sent a detachment of cavalry
with orders to manoeuvre in such a way that some of the
Romans might be enticed from their line. The emperor did
not fall into that trap; in fact, substantial reinforcements of
lightly-armed soldiers were moved to oppose them.

Both sides then indulged in some moderate skirmishing, but
Robert was quietly following these horsemen and the gap
between the two armies was already diminishing, when the
infantry and cavalry of Amiketas' group charged ahead of the
main body in an assault on the extremity of the line where
Nampites was. Our men resisted bravely and the enemy turned
back – for they were not all elite soldiers. They threw themselves
into the sea up to their necks and when they were near the
Roman and Venetian ships begged for their lives – but nobody
rescued them.

There is a story that Robert's wife Gaita, who used to accompany him on campaign, like another Pallas, if not a second
Athene, seeing the runaways and glaring fiercely at them,
shouted in a loud voice – words which were equivalent to those
of Homer, but in her own language: 'How far will ye run? Halt!
Be men!'[14] As they continued to flee, she grasped a long spear
and charged at full gallop against them. It brought them to
their senses and they went back to fight.

Meanwhile the axe-bearers and their leader Nampites had
advanced a fair distance from the Roman line, carried away by
their own inexperience and hot temper; they had gone too fast,
eager to clash with the Kelts who were just as eager themselves

former were passionately devoted to war, like the Kelts, in the matter of fighting were by no means their inferiors.) Robert noticed however that they were already tired and short of breath; their rapid advance, the distance they had covered and the weight of their arms were enough to convince him. He ordered a detachment of infantry to fall upon them. It seems that in their tired condition they were less strong than the Kelts. At any rate the whole barbarian force was massacred there, except for survivors who fled for safety to the sanctuary of the Archangel Michael;[15] all who could went inside the building; the rest climbed to the roof and stood there, thinking that would save their lives. The Latins simply set fire to them and burned the lot, together with the sanctuary.

The remnants of the Roman army carried on the battle with courage, but Robert, like some winged horseman, with the rest of his forces charged and pushed back the Roman line, in many places tearing it apart. In the end, some fell fighting on the field of battle; others looked to their own safety and fled. The Emperor Alexios, like an impregnable tower, stood his ground, though he had lost many of his companions, men distinguished alike for their birth and their experience in war. In that battle there fell Constantine, the son of the former emperor Constantine Doukas, who was born after his father had ceased to be a private citizen and so came into the world and was brought up in the *porphyra*; at the time he was honoured by his father with an imperial diadem. Nikephoros, surnamed Synadenos, a brave man and very handsome, who was impatient to surpass all others in that day's fighting, also died. The Constantine mentioned above often spoke to him about a marriage to his own sister. Other nobles fell, including Nikephoros the father of Palaiologos; Zakharias received a mortal wound in the chest and died instantly; Aspietes and many other fine soldiers were killed.

The battle was not yet finished when three Latins, seeing the emperor still holding out against the enemy, detached themselves from the rest and bore down on him at full gallop with long spears at the ready. One of them was the Amiketas I spoke of; the second was Peter, who described himself as the son of

Aliphas; the third was at least their equal. Amiketas missed the emperor because his horse swerved slightly. The emperor parried the spear of the second with his sword and with all his strength wounded him by the collarbone, severing his arm from his body. The third aimed a blow directly at the emperor's forehead, but with great presence of mind Alexios, coolly and not at all alarmed, recognized in a flash what he had to do in that split second: as the blow fell he leaned over backwards towards his horse's tail. The sword point just grazed his skin, immediately causing a slight cut, but was impeded by the rim of his helmet. It cut through the leather strap which fastened under his chin and knocked the helmet to the ground. The Kelt then rode on past him, thinking he was unseated, but the emperor drew himself upright and sat firmly in the saddle, with all his arms intact. In his right hand he held his unsheathed sword. He was dusty and bloodstained, bareheaded, with his bright red hair straggling in front of his eyes and annoying him (for his horse, frightened and impatient of the bit, was jumping about wildly and making the curls fall over his face), but even so he recovered as best he could and defied his adversaries.

He then saw the Turks running away too and even Bodin was withdrawing without a fight. Bodin had put on armour and had drawn up his troops in battle array; throughout the day he stood by, apparently ready to help the emperor at any minute in accordance with the agreements made with him. Really, it seems, he was watching anxiously to discover if victory was going to the emperor; if it did, he would join in attacking the Kelts; if not, he would quietly beat a retreat. From his actions it is clear that this was his plan, for when he realized that the Kelts were now sure of victory, he ran off home without striking a single blow. Alexios knew this and when he saw nobody coming to his aid, he also retired before the enemy. Thus the Latins put to flight the Roman army.[16]

7. Robert reached the sanctuary of St Nicholas, where was the imperial tent and all the Roman baggage. He then dispatched all his fit men in pursuit of the sovereign, while he himself stayed there, gloating over the imminent capture of the Roman emperor. Such were the thoughts that fired his arrogant spirit.

His men pursued Alexios with great determination as far as a place called by the natives Kake Pleura.[17] The situation was as follows: below there flows the River Kharzanes; on the other side was a high overhanging rock. The pursuers caught up with him between these two. They struck at him on the left side with their spears (there were nine of them in all) and forced him to the right. No doubt he would have fallen, had not the sword which he grasped in his right hand rested firmly on the ground. What is more, the spur tip on his left foot caught in the edge of the saddlecloth, which they call a *hypostroma*, and this made him less liable to fall. He grabbed the horse's mane with his left hand and pulled himself up. It was no doubt some divine power that saved him from his enemies in an unexpected way, for it caused other Kelts to aim their spears at him from the right. The spear points, thrust towards his right side, suddenly straightened him and kept him in equilibrium.

It was indeed an extraordinary sight. The enemies on the left strove to push him off; those on the right plunged their spears at his flank, as if in competition with the first group, opposing spear to spear. Thus the emperor was kept upright between them. He settled himself more firmly in the saddle, gripping horse and saddlecloth alike more tightly with his legs. It was at this moment that the horse gave proof of its nobility. Under any circumstances, it was unusually agile and spirited, of exceptional strength, a real warhorse (Alexios had actually taken him from Bryennios, together with the purple-dyed saddlecloth when he took him prisoner during the reign of Nikephoros Botaneiates). To put it in brief, this charger was now inspired by Divine Providence: he suddenly leapt through the air and landed on top of the rock I mentioned before, as if he had been raised on wings – or to use the language of mythology, as if he had taken the wings of Pegasos. Bryennios used to call him Sgouritzes.[18] Some of the barbarians' spears, striking at thin air, fell from their hands; others, which had pierced the emperor's clothing, remained stuck there and were carried off with the horse when he jumped. The emperor quickly cut away these trailing weapons.

Despite the terrible dangers in which he found himself, he

was not troubled in spirit, nor was he confused in thought; he lost no time in choosing the expedient course and contrary to all expectation escaped from his enemies. The Kelts stood open mouthed, astonished by what had happened, and indeed it was a most amazing thing. They saw that he was making off in a new direction and followed him once more. When he was a long way ahead of his pursuers, he wheeled round and, coming face to face with one of them, drove his spear through the man's chest. He fell at once to the ground, backwards.

Turning his horse about, the emperor continued on his way. However, he fell in with several Kelts who had been chasing Romans further on. They saw him a long way off and halted in a line, shield to shield, partly to rest their horses, but at the same time hoping to take him alive and present him as a prize of war to Robert. Pursued by enemies from behind and confronted by others, Alexios despaired of his life; but he gathered his wits and noting in the centre of his enemies one man who, from his physical appearance and the flashing brightness of his armour, he thought was Robert, he steadied his horse and charged at him. His opponent also levelled his spear and they both advanced across the intervening space to do battle.

The emperor was first to strike, taking careful aim with his spear. The weapon pierced the Kelt's breast and passed through his back. Straightway he fell to the ground mortally wounded, and died on the spot. Thereupon the emperor rode off through the centre of their broken line. The killing of this barbarian had saved him. The man's comrades gathered round when they saw him wounded and hurled to the ground, and tended him as he lay there. The others, pursuing from the rear, meanwhile dismounted from their horses and recognized the dead man. They beat their breasts in grief, for although he was not Robert, he was a distinguished noble, and Robert's second-in-command. While they busied themselves over him, the emperor was well on his way.

8. In the course of this account, partly because of the nature of the history and partly because of the great importance of these events, I have forgotten that it is my father whose successes I am writing of. Often, in my desire not to incur suspicion, in

the composition of my history I hurry over affairs that concern
him, neither exaggerating nor adding my personal observations.
I wish I were detached and free from this feeling that I have for
him, so that seizing on this vast material I might demonstrate
how much my tongue, when released from all restraint, could
delight in noble deeds. But the natural love I have for him
overshadows my personal wishes: I would not like the public
to imagine that I am inventing marvels in my eagerness to speak
about my own family. On many occasions when I recalled the
glorious deeds of my father, if I had written down and given a
full account of all the troubles he endured, I would have wept
away my very soul, and I could not have passed over the story
without lamentation and mourning. But so far as that part of
my history is concerned, I must avoid the subtleties of rhetoric,
and like some unfeeling stone or marble pass quickly over his
misfortunes. If I wanted to win a deserved reputation for loving
him, I should have included his disasters in an oath, like the
young man who swore: 'No, Agelaos, by Zeus and by my
father's woes.'[19] For I am certainly no worse than that young
man. But now we must leave my father's suffering; I alone must
marvel at them and weep, but the reader must return to the
narrative.

After this, the Kelts went on their way to Robert. When the
latter saw them empty-handed and learnt what had happened
to them, he bitterly censured all of them and one in particular,
whom he even threatened to flog, calling him a coward and an
ignoramus in war. The fellow expected the worst – because he
had not leapt on to the rock with his own horse and either
struck and murdered Alexios, or grabbed him and brought him
alive to Robert. For this Robert, in other respects the bravest
and most daring of men, was also full of bitterness, swift to
anger, with a heart overflowing with passion and wrath. In his
dealings with enemies he would either run through with his
spear any man who resisted him, or do away with him himself,
cutting the thread of destiny, so to speak.

However, the soldier whom he accused now gave a vivid
account of the ruggedness and inaccessibility of the rock: no
one, he added, whether on foot or on horseback, could climb

it without divine aid – not to mention a man at war and en[
in fighting; even without war it was impossible to vent[
ascent. 'If you can't believe a word I say,' he cried, [,
yourself – or let some other knight, however daring, have a go.
He will see it's out of the question. Anyway, if someone, I say
if someone should conquer that rock, not only minus wings
but even with them, then I myself am ready to endure any
punishment you like to name and to be damned for cowardice.'
These words, which expressed the man's wonder and amazement, appeased Robert's fury; his anger turned to admiration.

As for the emperor, after spending two days and nights in
travel through the winding paths of the neighbouring mountains and all that impassable region, he arrived at Akhris. On
the way he crossed the Kharzanes and waited for a short time
near a place called Babagora (a remote valley). Neither the
defeat nor any of the other evils of war troubled his mind; he
was not worried in the slightest by the pain from his wounded
forehead; but in his heart he grieved deeply for those who had
fallen in the battle and especially for the men who had fought
bravely. Nevertheless, he applied himself wholly to the problems of the town of Dyrrakhion, and it hurt him to recall that
it was now without its leader, Palaiologos, who had been unable
to get back into the town due to the rapid developments during
the battle. To the best of his ability the emperor ensured the
safety of the inhabitants and entrusted the protection of the
citadel to the Venetian officers who had migrated there. All
the rest of the town was put under the command of Komiskortes, an Albanian by origin,[20] to whom he gave profitable
advice in the meantime by letter.

BOOK V

1. Robert, without any trouble whatsoever, seized all the booty, as well as the imperial tent, and took up position on the plain where he had camped during the siege of Dyrrakhion. Full of pride he brought with him the trophies of victory. After pausing there for a short time he reviewed plans for the future, wondering if he should revive the assault on the walls, or whether he should defer it to the next spring,[1] in the meantime occupying Glabinitza and Ioannina, and wintering there with his whole army stationed in the valleys which dominate the plain of Dyrrakhion. The people of that town, as I have said, were mostly emigrants from Amalfi and Venice. When they learnt of the misfortunes of the emperor, the terrible carnage and the deaths of so many remarkable men, not to mention the withdrawal of the fleets and Robert's decision to renew the siege in the coming spring, they thought long and hard about how they could ensure their safety better in the future and about how they could avoid taking such risks again.

They gathered therefore, and after each man had expressed his own private opinion and when they failed to agree on a common course, they decided to resolve the impasse by submitting to Robert and surrendering the town. Instigated by one of the colonists from Amalfi[2] and in obedience to their advice, they opened the gates and allowed him to enter. Once master of the place, Robert called together his forces, separating them into their several nationalities. A careful check was made of those who had received serious injuries or chance skin-grazes from a sword; he inquired into the type and number of men killed in the previous battles; at the same time he took care, since winter was already at hand, to plan the recruiting of another mercenary force and the assembling of foreign contingents, so that on the arrival of spring he could march against the emperor at full strength.

Robert thus laid his plans and congratulated himself on his triumphs and victories. But he was not alone in preparing for the next campaign: despite this intolerable defeat, his own wound and the loss of so many noble comrades, the emperor was by no means cowed by fear; far from belittling his own chances or relaxing his efforts, he devoted himself entirely, with all his mental powers, to the avenging of defeat in the coming spring. Both leaders were prepared for all eventualities, able to comprehend at a glance every detail, acquainted with all the ruses of war; each was thoroughly familiar with siege tactics, the laying of ambushes, fighting in line of battle; in hand-to-hand combat bold and valiant, these two men, of all commanders under the sun, were worthy rivals, in wit and bravery well suited. The Emperor Alexios had a certain advantage over Robert, because he was still young and in no way the inferior of his adversary – although Robert was at the height of his powers and boasted that he could make the earth tremble, or nearly tremble, and cause terror among whole regiments by his battle cry alone. However, these matters must be reserved for other works; they will surely claim the attention of would-be encomiasts.

After resting for a little while at Akhris and recovering his spirits the Emperor Alexios came to Diabolis.[3] As best he could, he comforted the survivors, victims of battle fatigue; the rest he ordered through envoys to meet in Thessaloniki from all directions. Now that he had experience of Robert and the boldness of his great army, he condemned the extreme naivety and the cowardly behaviour of his own men. (I will not emphasize the fact that even the men there present with him were completely untrained and ignorant of a soldier's life.) It was essential therefore that he should acquire allies, but without money this was impossible. There was no money – the imperial treasury had been denuded by his predecessor on the throne, Nikephoros Botaneiates, and to no good purpose. So bare was it indeed that even the treasury doors were unlocked; anyone who wished to walk through them could do so unhindered, for everything had been frittered away. Thus the general situation was critical. Frailty and misery oppressed the Roman Empire simultaneously.

What then was this young emperor, having only just seized the helm of government, to do? Briefly, he had two courses open to him: he could either abandon all in despair and abdicate, to avoid imputations of incompetent and inept leadership, even though he was not responsible; or, of necessity, he could call on allies wherever available, collect from whatever source he could enough money to satisfy their demands and recall by means of largess his army now scattered to the four points of the compass. The men still with him would thus become more confident and hold on, while the absentees would be keener to return. Under those circumstances they might resist the Keltic hordes with greater boldness. Wishing to do nothing unworthy or inconsistent with his own knowledge of military science or for that matter his own bravery, he had two objects in view: first, to summon allies from all quarters, cleverly luring them with expectations of liberal gifts; and, second, to demand from his mother and brother the provision of money – from any source whatever.

2. Because they were unable to find another method of providing the money, they first collected their own available resources, in the form of gold and silver objects, and sent them to the imperial mint. The empress, my mother, took the lead: all that she had inherited from her father and mother was offered, in the hope that by doing this she might inspire others to follow her example. She was much concerned for the emperor, understanding just how difficult his position was. Afterwards there was a spontaneous and eager offering of available gold and silver by all the more loyal friends of these two rulers; they sent contributions partly to the allies, partly to the emperor.

Even so the amount was far from sufficient for their immediate needs. Some allies demanded favours on the grounds that they had fought on our side before; others – that is to say, the mercenaries – wanted higher pay. The emperor, despairing of the goodwill of the Romans, called for greater efforts and made fresh demands. His mother and brother, now in a state of utter perplexity, discussed many proposals, in public and behind closed doors – for they knew that Robert was arming again. They examined in their despair the ancient laws and canons on the alienation of sacred objects. Among other things they discovered that it is lawful to expropriate sacred objects from churches for the ransoming of prisoners of war (and it was clear that all those Christians living in Asia under barbarian rule and all those who had escaped massacre were thus defiled because of their relations with the infidels). In order to pay the soldiers and allies, therefore, they decided to convert into money a small quantity of such objects, which had long been idle and set aside as serving no purpose; in fact these objects merely tempted the majority to perform acts of sacrilege and irreverence.

Once this decision had been taken, the *Sebastokrator* Isaac went to the Great Church of God, where he had called together the Synod[4] and all the clergy. The members of the Holy Synod, who sit in council with the patriarch on ecclesiastical matters, were amazed to see him and asked why he came. 'I have come,' he replied, 'to inform you of a proposal which will help us in this terrible crisis and save our army.' Then he quoted the canons relating to sacred objects no longer in use, and after speaking at length on the matter, he added, 'I am forced to force those whom I do not wish to force.' The bold arguments he produced seemed likely to convince the majority.

He was opposed however by Metaxas, who raised certain specious objections and also poured ridicule on Isaac himself. Nevertheless the original proposal was passed. This became the subject of a very serious accusation against the emperors (for I do not hesitate to call Isaac emperor, although he did not wear the purple) not only on that occasion, but even later, right down to our own time. A certain Leo was then bishop of Chalcedon. He was not a particularly learned man nor a very wise one, but he had lived virtuously; unfortunately his manner was rough and disagreeable. When the gold and silver on the doors of the Khalkoprateia[5] were being taken away, he appeared in public and spoke freely, without the slightest concern for either the public finances or the laws relating to the sacred vessels. He behaved with inexcusable arrogance and even insubordination towards Alexios, for every time the emperor returned to the capital Leo abused his patience and courtesy. On the first occasion that the sovereign left Constantinople to fight Robert, Leo provoked the *Sebastokrator* Isaac's fury after the emperor's brother had been instructed to collect money from all available sources to general agreement and in accordance with the laws and wider justice.

After numerous defeats and thousands of daring attacks on the Kelts, the emperor by the grace of God came back crowned with the laurels of victory, but once again he heard that fresh hordes of enemies, by whom I mean the Scythians,[6] were setting out against him. For the same reasons as before there was a hurried collection of money. The bishop made a ruthless attack on the emperor, who was in the capital at the time. A long discussion followed on the issue of sacred objects. Leo maintained that the holy images were truly worshipped by us, not merely treated with reverence. On some points his arguments were reasonable and befitting a bishop, but on others he was unorthodox, whether because of his contentious spirit and hatred for the emperor, or through ignorance I do not know. He was incapable of expressing his ideas accurately and without ambiguity, because he was utterly devoid of any training in logic.

His attacks on the rulers became more and more reckless as he listened to the prompting of evil-minded men, many of whom at that time held places in the administration. They prodded him into such a state that he even became insolent and indulged in foolish calumnies, despite the fact that the emperor, who had already been commended by the more illustrious members of the Synod – men whom the bishop's supporters dubbed stooges – called on him to change his mind about the images and refrain from hostile acts against Alexios. Moreover, the emperor promised to restore to the sacred churches images more glorious than the originals and do everything necessary by way of reparation. In the end Leo was condemned and he lost his bishopric.[7] Far from cowering under the verdict or maintaining silence, he proceeded to stir up more trouble in the Church, gathering round him a considerable following made up of utterly stubborn and incorrigible men. Many years later he was unanimously condemned to exile. He retired to Sozopolis in Pontos, where every provision was made by the emperor for his comfort, although Leo afterwards refused to accept these courtesies, apparently because he nursed a grudge against him. There the story must end.

3. Recruits flocked to join the emperor (when they heard that he was safe). They were carefully trained in good horsemanship, in accurate shooting with the bow, in arms drill and in the best ways of setting an ambush. Envoys were once more sent to the king of Germany, led by the bishop of Methymna. In a letter Alexios urged him to delay no longer, but to invade Lombardy at once, in accordance with the treaty[8] concluded between them, thereby diverting Robert's attention. In the meantime, the emperor would benefit from this respite to gather new forces and foreign soldiers, hoping to use these to drive Robert from Illyrikon. If the king of Germany would do this, he said, not only would he be most grateful to him, but he confirmed that the marriage alliance promised by his ambassadors would be fulfilled.

After making these arrangements, Alexios left Pakourianos, the *megas domestikos*, in that area and returned to Constantinople to recruit foreigners from all quarters and to take certain other measures made necessary by the crisis and events that had occurred. The Manichaeans, Xantas and Kouleon,[9] with their men to the number of 2,500 had returned home in disorder. On many occasions they were recalled by the emperor, but although they had made promises, they were constantly putting off the day. Nevertheless he persisted, offering them gifts and honours. The offers were made in writing, but it was all to no avail.

While Roman preparations for war were going forward, someone came to Robert with the news that the German king was about to arrive in Lombardy. Robert was in an awkward position. When he crossed to Illyrikon he had left Roger in

charge of his realm, but so far no land had been apportioned
to the younger son Bohemond. Now, after considering many
possible courses, with many changes of mind, he summoned all
the counts and the leaders of the whole army to a meeting.
Bohemond Saniskos was invited to attend it. Seating himself in
front of them Robert made a speech:

'You know, counts, that when I was about to cross to Illyrikon I appointed my beloved son Roger, my eldest son, lord of
my realm. It would not have been right to go away on so
important a campaign and leave my own country without a
leader, a ready prey for anyone who cared to seize it. Now since
the king of Germany is already on the point of attacking it, we
must do our best to repel him, for it is wrong to lay claim to
the possessions of others and neglect one's own. That is why I
am going in person to protect my own country and to fight the
German. To this younger son of mine I entrust Dyrrakhion,
Avlona and the other towns and islands that I have won in war.
I give you an order and ask you to treat him as you would
myself; fight for him with all your heart and strength.

'And to you, my dear son,' he said, 'I give this advice: honour
the counts in every way, make use of their counsel at all times,
do not dictate, but always work with them. As for yourself,
make sure you do not neglect to follow up the war with the
Roman emperor; although he has suffered a great defeat and
barely escaped with his own life; although most of his armies
have been lost in war and he himself was almost taken alive (he
barely escaped with his life, and managed to slip through our
hands wounded) yet you must never relax. A respite might give
him the chance to recover his breath and take up the fight with
greater courage than ever. He is no ordinary enemy. From his
infancy he has been brought up amid wars and battles. He has
traversed the whole of the east and west, making prisoners of
all rebels against previous emperors – you have heard with your
own ears all about that often enough. In a word, if you lose
courage, if you fail to march against him with total determination, all my achievements, all my efforts will be brought to
nothing and you yourself will reap the fruits of your neglect in
full. As for me, I go now to fight the king, to expel him from

our territory, and thus confirm my beloved Roger in the position of authority I gave him.'

With these words he took his leave and embarking on a monoreme crossed over to Lombardy.[10] He quickly arrived at Salerno which had for a long time been set aside as the residence of those invested with the ducal office. He stayed there long enough to collect strong forces and as many mercenaries from other parts as he could. Meanwhile the German king, keeping his pledges to the emperor, hurried to occupy Lombardy. Robert knew this and lost no time in going to Rome; he wished to unite with the pope and frustrate the king's immediate aims. The pope was not reluctant and both set out against the German.

However, while the latter hastened to invade Lombardy he heard of the emperor's misfortunes: that he had lost a great battle; that some of his army had been wiped out, the rest had scattered in all directions; that Alexios himself, exposed to many dangers and fighting bravely, had been seriously wounded in various parts of his body, but thanks to his daring and courage had been miraculously saved. The king thereupon turned his horse back along the path by which he had come, seeing as something of a victory the fact that he had not personally taken any unnecessary risks. He then made for home. When Robert entered the king's camp, he was unwilling himself to pursue any further, but detached a strong body of his men and ordered them to hunt the Germans down. All the booty was seized and then Robert went back to Rome together with the pope.[11] The latter was enthroned by Robert and in return acclaimed him, after which Robert retired to Salerno in order to recover from the fatigue of his many battles.

4. Not long after Bohemond rejoined him; one could plainly read in his face the news of the defeat inflicted on him. How this came about I will now explain. Mindful of his father's recommendations, Bohemond, who was in any case a warlike man and loved danger, was tenaciously carrying on hostilities against the emperor. He had his own troops and was also accompanied by distinguished officers of the Roman army, as well as by governors of the regions and towns conquered by

Robert (these men, once they had given up on the emperor, had transferred their loyalty altogether to Bohemond). Bohemond now went through Bagenetia to Ioannina, where trenches were dug by the vineyards outside the town; all the soldiers were posted in vantage points while Bohemond established his headquarters inside the town walls. After making an inspection of the ramparts and recognizing that the citadel was in a dangerous condition, he not only did his best to restore it, but built another of great strength at a different section of the walls, where it seemed to him that it would be more useful. At the same time he oversaw the plunder of the towns and countryside in the surrounding area.

The emperor, informed of Bohemond's activities, without a moment's delay gathered all his forces and hurriedly left Constantinople in the month of May.[12] When he reached Ioannina the time was ripe for campaigning, but he was well aware of his own deficiencies: his army was vastly outnumbered and in any case the experience of the previous battle with Robert convinced him that the first charge of Keltic cavalry was irresistible. He decided therefore to begin operations by skirmishing with a small group of picked men; by doing this he would gain some indication of Bohemond's skill as a military commander, and these minor engagements would also give him an opportunity to discover the general situation; afterwards he would be able to use the intelligence to face the Kelt with more confidence. Both armies were impatient, eager for battle, but the emperor, fearing the first charge of the Latins, adopted a new strategy. Wagons, which were both lighter and smaller than usual, were made ready and on each four poles were fixed; armed infantrymen were stationed near them so that when the Latins made their assault on the Roman line at full gallop these men from underneath would push the wagons forward. In this way the continuous line of the enemy would be broken up.

When the hour of battle was nigh, just after the sun had risen above the horizon and was shining brightly, the emperor arranged his troops in combat order, and took his place at their centre. When the fighting began, however, it was clear that Bohemond had not been caught out by the emperor's plan; as

though he had foreknowledge of the Roman plan he had
adapted to the changed circumstances. His forces were divided
in two and swerving away from the chariots launched an attack
on either flank of the Roman line. There was a general melee
as the fighters met in head-on combat. The casualties on both
sides were heavy, but Bohemond won. As for the emperor, he
stood like some unshakeable tower under attack from all sides,
sometimes charging on horseback against the advancing Kelts
and when he closed with a group of them, striking, killing and
being struck, sometimes rallying the runaways with frequent
cries. But when he saw his regiments broken up and scattered,
he realized that he must look to his own safety, not to save his
own life or because he was overwhelmed by fear, as someone
might suggest, but in the hope that by avoiding the danger and
recovering his strength, he might resume the struggle with his
Keltic adversaries more bravely another day.

Fleeing with a handful of his men he happened on a party of
Kelts and once again showed himself a dauntless general. He
encouraged his comrades and in a death-or-glory charge himself
struck and killed one of the Kelts; his men, men of Ares all,
wounded many and chased the others away. Thus, after escaping fearful dangers beyond number, he reached safety again at
Akhris, passing through Strougai on his way there. At Akhris
he rested and when a considerable number of the defeated army
had been rounded up, he left them all in that district with the
megas domestikos while he himself went on to the Bardarios
river, but not to enjoy a period of leisure, since he never allowed
himself to indulge in royal pleasures and relaxations.

The armies were assembled once more and when the mercenaries were ready, he marched against Bohemond with a new
idea for victory. He had iron caltrops made and since he
expected the battle to take place on the next day, the evening
before scattered them over the plain between the two armies at
the point where he guessed that the Kelts would make a heavy
cavalry attack. The plan was to frustrate the first and irresistible
charge when the caltrops pierced the horses' hooves. The
Roman lancers in front of them were to ride forward at
measured distances, avoiding damage from the caltrops, but

split up to right and left, while the lightly-armed soldiers were to shoot arrows in a continuous stream at the Kelts from afar and the wings would fall on the enemy with terrific force from either flank.

Such was my father's scheme, but it did not deceive Bohemond. It happened thus: the emperor's plan was conceived in the evening and by the morning the Kelt had discovered it. Bohemond cleverly adapted to the situation with ease and accepted the challenge to fight, but his attack did not follow its usual course, for the emperor's plan was anticipated by a furious assault from the flanks, while the enemy centre remained immobile. In the hand-to-hand conflict which ensued, the Romans were defeated and fled from the Latins. In any case they were frightened before the battle started because of their previous disaster and did not dare to look their opponents in the face.

The Roman lines were thrown into confusion, although the emperor himself stood firm, gallantly resisting with all his strength and resolution. He wounded many, but was himself wounded. When all his army had melted away and he was left with few companions, he judged it to be his duty no longer to expose himself to senseless risks – for when a man has no more strength to fight after a great deal of suffering, he would be a fool to thrust himself into obvious peril. The right and left wings of his army had already taken to their heels when the emperor was still holding his ground, courageously carrying on the battle with Bohemond's men and bearing the whole brunt of the fight on his own shoulders. The danger became overwhelming and knowing that resistance was no longer possible, he came to the conclusion that he must save himself, in order to fight again and by really powerful opposition prevent Bohemond from enjoying the full fruits of victory.

That was very much Alexios' character, both in defeat and in victory, both in flight and in pursuit; he never cowered and was never caught in the depths of despair. The truth is that he had the greatest faith in God, making Him the centre of his own life in all things, but abstaining completely from taking oaths in His name. On this occasion, as I have said, he knew that the position was hopeless and fled, chased by Bohemond and picked counts. While this was going on he spoke to Goules, a servant of his father, and the others who were with him: 'How far shall we flee?' Then, wheeling round, he drew his sword and struck in the face the first adversary to catch up with him. The Kelts, seeing this and perceiving that he was quite reckless, halted and gave up the chase. They knew from long experience that such men are invincible. In this way he was free of his pursuers and escaped. Even in flight he did not lose heart altogether, but rallied some of those who had fled and mocked others, though most of them pretended not to know him. Having been saved from danger in this way, he returned to the capital, to recruit other armies and to march against Bohemond again.

5. When Robert returned to Lombardy, Bohemond took charge of operations against the emperor. He put into practice the advice of his father, ceaselessly conducting battles and wars. He sent Peter Aliphas with Pounteses to besiege various places. Peter at once seized the two Poloboi, while Pounteses made himself master of Skopia. Bohemond himself arrived quickly at Akhris in answer to an appeal from the townspeople there. After a short stay he departed without accomplishing anything because Ariebes was guarding the citadel there and went on to Ostrobos, where he was again repulsed. Empty-handed he left for Berroia, going through Soskos and Serbia. Although a number of assaults were made on several locations, he was unsuccessful and therefore went on through Bodena to Moglena, where he rebuilt a little fort long since in ruins. A count surnamed Sarakenos was left there with a strong garrison, but Bohemond moved to the Bardarios to a place called Asprai Ekklesiai. He remained there for three months and during this period three leading counts, Pounteses, Reynald and another called William were discovered plotting to desert to the emperor. Pounteses became aware of this and deserted to the emperor;[13] the other two were arrested and according to Keltic custom were freed to fight in single combat. William was defeated and was therefore condemned: he was blinded; the other, Reynald, was sent by Bohemond to his father in

Lombardy. Robert had him blinded too. Bohemond departed from Asprai Ekklesiai and went to Kastoria. On learning this, the *megas domestikos* made for Moglena, seized Sarakenos, put him to death immediately and razed the fort. Bohemond meanwhile left Kastoria and moved to Larissa with the intention of wintering there.

As for the emperor, after reaching the capital, as I said, he set to work at once, which is what one would expect of him, for he was a hard worker and never had his share of rest. He called on the sultan[14] to supply forces with leaders of long experience. The request was answered without delay: 7,000 men were sent with highly skilled officers, including Kamyres, who was the outstanding character thanks to his knowledge of war, acquired over a long period. While the emperor was making these preparations, Bohemond dispatched some of his men, all Kelts armed from head to foot, who took Pelagonia by assault, as well as Trikala and Kastoria. He himself with the whole army came to Trikala, but another detachment, all brave men, captured Tzibiskos without difficulty. He then moved on to Larissa, arriving in full force on the feast day of St George the Martyr.[15] The walls were invested and the siege began.

Leo Kephalas, the son of a former servant of the emperor's father, was governor of Larissa and for six months held out bravely against Bohemond's siege-engines. At the time he sent news of the barbarian's attack in letters to the emperor, but Alexios impatient though he was did not immediately set out on the road to Larissa; he was collecting more mercenaries from all directions and this delayed his departure. Later, when all were properly armed, he left Constantinople. As he drew near to the environs of the town and had crossed Mount Kellion, he left the public highway on his right and the hill called by the locals Kissabos and descended to Ezeban, a Vlakh village lying quite close to Andronia. From there he made his way to another small place commonly called Plabitza, situated fairly near the River ... and there, having dug a good entrenchment, he pitched camp. From there he went on in a hurry to the Gardens of Delphinas, then to Trikala.

At this point a messenger arrived with a letter from Leo

Kephalas, whom I have mentioned above. It was written with some frankness,[16] as follows: 'I would like you to know, Majesty, that I have till now preserved this fortress from capture through my own great efforts. But we are now deprived of victuals which Christian men may eat; we have even touched what is not lawful. Even that has failed us. If you are willing to hurry to our aid and can drive off our besiegers, thanks be to God. If not, I have already fulfilled my duty. From now on we are the slaves of necessity (for what can man do against nature and the tyranny she imposes?). We have a mind to surrender the place to the enemies who press us hard and are clearly strangling us. If this should be our unhappy lot – call down curses on me if you like, but I will speak boldly and frankly to Your Majesty: unless you hurry with all speed to deliver us from this peril (for we are unable to hold out for much longer), you, our emperor, if you do not bring aid quickly when you have the power to do so, you will be the first to be charged with treachery.'

Some other method, the emperor knew, must be found to defeat the enemy. He was absorbed in anxious calculations; indeed, he worked hard all through the day planning how to lay ambushes, pleading with God to help him. Help came in this way: he summoned one of the old men from Larissa and questioned him on the topography of the place. Turning his eyes in different directions and at the same time pointing with his finger, he carefully inquired where the terrain was broken by ravines, where dense thickets lay close to such places. The reason why he asked the Larissaean these questions was of course that he wished to lay an ambush there and so defeat the Latins by guile, for he had given up any idea of open hand-to-hand conflict; after many clashes of this kind – and defeats – he had acquired experience of the Frankish tactics in battle.

When the sun went down he retired to his bed after working all day. He had a dream. It seemed that he was standing in the sanctuary of the great martyr Demetrios,[17] and he heard a voice say: 'Cease tormenting yourself and complaining, for tomorrow you shall prevail.' He thought that the sound came to him from one of the icons suspended in the sanctuary, on which there was a painting of the great martyr Demetrios himself. When he awoke, overjoyed at the voice he had heard in this dream, he invoked the martyr and gave a pledge, moreover, that if it was granted to him to conquer his enemies, he would visit the shrine and dismounting from his horse some stades from the town of Thessaloniki he would come on foot at a slow pace and would venerate him in the appropriate fashion.

A council of generals, officers and all the relatives of the emperor was then called. Each man was asked to give his opinion. After that Alexios explained his strategy. He intended to hand over all the main forces to his kinsmen. Nikephoros Melissenos and Basil Kourtikios, also called Ioannikios, were appointed commanders-in-chief. Kourtikios was a famous soldier, renowned for his bravery and knowledge of warfare. He came originally from Adrianoupolis. Not only did the emperor entrust to them the army, but all the imperial standards. They were instructed to draw up the battle line according to the principles he himself had followed in former engagements; he advised them to test the Latin vanguard first by skirmishes, then to advance against them in full force with loud war cries; but as soon as the two lines came to close quarters, they were to turn their backs and pretend to run in a disorderly way in the direction of Lykostomion. While these orders were being given, all the horses of the army were suddenly heard to neigh – a sound which caused general consternation. To the emperor however and to all others of an inquiring mind it seemed a good omen.

After the meeting he left them to the right of Larissa, waited until sunset and with certain picked men, who were to follow him, passed through the defile of Libotanion, went round Rebenikon, through the place called Allage and arrived on the left of Larissa. The entire countryside was thoroughly reconnoitred and he found a low-lying spot; there he lay in ambush with his party. While the emperor was hurrying, as I explained, on his way and just about to enter the defile of Libotanion, the Roman commanders sent out a detachment against the Kelts. The plan was to distract the enemy by drawing attention to themselves and thus give them no chance of finding out the emperor's destination. These men went down on the plain and attacked; fighting went on for a long time until nightfall put an end to it. Thus the emperor was able to reach the set position. His men were ordered to dismount and kneel down, still holding the reins in their hands. He himself happened to alight on a bed of germander and there he spent the rest of the night, kneeling with reins in hand and his face turned towards the ground.

6. At sunrise, when Bohemond saw the Romans ranged in battle formation, the imperial standards, the silver-studded lances and the horses with the emperor's purple saddlecloths, he positioned his own army against them to the best of his ability, dividing his forces in two, one half commanded by himself, the other by Bryennius, a Latin of distinction who had the title of constable.[18] Bohemond used his normal tactics and launched a frontal attack where he saw the imperial standards, thinking that the emperor was there. He swooped down on the enemy like a whirlwind. For a little time they held out, then turned and fled. He drove on impetuously in pursuit, just as has been set out above. The emperor, seeing all this and judging that Bohemond was now far enough from his own camp, mounted his horse, bade his men do likewise and made for the Keltic camp. Once inside it he massacred many of the Latins and took up the spoils; then he looked round at those pursuing and fleeing alike.

When Alexios saw his troops escaping, being chased by Bohemond and behind him, Bryennius, he sent for George Pyrros, a famous archer, and some other brave lightly-armed soldiers and ordered them to drive hard on the heels of Bryennius but not to fight at close quarters; they were to shoot great numbers of arrows from a distance and at the horses rather than the riders. Catching up with the Kelts, therefore, they rained down arrows on their mounts and thus created a scene of chaos for the riders, for all Kelts when on horseback are unbeatable in a charge and make a magnificent show, but whenever they dismount, partly because of their huge shields, partly too because of the spurs on their boots and their ungainly walk, they become very easy prey and altogether different as their former enthusiasm dies down. It was this, I reckon, that led the emperor to suggest firing at the horses in particular.

Bryennius' men, as their chargers fell, began to circle round and round. As they congregated in a great mass, a thick cloud of dust rose high to the heavens, so that it might have been compared with the darkness over Egypt long ago,[19] a darkness that could be felt. The thick dust blinded their eyes and they were unable to find out from where the arrows came or who was firing them. Bryennius sent three Latins to tell Bohemond the whole story. They found him with a small group of Kelts on a tiny island in a river called the Salabrias and eating grapes. He was bragging loudly, full of his own vainglory. The remark he made is repeated even today and still parodied: he kept saying, with barbaric mispronunciation of Lykostomion, 'I've thrown Alexios to the wolf's mouth.'[20] That is what happens when excessive pride blinds people to what is right under their eyes and at their feet.

However, when he heard Bryennius' message and realized that the emperor had won a victory by a cunning ruse, he flew into a rage, but being the kind of man he was, by no means dismayed. A detachment of Keltic cavalry was sent off to the top of a mountain ridge opposite Larissa. The Roman soldiers, seeing them there, argued with great force and eagerness that they should fight them. The emperor tried to deter them, but they were many, a composite force from different contingents, and having climbed the ridge they put in an attack. The Kelts charged against them without hesitation and killed up to 500 of them. Afterwards, guessing the likely direction of Bohemond's march, the emperor sent Migdenos with some good soldiers of his own and a company of Turks to obstruct him, but as soon as they approached Bohemond charged and defeated them. He chased them as far as the river.

7. On the next morning when the sun rose Bohemond, with his attendant counts and Bryennius himself, rode along the said riverbank until he found a marshy area on the outskirts of Larissa. Between two hills there was a wooded plain ending in a rugged defile (their name for it is *kleisoura*). Going through this he pitched camp on the plain, which was called the 'Palace

of Domenikos'. On the following day at dawn the senior commander Michael Doukas, my maternal uncle, caught up with
him with the whole of the Roman army. Michael was renowned
for his prudence; he surpassed others of his generation in physical stature too, as well as fine looks; in fact he excelled all men
who ever lived in these respects (for everybody who saw him
was overcome with admiration). Endowed with extraordinary
and unrivalled powers of anticipation, he was no less capable
of discerning the main perils and of dealing with them.

The emperor gave him instructions not to allow his men to
enter this defile all at once; the main force was to remain outside
the entrance and only a few Turks and Sarmatians,[21] all skilled
bowmen, were to go in and they were to use no other weapons
but their arrows. After they had entered and were charging
against the Latins, the rest began to quarrel among themselves;
they were impatient to join them and the question was, who
should go. Bohemond, with his superb knowledge of military
tactics, ordered his men to stand firm in serried ranks, protecting themselves with their shields. The *protostrator*, noticing
that the Romans were slipping away one by one and going
into the mouth of the defile, went in himself. Bohemond rejoiced
like a lion which has chanced upon a mighty prey, in Homer's
words, when with his own eyes he saw Michael and his soldiers.
He hurled himself at them in a furious assault with all his
strength and they fled forthwith.

Ouzas,[22] who owed his name to his race, a man famed for
courage and one who knew how to wield the dried bull's hide
to right and left,[23] as Homer says, when he emerged from the
pass, swerved slightly to the right, swiftly turned and struck at
the Latin behind him. The man at once fell head first to the
ground. Nevertheless Bohemond chased them to the River
Salabrias. In the flight, however, Ouzas, whom I mentioned
already, speared Bohemond's standard-bearer, snatched the
insignia from his hands, waved it round a little and then pointed
it towards the ground. The Latins, puzzled by the sight of the
lowered standard, turned in confusion along another route and
arrived at Trikala, which had already been occupied by some of
the Kelts on their flight towards Lykostomion. They merged with

them and having set up camp for a while, went on to Kastoria.

The emperor meanwhile left Larissa and reached Thessaloniki. With his usual cleverness in such circumstances he lost no time in sending envoys to Bohemond's counts with many promises if they would demand from Bohemond the pay he had promised them. If he failed to produce the money, they were to persuade him to go down to the sea and get the pay from his father Robert, actually crossing to demand it in person. Alexios assured them that if they could bring this about they would all be honoured by him and receive countless benefits. Those who desired to serve with pay in the imperial army, would be placed on the rolls and enjoy good wages which they themselves could determine; on the other hand if they preferred to go home, he guaranteed their safe return through Hungary.

The counts followed the emperor's instructions, and vigorously demanded their pay for the last four years. Bohemond could not manage it and played for time. However, they pressed him harder, stressing that their demands were reasonable, and he in desperation left Bryennius there to guard Kastoria and Peter Aliphas[24] in charge of Poloboi, while he himself went to Avlona – whereupon the emperor returned in triumph to Constantinople.[25]

8. When he reached the capital, he found the affairs of the Church in disarray. Not for a brief moment was he able to enjoy a respite, for Alexios was a true representative of God and when he saw the Church troubled by the teaching of Italos, although he was planning operations against Bryennius (the Kelt who occupied Kastoria, as I explained), he did not disregard the plight facing true teaching. It was just at this time that the doctrines of Italos had gained wide popularity and had rocked the Church. This man Italos (his story needs to be told from the beginning) originally came from Italy and for a long time lived in Sicily, which is an island lying off Italy. The Sicilians had revolted against the Romans and when they decided to pursue a warlike policy called in the help of their Italian allies. Among the latter was the father of Italos accompanied by his son. Although not old enough to bear arms, he followed skipping along at his father's side. He was learning

the art of war as the Italians understand it. Such were his formative years and the first rudiments of his education.

But when the celebrated George Maniakes made himself master of Sicily in the reign of Monomakhos, it was with difficulty that father and son escaped from the island. They both became refugees in Lombardy, which was at that time still subject to the Romans. I am not sure how, but from there he moved to Constantinople, a not inconsiderable centre for all branches of learning and literary studies. In fact, from the reign of Basil *porphyrogennetos* until that of Monomakhos,[26] letters although treated with scant regard by most folk at least did not die out, and once again they shone in bright revival when under Alexios they became the object of serious attention, to those who loved philosophical argument.[27] Before then most men had lived a life of luxury and pleasure; because of their wanton habits they concerned themselves with quail hunting and other more disreputable pastimes, but all scientific culture and literature to them were of secondary importance.

Such was the character of the people whom Italos found here. He conversed with schoolmen who were both cruel and rough natured (for in those days there were men of that kind in the capital) and from them he received a literary education. Later he came into contact with the famous Michael Psellos,[28] who, because of his own native intelligence and quickness of apprehension, had not often attended the lectures of the great and the good. Psellos, moreover, had the help of God, apart from those mentors, for his mother with passionate supplication kept constant vigil in the sanctuary of the Lord before the sacred image of the Holy Mother of God,[29] with hot tears interceding for her son. He attained perfection of all knowledge, having an accurate understanding of both Hellenic and Chaldaean science, and so became renowned in those times for his wisdom. Italos, although he was a disciple of Psellos, was unable because of his uncouth and barbaric temperament to grasp the profound truths of philosophy; even in the act of learning he utterly rejected the teacher's guiding hand, and full of temerity and barbaric folly, believing even before study that he excelled all others, from the very start ranged himself against the great

Psellos himself. With fanatical zeal for dialectic he caused daily commotions in public gatherings as he poured out a continuous stream of subtle argument; subtle propositions were followed in turn by subtle reasons to support them.

The then emperor, Michael Doukas, was a friend of his, as were Michael's brothers, and although they considered him inferior to Psellos, they gave him their patronage and took his part in literary debate. The Doukas family were in fact great patrons of literature, the brothers of the emperor no less than Michael himself. Italos invariably regarded Psellos with a turbulent frenzy, but the other winged his way, like some eagle, far above the petty subtleties of Italos.

What happened next? In their struggle against the Romans, the Latins and Italians planned to take over the whole of Lombardy and indeed of Italy too. The same emperor, looking upon Italos as a personal friend, a good man and an expert on Italian affairs, sent him to Epidamnos. To cut a long story short, it was discovered that he was betraying our cause there and an agent was sent to remove him. Italos realized what was happening and fled to Rome. Then, true to character, he repented, appealed to the emperor and on his instructions was permitted to live in Constantinople at the Pege monastery and the Church of the Forty Saints. When Psellos withdrew from Byzantion after his tonsuration, Italos was placed in charge[30] of the teaching of philosophy as a whole, with the title 'Hypatos of the Philosophers'. He devoted his energies to the exegesis of Aristotle and Plato.

He gave the impression of vast learning, and it seemed that no other mortal was more capable of thorough research into the mysteries of the peripatetic philosophers, and more particularly of dialectic. In other literary studies his competence was not so obvious: his knowledge of grammar, for example, was defective and he was not capable of discerning the sweet nectar of rhetoric. For that reason his language was devoid of harmony and polish; his style was austere, completely unadorned. His writings wore a frown and in general reeked of bitterness, full of dialectic aggression, and his tongue was loaded with arguments, even more when he spoke in debate than when he wrote. So powerful was he in discourse, so irrefutable, that his opponent was inevitably reduced to impotent silence. He dug a pit on both sides of a question and cast interlocutors into a well of difficulties; all opposition was stifled with a never-ending string of questions, which confounded and obliterated reason, so skilled was he in the art of dialectic. Once a man was engaged in argument with him, it was impossible to escape his labyrinths.

In other ways, though, he was remarkably uncultured and temper was his master. That temper, indeed, vitiated and destroyed whatever virtue he had acquired from his studies; the fellow argued with his hands as much as his tongue; nor did he allow his adversary merely to end in failure – it was not enough for him to have closed his mouth and condemned him to silence – but at once his hand leapt to the other's beard and hair while insult was heaped on insult. The man was no more in control of his hands than his tongue. This alone would prove how unsuited he was to the philosopher's life, for he struck his opponent; the only philosophical feature about him was that after his anger calmed and his tears dried, clear signs of remorse filled him.

In case the reader may wish to know his physical appearance, I can say this: he had a large head, a prominent forehead, a face that was expressive, nostrils of a large capacity, a rounded beard, broad chest and robust limbs; he was of below average height. His accent was what one would expect from a Latin youth who had come to our country and studied Greek thoroughly but without mastering articulation; sometimes he mutilated his syllables. Neither his defective pronunciation nor the clipping of sounds escaped the notice of most people, and the better educated accused him of vulgarity in the way he spoke. It was this that led him to string his arguments with figures of speech, drawn from anywhere and everywhere. Such idioms were by no means exempt from faults of composition and there was in them a liberal sprinkling of solecisms.

9. This man then oversaw the teaching of philosophy and it was to his lectures that the young men flocked. (He elucidated the works of Proklos and Plato, the teachings of the two philosophers Porphyrios and Iamblikhos, and above all the technical

treatises of Aristotle.[31] He gave lectures on Aristotle's system to those who wished to use it for practical purposes; it was on the utility of his work that he prided himself especially and on this he spent much time.) Yet he was unable to help his students very much owing to his own hot temper and the general instability of his character.

Look at who his followers were: John Solomon, members of the Iasitas and Serblias families and others who maybe were industrious in their studies. Most of them were frequent visitors to the palace and I myself perceived later on that they had acquired no accurate systematic knowledge of any kind: they played the role of dialectician with chaotic changes and frenzied metaphors, but they had no sound understanding. They propounded their theories, even at that time putting forward their ideas on metempsychosis in rather veiled terms and on certain other matters of a similar nature and almost as monstrous.

Is there any sane person who has not seen the holy couple absorbed, day and night, deep in study of Holy Scripture? I am talking, of course, about my parents. I will digress here for a moment – the law of rhetoric will not grudge me that privilege. Many a time when a meal was already served I remember seeing my mother with a book in her hands, diligently reading the dogmatic pronouncements of the Holy Fathers, especially of the philosopher and martyr Maximos.[32] Inquiries into the physical nature of things did not interest her so much as the study of dogma, for she longed to reap the benefits of true wisdom. It often occurred to me to wonder at this, and as a result I once asked her: 'How could you of your own accord aspire to such sublimity? For my part, I tremble and dare not consider such things even in the smallest degree. The man's writing, so highly abstract and intellectual, makes the reader's head swim.' She smiled. 'Your reluctance is commendable, I'm sure,' she replied, 'and I myself do not approach such books without a tremble. Yet I cannot tear myself away from them. Wait a little and after a close look at other books,[33] believe me, you will taste the sweetness of these.' The memory of her words pierces my heart and plunges me into a sea of other reminiscences. But the law of history forbids me: we must return to the affairs of Italos.

When he was at the height of his popularity among his disciples, as I have already noted, he treated all with contempt; most of the thoughtless he incited to revolt and not a few were encouraged to become rebellious. I could have named many of them, had not age dimmed my memory. These events, you see, took place before my father was raised to supreme power. When he found here a general neglect of culture and literary skills, with the art of literature seemingly banished, he was eager to revive whatever sparks still remained hidden beneath the ashes. All those who had any inclination for learning were unceasingly urged by him to study (there were some, only a few, and those stood merely in the gateway to Aristotelian philosophy), but he did advise them to devote attention to Holy Scripture before turning to Hellenic culture.

Noting that Italos was everywhere causing trouble and leading many astray, he referred the man for preliminary examination to the *Sebastokrator* Isaac, who was himself a scholar and blessed with intelligence. Isaac, satisfied that Italos was indeed a troublemaker, publicly refuted him at this inquiry and later, on instructions from his brother, the emperor, committed him to appear before an ecclesiastical tribunal. It was impossible for Italos to conceal his ignorance and even before that gathering he belched out doctrines foreign to Church teaching; in the presence of Church dignitaries he persisted in ridicule and indulged in other things of a boorish and barbaric nature. At that time Eustratios Garidas presided over the Church and he, in order to convert him to a better frame of mind if he could, kept Italos in the precincts of the Great Church. But little good came of that, since rather than win him over to a truer doctrine, he became persuaded by the evils of the argument; and as a result, Italos made of Garidas his own devoted disciple.

What was the upshot of this? The whole population of Constantinople gathered as a crowd by the church looking for Italos. He would probably have been hurled from the galleries into the centre of the church if he had not hidden himself by climbing on to the roof and taken refuge in some hole. His evil doctrines were a common topic of conversation among many people in the palace and not a few nobles were corrupted by these pernicious ideas, to the great grief of the emperor. Accordingly his heretical teachings were summarized in eleven propositions and these were sent to the emperor. The sovereign ordered Italos to retract these propositions from the pulpit in the Great Church, bareheaded and in earshot of all the congregation, repeating the anathema.[34]

Although this was done, Italos proved to be incorrigible, and once more he openly preached these same doctrines in public and when he was warned by the emperor, rejected advice in barbaric and lawless fashion. He was therefore personally sentenced to excommunication, though afterwards, when he had recanted for a second time, the penalty was moderated. His teachings were anathematized, but his own name was inserted in a somewhat oblique manner, veiled and not easily recognized by the mass of people. Later he did indeed change his ideas about dogma and repented of his former errors. He repudiated the transmigration of souls and the ridicule of sacred images of the saints; he was eager to reinterpret the theory of ideas so that it should in some way be rendered orthodox, and it was clear that he condemned his early deviations from the truth.

BOOK VI

1. As we have noted, Bryennius occupied Kastoria.[1] The emperor, being determined to drive him out and seize the town himself, again called up his army. It was completely equipped for siege warfare and for fighting in open country. After preparations had been duly made, Alexios set out. The position of Kastoria is as follows: there is a lake, named after the place, and a promontory, broadening at the tip and ending in rocky cliffs, juts out into it; on the promontory towers and battlements had been built by way of fortifications – hence the name, Kastoria. The emperor found Bryennius in occupation and decided that he must first test the fortifications and the towers with siege-engines. However, as it was impossible for the soldiers to get near except from some base, he built a palisade to begin with and then wooden towers; the whole construction was held together tightly with iron chains to form a kind of stronghold, and from this he commenced operations against the Kelts.

Siege-engines and rock-throwing catapults were set up outside the walls and fighting went on all night and day. The circumference of the walls was breached, but the defenders resisted even more vigorously still (even though the rampart was smashed they still refused to surrender), and as he was unable to achieve his object, Alexios made a bold, and at the same time a wise, decision. His idea was to make war on two fronts simultaneously, from the mainland and from the lake; the lake assault would be made by soldiers from ships, but as they were negligible he had some skiffs transported on wagons and launched them in the lake from a small mole. He noticed that the Latins climbed up one side of the promontory quite quickly, but came down more slowly on the other side. He embarked George Palaiologos with fighting men, therefore, and ordered him to moor his skiffs at the foot of the rocks; he was also instructed to seize the summit in the rear of the enemy when he had seen the agreed signal, climbing up there by the unfrequented but easier route. Moreover, when he saw the emperor had attacked the Latins from the land side, he was to hurry on as fast as he could, for they would be incapable of fighting with equal determination against two attackers: resistance must grow feebler on one or the other front and at that point they would be vulnerable.

George Palaiologos moored off the cliffs and stood to under arms, with a sentry posted above to watch for the emperor's signal; he was to inform Palaiologos when he saw it. At daybreak the emperor's men charged into battle from the mainland, uttering their war cries. The scout, seeing the signal, passed it on to Palaiologos with one of his own. At once the latter secured the summit and drew up his ranks there.

Despite the fact that Bryennius knew he was under siege from the land and realized too that Palaiologos was gnashing his teeth against them from the other side, he still would not give in. In fact, he ordered the counts to fight back with greater courage. Their reply was shameful: 'You see how our troubles multiply. It is right then that each one of us should from now on look to his own safety, some by joining the emperor, others by returning to their native country.' Without hesitation they put their scheme into practice and asked the emperor to set up two standards: one, close to the sanctuary of the great martyr George (this church had been built there in the saint's honour), the other on the road to Avlona. 'Those of us who wish to serve under Your Majesty,' they said, 'will go to the standard close by the sanctuary, and those who prefer to return to their own country will approach the other, on the Avlona road.' With these words they promptly went over to the emperor. Bryennius, however, was a brave man and had no intention of joining him, but he did swear never to take up arms against him, provided that safe conduct was granted him as far as the fron-

tiers of the empire and if permission was given to return freely
to his home. The emperor very readily agreed. After that he
took the road to Byzantion, a glorious victor.

2. At this point I must interrupt the narrative briefly to
describe how he also overcame the Paulicians.[2] To him it was
intolerable not to put down these rebels before entering the
palace again. One success, he thought, should be followed by
another and the people of the Manichaeans[3] should be made to
round off the cycle of his triumphs. To allow these men,
descended from the Paulicians, to constitute a blot, as it were,
on the splendid roll of his victories over the western enemies,
was unbearable. Nevertheless, he did not wish to bring this
about by war and battle, because many men on either side
might well be wiped out in the fighting. He knew them of old
as desperate warriors, full of loathing for their opponents. It
was desirable that the ringleaders should be punished, but he
hoped to enrol the others in his own army.

He set about the task with a trick. Recognizing their love of
danger and their incurable delight in wars and battles, he was
afraid they might in a crisis meditate some awful crime. At the
moment they were quietly living in their own territories and so
far they had not turned to robberies or to other plundering
raids. On his return to Byzantion therefore, he summoned them
in letters full of promises. For their part, they had heard of his
victory over the Kelts and feared his letters were merely flattering them with fine hopes. However, much against their will,
they came to him.

After reaching Mosynopolis, he had halted in the vicinity,
pretending to stay on there for some other reasons but really to
await their arrival. When they did arrive he feigned a desire to
meet them personally and enter their names in the register. He
took his seat in front of them, a most impressive figure,[4] and
directed that their leaders should come forward, not in a disorderly fashion, but in groups of ten. Arranged thus they were
to be registered and then enter the gates of the town. A general
review of the rest was promised for the next day. Men had
already been posted to relieve them of their horses and arms,
to restrain them and lock them up in selected prisons, but the

groups, following in due order, had no knowledge whatever of this. They went inside ignorant of their fate.

So he arrested them, confiscated their property and divided it up among the brave men who had shared his privations in the battles and perils of the past. The officer in charge of this duty left to drive the Manichaean women from their homes and held them in custody in the citadel. Not long after, however, the emperor thought it right to exercise clemency and all those who preferred holy baptism were not denied it. After a thorough investigation the ringleaders were identified – those responsible for their absurd behaviour – and these he condemned to exile and imprisonment on islands. The others were granted an amnesty and allowed to go away[5] wherever they wished. They chose their own country above all others and returned there at once to manage their affairs as best they could.

3. The emperor went back to the Queen of Cities.[6] He was not unaware of the whispering campaign against himself in the highways and byways of the city, but it hurt his feelings to hear these things. After all, the deed was not so very heinous. Yet the number of his accusers, eager to bring charges, was greatly multiplied. His offence had been committed under the pressure of chaotic circumstances, when the imperial treasury had failed him, and he regarded the money as a loan; to him the transaction was neither brigandage, as his detractors claimed, nor the treacherous plot of a tyrant. His intention had been, after winning the wars that menaced him then, to restore the precious objects taken from the churches back to them.

Now that he had returned to the capital the thought that would-be critics of his acts had any credibility was unbearable. Accordingly he announced that a most important meeting would take place in the Palace of Blakhernai, at which he proposed to appear as defendant and so offer his own explanation. There were present the whole Senate, military commanders and all the dignitaries of the Church, all impatient to know the purpose of a full assembly. It was in fact nothing more than the emperor's reply to the rumours against him. On this occasion, therefore, the priors of the sacred monasteries attended and the books (commonly called *brevia*) were produced for inspection;

in these the treasures held by each sanctuary were recorded. One would imagine that the emperor, seated on the imperial throne, was presiding as judge but in reality he was about to subject himself to cross-examination. The objects presented to the sacred houses by many persons long ago were scrutinized in the records, to see if they had been removed by the said persons later on or by the emperor himself.

It was proved however that nothing had been taken, with one exception: the gold-and-silver ornament that had lain on the coffin of the famous Empress Zoe,[7] and certain other small objects no longer in use at divine worship. Thereupon the emperor publicly submitted himself to judgement, accepting the verdict of anyone present who was willing to serve as juror. Then, after a short pause, he went on with a change of tone: 'It was my misfortune to find the empire surrounded on all sides by barbarians, with no defence worthy of consideration against the enemies who threatened it. You know the many dangers I faced, almost myself becoming a victim of the barbarian's sword. Those who shot arrows at us from east and from west vastly outnumbered our forces – you cannot be ignorant of the Persian invasions and the raids of the Scythians; you cannot have forgotten the sharp-pointed spears of Lombardy. With the arms we provided our money disappeared and the circle of empire was drawn close, indeed to its irreducible limit. You are aware how our entire army was built up, recruited from all sides and trained, and there is no one here who does not know that all these things involved great expenditure of money; what was removed has been spent on necessities, following the example of Perikles, and it has been used to safeguard our honour.

'However, if the censorious see in our actions some offence against the canons, that is not surprising. For we hear that even the prophet-king David, when he was reduced to the same necessity, ate of the sacred bread with his warriors, although it was forbidden for an ordinary person to touch the food reserved for the priests. Anyway, the sacred canons palpably allow the holy objects to be sold for the ransoming of prisoners of war, among other things. But if the whole country is being taken prisoner, if its towns and Constantinople itself are already in danger of becoming captives, if then we, in such a moment of peril, laid our hands on a few objects, not really worthy of the name sacred, and used them to secure our freedom, surely we leave no reasonable excuse to our detractors for charging us.'

Having said this he altered the argument, assumed responsibility for what had occurred and condemned himself; after which he told those who had the inventories to read them again, so that it might be quite clear what had been removed. He then immediately calculated an adequate sum of gold to be paid annually by the treasury officials to the office of the Antiphonetes – a custom which has persisted without interruption even to this day. It was there that the coffin of the empress whom we mentioned above lay. To the church in the Khalkoprateia he ordered a yearly income of gold to be allotted from the treasury for payment to those who usually sing hymns in the holy sanctuary of the Theometor.[8]

4. Meanwhile it became apparent that a plot was being made against the emperor by leading members of the Senate and the great military commanders. He was at once informed. Accusers came before him and the conspirators were convicted. Although their guilt was established and the penalty laid down by law was the ultimate sanction, the emperor was against passing the full sentence: the ringleaders were merely condemned to lose their property and go into exile. He pursued the matter no further than that. However, let us return to the point where we digressed.

When Alexios was promoted to the rank of *domestikos* by Nikephoros Botaneiates, he had taken with him a certain Manichaean called Traulos[9] and made him one of his family servants. The man was considered worthy of holy baptism and was married to one of the empress's maids. Traulos had four sisters and when he found out that they had been carried off to prison with the others and deprived of all their possessions, he could not contain his indignation. He sought a way of escaping from the emperor's service. His wife had by now discovered his plan and seeing that he was about to run away, told the man who was at that time charged with supervision of the Manichaeans.

Traulos knew what she had done and straightway called on

his confidants to meet him in the evening. All those who were relatives obeyed and together they went off to Beliatoba, which is a small place on the ridge which dominates the valley of the same name. They found it uninhabited, looked upon it as their own and proceeded to make their dwelling there. Every day they made sorties and returned with much booty from as far away as our Philippopolis.

But Traulos was not satisfied with these achievements. He made a treaty with the Scythians of Paristrion and won the friendship of the chiefs in Glabinitza, Dristra and the neighbouring area.[10] At the same time he married the daughter of a Scythian chieftain. By every means he strove to foster a Scythian invasion in order to hurt the emperor. Daily reports of his deeds kept the emperor informed and he did his best to avert catastrophe. He foresaw the evil likely to result and wrote conciliatory letters full of promises. He even sent a chrysobull guaranteeing Traulos an amnesty and full liberty. But the crab refused to learn how to walk straight: he remained what he had been the day before and the day before that, intriguing with the Scythians, sending for more of them from their own lands and plundering all the vicinity.

5. In the end the emperor, who had regarded the Manichaean affair as of minor importance, again brought them under his control.[11] But Bohemond was still waiting at Avlona. Let us get back to him. When he heard of the fate of Bryennius and the other counts, some of whom had chosen to serve under the emperor, while the rest dispersed in all directions, he left for his own country and crossed to Lombardy. At Salerno he met his father Robert, as I have already described, and with many charges he tried to stir up resentment against the emperor. Robert, who saw the terrible news in his son's face and knew that the glorious hopes he had placed in him had gone completely astray, like a coin falling wrong way up, stood for a long time speechless, as if struck by a thunderbolt. When he had learnt all and fully realized how his expectations had been disappointed, he was in the depths of despair. Yet no ignoble thought unworthy of his own bravery and daring entered his head. On the contrary he was more than ever eager for battle,

more occupied with plans and ideas for war. Robert was a determined champion of his own designs and prejudices, absolutely resolved never to give up a decision once he had taken it: in a word, he was indomitable – for he believed that his first assault could achieve anything.

He quickly regained his composure; his terrible gloom passed. Heralds were sent everywhere proclaiming a general mobilization and a fresh attack on the emperor in Illyrikon.[12] All men were required to join Robert. So a host of soldiers, cavalry and infantry, soon gathered from all directions, all finely armed, thinking only of battle. They flocked to join him from the neighbouring towns and no less from foreign countries, coming as Homer would have said like buzzing swarms of bees.[13] Robert therefore had the military power to avenge his son's defeat. Now that sufficient forces had assembled he sent for the two other sons, Roger and Guy. (The Emperor Alexios had secretly made overtures to Guy, with offers of a marriage alliance and the prospect of exceptional honour and a generous financial reward. He hoped to tempt him from allegiance to his father. Guy listened to the proposals and accepted, but for the moment kept his own counsel.) To Roger and Guy, then, Robert handed over all his cavalry and sent them off to seize Avlona without delay; they crossed over and took the town at once.[14] They left a handful of soldiers there to protect the place and with the rest went on to Butrint and captured that too without any difficulty.

As for Robert, he sailed with his whole fleet along the coast opposite Butrint until he reached Brindisi, intending to cross from there. However, when he discovered that the voyage would be shorter from Otranto,[15] he sailed from that place to Avlona. After coasting along as far as Butrint he rejoined his sons. Corfu, previously subdued by him, had again rebelled; accordingly he left Roger and Guy[16] in Butrint and himself sailed to the island.

So much for Robert. The emperor meanwhile was informed of his movements, but was far from shaken. He urged the Venetians to equip a strong naval expedition, having convinced them to do battle with Robert. He promised that they would be reimbursed; he would pay their expenses many times over.[17] He himself made ready biremes, triremes and all kinds of raiding vessels. With soldiers on board experienced in naval warfare they sailed against Robert.

The hostile manoeuvres of these fleets were known to Robert and, characteristically, he seized the initiative: weighing anchor he sailed with his entire force to the harbour of Kassiopi. The Venetians had not been long in the harbour of Passaron before they heard of his move. Immediately they too made for Kassiopi. In the tremendous struggle that took place at close quarters Robert was defeated, but remained utterly undaunted. He prepared for a second conflict of even greater ferocity – it was typical of the man's combative, war-loving spirit. The commanders of the allied navies, knowing of his preparations, but confident after their own triumph, attacked him three days later and won a resounding victory, after which they withdrew again to the harbour of Passaron.

It may be that they overestimated the importance of their successes, under the circumstances a reaction normal enough, or perhaps they believed their opponents were really down and out; anyway, they relaxed as if the business was completely finished and treated Robert with thorough contempt. A squadron of fast ships was dispatched to report these events and describe the absolute rout of the enemy in Venice. A certain Venetian called Peter Contarini, who had recently taken refuge with Robert, told him what they had done. The news plunged him into a worse despair; for a time he lost all energy, but better counsels prevailed and once more he assailed the Venetians. The latter were astounded by his unexpected arrival, but lost no time in linking their bigger vessels with iron chains in the port of Corfu with the smaller ships inside this compact circle, the so-called 'sea harbour'. All anxiously awaited his onslaught under arms.

In the ensuing battle – terrible and more violent than the two previous encounters – both sides fought with unprecedented passion and neither would give way; indeed they collided head-on. The Venetians had already exhausted their supplies, however, and there were no reserves of men – they had only the soldiers on the ships. The latter, because they had no cargo, floated on the surface as if buoyed up by the waves – indeed the water did not even reach the second line on their hulls – so that when the men all rushed to one side to oppose the enemy, the boats immediately sank. Up to 13,000 were drowned. The other vessels were captured, with their crews.[18]

Robert behaved in cruel fashion after his famous victory. Many of the prisoners were treated with hideous savagery: some were blinded, others had their noses cut off, others lost hands or feet or both. As for the remainder, he sent heralds to their fellow-countrymen widely advertising their sale: anyone who wished to buy a relative for a price could come and do so with impunity. At the same time he had the effrontery to suggest negotiations for peace. They rejected the idea: 'Duke Robert, you can be sure of this: even if we saw our own wives and children having their throats slit, we would not denounce our treaty with the Emperor Alexios. What is more, we will certainly not cease to help him and fight bravely on his behalf.'

A short time afterwards they made ready warships, triremes and some other small and fast ships and attacked Robert with a larger force. They caught up with him off Butrint, where he was camped, and joined battle. The Venetians won a conclusive victory, killing many of their adversaries and throwing more into the sea. They very nearly captured Robert's own son Guy, as well as his wife. The report of this fine success was sent in full to the emperor.

He rewarded them with many gifts and honours. The Doge of Venice was personally honoured with the rank of *protosebastos* and the appropriate pension. The patriarch, too, received the title of *hypertimos*, also with the corresponding pension. Apart from that, all the churches in Venice were allotted an annual payment of gold – a considerable sum – from the imperial treasury on the emperor's orders. To the Church of St Mark the Apostle and Evangelist,[19] all the Amalfitans[20] who had workshops in Constantinople were to pay tribute; and he made a present to this church of the workshops from the ancient quay of the Hebrews as far as the Vigla, including the anchorages between these two points, not to mention the gift of much real property both in the capital and in the town of Dyrrakhion and wherever else the Venetians demanded it. But the main reward was the free market he afforded them in all provinces under Roman control, so that they were allowed to trade without interference as they wished; not a single obol was to be exacted by way of customs duties or any other tax levied by the treasury. They were completely free of Roman authority.[21]

6. Now we must go back to the point where we digressed and take up the main thread[22] of the narrative. Even after this defeat Robert did not return to peaceful ways. He had already sent some of his ships, under the command of his son Roger, against Kephalenia. He was eager to capture the town. The rest of the fleet anchored off Vonitsa with all the army. He himself boarded a galley with one bank of oars and sailed to Kephalenia, but before he could join the other forces and his son, while he was still waiting near Ather, a promontory of the island, he was attacked by a violent fever. Unable to bear the burning heat, he asked for some cold water. His men, who had dispersed everywhere in search of water, were told by a native: 'You see the island of Ithaka there. On it a great city was built long ago called Jerusalem, now in ruins through the passage of time. There used to be a spring there which always gave cold drinkable water.'

Robert, hearing this, was at once seized with great dread, since the connection between Ather and Jerusalem made him realize that his death was close by. A long time before some individuals had uttered a prophecy in the way that sycophants usually make to the great: 'As far as Ather you will subdue everything, but on your way from there to Jerusalem, you will obey the claims of necessity.' Whether it was the fever that carried him off, or whether he suffered from pleurisy I cannot say with certainty. He lingered on for six days and then died.

His wife Gaita reached him as he was breathing his last, with his son weeping beside him. The news was given to the other son,[23] whom he had named heir to his domains previously. He was heart-broken at the time, but reason prevailed and when he had recovered his self-composure, he called a general meeting. First of all, he announced what had happened, shedding tears copiously over his father's death; then he compelled all to take the oath of allegiance to himself. He crossed with them to Apulia but even though it was summer, ran into a terrific storm on the voyage. Some ships were sunk, others were cast up on the beach and wrecked. The vessel carrying the dead man was half-destroyed; it was with difficulty that his friends saved the coffin with the body inside and brought it to Venosa. He was buried in the monastery built long ago in honour of the Holy Trinity, where his brothers had also been laid to rest before him. Robert died in the twenty-fifth year of his ducal reign, having lived in all seventy years.[24]

The emperor was relieved at the news of Robert's sudden death, like a man throwing off a great load from his shoulders. He immediately set about the enemies still occupying Dyrrakhion, attempting to sow dissension among them by letters and every other method. He hoped that by doing this he would capture the town easily. He also persuaded the Venetians resident in Constantinople to write to their fellow-countrymen in Epidamnos, and to the Amalfitans and all other foreigners there, advising them to yield to his wishes and surrender the place. Unceasingly, with bribes and promises, he worked to this end. The inhabitants were in fact persuaded (for all Latins lust after money: for one obol they would sell even their nearest and dearest). In their desire for great rewards they formed a conspiracy, wiped out the man who first led them to betray the town to Robert and killed his partisans with him. They then approached the emperor and handed over the town;[25] in return they were granted a complete amnesty.

7. A certain scholar called Seth,[26] who boasted loudly of his knowledge of astrology, had foretold Robert's death, after his crossing to Illyrikon. The prediction, set out by an oracle on paper and before being sealed, was handed to some of the emperor's closest friends. Seth told them to keep the document for some time. Then, when Robert died, on his instructions they opened it. The oracle ran thus: 'A great enemy from the west, who has caused much trouble, will die suddenly.' All wondered at the skill of the man; he had indeed reached the peak of this science.

For a brief moment let us leave the main narrative for a short digression on the nature of oracles. The art of divination is a rather recent discovery, unknown to the ancient world. In the time of Eudoxos, the distinguished astronomer, the rules for it did not exist, and Plato had no knowledge of the science; even Manetho[27] the astrologer had no accurate information on the subject. In their attempts to prophesy they did at least establish the ascendant and fix the cardinal points; they understood how to observe the position of the stars at one's birth and how to do all the other things that the inventor of this system bequeathed to posterity, things that are intelligible to the devotees of such nonsense.

I myself once dabbled a little in the art, not in order to make use of any such knowledge (Heaven forbid!), but so that being better informed about its futile jargon I might confound the experts. I write this not to glorify myself, but to point out that in the reign of this emperor many sciences made progress. He honoured philosophers and philosophy itself, although it was obvious that he adopted a somewhat hostile attitude towards this study of astrology, because I suppose it diverted most of the more simple-minded from hopes that come from above to a blind belief in the influence of the stars. That was the reason for Alexios' war on the pursuit of astrology.

There was certainly no dearth of astrologers in this period – far from it. Seth, whom I have already mentioned, flourished then and there was the famous Egyptian from Alexandria[28] who devoted much of his time to the revelation of the mysteries of astrology. Many people interrogated him and he gave extra-ordinarily accurate forecasts in some cases without using an astrolabe; he relied for his predictions on some form of divination. There was no magic whatever in this, but merely a certain numerical skill on the part of the Alexandrians. When the emperor saw young people flocking to consult him as though he were a prophet, he himself put questions to him on two occasions and each time received a correct reply. Afraid that Seth might do harm to many and that the public might turn to the unprofitable pursuit of astrology, he banished him from the city and made him live at Rhaidestos, but took great care that his needs should be generously provided for at the expense of the imperial treasury.

Then there was the case of the famous dialectician Eleutherios,[29] another Egyptian, who attained great proficiency in the art, which he practised with a wonderful skill. He was undoubtedly the supreme exponent. In later times, too, there was an Athenian, one Katanankes,[30] who came from his native city to Constantinople with the ambition to surpass all his predecessors. He was asked by some people about the emperor, inquiring as to when he would die. He forecast the date according to his calculations, but proved to be wrong. However, it happened at that moment that the lion living in the palace breathed its last after suffering from a fever for four days, and most people thought that Katanankes' prediction was thereby fulfilled. Some time afterwards he again foretold the emperor's death wrongly, but on the very day he had mentioned the Empress Anna, his mother, died. Although the man had been wrong as often as he had been right, the emperor was unwilling to remove him from the city, even if he was erratic; moreover, he wished to avoid any appearance of resentment.

It is time now for us to return to the narrative so that I do not seem like someone whose head is in the clouds, and so that I do not obscure the main theme of my history with the names of astrologers.[31] It was generally agreed and some actually said that Robert was an exceptional leader, quick-witted, of fine appearance, courteous, a clever conversationalist with a loud voice, accessible, of solid build, with hair invariably of the right length and a thick beard; he was always careful to observe the customs of his own race; he preserved to the end the youthful bloom which distinguished his face and indeed his whole body, and was proud of it – he had the physique of a true leader; he treated with respect all his subjects, especially those who had served him with unswerving loyalty.[32] On the other hand, he was niggardly and grasping in the extreme, a very good businessman, most covetous and full of ambition. Dominated as he was by these traits, he attracted much censure from everyone.

Some people blame the emperor for losing his head and starting the war with Robert prematurely.[33] According to them, if he had not provoked Robert too soon, he would have beaten him easily in any case, for Robert was being shot at from all directions, by the Albanians and by Bodin's men from Dalmatia. But of course fault-finders stand out of weapon range and the acid darts they fire at the contestants come from their tongues. The truth is that Robert's manliness, his marvellous skill in war and his steadfast spirit are universally recognized. He was an adversary not readily vanquished, a very tough enemy who was more courageous than ever in the hour of defeat.

8. The emperor, accompanied by the Latins of Count Bryennius who had deserted to him, returned to the capital with the laurels of victory. The date was the first of December in the seventh indiction.[34] He found the empress in the throes of childbirth, in the room set apart long ago for an empress's confinement. Our ancestors called it the *porphyra* – hence the world-famous name of the *porphyrogennetoi*. At dawn (it was a Saturday) a baby girl was born to them, who resembled her father, so they said, in all respects. I was that baby.

On several occasions I have heard my mother tell how, two days before the emperor's return to the palace (he was coming back then after his battle with Robert and his other numerous wars and labours), she was seized with the pains of childbirth and making the sign of the cross over her womb, said, 'Wait a while, little one, till your father's arrival.' Her mother, the *protovestiaria*, so she said, reproached her soundly: 'What if he comes in a month's time? Do you know when he'll arrive?' she said angrily. 'And how will you bear such pain?' So spoke her mother; but her own command was obeyed – which very clearly signified even in her womb the love that I was destined to have for my parents in the future. For thereafter, when I grew to womanhood and reached years of reason, I had beyond all doubt a great affection for both of them alike. Many folk, certainly all those who know my history, are witnesses of this deep feeling of mine and their evidence is supported by the numerous struggles and labours I have endured on their behalf, as well as those dangers to which I have exposed myself because of that love, unconcerned by honour, money, or life itself.

My love for them burned so fiercely that many a time I was ready to sacrifice my very soul for them. But it is not time to speak of that yet. I must tell the reader of the events that followed my birth.

When all the ceremonies which are usually performed at the birth of imperial children had taken place, by which I mean the acclamations, the gifts and honours presented to the leaders of the Senate and army, there was, I am told, an unprecedented outburst of joy; everyone was dancing and singing hymns, especially the close relatives of the empress, who could not contain themselves for delight. After a certain period of time my parents honoured me too with a crown and imperial diadem. Constantine, the son of the former emperor Michael Doukas, who has on many occasions been mentioned in this history, was still sharing the throne with my father; he signed notices of donations with him in purple ink, followed him with a tiara in processions and was acclaimed after him.[35] So it came about that I too was acclaimed and the officers who led the acclamations linked the names of Constantine and Anna. Often in later times I have heard my relatives and parents say that this practice continued in fact over a long period. Maybe it foreshadowed what was about to befall me afterwards, for good or ill.

When a second daughter was born, very like her parents and at the same time showing clear signs of the virtue and wisdom which were to distinguish her in later years, they longed for a son and he became the object of their prayers. Thus in the eleventh indiction a boy[36] was indeed born to them – an event immediately followed by great rejoicing; not a trace of disappointment remained now that their desire was fulfilled. The entire people, seeing the pleasure of their rulers, made merry; everyone was pleased and all together were glad. The palace then was a place of perfect happiness, all sorrow and worries of all kinds banished, for their supporters showed a genuine, heartfelt pleasure, and the rest pretended to share their joy. For ordinary folk are in general not well-disposed to their rulers, but usually feign loyalty and by flattery win the favour of their betters. Anyway on this occasion the universal delight was there for all to see.

The little boy was of a swarthy complexion, with a broad forehead, rather thin cheeks, a nose that was neither flat nor aquiline, but something between the two, and darkish eyes which, as far as one can divine from the appearance of a new-born baby, gave evidence of a lively spirit. Naturally my parents wanted to promote the little one to the rank of emperor and leave to him the empire of the Romans as a heritage; in the Great Church of God, therefore, he was honoured by the rite of holy baptism and crowned. Such were the events that befell us, the *porphyrogennetoi*, from the very moment of our birth. What happened to us later on will be told in the appropriate place.

9. As I have said before, after driving the Turks from the coastal districts of Bithynia and the Bosphorus itself, as well as from their hinterlands, the emperor Alexios concluded a peace treaty with Solymas.[37] He then turned to Illyrikon, thoroughly defeated Robert and his son Bohemond, albeit not without much suffering, and rescued the provinces of the west from utter disaster. On his return from that campaign he found that the Turks of Apelkhasem[38] were not merely invading the east again, but had even reached the Propontis and the places on the coast there. I must now describe how the Emir Solymas, having left Nicaea, appointed this Apelkhasem governor of the city; how Pouzanos was sent by the Persian sultan to Asia and vanquished by the brother of the sultan, Toutouses;[39] and how he was killed by him, but Toutouses after the victory was strangled by Pouzanos' cousins.

An Armenian called Philaretos, highly respected for his bravery and intelligence, had been promoted to the rank of *domestikos* by the former emperor Romanos Diogenes, and when he saw Diogenes' downfall and knew moreover that he had been blinded, it was more than he could bear, for he had a deep affection for this emperor. He organized a rebellion[40] and seized power for himself in Antioch. As the Turks plundered the area round the city every day and there was no respite at all, Philaretos decided to join them and offered himself for circumcision, according to their custom. His son violently opposed this ridiculous impulse, but his good advice went unheeded. After a journey of eight days he arrived in a state of extreme distress at Nicaea and approached the Emir Solymas, who at that time had been accorded the rank of sultan. He urged him to besiege Antioch and prosecute the war against his father. Solymas agreed and as he was about to leave for Antioch, appointed Apelkhasem governor of Nicaea with overriding authority over all other military commanders. After a march of twelve nights – undertaken to avoid detection (and necessitating rest by day) – Solymas and Philaretos' son reached Antioch and took it at the first assault.

Meanwhile Kharatikes, who had discovered that a large sum of gold and currency from the imperial treasury had been deposited in Sinope, made an unexpected attack on the place and captured it. Toutouses, the brother of the great sultan,[41] ruler of Jerusalem, the whole of Mesopotamia, Aleppo and the territory as far as Baghdad, also coveted Antioch, and when he saw the Emir Solymas in revolt and laying claim to the governorship of that city, he took up position with his whole army between Aleppo and Antioch. Solymas advanced to meet him and a fierce war broke out at once. However, when it came to fighting at close quarters Solymas' troops turned and fled in disorder. He made strenuous efforts to inspire them with courage, but in vain, and seeing that his life was in imminent danger he left the battlefield. Maybe because he felt that he was now safe, he put his shield on the ground and sat down there beside it. But his fellow-countrymen had seen him. Some of the satraps came near and told him that his uncle Toutouses was sending for him. Suspecting some danger from this invitation he refused. They pressed him and as he had no power to offer any resistance given he was on his own, he drew the sword from his sheath and thrust it into his own entrails. The sword passed clean through him and the wretched man perished wretchedly.[42] His death was inevitably the signal for his surviving forces to join Toutouses.

This news alarmed the great sultan – Toutouses was becoming too strong – and he dispatched Siaous to the emperor with proposals for a marriage alliance; he promised that if this were arranged he would force the Turks to withdraw from the coastal regions and hand over to the emperor the fortified places; he would lend his wholehearted support. The emperor received Siaous and read the sultan's letter. Then without even referring to the question of a marriage, and having noticed that Siaous was a sensible man, Alexios asked him where he came from and who his parents were. His mother, he said, was from Iberia, although he did admit that his father was a Turk. The emperor was much concerned to have him baptized and Siaous consented to this. He gave pledges, moreover, that he would not return to the sultan once he had obtained the grace of that holy rite.

He had a written order from the sultan which gave him the right to remove all satraps from the coastal towns they had occupied. All he had to do was to produce this document, if the emperor showed himself willing to conclude the marriage agreement. The emperor suggested to Siaous that he should make use of the sultan's order, and when he had by means of it removed the satraps, he should come back to the capital. With great enthusiasm Siaous visited Sinope first, revealed the sultan's letter to Kharatikes and made him leave the place without taking possession of a single obol of the imperial money. Then the following incident took place. As Kharatikes left Sinope he smashed the sanctuary built in honour of the Mother of God, our Immaculate Lady, and by Divine Providence he was delivered to a demon, as to some avenger, and fell to the ground frothing at the mouth. And thus he left, possessed by a devil.

Siaous then handed over Sinope to its new governor, Constantine Dalassenos, who had been sent by the emperor for that very purpose. In the same way Siaous visited the other towns, showing the sultan's order, removing the satraps and reinstating the emperor's satraps in their place. Having completed his task, he came back to the emperor, received holy baptism and was showered with many gifts and then handed the position of *doux* of Ankhialos.[43]

10. When the murder of the Emir Solymas became known throughout Asia, all those satraps who happened to be governors of towns or fortresses seized the places for themselves. For at the time when Solymas departed for Antioch, he had left

the protection of Nicaea in the hands of Apelkhasem, and various other satraps, so it is said, were entrusted with the coastal region, with Kappadokia and with the whole of Asia, each being required to guard his own particular area until Solymas' return. But Apelkhasem was at the time archisatrap of Nicaea and having control of this town, which also happened to be the headquarters of the sultanate, and having ceded control of the region of Kappadokia to his brother Poulkhases,[44] he had no qualms in claiming for himself the title of sultan: indeed, he believed he already had power in his hands. He was a clever man, prepared to run risks and his ambition was by no means satisfied. He sent out raiding parties to plunder the whole of Bithynia right down to the Propontis.

The emperor pursued his former policy: the raids were checked and Apelkhasem was constrained to seek terms of peace. But Alexios knew well enough that the man continued to cherish secret designs against himself and deferred the signing of any treaty; it was clearly necessary to send out a really strong force to make war on him. He therefore sent Tatikios, who has been mentioned many times in this history, with a powerful army to Nicaea with instructions to engage whatever enemies he met outside the walls but to do so with circumspection. Tatikios set off and when he was just outside the town, as no Turks appeared then, marshalled his troops in battle array. Suddenly a band of 200 Turks rode out against him. The Kelts (who were present in good numbers) caught sight of them, and armed with long lances charged into them head-on with terrific force; they wounded many and drove the rest back into the citadel.

Tatikios stood to arms in the same formation until sunset, but as no Turk showed himself outside the gates, he moved away to Basileia and pitched camp there, twelve stades from Nicaea. During the night a peasant came to him to assure Tatikios that Prosoukh was on the way there with 50,000 men sent by the new sultan Pargiaroukh.[45] The news was confirmed by others and since Tatikios was greatly inferior in numbers he altered his plans: it seemed more desirable to look to the safety of his whole army than to lose all his troops against heavy odds and against a braver force. His intention was to retire to the capital through Nikomedia.

From the town ramparts Apelkhasem saw him making for Constantinople and therefore left the town in pursuit, with the idea of attacking when he camped in a place which gave the Turks an advantage. He caught him at Prenetos, took the initiative and engaged in a violent conflict. Tatikios was very quick in drawing up a battle line and ordered the Kelts, in reply to this onslaught, to make the first cavalry charge against the barbarians. With their long lances at the ready they swept down on the enemy at full gallop like a flash of lightning, cut through their ranks and put them into headlong flight. Thus Tatikios returned to the capital through Bithynia.

Apelkhasem, however, did not want to rest under any circumstances. He coveted the sceptre of the Roman Empire, or failing that control of the whole seaboard and even of the islands. With this in mind, he decided first to build pirate vessels, since he had captured Kios (a town situated on the coast of Bithynia). While the ships were being completed, his scheme was going well or at least he thought so, but the emperor was not unaware of his activities. A fleet of the available biremes, triremes and other ships was made ready; then naming Manuel Boutoumites as *doux*, he sent him against Apelkhasem with orders to lose no time in burning his half-built navy, in whatever condition they found it. Tatikios was also to attack him with a strong force by land.

Both commanders left the city. Apelkhasem, seeing that Boutoumites was already on his way by sea and crossing at great speed, and learning moreover that other enemies were arriving by land, considered that the place where he was based was poorly suited to battle – it was too rugged and narrow, and at the same time, not suited to archers, leaving them unable to become involved against the Roman cavalry charges. As a result, he raised camp and decided to seek a better location, which was more advantageous for him. The new place was called by some Halykai, by others Kyparission.

Once he was over the sea Boutoumites very quickly burnt Apelkhasem's ships. On the day after, Tatikios also arrived, from the land side, pitched camp in a good strategic position and for fifteen whole days, from early morning till evening, kept up unceasing attacks on Apelkhasem, sometimes skirmishing, sometimes in regular battles. Apelkhasem never gave in; in fact he resisted vigorously, to the discomfiture of the Latins, who begged Tatikios to let them fight the Turks on their own despite the unfavourable terrain. It seemed to him an unwise move, but he knew that every day the Turks were reinforcing their general. He yielded to the Latins. About sunrise he drew up his forces and joined battle. Many of the Turks were killed in this engagement, very many were taken prisoners, but the majority fled without a thought for their baggage. Apelkhasem himself drove straight for Nicaea and barely escaped with his life. Before they returned to their own camp, the men serving with Tatikios had helped themselves to much booty.

The emperor, expert in winning the heart of a man and softening the hardest nature, at once sent Apelkhasem a letter in which he advised him to give up such useless schemes, to stop beating the air and make terms; by doing this he would relieve himself of much labour and enjoy instead liberal gifts and honours. Once Apelkhasem had learnt that Prosoukh was besieging the strongpoints held by some satraps and would soon approach Nicaea to lay siege to that town too, he made a virtue of necessity, as they say, and welcomed peace with the emperor confidently, for he had a shrewd idea of his intentions. A treaty of peace was concluded between them, but Alexios was eager to obtain a further advantage, and since there was no other way of achieving his goal, invited the Turk to the capital; he would receive money, sample the delights of the city to his heart's content, and thus rewarded go home.

Apelkhasem accepted the offer and was welcomed in the capital with every mark of friendship. Now the Turks who controlled Nicaea had also occupied Nikomedia (the capital of Bithynia), and the emperor wished to eject them; in order to do so, he thought it was essential to build a second stronghold by the sea, while the 'love scene' was being played out in Constantinople. All the construction materials needed for the building of this fortress, together with the architects, were put

on board transport ships and sent off under the command of
Eustathios, the *droungarios* of the fleet, who was to be responsible for the building and to whom the emperor confided his
secret plan. Eustathios was to receive in the most friendly
fashion any Turks who happened to pass that way, supply
their needs with the utmost generosity and inform them that
Apelkhasem knew of the project; all ships were to be barred
from the coastal areas of Bithynia, to prevent him from finding
out what was happening.

Every day the emperor continued to give Apelkhasem presents of money, to invite him to the baths, to horse races and
hunts, to sightseeing tours of the commemorative columns set
up in public places; to please him the charioteers were ordered
to organize an equestrian display in the theatre built long ago
by Constantine the Great, and he was encouraged to visit it
daily and watch the horses parade for inspection – all in order
to waste time and allow the builders a free hand. When the
fortress was finished and his aim achieved, Alexios presented the
Turk with more gifts, honoured him with the title of *sebastos*,[46]
confirmed their agreement in greater detail and sent him with
every sign of courtesy back over the sea.

When Apelkhasem eventually heard about the building,
although he was deeply distressed, he pretended ignorance and
maintained a complete silence on the subject. A similar anecdote
is recorded about Alkibiades.[47] He too in the same way deluded
the Spartans, when they had not agreed to the rebuilding of
Athens after its destruction by the Persians. He told the
Athenians to rebuild the city, then went away to Sparta as an
envoy. The negotiations took time and gave the restorers a
good opportunity. The Spartans only heard of the restoration
of Athens after the ruse had fully succeeded. The Paeanian,[48] in
one of his speeches, recalls this beautiful trick. My father's
scheme was indeed like it, but it was much more strategically
astute than that of Alkibiades, for by humouring the barbarian
with horse races and other pleasures and by putting off his
departure from day to day, he allowed the job to be finished,
and then, when the whole work was completed, he let the man
go free from the capital.

11. According to expectations Prosoukh arrived with an impressive force to besiege Nicaea,[49] exactly as Tatikios' night visitor had said, and for three months he never relaxed his efforts. The inhabitants of the town, and indeed Apelkhasem himself, saw that their condition was really desperate – it was impossible to hold out against Prosoukh any more. They got a message through to the emperor asking for help, saying that it was better to be called his slaves than to surrender to Prosoukh. Without delay the best available troops were sent to their aid, with standards and silver-studded sceptres.

Alexios' aim in this was not to help Apelkhasem directly, but he calculated that providing help would bring about the ruin of Apelkhasem. For when two enemies of the Roman Empire were fighting one another, it would pay him to support the weaker – not in order to make him more powerful, but to repel the one while taking the town from the other, a town that was not at the moment under Roman jurisdiction but would be incorporated in the Roman sphere by this means; little by little a second would be taken, and then another, so that Roman influence, which was then reduced to almost nothing, especially since Turkish military strength had increased, would be much extended.

There was a time when the frontiers of Roman power were the two pillars at the limits of east and west – the so-called Pillars of Herakles in the west and those of Dionysos[50] not far from the Indian border in the east. As far as its extent was concerned, it is impossible to say how great was the power of Rome: it included Egypt, Meroë, all the land of the Troglodytes, the countries near the Torrid Zone;[51] on the other side, the famous Thule and all the peoples who live in the region of the north, over whom is the Pole Star. But at the time we are speaking of, the boundary of Roman power on the east was our neighbour the Bosphorus, and on the west the town of Adrianoupolis. The Emperor Alexios, fighting two-fisted against barbarians who attacked him on either flank, manoeuvred round Byzantion, the centre of his circle as it were, and proceeded to broaden the empire: on the west the frontier became the Adriatic Sea, on the east the Euphrates and Tigris.

He would have revived the ancient prosperity of the empire, too, had not a succession of wars and constant dangers and troubles checked his ambitions (for he was always taking risks and playing with high stakes).

However, as I said at the beginning of this episode, when he sent an army to Apelkhasem, the ruler of Nicaea, it was not to rescue him, but to win a victory for himself. Nevertheless, fortune did not smile on his efforts. It happened like this. The expeditionary force reached the place called St George and the Turks without hesitation opened the gates to them. The soldiers climbed up to the ramparts above the east gate and put their standards and sceptres all together there, at the same time making a great hullabaloo and shouting their war cry over and over again. The besiegers outside were terrified by these noises and thinking that the emperor had come in person they went away in the night. But the Roman army returned to the capital, too outnumbered to resist another Persian invasion expected from the deep interior of the Turkish Empire.

12. The sultan waited for the return of Siaous,[52] but when he saw how painfully slow he was and then learnt what had happened to him: how he had driven Kharatikes out of Sinope by a trick, how he had received holy baptism and how he had been sent to the west by the emperor with the title *doux* of Ankhialos; he was annoyed and distressed. Anyway he decided that Pouzanos must this time be sent to attack Apelkhasem. At the same time he entrusted to him a letter addressed to the emperor about a marriage alliance. The message read as follows: 'I have heard, Emperor, of your troubles. I know that from the start of your reign you have met with many difficulties and that recently, after you had settled the Latin affairs, the Scythians were preparing to make war on you. The Emir Apelkhasem, too, having broken the treaty that Solymas concluded with you, is ravaging Asia as far as Damalis itself. If therefore it is your wish that Apelkhasem should be driven from those districts and that Asia, together with Antioch, should be subject to you, send me your daughter as wife for the eldest of my sons. Thereafter nothing will stand in your way; it will be easy for you to accomplish everything with my aid, not only in

the east, but even as far as Illyrikon and the entire west. Because
of the forces which I will send you, no one will resist you from
now on.'

So much for the Persian sultan's[53] proposal. Pouzanos meanwhile reached Nicaea. Several attempts were made on the town
without success, for Apelkhasem fought back bravely; he asked
for and obtained help from the emperor. In the end, Pouzanos
left hurriedly to attack the other towns and fortresses. He
pitched camp by the Lampe, a river near Lopadion. When he
had gone, Apelkhasem loaded gold on fifteen mules, as much
as they could carry, and went off to the Persian sultan, hoping
that with this bribe he would not be relieved of his command.
He found him bivouacking near Spakha.

Since a personal meeting was denied him, he sent intermediaries who pleaded earnestly on his behalf. The sultan replied:
'I have given authority, once and for all, to the Emir Pouzanos;
it is not my wish to deprive him of it. Let Apelkhasem take his
money then and give it to him. Let him tell Pouzanos whatever
he likes. What Pouzanos decides will be my decision.' So, after
waiting there for a long time and after much suffering and
nothing accomplished, he set off to find Pouzanos. On the way
he met 200 leading satraps sent out by the latter to arrest him
– Apelkhasem's departure from Nicaea had not gone unnoticed.
These men seized him, made a noose of twisted bowstring, put
it round his neck and strangled him.[54] In my opinion the whole
business was not the doing of Pouzanos but of the sultan, who
gave orders to deal with Apelkhasem in this way.

So much for him. Having read the sultan's letter the emperor
had no intention whatever of accepting his proposal. How
could he? His daughter, the bride sought for the barbarian's
eldest son, would have been wretched indeed if she had gone
to Persia, to share a royal state worse than any poverty. But
that was not the will of God, nor did the emperor dream of
going so far, however desperate his position. At the first reading
of the letter he immediately burst into laughter at the Turk's
presumption, muttering, 'The Devil must have put that into his
head.' Despite his attitude to the marriage, he still thought it
advisable to keep the sultan in suspense by offering vain hopes.

He summoned Kourtikios with three others and sent them as envoys furnished with letters in which he welcomed the idea of peace and agreed with the sultan's propositions; at the same time he himself made certain demands which would prolong the negotiations. Actually the ambassadors from Byzantion had not yet arrived in Khorosan when they heard that the sultan had been murdered.[55] They returned home.

Toutouses was full of arrogance after the killing of Emir Solymas, his own son-in-law, who had marched against him from Arabia. He had heard that the sultan was already seeking peace terms with the emperor and he now planned to murder him, even though he was his own natural brother. To this end he summoned twelve bloodthirsty individuals called in the Persian dialect 'Khasioi'[56] and sent them at once as envoys to him. He gave them instructions as to the killing: 'Go,' he said, 'and first of all make an announcement that you have certain secret information for the sultan, and when you are granted the right of entry, approach as if you desire to speak with him privately, and massacre my brother then and there.'

The ambassadors, or rather murderers, most gladly departed to commit this crime, as if setting out for some dinner or festive occasion. They found the sultan in a state of drunkenness and everything favourable to their plans, since his guards were standing some way off; they came up to him, drew their swords from under their armpits and straightway cut the wretched man to pieces. The Khasioi delight in that sort of bloodshed; their idea of pleasure is merely the plunging of a sword into human entrails. Furthermore, should anyone happen to attack them at the very same moment and cut them up into mincemeat, they regard such a death as an honour, passing on these bloody deeds from one generation to another like some family heritage. At all events, not one of them returned to Toutouses, for they paid for their crime with their own violent deaths.

At the news Pouzanos retired to Khorosan with all his forces. The brother of the murdered man, Toutouses, met him as he was nearly at the end of his journey. A battle was fought at once at close quarters, both armies showing great spirit and neither yielding the victory to the other. Pouzanos played a

gallant part in the struggle and spread confusion in the enemy
ranks everywhere, but fell mortally wounded. His men, each
looking to his own safety, fled in all directions, so that Toutouses returned in triumph to Khorosan as if he had already
won the title of sultan. In reality, he was in imminent peril.
Pargiaroukh, son of the murdered Sultan Taparas, encountering
him like a lion rejoicing when he lights upon some mighty prey,
as the poet says, and made a powerful attack on him and tore
his army apart. Toutouses himself, who was puffed up with the
pride of Nauatos,[57] was killed.

At the time when Apelkhasem went off with the money to
the Sultan of Khorosan, as I have already explained, his brother
Poulkhases came to Nicaea and occupied it. The emperor, hearing of this, offered extremely generous bribes if he would hand
over the town and leave. Poulkhases was willing, but kept
putting off the decision, again looking to Apelkhasem; a continuous stream of messages to the emperor left him in suspense,
but in fact the man was waiting for his brother's return. While
this was going on, an incident took place which I will outline
as follows: the sultan of Khorosan who was murdered by the
Khasioi had previously held the two sons of the great Solymas;
after his death they fled from Khorosan and soon arrived in
Nicaea. At the sight of them the people of Nicaea ran riot with
joy, and Poulkhases gladly handed over the town to them, as if
it were a family inheritance. The elder son, Klitziasthlan[58] by
name, received the title of sultan. He sent for the wives and
children of the soldiers present in Nicaea and they set up home
there; the town became what one might call the official residence of the sultans. After arranging the affairs of Nicaea thus,
Klitziasthlan forced Poulkhases to resign his governorship,
appointed Muhammad in charge of Nicaea and of all the satraps, and leaving him in command, marched on Melitene.

13. Such was the history of the sultans. Elkhanes[59] the archisatrap with his men occupied Apollonias and Kyzikos (both
these towns are on the coast) and ravaged all the districts by
the sea. This led the emperor to equip a fair number of the
available boats (the fleet was not yet ready) and put on board
siege-engines and good fighting men under the command of

Alexander Euphorbenos, an illustrious man and famed for his
bravery. The object of the expedition was to come to grips with
Elkhanes. They arrived at Apollonias and at once began to
besiege it. At the end of six consecutive days, during which the
assault on the walls continued even during the night, Euphorbenos controlled the outer periphery of the citadel, which is
nowadays usually called the *exopolon*, but Elkhanes stubbornly
defended the acropolis, hoping for reinforcements from outside.

When Alexander saw a barbarian force of considerable
strength on its way to help and as his own army was equivalent
to a mere fraction of the enemy, he thought it wiser, if he could
not win, to keep his own troops out of danger. His position
was one of extreme peril and it was impossible to achieve any
safety there. He decided to make for the sea, embarked his men
on the ships and sailed down the river. Elkhanes, however, had
guessed his plan. He anticipated it by seizing the entrance to
the lake and the bridge over the river, at the place where in
olden times a sanctuary had been built by St Helena in honour
of the great Constantine – hence the bridge's name, which still
persists to this day. At the entrance to the lake, then, and on
the bridge itself, to right and left he posted his most experienced
soldiers with orders to surprise the Roman ships on their way
through. In fact they all fell into the trap as they reached that
point in small boats. When they saw the danger, they made for
the shore in desperation and leapt from the boats on to dry
land, but the Turks caught up with them and a fierce battle
ensued. Many of the officers were captured; many fell into the
river and were swept away by the current.

The news of this disaster annoyed the emperor intensely; he
sent a powerful force under Opos overland against the Turks.
Opos reached Kyzikos and took the place at the first assault,
then detached from his own regiments about 300 men who
were siege specialists and ready to face any danger, for an
attempt on Poimanenon. That too was easily captured; some of
the defenders were killed there, others were taken prisoner and
sent to Opos, who promptly forwarded them to the emperor.
Then, leaving Poimanenon, he went on to Apollonias and began
a determined siege.

Elkhanes had too few men there to resist and voluntarily surrendered the town. Together with his closest relatives he deserted to the emperor and was rewarded with countless gifts, including the greatest of all – the holy rite of baptism. All those unwilling to follow Opos, Skaliarios, for example, and . . . who was afterwards honoured with the title of *hyperperilampros* (they were archisatraps and distinguished men), when they heard of the emperor's friendly overtures to Elkhanes and how generous he had been, also came to Alexios and received what they wanted. One can truly say that the emperor was a most saintly person, both because of his virtues and in his manner of speaking – a high priest, as it were, of perfect reverence. He was an excellent teacher of our doctrine, with an apostle's faith and message, eager to convert to Christ not only the nomad Scythians, but also the whole of Persia and all the barbarians who dwell in Egypt or Libya and worship Muhammad in their extraordinary ways.

14. That is enough about these matters. As I now wish to describe a more terrible and greater invasion of the Roman Empire, it will be advisable to tell the story from its beginning, for these invaders followed one another in succession like the waves of the sea. A Scythian tribe, having suffered incessant pillaging at the hands of Sarmatians, left home and came down to the Danube. As it was necessary for them to make peace with the people living near the river and everyone agreed, they entered into negotiations with the chiefs: Tatou, also called Khales; Sesthlavos and Satzas (I have to mention the names of their leading men, even if it spoils the tone of my history). One controlled Dristra, the latter two Bitzina and the remaining areas. A treaty was concluded and the Scythians in future crossed the Danube with impunity and plundered the country near it, so that they even seized some fortresses. Later, as they enjoyed a period of peace, they tilled the soil and sowed millet and wheat.

But the notorious Traulos, the Manichaean, with his followers and some men of the same religious persuasion who had occupied the stronghold on the hilltop of Beliatoba[60] – a fuller account of this was given earlier in the history – learning about the activities of these Scythians, brought to light a scheme which they had been mulling over for a long time: they manned the rough tracks and mountain passes, called in the Scythians and proceeded to ravage Roman territory. The Manichaeans, of course, are by nature a bellicose people, always ravening like dogs to gorge on human blood.

The Emperor Alexios, being informed of this, ordered the *domestikos* of the western provinces, Pakourianos, an excellent commander and skilled at drawing up his forces in battle formation and for free combat, to march with his army against them. Branas, himself a first-class soldier, was to accompany him. Pakourianos discovered that the Scythians had passed through the defiles and pitched camp not far from Beliatoba, in such vast numbers that taking them on was out of the question: the very thought of it numbed him. The more profitable course, he believed, was to keep his troops out of harm's way for now without risking an engagement; better that than to fight a losing battle and suffer annihilation. But Branas, who was bold and daring, disapproved; the *domestikos*, to avoid any imputation of cowardice if he refused the challenge, gave way to his impulsive colleague. Everyone was ordered to arm. When the preparations for battle were complete, they advanced against the Scythians, with Pakourianos at the centre of the line. The Romans were vastly outnumbered and the sight of the enemy filled all of them with dread. Nevertheless they attacked. Many were slain and Branas was mortally wounded. The *domestikos*, fighting furiously and charging the Scythians with great violence, crashed into an oak tree and died on the spot. After that the rest of the army dispersed in all directions.

The emperor mourned all those who had fallen, individually and as a body, but in particular he lamented the death of Pakourianos, for even before his accession he had loved him dearly. He shed many tears for the *domestikos*. However, there was no lessening of effort on that account. Tatikios was sent with large sums of money to Adrianoupolis both to pay the soldiers their annual wages and to draw recruits from everywhere for a new army, worthy of battle. Houmpertopoulos was to hurry, with only the Kelts, to join Tatikios, and he was to

leave a moderate garrison in Kyzikos. Tatikios, full of confidence on the arrival of these Latins and their commander, lost
no time, once the force was strong enough, in marching against
the Scythians.

He pitched camp near Philippopolis, by the banks of the river
which flows past Blisnos, but before all the baggage could be
stored inside the entrenchments, the enemy came into sight on
their way back from a marauding raid with much booty and
many prisoners. A powerful detachment was sent against them;
Tatikios followed later with the main body, all fully armed and
arranged in line. When the Scythians joined the rest of their
forces near the banks of the Euros[61] with their spoils and captives, the Romans were divided in two and ordered to shout
their war cry. The attack went in from either flank with tremendous yells and clamour. Most of the Scythians fell in the bitter
fighting, but many saved their lives in scattered flight. Tatikios,
with all their booty, returned triumphantly to Philippopolis.

Having established his whole army there, he planned a second
attack; the question was, from where and how was it to be
launched. The Scythians had enormous resources of manpower.
Tatikios, realizing this, deployed his scouts in all directions –
he wanted continuous information of all their movements. The
scouts reported the presence of a large number of Scythians
gathered near Beliatoba who were plundering the surrounding
region. Despite his complete inability to match their numbers,
Tatikios awaited the Scythian onslaught, but he was really at
his wits' end and in a most embarrassing situation. However,
he sharpened his sword and encouraged his men before the
fight. At that point someone came to announce that the barbarians were on the march and emphasized that they were near.

He immediately donned his armour, gave the general call to
arms and at once crossed the Euros. On the far side the line
was drawn up for battle, with the battalions in due order.
He personally commanded the centre. The enemy arranged
themselves in their Scythian fashion, obviously spoiling for a
fight and provoking the Romans. Even so, both armies were
afraid and put off the moment of conflict, the Romans because they trembled before the overwhelming numbers of the

Scythians; the Scythians because they feared the sight of all those breastplates, the standards, the glory of the Roman armour and the brightness reflected from it like rays of starlight. Of all those men only the Latins were brave and daring enough to seize the initiative, sharpening teeth and sword alike, as they say. But Tatikios restrained them – he was a level-headed man and knew well what was likely to happen. Thus both sides stood firm, waiting for their adversaries to make the first move. Not a man from either line dared to ride out into the no-man's-land between them, and when the sun was going down both generals went back to their camps. This was repeated on the two following days. The leaders prepared for combat and each day the troops were drawn up in battle order, but, since no one had the courage to attack, at dawn on the third day the Scythians withdrew. Thereupon Tatikios at once set out in pursuit,[62] but it was a case of the proverbial footslogger chasing the Lydian chariot. The Scythians first crossed the Sidera, which is the name of a valley, and since Tatikios was not able to catch up with them, he retired with his whole army to Adrianoupolis. He left the Kelts in that area, and having sent his soldiers home, went back to the imperial capital with a detachment of his army.

BOOK VII

1. At the beginning of the spring Tzelgou (the supreme leader of the Scythian army) crossed the upper Danube valley at the head of a diverse force made up of around 80,000 men, Sarmatians, Scythians and a large contingent of Dacians led by one Solomon.[1] Tzelgou proceeded to ravage the towns of the Kharioupolis area, and even reached Kharioupolis itself. After taking much plunder he established himself in a place called Skotinos. When Nicholas Maurokatakalon heard of this, he and Bempetziotes (who revealed with his name the country of his origin) occupied Pamphilon with their own forces. When they saw that the villagers from the surrounding districts were hurrying to the towns and strongholds in panic, they withdrew from the said Pamphilon and redeployed the whole of their army to the village of Koule. Behind them came the Scythians, who had realized that the Romans were hacked off (to use an expression known to soldiers) and they closely followed their tracks.

It was already light when Tzelgou drew up his forces to fight Maurokatakalon. The latter climbed up to a narrow defile with some officers which dominated the plain, so that he could observe the barbarian army. When he saw the size of the Scythian host, he decided to postpone engaging them – even though he was eager for battle – since the Roman forces were massively outnumbered by those of the enemy. However, on his return to camp he consulted the officers of the whole army including Ioannikios about whether an attack should be made. They encouraged him to do so, and as he was more inclined to that course anyway, he divided the Roman forces into three, gave the order to sound the attack and engaged the barbarians. In the struggle many of the Scythians fell wounded; no fewer were killed. Among them was Tzelgou, who received a mortal blow and gave up his spirit, having fought bravely and spread confusion everywhere in the Roman ranks. Most of the enemy fell in their flight into the mountain torrent between the place known as Skotinos and Koule, were trampled under foot by their own comrades and drowned. After this glorious victory, the emperor's men entered Constantinople, where they received appropriate rewards and honours from the emperor. Then they retired from the city with Adrian Komnenos, the emperor's own brother, now promoted to the rank of *megas domestikos* of the West.

2. Although the enemy had been driven from Macedonia and the area round Philippopolis, they returned to the Danube and made their camp there. Living alongside our territories they treated them as their own and plundered with complete licence. The news that the Scythians were living inside the Roman borders was reported to the emperor. He thought the position was intolerable, but he was also afraid they might make their way over the mountain passes again and turn bad to worse. Accordingly preparations were made and the army was well equipped before he made for Adrianoupolis; from there he went on to Lardeas, which lies between Diampolis and Goloe. At Lardeas, Alexios appointed George Euphorbenos to a command position and sent him by sea to Dristra.

The emperor himself spent forty days in the district, summoning forces from all parts. When he had collected a large army, he deliberated whether he should cross the mountain passes and begin an offensive against the Scythians. 'It is essential,' he said, 'that no respite be given to the Scythians' – a reasonable remark to make about these barbarians. For Scythian incursions did not begin in any one of the four seasons only to end in the next, lasting from the start of summer, for example, till autumn, or even to late autumn and the cold weather; the Scythians did not limit their evil activities to a whole year even, but in fact troubled the Roman Empire over a long period, although I have mentioned only a few of many such invasions. Specious arguments failed to divide them and, despite the emperor's repeated efforts to win them over by all kinds of enticement, no deserter came to him, even in secret, so inflexible was their determination.

Nikephoros Bryennios and Gregory Maurokatakalon, who had of course been ransomed by the emperor for 40,000 *nomismata*, were by no means in favour of making war on them in the Paristrion. On the other hand, George Palaiologos and Nicholas Maurokatakalon and all the other young and vigorous officers endorsed the emperor's plan and urged him to cross the pass over the Haimos² and join battle with them in Paristrion. The two sons of the Emperor Diogenes, Nikephoros and Leo, were also of the same opinion.

They had been born in the *porphyra* after their father's elevation to the throne and for that reason had the title *porphyrogennetoi*. This *porphyra* is a room in the palace built in the form of a complete square from floor to ceiling, but the latter ends in a pyramid. The room affords a view of the sea and harbour where the stone oxen and the lions stand. Its floor is paved with marble and the walls are covered with marble panels. The stone used was not of the ordinary kind, nor marble which can be more easily obtained but at greater expense; it was in fact casually acquired in Rome by former emperors. This particular marble is generally of a purple colour throughout, but with white spots like sand sprinkled over it. It was for this, I suppose, that our forefathers called the room *porphyra*.

Anyway, to return to the subject, when a loud blast from the trumpet gave the signal to cross the Haimos, Bryennios tried hard to dissuade the emperor from the enterprise. When all his arguments failed, he ended solemnly with these words: 'I tell you this, my Emperor: if you cross the Haimos, you will appreciate the fastest horses.' Someone asked him what he meant. 'For when you flee,' he replied, 'all of you.' This Bryennios, although he had lost his eyes because of a revolution, was recognized to be a foremost authority and expert on strategy and tactics. If anyone wants to know in greater detail how he lost his eyes, through some revolt or uprising against the Emperor Botaneiates, and how he was taken prisoner by

Alexios Komnenos, at that time *megas domestikos* of the western and eastern forces, and afterwards handed over to Borilos with his sight undamaged, then we must refer him to the illustrious *Kaisar* Nikephoros.

He became the son-in-law of Alexios when the latter already held the sceptre of the Romans; the former, of course, was the son of the famous Bryennios. But these memories upset me; my heart is filled with sorrow. The *kaisar* was a man of learning and an extremely intelligent writer. Everything – strength, agility, physical charm, in fact all the good qualities of mind and body – combined to glorify that man. In him Nature brought to birth and God created a unique personality, outstanding in every way; just as Homer sang the praises of Akhilles among the Achaeans, so might one say that my *kaisar* excelled among all men who live beneath the sun. He was a magnificent soldier, but by no means unmindful of literature; he read all books and by closely studying every science derived much wisdom from them, both ancient and modern. Later on he devoted himself to writing and even produced a history which is a work of real value and deserves to be read. He did this on the order of my mother, the Empress Eirene, and in it gave an account of my father's exploits before he seized the reins of power. He describes in detail the Bryennios episode, telling the story of his own father's sufferings and at the same time writing of the noble deeds of his father-in-law. As a relative of the one by marriage and of the other by blood, he certainly did not lie about these two men. I too have mentioned these matters in the early books of this history.

So, the Scythians saw George Euphorbenos coming down the Ister against them, accompanied by a strong naval and military force. This river flows from high ground in the west and after a series of cataracts issues through five mouths into the Black Sea; it is long and wide, traversing vast plains, and it is navigable, so that even the biggest ships, loaded with heavy cargoes, can sail on it. It has not one name, but two: the upper reaches to the source are called Danube; the part near the mouth and the lower reaches have the name Ister. The Scythians saw George Euphorbenos making his way up the river; they also learnt that the emperor was on the march by land with a very large army. As they realized that to fight both was impossible, they looked for a way of escape – the danger was acute. Ambassadors were therefore sent, 150 Scythians who were to ask for peace terms, but at the same time to convey threats in their representations; they might even make occasional promises to aid the emperor, whenever he so wished, with 30,000 horsemen – provided that he agreed to their demands.

The emperor saw through the Scythian fraud: their embassy was an attempt to evade the imminent peril, and, if they were granted a general amnesty, it would be a signal for the underlying spark of evil to be kindled into a mighty conflagration. He refused to hear the envoys. While these exchanges were taking place, a man called Nicholas, a *hypogrammateus*, approached the emperor and gently whispered in his ear, 'Just about this time, Sir, you can expect an eclipse of the sun.'[3] The emperor was completely sceptical about it, but the man swore that he was not lying. With his usual quick apprehension, the emperor turned to the Scythians. 'The decision,' he said, 'I leave to God. If some sign should clearly be given in the sky within a few hours, then you will know for sure that I have good reason to reject your embassy as suspect, because your leaders are not really negotiating for peace; if there is no sign, then I shall be proved wrong in my suspicions.' Before two hours had gone by there was a solar eclipse; the whole disc of the sun was blotted out as the moon passed before it.

At this the Scythians were amazed. As for the emperor, he handed them over to Leo Nikerites with instructions to escort them under strong guard as far as the Queen of Cities. This Nikerites, a eunuch, had spent his life among soldiers from his earliest years and was a man who was widely respected. He set off for Constantinople with due caution. But the barbarians, who were determined to recover their own freedom, murdered their negligent guards at night when they arrived at Little Nicaea and made their way back to those who had sent them. Nikerites and three companions barely escaped with their lives and rejoined the emperor at Goloe.

3. The news alarmed the emperor. He was afraid that the

Scythian ambassadors would stir up their whole army against him and launch an attack. Unlike Atreus' son Agamemnon he needed no dream to urge him to battle[4] – he was longing for a fight. He crossed the Sidera with his troops and set up camp near the Bitzina, a river which flows down from the neighbouring mountains. Many Romans who left the encampment there in search of food went too far and were massacred; many others were captured. The emperor left hurriedly for Pliskoba about first light and from there climbed a ridge called Symeon's, which the local people call the Assembly of the Scythians. Those who went far from the camp for supplies suffered the same fate as their comrades.

On the next day he came to a river that flows close by Dristra and there, at a distance of about twenty-four stades, put down his baggage and pitched camp. Suddenly the Scythians made an attack from the rear on the emperor's tent; several lightly-armed soldiers were killed, and some of the Manichaeans, who fought with exceptional fury, were taken captive. There was much confusion and uproar among the soldiers because of this, and the imperial tent actually collapsed when the horses galloped about in panic – a sure sign of ill omen to those not well disposed to the emperor. However, the emperor drove off the barbarians far from the tent, with a group of men, and then, to quell the tumult, mounted his horse, restored order and marched out with his forces in disciplined ranks to Dristra, which he intended to besiege with siege-engines. (Dristra is the best-known of the towns situated by the Ister.) The work was indeed begun. The town was invested on all sides and a breach was made at one point, and the emperor gained access there with the whole of his army.

However, the two citadels of Dristra still remained in the hands of kinsmen of Tatou, who himself had set off by then to win over the Cumans and hoped to bring them back with him to help the Scythians. At his departure, when he took leave of his comrades, he told them: 'I know well that the emperor will besiege this town. When you see him marching on to the plain, make sure you seize the ridge that dominates it before he can do so. It's the finest position of all. Make your camp there. In that way he will not have a free hand in besieging the garrison; he'll be forced to look out for his rear, watching for trouble from you. Meanwhile do not stop incessant attacks, all day and all night, sending warriors against him.' The emperor had to yield to necessity. The investment of the citadels was abandoned and after withdrawing back through the fortifications, he set up camp not far from the Ister by a mountain stream. There he took counsel as to whether he should attack the Scythians.

Palaiologos and Gregory Maurokatakalon were for deferring a war with the Patzinaks; they advised a military occupation of the great town of Peristhlaba.[5] 'If the Scythians see us marching fully armed as we are and in good order,' they said, 'they will certainly not dare to attack us. And if their cavalry were to risk an engagement without chariots, you can be sure that they will be defeated, and we shall take permanent possession of Great Peristhlaba. It will be an impregnable stronghold.' This town is a famous place, lying near the Ister. Originally it did not have this barbaric name, but rather had a Greek name 'Great City', which indeed it was. But after Mokros, the king of the Bulgars, and his descendant Samuel, the last of the Bulgar dynasty as Zedekiah was the last of his dynasty among the Jews – invaded the west, the name was changed. It became a compound of the Greek word for 'great' and a word from the language of the Slavs; the addition made it 'Great Peristhlaba' and everybody thereabouts calls it by that name.

Mavrokatakalon's supporters continued: 'If we use this place as a secure base of operations, we shall inflict continual losses on them with daily guerrilla warfare. They will never be allowed to leave their own camp to get provisions or collect supplies.' The discussion was still going on when Diogenes' sons, Nikephoros and Leo, dismounted from their chargers, took away their bridles, gave them a slap and drove them off to graze in the millet. They were young men and for that reason had no experience of the misery of war. 'Have no fear, Sir,' they said, 'we'll draw our swords and cut them to pieces.'

The emperor himself loved to take risks and was naturally inclined to provoke battle; he completely ignored the arguments for restraint, entrusted the imperial tent and all the baggage to

George Koutzomites and sent him off to Betrinos. Having done this he gave orders that no lamp, no fire whatsoever was to be lit in camp that night; the army was to have the horses ready and stay awake until sunrise. About first light he left the camp, divided his forces and drew up his ranks for battle. After that he reviewed them quickly. He stationed himself at the centre of the line with a group of those to whom he was related by blood or marriage, including his brother Adrian, at that time in command of the Latins, as well as other brave warriors. The left wing was directed by the *kaisar*, Nikephoros Melissenos, who had married a sister of the emperor. On the right the leaders were Kastamonites and Tatikios, but the allies were commanded by Ouzas and Karatzas, the Sarmatians. Six men were picked out by the emperor to act as a personal body-guard; they were told to watch him and pay attention to no-body else at all. The men chosen were Romanos Diogenes' two sons; Nicholas Maurokatakalon, who had long and varied experience in war; Ioannikios; Nampites, the commander of the Varangians; and a certain Goules, who was a retainer of the family.

The Scythians also prepared for the battle. War is in their blood – they know how to arrange a phalanx. So, after placing ambushes, binding together their ranks in close formation, making a sort of rampart from their covered wagons, they advanced en masse against the emperor and began skirmishing from a distance. The emperor drew up his forces into squadrons and gave clear orders that no soldier was to advance in front of the line, which must remain unbroken, until the Romans were near the Scythians; then, when they saw the distance between the two charging lines was no more than enough to rein in a horse, they were to close with the enemy.

The emperor's preparations were actually still going on when the enemy appeared in the distance with their covered wagons, their wives and their children. Battle was joined and from early morning till late in the evening the casualties on both sides were extremely heavy. Leo, Diogenes' son, charged furiously against the enemy and being swept on further than he should have been in the direction of the wagons was mortally wounded. Adrian, the emperor's brother and at that time commanding the Latins, seeing that it was impossible to stem the Scythian onslaught, rode at full gallop and forced his way right up to the wagons. After a gallant struggle he returned with only seven survivors; all the others had either been slain or were captured. The battle was still evenly balanced, with both armies fighting bravely, when some Scythian officers appeared in the distance with 36,000 men.[6] At last the Romans gave ground; further resistance in the face of so many was out of the question.

The emperor, however, still stood with sword in hand ahead of his own front line. In the other hand he grasped like a standard the *Omophoron* of the Mother of the Word.[7] He had been left behind with twenty horsemen, all brave men. They were Nikephoros, the other son of Diogenes, the *Protostrator* Michael Doukas, brother of the empress, and some family servants. Three Scythian foot soldiers leapt upon them. Two seized his horse's bit, one on either side; the third grabbed him by the right leg. Alexios immediately cut off the hand of one and raising his sword and roaring loudly put him to flight. The man who was clinging to his leg he struck on the helmet. He only struck him rather lightly, however, rather than with full force since he feared one of two things would happen if he hit him too hard: either he might strike his own foot, or he might hit his horse – with the result that he would then be captured by the enemy. He delivered a second blow, but this time took careful aim. In all his deeds and words and movements Alexios let reason be his guide; he was never carried away by anger or swept off his feet by passion. At the first blow the Scythian's helmet had been thrust backwards and he now struck at the man's bare head. In a second he was lying on the ground without having had a chance to utter a cry.

At this point the *protostrator*, who had seen the disorderly flight of the Romans (the lines were by now completely broken up and the rout was uncontrollable), addressed the emperor. 'Why, Sir,' he said, 'are you trying to hold out here any longer? Why lose your life, without a thought for your own safety?' The emperor replied that it was better to die fighting bravely than win safety by doing something unworthy. But the *proto-*

strator persisted, 'If you were just an ordinary soldier, those would be fine words; but when your death involves danger for everybody else, why not choose the better course? If you are saved, you will make war again, and win.' The emperor saw the danger that now threatened him; the Scythians were boldly attacking and all hope of saving the day had gone. 'This is the moment,' he said, 'when with God's help we must look to our own safety. But we must not go by the same way as the rest; the enemy might meet us on their return from the pursuit.' Then, waving his hand toward the Scythians standing at the end of their line, 'We must ride hell for leather at them. With God's aid we'll get round behind and go by another route.' So, after encouraging the others, he led the way himself, charging at the enemy like a flash of lightning. He struck at the first man to meet him. The fellow was unhorsed and fell instantly to the ground. In this way they cut through the Scythian line and reached a place in their rear.

So much for the emperor. The *protostrator* had the ill luck to fall when his horse slipped, but one of his servants at once gave him his own mount. He rejoined the emperor and from that point, did not leave his side by more than a foot – so great was his affection for his brother-in-law. In the great confusion, with some fleeing and others chasing, other Scythians again caught up with the emperor, who quickly wheeled round and hit the pursuer who was closest to him. Nor was he the only one to be killed by the emperor; according to the evidence of eyewitnesses, others met the same fate. One Scythian came up on Nikephoros Diogenes from behind and was about to strike, when the emperor saw him and shouted to Diogenes, 'Look out! Behind you, Nikephoros!' Turning swiftly Nikephoros hit hard at the man's face. In later years we have heard Alexios tell that story; never, he said, had he seen such agility and speed of hand. 'If I had not been holding the standard that day,' he went on, 'I would have killed more Scythians than I have hairs on my head' – and he was not bragging.[8] Was there ever a man who took modesty to such degrees? However, when the conversation and the subject of discussion compelled it, he would sometimes tell of his adventures to us, his relatives, in our own circle, especially if we put much pressure on him to do so. But nobody ever heard the emperor say anything boastful in public.

A strong wind was blowing and with the Patzinaks charging against him, he no longer had the strength to hold the standard firmly. One of the Scythians grasped a long spear in both hands and struck him on the buttock. The blow did not break the skin in any way, but caused excruciating pain which persisted for many years afterwards. In his agony he had to hide the standard in a bush of germanders, where it could no longer be seen by anyone. During the night he arrived safely in Goloe and the next day went on to Berroe[9] where he stopped because he wanted to ransom the prisoners.

4. On the same day that the Romans were defeated and put to flight, Palaiologos was thrown from his horse which he then lost. It was a precarious situation for him; he realized the danger and looked everywhere around him in case he might catch sight of his mount. Then he saw the Bishop of Chalcedon, Leo, whom we have mentioned before. He was dressed in his priestly robes and was offering him his own horse. On that Palaiologos[10] made his escape. He never set eyes on the reverend bishop again. Leo was a man who spoke his mind, in very truth a leader of the Church, but he was a rather simple-minded man and his enthusiasm was occasionally based on insufficient knowledge; he had not even a profound grasp of the sacred canons. It was for that reason that the disgrace I mentioned before came upon him and he was dethroned. Palaiologos always regarded him with affection and continued to honour him greatly for his outstanding virtue. Whether it was because of his passionate belief in this man that Palaiologos was favoured with a divine visitation, or whether the apparition was in some other way concerned with this archbishop and due to the mysterious working of Providence, I cannot say.

Anyway Palaiologos arrived at a marshy area covered with trees, still pursued by the Patzinaks. There he found 150 soldiers, surrounded by Scythians and in a desperate position. Seeing that they were not strong enough to resist such a multitude, they depended on him for advice. In the past they had recognized his fortitude and the dauntless spirit of the man. He

advised them to attack, utterly regardless of their own personal
safety – no doubt by that they would ensure it. 'But,' he added,
'we must confirm this plan by oaths: no one must shirk the
attack against the enemy. We are now all of one mind, we must
look upon the safety or danger of all as the concern of each one
of us.' He himself charged on horseback furiously and struck
the first man to stand in his path; stunned by the blow he
fell at once to the ground. But Palaiologos' companions rode
half-heartedly with the result that some were killed, and the
remainder returned to the dense undergrowth, as if it were a
hole in the ground, and saved themselves by hiding there.

While Palaiologos, again chased by Patzinaks, was riding to
a hilltop, his horse was wounded and fell, but he escaped to the
nearby mountain. For eleven days he wandered seeking a way
to safety – no easy task – but finally met a soldier's widow and
found lodging with her for some time. Her sons, who had
themselves escaped danger, showed him the path to freedom.

Such were the adventures of Palaiologos. Meanwhile the
Scythian leaders planned to kill their prisoners, but the majority
of the ordinary warriors opposed the idea altogether: they
wanted to sell them for ransom, and this scheme was approved.
The emperor was notified through letters from Melissenos, who
although he was a prisoner himself did much to provoke the
Scythians to take this decision. The emperor, who was still in
Berroia, sent for a large sum of money from the Queen of Cities
and bought back the men.[11]

5. At this moment Tatou reached the Ister with the Cumans[12]
he had won over. When they saw the enormous booty and the
multitude of prisoners, they told the Scythian chieftains, 'We
have left our homes. We have come a great distance to help
you, with the purpose of sharing your danger and your victory.
Now that we have contributed all that we could, it is not right
to send us away empty-handed. It was not from choice that we
arrived too late for the war, nor are we to be blamed for
that: it was the emperor's fault – he took the offensive. Either
therefore divide up all the booty in equal shares with us, or
instead of allies you will find us as deadly enemies.' The
Scythians refused and, as the Cumans thought that unbearable,

a fearful battle took place, in which the Scythians suffered complete disaster and barely saved themselves by fleeing to Ozolimne.

The lake now called by us Ozolimne is in diameter and circumference very big, in surface area not inferior to any other lake described by geographers. It lies beyond the 'Hundred Hills' and into it flow very great and noble rivers; many ships and large transport vessels sail on its waters, from which one can deduce how deep the lake is. It has been called Ozolimne, not because it emits an evil or unpleasant odour, but because an army of Huns once visited the lake (those who used to be called Huns are now commonly known as Ouzes) and camped by its banks. The name Ouzolimne was given to it, with the addition of the vowel 'u'. No congregation of Huns in that area has ever been mentioned by the ancient historians, but in the reign of the Emperor Alexios there was a general migration there from all directions – hence the name.

However, let us leave the question of the lake with some such explanation. I am the first to write about it in this book, and I did so in order to demonstrate how places acquired many names because of the frequent and widespread expeditions of the emperor. Some were named after him, some after the enemies who assembled to fight him. I understand that some such thing happened in the time of Alexander, the Macedonian king: Alexandria in Egypt and the Indian Alexandria were both named after him. We know too that Lysimakheia got its name from one of his generals, Lysimakhos. I would not wonder, then, if the Emperor Alexios, rivalling him, bestowed new names on places, either from the peoples who united against him, or were summoned by him, or because of his exploits gave his own name to them. So much for this Ozolimne – supplementary details of some historic interest. There they were hemmed in by the Cumans for a long time, not daring to move. When the Cumans' provisions were exhausted, they went home. They intended to return, after making up their deficiencies, to fight the Scythians.

6. In the meantime the emperor was concentrating his forces at Berroe, his headquarters. The prisoners of war and all the rest

of the army were thoroughly equipped. The count of Flanders,[13] who was then on his way back from Jerusalem, met the emperor and gave him the traditional oath of the Latins: he promised that on his arrival in his own country he would send the emperor allies, 500 horsemen. The emperor received him with honour and sent him on his journey satisfied. The emperor then set out and went on to Adrianoupolis with the forces he had reassembled.

The Scythians had crossed the valley between Goloe and Diampolis, and fixed their camp near Markella. They were expected to return, but news of their movements alarmed the emperor. He summoned Synesios, furnished him with a chrysobull for the Scythians and sent him to find them. The instructions were as follows: if the enemy could be persuaded to negotiate and give hostages, Synesios was to prevent their further advance, to make sure that they remained in the area already occupied by them, and provided these terms were acceptable, to give them ample supplies at his expense. The emperor's policy was to make use of the Scythians against the Cumans, if the latter again approached the Ister and tried to seize territory beyond it. On the other hand, if the Scythians proved obdurate, Synesios was to leave them there and return to camp.

The envoy made contact and after the formalities had been concluded, persuaded them to make a truce with the emperor;[14] he stayed with them for some time, treated all of them with courtesy, and avoided every pretext for offence. The Cumans did return, again prepared to fight the Scythians, and when they failed to meet them, learnt that they had gone over the passes and on their arrival at Markella had concluded a treaty with the emperor, they demanded the right to pursue and attack them. Alexios refused, because peace had been made. He sent his reply: 'We do not for the present require your help. Take these gifts and go home.' Their ambassadors were honourably received and before they were dismissed peaceably generous gifts were handed over to them. Emboldened by this the Scythians broke the treaty. With their old savagery they murdered the neighbouring towns and country districts. The truth is, all barbarians are usually fickle and by nature are unable to keep their pledges.

Synesios witnessed their actions and of his own free will came back to inform the emperor of the ingratitude of the Scythians and of their transgression. The news that they had seized Philippopolis was embarrassing: the forces at the emperor's disposal were insufficient to start a general war against such overwhelming numbers. But, being the kind of man who in difficulties finds ways and means, having accustomed himself never to lose heart, however hard the circumstances, he decided to practise the art of destroying the enemy by skirmish and ambushes. He second-guessed which places and towns they were likely to occupy in the morning, and took up position accordingly the evening before; if he discovered that they were going to seize a place in the evening, he got there before them in the morning. Thus by guerrilla tactics and making best use of his forces he made war on them at a distance; they were unable to get possession of the forts. Now it happened that both the emperor and the Scythians reached Kypsella at precisely the same time.

As the expected mercenaries had not arrived yet, the emperor was in a tight spot. He knew that the Scythians could move very fast; he also saw that they were already on their way to Constantinople itself, at great speed; he was, moreover, vastly outnumbered and battle was out of the question. Calculating that the lesser of two evils is the better, he once more sought refuge in peace talks. Envoys were sent to confer and for a second time the barbarians yielded to his wishes.[15] Before the truce was made, however, Neantzes deserted to the Romans.

Meanwhile Migidenos was sent to collect recruits from the neighbouring districts. It was his son who in the war which broke out later charged fiercely against the Patzinaks at ... As he swept past, he was dragged by an iron grapple inside the circle of wagons by a Scythian woman and so made prisoner. His severed head was bought by the emperor at his father's request, but Migidenos, unable to bear his affliction, died after beating his breast for three days and nights with a huge block of stone. The Scythians were not content with peace for long:

like dogs they came back to their own vomit. Setting out from
Kypsella they seized Taurokomos, where they spent the winter
ravaging the nearby villages.

7. At the beginning of spring[16] they went on from there to
Kharioupolis. The emperor was at that time in Boulgarophygon, but he hesitated no longer. A considerable part of the
army was detached, all soldiers called *Arkhontopouloi*, all with
beards barely grown, but irresistible in attack. Alexios ordered
them to attack the Scythians from the rear, since the latter were
standing on their wagons. This company of *Arkhontopouloi*
was first recruited by Alexios. Because of the neglect of preceding emperors the Romans tolerated exemption from military
service, but he regularly enrolled sons of soldiers who had lost
their lives, trained them in arms and war, and gave them this
name, as if they were sons born of leaders. The name would
inspire them to emulate the nobility and valour of their forefathers; they would be mindful of the furious battle-spirit and
when the moment called for daring and strength they would
fight all the more bravely. Such in brief was the company of
Arkhontopouloi, made up to the number of 2,000 men, like
the Sacred Band of the Spartans.[17]

The newly recruited *Arkhontopouloi* went off in full fighting
order, but the enemy were lying in ambush at the foot of a
hill watching their advance and, when they saw them rushing
against the wagons, charged into them with terrific impetus. In
a hand-to-hand struggle about 300 *Arkhontopouloi* fell fighting
valiantly. For a long time the emperor grieved deeply for them,
shedding hot tears and calling upon each one by name as if they
were just missing.

After defeating these opponents the Patzinaks went through
Kharioupolis and then turned off to Apros, ravaging everything on the way. The emperor followed the same system as
before, getting to Apros first – as I have said more than once,
he did not have adequate forces to take on the enemy in open
battle. He knew the Scythians left their camp to forage about
sunrise. So Tatikios, with the bravest of the young soldiers, all
the Latins and the elite of Alexios' own personal bodyguard,
was ordered to keep careful watch on the Scythian movements

just before dawn; when it was reasonable to suppose that the Scythians were well away from camp on their foraging expedition, they were to charge down on them at full gallop. Tatikios carried out his instructions, killed 300 and took numerous prisoners.

What happened next? Later on the elite knights sent by the count of Flanders arrived;[18] there were about 500 of them and they brought a gift for the emperor, 150 outstanding horses. What is more, they sold to him all the other horses not required by themselves for immediate use. They were received with due honour and warmly thanked. As news came from the east that Apelkhasem, the governor of Nicaea, commonly called a satrap by the Persians and emir by the Turks who are now masters of the Persian lands, was preparing an offensive against Nikomedia, the emperor sent them to protect that area.

8. At this moment Tzakhas,[19] being informed of the emperor's manifold difficulties in the west and of his frequent encounters with the Patzinaks, decided that the circumstances were favourable and that he should create a fleet. He met a certain man from Smyrna and entrusted to him the task of constructing pirate ships, since he had considerable experience in this. In addition to the pirate vessels there were forty decked ships and on them crews of efficient sailors. They put to sea and dropped anchor again off Klyzomenai, which was at once captured. From there Tzakhas went on to Phokaia. That was also taken at the first assault. A messenger was then dispatched to Alopos, the curator appointed to govern Mitylene. He was threatened with the most frightful vengeance if he did not immediately abandon Mitylene; Tzakhas added that he wished him well and because of that was forewarning him of the terrible fate which would follow disobedience. Alopos, thoroughly scared by these intimidations, boarded a ship in the night and made for Constantinople. Not a moment was lost by Tzakhas at this news. He landed at once and took the town by storm.

However, Methymna, which is situated on a promontory of the same island, did not come over to Tzakhas and this was made known to the emperor. He at once sent a powerful force by sea and strongly fortified the place. Contrary to expectations Tzakhas ignored Methymna and making straight for Khios took it immediately. At this news the emperor sent a powerful force against him under the command of Niketas Kastamonites. Niketas had enough men and ships to fight the enemy. In the ensuing engagement, however, he was promptly worsted and many of the ships which had put to sea with him were captured by Tzakhas.

When news came of Kastamonites' misfortune, the emperor sent another fleet, this time with Constantine Dalassenos as *doux* of the fleet, a valiant fighter and a relative on his mother's side. As soon as he had landed on the shore of Khios, he invested the fortress with great spirit, hurrying to take the town before Tzakhas arrived from Smyrna. The walls were battered with a host of siege-engines and stone-throwing catapults, and the ramparts between two towers were destroyed, but the Turks inside, knowing what had happened and realizing that further resistance was impossible, began to call upon the Almighty to have pity on them, uttering their prayers in the Roman tongue. The soldiers of Dalassenos and Opos could not be held back in their eagerness to break into the citadel, though their leaders tried to restrain them, fearful no doubt that once inside they might lay hands on all the booty and wealth previously deposited there by Tzakhas. 'You can hear the Turks,' they said, 'clearly acclaiming the emperor already; they have surrendered to us. It is wrong then that you should go in and massacre them without mercy.' Since the whole of that day had pretty much passed and it was almost nightfall, the Turks set about putting up another wall to replace the ruined battlements. On the outside of it they hung mattresses, hides of leather and all the clothing they could gather, so that the force of the bombardment might be deadened, however little.

Tzakhas meanwhile made ready his fleet, enlisted some 8,000 Turks and set them on the road to Khios by land. The fleet followed him, keeping close to the coast. Dalassenos, aware of this, ordered his ship's captains to take on board a large number of soldiers with their leader Opos and to weigh anchor. He wanted to join battle with Tzakhas wherever he might meet him at sea. Tzakhas left the mainland and sailed directly to Khios; when Opos did meet him, about midnight, it was clear that the enemy had adopted a new form of anchorage. (By means of a very long chain Tzakhas had tied together all his ships, so that those who were minded to escape could not do so, nor could the others who wanted to sail out in front break up the line of vessels.) Opos was terrified at the sight. He had not the confidence even to approach them, and making a complete turn sailed back to Khios.

Tzakhas cleverly followed him, rowing without a rest. When they were both nearing Khios, Opos was first to anchor his ships in the harbour (Dalassenos had already occupied it), but Tzakhas sailed past and brought his own ships to land by the wall of the fortress. It was the fourth day of the week. On the Thursday he disembarked all his men, counted them and entered their names on a list. Dalassenos for his part found a small village by the harbour and took up position there. First he destroyed his old entrenchment and dug another, with a wide ditch, at this place. Then he moved his army there. On the following day both forces, in full armour, prepared for action. The Romans stood immobile since Dalassenos had given orders that the battle line must remain intact. Tzakhas, on the other hand, prompted the bulk of his infantry to attack, with a small body of horsemen in support. The Latins, seeing this, charged the Turks with their long lances. It was not at the Kelts, however, that the enemy fired their arrows, but at their horses; some were also wounded by spear-thrusts. Casualties were very heavy and the cavalry were driven back in a crowd inside their own entrenchment; from there they rushed into the ships in headlong panic.

The Romans witnessed the disorderly retreat of the Kelts and in great alarm withdrew slightly to the wall of the fort and paused. Thereupon the barbarians came down to the shore and seized some of the ships. The crews slipped the stern cables, pushed off from land, dropped anchor again and stood off waiting anxiously to see what happened. Dalassenos ordered them to sail along the coast westwards to Bolissos and wait for him there; Bolissos is a small place near the promontory of

Khios. But some Scythians came to Tzakhas and told him beforehand of Dalassenos' plan. Tzakhas immediately sent out fifty scouts, with orders to give him warning instantly when the Roman fleet was ready to sail. After that he sent a message to Dalassenos, perhaps because he wanted to discuss terms of peace; in my opinion he had given up all hope of victory when he saw his brave opponent was prepared to face danger. The latter promised Tzakhas that he would come to the edge of his camp the next day to discuss whatever terms might be agreeable to both.

The barbarian accepted the offer and early in the morning the leaders met. Tzakhas, addressing Dalassenos by name, began the conversation: 'You should know that I am the young man who used to make incursions into Asia. I fought with great spirit, but because of my inexperience I was deceived and captured by the famous Alexander Kabalikas. He offered me as a prisoner of war to the Emperor Nikephoros Botaneiates. I was at once honoured with the title of *protonobellisimos*[20] and after being rewarded with liberal gifts I promised obedience to him. But ever since Alexios Komnenos seized power, everything has gone wrong. That is why I have come in person now to explain the reason for my enmity. Let the emperor know this, and if he wishes to put an end to the hostility which has sprung up, let him restore to me in full the rightful possessions of which I have been deprived. As for you, if you approve of a marriage alliance between our families, let the marriage contract be committed to writing, agreeable to both parties, as is the custom of the Romans and of us barbarians. After that, when all the terms I have mentioned have been fulfilled, I will hand over to the emperor, through you, all the islands invaded by me and taken from the Roman Empire; moreover, when I have observed all the conditions of my treaty with him, I will return to my own country.'

Dalassenos thought this proposal specious, knowing the treacherous nature of the Turks, and so he deferred for the time being the ratification of his demands. Nevertheless, he laid bare his suspicions: 'You,' he said, 'will neither restore the islands to me, as you are promising; nor can I, without the emperor's consideration, decide the terms which you ask for from him and from me. But when John, the *megas doux* and the emperor's brother-in-law, arrives shortly[21] with all the fleet, bringing with him massive forces by land and by sea, let him hear your proposition. Under those circumstances you can be sure that a treaty will be successfully concluded with the emperor – provided that John acts as arbitrator to bring about the peace.'

This John had been sent by the emperor to Epidamnos with a considerable army, for two purposes: to concern himself diligently with the protection of Dyrrakhion, and to make war on the Dalmatians. A certain man called Bodin, a combative and thoroughly unprincipled rascal, had refused to stay inside his own borders and made daily attacks on the towns nearest to Dalmatia. These he annexed. For eleven years John Doukas had remained in Dyrrakhion. He recovered many of the defended places under the control of Bolkan, and many Dalmatian prisoners were sent to the emperor. In the end he clashed with Bodin in a fierce battle and took him too. Thus the emperor had good reason to recognize the warlike qualities of this John Doukas; he knew his skill as a strategist, he knew also that John would under no circumstances disregard his instructions. Since he needed such a man to deal with Tzakhas, he recalled him from Dyrrakhion and sent him as *megas doux* of the fleet with strong land and naval forces to make war on him. How many battles he fought with Tzakhas and to what dangers he exposed himself before emerging undisputed victor will be explained in the subsequent pages of this history.

While Dalassenos waited for his arrival, he made it clear in his conversations with Tzakhas that the whole business was to be referred to Doukas. Tzakhas gave the impression that he was quoting Homer's line, 'Night is already upon us: it is good to heed the night.'[22] He promised that when day broke he would furnish much of the provisions. However, it was all a lie and deceit. In fact, Dalassenos was not far from the mark in his judgement, for in the grey of the dawn Tzakhas went secretly down to the shore of Khios and as the wind was favourable, set sail for Smyrna, to collect greater forces and return to the island. His opponent, though, was no less crafty: he embarked with his men on the available ships and made for Bolissos; he acquired a fleet, made ready other siege-engines, and after giving his soldiers a rest and recruiting more of them, he went back to his original starting point. There followed a bitter clash with the Turks, in which the ramparts were destroyed and the town fell into Dalassenos' hands. Tzakhas was still in Smyrna. Afterwards, when the sea was calm, Dalassenos sailed on a straight course to Mitylene with his whole fleet.

9. Such was the action taken by the emperor against Tzakhas. Next he discovered that the Scythians were again on their way to Rousion and had pitched camp at Polyboton. Without hesitation he left Constantinople and arrived at Rousion, accompanied by the renegade Neantzes, who was devising a terrible and deep-laid plot against him, and also by Kantzes and Katranes, experienced soldiers who had a great affection for the emperor. At a distance a fairly large detachment of Scythians was sighted and the emperor prepared to do battle. In the fighting many Romans fell, some were taken prisoner and later put to death by their captors, but several got as far as Rousion.

However, that was merely a skirmish with Scythian foragers. The arrival of the so-called Maniakatoi Latins put new heart into the emperor and he decided to fight a pitched battle on the next day. As the space between the two armies happened to be rather small, he dared not allow the trumpet to sound the alert, for he wanted to take the enemy by surprise. The man in charge of the imperial falcons, one Constantine, was summoned and told to obtain a drum in the evening; all night long he was to walk round the camp beating this drum, warning all to be ready because at sunrise the emperor planned to do battle with the Scythians and there would be no trumpet call. The enemy, coming from Polyboton, had already reached a place called Hades and made camp there. On the Roman side preparations went on from the evening. When the sun rose, the emperor arranged his army in companies and ranks for the battle.

The struggle had not yet begun with both armies still forming up, when Neantzes climbed a hill in the vicinity in order, as he said, to spy out the Scythian lines and bring back information to the emperor. In fact his intention was quite different. He advised the enemy, speaking in his native language, to set their wagons in rows and not to be afraid of Alexios: he had been defeated before and was beaten and ready to run now, he said, with too few soldiers and not enough allies. Having delivered this message he returned to our lines. But a half-caste who knew the Scythian language had understood Neantzes' conversation with them and reported the whole matter to the emperor. Neantzes heard of this and demanded proof. The half-caste unashamedly came forward and proceeded to give proof in public. All at once Neantzes drew his sword and cut off the man's head, in the presence of the emperor and with ranks of soldiers on either side of him.

In my view, Neantzes brought suspicion on himself by killing the informer – even though he had been wanting to achieve the opposite. Otherwise why did he not wait for the proof? His desire to quash in advance the evidence of his own treachery, it seems to me, caused him to do something even more perilous and daring, a deed worthy of a barbarian, but as foolhardy as it was suspicious. Nevertheless the emperor did not immediately take action against Neantzes, nor punish him according to his deserts, but for the moment he controlled his rising indignation and anger; he did not want to frighten away his prey too soon and upset the soldiers, but his anger at Neantzes, though concealed, was reserved for the future – from former actions of the man, and for other reasons, he had foreseen his treachery and insubordination. The war stood in the balance and on account of that he checked his consuming rage temporarily, not knowing what to do with him for the time being.

For all that Neantzes soon afterwards approached him, dismounted from his horse and asked the emperor for another; without hesitation Alexios gave him one, a fine beast, with the imperial saddle. Neantzes mounted it, waited until the two lines were already marching towards one another across the battlefield and then made a pretence of charging. With spear point reversed he went over to his fellow-countrymen and gave them much information about the imperial army.

They made use of his advice, and in a tough battle against the emperor routed his forces. Seeing the lines broken and all the soldiers fleeing, Alexios was extremely concerned, since he was not willing to take any foolish risks. Therefore, he turned his horse's head and rode off to the river which flows near Rousion. There he drew rein and with some chosen soldiers drove off his pursuers as best he could. Charging on horseback he actually killed many of them, but also suffered injury himself. When from another direction George Pyrros fled to the river, the emperor rebuked him and called him back. Later, when he saw how reckless the enemy were and how hour by hour their numbers grew as others came to their aid, he left this same George on the spot with the remainder of his troops, telling him to resist with discretion until he himself returned. Then, quickly turning his horse's bridle, he crossed the river and entered Rousion. All fugitive soldiers found there, the whole native population capable of bearing arms and even the peasants with their own wagons were ordered to leave the town at once and take up position on the riverbank. This was done quicker than it can be explained. The emperor drew them up in a line and then recrossed the river, hurrying back to George even though he was troubled by a quartan fever, so bad that his teeth chattered from the shivering cold.

By now the whole Scythian army had concentrated, but when they saw a double line and the emperor exerting himself in this way, they halted, not daring to risk a clash with him. They knew that he was prepared to face dangers and that both in victory and in defeat he remained true to himself; his attack would be overwhelming. The emperor was restrained to a certain extent by his shivering, but was above all impeded by the fact that not all the fugitives had rejoined him yet. He too stayed where he was, but rode slowly up and down the ranks and displayed his own confidence before the enemy. Thus it came about that both armies held their positions until evening. When night was actually falling, each side withdrew to its own camp without fighting, afraid to engage in a battle which seemed too hazardous. Little by little the men who had scattered in all directions after the first battle came back to Rousion;

the majority of them had taken no part at all in the fighting. Monastras, Ouzas and Synesios, men dear to Ares and fine warriors, went through Apros at this time, and they also arrived at Rousion without striking a blow against the enemy.

10. The emperor was afflicted by fever, as I have mentioned, and in order to get relief was forced to take to his bed for a while. Nevertheless, ill though he was, he never ceased making plans for the next day. Tatranes approached him with an idea. (This man was a Scythian who had deserted to the emperor on many occasions and later gone back to his home; each time he was pardoned and because of the emperor's extraordinary forbearance Tatranes conceived a great affection for him. Tatranes in fact was for the rest of his life wholly devoted, body and soul, to Alexios.) 'I expect, Sir,' he said, 'that the Scythians will surround us tomorrow and having done that they will challenge us to battle. If that is so, we must be outside the walls by sunrise with the battle line ready before they come.' The emperor commended him, adopted his plan and agreed to put it into operation at dawn. Tatranes then went off to the Scythian commanders and spoke to them: 'Don't be elated,' he said, 'by the previous disasters suffered by the emperor and when you see how outnumbered we are, don't go into battle full of confidence. His power is invincible; even now he awaits the arrival of a strong mercenary force. If you won't make peace with him, birds of prey will feast on your corpses.'

So much for Tatranes. Meanwhile the emperor considered the possibility of seizing their horses, which were grazing on the plain (and which were very numerous), for the Scythians were raiding our territory every single day and night. He sent for Ouzas and Monastras. They were to take picked horsemen, he said, and make their way to the rear of the enemy; about first light they must be on the plain and capture all the horses and other animals, together with their herdsmen. 'Don't be afraid,' he added, 'we shall be attacking from the front. You will easily carry out this order.' Nor was he wrong – the plan was immediately successful.

He had no sleep that night as he awaited the Scythian onslaught; there was not even any dozing. Throughout the

hours of darkness he was summoning his soldiers, especially the
expert archers. He talked much with them about the Scythians,
stirring them for battle. He gave them useful advice for the
struggle expected to take place the next day – how to bend their
bows and fire their arrows, when to rein in a horse, when to
relax the bridle, and when to dismount, if indeed they had to.
This went on during the night, but he did have a brief nap
before; as day was now breaking, the elite of the Scythian army
crossed the river en masse, apparently provoking the Romans
to battle. The emperor's prediction was already proving correct.
(He had indeed great prescience of the future, acquired from
long experience of continual warfare.) At once, he mounted his
horse, ordered the trumpeter to sound the alert and drew up
his ranks, with himself in front. Seeing that the Scythians were
attacking with more boldness than before, he commanded the
archers to dismount without delay and advance on foot, pour-
ing volleys of arrows into the Scythians all the time. The rest of
the line followed behind, with the emperor in person commanding the centre of the line. The archers therefore bravely pressed
on against the Scythians.

The battle was sternly contested, but the enemy, partly because of the continuous showers of arrows, partly because they
saw the unbroken line of the Romans and the emperor himself
engaging in fierce conflict, turned back in flight, panic-stricken
and hurrying to cross the river behind them to find refuge in
their covered wagons. The Roman line pursued at full gallop,
some piercing the enemies' backs with spears, others shooting
at them with arrows. Many perished before they ever reached
the bank of the river; many others fled in haste, but fell into
the whirling streams and were swept away by the water and
drowned. On that day the emperor's retinue surpassed all others
in valour; they were tireless, all of them. As for the emperor,
he was clearly the bravest of all. He returned to his own camp,
the undisputed victor on that battlefield.

11. For three days he had a rest in that area, then left for
Tzouroulos. Thinking it was essential not to move from there
quickly, he had a trench dug towards the east side of the village
big enough for the forces he had with him, and placed the

imperial tent and all the baggage within it. The Scythians also advanced on Tzouroulos, but when they heard that he had anticipated them, they crossed the river flowing through the plain not far from the village (the natives call the place Xero-gypsos) and pitched camp between the river and Tzouroulos. The Scythians surrounded the camp, so that the emperor was cut off and effectively under siege. When night came, 'the others, both gods and warriors with horsehair crests, slept', to quote Homer's muse, but 'sweet sleep did not embrace'[23] the Emperor Alexios. He lay awake, turning over in his mind schemes by which he might outwit and overcome the boldness of the barbarians.

He noticed that this village Tzouroulos had been built on a steep hill and the entire barbarian force was camped down below on the plain. It was impossible for him to fight with any confidence in close combat, for he was greatly outnumbered, but he conceived a most ingenious plan. He requisitioned the wagons of the inhabitants, removed their wheels and axles, and had them carried up to the ramparts. They were then suspended by ropes, just as they were, on the outside of the wall in a row from the battlements; the ropes were made fast to the parapets. No time was wasted in putting the plan into action: in one hour the wheels, with the axles, hung round the wall like a series of circles, touching each other and still attached to the axles.

The emperor rose early next morning, armed himself and his men, led them away from the wall and set them directly in front of the Scythians. It happened that our men took up position on the side where the wheels had been suspended; just opposite them were the enemy in one line. At this point the emperor, standing in the centre, warned his men: when the trumpet sounded the attack, they were to dismount and advance slowly on foot towards the enemy, shooting at them with their bows again and again, skirmishing at a distance and provoking the Scythians to attack. When they saw them moving forward and shouting at their horses to charge, then the Romans were to turn away in disorder, splitting into two groups, right and left, and giving ground to the Scythians until they came up close to the wall. Orders had been given to men standing on the walls that when this happened – that is, when they saw the ranks moving apart – they were to cut the ropes with their swords and let wheels and axles crash headlong down.

This was done, just as the emperor ordered. The Scythian horsemen bursting out in a mass descended on our lines with barbaric yells. The Romans were advancing on foot and slowly, all together, with only the emperor on horseback. Little by little, following the emperor's plan, they slowly changed knee for knee,[24] and like men on a retreat became separated from each other, to the enemies' surprise, as if opening up a wide door for them to enter. When the Scythians were in fact inside this gap, with our lines on either side, the wheels crashed down with a loud whirring noise, all of them rebounding more than a cubit from the rampart as the curving wheels were thrust away like bullets from a sling, and down they rolled into the midst of the barbarian horsemen as they gathered additional impetus. The normal weight of the wheels, falling in this mass descent, acquired tremendous momentum from the downward incline of the ground. They toppled down on the barbarians with great violence, crushing them in all directions and cutting off their horses' legs like mowers in a harvest field; with fore- or hindlegs severed, depending if they were struck from the front or from the rear, the horses sank down and threw their riders forward or backward. The horsemen fell in great numbers, one after another, and our infantry fell on them from both flanks. The Scythians were threatened on all sides by the terrors of battle. Some were massacred by flying arrows, others were wounded by our lances, but of the remainder most were hurtled in a crowd by the violent downrush of the wheels to the river and there drowned.

On the next day, seeing the survivors preparing to renew the conflict, the emperor mobilized all his army – he knew they were confident now. He himself donned armour and after arranging the line went down to the plain. Then he turned his forces to face the enemy and waited, ready to join battle as best he could. He was at the centre of the line. It was a bitter contest, but the Romans won the day against expectations and pursued the Scythians madly. When he realized the chase had gone far enough, the emperor was concerned that some enemy, lying in ambush, might suddenly fall upon them and turn the Scythian rout into a victory for them; with the reinforcement of the fugitives they might bring the Roman army into great peril. So he kept riding to his men, urging them to rein in their horses and let them draw breath.

At any rate, that is how the two forces parted that day, one in flight, the other returning to camp rejoicing in a notable triumph. After their crushing defeat the enemy pitched tents between Boulgarophygon and Little Nicaea. Winter had now started and the emperor decided that he must return to Constantinople; both he and most of his army were in need of rest after their many struggles. Having divided his forces in two, therefore, he picked out the most courageous fighters to watch the enemy. They were under the command of Ioannikios and Nicholas Maurokatakalon, who have been mentioned in this history many times already. These last two were instructed to bring into each town enough soldiers to protect the place and to round up infantry from the whole district, with wagons and their ox teams. He intended to carry on the war with more vigour at the approach of spring. He was already planning and making preparations essential for the victory. When all these arrangements were complete, he returned to Byzantion.[25]

BOOK VIII

1. The emperor learnt that the Scythian leaders had sent a contingent against Khoirovakhoi and that their arrival was imminent. Always prepared even when faced with the unexpected, and without having had even a week's peace at the palace, with no chance to bathe or shake off the dust of battle, the emperor assembled the garrison troops with characteristic speed and all the new recruits, about 500 in number, and spent the whole night attending to their equipment. About first light on the next morning he left the city. At the same time he informed his kinsmen by blood or marriage and all the nobles enrolled in the army that he was going out to do battle with the Scythians. The following instructions were issued to them (it was then the Friday of Carnival week[1]): 'I have been informed that the Scythians are moving swiftly on Khoirovakhoi. I am leaving now, but you will join us in Cheese week. I am allowing you a short rest, so as not to seem harsh and unreasonable, during the period between the Friday of Carnival week and the start of the week of Cheese week.'

He then rode straight for Khoirovakhoi, entered the gates of the town and locked them; he himself kept the keys. On the battlements he stationed all the servants loyal to himself and told them not to relax, but to stay vigilant and patrol the walls; nobody must be allowed to climb up there, or lean over and talk with the Scythians.

At daybreak the enemy arrived, as expected, and took up position on a high place near to the wall. About 6,000 of them then separated from the rest and dispersed to look for plunder, getting as far as Dekatos, which is about ten stades from

Constantinople – hence, I suppose, its name.[2] The remainder of the Scythians stayed in the district of Khoirovakhoi. The emperor climbed to the parapet to examine the plains and hills in case another force was on its way to reinforce them; maybe the Scythians had laid ambushes to trap any potential attacker. There was no evidence of any such thing, but about the second hour of the day he noticed that they were in no state for battle; they were in fact getting ready for a meal and a rest. Because of their great numbers he knew that a fight at close quarters was out of the question, but the thought that they might ravage the countryside and approach the walls of the capital itself horrified him – especially as he had set out in person to scare them away.

At once therefore he called together his soldiers to address them, seeking to test their confidence, and said: 'We must not be overawed by Scythian numbers, but put our trust in God and fight them. If we are all of one mind, I am absolutely confident of victory.' When they rejected the idea out of hand and refused to listen, he struck greater fear into them; trying to rouse them to face facts, he went on: 'If those who went off to plunder come back again and unite with the Scythians here, the danger is obvious: either the camp will be captured and we shall be massacred, or they will treat us as of no consequence, march to the walls of the capital and prevent us from entering by setting up camp by the city's gates. We have to deal with the danger confronting us rather than die like cowards. For my part I am going out now. I shall ride on ahead and burst into the enemy's midst. All you who are willing can follow me; those who either cannot or do not want to, must not move outside the gates.'

With that, he rode out through the gate opposite the lake, in full armour. He moved fast along the walls, then making a slight detour, climbed the hill from the far side, for he was certain that his army would not fight the enemy in close combat. At the head of his men he seized his spear and threw himself into the centre of the Scythians, striking the first man who opposed him. The others were no less eager to fight, killing many and capturing others besides. Then, resourceful as ever, the emperor clothed his soldiers in the Scythian uniforms and told them to ride the Scythian horses, handing to some of the more reliable men Roman standards and the severed heads of Scythian victims, with instructions to take them back to the fort and await him there. Having taken these precautions, he went down with the Scythian standards and his men dressed as Scythians to the river which flows near Khoirovakhoi. He thought the enemy would cross at this point on their return from plundering. The Scythians saw them standing there and believing that they were fellow-countrymen ran towards them without reconnoitring first. Some were massacred, others were captured.

2. When evening fell (it was the Saturday), the emperor returned with his prisoners. The next day he rested, but at sunrise on the Monday he left the fort. The army was divided: in front were the men holding the Scythian standards, in the rear the captives, each guarded by natives of the country; others held aloft the severed heads on spears. Such was the order of march. Behind these again, at a moderate distance, came the emperor himself with his men and the usual Roman standards.

Early in the morning of the Sunday of Carnival week,[3] Palaiologos, eager for military fame, left Byzantion at the head of other troops. Knowing the unpredictable nature of the Scythians, he marched with circumspection: a few of his retinue were detached with orders to go on ahead and reconnoitre the plains and woods and roads of the district; if any Scythians appeared, they were to turn round quickly and report to him. The march was proceeding in this formation when they saw men clothed in Scythian uniforms and carrying Scythian standards, at what is known as the plain of Dimylia; so, turning back, they reported that the Scythians were already on the way. At once Palaiologos took up arms. Close on their heels came another messenger who insisted that behind the men who purported to be Scythians, appeared to be Roman standards and soldiers following them at a fair distance.

The messengers were of course partly right and partly wrong, for the army at the rear was truly Roman, in appearance and in fact, was led by the emperor himself; but the vanguard, dressed like Scythians, was also indeed wholly Roman, since according to the emperor's instructions they were wearing the same garb as they had when the real Scythians were deceived, just as was explained previously. On this occasion the use of Scythian uniforms tricked and deceived our own folk. Alexios did it so that the first men to meet our troops might be filled with dread, thinking they were Scythians – a joke black with humour because before they became really scared, they were reassured at the sight of the emperor following on at the rear. Such was the way that the emperor used to catch out those he met.

The rest were upset by what they saw, but Palaiologos, who had far more experience than anyone else and knew Alexios' inventive genius, immediately realized that this was one of his stratagems; he recovered his own nerve and told the others to do the same. By now all the crowd of kinsmen and relatives of the emperor had joined them from the rear; they were hurrying, as they imagined, to meet him according to the arrangements made previously – that is, after the week of abstinence from meat in Cheese week. In fact they had not yet left the city when he returned in triumph. Meeting him under these circumstances they could not believe that he had won a victory and returned with the trophies so quickly, until they saw for themselves the Scythian heads impaled on the end of spears and the survivors, not yet beheaded, being led with hands tied behind their backs and in chains, driven and trailing along one after the other.

The rapidity of this campaign caused a sensation. I heard that George Palaiologos (eyewitnesses related this to us) complained angrily and was annoyed with himself for being too late to fight in the war; he would have liked to be with the emperor when he won such glory with this unexpected triumph against the barbarians. He had longed with all his heart to share in such fame. As for the emperor, one might say that on this occasion the verse of Deuteronomy was visibly fulfilled in him: 'How should one chase a thousand, and two put ten thousand to flight?'[4] For in that crisis the Emperor Alexios, by opposing himself to so great a multitude of barbarians, gloriously bore almost the whole brunt of the war, up to the moment of victory itself. In fact, if one considers the soldiers who were with him and reflects on their numbers and quality, and then compares with them the stratagems of the emperor, his versatility, his strength, and his bravery in the face of all the barbarian host and its might, one would conclude that Alexios alone brought about the victory.

3. That at any rate was how God gave the victory – an extraordinary one – to our ruler that day. When the Byzantines witnessed his arrival in the city they rejoiced. Amazed by the speed, the audacity the skilfulness of the enterprise, as well as the suddenness of his triumph, they sang, they danced, they praised God for providing them with such a saviour and bene-factor. Nikephoros Melissenos, though, was hurt by these dem-onstrations and could not bear them – such is human nature. 'This victory was a joy without any benefit,' he said, 'while for the enemy it was a meaningless blow.' In fact, the Scythians, who were countless in number and spread throughout the whole of the western provinces, continued to ravage everything, and nothing whatever of the mishaps that had befallen them checked their brazen audacity. In several parts of the west they seized some small towns, not even sparing the larger places near Constantinople. They got as far as the place known as Deep Torrent, where there is a church built in honour of Theo-dore, the greatest of all martyrs. Many people used to visit this place every day in order to pray to the saint, and when Sunday[5] came round the devout made their way in crowds to the holy shrine; all day and all night they would remain there, either outside the building, or in the vestibule, or in the back of the church. But the unchecked violence of the Scythians had such an overwhelming effect that those who wanted to visit the shrine dared not even open the gates of Byzantion because of these frequent assaults of the Scythians.

Such were the terrible disasters which fell upon the emperor in the west; on the sea, too, there was no respite from trouble, for Tzakhas had acquired a new fleet and was overrunning the whole coastline. The threats coming from all directions caused the emperor deep concern and annoyance. The news came that Tzakhas' fleet, recruited from the maritime districts, was bigger than ever; the rest of the islands previously taken by him had been sacked; worse, he planned to attack the western provinces and had sent envoys to the Scythians advising them to occupy the Kherronesos. He would not let the mercenary force of Turks from the east, who had come to the emperor's aid, keep their treaty with the emperor inviolate, instead promising them fine rewards if they abandoned the emperor and came over[6] to him instead – once he got his nose in the trough, that is.

Things were not going well for Alexios either by sea or on land, and the severe winter did not help; in fact, the doors of houses could not be opened for the heavy weight of snow (more snow fell that year than anyone could remember in the past). Still, the emperor did all that he could by summoning mercenaries by letter from all quarters.

Just after the spring equinox,[7] when the threat of war from the clouds had vanished and the sea lost its fury, although his enemies attacked on two fronts, he thought it wiser to get control of the sea coast first; by doing that he could easily withstand the onslaught of enemy fleets and conveniently dispose of attacks by land. At once, therefore, he sent a message to the *Kaisar* Nikephoros Melissenos, calling on him to take Ainos. Before this he had sent written instructions to him to recruit as many men as he could, not from the veterans (for he had already dispersed them generally among the towns of the west, to guard the more important places), but to enrol men from the Bulgars and those who live a nomadic life (commonly called Vlakhs) and any others who came from any and every province, both cavalry and infantry.

The emperor himself summoned the 500 Kelts of the count of Flanders from Nikomedia, and leaving Byzantion with his kinsmen quickly arrived at Ainos. There he boarded a boat and explored the geography of the river from end to end, thoroughly examining the bed of the stream from both banks and deciding where it was best to camp. Then he returned. During the night he called a meeting of the army officers and gave them a lecture on the river and the conditions on either bank. 'You must cross the river tomorrow,' he said, 'and carefully reconnoitre the whole plain. Maybe you will find the place I have suggested to you would not be unsuitable for a camp.' All agreed and at daybreak the emperor was the first to make the crossing; he was followed by the whole army. Again, with the officers, he examined the banks of the river and the adjacent plain. He pointed out to them the place he had chosen (near a small town called by the natives Khoirenoi, with the river on one side and on the other a swamp). As the position seemed to everyone satisfactory, a trench was quickly dug and the whole force settled down inside it. Alexios himself went back to Ainos with a strong body of lightly-armed soldiers to repel Scythian attacks from that quarter.

4. When the men who were dug in at Khoirenoi heard that countless hordes of the enemy had arrived, they warned the emperor who was still at Ainos. He at once boarded a patrol boat, sailed along the coast and after crossing the river mouth rejoined the others. He saw that his own forces were incapable of matching even a tiny part of the Scythian multitude; with no glimmer of hope – at least from human sources – he was in a serious and frightening situation. Nevertheless, there was no loss of heart, no weakening of resolve; on the contrary, his mind was bubbling over with ideas.

However, four days later a Cuman army of about 40,000 was sighted in the distance coming towards him from another direction. If they joined the Scythians, they might wage a fearful war on himself (the outcome of which could be nothing but total destruction). To avoid this, he thought it imperative to win them over. He took the initiative by calling on them to meet him. In the Cuman army there were numerous chiefs, but the outstanding leaders were Togortak, Maniak and some others noted for their warlike qualities. The sight of the multitude of Cumans who had already assembled was distinctly alarming, for the emperor had long experience of their vacillation: these allies might well become enemies, and the emperor feared that as adversaries they could be the cause of very considerable harm.

It would be more prudent, he decided, to cross with all his army to the other bank of the river, but it was imperative to summon their leaders first. They soon accepted the invitation, with Maniak following later than the others, after he had first refused to join them. The emperor ordered the cooks to put before them a splendid banquet, and after they had feasted, he treated them with cordiality and gave them all kinds of presents. Then he requested them to take an oath and give hostages, distrusting their unreliable nature. They readily complied with this demand and gave the pledges. They asked to be allowed to make war on the Patzinaks for three days, and promised that if God granted them victory, they would divide all the booty that fell to them and set aside one half of it for the emperor. He gave them permission to attack the Scythians not merely for three days, but for ten whole days if they so wished, and if God did indeed grant them the victory, he would relinquish all claim on the booty.

Thus, the Scythian and Cuman forces remained where they were, but the latter tested their opponents with skirmishing raids. Before three days had passed the emperor sent for Antiokhos (one of the nobles and a man distinguished among his fellows for his lively intelligence). He was ordered to build a bridge. It was quickly constructed by means of boats fastened together with very long planks of wood. After that the *Protostrator* Michael Doukas, the emperor's brother-in-law, and Adrian, the emperor's brother and *megas domestikos*, were summoned. They were ordered to take up position on the riverbank and prevent infantry and cavalry crossing over in general confusion: the infantry was to have precedence with the baggage wagons and pack mules. When the infantry had crossed, the emperor, fearing the powerful Scythian and Cuman armies and suspicious of the secret plans of the latter, had a trench dug at great speed. Inside it all his men were then gathered. After that the cavalry were given the signal to cross. Alexios himself stood by the bank and watched the whole operation.

In the meantime, in accordance with the emperor's written instructions, Melissenos had collected recruits over a wide area. The foot soldiers whom he rounded up from the vicinity piled their baggage on ox wagons, together with all necessary supplies, and were sent in haste to the emperor, but when they were just near enough for a man to see them, they were thought by most of the scouts to be a detachment of Scythians on their way to attack the Romans. One scout pointed them out to the emperor and confidently declared them to be Scythians. The emperor believed him, and because he was heavily outnumbered was at a loss what to do. Rodomeros (a nobleman of Bulgarian extraction and a relative on the maternal side of our own mother the empress) was immediately sent to spy on the approaching force. He soon returned with the news that they were sent by Melissenos, to the intense joy of the emperor, who after awaiting their arrival for a short time crossed over the bridge with them and without delay increased the area of the entrenchment, for they joined the rest of the army.

The Cumans soon reached the camp that the emperor had abandoned before he crossed the river, and set themselves up there. On the next day Alexios left with the idea of seizing a ford downstream, called Philokalos by the locals, but he came across a strong body of Scythians. He attacked at once and a bitter fight ensued. Many men on both sides were killed, but the Scythians were heavily defeated. After the struggle, both armies withdrew to their own camps. The Roman army stayed on in the area all through that night, but at daybreak they left for a place called Lebounion, a hill dominating the plain. The emperor climbed it, but finding that the hilltop could not accommodate all the army, he had a trench dug round the lower slopes. The whole of his force was established inside this entrenchment, which was big enough to protect them all. It was at this moment that the deserter Neantzes again presented himself to the emperor, accompanied by a few Scythians. The emperor was reminded of his betrayal, and, considering other issues too, had him and his companions arrested and thrown into chains.

5. While the emperor was engaged in these operations, the Scythians, encamped by a mountain stream called Mauro-potamos, secretly tried to win over the Cumans. Despite this they did not cease making peace proposals to the emperor. Guessing their unscrupulous dealings, he gave them appropriate

replies; he hoped to keep them in suspense until the mercenaries expected from Rome could reach him. The Cumans, finding the Patzinak pledges ambiguous, were by no means inclined to support them. One evening they notified the emperor: 'How long are we to put off the battle? Be sure of this: we will not wait any longer. At sunrise we intend to decide the matter, one way or the other.'[8] Hearing these words the emperor, who thoroughly understood the implications of what the Cumans had said, no longer deferred the contest. He gave his word that on the next day battle would be joined with the enemy, and that day, he determined, would be the decisive point of the whole war. Without delay the officers, commanders of units of fifty men and others were told to spread throughout the camp the news that battle was fixed for the next day.

In spite of these arrangements he still feared the countless hordes of Patzinaks and Cumans; he suspected a covenant between them. The emperor was still examining that possibility when some highlanders came to join him, bold men full of warlike frenzy. As many as 5,000 of them joined up with him in order to fight.

When there was no longer reason to delay further, the emperor invoked the aid of God. As the sun was setting he led the prayers; a brilliant torch-light procession took place and suitable hymns, also led by him, were chanted to the Lord. Nor did the emperor allow the rest of the camp to enjoy repose: the more cultivated were enjoined to follow his example, the more boorish he commanded to do so. At the moment when the sun set below the horizon, one could see the heaven lit up, not with the light of one sun, but with the gleam of many other stars, for everyone lit torches, or candles, according to what they had available, fixed on their spear points. The prayers offered up by the army no doubt reached the very vault of heaven, or shall I say that they were borne aloft to the Lord God Himself. The fact that the emperor did not believe he could attack the enemy without the help of God is proof, I think, of his piety, for his confidence was stayed neither on men nor on horses nor on machines of war, but all his faith was placed in the hands of Divine Providence.

These ceremonies went on until the middle of the night. Then, after resting for a short time, he leapt up from his sleep to arm the light troops for battle. In some cases he even provided cuirasses and caps made out of silken garments, since there was insufficient iron for all, and the silk resembled iron in colour, equipping some men with these. The preparations were completed, and just as the morning sun began to shine brightly, he left the entrenchment, after ordering the alert to be sounded.

At the foot of Lebounion (the name of this place) the army was divided up and the ranks were massed. He himself took his place in front breathing the fierce spirit of battle.[9] On the right and left wings George Palaiologos and Constantine Dalassenos were in command. To the right of the Cumans, Monastras stood in full armour with his men on higher ground. The Cumans, seeing the emperor drawing up the Roman ranks, were already arming their own forces and preparing the battle line according to their own fashion. On their left was Ouzas and towards the west Houmpertopoulos with the Kelts. Thus the emperor's army was like a bastion, with its ranks of infantry tightly enclosed by squadrons of cavalry on either wing. Once again the trumpeter was ordered to sound the call to battle. In their dread of the numberless host of Scythians and their terrifying covered wagons, which served as ramparts for them, the Romans called upon the Lord of all with one voice to have pity and then, at full gallop, rushed to do battle with their enemies. Riding in front of everyone was the emperor.

When the line had become crescent-shaped, as if at one word of command, the whole army, including the Cumans, surged forward against the enemy. One of the leading Scythian chieftains, anticipating the outcome of the struggle, seized the opportunity to save his own life and approached the Cumans, whose language he spoke with a few others. Although these too were engaged in a ferocious conflict with his people, he had more faith in them than in the Romans. He surrendered, hoping they would act as intermediaries with the emperor. Now Alexios saw this incident and he was afraid that other Scythians might come over to the Cumans too and persuade them to turn their loyalties – and their horses – against the Romans. He was the kind of man who quickly decides in a crisis what needs to be done. So, without losing a moment, he ordered the ensign to take up position with the Cuman army, grasping in his hands the imperial standard.

By this time the Scythian line was in complete disarray, and as each army fought at close quarters there was slaughter such as no one had ever seen before. While the Scythians, like men already forsaken by Almighty God, were being terribly massacred, their slayers grew weary, worn out with the violent, continual sword blows, and they began to lose impetus. But the emperor, charging into the midst of the enemy, threw the enemy ranks into confusion, hacking at his immediate adversaries and with loud cries striking terror into those far off.

However, when at midday he saw the sun shedding its rays directly overhead, he had the good sense to take the following precaution: he sent a number of men to order the peasants to fill wineskins with water, load them on their own mules and bring them to the army. Their neighbours, even those not bidden to do this, followed their example, eager to refresh with water those who delivered them from the terror of the Scythians, some with water jars, some with wineskins, others with whatever vessel came to hand. The fighters sipped a drop of water, then returned to the fray. It was an extraordinary spectacle. A whole people, numbered not in their tens of thousands, but in countless multitudes, with their women and children, was utterly wiped out on that day. It was the twenty-ninth of April,[10] a Tuesday. Hence the ditty chanted by the Byzantines: 'All because of one day the Scythians never saw the month of May.'

When the sun was just about to set and all had been smitten by the sword, and I include children and mothers in this number, and many also had been taken captive, the emperor ordered the recall to camp. It was an amazing sight to anyone who recollects how in the old days our soldiers left Byzantion to fight these Scythians, buying ropes and straps with which to bind their Scythian prisoners, only to be captured themselves and made prisoner by the enemy. That was what happened when we fought them near Dristra,[11] for on that occasion God humbled the pride of the Romans; but later, at the time I am now dealing with, knowing that they were fearful, that they had lost hope of safety, helpless in the face of such multitudes, He granted them the victory beyond all expectation, so that they bound and massacred and took the Scythians into captivity. Nor was that all – such outcomes are not uncommon in minor clashes – but in this case a whole people, comprising myriads of men, women and children, was exterminated in one single day.

6. The Cuman and Roman forces separated and as darkness fell the emperor prepared to dine. An angry Synesios appeared before him. 'What's this nonsense? What's the meaning of it?' he cried. 'Every soldier has up to thirty and more Scythian prisoners. The Cumans are near us and if the soldiers fall asleep, as they no doubt will, as they are completely worn out, and the prisoners set each other free, draw their daggers and kill them, what will happen then? I demand that you order most of the prisoners to be executed at once.' The emperor looked at him sternly. 'Scythians they may be,' said he, 'but they are human beings all the same; enemies, but worthy of pity. I don't understand what makes you talk such rubbish.' Synesios persisted and Alexios angrily dismissed him.

However, he did issue a proclamation throughout the camp: every weapon was to be taken from the Scythians and deposited in one place; the captives were to be securely guarded. After issuing that decree he spent the rest of the night in peace. Sometime in the middle watch the soldiers, as if acting under orders, killed nearly all of them. Whether they did this in response to some divine bidding, or how they came to do it, I cannot say. The emperor heard about it at dawn and immediately suspected Synesios. He was at once called. Alexios blamed him and uttered violent threats. 'This is your doing,' he said. Although Synesios protested on oath that he knew nothing about it, he had him arrested and thrown into chains. 'Let him learn,' he said, 'how horrible it is merely to be chained, so that he never again passes such a verdict against his fellow men.' Maybe he would have punished him further, had not the leading

officers, close relatives of the emperor's, intervened and all
pleaded for mercy for Synesios.

Meanwhile most of the Cumans, fearful of the emperor's
intentions, since they thought he might plot some evil against
themselves in the night, took up all the booty and went off in
the darkness on the road to the Danube. As for the emperor,
he also departed at daybreak because of the abominable
stench of the corpses. He left for a place called Kala Dendra,
eighteen stades from Khoirenoi. While he was on his way there
Melissenos joined him. He had not been able to take part in
the battle, because he was busily engaged in sending off the
multitude of new recruits. They greeted one another with
mutual congratulations and naturally spent the rest of the
march in conversation about the events which led up to the
Scythian defeat.

When he reached Kala Dendra, Alexios heard of the departure of the Cumans. Mules were loaded with everything that
they had been promised in the agreements with the emperor
and were sent after them. Instructions were given that the
Cumans must be found quickly and the property delivered,
even on the far side of the Danube if possible. To Alexios, lying,
or even seeming to lie, was a very serious thing and he often
denounced in public the practice of lying. So much for the
fugitive Cumans. The rest, who followed him, were entertained
at a magnificent banquet for the remainder of the day, but he
thought it wiser not to give them their due rewards at that
moment; after a sleep, when the effects of the wine had worn
off, with their wits fully recovered, they could better appreciate
what was being done. Next day they were all assembled and
given not only what they had been promised, but far more than
that. He wished to send them home, but was anxious lest
they should roam widely in search of loot and so damage the
inhabited areas on their route home. So he took hostages. They
in their turn asked for assurances of safe conduct. He gave them
Ioannikios (a man of outstanding bravery and prudence); he
was to arrange everything and make certain that the Cumans
reached Zygos[12] unharmed.

So the emperor's affairs prospered in every way, thanks to

Divine Providence. When all was fully settled, he returned to Byzantion during the month of May, a triumphant victor. At this point I must leave the history of the Scythians, although I have only repeated a fraction of the events which I might have done, as though I had dipped just one finger into the water of the Adriatic Sea. As to the emperor's glorious victories, the partial setbacks at the hands of his enemies, his individual feats of valour, the events that occurred meanwhile, the way in which he adapted himself to every circumstance and by different means broke up the terrors which threatened us, not even a second Demosthenes, nor indeed the whole chorus of orators, nor all the Academy and Stoa united in one effort to do justice to the deeds of this emperor, would have had the ability to capture his achievement.

7. Not many days after his return to the palace, the Armenian Ariebes and the Kelt Houmpertopoulos (both distinguished officers and brave men) were discovered in the act of conspiring[13] against him. They dragged into their plot quite a large number of other men of not ignoble birth. The proofs were there and the truth was freely acknowledged. They were convicted and condemned to exile; their property was to be confiscated at once, but the emperor resolutely opposed the extreme penalty demanded by the laws.

The emperor also heard talk of a Cuman invasion at this time, together with reports that Bodin and his Dalmatians planned to violate their treaty and march on our territory. It was difficult to decide which of the two enemies he should move against first. He judged it essential to deal with the Dalmatians first; he must seize the initiative by making as safe as possible the valleys between their lands and our own. A general conference was called, at which he explained his purpose, and as everyone agreed, he left the capital to settle affairs in the west.

On his arrival soon after at Philippopolis, he received letters from the then archbishop of Bulgaria[14] who gave him advice about his nephew John, son of the *Sebastokrator* Isaac and *doux* of Dyrrakhion. He was accused of plotting a revolt. All that night and all day long the emperor was tormented by this news. Because of John's father he was for putting off the inquiry into the affair; on the other hand, he feared that the rumour was true. John was only a youth, and the emperor knew that such persons are usually the victims of overwhelming impulses, so that he had reason to suspect some revolt. The youth could be the cause of unbearable grief to both father and uncle. It was necessary, therefore, to thwart the plan quickly by any method, for he had a very real affection for the boy.

He sent for the officer who was *megas hetairiarkhes* at that time, Argyros Karatzas, a Scythian by birth, but a man of wisdom, a lover of virtue and truth, and to him he entrusted two letters. One, addressed to John, read as follows: 'Having learnt of the hostile movement of barbarians through the passes, I, your emperor, have left the City of Constantine to ensure the frontiers of the Roman Empire. You are required to come in person to render account of the province under your government (for I worry that Bolkan is our enemy and is scheming against us). You must also inform us about affairs in Dalmatia and report whether this Bolkan remains true to the agreements made with him (for the information that reaches us is not encouraging). When we have a clearer picture of what is going on, we can prepare more fully to combat his schemes and after advising you on the proper course of action send you back to Illyrikon. Thus, with God's aid, fighting our enemies on two fronts, we may have the victory.'

Such was the gist of the letter written to John. The second, to be delivered to the magistrates of the town of Dyrrakhion, ran thus: 'Since we have learnt that Bolkan is again plotting against us, we have left Byzantion to ensure the safety of the valleys between Dalmatia and our frontiers, and at the same time to obtain accurate information about the activities of the man and his people. For these reasons we deemed it necessary to summon your *doux*, the beloved nephew of your emperor. We have therefore sent this envoy who delivers to you this letter and have promoted him to the rank of *doux*. Receive him therefore and in every way obey his commands.' These letters were then placed in the hands of Karatzas who was told first of all to give John the letter addressed to him when he arrived, and if the latter willingly followed its instructions, to send him on in peace. Karatzas was then to assume the government of the country until such time as John returned. If, however, John remonstrated and would not obey, Karatzas was to call for the leading citizens of Dyrrakhion and secretly read to them the second letter, so that they might help in arresting John.

8. As soon as the *Sebastokrator* Isaac heard these things while in Constantinople, he left the city in haste and after a journey of two days and two nights arrived at Philippopolis. The emperor was sleeping in his imperial tent, but Isaac went in noiselessly and lay down on the second of his brother's beds, and after making a sign with his hand to the chamberlains to be quiet, he fell asleep too. When the emperor awoke, he was surprised to see his brother, but said nothing for a while and ordered the others who happened to be there to do likewise. Later Isaac woke up, to find his brother the emperor had already risen and was watching him. They embraced and greeted one another. The emperor asked what on earth he wanted and why he had come. 'You,' he replied, 'are the reason for my visit.' 'You have worn yourself out with all this exertion to no purpose,' said Alexios.

The *sebastokrator* had no answer to this for some time – he was deep in thought about information he expected from Dyrrakhion. As soon as he had heard the rumours about his son, he had sent a messenger with a short note urging him to visit the emperor soon; he himself had left the capital at the same time as this envoy and was hurrying to Philippopolis to refute the accusations made against John; he intended to talk with the emperor and suggest likely reasons for them; meanwhile he would await John's arrival there. Isaac took his leave of the emperor and withdrew to the tent specially assigned to himself. But not long afterwards the messenger arrived from Dyrrakhion in haste with the news that John was on his way.

The *sebastokrator*, relieved at once of his suspicions, recovered his self-confidence. Full of anger with those who had first denounced his son, he appeared before the emperor in a highly agitated frame of mind. The moment he saw him Alexios knew the cause of it, but merely asked him how he was. 'Rotten!' replied Isaac. 'And it's your fault.' The truth is that he was boiling over with uncontrollable anger, misled by a chance phrase unsupported by evidence. 'I'm not so much hurt by Your Majesty as by him,' he said, pointing at Adrian, 'and by his barefaced lies.' The emperor, a mild and gentle man, made no reply whatever to this, for he knew a better way to check his brother's seething rage. Both of them sat down together with Nikephoros Melissenos and certain other close relatives, and had a private conversation about the charges brought against John. But when Isaac saw Melissenos and his own brother Adrian attacking his son in a sly, affected way, he was once again unable to restrain his boiling rage. Fixing a furious gaze on Adrian, he threatened to tear out his beard: he would teach him not to try to drive a wedge between the emperor and his family by such unpleasant fabrication.[15]

In the midst of this John arrived and was straightway ushered into the imperial tent. He heard all the accusations made against him. However, he was not subjected to any inquiry at all. The accused stood free while the emperor addressed him: 'In consideration of your father, my brother, I cannot bring myself to listen to these rumours. Consider this all in the past as from now on.' All this was said inside the imperial tent; only relatives were present, no strangers. What was said, there-fore, or what maybe was intended, was hushed up, but the emperor certainly did send for his brother, by whom I mean Isaac the *sebastokrator*, and his nephew John. After a long conversation, he said to Isaac, 'Go in peace now to the capital and tell our mother what has passed between us. As for this young man (and here he pointed to John), I shall again, as you see, send him out to Dyrrakhion, to devote his energies faith-fully to the affairs of his own province.' So they parted, Isaac leaving for Byzantion on the next day, and John being sent to Dyrrakhion.

9. However, that was not the end of the emperor's troubles. Theodore Gabras[16] was living in the capital and the emperor, knowing his passionate nature and love of action, was keen to

get him away from the city. He was promoted *doux* of Trapezous, a town which he had previously recaptured from the Turks.
This man Theodore Gabras came originally from Khaldia and
its upper regions. He was a famous soldier, of exceptional
intelligence and bravery. Whatever he attempted, he was almost
always successful, and he was victorious in all his wars. After
capturing Trapezous he regarded the town as his own property
and was invincible.

The *Sebastokrator* Isaac Komnenos had destined Gabras' son
Gregory to marry one of his own daughters, but as both were
merely children the union for the time being was only promised.
Gabras entrusted Gregory to the care of the emperor, so that
when the children attained the legal age, the marriage might be
celebrated. He then took his leave of the emperor and returned
to his own country. Not long after his wife died and he married
a second time. The new wife was an Alan, of noble blood. It
happened that she and the *sebastokrator*'s wife were daughters
of two brothers. When this became known, since by law and
the canons of the Church the union of the children was forbidden, the putative marriage contract was broken. The
emperor was aware of Gabras' military reputation and of the
great harm he could cause. Consequently he was unwilling that
Gregory should return to his father once the engagement had
been called off. He wished to keep him in Constantinople, for
two reasons: first, he could hold him as a hostage; and, secondly, he might win Gabras' friendship. Thus, if Gabras did
harbour some evil design, he might frustrate it. He intended to
marry Gregory to one of my sisters.[17] These were the reasons
why the boy's departure was delayed.

The elder Gabras again visited Constantinople and ignorant
of the emperor's plans looked for a secret way of recovering his
son. You see, although the emperor had hinted at what his idea
was and had partially clarified the situation, he remained to all
intents and purposes silent. Gabras, whether because he did not
know, or because he had grown indifferent after the recent
breakdown of the former marriage contract, I am not sure
either way; whatever the case, when he was about to return

home, he demanded that his son be handed over to him. The emperor refused.

Gabras then pretended to leave him behind voluntarily and in deference to the emperor's wishes allow the latter to settle the boy's affairs. Having taken leave of the emperor, Gabras was just about to leave Byzantion when he was received hospitably by the *sebastokrator*, partly because of their marriage ties and also because of the intimacy to which it led. He entertained Gabras in a very beautiful house in the suburbs near the Propontis, where the church of the great martyr Phokas is built. After enjoying a magnificent banquet there, Isaac was returning to the capital when Gabras asked that his son might be allowed to be with him on the next day. Isaac at once consented. However, as he was about to be parted from the boy, our much-mentioned Gabras begged his son's tutors to accompany him as far as Sosthenion, for he intended to rest there. They agreed and went with him. Then, in the same way, as he was again about to take his leave, he begged that his son should go with him to Pharos. They refused to allow this. He therefore made excuses – a father's affection, a long separation and so on – and his persistence so touched the hearts of the tutors that they again gave in to his arguments and continued the journey. When he arrived at Pharos, though, he brought his plan into the light, took up the boy, put him on board a merchantman and committed both himself and Gregory to the waves of the Black Sea.

When the emperor heard of it, he immediately dispatched fast boats after him, with instructions to deliver letters to Gabras and bring back the boy with his father's consent; if he objected, Gabras must be made to realize that the emperor was his enemy. They caught up with him after leaving the town of Aiginoupolis, near a place known locally as Karambis. The imperial letters were delivered, in which the emperor disclosed that he desired the boy to marry one of my sisters, and after a long discussion Gabras was finally persuaded to hand over his son.

The marriage contract was soon ratified in the usual legal terms – nothing more – and Gregory was then entrusted to

a tutor, one of the empress's retinue, the eunuch Michael.
Spending his time thus in the palace he was honoured with
much attention; he was given a good moral education and a
thorough grounding in all aspects of military science. But as is
the way with the young, he absolutely refused to be subject to
anyone; he felt aggrieved, because he was not treated with the
respect which he considered proper to him. At the same time
he was at loggerheads with his tutor. He made up his mind
therefore to abscond to his father, although he should have
been grateful rather for the great care lavished on him. He did
not only mull over such a plan, but actually put it into action.
He approached certain persons and confided in them. These
gentlemen were George Dekanos, Eustathios Kamytzes and
Michael the Cup-bearer, usually called *pinkernes*[18] by the
courtiers at the palace. They were all great warriors, among the
closest associates of the emperor. One of them, Michael, went
to the emperor and told him everything. Alexios was quite
unable to believe the story. When Gabras insisted on hastening his escape, those who remained loyal to the emperor told
him, 'Unless you confirm your plan to us by an oath, we will
not help you.' He agreed, and they secretly indicated to him
where the Sacred Nail[19] with which the impious pierced my
Saviour's side was located. They planned to remove it and bring
it out so that Gabras might swear in the name of Him who
was wounded by it.

Gabras was persuaded by them, and therefore entered the
place in question and stealthily removed the Holy Nail. Then
one of those who had before informed the emperor of the plot
ran to him and said: 'Behold Gabras, with the Nail hidden in
his clothes.' At once the emperor commanded him to be led in
and the relic was extracted at once from its hiding place in his
clothes. He was questioned and without hesitation admitted
everything; he gave the names of his accomplices and confessed all his plans. The emperor condemned him and handed
him over to the *doux* of Philippopolis, George Mesopo-
tamites, with instructions to keep him under guard and in
chains in the citadel. George Dekanos he sent with letters to
Leo Nikerites, who was at that time *doux* of Paristrion.

Apparently he was to assist him in protecting the Danube area, but in fact he was sent so that Nikerites might keep an eye on him. Eustathios Kamytzes himself and the rest were banished and imprisoned.

BOOK IX

1. Having settled the affairs of John and of Gregory Gabras, the emperor left Philippopolis for the valleys lying between Dalmatia and our own territory. He traversed the whole ridge of the Zygos, as it is known locally, not on horseback but on foot (for the country was very rugged, full of ravines, covered with forests and almost impassable). He visited all parts and saw everything with his own eyes, lest any point should inadvertently be left unguarded to give the enemy easy access to our side. At one place he commanded trenches to be dug, at another wooden towers to be erected; where the terrain permitted, small forts were to be built of brick or stone, and he personally fixed their size and the distance between them. At some points he ordered very tall trees to be felled at the roots and laid across the enemies' path. Then he returned to Constantinople.

My account might sound as if these measures were simple, but many eyewitnesses, still alive today, bear evidence to the strain caused by that tour on the emperor. Soon after he had come back, more detailed intelligence arrived of Tzakhas. It was reported that defeat by land and sea had not diverted him from his previous intentions: he was wearing the imperial insignia, calling himself emperor and living at Smyrna as though it were an imperial residence. A fleet was being equipped to ravage the islands afresh, for Tzakhas hoped to reach Byzantion itself and attain supreme power, if that were possible.

Every day the emperor received confirmation of these reports. Under the circumstances, it was clearly essential that there should be no weakening, no relaxation of effort; he would have to make preparations from the end of spring to the following winter in order to oppose Tzakhas with strong forces in the spring after that. The man's ambitions, his plans, his hopes, his enterprises would have to be quickly and completely crushed; he must be driven out of Smyrna itself, and all the other places he had seized in the past must be wrenched from his grasp. At the conclusion of winter, therefore, when the fine weather of spring began, John Doukas, the emperor's brother-in-law, was summoned from Epidamnos[1] and appointed *megas doux* of the fleet. He was given an army of picked landsmen and ordered to march against Tzakhas by the overland route, while Constantine Dalassenos was to control the fleet and sail along the coast. The idea was that they should arrive simultaneously at Mitylene and converging on Tzakhas by land and sea, make war on him.

The moment Doukas reached Mitylene he had wooden towers constructed and using this as a base of operations began the campaign in earnest. Tzakhas had left his brother Galabatzes in charge of the garrison there, and since he knew that the latter's force was inadequate for battle against so experienced an opponent, he hurried back, formed a line and attacked. It was a stern contest, but night put an end to it. For three revolutions of the moon, daily assaults were made on the walls of Mitylene; from dawn to sunset continual war was waged on Tzakhas.

For all his great efforts though, Doukas made no progress. The emperor was becoming annoyed and exasperated. Then one day he questioned a soldier on leave from Mitylene and having discovered that Doukas did nothing but fight and make war, he asked the man about the circumstances: 'At what time of the day do these battles with Tzakhas take place?' – 'About sunrise.' – 'And which side faces the east?' – 'Ours,' said the man. At once the emperor recognized the reason for their failure and, as usual, found the solution in a moment. He dashed off a letter to Doukas, advising him to refrain from dawn encounters with the enemy, and not to fight against two enemies at the same time – that is, against the sun's rays and against Tzakhas too. He told him that when the sun had passed

the meridian and was inclining to the west, that was the time
to attack. This letter was put in the soldier's hands, with many
recommendations; finally, the emperor said with emphasis, 'If
you make the assault on the enemy as the sun goes down, you
will win at once.'

Doukas received the message from this soldier, and as he
never neglected the emperor's advice, even on quite ordinary
matters, when the barbarians on the next day armed for battle
in the normal way, no opponents were to be seen (for the
Roman troops were resting in accordance with the emperor's
suggestion); the enemy gave up all hope of a clash for that day,
piled their arms and stayed where they were. But Doukas was
not resting. When it was midday he and all his men were ready,
and as the sun began to decline they were in battle formation.
He charged the barbarians suddenly, with tremendous war cries
and shouts. It appears, however, that Tzakhas was not caught
unawares. He called his men to arms and without delay joined
in a fierce counter-attack. At the time a strong wind was blowing and when they came to close quarters, a dust cloud rose
high in the air. The barbarians had the sun glaring into their
faces and the dust, blown into their eyes by the wind, partly
blinded them; what is more, the Roman attack was more vigorous than ever. They were defeated and fled.

After that, Tzakhas was unable to support the siege any more
and was too weak to carry on incessant warfare, so he sued for
peace, asking only to be allowed to sail away unharmed to
Smyrna. Doukas agreed and took as hostages two of the leading
satraps. Tzakhas asked Doukas for hostages too, saying that
this would guarantee him safe passage to Smyrna, while he in
turn would wrong none of the Mitylenians when he left, nor
take them away with him to Smyrna. Doukas gave him Alexander Euphorbenos and Manuel Boutoumites, who were both
excellent fighters and men of courage. Having exchanged satisfactory promises, no doubts remained with Doukas happy that
Tzakhas would not harm the Mitylenians, and the latter satisfied that the Roman fleet would not impede him on his journey.

But the crab never learns to walk straight, and Tzakhas could
not help but return to his former wickedness. He tried to carry

off all the people of Mitylene, including the women and children. While this was going on, Constantine Dalassenos, *thalassokrator* at that time, had not yet arrived, but had moored his ships off a promontory as he had been ordered by Doukas. Seeing now what Tzakhas had done, he came to Doukas and begged to be allowed to fight him. Doukas, out of respect for the oath he had taken, put off any decision for the time being. But Dalassenos persisted. 'You have sworn an oath,' he said, 'but I was not present. As far as you are concerned, keep the assurances you gave inviolate. But I will prepare for action against Tzakhas, on the basis that I was not present and gave no undertaking; I know nothing of what you two agreed.' Tzakhas, weighing anchor, made straight for Smyrna, but Dalassenos set off after him, attacking while giving chase. The rest of the enemy fleet was caught as it was weighing anchor; Doukas captured their ships and rescued all the prisoners of war and other captives held by the barbarians in chains. Dalassenos took many of Tzakhas' pirate vessels too and had their crews executed, including the rowers.

Tzakhas himself would also have been made prisoner, had not the rascal, foreseeing what was likely to happen, boarded one of the faster ships and thus, unseen and unsuspected, got safely away. Because he had guessed the outcome, he had Turks standing by on a headland watching for him until he reached Smyrna without mishap; if, on the other hand, the Romans should intercept him, he would steer his boat towards these Turks and so find refuge. He was successful, too, for he came to anchor there, linked up with the Turks and finally made his way back to Smyrna. Dalassenos, his conqueror, rejoined the *megas doux*. Doukas strengthened the defences of Mitylene, and after Dalassenos returned home, detached an important part of the Roman fleet to liberate the places held by Tzakhas (he had already gained control of a fair number of islands). Having taken Samos at the first attempt and certain other islands too, Doukas withdrew to Constantinople.

2. Not many days later it was reported that Karykes had revolted and had seized Crete, and also that Rhapsomates had

taken Cyprus.[2] The emperor therefore sent Doukas with a large
fleet against them. When the Cretans received the news that
Doukas had arrived at Karpathos, which they knew was not
far away, they attacked Karykes and cruelly murdered him,
after which they handed over the island to the *megas doux*.
Having made sure that Crete was now secure, Doukas left a
force strong enough for a garrison and sailed on to Cyprus. As
soon as he landed, Kyrenia was captured at the first assault.
However, when Rhapsomates heard this, he began making
major preparations against him. It was for this reason that he
left Nicosia and occupied the heights above Kyrenia; in that
area he pitched camp, but for the time being refused to fight –
which proved his inexperience of war and ignorance of the art
of strategy, for he should have fallen upon his adversaries while
they were unready. His procrastination was not due to any lack
of preparedness on his side; it was not that he was ill-fitted for
the clash (in fact he was very well prepared and had he wished
he could have waged war at once). The truth is that he did not
want to commit himself to hostilities at all; he had started the
war as a game, like small boys at play. Feebly he kept sending
envoys, apparently expecting to win them over with soothing
phrases.

In my opinion he did this because of his ignorance, for
according to the information I received about him, he had only
recently laid hand on a sword and spear and did not even know
how to mount a horse; if by some chance he managed to get
on and then attempted to ride, he was seized with panic and
vertigo. That shows how inexperienced Rhapsomates was in
soldiering. Anyway he lost his head, whether for these reasons
or because he was completely taken by surprise when the
imperial forces attacked. Somewhat disheartened, he did make
an attempt to fight, but things did not go well for him, for
Boutoumites enticed away some of his soldiers and when they
deserted, he enrolled them in his own army. On the following
day Rhapsomates arranged his line and challenged Doukas to
battle, marching at a slow pace down the slope of a hill. When
the two armies were only a short distance apart, a group of
Rhapsomates' men, a hundred strong, broke away, seemingly

with the intention of charging against Doukas, but they reversed their spears and went over to the Romans.

At this Rhapsomates immediately galloped off at full speed towards Nemesos, hoping no doubt to find a ship there on which he could flee to Syria, and thereby find safety. But Manuel Boutoumites pressed hard on him in pursuit. His ambitions thwarted and with Manuel close on his heels, he reached the mountain on the other side and took refuge in the ancient Church of the Holy Cross. Boutoumites (whom Doukas had assigned the task of pursuing him) caught up with him near there, spared his life and took him back to the *megas doux*. Later they all arrived at Nicosia and after subduing the whole island assured its defence as far as they could. A full account of the campaign was sent to the emperor.

He was delighted by their efforts, but realized that the security of the island required special attention. Kalliparios was forthwith appointed *krites* and *exisotes*. He was not a nobleman, but had given ample proof of fair dealing; he was both modest and incorruptible. A military governor was also needed; thus Eumathios Philokales was designated *strato-pedarkhes* and given responsibility for its defence by land and sea. He was given warships and cavalry. As for Boutou-mites, he returned to Doukas with Rhapsomates and the Immortals who had rebelled with him, and then made his way to Constantinople.

3. Such were the events that took place in the islands, that is to say Cyprus and Crete. Tzakhas, on the other hand, was too warlike and enterprising to remain inactive. After a short while, therefore, he attacked Smyrna and established himself there. Again pirate vessels were thoroughly equipped, as well as war-ships, biremes, triremes and other fast ships, with the same plan in mind. The news, far from discouraging the emperor or causing him to delay, convinced him that Tzakhas must be speedily crushed by land and sea. So Constantine Dalassenos was appointed *thalassokrator* and sent to sea with all the fleet against Tzakhas.

Alexios also thought it would be expedient to stir up trouble for him with the sultan through letters. He therefore sent the

following: 'Most Illustrious Sultan Klitziasthlan,³ you know
that the dignity of sultan is yours by right of inheritance.
But your kinsman Tzakhas, although apparently preparing for
war against the Roman Empire and calling himself emperor, is
in reality using this as a pretext – an obvious pretext, for he is
a man of experience and he knows perfectly well that the
Roman Empire is beyond him and that it would be impossible
for him to grasp so great a realm. The whole mischievous
plan is directed against you. If you are wise, therefore, you will
not endure this. There is no need for despair, however, but
rather for vigilance; otherwise you will be driven from your
sultanate. For my part, I will with God's help expel him from
Roman territory, and as I care for your interests, I would advise
you to consider your own authority and power, and quickly
bring him to heel, by peaceful means or, if he refuses, by the
sword.'

After the emperor had taken these precautions Tzakhas
appeared with an army on the landward side of Abydos and
laid siege to the place with siege-engines and all kinds of rock-
throwing engines. He could do no more, for his pirate ships,
not yet ready for action, were not accompanying him. Dalassenos, who loved a fight and was a courageous man, marched
with all his forces along the Abydos road. The Sultan Klitziasthlan also set out with his army to engage Tzakhas immediately after receiving the emperor's message. Such is every
barbarian – constantly lusting after massacre and war.

When the sultan drew near, Tzakhas saw himself menaced
by land and sea; he had no ships, because his navy was still
unseaworthy; his land forces were outnumbered by the Romans
and the army of his kinsman Klitziasthlan; his position was
desperate. He was afraid, too, of the inhabitants of Abydos, as
well as its garrison, and therefore he decided that it was better
to approach the sultan, knowing nothing himself of the
emperor's intrigue with him. The sultan received him graciously
with a pleasant smile, and when his table was laid ready in the
usual way, he shared it with Tzakhas at dinner and encouraged
him to drink heavily. Then, seeing him in a fuddled state, he
drew his sword and thrust it into his side. Tzakhas fell dead on

the spot. The sultan then made overtures to the emperor for peace in the future and these did not fail to meet with success. The emperor consented and when a treaty had been concluded in the normal way, peace was restored to the maritime provinces.

4. However, before the emperor could find relief from these great anxieties or purge away the ill effects caused by Tzakhas (for even if he had not been personally involved, he had nevertheless played his part in making decisions and plans), he was hurried into fresh troubles. Bolkan (who was ruler of all Dalmatia, and a man highly capable both in word and in deed) crossed his own frontiers and ravaged the neighbouring towns and districts, two solar years[4] after the destruction of the Scythians. He even got as far as Lipenion, which he deliberately burnt down.

The emperor was informed of this and decided that the situation was unbearable. Collecting a strong army he marched against the Serbs on the direct route to Lipenion, a small fortified post lying at the foot of the Zygos mountains, which separate Dalmatia from Roman territory. He intended, if he had the opportunity, to meet Bolkan in battle and, provided that God gave him the victory, to rebuild Lipenion and restore all the other places to their former condition.

When Bolkan heard of the emperor's arrival, he left for Sphentzanion, a fort north of the aforementioned Zygos mountains lying in the no-man's-land between Roman and Dalmatian territory. After the emperor reached Skopia, however, Bolkan sent ambassadors to arrange peace terms. At the same time he protested that he himself was not responsible for all that had happened; he laid all the blame on the Roman satraps. 'Unwilling to remain inside their own borders,' he said, 'they make repeated raids and have brought no little trouble on Serbia. As far as I am concerned, nothing of this kind will happen again, for I will go home, send members of my own family as hostages to Your Majesty, and never cross the boundaries of my land in the future.' The emperor accepted this explanation and after leaving men behind to rebuild the ruined towns and take hostages, he went back to Constantinople.

But despite the demand for hostages, Bolkan did not hand them over. Day after day he procrastinated and when less than twelve months had passed, he again invaded Roman territory. He received several letters from the emperor reminding him of the treaty and promises made by him, but he was still unwilling to fulfil his obligations. Accordingly, the emperor summoned John, son of his brother the *sebastokrator*, and sent him with a powerful army against Bolkan. John had no experience in war and like all young men was impatient to get at the enemy. He crossed the river which flows past Lipenion and pitched camp by the foothills of the Zygos mountains opposite Sphentzanion. His movements were noted by Bolkan, who once again inquired about terms of peace. Bolkan went on to promise that the hostages would be delivered and in future peace with the Romans would be scrupulously respected. In fact, these were nothing more than empty pledges; he was arming to attack us unawares.

While Bolkan was on the march against John, a monk came on ahead and warned John of his plot; he told him emphatically that the enemy was already near. John angrily dismissed him, calling him a liar and a humbug. But facts soon proved that the monk was right, for during the night Bolkan did attack and many soldiers were massacred in their tents; many others fled in haste and being caught up in the eddies of the river in the ravine below were drowned. The more steadfast made for John's tent and after some hard fighting managed to save it. Most of the Roman army by then had perished. Bolkan rallied his own men, climbed to the ridge of the Zygos mountains and established himself in Sphentzanion.

John's staff, who were so few in number that they could not possibly engage with so many, advised him to recross the river. Having done this, they reached Lipenion, about twelve stades further on. After such heavy casualties more resistance would have been impossible. So he set out on the road to the capital. His adversary, much encouraged because no one had been left behind to oppose him, proceeded to plunder the surrounding countryside and its towns. He demolished the environs of Skopia completely and even burnt some part of it. Not content with that, he went on to Polobos and as far as Branea, destroying everything and carrying off vast quantities of booty. He then returned to his own country.

5. When he learnt of the situation, the emperor decided it was intolerable and therefore immediately equipped another expedition; unlike Alexander, who waited for the high-pitched strain of the 'Orthian' mode, he needed no urging from the flute-player Timotheos. So he strapped his armour back on and armed all other available troops in the city, then marched quickly by the direct route to Dalmatia. His object was twofold: to rebuild and restore to their former condition the ruined forts, and to take strong reprisals against the fellow who was responsible for the problems. He started from the capital, reached Daphnoution, an ancient town forty stades away, and waited there for those of his relatives who had not yet arrived.

On the following day Nikephoros Diogenes arrived, in a thoroughly bad mood and brimming with arrogance, but as usual putting on a cheerful expression; the sly fox pretended that he was behaving sincerely in his dealings with the emperor. However, he had his tent pitched, not at the customary distance from the emperor's sleeping quarters, but close to the passage leading up to it. When Manuel Philokales observed this, he was like a man struck by lightning and stood there dumbfounded, for he was not unaware of Diogenes' schemes. With great difficulty he recovered his presence of mind and lost no time in reporting to the emperor. 'It seems to me,' he said, 'that there is something not right here. I am afraid that an attempt may be made on Your Majesty's life in the night. Anyway, I will have a talk with him and see that he moves.' But the emperor, imperturbable as ever, would not allow him to interfere. Philokales became more insistent. 'Leave him alone,' said Alexios. 'We must not afford him a pretext against me. He alone must be responsible, before God and man, for the evil he plans.' Philokales left the tent in anger, wringing his hands and declaring that the emperor had grown foolish.

Not long after, when the emperor and the empress were

peacefully asleep, about the middle watch of the night, Diogenes rose, came to the threshold of their tent and stood there, with a sword concealed under his arm. When this emperor was sleeping, the doors were not fastened nor was a guard on duty outside. Such was the position the emperor found himself in. Nikephoros, though, was deterred from the crime at that moment by some divine force. He caught sight of the little girl who was fanning the imperial couple and driving away mosquitoes; at once 'a trembling seized on his limbs and a pale hue spread over his cheeks',[5] as the poet says. He put off the assassination for another time.

Unceasingly he plotted the murder of the emperor, although he had no excuse for it, but his schemes were by no means undetected: the maid soon went to the emperor and told him what had happened. In the morning he left that place and began the day's march, but pretended to know nothing; in fact, though, enough precautions were taken to ensure his safety without at the same time giving Nikephoros any reasonable cause for complaint. When he arrived in the area of Serrai, Constantine Doukas[6] the *porphyrogennetos*, who was accompanying the emperor, invited him to stay on his personal estate, a delightful place with a good supply of cold, drinkable water and apartments big enough to receive an emperor as guest (its name was Pentegostis). The emperor accepted the invitation and stayed there. He wanted to leave on the following day, but the *porphyrogennetos* would not hear of it: he begged him to stay on, at least until he had recovered from the fatigue of his march and bathed so as to wash off the dust of travel. A costly banquet had in fact also already been prepared in his honour. Once more the emperor let himself be persuaded by the entreaties of the *porphyrogennetos*.

Nikephoros Diogenes had lusted after power for a long time, so when he heard that the emperor had washed and left the bath, he realized he had the chance to commit the murder himself, and therefore strapped on a short sword and went into the house, as if he were returning from hunting in the usual way. Tatikios saw him and because he had known for a long time what Nikephoros was planning, pushed him away. 'What's the meaning of this? Why do you come here in this distinctly odd fashion? – and wearing a sword? This is the time for bathing, not for marching or hunting or battle.' So Nikephoros went and his opportunity was lost. He realized that he was now a marked man (conscience is a terrible accuser) and decided to save his skin by running away to the estates of the Empress Maria in Khristoupolis, either to Pernikos or Petritzos; while there, he could always restore his fortunes as circumstances permitted. Maria had taken a personal interest in him, because he was the brother of her husband, the former Emperor Michael Doukas, on the mother's side, though they had different fathers.

Three days later, the emperor set out from there, but Constantine remained behind to rest; the emperor was concerned for the young man's delicate constitution – he was unused to military expeditions and this was his first real expedition. He was also his mother's only son and a particular favourite of the emperor, who allowed him to enjoy all the rest he needed with her. He loved him deeply, as if he were really his own son.

6. In order to avoid confusion at this point in the history, I will relate the story of Nikephoros Diogenes from its very beginning. The elevation of his father Romanos to the imperial throne and the manner of his downfall have been described by several historians, and anyone who wishes to read about him will find the details in their works. In any case Romanos died when Leo and Nikephoros were still children. At the outset of his reign the Emperor Alexios found them reduced to the status of ordinary citizens (for when Michael ascended the throne, although he was their brother, he deprived them of the purple sandals, took away their diadems and exiled them with their mother, the Empress Eudokia, to the monastery of Kyperoudes[7]). Alexios thought it right to give them every consideration, partly in pity for their sufferings, partly because they were exceptionally handsome and strong, on the threshold of manhood, tall and finely proportioned, with all the promise of youth; their very appearance, to anyone not blinded by prejudice, manifested a spirit that was both passionate and brave. They were like lion cubs.

Moreover, as Alexios was not a man to judge anyone super-

ficially, being neither blind to the truth nor a prey to base
passions, but the kind of person who weighs facts in the fair
balance of his own conscience, he took into account the degra-
dation they had endured. He nurtured them as though they
were his own children. Did he ever miss the chance to speak
well of them? Did he ever fail to promote their welfare and
provide for their future? And this despite the fact that the
envious continually attacked them. Many people, indeed, tried
to provoke him to enmity against the young men, but that made
him more than ever determined to help them in every way;
invariably he had a smile for them, apparently taking a real
pride in their achievements, and always giving advice which
looked to their best interests.

Another would probably have regarded them with suspicion
and made it his business to put power out of their reach completely, but this emperor made light of the charges brought by
many against these two. He had a deep affection for their
mother Eudokia whom he honoured with suitable gifts and
from whom he did not withhold any honour befitting of an
empress. Nikephoros himself was made governor of the island
of Crete[8] to treat as his own private property.

Such were the arrangements of the emperor. As to Leo, he
was a good-hearted man, of a generous disposition, conscious
of the emperor's benevolent attitude to himself and his brother,
and grateful for his lot. He accepted the old saying, 'Sparta is
your inheritance; glorify her.'[9] He was content to remain as he
was. But Nikephoros was an ill-tempered, acrimonious fellow,
harbouring secret designs against the emperor, incessantly
scheming for power; nevertheless, his plan remained a secret.
However, when it was time to put it into practice, he spoke
more freely about it to some of his companions; a great many
people got to hear of it and through them it reached the ears
of the emperor. Alexios reacted in rather an original way:
he summoned the conspirators at appropriate intervals and
although he did not let on what he had heard, dropped hints
and offered some friendly advice. The more he got to know of
the conspiracy, the more liberal his treatment of them became;
it was in this way that he hoped to make progress. But the

Ethiopian cannot turn himself into a white man.[10] Nikephoros remained what he was and communicated infection to all with whom he came in contact, winning over some by oaths, others by promises.

He was not so much concerned with the ordinary soldiers, for they already favoured him to a man, but he devoted all his energies to canvassing the aristocracy, paying special attention to the senior officers and to leading members of the Senate. He had a mind sharper than a two-edged sword, but he was extremely fickle – except in one respect: he displayed uncompromising resolution in his quest for power. He was a charming conversationalist, pleasant in his social life, sometimes wearing a cloak of modesty to deceive, occasionally showing the spirit of a lion. He was physically strong and boasted that he rivalled the Giants; a broad-chested, blond man, a head taller than others of his generation. People who saw him playing polo on horseback, shooting an arrow or brandishing a spear at full gallop, stood open mouthed, almost rooted to the spot, thinking they were watching a genius never seen before. It was this, more than anything else, that won him the favour of the people. His advance to the coveted goal prospered so well that he even managed to win over the husband of the emperor's sister, Michael Taronites, who had been honoured with the title of *panhypersebastos*.

7. But we must return to the point at which we digressed and follow the chain of events. When he discovered Diogenes' conspiracy, the emperor reviewed the whole situation; he recalled his treatment of the brothers from the beginning of his reign, the kindness and care he had lavished on them for so many years. None of this had changed Nikephoros for the better. This made him despair. The emperor took stock of all that had happened, recalling Nikephoros' second attempt to get close to him after an initial failure, his repulse by Tatikios, the knowledge that he was sharpening his murderous weapon, eager to stain his hands with innocent blood, still lying in wait, watching by night for an opportunity to commit his crime and now openly pursuing it. He did not want to punish Diogenes in any way because he was very fond of him; he had in fact an

extraordinary affection for the man. But when he summed it all up, realizing the depths of the problem and knowing that imminent danger threatened his own life, his heart grew heavy with pain.

After weighing up all the evidence, he decided that he must be arrested. Nikephoros was hurrying on with preparations for his flight, and as he wished to take the road to Khristoupolis by night, in the evening he sent a messenger to Constantine *porphyrogennetos* to beg the loan of the racehorse given to him by the emperor. Constantine refused, saying that he could not let a gift of such value from the emperor go to someone else – and certainly not on the same day that he had received it from the emperor.

In the morning the emperor set out on the day's march and Diogenes followed him with the rest. God, who frustrates plans and reduces to nothing the designs of whole peoples, confounded this man too, for after debating in his mind the question of flight, he put it off from hour to hour. Such are the judgements of God. So Diogenes encamped near Serrai where the emperor also was. As usual he imagined that he was already a marked man and became fearful of the future. At this point Alexios called for his brother Adrian, the *megas domestikos*. It was the evening on which honour is paid to the memory of the great martyr Theodore.[11] Alexios again communicated to him the facts about Diogenes which Adrian actually already knew: he spoke of Diogenes' armed intrusion into the house, his repulse from the door, his eagerness to commit even now, if possible, the deed he had so long planned. Thus, he instructed the *domestikos* to invite Diogenes to his own tent, to persuade him with kind words and all manner of promises to reveal the whole plot; he was to guarantee him an amnesty, with full forgiveness for his crimes in the future, if only he would uncover everything, including the names of all his accomplices.

Adrian was full of despair, but carried out the order. He used threats, he made promises, he gave advice, but he failed completely to induce Diogenes to reveal even one part of his plans. What was the upshot? The *megas domestikos* grew angry and worried, having a good idea of the dangers which

Nikephoros was exposing himself to. Diogenes had in the
past chosen him as husband for the youngest of his stepsisters,
and because of this relationship he persisted, even entreating
him with tears, but there was no success whatever, despite
reminiscences of the past.

Adrian reminded him how one day the emperor was playing
polo in the riding school of the Great Palace when a barbarian
of mixed Armeno-Turkish descent approached him with a
sword hidden in his clothes. He saw that the emperor had been
left by the other players when he drew rein to give his panting
horse a rest; he fell on his knees and pretended to ask a favour.
The emperor immediately stopped his horse, turned round and
inquired what he wanted. The murderer – for that is what he
was, rather than a suppliant – thrust his hand under his clothes,
grasped his sword and tried to draw it from the scabbard, but
it would not budge. Again and again he tugged at it while
mouthing out a series of imaginary requests, then in desperation
threw himself to the ground and lay there begging for mercy.
The emperor turned his horse round towards him and asked
for what he was begging forgiveness. The barbarian then
showed him the sword still in its scabbard; at the same time he
beat his breast and in his distress cried in a loud voice: 'Now I
know that you are a true servant of God; now I have seen with
my own eyes the Almighty protecting you. For I got ready this
sword here to murder you; I brought it from home and here I
am, prepared to plunge it into your heart. Once, twice, then
once again I tugged at it, but it wouldn't yield to force.'

The emperor meanwhile stood there in the same position,
unafraid, as though he had not heard anything unusual, but all
the others ran up to him in haste, some to hear what was being
said, others in alarm. The more loyal men tried to tear the man
to pieces and would have done it too, if the emperor had not
prevented them by making signs and gestures and frequent
rebukes. And what came of this? The assassin was granted a full
pardon on the spot, and not only forgiveness, but magnificent
presents; but above all, he was allowed to enjoy his freedom.
At that many declared forcefully that the murderer should be
expelled from the capital, but to no avail. 'Unless the Lord

guards the city,' said the emperor, 'the sentinels keep vigil in vain. In future, then, we must pray to God and implore Him to grant us safety and protection.'

Some whispered that the attempt on his life by this man had been made with the support of Diogenes. The emperor himself refused altogether to listen to these rumours; in fact, he became more angry than ever, so tolerant of Nikephoros that he feigned ignorance until the dagger point was almost at his throat. So much for that incident. The *megas domestikos* reminded Diogenes of this, but made no impression on him, so he went to the emperor and told him of the man's stubbornness. Again and again he begged Diogenes to speak, said Adrian, but he was absolutely determined to say nothing.

8. The emperor called for Mouzakes and ordered him with other armed men to remove Diogenes from the *megas domestikos'* tent to his own and there detain him in safe custody, but without putting him in chains or ill-treating him in any way. The order was carried out without delay. All through the night Mouzakes pleaded with Diogenes and warned him, but his efforts failed; worse, he found the man's behaviour really offensive. In the end he became very angry and was driven to exceed the emperor's commission, for he thought fit to torture him. The process had hardly begun when Diogenes, incapable of resisting even the gentlest probing, declared that he would admit everything. He was at once set free from his chains and a secretary was called, pen in hand. (The man's name was Gregory Kamateros, recently appointed as *hypogrammateus* to the emperor.) Diogenes confessed all, including the attempted murder.

In the morning Mouzakes collected the written confession, as well as other documents found when he searched him. They were addressed to Diogenes by certain people and from them it was clear that the Empress Maria knew of the conspiracy, but strongly disapproved of the plan to murder Alexios; she was obviously trying hard to dissuade him, not merely from the crime, but from the very thought of it. Mouzakes conveyed these papers to the emperor, who read them privately and when he discovered the names of several suspects mentioned in them

– they were all persons of distinction – he found himself in a difficult situation. Diogenes had not cared much about the rank and file – to them he had long been a hero and they gazed on him with open-mouthed admiration – but he had been anxious to conciliate all leaders of the army and prominent civilians. The emperor decided that the references to the Empress Maria should remain secret, although he carefully examined them. He pretended to know nothing because of the faith he had in her and a bond of sympathy which he had felt even before his accession to the throne. A general rumour was spread that Constantine *porphyrogennetos*, her son, had informed the emperor of the plot, although this was not so, for the facts were supplied piecemeal by the accomplices themselves.

After Diogenes had been convicted, put in chains and exiled, those ringleaders who had not been arrested, knowing that they were under suspicion, showed every sign of alarm as they considered the next step. The emperor's intimates noted their perturbation, but seemed themselves to be in difficulties. The emperor, they knew, was in extreme peril; his supporters were now limited to a handful of men and his life was in danger.

The emperor was also seriously disturbed when he cast his mind over all these events – the numerous attempts by Diogenes to kill him, frustrated by Divine Power, and the fact that Diogenes had tried to assassinate him with his own hands. There was much to worry him. Time after time he altered his plans as some new idea occurred to him. He realized that both civilians and military had been thoroughly corrupted by the seductions of Diogenes; he was aware too that his own forces were inadequate to guard so many prisoners; he was certainly unwilling to mutilate a great host of people. In the end he banished Diogenes and Kekaumenos Katakalon, the principal conspirators, to Kaisaropolis, to be kept in chains there and under guard. No further punishment was contemplated, although everyone advised him to have them mutilated. (Alexios would not agree, for he had a great love for Diogenes, and was still concerned as ever for his welfare.) Michael Taronites, his sister's husband, was also sent into exile and . . . Their property was confiscated. As for the others, he judged the safe course would be not to

examine them at all, but rather to win them over by a show
of mercy. In the evening therefore each of the exiles reached
the place allotted to them. Diogenes was to go to Kaisaropolis;
of the rest, none left their own homes: all remained where
they were.

9. In the midst of this crisis the emperor decided to call a
general meeting for the next day and effect his plan. All his
relatives, by blood or marriage, were present – those, that is,
who were really devoted to him – and all the family servants.
They were tough men, quick to gauge the outcome, with enough
shrewdness to achieve in the shortest possible time the most
profitable result. They were afraid that when the crowd
assembled on the following day some men might rush against
the emperor and cut him to pieces on the throne, for people
like this often carried daggers under their clothes, just like the
individual who approached him in the guise of a suppliant
when he was playing polo. (There was only one way to prevent this – to dash the people's hopes, which were centred on
Diogenes, by spreading a rumour that he had been secretly
blinded.) Men were collected and sent to quietly spread this
rumour everywhere, though Alexios had nothing like this in
mind. However bare the rumour was at the time, it succeeded
in its purpose, as this history will demonstrate below.

When the sun peeped over the horizon and leapt into the
sky in glory, all those members of the imperial retinue not infected with Diogenes' pollution, as well as the soldiers who had
long served as the emperor's bodyguard, led the procession to
his tent; some wore swords, others carried spears, others had
heavy iron axes on their shoulders. At some distance from
the throne they arranged themselves in a crescent-shaped
formation, thereby surrounding the emperor. They were all
moved by anger and if their swords were not ready to go to
work, their souls certainly were. Near the throne on either side
stood the emperor's relatives, and to right and left were
grouped the armour-bearers. The emperor, looking formidable,
took his seat, dressed rather as a soldier than an emperor.
Because he was not a tall man, he did not tower above the rest.
Nevertheless it was an impressive sight, for gold overlaid his

throne and there was gold above his head. He was frowning and the ordeal had brought an unusual tinge of red to his cheeks; his eyes, fixed in concentration, gave a hint of the troubles that beset him.

Everybody hurried to the tent, all in a state of alarm and almost on the point of collapse through fear, some pricked by an evil conscience more effectively than by any sharp weapon, others dreading unwarranted suspicion. Not a sound was heard from any of them as they stood with beating hearts, their eyes fixed on the officer in charge by the tent's door – a man who was articulate and a powerful man of action – his name was Tatikios. With a glance the emperor signalled to him to admit those outside. He immediately did so. Frightened, they came in with eyes averted, walking slowly. When they had been marshalled in lines, they waited anxiously, each fearful lest his own last moment was at hand.

The emperor himself was not altogether confident (humanly speaking, for he had committed his fate entirely to God). He was apprehensive lest in so disparate a gathering there might be some who planned another horrible and unforeseen crime. However, composing himself and at last ready for the challenge, he began his address to them. (They meanwhile were as silent as fish, as if their tongues had been cut out.) 'You know,' he said, 'that Diogenes has never suffered ill at my hands. It was not I who deprived his father of this empire, but someone else entirely. Nor have I been the cause of evil or pain of any sort so far as he is concerned. Moreover, when, by the will of God alone, I became ruler of the empire not only did I give my protection equally to him and his brother Leo, but I loved them and treated them as my own children. Every time that I caught Nikephoros plotting against me I forgave him. Even though he never mended his ways, I bore with him and concealed most of his offences, in the knowledge that they would have met with widespread contempt. Yet none of my favours has succeeded in altering his perfidy. Indeed, by way of gratitude he sentenced me to death.'

At these words they all shouted that they would not wish to see anyone else in his place on the imperial throne; most of them did not mean it, but they flattered, hoping thereby to escape the immediate danger. The emperor seized on the opportunity and proclaimed a general amnesty for the majority of them, since those responsible for the plot had been condemned to banishment. Thereupon a great clamour arose, such as none of those present there had ever heard before and have never heard since, at least to judge from those who were there; some praised the emperor and marvelled at his kindness and forbearance, while others abused the exiles, insisting that they should be punished by death. Such is the way of men – today they cheer, escort, treat with honour, but once they see the fortunes of life reversed, they act in the opposite manner, without a blush.

The emperor silenced them with a gesture and continued. 'There is no need for commotion, nor must you confuse the issue. As far as I am concerned, as I said, I have granted a general amnesty, and I shall treat you just as I did before.' While he was pardoning them, certain men who had made the infamous decision sent emissaries, without the emperor's knowledge, to blind Diogenes. The same decision was made in respect of Kekaumenos Katakalon, because he had conspired alongside him. It was the day on which the memory of the Great Apostles[12] is celebrated. These events have been the subject of controversy ever since. Whether the emperor was informed of the plan by them and then gave his consent, or was himself the author of the whole idea, God alone knows. For my own part, I have been unable so far to discover anything for certain.

10. Such were the troubles which befell the emperor because of Diogenes. He was rescued from instant peril contrary to all expectations by the invincible hand of the Lord on High. Despite all this, he did not lose his nerve. Instead, he drove straight for Dalmatia.[13] When Bolkan learnt of the emperor's arrival at Lipenion and saw with his own eyes that he had occupied it, and was unable to contemplate the Roman battle lines, their famous formation and their military equipment, he dispatched envoys without delay to offer terms of peace, promising at the same time to deliver the hostages he had agreed to hand over before, and to cease hostilities in the future. The

emperor gladly accepted the proposal, for he was weary and
loathed civil war. The men may have been Dalmatians, but they
were still Christians. Soon Bolkan presented himself confidently
before the emperor, accompanied by his kinsmen and the leading
župans. He promptly handed over his own nephews Uresis
and Stephen Bolkan[14] as hostages with others, bringing the total
to twenty. The truth is, of course, that he could not make any
other arrangements for the future. Thus the emperor had settled
by peaceful means all that is normally accomplished by war
and strife. He returned to Constantinople.

In spite of everything he still cared much for Diogenes. Often
he was seen in tears and heard sighing deeply because of the
young man's misfortunes. He displayed great friendship for
him and in his anxiety to relieve Diogenes' sufferings installed
him again in most of his confiscated property. Frantic with
pain and reluctant to live in the great city, Diogenes found
satisfaction on his own estates, devoting all his energies to the
study of ancient literature, read to him by others. Deprived of
his own sight, he relied on the eyes of others, who would read
to him. He was a man of such extraordinary ability that, blinded
though he was, he could readily comprehend things which
sighted people found hard to understand. Later he covered the
whole syllabus of education and even studied the famous science of geometry, an extraordinary thing really, getting a philosopher he had met to prepare figures in relief. By touching
these with his hands he acquired knowledge of all the geometri-
cal theorems and figures. Thus he rivalled Didymos,[15] who by
sheer intellectual power and despite his blindness attained the
highest standards in the arts of geometry and music; unfortunately after this achievement Didymos was driven into an
absurd heresy, his mind darkened by conceit as his eyes were
by disease. Everyone who hears this about Diogenes is astonished, but I myself have seen the man and marvelled at him as
he talked about these things. As I too am not altogether
untrained in such matters, I recognized in him an accurate
understanding of the theorems.

Yet, busied as he was with literary studies, he would not
forget his old antipathy, but to the end maintained that smoul-

dering lust for power. However, he confided his secret once more to certain individuals, one of whom went to the emperor and told of his plans. Diogenes was summoned and questioned about the plot and his accomplices. He immediately confessed everything and was immediately forgiven.[16]

BOOK X

1. Not long after the dogmas of Italos had been condemned, the infamous Neilos[1] appeared, descending on the Church like some evil flood, to the great consternation of all. Many were swept away in the currents of his errors. He was a man with a particular skill of dissimulating and of seeming virtuous. I do not know where he sprang from, but for a time he frequented the capital, living in obscurity alone, no doubt, with God and himself. All his time was devoted to the study of the Holy Scriptures. He had never been initiated into Hellenic culture, nor had he any tutor to give him even an elementary insight into the deeper meaning of the divine texts. The result was that he examined the works of the Saints, but as he was completely devoid of a training in logic, his interpretation of Scripture was extremely erratic.

However, he did attract a not inconsiderable band of adherents and wormed his way into illustrious households as a self-appointed teacher, partly because of his own apparent virtue and austere way of life, partly maybe because of the knowledge with which he was supposed to be secretly endowed. Neilos' ignorance led him to misapprehend the union of the human and divine natures in the one Person of Christ as taught in our doctrine. He could not clearly understand the meaning of 'union', nor had he any idea at all of the meaning of 'person', nor had he learnt from holy men how the flesh assumed by Our Lord was made divine. Thus he erred far from the truth and in his delusion supposed that His flesh changed its nature and thus became divine.

The heresy did not escape the emperor's notice, and when he

realized what was going on he lost no time in applying a remedy. The man was called into his presence; his boldness and ignorance were severely censured. On several points he was refuted and Alexios taught him clearly the meaning of the union of divine and human in the Person of the Word; he set before him the interpretation of the two natures, how they were united as one indivisible Person and how the human flesh assumed by Christ was made divine by the grace from above. But Neilos clung rigidly to his own false teaching and was quite prepared to undergo any ill-treatment – torture, imprisonment, mutilation – rather than give up his doctrine that the human flesh altered its nature.

At that time there were in the capital many Armenians, for whom Neilos' doctrines acted as a spur to their own further impieties, since he held frequent conferences with the notorious Arsakes and Tigranes.[2] And what came of all this? The emperor understood that this evil was corrupting many souls; that Neilos and the Armenians were equally involved, proclaiming openly on all occasions that the human part of Christ had been deified in nature; that the pronouncements of the holy fathers on this subject were being put aside and that the doctrine of the two natures united in one Person was being almost unrecognized. So he decided to counteract the violent course of the heresy. The leading members of the Church were brought together with the idea of holding a public synod to debate the matter.

At this meeting the full complement of bishops was present, together with the Patriarch Nicholas. Neilos, accompanied by the Armenians, appeared before them and his doctrines were revealed to all those assembled. In a clear voice he expounded and vigorously defended them at greater length than before. With what result? In the end the synod, in order to save many souls from this corrupt teaching, imposed on Neilos eternal anathema and proclaimed categorically on the issue of the union of the two natures according to the tradition of the Saints.

Afterwards, or to be more exact, about the same time, Blakhernites was also condemned[3] for holding irreverent views contrary to Church teaching, even though he was himself an ordained priest. He had in fact had dealings with the Enthusiasts and, after becoming infected with their impurity, was deceiving many, undermining great houses in the capital and transmitting his evil dogma. On several occasions he was urgently summoned by the emperor, who personally instructed him, but since he absolutely refused to abandon his particular brand of heresy, he too was brought before the Church. The bishops examined his case in more detail, and when they recognized the incorrigibility of the man, eternal anathema was put on him and his teachings also.

2. In this way the emperor like a good helmsman guided his craft safely through constant battering of the waves. Scarcely had he cleansed himself of the thick layers of brine and set in good order the affairs of Church and State than he was called upon to embark on fresh seas of tribulation. Indeed, there was a never-ending succession of woes – an ocean of trouble, as it were – so that he was allowed no chance to breathe nor even to rest his eyes. The briefest outline of a few of his deeds in this crisis might well be compared to a tiny drop from the whole Adriatic Sea, for he braved all tempests, all storms, till he brought the ship of state to a calm anchorage with a following breeze. Could the fine voice of Demosthenes, Polemo's[4] impassioned style or all the Muses of Homer do justice to his exploits? I myself would say that neither Plato himself, nor the whole of the Stoa, nor the Academy acting in unison would have proved equal to the task of describing the emperor's spirit, for before the storms had time to die down and the tempests had done their worst, before the convoluted wars had ended, he was faced with another storm as bad as any before it.

A man, not a member of the aristocracy, but a person of humble origin, an ordinary soldier, announced that he was the son of the Emperor Diogenes – although that son had been killed long ago when Isaac Komnenos, the emperor's own brother, fought against the Turks by Antioch. (Anyone wishing to know the details of how he met his death can find these in the writings of the illustrious *kaisar*.) Many people tried to gag him, but their efforts came to nothing. This individual had come from the east, penniless and clothed in skins, a villain

through and through and a shifty one at that, who went around
Constantinople, street by street and quarter by quarter, boasting about himself and saying that he was the famous Leo, son
of the former emperor Diogenes who was reported to have died
of an arrow wound[5] at Antioch. At any rate the fellow brought
Leo to life again and boldly adopted his name. It was obvious
that his aim was imperial power. What is more, he succeeded
in winning over the light-headed with this talk. Such then was
the new danger to add to the emperor's difficulties. Fortune,
one might say, was composing a new tragic play on this ill-
starred fellow for the emperor's viewing. Just as gourmets, I
understand, after eating their fill have honey cakes brought on
for dessert, so now it was the destiny of the Roman people,
after triumphing over many evils and being sated with disaster,
to tantalize their emperor with fake pretenders to the throne.

All these rumours were treated with contempt by the
emperor, but when this charlatan persisted in his folly, losing
no opportunity to spread these stories in every street and on
every highway in the city, the matter came to the ears of Theodora, the emperor's sister, who was the widow of Diogenes'
murdered son. This rubbish was more than she could bear; she
was very annoyed. After her husband's death she had chosen
to live as a nun, following a regimen of the strictest self-denial
and total dedication to God. As the fool still would not hold
his tongue after a second and third warning, the emperor sent
him off to Kherson and ordered that he be imprisoned. While
he was there the pretender climbed to the ramparts during the
night and leaning over them had talks with the Cumans who
regularly visited the place to trade with the locals and to pur-
chase necessities. They exchanged pledges with him and one
night he let himself down from the wall by ropes.

The Cumans took him with them to their own country and
he lived with them there for a fairly long time, gaining their
confidence to the extent that they soon addressed him as
emperor. The Cumans, who were longing to gorge themselves
on human blood and human flesh and were more than ready
to amass booty from our territories, found that they had in him
a Patroklos-excuse; they decided to march in full force against

the Roman Empire, on the pretext of re-establishing him on the ancestral throne. This plan had been brewing for some time; the emperor, however, was not unaware of it. Accordingly he armed his troops as best he could and made preparations for war. As I have said before, the mountain passes, known commonly as *kleisourai*, had already been fortified. Some time later, when Alexios discovered ·that the Cumans had occupied Paristrion with the pretender, he assembled the leading officers of the army, together with his own relatives by blood or marriage, and debated the advisability of taking the initiative against them. They opposed the idea unanimously.

Alexios, though, felt unable to trust his own judgement and was unwilling to rely on his own unaided calculations. So he referred the whole matter to God and asked Him to decide. All the churchmen and soldiers were summoned to an evening meeting in the Great Church. The emperor himself attended and so did the Patriarch Nicholas, who had succeeded to the patriarchal throne in the course of the seventh indiction in the year 6592,[6] after the abdication of Eustratios Garidas. The emperor wrote a question out on two tablets: should he set out to attack the Cumans; or not. They were then sealed and the patriarch was commanded to place them on the Holy Table. After hymns had been sung all through the night, Nicholas went to the altar, picked up one of the papers and brought it out. In the presence of the whole company he broke it open and read aloud what was written on it. The emperor accepted the decision as though it derived from some divine oracle. All his energies were now concentrated on the expedition, with the army being summoned by letters from all parts of the empire.

When everything was ready he set out to fight the Cumans.[7] At Ankhialos, which he had reached with all his forces, he sent for his brother-in-law, the *Kaisar* Nikephoros Melissenos, and George Palaiologos, and his nephew John Taronites. They were dispatched to Berroia, with instructions to keep watch there and make sure that not only the town but also the neighbouring districts were secure. He then divided his forces, appointing Dabatenos, George Euphorbenos and Constantine Houmperto-poulos[8] as commanders of separate detachments, which were to protect the passes through the Zygos mountains. Alexios went on to Khortarea, itself a pass in that area, and inspected the whole range to see if all his previous orders had been faithfully carried out by the officers entrusted with the task; where the fortifications were half-finished or incomplete, he insisted that they should put things right, so that the Cumans would not find an easy passage. When all precautions had been taken, he returned from Khortarea and pitched camp by what is known as the Holy Lake near Ankhialos. During the night a certain Poudilos, one of the leading Vlakhs,[9] came and reported that the Cumans were crossing the Danube. The emperor thought it essential to hold a council of war with the more important of his kinsmen and the officers. At daybreak, therefore, they were sent for. Since all agreed that Ankhialos must be occupied, he personally set out for the town after dispatching Kantakouzenos and Tatikios with some mercenaries, Skaliarios Elkhanes and other elite troops, to a place called Therma. They were to secure the safety of that district. He himself made for Ankhialos.

At this point, however, information was received that the Cumans were making for Adrianoupolis. Alexios sent for all the leading citizens. Prominent among them were Katakalon surnamed Tarkhaneiotes and Nikephoros, son of the Bryennios who had once aspired to the throne and who had been blinded in his attempt to gain it. They were ordered to guard the citadel with great determination; if the Cumans did come, they must be engaged in battle with no half-hearted measures; he advised them to take careful aim, shoot their arrows at long range and keep the gates closed as far as possible. Many rewards were promised if these instructions were properly carried out. Bryennios and his companions returned to Adrianoupolis full of confidence. Written orders were also sent to Constantine Euphorbenos Katakalon. He was to take Monastras (a barbarian half-caste with considerable fighting experience) and Michael Anemas, together with the forces under their command, and when they heard that the Cumans had passed through the defiles they were to follow them closely and to attack them when they least expected it.

3. As it happened the Cumans were shown the way through the passes by the Vlakhs and so crossed the Zygos mountains with ease. As soon as they approached Goloe the inhabitants threw into chains the commander of the garrison and handed him over to the Cumans, whom they welcomed with cries of joy. But Constantine Katakalon, with the emperor's instructions still fresh in his mind, fell in with a party of Cumans who were on a foraging raid and after launching a vigorous attack took a hundred prisoners or so. He was honoured on the spot by the emperor in person with the title of *nobellisimos*. The people of the neighbouring towns, Diampolis and the rest, however, saw the Cumans had gained possession of Goloe; they therefore capitulated, welcomed them with pleasure, surrendered and what is more, acclaimed pseudo-Diogenes. Once control of all these places was assured, the imposter marched with the entire barbarian army on Ankhialos, intending to make an immediate assault on the fortifications.

The emperor was inside the town. A lifelong experience of war told him that the Cumans would be deterred by the natural strength of the town's position, which made the walls even more impregnable. He divided his forces, opened the gates of the citadel and drew up his companies in close formation outside the walls. One part of the Roman army hurled itself on the extremity of the Cuman line with terrible cries, routed them and pursued them all the way to the sea. The emperor saw what had happened, but knowing that his forces were hopelessly outnumbered and quite unable to withstand the enemy, he gave orders that the serried ranks should remain absolutely unbroken and stay inintact. The Cumans took up position in line opposite the Roman forces, but they too made no move to attack. For three days from early morning to evening this arrangement was repeated; however eager the enemy were for battle, they feared the unfavourable terrain and were put off because no Roman broke ranks to charge out against them.

The fortress of Ankhialos was situated thus: on the right lay the Black Sea; on the left rough ground, impassable and overgrown with vines, affording no opportunity for cavalry manoeuvres. How did this go on? In view of the emperor's

stubbornness, the barbarians abandoned their plans in desperation and took the road to Adrianoupolis. The pretender
had deceived them in this matter, telling them: 'The moment
Nikephoros Bryennios finds out that I have come to
Adrianoupolis, he will open the gates of the town and receive
me with delight. He will give me money and show every sign
of friendship. He used to look on my father as a brother, though
he was not actually related by birth. Yet he chose to regard him
as such. And when the citadel is handed over to us, we shall
resume our march to the capital.' He used to call Bryennios his
uncle. It was untrue, but there was some foundation for it in
fact: the former emperor Romanos Diogenes had recognized
Bryennios' quite outstanding judgement; he knew with good
reason that he was straightforward and absolutely sincere in
word and deed. It was his desire therefore to adopt Bryennios
as his own brother. Both parties were willing and the adoption
was confirmed. These facts are undisputed and common knowledge, but the impostor had the supreme effrontery to address
Bryennios as his real uncle.

So much for the schemes of the imposter. The Cumans, like
all barbarians, being fickle and inconsistent by nature, were
persuaded by his arguments and reached Adrianoupolis. They
set up camp outside the town. For forty-eight days there were
daily clashes (as the young men, eager for action, regularly went
out to fight the barbarians). During this time the pretender, at
the foot of the wall, asked to see Bryennios. The latter leant
over the rampart and declared that as far as he could judge
from the man's voice he was not the son of Romanos Diogenes,
who, as I have said, was his adopted brother – a practice which
was not uncommon; and Diogenes' real son had undoubtedly
been killed at Antioch. With these words he rejected the usurper
with ignominy.

However, as time went on provisions in the town began to fail
and help had to be requested from the emperor through a letter
sent to him. He immediately ordered Constantine Euphorbenos
to take a strong detachment of counts who were under his
command and make his way by night into Adrianoupolis from
the side of Kalathades. Katakalon was soon on the road to

Orestias, confidently expecting that he would escape detection by the Cumans. But he was wrong; they saw him and charged on horseback in overwhelming numbers, driving him back and setting off in hot pursuit. His son Nikephoros – who afterwards became my brother-in-law when he married my younger sister the *Porphyrogennetos* Maria – seized a long spear, wheeled round and met his Scythian pursuer face-to-face. He struck him in the chest and the man fell dead on the spot. Nikephoros was an expert with the lance and knew how to protect himself with a shield. On horseback he gave the impression that he was not a Roman at all, but a native of Normandy. The young man was certainly remarkable for his horsemanship – a natural genius, in fact. Nikephoros was extremely devout, and in dealings with his fellow men was courteous and pleasant.

Before forty-eight days had passed, Nikephoros Bryennios (who was invested with supreme command of Adrianoupolis) ordered the gates to be thrown open suddenly and fighting men went out to do battle with the enemy. It was a bitter conflict and although many Romans fell in the struggle, risking their lives with no thought for their own safety, at least they killed more of the Cumans. Marianos Maurokatakalon caught sight of Togortak (the commander-in-chief of the Cuman army), and armed with a long spear charged him at full gallop. He would almost undoubtedly have killed him, had not his Cuman body-guard rescued him in time – nearly killing Marianos in the process. This Marianos was only a youth, who had recently taken his place among the young men, but he often made sorties from the gates of the town and every time wounded or killed some enemy and returned in triumph. He was a really fine soldier, worthily upholding the ancestral reputation for bravery, the most courageous member of a very courageous family. Full of rage at his narrow escape from death, he now made his way towards pseudo-Diogenes, who was standing on the far bank of the river just where Marianos had fought with the barbarians. Seeing him clothed in purple, with the insignia of an emperor but deserted by his bodyguard, Marianos raised his whip and beat him mercilessly about the head, at the same time calling him a false emperor.

4. Reports of Cuman obstinacy before Adrianoupolis and the frequent battles there convinced the emperor that he must leave Ankhialos and go to help in person. The senior officers and leading citizens were summoned to a council of war, which was interrupted by a man called Alakaseus. 'It so happens,' he said, 'that my father was friendly in the old days with the imposter's father. If I go there, I can take advantage of this. I will get him inside one of the fortresses and detain him.' He was asked how he could pull this off; he suggested to the emperor that he would imitate the trick of Zopyros in Cyrus' reign:[10] he would disfigure himself, shave off his hair and beard, and then present himself to pseudo-Diogenes as a victim of the emperor's punishment.

He kept his word too, for no sooner was the plan approved by the emperor than he shaved himself completely, maltreated his body and went off to the pretender. Among other things, he reminded him of their old friendship, adding these words: 'I have endured many outrages at the hands of the Emperor Alexios. That is why I have come to you now, trusting in the ancient friendship between my father and Your Majesty, to help you in your enterprise.' He thought that flattery was a more effective way of winning him over. In order to elaborate on Alakaseus' activities, I should remark here that he took with him a safe-conduct document from the Emperor Alexios and a letter for the military governor of a stronghold called Poutza which read as follows: 'Pay attention to the bearer of this note and do promptly whatever he proposes.' (The emperor had guessed correctly that the Cumans would make for this place when they left Adrianoupolis.) When these arrangements had been completed, Alakaseus appeared, just as we have said, before the imposter. 'It is because of you,' he said, 'that I have suffered so terribly. Because of you I have been insulted and thrown into chains. Because of you I was imprisoned for many days – in fact, ever since you crossed the Roman frontiers – for on account of my father's friendship for you I was suspected by the emperor. I escaped and now I have fled to you, my lord, after freeing myself from my bonds. I bring you advice that will be profitable.'

The man received him warmly and asked what steps he should take to achieve his aim. 'You see this fortress of Poutza,' answered Alakaseus, 'and this broad plain. There is enough pasture to feed your horses here for as long as you choose to rest yourself and your army. Well, for the time being we should go no further than this. Stay here for a little while, seize the fortress and rest. Meanwhile the Cumans can go out to forage and afterwards we can set out for Constantinople. If you agree I will see the garrison commander, who has been devoted to me for a very long time, and I will arrange for him to surrender the place to you without bloodshed.'

The idea pleased Diogenes. So, during the night, Alakaseus tied his letter to an arrow and fired it into the citadel. The governor read it privately and prepared to hand over the place. Early next morning Alakaseus approached the first of the gates. He pretended to chat with the governor, having formerly arranged a signal with Diogenes; when he saw it he was to march straight into the fort. After Alakaseus had carried on his feigned conversation for a reasonable time, he gave the signal. Diogenes thereupon took with him a few soldiers and boldly entered the gates. The inhabitants received him with delight and the commander of Poutza invited him to take a bath. On the advice of Alakaseus he immediately accepted the invitation. Later, a magnificent banquet was made ready for him and the Cumans who formed part of his entourage. They all feasted together to their hearts' content and after drinking their fill of wine, gulping it down from full wineskins, they lay down and snored. Alakaseus, the commander and some others then went round, took away their horses and arms, left Diogenes himself where he was, snoring away, but killed his attendants and summarily hurled them into trenches which served as natural graves.

Meanwhile Katakalon, who was following the Cuman army as the emperor had ordered, saw that the pretender had gone into the fort and saw too that the Cumans had dispersed to look for plunder. He therefore left for a place nearby and pitched his camp. With Cumans scattered all over the countryside, Alakaseus dared not report his capture to the emperor, but took Diogenes off with him and drove straight for Tzouroulos on his way to the capital. Nevertheless, the emperor's mother, acting as regent in the palace, heard about it and sent the *droungarios* of the fleet, the eunuch Eustathios Kymineianos, in great haste to arrest the prisoner and bring him to Constantinople. The *droungarios* had a Turk called Kamyres with him to whom he entrusted the task of blinding the prisoner.

As for the emperor, he was still waiting at Ankhialos, but hearing that Cumans were roaming all over the neighbouring districts in search of booty he went on to Little Nicaea. There he was informed that Kitzes, one of the Cuman leaders, with a force of 12,000 men engaged in general pillaging had collected all his booty and occupied the ridge of Taurokomos. Alexios thereupon led his own forces down to the bank of the river which flows across the plain below it, a place covered with germander bushes and young trees. He halted his men there. A strong contingent of expert Turkish archers was sent to join battle with the Cumans and entice them on to level ground by making charges on horseback. In fact, the Cumans took the initiative and pursued them hotly as far as the main host of the Roman army. At this point they reined in their horses a bit, re-formed their ranks and made ready for an assault.

The emperor spied a Cuman horseman arrogantly leap ahead of his own line, ride along their ranks and apparently all but challenge anyone to come and fight him. The Romans on the right and left did nothing, but the emperor impatiently galloped out in full view of all and struck the first blow. He used his spear, then drove his sword right through the Cuman's chest and knocked him down from his horse. Thus on this occasion he showed himself more of a soldier than a general. Anyway the deed at once put great heart into the Romans and induced a corresponding dread in the Scythians,[11] so that moving towards them like a tower of strength, he broke the army up; they scattered in all directions as the line was torn apart and fled pell-mell. In the battle the Cumans lost some 7,000 men; another 3,000 were taken into captivity.

Their entire booty was seized by the Romans, who were not

allowed to share it out among themselves in the normal manner; it had only recently been stolen from the natives of the district and had to be restored to them. The news of this imperial decree spread like wildfire throughout all the countryside and individuals who had been robbed came to the camp, recognized their possessions and took them away. Beating their breasts and raising their hands in supplication to heaven they prayed for the emperor's prosperity; the loud cries of men and women alike might well have been heard on the moon itself.

So ended this episode. As for the emperor, he joyfully returned with his men to Little Nicaea and after staying there for a couple of days, on the third left for Adrianoupolis, where he remained for some time in the house of Silvester. It was at this moment that every single one of the Cuman leaders separated from the rest of their army and came to the emperor, really hoping to deceive him, but pretending to be deserters anxious for an immediate peace settlement. Their idea was that negotiations would waste time; their fellow-countrymen would thus get a flying start on their march. So having waited three days, on the night of the third they set out for home.

As soon as he realized he had been deceived, Alexios sent fast couriers to warn the officers on guard at the paths over the Zygos mountains: they were to be constantly alert for an opportunity to intercept them; there must be no relaxation. But once news came that the whole Cuman army was already well on its way, the emperor gathered all available Romans, and rushed to a place called Skoutarion, eighteen stades from Adrianoupolis; the next day he arrived at Agathonike. There Alexios discovered that the enemy were still in the Abrilebo district (not very far from both these places). Accordingly he went in that direction and from a long way off he saw innumerable campfires which they had lit. After reconnoitring the position he called for Nicholas Maurokatakalon and other senior officers, and debated with them about what he should do. It was decided to summon the leaders of the mercenaries, Ouzas (a Sarmatian), Karatzas, who was a Scythian, and the half-caste Monastras. They were instructed to have fifteen or more watchfires lit at every tent so that when the Cumans saw them they would believe the Roman army was enormous; they would then become panic-stricken and lose heart for any future attack. The orders were carried out and the Cumans were duly frightened. Early next morning the emperor armed himself and began the battle with an assault. Both sides fought well, but eventually the Cumans turned away. The emperor therefore divided the army: the light-armed were sent on ahead to pursue the enemy, while he himself also took up the chase with gusto. He caught up with them near the Sidera pass. He massacred a great many, but captured most of them alive.

The Roman vanguard returned with all of the booty that had been taken by the Cumans. The emperor spent the whole of that night on the mountain ridge of the Sidera while a violent storm raged, but he reached Goloe once it was light. He stayed there for a day and a night in order to honour all those who had distinguished themselves in the battle; they were handsomely rewarded. Now that the plan had been successfully accomplished, he cheerfully dismissed them all to their respective homes, and two days and nights later he was back in the palace.

5. After a brief rest from his many labours, the emperor discovered that the Turks were engaged in general plunder, overrunning the interior of Bithynia. At the same time, the situation in the west claimed his attention, but he was more concerned with the former problem (since the trouble there was more urgent). To deal with it he conceived a project of really major importance, worthy of his genius: the plan was to protect Bithynia against Turkish incursions with a canal. It is worthwhile to describe how it was done.

The River Sangaris and the coastline that runs to the village of Khele and which extends north enclose a considerable tract of land. Because there was no one to oppose them the Ishmaelites, who have been troublesome neighbours to us for a long time, easily ravaged it. They made their incursions through the lands of the Maryandenoi[12] and of those who live by the Sangaris river. Nikomedia in particular suffered from their attacks after they had crossed the river. Naturally the emperor wished to check such raids and prevent the devastation; above all he wanted to ensure the safety of Nikomedia. South of Lake

Baane he noticed a very long trench and when he followed its course to the end he concluded from its position and shape that the excavation was not accidental, nor was it the result of some natural process, but the deliberate work of some human hand. After much investigation he was told by some persons that it was Anastasios Dikouros[13] who had been responsible for this work. What his purpose had been they could not say. To Alexios anyhow it seemed clear that Anastasios had wanted to divert water from the lake into this artificial gully. Once he had the same idea he ordered the trench to be dug to a great depth.

Fearing that at the point where lake and canal met it might be possible to get across, he built an extremely strong fort there, completely secure and impregnable, not only because of the water, but also because of the height and thickness of its walls – for which reason it was called the Iron Tower. Even today it constitutes a town in front of a town, an outlying bastion to protect a wall. The emperor himself directed its construction from early morning till evening, despite the soaring temperatures caused by the sun passing the summer solstice. He had to endure both scorching heat and the dust. Enormous sums of money were spent to ensure that the walls should be really strong and impregnable. He paid generous wages to the men who dragged the stones, one by one, even if fifty or a hundred workers were involved at a time. The money attracted not casual labourers, but all the soldiers and their servants, natives and foreigners alike; they were glad to move stones for such liberal pay under the direction of the emperor in person. To them he seemed like a prize-giver at an athletic competition. He made skilful use of the crowds who flocked to help, and the transport of these huge blocks of stone was made easier. It was typical of Alexios: he thought deeply about a project and then worked with tremendous energy to execute it properly.

Such were the events of the emperor's reign up to the ... indiction of the ... year.[14] He had no time to relax before he heard a rumour that countless Frankish armies were approaching. He dreaded their arrival, knowing as he did their uncontrollable passion, their erratic character and their unpredictability, not to mention the other characteristics of the Kelt,

with their inevitable consequences: their greed for money, for
example, which always led them, it seemed, to break their own
agreements without scruple. He had consistently heard this said
of them and it was abundantly justified. So far from despairing,
however, he made every effort to prepare for battle if need
arose. What actually happened was more far-reaching and terrible than rumours suggested, for the whole of the west and the
entire people living between the Adriatic and the Straits of
Gibraltar migrated in a body to Asia, marching from one end
of Europe to another with their whole households in tow. The
reason for this mass movement is the following.

A Kelt, by the name of Peter and known too as Koukoupetros,[15] left to worship at the Holy Sepulchre and after suffering much ill-treatment at the hands of the Turks and Saracens
who were plundering the whole of Asia, returned home with
great difficulty. Unable to admit defeat, he wanted to make a
second attempt by the same route, but realizing the folly of
trying to do this alone for fear that even worse things might
happen to him, he worked out a clever scheme. He decided to
preach in all the Latin countries. 'A divine voice,' he said, 'has
commanded me to proclaim to all the counts in France that all
should depart from their homes, set out to worship at the Holy
Sepulchre, and with all their soul and might, strive to liberate
Jerusalem from the hands of the Agarenes.'

He proved very successful. It was as if he had inspired every
heart with some divine command. Kelts assembled from all
parts, one after another, with arms and horses and all the
other equipment for war. Full of enthusiasm and ardour they
thronged every highway, and with these warriors came a host of
civilians, outnumbering the sand of the seashore or the stars of
heaven, carrying palms and bearing crosses on their shoulders.
There were women and children, too, who had left their own
countries. Like tributaries joining a river from all directions they
streamed towards us in full force, mostly through Dacia.

The arrival of this mighty host was preceded by locusts,
which abstained from the wheat but completely ravaged the
vines. The prophets at the time interpreted this as a sign that
the Keltic army would refrain from interfering in the affairs

of Christians but bring dreadful affliction on the barbarian
Ishmaelites, who are slaves to drunkenness, wine and Dionysos.
The Ishmaelites are indeed dominated by Dionysos and Eros;
they indulge readily in every kind of sexual licence, and if they
are circumcised in the flesh they are certainly not so in their
passions. In fact, the Ishmaelites are nothing more than slaves
– trebly slaves – of the vices of Aphrodite. Hence they revere
and worship Astarte and Ashtaroth, and in their land the figure
of the moon and the golden image of Khobar[16] are considered
of major importance. Corn (because it is not heady and at the
same time is very nourishing) is thought of as the symbol of
Christianity. In the light of this the diviners interpreted the
references to vines and wheat.

So much for the predictions. The incidents of the barbarians'
advance followed in the order I have given and there was something strange about it, which intelligent people at least would
notice. The multitudes did not arrive at the same time, nor even
by the same route (how could they cross the Straits of Lombardy
simultaneously after setting out from different countries in such
great numbers?). There was a first group, and then a second,
followed by another after that, until all had made the crossing,
and then they began their march across the mainland. Each
army, as I have said, was preceded by a plague of locusts, so
that everyone, having observed the phenomenon several
times, came to recognize locusts as the forerunners of Frankish
battalions.

They had already begun to cross the Straits of Lombardy in
small groups when the emperor summoned certain leaders of
the Roman forces and sent them to the area round Dyrrakhion
and Avlona, with instructions to receive the voyagers kindly
and to supply them abundantly with provisions gathered from
all over along their route; they were then to watch them carefully and shadow their movements, so that if they saw them
making raids or running off to plunder the neighbouring districts, they could check them by light skirmishes. These officers
were accompanied by interpreters who understood the Latin
language; their duty was to quell any incipient trouble that
might arise.

I would like here to give a clearer and more detailed account of the matter. According to widespread rumours, the first to sell his land and set out on the road to Jerusalem was Godfrey.[17] He was a very rich man, extremely proud of his noble birth, his own courage and the glory of his family – every Kelt is anxious to outdo his peers. The upheaval that ensued as both men and women took to the road was unprecedented within living memory. The simpler folk were led on by a genuine desire to worship at Our Lord's tomb and visit the holy places, but the more villainous characters, in particular Bohemond and his like, had an ulterior motive, for they hoped on their journey to seize the imperial capital itself, looking upon its capture as a natural consequence of the expedition. Bohemond disturbed the morale of many nobler men because he still cherished an old grudge against the emperor. Peter, after his preaching campaign, was the very first to cross the Straits of Lombardy,[18] with 80,000 infantry and 100,000 horsemen. He reached the capital via Hungary. The Kelts, as one might guess, are in any case an exceptionally hotheaded race and passionate, but once they are motivated they become irresistible.

6. The emperor was aware what Peter had suffered before from the Turks and advised him to wait for the other counts to arrive. He refused, however, confident in the number of his followers. He crossed the Sea of Marmora and pitched camp near a small place called Helenopolis. Normans, numbering 10,000 in all, joined him but detached themselves from the rest of the army and ravaged the outskirts of Nicaea, acting with horrible cruelty to the whole population; babies were hacked to pieces, impaled on wooden spits and roasted over a fire; old people were subjected to every kind of torture.

The inhabitants of the town, when they learnt what was happening, threw open their gates and charged out against them. A fierce battle ensued, in which the Normans fought with such spirit that the enemy was forced to retire; they in turn therefore returned to Helenopolis with all the booty. An argument erupted between them and those who had not gone on the raid – the usual quarrel in such cases – for the latter were green with envy. That led to brawling, whereupon the daredevil

Normans broke away for a second time and took Xerigordos by assault.

The sultan's reaction was to send Elkhanes with a strong force to deal with them. He arrived at Xerigordos and captured it; of the Normans some were put to the sword and others taken prisoner.[19] At the same time Elkhanes made plans to deal with the remainder who had stayed back with Peter the Hermit. He laid ambushes in suitable places, hoping that the enemy would fall into the trap unawares on their way to Nicaea and be killed. Knowing the Keltic love of money he also enlisted the services of two determined men who were to go to Peter's camp and announce that the Normans, having seized Nicaea, were sharing out all the spoils of the town.

This story had an immediate effect on Peter's men, and threw them into a state of great confusion; without a moment's hesitation they set out on the Nicaea road in complete disorder, without regard to military discipline appropriate to men setting off to war. As I have said before, the Latin race at all times is unusually greedy for wealth, but when it plans to invade a country, neither reason nor force can restrain it. They set out neither in rank nor in file, but near the River Drakon they fell into the Turkish ambushes and were miserably slaughtered. So great a multitude of Kelts and Normans died by the Ishmaelite sword that when they gathered the remains of the fallen, lying on every side, they heaped up, I would not call it a great ridge or a hill or a peak, but a mountain of considerable height and depth and width, so huge was the mass of bones. Some men of the same race as the slaughtered barbarians used the bones of the dead as mortar to fill up the cracks in walls which they built some time later, thereby making a tomb for them rather like a town. To this very day it stands with its encircling wall built of mixed stones and bones.

When the killing was over, only Peter and a handful of men returned to Helenopolis. The Turks, wishing to capture him, again laid an ambush, but the emperor, who had heard of this and indeed of the terrible massacre, was extremely concerned by the thought that Peter himself might have been captured. Constantine Euphorbenos Katakalon, already mentioned many times in this history, was accordingly sent with a powerful force in warships across the straits to help him. At his approach the Turks took to their heels. Without delay Katakalon picked up Peter and his companions of whom there were only a few and brought them in safety to Alexios.

The emperor reminded Peter of his recklessness at the outset and added that these great misfortunes had come upon him through not listening to his advice. Far from accepting responsibility, with characteristic Latin arrogance, Peter blamed his men, stating that they had been disobedient and had followed their own whims. He called them brigands and robbers. This was why they had not been allowed by the Saviour to worship at the Holy Sepulchre.

Others among the Latins, who like Bohemond and his cronies, had long coveted the Roman Empire and wished to acquire it for themselves, found in the preaching of Peter the opportunity they had been looking for and caused this great upheaval by deceiving more innocent people. They sold their lands on the pretence that they were leaving to fight the Turks and liberate the Holy Sepulchre.

7. A certain Hugh,[20] brother of the king of France, with all the pride of Nauatos in his noble birth, his riches and his power, was about to leave his native country in order to journey to the Holy Sepulchre; he sent an absurd message to the emperor seeking to ensure that he would be received with a magnificent reception: 'Know, Emperor, that I am the King of Kings, the greatest of all beneath the heavens. It is fitting that I should be met on my arrival and received with the pomp and ceremony appropriate to my noble birth.'

When the emperor learnt of this, John[21] the son of Isaac the *sebastokrator*, whom we have mentioned before, happened to be *doux* of Dyrrakhion, and Nicholas Maurokatakalon, commander of the fleet, had anchored his ships at intervals round the harbour of Dyrrakhion. From this base he made frequent voyages of reconnaissance to prevent pirate ships sailing by unnoticed. The emperor now sent these two men urgent instructions: the *doux* of Dyrrakhion was to keep watch by land and sea for Hugh's arrival and inform the emperor immediately when he came; he was also to receive him with great pomp; the *doux* of the fleet was exhorted to keep a constant vigil without the slightest let-up.

Hugh reached the coast of Lombardy safely and forthwith dispatched envoys to the *doux* of Dyrrakhion. There were twenty-four of them in all, armed with breastplates and greaves of gold and accompanied by Count Tzerpenterios[22] and Elias, who had deserted from the emperor at Thessaloniki. They addressed the *doux* as follows: 'Be it known to you, *Doux*, that our Lord Hugh is almost here. He brings with him from Rome the golden standard of St Peter. Understand, moreover, that he is supreme commander of the Frankish army. See to it then that he is accorded a reception worthy of his rank and yourself prepare to meet him.'

While the envoys were delivering this message to the *doux*, Hugh, who had come down via Rome to Lombardy, as I have said, had set sail for Illyrikon from Bari. He was caught by a tremendous storm. Most of his ships, with their rowers and crews, were lost. Only one ship, as luck would have it his own, was thrown up on the coast somewhere between Dyrrakhion and a place called Pales, and that was half-wrecked. Having been saved miraculously in this way, he was spotted by two of the men who were on the lookout for his arrival. They called to him, 'The *doux* is anxiously waiting for your coming. He is very eager to see you.' At once he asked for a horse and one of them dismounted and gave him his own gladly.

When the *doux* saw him, saved in this way, he greeted him and asked about the voyage, about where he had come from and about the storm which had wrecked his ships. He encouraged Hugh with fine promises and entertained him at a magnificent banquet. After the feasting Hugh was allowed to rest, but he was not granted complete freedom. The *doux* had immediately informed the emperor what was going on and was now awaiting further instructions. After being briefed, the emperor straightaway sent Boutoumites to Epidamnos, which we have on numerous occasions called Dyrrakhion, to escort Hugh, not by the direct route but on a detour through Philippopolis to the capital. He was afraid of the armed Keltic hordes coming on behind him. Hugh was welcomed with honour by the emperor, who showed him much kindness, and after giving him an abundant gift of money, persuaded him then and there to become his liegeman and take the customary oath of the Latins.

8. The episode concerning Hugh was just the start of it. Barely fifteen days later Bohemond, whom we have mentioned on many occasions already, made the crossing to the coast of Kabalion with various counts and an army which defied enumerating. This place is near Bousa. Kabalion and Bousa are names of towns in that area. I hope that nobody will rebuke me for using such barbaric names, thereby defiling the text of my history. Even Homer did not object to using the names of Boetians as well as of a number of barbaric islands for the sake of historical accuracy.

Hard on Bohemond's heels came the Count Prebentzas.[23] He too reached the Lombardy coast and wanting to cross over to Illyrikon, hired a three-masted pirate vessel of large tonnage for 6,000 gold staters. She carried 200 rowers and towed three ship's boats. This count did not make for Avlona, as the other Latin armies had done, but because of the fact that he feared the Roman fleet, weighed anchor, changed direction a little and with a favourable wind sailed straight for Khimara.

However, in escaping the smoke he fell into the fire: he avoided the ships lying in wait at different points in the Lombardy straits but crossed the path of none other than the *doux* of the whole Roman fleet, Nicholas Maurokatakalon himself. The latter had heard of this pirate vessel some time before and had detached biremes, triremes and some fast cruisers from the main force; with these he moved from his base at Ason to Kabalion and took up station there. The so-called second count was sent with his own galley, known as an *exkoussaton* by the ordinary seamen; he was to light a torch when he saw the rowers loose the stern cables of the enemy ship and throw them into the sea. Without delay the order was carried out.

When Nicholas saw the signal, he hoisted sail on some of his ships, while others were rowed with oars – they looked like millipedes – against the count, who was now at sea. They caught

him before he had sailed three stades from the land, hurrying to reach the opposite coast by Epidamnos. He had 1,500
soldiers on board, plus eighty horses belonging to the nobles.
The helmsman, sighting Nicholas, reported to the Count
Prebentzas: 'The Syrian fleet is on us. We're in danger of being
killed by dagger and sword.' The count at once ordered his men
to arm and put up a good fight.

It was midwinter – the day sacred to the memory of
Nicholas,[24] greatest of pontiffs – but there was a dead calm and
the full moon shone more brightly than in the spring. As the
winds had fallen completely, the pirate ship could no longer
make progress under sail; it lay becalmed on the sea. At this
point in the history I should like to pay tribute to the exploits
of Marianos. He immediately asked the *doux* of the fleet, his
father, for some of the lighter vessels and then steered straight
for the leader's ship. He fell upon the prow and tried to board
her. The warriors rushed there and found that he was fully
armed for battle. But Marianos, speaking in their language,
told the Latins there was no need for alarm; he urged them not
to fight against fellow Christians. Nevertheless one of them
fired a *tzangra* and hit his helmet.

The *tzangra*[25] or crossbow is a weapon of the barbarians,
absolutely unknown to the Greeks. In order to stretch it one
does not pull the string with the right hand while pushing the
bow with the left away from the body; this instrument of war,
which fires weapons to an enormous distance, has to be
stretched by lying almost on one's back; each foot is pressed
forcibly against the half-circles of the bow and the two hands
tug at the bow, pulling it with all one's strength towards the
body. At the midpoint of the string is a groove, shaped like a
cylinder cut in half and fitted to the string itself; it is about the
length of a fair-sized arrow, extending from the string to the
centre of the bow. Along this groove arrows of all kinds are
fired. They are very short, but extremely thick with a heavy
iron tip. In the firing the string exerts tremendous violence and
force, so that the missiles do not rebound when they hit a target;
in fact they pierce a shield, cut through a heavy iron breastplate
and resume their flight on the far side, so irresistible and violent

is the discharge. An arrow of this type has been known to go straight through a bronze statue, and when fired at the wall of a very great town, its point either protruded from the inner side or buried itself in the wall and disappeared altogether. Such is the *tzangra*, a truly diabolical machine. The unfortunate man who is struck by it dies without feeling anything, so strong is the force of the blow.

The arrow fired from this *tzangra* drove clean through the top of it without touching a hair on Marianos' head – Providence thwarted it. Another arrow was quickly fired at the count, striking him on the arm; it pierced his shield, bored through his breastplate of scale-armour and grazed his side. A certain Latin priest who happened to be standing in the stern with twelve other fighting men saw what had occurred and shot several times with his bow at Marianos. Even then he refused to give up, fighting bravely and encouraging his men to follow his example, so that three times the priest's comrades had to be relieved because of wounds or fatigue. The priest, too, although he had been hit again and again and was covered with streams of blood from his wounds, still was undaunted.

The Latin customs with regard to priests differ from ours. We are bidden by canon law and the teaching of the Gospel, 'Touch not, grumble not, attack not – for thou art consecrated.' But the barbarian Latin will at the same time handle sacred objects, fasten a shield to his left arm and grasp a spear in his right. He will communicate the sacred Body and Blood while at the same time gazing on bloodshed and become himself a man of blood as it says in the Psalm of David. Thus this barbarian race is no less devoted to religion than to war. This priest, then, more man of action than holy man, wore priestly garb and at the same time handled an oar and ready for naval action or war on land, fought sea and men alike. Our rules, as I have just said, derive from Aaron, Moses and our first high priest.

After a bitter contest which had gone on from evening till the middle of the following day, the Latins surrendered to Marianos, much against their will, having asked for and obtained an amnesty from him. But that most war-hungry of priests did not cease from fighting, even once the peace had been agreed. After emptying his quiver of arrows, he picked up a sling-stone and hurled it at Marianos, who protected his head with his shield, but that was broken into four and his helmet was shattered. The blow stunned him; he lost consciousness at once and for some time lay speechless, just as the famous Hector lay almost at his last gasp when struck by Ajax's stone. Having recovered his senses with some difficulty, he pulled himself together and fired a series of arrows against his enemy, wounding him three times. This man, more commander than priest, was far from sated, even though he had exhausted his stones and arrows and was at a loss what to do and how to defend himself against his adversary. He grew impatient, on fire with rage, like a wild animal angrily trying to chase its own tail. He was ready to use whatever came to hand. So when he found a sack full of barley cakes, he threw them like stones, taking them from the sack. It was as if he were officiating at a ceremony, celebrating as though war was a holy ritual. He picked up one cake, hurled it with all his might at Marianos' face and hit him on the cheek.

So much for the story of the priest, the ship and its crew. As for Count Prebentzas, he put himself in the hands of Marianos, together with his ship and her crew, and followed him willingly. When they reached land and were disembarking, the priest kept on making inquiries about Marianos and not knowing his name, described him by the colour of his garments. When at last he found him, he threw his arms round him and with an embrace boasted, 'If you had met me on dry land, many of you would have died at my hands.' He drew out a large silver cup, worth 130 staters, and gave it to Marianos and having uttered these words, promptly left this world to meet his maker.

9. It was at this time that Count Godfrey also made the crossing[26] with some other counts and an army of 10,000 horsemen and 70,000 infantry. When he reached the capital he quartered his men in the vicinity of the Propontis, from the bridge nearest the Kosmidion as far as the Church of St Phokas. But when the emperor urged him to go over to the far side of the Propontis, he put off the decision from one day to the next, blaming this on a series of excuses. In fact, of course, he was

waiting for Bohemond and the rest of the counts to arrive. Peter
had in the beginning undertaken his great journey to worship
at the Holy Sepulchre, but the other counts, and in particular
Bohemond, were nursing an old grudge against the emperor
and were looking for a good opportunity to avenge the glorious
victory which the emperor had won at Larissa[27] against
Bohemond. They were all of one mind and in order to fulfil
their dream of taking Constantinople, they adopted a common
policy, which I have often referred to before: to all appearances
they were on pilgrimage to Jerusalem; in reality they planned
to dethrone the emperor and seize the capital.

The emperor, however, had been aware of their perfidy for a
long time. He gave written orders to move the auxiliary forces
with their officers from Athyras to Phileas en masse (Phileas is
a place on the coast of the Black Sea). They were to lie in wait
lest Godfrey send anyone to Bohemond or to the other counts
coming behind him, or vice versa; all communications were
thus to be intercepted.

Meanwhile the following incident took place. Some of the
counts who were close to Godfrey were invited by the emperor
to meet him, so he could encourage them to advise Godfrey to
take the oath of allegiance. The Latins, however, wasted time
with their usual verbosity and love of long speeches, so that a
false rumour did the rounds that their counts had been arrested
by the emperor. Immediately they marched in serried ranks on
Byzantion, starting with the palaces near the Silver Lake; they
demolished them completely. An assault was also made on the
city walls, not with a siege-engine, as they had none, but trusting
in their great numbers they had the effrontery to try to set fire to
the gate below the palace, near the sanctuary of the great pontiff
Nicholas,[28] which was built long ago by one of the emperors.

The vulgar mob of Byzantines, who were utterly craven, with
no experience of war, were not the only ones to weep and wail
and beat their breasts in impotent fear when they saw the Latin
ranks; even more alarmed were the emperor's loyal supporters,
who recalled the Thursday on which the city had been captured[29] and feared that the day had come where vengeance
would be taken for what had happened then. All the trained

soldiers hurried to the palace in disorder. But the emperor did not trouble to arm himself; he did not buckle on his cuirass of scale-armour, did not pick up his spear nor his sword. He sat implacably on the imperial throne, giving hope to all with his calmness and filling their hearts with confidence, while taking counsel with his kinsmen and with the commanders of the army about what should be done.

In the first place he insisted that no one whatever should leave the ramparts to attack the Latins, for two reasons: because of the sacred character of the day (it was the Thursday of Holy Week,[30] in which the Saviour suffered an ignominious death on behalf of all mankind); and secondly, because he wished to avoid bloodshed between fellow men. On several occasions he sent messages to the Latins advising them to desist from such an undertaking. 'Have reverence,' he said, 'for God on this day was sacrificed for us all, refusing neither the Cross, nor the Nails, nor the Spear which were used on common criminals. If you must fight, we too shall be ready, but after the day of the Saviour's resurrection.'

Far from listening to his words, the Latins instead reinforced their ranks, and so thick were the showers of their arrows that even one of the emperor's retinue, standing near the throne, was struck in the chest. At this, most of those who were standing on either side of the emperor began to withdraw, but he remained seated and unruffled, comforting them and cajoling them in a gentle way – to the wonder of all. However, as he saw the Latins brazenly approaching the walls and rejecting sound advice, he took active steps, first of all summoning his son-in-law Nikephoros, my *kaisar*. He was ordered to pick out the best fighters, expert archers, and post them on the ramparts; they were to fire volleys of arrows at the Latins, but without taking aim and mostly off-target, so as to terrify the enemy by the weight of the attack, but at all costs to avoid killing them. As I have said, he was anxious to respect the spiritual importance of that day and he wished to prevent fratricide.

Other elite troops, most of them carrying bows, but some wielding long spears, were ordered to throw open the gate of St Romanos and make a show of force with a violent charge against the enemy; they were to be drawn up in such a way that each lancer had two lightly-armed soldiers to protect him on either side. In this formation they were to advance at a walking pace, sending on ahead a few skilled archers to shoot at the Kelts from a distance and alter their position from time to time; when they saw that the space between the two armies had been reduced to a narrow gap, then the officers were to signal the archers accompanying them to fire thick volleys of arrows at the horses, not at the riders, and advance at full speed against the Latins. The idea was to break the full force of the Keltic attack by wounding their mounts so that they would not find it easy to ride out against them in this condition, but most importantly, to avoid the killing of Christians. The emperor's instructions were gladly followed. The gates were flung open; now the horses were given their head, now reined in. Many of the enemy were slain, but only a few of ours were wounded that day.

Enough about them. Having taken his practised bowmen with him, as I said, my lord the *kaisar* set them on the towers in order to fire at the barbarians. Every man had a bow that was accurate and far-shooting. They were all young, as skilled as Homer's Teucer in archery. The *kaisar*'s bow was truly worthy of Apollo. Unlike the famous Greeks of Homer he did not pull the bowstring until it touched his breast and draw back the arrow so that the iron tip was near the bow;[31] he was making no demonstration of the hunter's skill, like them. But like a second Herakles, he shot deadly arrows from deathless bows and hit the target at will. At other times, when he took part in a shooting contest or in a battle, he never missed his aim: at whatever part of a man's body he shot, he invariably and immediately inflicted a wound there. With such strength did he bend his bow and so swiftly did he let loose his arrows that even Teucer and the two Ajaxes were not his equal in archery. Yet, despite his skill, on this occasion he respected the holiness of the day and kept in mind the emperor's instructions, so that when he saw the Latins recklessly and foolishly coming near the walls, protected by shield and helmet, he bent his bow and put the arrow to the bowstring, but purposely shot wide, shooting sometimes beyond the target, sometimes falling short.

Because of the importance of that day, he refrained from shooting straight at the Latins; yet whenever a Latin was so arrogant and foolish as to fire at the defenders on the ramparts, but appeared to unleash a volley of insults in his own language, then did the *kaisar* bend his bow. Nor did the dart fly in vain from his hand, but pierced the long shield and cleft its way through the corselet of mail, so that arm and side were pinned together. Straightway he fell speechless to the ground,[32] as the poet says, and a cry went up to heaven as one side cheered their *kaisar* while the other bewailed their fallen warrior. Outside, the cavalry was fighting just as bravely as the men on the ramparts, so it was a grim battle which broke out between the two armies. Finally, however, the emperor threw in his personal guards, and put the Latin ranks to flight.

On the next day Hugh advised Godfrey to yield to the emperor's wish and to take an oath of allegiance to him, unless he wanted to learn how experienced a general Alexios was for a second time. He should take an oath, he said, to bear his true allegiance. But Godfrey rebuked him sternly. 'You left your own country as a ruler,' he said, 'with all that wealth and a strong army; now from the heights you've brought yourself to the level of a slave. And then, as if you had won some great success, have you come here to tell me to do the same?' 'We ought to have stayed in our own countries and kept our hands off other people's,' replied Hugh. 'But since we've come thus far and need the emperor's protection, no good will come of it unless we obey his orders.' Hugh was sent away with nothing achieved. Because of this and reliable information that the counts coming after Godfrey were already near, the emperor sent some of his best officers with their troops to try to persuade him once more or otherwise to compel him to cross the straits. No sooner had the Latins caught sight of them than they attacked without a moment's hesitation, not even waiting to ask them what they wanted. In this fierce engagement many on both sides fell, and all the emperor's men who had attacked with such recklessness were wounded. As the Romans showed greater spirit the Latins gave way.

Thus, not long afterwards, Godfrey submitted to the emperor's will; he came to the emperor and swore on oath as he was directed that whatever towns, lands or forts he might in future subdue that had in the first place belonged to the Roman Empire would be handed over to the officer appointed by the emperor for this very purpose. Having taken the oath he received generous amounts of money, and he was invited to share the emperor's hearth and table, and was entertained at a magnificent banquet, after which he crossed over to Pelekanos and pitched camp there. The emperor then gave orders that plentiful supplies should be made available for his men.

10. In the wake of Godfrey came Count Raoul, with 15,000[33] cavalry and foot soldiers. He camped with his attendant counts by the Propontis near the Patriarch's Monastery; the rest he quartered as far as Sosthenion along the shore. Following Godfrey's example he procrastinated, waiting for the arrival of those coming after him. The emperor was very anxious, and guessing what was likely to happen, used every possible means to hurry them into crossing the straits. He therefore summoned Opos – a man of noble character, unsurpassed in his knowledge of things military – and when he presented himself before the emperor he was dispatched overland with other brave men to Raoul, in order to force him to cross over to the other side. When it was clear that the latter had no intention of doing so and what is more that he had adopted an insolent and quite arrogant attitude to the emperor, Opos took up arms and set his men in battle order, perhaps to scare the barbarian. He thought this might persuade him to set sail for the shore on the other side. Quicker than you can say it, Raoul drew up the Kelts who were with him in formation, and like a lion who rejoices when he has found a huge prey, kicked off an almighty battle with Opos.

At this moment, Pegasios arrived by sea to transport them to the other side and when he saw the fight on land and the Kelts throwing themselves headlong at the Roman ranks, he disembarked and himself joined in the conflict, attacking the enemy from the rear. In this fight many men were killed, but a far greater number were wounded. The survivors asked to be taken over the straits; reflecting that if they joined Godfrey and told him of their misfortunes he might be stirred to action against the Romans, the emperor prudently granted their request. He therefore gladly put them on ships and had them transported by sea to the Holy Sepulchre, especially since they themselves wanted this. Friendly messages, offering great expectations, were also sent to the counts whom they were awaiting. Consequently, when they arrived, they willingly carried out his instructions.

So much for Count Raoul. After him came another contingent of innumerable size, a diverse host gathered together from almost all the Keltic lands with their leaders – kings and dukes and counts and even bishops. With his trademark skill of forseeing the future and taking the appropriate action accordingly, the emperor sent envoys to greet them as a mark of friendship and to give them messages of comfort. Officers appointed for this particular task were ordered to provide victuals to the new arrivals on their journey, so that there could be no excuse for complaint for any reason whatsoever. These pressed on to the capital. One might have compared them for number to the stars of heaven or the grains of sand poured out over the shore; as they hurried towards Constantinople they were indeed numerous as the leaves and flowers of spring,[34] in the words of Homer.

For all my desire to name their leaders, I prefer not to do so. The words fail me, partly through my inability to make the unpronounceable barbaric sounds and partly because I am put off by just how many of them there were.[35] In any case, why should I try to list the names of so enormous a multitude, when even their contemporaries became indifferent at the sight of them? When they did finally arrive in the capital, on the emperor's orders they established their troops near the monastery of Saint Kosmas and Saint Damian, reaching as far as the Hieron.

It was not nine heralds who restrained them with cries in the classical Greek tradition, but a considerable number of soldiers who accompanied them and persuaded them to obey the emperor's commands. With the idea of enforcing the same oath that Godfrey had taken, the emperor invited them to visit him separately. He talked with them in private about his wishes and used the more reasonable among them as intermediaries with the more reluctant. When they rejected advice because of the fact that they were waiting for Bohemond to arrive, and found ingenious methods of evasion by making new demands, he refuted their objections with no difficulty at all and using a range of arguments, cajoled them into taking the oath. Godfrey himself was invited to cross over from Pelekanos to witness these being given.

When all were assembled including Godfrey himself and the oath had been sworn by every count, one nobleman dared to seat himself on the imperial throne. The emperor endured this without a word, knowing of old the arrogance of the Latins. However, Count Baldwin[36] went up to the man, took him by the hand and made him rise. He gave him a severe reprimand: 'You ought never to have done such a thing, especially after promising to be the emperor's liegeman. Roman emperors don't let their subjects sit with them. That's the custom here and sworn liegemen of His Majesty should observe the customs of the country.' The man said nothing to Baldwin, but with a bitter glance at the emperor muttered some words to himself in his own language: 'What a peasant! He sits alone while generals like these stand beside him!'

The emperor saw his lips moving and calling one of the interpreters who understood the language asked what he had said. Being told the words he made no comment to the man at the time, but kept the remark to himself. However, when they were all taking their leave of him, he sent for the arrogant, impudent fellow and asked who he was, where he came from and what his ancestry was. 'I am a pure Frank,' he replied, 'and of noble birth. One thing I know: at a crossroads in the country where I was born is an ancient shrine; anyone who wishes to engage in single combat goes there prepared to fight; he then prays to God for help and there he stays awaiting the man who will dare to answer his challenge. I myself have spent time by that very crossroads, waiting and longing for the man who would fight – but there was never one who dared.' To this the emperor said, 'If you didn't get your fight then, when you looked for it, now you have a fine opportunity for many. But I strongly recommend you not to take up position in the rear of the army, nor in the van; stand in the centre with the junior officers. I know the enemy's methods and have had much experience of combat with the Turks.' The advice was not given to him alone, but as they left he warned all the others of the manifold dangers they were likely to meet on the journey. He advised them not to pursue the enemy too far, if God gave them victory, lest falling into traps set by the Turkish leaders they should be massacred.

11. So much for Godfrey, Raoul and those who came with them. Bohemond arrived at Apros with the other counts. Recognizing that he himself was not of noble descent, with no force of any significant kind because of his lack of resources, he wished to win the emperor's goodwill, but at the same time to conceal his own hostile intentions against him. He separated ten Kelts only from the other counts and hurried on to the capital. The emperor had long experience of Bohemond's deceitful and treacherous nature and desired to talk with him before the other counts arrived; he wanted to hear what Bohemond had to say and thought he could convince him to cross over before he had the chance to join up with those behind him or to corrupt their minds. When Bohemond came into his presence, Alexios smiled at him and inquired about his journey and asked where he had left the counts.

Bohemond replied to all these questions as best he could, while the emperor joked about his daring deeds at Larissa and Dyrrakhion; he also recalled Bohemond's former hostility. 'I was indeed an enemy and foe then,' said Bohemond, 'but now I come of my own free will as Your Majesty's friend.' The emperor talked at length with him trying to gauge the man's real feelings, and when he concluded that Bohemond would be prepared to take the oath of allegiance, he said to him, 'You are tired now from your journey. Go away and rest. Tomorrow we can discuss matters at length.'

Bohemond went off to the Kosmidion, where an apartment had been made ready for him and a rich table was laid full of delicacies and food of all kinds. The cooks also brought in meat and flesh of animals and birds, uncooked. 'The food, as you see, has been prepared by us in our customary way,' they said, 'but if that does not suit you here is raw meat which can be cooked in whatever way you like.' In doing and saying this they were carrying out the emperor's instructions. Alexios was a shrewd judge of a man's character, cleverly reading the innermost thoughts of his heart, and knowing the spiteful, malevolent nature of Bohemond, he rightly guessed what would happen. It was in order that Bohemond might have no suspicions about his own motives that he ordered raw meat to be set before him at the same time, and it was an excellent move.

The cunning Bohemond not only refused to taste any of the food, but did not even touch it with his fingertips; he rejected it outright, dividing it all up instead among the attendants, without a hint of his own secret misgivings. It looked as if he was doing them a favour, but that was mere pretence: in reality, if one considers the matter rightly, he was mixing them a cup of death. There was no attempt to hide his treachery, for it was his habit to treat servants with utter indifference. However, he told his own cooks to prepare the raw meat in the usual Frankish way. On the next day he asked the attendants how they felt. 'Very well,' they replied and added that they had suffered not the slightest harm from it. At these words he revealed his hidden fear: 'For my own part,' he said, 'when I remembered the wars I have fought with him, not to mention the famous battle, I was afraid he might arrange to kill me by putting a dose of poison in the food.' Such were the actions of Bohemond. I must say I have never seen an evil man who in all his deeds and words did not depart far from the path of right; whenever a man leaves the middle course, to whatever extreme he inclines he takes his stand far from virtue.

The emperor summoned Bohemond and required of him that he take the customary Latin oath. Knowing what his position was he acquiesced gladly enough, for he had neither illustrious ancestors nor great wealth and therefore lacked a substantial following, and had only a very modest contingent of Kelts with him. In any case Bohemond was by nature a liar. After the ceremony was over, the emperor set aside a room in the palace and had the floor covered with all kinds of wealth: clothes, gold and silver coins and objects of lesser value filled the place so completely that it was impossible for anyone to walk in it. He ordered the man deputed to show Bohemond these riches to open the doors suddenly. Bohemond was amazed at the sight. 'If I had had such wealth,' he said, 'I would long ago have become master of many lands.' 'All this,' said the man, 'is yours today – a present from the emperor.'

Bohemond was overjoyed. After accepting the gift and thanking him for it, he went off to rest in his quarters. Yet when the things were brought to him, he had changed his tune, even though he had previously expressed such admiration. 'I never thought I should be so insulted by the emperor,' he said. 'Take them away. Give them back to the person who sent you.' The emperor, who was familiar with the erratic disposition of the Latins, quoted a popular saying: 'His mischief shall come back to haunt him.' Bohemond heard about this, and when he saw the servants carefully assembling the presents to carry them away, he changed his mind once more; instead of sending them off in anger he smiled on them, like a chameleon, which transforms itself in a minute. The truth is that Bohemond was a habitual rogue, quick to react to fleeting circumstance; he far surpassed all the Latins who passed through the Roman Empire at that time in his villainy and sheer gall, just as he was outshone by them in wealth and resources. He was the supreme mischief-maker. As for inconstancy, that followed automatically – a trait common to all Latins. It was no surprise then that he would be so pleased to receive the money he had formerly refused.

He was a bitter man, for as he had no inheritance at all to speak of, he had set out from his native land, in theory to worship at the Holy Sepulchre, but he had really done so in order to win power for himself – and better, if possible, to seize the Roman Empire itself, as his father had suggested. He was prepared to go to any length, as they say, but a great deal of money was required. The emperor, aware of the man's disagreeable, ill-natured disposition, cleverly sought to remove everything that contributed to Bohemond's secret plans. When therefore Bohemond demanded the position of *domestikos* of the East, he was not granted his request; he could not 'out-Cretan the Cretan'.[37] The emperor was afraid that once possessed of authority he might use it to subjugate all the other counts and thereafter convert them easily to any policy he chose. At the same time, because he did not wish Bohemond to suspect in any way that his plans were already detected, he flattered him with fine hopes. 'The time for that is not yet ripe, but with your energy and loyalty it will not be long before you have even that honour.'

After a conversation with the Latins and after showing his friendship for them with all kinds of presents and honours, he took his seat the next day on the imperial throne. Bohemond and the others were sent for and warned about the things likely to happen on their journey. He gave them profitable advice. They were instructed in the methods normally used by the Turks in battle; told how they should draw up a battle line, how to lay ambushes; advised not to pursue far when the enemy ran away in flight. In this way, by means of money and good advice, he did much to soften their ferocious nature. Then he proposed that they should cross the straits.

Alexios had a deep affection for St Gilles[38] because of the count's superior intellect, his untarnished reputation and the purity of his life. He knew moreover how greatly St Gilles valued the truth, which he valued above all else, whatever the circumstances. In fact, he outshone all Latins in every quality, as the sun outshines the stars. It was for this reason that the emperor detained him for some time. Thus, when all the others had taken their leave of him and made the journey across the straits of the Propontis to Damalion,[39] and when he was now relieved of their troublesome presence, he sent for Raymond on many occasions. He explained in more detail the adventures that the Latins must expect to meet with on their march; he also laid bare his own suspicions of the plans of the Franks. In the course of many conversations on this subject he unreservedly opened the doors of his soul, as it were, to the count; he warned him always to be on his guard against Bohemond's perfidy, so that if attempts were made to break the treaty he might frustrate them and in every way thwart these schemes.

Raymond replied to the emperor: 'Bohemond inherited perjury and guile from his ancestors. It will be a miracle if he keeps his word. As far as I am concerned, however, I will always try to the best of my ability to observe your commands.' With that he took his leave of the emperor and went off to join the main Keltic army.

The emperor would have liked to share in the expedition of the Kelts against the barbarians too, but he feared the enormous numbers of them. He did think it wise, though, to move to Pelekanos. From there, being close to Nicaea, he could obtain information about the Kelts and their progress and at the same time could learn about Turkish sorties from the town, as well as about the condition of the inhabitants inside Nicaea. It would be shameful, he believed, if in the meantime he did not himself win some military success. When a favourable opportunity arose, he planned to capture Nicaea himself; that would be preferable to receiving it from the Kelts, according to the agreement already made with them. Nevertheless he kept the idea to himself. He kept whatever plans and intentions he had to himself, although he did let Boutoumites, his sole confidant, in on it. The latter was instructed to win over the barbarians in Nicaea by all kinds of guarantees and the promise of a complete amnesty, but also by holding over them the prospect of this or that retribution – even massacre – if the Kelts took the town. He was more than familiar with Boutoumites' unswerving loyalty and of his competence in such matters. This is how the events took place then from the very beginning.

BOOK XI

1. Bohemond and all the counts met at a place from which they intended to sail across to Kibotos, and with Godfrey they awaited the arrival of St Gilles. However, their numbers were so immense that further delay became impossible due to problems of provisioning, so they divided their army in two, even though they were still waiting for the arrival of St Gilles and the emperor who was with him, so that they could set out for Nicaea together. One group drove on through Bithnyia and Nikomedia towards Nicaea; the other crossed the strait to Kibotos and assembled there. Having approached Nicaea in this manner they allocated the towers and intervening battlements among them. The idea was to make the assault on the walls according to these dispositions; rivalry between the various contingents would be provoked and the siege pressed with greater vigour. The area allotted to St Gilles was left vacant until he arrived. At this moment the emperor reached Pelekanos, with his eye on Nicaea, as has already been pointed out.

The barbarians inside the town meanwhile sent repeated messages to the sultan[1] asking for help, but he was still taking his time, and as the siege had already gone on for many days, from sunrise right up to sunset, their condition was obviously becoming extremely serious. They gave up the fight, deciding that it was better to make terms with the emperor than to be taken by the Kelts. Given the circumstances they summoned Boutoumites, who had often promised in a never-ending stream of letters that this or that favour would be granted by the emperor, if only they surrendered to him. He now explained in more detail the emperor's friendly intentions and produced written guarantees. He was gladly received by the Turks, who had despaired of holding out against the overwhelming strength of their enemies; it was wiser, they thought, to cede Nicaea voluntarily to the emperor and receive gifts and honourable treatment, than to fall victim to the sword for the sake of it.

Boutoumites had not been in the place more than two days before St Gilles arrived, determined to make an attempt on the walls without delay; he had siege-engines ready for the task. Meanwhile a rumour spread that the sultan was on his way. At this news the Turks, inspired with courage again, at once expelled Boutoumites. As for the sultan, he sent a detachment of his forces to observe St Gilles's offensive, with orders to fight if they met any Kelts. They were seen from a distance by St Gilles' men who took the battle to them. As soon as the other counts and Bohemond himself learnt of the engagement, each set aside up to 200 men from their own company, thus making up a considerable army, and sent them immediately to help St Gilles's men. They routed the barbarians and pursued them till nightfall.

Nevertheless, the sultan was far from downcast at this set-back; at sunrise the next morning he was in full armour and with all his men occupied the plain outside the walls of Nicaea. When the Kelts heard about his arrival, they too armed themselves for battle, before descending on their enemies like lions. The struggle that then ensued was ferocious and terrible. All through the day it was indecisive, but when the sun went down the Turks fled. Night had ended the contest. On either side many fell and most of them were killed; the majority of the survivors were wounded.

Having won so glorious a victory, the Kelts stuck heads of the enemy on the ends of their spears and returned carrying these like standards, so that the barbarians would recognize from a distance what had happened and being frightened by this defeat at their first encounter, would not be so eager for battle in future. So much for the ideas and actions of the Latins. The sultan, realizing how numerous they were and after this onslaught aware of their self-confidence and daring, gave a hint to the Turks in Nicaea: 'From now on do just what you consider

"So much for..."

best.' He already knew that they preferred to deliver up the town to the emperor than to become prisoners of the Kelts.

Meanwhile St Gilles, setting about the task allotted to him, was constructing a wooden tower, circular in shape; inside and out he covered it with leather hides and filled the centre with intertwined wickerwork. When it was thoroughly strengthened, he approached what is known as the Gonatas Tower. This building acquired its name long ago, when the famous Manuel, father of the previous emperor Isaac Komnenos and his brother John, my grandfather on the paternal side, was promoted commander-in-chief of all the east by the then emperor Basil. His purpose was to put an end to hostilities with Skleros,[2] either by opposing him with force, or by driving him to seek peace terms through reason. However, as Skleros was a man of war and delighted in bloodshed, he inevitably welcomed battle rather than peace, so day by day there were violent clashes. Not only did Skleros reject a truce, but he even fought bravely to capture Nicaea with siege-engines and battered down the ramparts. The greater part of this tower was cut away at its base and it sank down: it seemed to be bending its knee – hence its name.

But enough about the Gonatas Tower. When St Gilles, who was highly experienced in these matters, had built the wooden tower I have mentioned, which is called a 'tortoise' by specialists in siege warfare, he manned it with soldiers whose job was to batter the walls and also with expert sappers, equipped with iron tools to compromise from below; the former would engage the defenders on the ramparts above, while the latter mined from below. In place of the stones they prised out, logs of wood were put in and when their excavations reached the point where they were nearly through the wall and a gleam of light could be seen from the far side, they set light to these logs and burnt them. After they had turned to ashes, Gonatas inclined even more, so that its name was still entirely appropriate. The rest of the walls were surrounded with a girdle of battering rams and tortoises; in the twinkling of an eye, so to speak, the outer ditch was filled with dust, level with the flat parts on either side of it. Then the Kelts committed themselves to the siege with all their might.

2. The emperor, who had thoroughly investigated Nicaea, and on many occasions, judged that it could not possibly be captured by the Latins, however overwhelming their numbers. In his turn he constructed siege-engines of several types, but mostly to an unorthodox design of his own which was much admired. He had these sent to the counts. He had, as we have already remarked, crossed with the available troops and was staying at Pelekanos near Mesampela, where in the old days a sanctuary was built in honour of George, the great martyr.

The emperor would have liked to accompany the expedition against the godless Turks, but abandoned the project after carefully weighing the arguments for and against: he noted that the Roman army was hopelessly outnumbered by the enormous host of the Franks; he knew from long experience, too, how untrustworthy the Latins were. Nor was that all: the unreliability of these men and their faithless nature might well sweep them again and again, like the tides of Euripos, from one extreme to the other; through love of money they were ready to sell their own wives and children for next to nothing. So this was why the emperor decided against joining the enterprise at that time. However, even if his presence was unwise, he realized the necessity of giving as much aid to the Kelts as if he were actually with them.

The great strength of its walls, he was sure, made Nicaea impregnable; the Latins would never take it. But when it was reported that the sultan was bringing strong forces and all necessary food supplies across the lake,[3] with no difficulty at all, and these were finding their way into the town, he determined to gain control of the lake. Light boats, capable of sailing on its waters, were prepared, hoisted on wagons and launched on the Kios side. Fully-armed soldiers were put on board, under the command of Manuel Boutoumites. In order that they might seem more numerous than they really were, the emperor gave them more standards than usual – and also trumpets and drums.

Such then were the measures the emperor took with regard to the lake. As far as the mainland goes, he sent for Tatikios and the man known as Tzitas together with a force of around 2,000 lightly-armed soldiers who were dispatched to Nicaea;

their orders were to load their very generous supply of arrows on mules as soon as they had disembarked and seize the fort of St George; at a good distance from the walls of Nicaea they were to dismount from their horses, go on foot straight for the Gonatas Tower and there take up position; they were then to form ranks with the Latins and acting under their orders assault the walls. As soon as Tatikios was in position with his force, he briefed the Kelts as to the emperor's orders. At this, everyone put on their armour and attacked with loud shouts and war cries.

Tatikios' men fired their arrows in great volleys while the Kelts made breaches in the walls and kept up a constant bombardment of stones from their catapults. On the side of the lake the enemy were panic-stricken by the imperial standards and the trumpets of Boutoumites, who chose this moment to send a message to the defenders, setting out the emperor's promises. The barbarians were reduced to such straits that they dared not even peep over the battlements of Nicaea. At the same time they gave up all hope of the sultan's coming, and decided therefore it was better to hand over the town to the emperor and to start negotiations with Boutoumites to that end. After the usual courtesies Boutoumites showed them the chrysobull entrusted to him by the emperor, in which they were not only guaranteed an amnesty, but also a liberal gift of money and honours for the sister and wife of the sultan (the latter, it was said, the daughter of Tzakhas). These offers were extended to all the barbarians in Nicaea without exception. With confidence in the emperor's promises, the inhabitants allowed Boutoumites to enter the town. At once he sent a message to Tatikios: 'The quarry is now in our hands. Preparations must be made for an assault on the walls. The Kelts must be given that task too, but leave nothing to them except the wall-fighting round the ramparts. Invest the town at all points, as necessary, and make the attempt at sunrise.'

This was in fact a trick to make the Kelts believe that the town had been captured by Boutoumites through combat; the drama of betrayal carefully planned by the emperor was to be concealed, for it was his wish that the negotiations conducted by

Boutoumites should not be divulged to the Kelts. On the next day the call to battle was sounded on both sides of the town: on one, from the mainland, the Kelts furiously pressed the siege; on the other Boutoumites, having climbed to the battlements and set up the imperial sceptres and standards there, acclaimed the emperor to the accompaniment of trumpets and horns. It was in this way that the whole Roman force entered Nicaea.

Nevertheless, knowing the enormous size of the Keltic host, as well as their fickle nature and passionate, impulsive whims, Boutoumites guessed that they might well seize the citadel if they once got inside. The Turkish satraps in Nicaea, moreover, were capable, if they wished, of taking his own forces prisoner, or even of massacring them, since they outnumbered him. He therefore took possession of the keys of the town gate at once. There was only one point of entry and exit to the town at that moment, the others having been closed through fear of the Kelts who were camped just beyond the walls. With the keys of this particular gate in his hands, he determined to reduce the number of satraps by a ruse, in order to have them at his mercy, and to avoid something terrible happening to him. He sent for them and advised a visit to the emperor, if they wanted to receive from him large sums of money, to be rewarded with high distinctions and to find their names on the lists of those receiving an annual payment. The Turks were persuaded and during the night the gate was opened; they were let out, a few at a time and at frequent intervals, to make their way across the nearby lake to Rodomeros and the half-caste Monastras, who were stationed by St George's fort. From there, they were to be hurried on to the emperor as soon as they had disembarked; they were not to be detained even for a brief moment, lest they join up with the Turks sent on behind them, and then plot some mischief.

This was in fact a simple prediction, an intuitive proof which could only be put down to the man's long experience, for as long as the new arrivals were quickly sent on to the emperor, they were secure and could pose no danger whatsoever, but were the vigilance to be relaxed in any way, they would find themselves in peril from the barbarians whom they kept back.

As they were great in number, the Turks planned to take one of two courses: either they would attack and kill the Romans under the cover of night, or they would bring them as prisoners to the sultan. The latter was unanimously considered to be the better idea. They did attack in the night and took them away as their captives, as planned and then made for the hilltop of Azala (. . . stades from the walls of Nicaea). When they got there, they naturally dismounted to rest their horses.

Now Monastras was a half-caste and understood the Turkish dialect; Rodomeros, too, having been captured by the Turks long ago and having lived with them for a considerable time, was himself not unacquainted with their language. They tried hard to move their captors with persuasive arguments. 'Why are you mixing the cup of death for us, without deriving the slightest benefit for yourselves? When every single one of the others is enjoying great rewards from the emperor and having their names enrolled for annual salary payments, you will be cutting yourselves off from all these privileges. Well now, don't be such fools, especially when you can live in safety without interference and return home exulting in riches. You may perhaps acquire new territory. Don't throw yourselves into certain danger. Maybe you'll meet Romans lying in ambush over there,' pointing to mountain streams and areas of marshland; 'if you do, you'll be massacred and lose your lives for nothing. There are thousands of men lying in wait for you, not only Kelts and barbarians, but a multitude of Romans as well. Now if you take our advice, you will turn your horses' heads and come to the emperor with us. We swear, as God is our witness, that you will enjoy countless gifts at his hands, and then, when it pleases you, you will leave as free men, without hindrance.'

These arguments convinced the Turks. Pledges were exchanged and both parties set out on their way to the emperor. On their arrival at Pelekanos, all were received by the emperor with a cheerful smile, although inwardly he was very angry with Rodomeros and Monastras. For the present they were sent off to rest. The next day all those Turks who were eager to serve him received numerous benefits; those who desired to go home were permitted to follow their own inclination – and they too

departed with not a few gifts. It was only after this that the
emperor severely rebuked Rodomeros and Monastras for their
folly, but seeing that they were too ashamed to look him in the
face, he altered his attitude and with words of forgiveness strove
to conciliate them. We will leave Rodomeros and Monastras
there. When Boutoumites was appointed *doux* of Nicaea at
that time by the emperor, the Kelts asked him for permission
to enter the town:[4] they desired to visit the sacred churches
there and worship. Boutoumites, as I have already remarked,
was well aware of the Keltic disposition and a visit en masse
was refused. However, he did open the gates for groups of ten.

3. The emperor was still in the vicinity of Pelekanos. He
wished those counts who had not yet sworn allegiance to give
their pledges to him. Written instructions were issued to
Boutoumites therefore to advise all counts not to begin the
march to Antioch before doing homage to the emperor; this
would be another opportunity for them to accept an array of
gifts. Hearing of money and gifts, Bohemond was the first to
pay heed to Boutoumites' comments, and immediately counselled all of them to return to see the emperor. Bohemond was
like that – so uncontrollable was his lust for money. The
emperor welcomed them with great splendour when they
arrived at Pelekanos, and treated them with great care. Then
he called them together and said: 'Remember the oath you have
all sworn to me and if you really intend not to transgress it,
advise any others you know, who have not sworn, to take this
same oath.' They at once sent for these men and all assembled
to pay homage.

But the nephew of Bohemond, Tancred,[5] was a man of independent spirit, and protested that he owed allegiance to one
man only, Bohemond, and that allegiance he hoped to keep till
his dying day. He was pressed by the others, including even the
emperor's kinsmen. With apparent indifference, he fixed his
gaze on the tent in which the emperor held the seat of honour
(a tent more vast than any other in living memory), as he said,
'If you fill it with money and give it to me, as well as the sums
you have given to all the other counts, then I too will take the
oath.' But Palaiologos, acting zealously on the emperor's behalf,

found Tancred's words contemptible and hypocritical, and pushed him away with scorn. Tancred recklessly darted towards him, whereupon the emperor rose from his throne and intervened. Bohemond, for his part, calmed down his nephew, and said to him: 'It is not fitting to behave in so disrespectful a way towards the kinsmen of the emperor.' Tancred was ashamed of having acted like a drunken lout with Palaiologos and yielding to the arguments of Bohemond and the others, took the oath.

When all had taken their leave of the emperor, Tatikios, at that time *megas primikerios* together with the forces under his command was attached to the main army, both in order to help and protect them on all occasions and also to take over from them any towns they captured, if indeed God granted them that favour. Once more therefore the Kelts made the crossing on the following day and all set out for Antioch. The emperor assumed that not all their men would necessarily follow the counts; he accordingly notified Boutoumites that all Kelts left behind were to be recruited to guard Nicaea.

Tatikios, with his forces, and all the counts, with their numberless hosts, reached Leukai in two days. At his own request Bohemond was placed in command of the vanguard, while the rest followed in column of march at a slow pace. When some Turks saw him moving rather fast on the plain of Dorylaion, they thought they had chanced upon the whole Keltic army and treating it with disdain they at once attacked. That crazy idiot, Latinos, who had dared to seat himself on the imperial throne, forgetting the emperor's advice, stupidly rode out to the front of Bohemond's lines, and galloped on ahead of the rest. Forty of his men were killed while he himself, having been seriously wounded, turned in flight and hurried back to the centre – proving in his actions, if not in words, just how wise the emperor's advice had been.

Bohemond, seeing the ferocity of the Turks, sent for reinforcements, which quickly arrived. An almighty and terrible battle followed. Victory though belonged to the Roman and Keltic army. After that they continued on in marching order, and near Hebraike encountered the Sultan Tanisman[6] and Hasan, who alone commanded 80,000 fully-armed infantry. It was a hard-fought battle, not only because of the vast numbers involved, but also because neither side would give way. However, the Turks were fighting with more spirit and Bohemond, commanding on the right wing, realized this. So, detaching himself from the rest of the army, he made a headlong onslaught on Klitziasthlan himself, charging like a lion exulting in his might,[7] as the poet says. This had a terrifying effect on the Turks, causing them to flee before the Keltic force.

The Kelts themselves, remembering the emperor's instructions, did not pursue them very far, but occupied the Turkish entrenchment and regrouped there for a short time. They again fell in with the Turks near Augoustopolis, attacked and routed them completely. After that the barbarians faded away. The survivors from the battle were scattered in all directions, leaving behind their women and children; they no longer had the capability to engage with the Latins, and instead sought to save themselves by fleeing home.

4. What happened then? Well, the Latins with the Roman army reached Antioch by what is called the Quick March, ignoring the lands to either side of this. Near the walls of the city a ditch was dug, in which the baggage was deposited, and the siege of Antioch began. It lasted for three lunar months.[8] The Turks, who were extremely anxious about the difficult position in which they found themselves, sent a message to the sultan of Khorosan,[9] imploring him to supply enough men to help them reinforce those defending Antioch and drive off the besieging Latins.

Now it so happened that a certain Armenian[10] was on a tower of the city, watching that part of the wall allotted to Bohemond. This man often used to lean over the parapet, and so Bohemond took the opportunity to tempt him with many promises and convinced him to agree to hand over the city. The Armenian said to him: 'Whenever you like to give me the sign from outside, I will at once hand this tower over to you. Only make sure that you and all the men under you are ready, with ladders at the ready. Nor must you alone be ready: all the men should be in armour, so that as soon as the Turks see you on the tower and hear you shouting your war cries, they panic and flee.'

However, Bohemond kept this arrangement to himself. While this was going on, a man came with the news that a very large force of Agarenes was on the point of arriving from Khorosan under the command of Kourpagan,[11] to attack them. Bohemond was informed and being unwilling to hand over Antioch to Tatikios, as he was bound to do if he kept his oaths to the emperor, and coveting the city for himself, he devised an evil scheme for removing Tatikios against his will. He went to find him and said: 'I wish to reveal a secret to you, which has to do with your personal safety. A report has reached the ears of the counts, which has seemed to agitate them profoundly, revealing that the sultan has sent these men from Khorosan against us at the emperor's bidding. The counts believe the story is true and they are plotting to kill you. Well, I have now done my duty in warning you about this threat: the danger is imminent. The rest is up to you. You must look after your own interests and take thought for the lives of your men.' Tatikios had other worries apart from this: there was a severe famine (an ox head was selling for three gold staters) and he despaired of taking Antioch. He left the place, therefore, boarded the Roman ships anchored in the harbour of Soudi and sailed for Cyprus.[12]

After his departure Bohemond, who was still keeping the Armenian's promise secret and was buoyed up by the hope of gaining Antioch for himself, addressed the counts: 'You see how we have already spent a long time here in misery, without making any progress whatsoever. Quite the opposite; we will soon become the victims of famine, unless we make provision for our safety.' When they asked him what he suggested, he went on: 'Not all victories are granted by God through the sword, nor are such results invariably achieved through battle. What the turmoil of war has not produced is often gladly given through negotiation, and friendly diplomatic manoeuvres many a time have set up finer trophies. Let us not waste time in vain, but rather hurry to come up with a cunning and bold scheme to save ourselves before Kourpagan arrives. I suggest that each of us should try hard to win over the barbarian watching his particular section. And if you approve, let a prize be awarded to the first man who succeeds in this – the governorship of the city, say, until the arrival of the emperor's nominee, who will take over from us. Of course, even in this we may not make any good progress.'

The cunning Bohemond loved power, not for the sake of the Latins or their common interests, but for his own self-grandeur. His plans and intrigues and deceptions did not disappoint, as the account which follows will make clear. The counts unanimously approved of his scheme and set to work. As day broke Bohemond immediately went off to the tower; the Armenian, according to his agreement, opened the gates. Bohemond leapt at once to the top of the tower as fast as he could, followed by his comrades. Besiegers and besieged alike saw him standing there on the battlements and ordering the trumpeter to sound the call to battle. An extraordinary sight could then be seen: the Turks, panic-stricken, without more ado fled through the gate at the other side of the city; a mere handful, brave warriors, were left behind to guard the citadel; the Kelts outside followed in the steps of Bohemond as they climbed the ladders to the top and straightway occupied the city. Tancred, with a strong force of Kelts, lost no time in pursuing the runaways, killing and wounding many of them.

When Kourpagan arrived with his countless thousands to help relieve Antioch, he found the place already in the hands of the enemy. He made camp, dug a trench and deposited his baggage, and prepared to invest the city. Before he could begin the Kelts made a sortie and attacked him. There was a tremendous struggle, in which the Turks were victorious; the Latins were penned up inside the gates, exposed to danger from two sides – from the defenders of the citadel (which the barbarians still controlled) and from the Turks encamped beyond the walls. Bohemond, being a shrewd man and wishing to secure for himself overlordship of Antioch, again addressed the counts: 'It's not right,' he said, 'that the same men should have to fight on two fronts, with enemies outside and in the city at the same time. We ought to divide up our forces in two unequal groups, proportionate to the enemies opposed to us, and then take up the challenge against them. My task will be to fight the defenders of the citadel, if, that is, you agree. The others will be concerned with the enemy outside. They will launch a violent attack on them.'

Everyone agreed with this idea of Bohemond's. He immediately built a small counter-wall facing the citadel and cutting it off from the rest of Antioch, which would be a sturdy line of defence if the war went on. After it was completed he established himself as its guardian, and maintained unceasing pressure on the defenders at every available opportunity (and showing great bravery in doing so). The other counts devoted careful attention to their own sectors, protecting the city at all points, examining the parapets and the battlements that crown the walls, making sure that no barbarians from outside should climb up by ladders and so capture the city, that no one from inside should furtively make his way on to the walls and then, after parley with the enemy, arrange to betray it.

5. While these events were taking place at Antioch, the emperor was very eager to bring help personally to the Kelts, but the despoiling and utter destruction of the towns and of the coastal regions held him back, despite his impatience. For Tzakhas held Smyrna[13] as though it were his own private property, and the individual known as Tangripermes retained Ephesos, where a church had once been built in honour of the apostle St John the Divine. One after the other the satraps occupied fortified locations, treating the Christians like slaves and ravaging everything. They had even taken the islands of Khios and Rhodes and all the others besides and were building pirate vessels there. As a result of these activities the emperor thought it best to attend first to the seaboard and Tzakhas. He decided to leave sufficient forces on the mainland, with a strong fleet; they would serve to throw off and contain barbarian incursions. With the remainder of the army he would take the road to Antioch and fight the barbarians on the way as chance offered.

He therefore sent for John Doukas,[14] his brother-in-law, and entrusted him with troops drawn from different countries and enough ships to lay siege to the coastal towns; he also gave him charge of Tzakhas' daughter, who had been taken prisoner along with the others who happened at that time to be in Nicaea. Doukas was to make a general proclamation of the capture of Nicaea; if it was not believed, he was then to exhibit

the lady herself to the Turkish satraps and the barbarians living
in the coastal areas, so that those who occupied the towns
mentioned above would be convinced by seeing her that Nicaea
had indeed fallen and would therefore become disheartened
and surrender the towns without a fight. So John was sent, well
equipped with supplies of all kinds. How many triumphs he
achieved in the fight against Tzakhas and how he dealt with
him and drove him away will be described here.

The *doux* took his leave of the emperor, left the capital
and crossed at Abydos; he called for Kaspax, who was given
command of the fleet, with total responsibility for the naval
expedition. John promised him that if he fought well he would
be appointed governor of Smyrna itself when that town was
taken and of all the neighbouring districts. While Kaspax sailed
as *thalassokrator* of the naval forces, John remained on land in
command of the armed forces. The inhabitants of Smyrna saw
Kaspax and John approaching simultaneously with the fleet
and by land respectively; Doukas pitched camp a short distance
from the walls, while Kaspax anchored his ships in the harbour.
The inhabitants of Smyrna already knew that Nicaea had fallen
and were in no mood for fighting: they preferred to start negotiations for peace, promising to give up their town to John without a struggle and with no bloodshed if he would swear on
oath to let them go home unharmed. Doukas agreed, giving his
word that Tzakhas' proposal would be carried out to the letter.
Thus the enemy was peacefully expelled and Kaspax was
installed in Smyrna with full authority. At this point an incident
took place which I will outline now.

When Kaspax had left John Doukas, a man from Smyrna
came to him, complaining that 500 golden staters had been
stolen from him by a Saracen. Kaspax ordered the two parties
to appear before him for judgement. The Syrian was forcibly
dragged in and thought he was being hauled off to execution.
In desperation for his life he drew his dagger and plunged it
into Kaspax's stomach; then, wheeling round, he struck at the
governor's brother and wounded him in the thigh. In the great
confusion that followed the Saracen ran off, but all the sailors
of the fleet including the rowers entered the town in a disorgan-

ized mob and massacred everyone without mercy. It was a
pitiable sight – some 10,000 slain in the twinkling of an eye.
John Doukas, deeply moved by the murder of Kaspax, once
again, and for some time, devoted his whole attention to the
affairs of Smyrna. He came to the town, made a thorough
inspection of its defences and received accurate information
from experts about the feelings of its people. The situation
called for a man of courage and so Hyaleas was appointed *doux*
of Smyrna, as he was the best candidate; what is more, he was
a military man.

All the fleet was left behind to protect Smyrna, but Doukas
himself advanced with his force on Ephesos, which was held by
the satraps Tangripermes and Marakes. When the barbarians
realized he was approaching, they arranged their forces, fully
armed and in battle formation, on the plain outside the place.
Losing not a minute the *doux* bore down on them with his men
in disciplined order. The battle that ensued lasted for most of
the day. Both sides were locked in combat and the issue was
still undecided, when the Turks turned away and fled at speed.
Many of them were killed there and prisoners were taken, not
only from among the ordinary soldiers, but from the satraps,
most of whom were captured, with the total number as high as
about 2,000. When the emperor heard of this victory, he gave
orders that they were to be scattered among the islands. The
Turkish survivors went off across the River Maiandros towards
Polyboton, thinking they had seen the last of Doukas. But it
did not turn out like that. Doukas left Petzeas to govern the
town and taking with him all the infantry at once set out in
pursuit, not chaotically, but in disciplined fashion just as would
be expected of a highly experienced general and furthermore,
as ordered by the emperor.

The Turks, as I have said, had made their way across the
Maiandros and through the towns in that vicinity; they reached
Polyboton. The *doux*, however, did not take the same route:
he followed a shorter track, seizing Sardeis and Philadelphia by
surprise, and detailing Michael Kekaumenos to guard the latter
afterwards. When Doukas arrived at Laodikeia the whole population immediately came to meet him, and as a result, he treated

them kindly since they had joined him of their own accord; he
therefore allowed them to carry on peacefully without even
appointing a governor. From there he went through Khoma to
Lampe, where Eustathios Kamytzes was appointed *strategos*.
When he finally came to Polyboton he found a strong body of
Turks. An attack was launched on them just after they had
deposited their baggage, and in a brief encounter he won a
decisive victory, killing many, and taking the kind of booty one
would expect from a group of this considerable size.

6. John Doukas had not yet returned and was still continuing
his efforts against the Turks when the emperor was ready to
march to the aid of the Kelts in the Antioch region. After wiping
out many barbarians en route and sacking many towns that
they had been occupying, he arrived at Philomelion with his
whole army. It was here that he was joined by William of
Grantmesnil, Stephen, count of France, and Peter Aliphas, who
had come from Antioch.[15] They had been let down by ropes
from the battlements of the city and had come by way of Tarsos.
They assured him that the Kelts had been reduced to a state of
extreme peril, and went on to swear that they were utterly
doomed.

The emperor was all the more anxious to hurry to their aid
as a result of this, despite the general opposition to the enterprise. But there was a widespread rumour that countless hordes
of barbarians were about to attack him (the Sultan of Khorosan,
learning that the emperor had set out to help the Kelts, had
sent his son Ishmael with very strong forces from Khorosan
and even more distant parts, all well armed, with orders to
tackle the emperor before he could reach Antioch). And so the
news brought by the Franks from Antioch and information
received about Ishmael's approach checked the plans for rescuing the Kelts, however much the emperor longed to wipe out
the Turks who were fighting so furiously and above all their
leader Kourpagan. As to the future, he drew the conclusion one
would expect: to save a city recently captured by the Kelts, but
still unsettled and immediately besieged by the Agarenes, would
be impossible; the Kelts moreover had given up hopes of saving
themselves and were planning to desert the fortifications and

hand them over to the enemy, intent simply on saving their own lives by running away.

The truth is that the Keltic race, among other characteristics, combines an independent spirit and imprudence, not to mention an absolute refusal to cultivate a disciplined art of war; when fighting and warfare are imminent, inspired by passion they are irresistible, evident not only in the rank and file, but in their leaders too, charging into the midst of the enemy's line with overwhelming abandon – provided that the opposition everywhere gives ground; but if their foes chance to lay ambushes with soldier-like skill and if they meet them in a systematic manner, all their boldness vanishes. Generally speaking, Kelts are indomitable in the opening cavalry charge, but afterwards, because of the weight of their armour and their own passionate nature and recklessness, it is actually very easy to defeat them.

The emperor, having neither sufficient forces to resist their great numbers, nor the power to change the Keltic character, nor the possibility of diverting them to some expedient policy by more reasonable advice, thought it wise to go no further. He might lose Constantinople as well as Antioch in his eagerness to relieve them. He was afraid that if the enormous hosts of Turks came upon him now, the people living in the area of Philomelion might fall victims to the barbarian sword. Under the circumstances he decided to make a general proclamation announcing the arrival of the Agarenes. It was immediately announced that every man and woman should leave the place before their arrival, thus saving their own lives and as much of their possessions as they could carry.

Without delay the whole population, men and women alike, chose to follow the emperor ... Such were the measures taken by the emperor with regard to the prisoners. One part of the army was detached and then subdivided into many companies; they were sent out in several directions to fight the Agarenes, with orders to attack whenever they discovered the Turks making forays, and to hold up their progress against the emperor. Alexios himself, with all the barbarian prisoners and the Christians who had joined him, prepared to return to the imperial capital.

The Archisatrap Ishmael had been informed of the emperor's departure from Constantinople, of the great slaughter that followed it and of the utter destruction of many townships on his march; he also knew that the emperor was about to return to the capital with much booty and many captives. Ishmael was in a difficult position: there was nothing left for him to do – he had lost the quarry, as it were. He changed his line of march and decided to besiege Paipert, which had been taken and occupied shortly before by the famous Theodore Gabras. The whole Turkish force halted by the river which flows near this place. Gabras took stock of this, and set about planning a surprise attack under the cover of nightfall. We should save the story of the culmination of the Gabras affair, the background of this individual and his character for later in this history; we must now resume the narrative.

The Latins were dreadfully harassed by famine and by the unrelenting siege, and went to approach Peter, their bishop,[16] who had been defeated formerly at Helenopolis, as I have already made clear, to ask for his advice. 'You promised,' he replied, 'to keep yourselves pure until you arrived at Jerusalem. But you have broken that promise, I think. For that reason God no longer helps us as He did before. You must turn again to the Lord and weep for your sins in sackcloth and ashes, with hot tears and nights passed in intercession, to prove your repentance. Then, and only then, will I join in seeking God's favour for you.' They listened to the high priest's counsel. Some days later, moved by some divine oracle, he called to him the leading counts and recommended them to dig to the right of the altar and there, he said, they would find the Holy Nail. They did as he said, but found nothing, and returning to him in dismay told him of their failure. He prayed even more earnestly and commanded them to make a close examination with greater care. Again they carried out his orders exactly. This time they found what they were looking for and running brought it to Peter, overcome with joy and awe.

After that the revered and Holy Nail was entrusted by them to St Gilles to carry with him in battle, for he was purer than the rest. On the next day they made a sortie from a secret gate against the Turks. This was the occasion when the one named Flanders[17] asked the others to grant him one request – to be allowed to ride out at the head of their force against the enemy, with only three companions. The request was granted, and when the rival armies were drawn up in ranks ready for battle, he dismounted, knelt down on the ground, and three times in prayer implored God for help. And when all cried aloud, 'God with us!', he charged at full gallop at Kourpagan, who was standing on a hilltop. Those who opposed them were straightway speared and hurled down. This struck terror into the hearts of the Turks and before battle was even begun they fled, since a divine force was so obviously aiding the Christians. What is more, in the confusion of their flight most of the barbarians were caught up in the currents of the river and drowned; their bodies served as a bridge for those who came after them.[18]

When the pursuit had gone on for a fair distance, the Kelts returned to the Turkish entrenchment, where they found the barbarians' baggage and all the booty they had brought with them. They would have liked to take it up at once, but it was so enormous that thirty days would not have been enough to get it all back to Antioch. For a short while they remained there, recovering from the tribulations of war. At the same time they were concerned for Antioch, for a new governor had to be appointed. Their choice fell on Bohemond, who had been after this position even before the fall of the city. After he had been invested with overriding authority of Antioch,[19] the army set out on the road to Jerusalem. Many coastal strongpoints were captured along the route, but the most powerful places, which would require a longer siege, were for the time ignored, as they hurried on to reach Jerusalem. The walls were encircled and repeatedly attacked, and after a siege of one lunar month it fell.[20] Many Saracens and Jews in the city were massacred. When submission was complete, when all opposition ended, Godfrey was invested with supreme power and nominated king.

7. Amerimnes, *exousiastes* of Babylon, was informed of the Keltic invasion, of how Jerusalem had been taken, of how they had occupied Antioch itself as well as many other towns in that

region. Accordingly he collected a huge force composed of Armenians, Arabs, Saracens and Agarenes, and sent these off against the Kelts. Godfrey informed them about this, so they at once took up arms and descended to Jaffa to await the attack. From there they then moved to Ramleh, the place where the great martyr George suffered his martyrdom, and there they fought a battle against the army of Amerimnes which had arrived to attack them. The Kelts quickly won a victory.

On the next day, however, when the enemy's vanguard caught them from the rear, the Latins were beaten and escaped with their lives to Ramleh. The only count not present was Baldwin; he had escaped, not from cowardice, but to find some better means of securing his own safety and that of the army against the Babylonians. The Babylonians themselves moved on Ramleh,[21] and, having encircled it and submitted it to a short siege, took it. Many of the Latins were killed at the time, but more were sent as prisoners to Babylon. From Ramleh the whole enemy force was hurriedly diverted to the siege of Jaffa – a typical manoeuvre of the barbarians. Baldwin visited all the townships captured by the Franks and raised a not inconsiderable number of cavalry and infantry troops, a force to be reckoned with. He marched on the Babylonians and routed them severely.

The news of the Latin disaster at Ramleh was a grievous shock to the emperor; the thought of the counts being held in captivity was intolerable. To him these men, in the prime of life, at the height of their strength, of noble lineage, seemed to rival the heroes of old. He could not stand that they remain prisoners in a foreign land. He called for a man named Bardales, gave him plenty of money to ransom them, and dispatched him to Babylon with letters addressed to Amerimnes about the counts. Amerimnes read the messages from the emperor and as a result released the captives without accepting a ransom, gladly freeing them all – except Godfrey,[22] who had already been sold at a price to his brother Baldwin. The counts were received with honour by the emperor at Constantinople. He gave them large sums of money, and after they had rested sufficiently sent them home, delighted with the treatment they had received at his hands. As for Godfrey, once he had been restored as king of Jerusalem, he sent Baldwin to Edessa.[23]

At this point the emperor instructed St Gilles to hand over Laodikeia to Andronikos Tzintziloukes and the districts of Marakes and Balaneus to the officers of Eumathios, who was then *doux* of Cyprus, while he himself was to proceed further and fight to the best of his ability for control of the other fortified places. St Gilles did so, following the emperor's instructions to the letter.[24] After handing over the places to the aforementioned officers, he departed for Antarados which he took without resorting to force. News of this spurred Atapakas of Damascus[25] to march against him with a strong force. St Gilles did not have enough men to stand up to so numerous a foe, but devised a plan notable rather for its ingenuity than for any show of bravery. Putting his faith in the inhabitants of Antarados, he said to them: 'As this fortress is so large, I will hide myself away in a corner somewhere. When Atapakas arrives, you must not tell him the truth, but assure him that I fled because I was so scared.'

Well, Atapakas came and asked about St Gilles; he was persuaded that he had indeed run away. Then, tired out after his march, he pitched his tent near the walls. As the natives showed him every mark of friendship, the Turks had no reason whatever to suspect any hostile intentions from them, and confidently set their horses free on the plain. At midday, when the sun's rays were directly overhead, St Gilles and his men (who numbered up to four hundred) prepared themselves in full armour, suddenly opened the gates and charged through the middle of the enemy camp. Those of the Turks who normally fought valiantly stood up and gave battle, forgetful of their own lives, but the rest attempted to escape to safety by fleeing. The width of the plain and the absence of any marsh or hill or ravine betrayed them all into the hands of the Latins; they were all slain by the sword, except for a few who were captured. St Gilles, having outwitted the Turks in this manner, went on to Tripolis.

As soon as he arrived, he climbed and seized the summit of the hill which lies opposite Tripolis and which forms a part of

the Lebanon, in order to use it as a fortress and therefore cut
off the water supply flowing down from the Lebanon into
Tripolis over the slopes of this hill. After informing the emperor
of these actions, St Gilles asked him to build a very strong fort
there before bigger forces turned up from Khorosan, against
which he would have to fight. The emperor entrusted to the
doux of Cyprus the task of building this fortress and instructed
him to use the fleet to supply whatever materials as well as
manpower were necessary to build it in the position identified
by St Gilles. Such was the situation up to this point.

St Gilles was camped outside Tripolis, relentlessly straining
every nerve to capture the place.[26] But Bohemond, on the other
hand, vented the hatred he had long held against the emperor
once he found out that Tzintziloukes had reached Laodikeia,
and sent his nephew Tancred to besiege that town with a substantial force. A rumour of this soon reached St Gilles and he
lost not a minute in coming himself to Laodikeia and entering
into negotiations with Tancred to try to convince him through
every and any argument to give up the siege. However, once it
became clear, after numerous meetings, that Tancred was not
to be convinced and that he might as well have been singing to
the deaf, he returned to Tripolis. Without the slightest relaxation Tancred pressed the siege. Tzintziloukes, who realized
that his position was critical and was impressed by Tancred's
determination, appealed for aid from Cyprus. It came too
slowly and so, reduced to helplessness partly because of the
siege, but also because of the distress brought about by famine,
he decided to surrender the town.[27]

8. While these things were going on, Godfrey had died, and
since it was essential to choose a successor, the Latins in Jerusalem at once sent for St Gilles from Tripolis, wanting to make
him king of Jerusalem.[28] But he kept putting off his departure.
Later he went to their capital and as the people of Jerusalem
realized that he was still obdurate, they sent for Baldwin, who
was then in the district of Edessa, and elected him king of
Jerusalem. The emperor had gladly welcomed St Gilles, but
when he learnt that Baldwin had become ruler of Jerusalem, he
kept the former with him. It was at this moment that the army

of Normans arrived under the command of the two brothers named Flanders.[29]

The emperor repeatedly advised these individuals to follow the same route as their predecessors and to pass through the coastal areas to reach Jerusalem and thereby link up with the rest of the Latin army in Jerusalem. He found that they would not listen and were reluctant to join the Franks. They wanted to take a different route to the east, going straight towards Khorosan, which they intended to conquer. The emperor knew their plan would be utterly disastrous, but since he was unwilling to see an army so numerous suffer extinction (there were 50,000 cavalrymen and 100,000 infantry) and since persuasion was impossible, he tried a new tack, as they say, and summoned St Gilles and Tzitas, sending them off with them in order to give suitable advice and as far as they could restrain them from foolish enterprises. So they crossed the straits to Kibotos, hurried on to the Armeniakon and took Ankyra[30] by surprise. Crossing the River Halys they reached a small fort. Since this was held by the Romans, the priests there went out to greet them in their sacred vestments and carrying the gospel and crosses, since they were Christians after all. But the invaders not only massacred the priests with inhuman cruelty, but the rest of the Christians too. Then without the slightest concern for what they had done, they simply carried on with their march in the direction of Amaseia.

The Turks, who are skilled in warfare, occupied all the villages on their route and burnt all food supplies before they arrived, then quickly attacked them. It was on a Monday[31] that the Turks overwhelmed them. On that day they set up camp locally, and having dug trenches, set their baggage inside. The following day battle was renewed. The Turkish encampment surrounded their enemy, so that opportunity for foraging was denied them; nor could they lead out their horses and baggage animals to water. By now the Kelts saw with their own eyes that annihilation awaited them and with utter disregard for their own safety, took up arms the following day, a Wednesday, and engaged the barbarians in a fierce battle. The Turks, having them in their grip, no longer relied on lance or bow, but drew their swords to fight at close quarters, and routed the Normans. The latter withdrew to their own camp to consider what they could do.

The outstanding emperor, who had put before them a better course and whom they had refused to listen to, was not with them any more. Their only recourse was to ask the opinions of St Gilles and Tzitas. At the same time they inquired whether there was any territory in that area under the emperor's control where they might find refuge. In the end they abandoned baggage, tents and all the infantry, mounted their horses and galloped off as fast as they could to the coastal regions of the Armeniakon and Paurae. The Turks made a mass attack on their encampment and took away everything. Afterwards they pursued and caught up with stragglers; all were massacred, except for a handful of men who were carried off to Khorosan to be exhibited.

So much for the exploits of the Turks in their battles against the Normans. As for St Gilles and Tzitas, they made their way to Constantinople with the few surviving knights.[32] The emperor received them there and after presenting them with generous gifts of money and allowing them to rest, he asked them where they would like to go for the future. They chose Jerusalem. He lavished more presents on them, and sent them off by sea, just as they had wanted. St Gilles left Constantinople also, to rejoin his own army at Tripolis, which he was eagerly seeking to capture. Later he met with a fatal illness[33] and as he was breathing his last sent for his nephew William, to whom he set out his legacy, namely all the strongpoints which he had taken, and appointed him lord and commander of all his forces. At the news of his death the emperor at once wrote to the *doux* of Cyprus, instructing him to send Niketas Khalintzes with large sums of money for William, in order to win him over and persuade him to take a firm oath of allegiance to the emperor, an allegiance which his dead uncle St Gilles had faithfully observed to the end of his life.

9. News also reached the emperor of Tancred's occupation of Laodikeia. He sent a letter to Bohemond, which ran thus: 'You know full well of the oaths and promises made to the

Roman Empire, not by you alone, but by all the other counts. Now you are the first to break faith. You have seized Antioch and gained possession of other fortified places too, including Laodikeia itself. I bid you withdraw from the city of Antioch and all other places, thereby doing what is right, and do not try to provoke fresh hostilities and battles against yourself.' Bohemond read the imperial missives.[34] It was no longer possible to defend himself with his usual deceit, for his deeds bore clear evidence of the truth; in theory, therefore, he admitted the letter was justified, but blamed the emperor for his own evil doings. 'I myself,' he wrote, 'am not responsible for these things, but you. You promised to follow us with a strong force, but you were unwilling to back your pledges by action. As for us, after our arrival at Antioch, for three months we endured great suffering, contending with the enemy as well as with a famine worse than any in living memory, one so bad that most of us were even reduced to eating meats forbidden by law. Nevertheless, we held on as best we could, and while we were doing that, Your Majesty's most faithful servant Tatikios, who had been appointed to help, abandoned us in our peril and went away. Contrary to expectation we did take the city and routed the forces which came from Khorosan to aid the inhabitants of Antioch. How, tell me, can it be right for us to renounce so easily what we have won by our own sweat and toil?'

When the emperor's ambassadors returned and he read Bohemond's reply, he realized that Bohemond was his old self again, incorrigible as ever; clearly the frontiers of the Roman Empire must be firmly held and Bohemond's unbridled ambition must somehow be checked. For these reasons Boutoumites was dispatched with numerous troops[35] to Kilikia, with elite forces, all magnificent fighters, every one a follower of Ares; also with him were Bardas and Michael, the *arkhioino-khoos*, both in the prime of life, and just growing their first beards. When these young men were small children the emperor had taken them under his personal protection and had given them a good military education. He sent them with Boutoumites together with thousands of other fine soldiers, both Keltic and Roman, since he thought they were more reliable than their companions. They were to accompany Boutoumites and obey him in everything, but at the same time the emperor relied on them to keep him informed by secret letters about what was going on. He was anxious to secure the whole of Kilikia; it would be easier then to prepare for operations against Antioch.

Boutoumites therefore set out with all his forces and had reached Attaleia when he discovered that Bardas and Michael were not obeying his orders. To prevent a mutiny among the soldiers – which would cause all his enthusiasm to end in nothing and force him to evacuate Kilikia without accomplishing anything – he at once informed the emperor of their activities. He begged to be relieved of their company. The emperor, aware of the damage likely to be done by such men, promptly diverted them and all the other suspects to a different task. They were told in writing to report without delay to Cyprus where Constantine Euphorbenos was at that time *doux*, and to obey whatever orders he gave them. The young men gladly read their instructions and sailed with all speed to Cyprus. They had only spent a short time with the *doux* of Cyprus there before they were behaving with their usual arrogance towards him also. Naturally he regarded them with suspicion. They remembered the affection which the emperor had shown them and wrote to him, denigrating the *doux* and demanding his recall. The emperor was alarmed by their letters: with them in Cyprus were certain nobles whose loyalty he doubted and whom he had exiled; it was possible that these men might also be disaffected by their bad feeling. Because of this he at once ordered Kantakouzenos to take the young men with him. He came to Kyrenia, summoned them and took them away.

Such was the story about these men, by whom I mean Bardas and Michael, the *arkhioinokhoos*. As for Boutoumites, he arrived in Kilikia with Monastras and the other commanders who had been left behind with him, and when he found that the Armenians had come to terms with Tancred, he modified his route to go past them and went on to Marash, which he took together with all the neighbouring townships and small places. A force capable of guarding the whole countryside was left under the command of the semi-barbarian Monastras, who has often been mentioned in this account, while Boutoumites himself returned to the capital.

10. When the Franks set out for Jerusalem with the intention of conquering the towns of Syria, they made fine promises to the bishop of Pisa,[36] if he would help them to attain their goal. He was convinced by their arguments and incited two of his colleagues living by the sea to the same course of action. There was no delay. He equipped biremes, triremes, warships and other fast vessels to the number of 900, and set off for Syria. A fairly strong squadron of this fleet was sent to ravage Corfu, Leukas, Kephalenia and Zakynthos.

The emperor thereupon ordered all provinces of the Roman Empire to provide ships. Many were also made ready in Constantinople itself. From time to time he used to board a ship with one bank of oars and give advice himself to the shipwrights about their construction. He knew the Pisans were masters of naval warfare and he feared a sea battle with them. Accordingly, he affixed on the prow of each vessel the heads of lions and other land animals; they were made of bronze or iron with wide-open jaws; the thin layer of gold with which they were covered made the very sight of them terrifying. Greek fire[37] to be hurled at the enemy through tubes was made to issue from the mouths of these figureheads in such a way that they appeared to be belching out the fire. When all was ready, the emperor sent for Tatikios, who had just come from Antioch, and entrusted this fleet to him with the title of *periphanestatos kephale*; Landulph, however, was put in charge of the whole navy, and promoted to the rank of *megas doux*,[38] because he was the greatest expert in warfare at sea.

They left the capital in the latter half of April[39] and arrived at Samos, with the Roman fleet. They came ashore, then hauled their boats up on to land, tarring them thoroughly so as to make them more seaworthy. When they heard that the Pisans were close by, they cast off and chased them as far as Kos. While the Pisans reached the island in the morning, they arrived in the evening. Finding no Pisans, they sailed away to Knidos, which lies off the Anatolian mainland. Although they had missed their prey, they discovered a few Pisans who had been left behind and asked them where the Pisan fleet had gone. They said that they had gone to Rhodes. At once the Romans cast off again and soon caught up with them between Patras and Rhodes. Spying the enemy the Pisans immediately made ready for battle, with sharpened swords and hearts prepared for combat. The Roman fleet drew near and a Peloponnesian count called Perikhytes, an expert navigator, rowed hard and fast in his monoreme against the enemy as soon as they came in sight. He went through the Pisan centre like a flash of light-ning and returned to the Roman fleet.

Unfortunately, the latter did not enter the battle in a disci-plined manner, but made sharp, disorderly attacks. Landulph himself was the first to make contact with the enemy, but his fire missed the target and all he did was to squander the fuel. The count called Eleemon boldly made for a very large vessel by the stern, but fouled its rudders and found it hard to dis-engage. He would have been caught, too, if he had not quickly remembered the fuel prepared for his tubes and scored a direct hit with Greek fire. He then deftly manoeuvred his ship round and immediately set light to three very big barbarian vessels. At the same time there was a sudden squall of wind which descended violently on the sea and whipped it up; the ships were dashed together and all but threatened to sink – the waves crashed down on them, the yardarms creaked and the sails were torn. The barbarians were frightened out of their wits, partly because of the fire being directed at them (they were unaccus-tomed to such equipment: fire naturally rises upwards, but this was being shot in whatever direction the Romans wished, often downwards and sideways, to port or starboard), partly because they were thrown into confusion by the heavy seas. They decided to flee.

So much for the barbarians. As for the Roman fleet, it made for a tiny island with a name something like Seutlos. When day broke, the Romans sailed on to Rhodes. They disembarked there and led out their prisoners, among whom they found the nephew of Bohemond himself. They tried to scare them with threats that they would sell them all as slaves or kill them.

When they saw that this had no effect on them and the prospect of slavery made no impression at all, they wasted no more time – they massacred them with swords.

The survivors of the Pisan expedition turned to plundering the islands that lay on their course, not least Cyprus. Eumathios Philokales happened to be there and attacked them. Their naval crews, overcome by fear and without a thought for their ship-mates who had gone ashore to find booty, abandoned most of them on the island and weighing anchor in a state of panic sailed away to Laodikeia with the idea of rejoining Bohemond. In fact they did reach the place and went to him, declaring their desire for friendship. He, being Bohemond, was pleased to receive them. Those who had been marooned while they pil-laged returned to find their fleet had gone, recklessly hurled themselves into the sea and were drowned.

The Roman commanders and Landulph held a conference once they reached Cyprus about the possibility of suing for peace. As they were all agreed that such a course was desirable, Boutoumites was sent to Bohemond. He was detained by him for fifteen whole days. Laodikeia was now in the grip of famine and Bohemond being Bohemond, not changed a jot, a man who had never learned what it was to keep the peace. He sent for Boutoumites. 'It wasn't for friendship's sake nor in search of peace that you came here,' he said, 'but to set fire to my ships. Be off with you – and think yourself lucky that you're allowed to go away in one piece.'

So Boutoumites went off back to those who had sent him in the harbour of Cyprus. Bohemond's wicked intentions were now much clearer after these revelations and a treaty with the emperor was obviously out of the question. The Romans therefore weighed anchor again and crammed on all sail for the capital over watery ways. Off Syke, however, in a tremendous storm which lashed the waves into fury, the ships were cast up on the beach, all being half-wrecked, except those commanded by Tatikios.

Such were the events concerning the Pisan fleet. Meanwhile Bohemond, being himself a thorough rogue, was afraid that the emperor might anticipate him and seize Kourikos, moor a

Roman fleet in the harbour, guard Cyprus and thus prevent
the approach of hoped-for allies from Lombardy along the
Anatolian seaboard. Under the circumstances he decided to
rebuild Kourikos and occupy the harbour. In former times it
had been a very strong town, but later fell into ruin. Now the
emperor, foreseeing Bohemond's strategy, had taken his own
precautions. The eunuch Eustathios was promoted from the
office of *kanikleios* to that of *megas droungarios* of the fleet
and was sent with instructions to seize Kourikos without delay.
He was to lose no time in rebuilding the place itself and also
the fort of Seleukeia, six stades away; in both places a strong
force was to be left, and Strategios Strabos was to be appointed
doux, physically a small man but in the arts of war a person
with a profound amount of experience. Moreover, an adequate
fleet was to lie at anchor in the harbour and a proclamation
was to be made warning sailors to be on their guard, to lie in
wait for Bohemond's reinforcements coming from Lombardy
and to give help to Cyprus.

The *droungarios* of the fleet set sail, thwarted Bohemond's
schemes and restored Kourikos[40] to its former condition. At
once, too, Seleukeia was rebuilt and strengthened with ditches
all round the town. Strategios had enough men to deal with the
situation. He then returned to the capital, to be highly praised
and generously rewarded by the emperor.

11. Such were the actions taken at Kourikos. A year later[41]
the emperor learnt that a Genoese expedition was about to sail
to the help of the Franks. He foresaw that the Genoese, like the
others, would cause no little trouble to the Roman Empire.
Kantakouzenos was accordingly sent overland with a considerable army while Landulph was dispatched with a hastily
equipped fleet, and instructed to make full speed to the southern
coast, in order to attack the Genoese as they sailed past. Both
went off to their appointed tasks, but a terrible storm overwhelmed and broke up many of the ships. They were hauled
up on the beach again and carefully treated with liquid pitch.

While this was going on, Kantakouzenos was informed that
the Genoese fleet was in the neighbourhood. He suggested that
Landulph should take eighteen ships (as it happened they were

the only ones seaworthy at the time – the rest had been pulled up out of the sea) and sail for Cape Maleos; he could moor the ships there, just as the emperor had advised. When the enemy sailed by, he could attack at once if he felt confident enough to risk battle; if not, he could look to his own safety and that of his ships and crews by landing at Korone. Off he went and seeing the huge Genoese fleet he decided not to fight. Instead he sailed quickly to Korone.

Kantakouzenos took command of the whole Roman naval force, exactly as he needed to do, loaded what troops he had with him and pursued the Genoese as fast as he could. He failed to overtake them, but reached Laodikeia, eagerly looking forward to a trial of strength with Bohemond. He set to work occupying the harbour and keeping up ceaseless attacks on the walls[42] by day and night.

However, no progress was made. Hundreds of assaults were made and hundreds were repelled; his attempts to win over the Kelts were frustrated, his battles against them failed. In the end he spent three days and nights building a small circular wall of dry rocks between the sands and the walls of Laodikeia. When it was completed, he used it as a protective covering while another strongpoint of whatever materials he could find was erected inside it, a base of operations for even fiercer attacks on the town defences. Two towers, moreover, were set up on either side of the harbour mouth and an iron chain was stretched across the space between them to prevent the Kelts from providing relief by sea. At the same time he seized many of the forts along the coast: the place known as Argyrokastron, Markhapin, Gabala and certain others as far as the borders of Tripolis; these were places which formerly paid tribute to the Saracens, but eventually, thanks to the emperor, were recovered by the Roman Empire at the cost of much sweat and toil.

The emperor reckoned that Laodikeia should be invested from the land side as well. He had long experience of Bohemond's cunning and his stratagems, and thanks to his genius for appreciating a man's character quickly, he understood all too well the traitorous, rebellious nature of this individual. Monastras was therefore sent overland with a powerful

contingent to besiege Laodikeia from land while Kantakouzenos shut it in by sea. But before Monastras arrived, his colleague had occupied both harbour and town; only the citadel,
nowadays commonly referred to as the *koula*, was still in the
hands of 500 Keltic infantry and a hundred knights.

Bohemond heard of this and he was also told by the count
responsible for the defence of the citadel that provisions were
running low. He concentrated all his own forces, therefore,
with those of Tancred and St Gilles and all kinds of supplies
were loaded on mules. When he reached Laodikeia it was not
long before they were transported to the *koula*. Bohemond also
had an interview with Kantakouzenos. 'What's the idea of
building these earthworks?' he asked. 'You know,' replied Kantakouzenos, 'that you and your fellow counts swore to serve
the emperor and agreed under oath to hand over to him whatever towns were captured by you. Later on you lied about the
oaths, and even disregarded the treaties of peace; you took this
town and handed it over to us, then changed your mind and
kept it, so that when I came here to accept the towns taken by
you my visit was useless.' 'Have you come here hoping to take
it from us with money or by force?' asked Bohemond. 'Our
allies have received the money,' came the reply, 'for their gallan-
try in battle.' Bohemond was filled with rage. 'Be sure of this:
without money you wouldn't be able to capture even a watch-
post.' Whereupon he provoked his troops to gallop right up to
the gates of the town.

Kantakouzenos' men, who were guarding the ramparts, fired
arrows thick as snowflakes at the Franks as they came closer to
the walls. Bohemond promptly rallied all his men and they made
it into the citadel. Bohemond was uneasy about the loyalty of
the count who had been in charge of the defence of the town,
as well as that of the Kelts serving him, so he summarily dismissed them and appointed a new commander. At the same
time he destroyed the vineyards near the walls, so that the Latin
cavalry should have freedom of movement. Then, having made
these arrangements, he left the town and went off to Antioch.
As for Kantakouzenos, he carried on the siege by every means
available; thousands of devices were tried, sudden assaults were

made and siege-engines brought up to confound the Latins in
the citadel. Monastras was also busy. Coming overland with
the cavalry he occupied Longinias, Tarsos, Adana, Mamistra
and indeed the whole of Kilikia.[43]

12. Bohemond shuddered at the emperor's threats. Without
means of defence (for he had neither an army on land nor a
fleet at sea, and danger hung over him on both sides), he came
up with a plan[44] which, while not very elegant, was amazingly
crafty. First he left the city of Antioch in the hands of Tancred,
the son of the marquis and his own nephew; then he spread
rumours everywhere about himself to the effect that Bohemond
was dead; even though he was very much still alive, he convinced the world that he had passed away.   *Metaphor*

Faster than the beating of a bird's wings the story was fanned
in all directions that Bohemond was a dead man. When he
thought that the story had done the rounds, a wooden coffin
was made and a bireme prepared. The coffin was placed on
board and he, the living dead, sailed away from Soudi, which
is the port of Antioch, for Rome. He was being transported by
sea as a corpse, since to outward appearances, the coffin and
the behaviour of his companions suggested clearly that he was
a corpse (as did the fact that at each stop the barbarians tore
out their hair and paraded their mourning). But inside the coffin
Bohemond, stretched out at full length, was a corpse in terms
of physical pose only; in other respects he was alive, breathing
air in and out through hidden holes. That is how it was at the
coastal places, but when the boat was out at sea, they shared
their food with him and gave him attention; then once more
there were the same dirges, the same tomfoolery.

However, in order that the corpse might appear to be in a
state of rare putrefaction, they strangled or cut the throat of a
cock and put that in the coffin with him. By the fourth or fifth
day at the most, the horrible stench was obvious to anyone who
could smell. Those who had been deceived by the outward
show thought the offensive odour emanated from Bohemond's
body, but Bohemond himself derived more pleasure than anyone from his imaginary misfortune. For my part I wonder how
on earth he endured such a siege on his nasal faculties and

still continued to live while being carried along with his dead companion. But that has taught me how hard it is to check all barbarians once they have set their hearts on something: there is nothing, however objectionable, which they will not bear when they have made up their minds once and for all to undergo self-inflicted suffering. This man Bohemond was not dead – he was dead only in pretence – yet he did not hesitate to live alongside dead bodies. In the world of our generation this ruse of Bohemond's was unprecedented and unique, and its purpose was to bring about the downfall of the Roman Empire. Before it no barbarian or Greek devised such a plan against his enemies, nor, I fancy, will anyone in our lifetime ever see its like again.

When he reached Corfu, as if he had reached some mountain peak, as if the island were a place of refuge and he was now free from danger, he rose from his state of presumed death, left the coffin where his corpse had lain, and enjoying the sunshine to the full, breathed in a cleaner air and walked round the town of Corfu. The inhabitants, seeing him dressed in outlandish, barbarian clothes, inquired about his family, his condition, his name; they asked where he came from and to whom he was going.

Bohemond treated them all with lofty disdain and demanded to see the *doux* of the town. He was in fact a certain Alexios originally from the Armeniakon. Coming face to face with him, Bohemond, arrogant in look and attitude, speaking with an arrogant tongue in completely barbaric language, ordered him to send this communication to the Emperor Alexios: 'To you I, Bohemond, famous son of Robert, send this message. The past has taught you and your empire how formidable my bravery and my opposition both are. When I turn the scales of fortune, as God is my witness I will not leave unavenged the evils done to me in the past. Ever since I took Antioch on my march through Roman territory and enslaved the whole of Syria with my spear, I have had my fill of misery because of you and your army; my hopes, one after another, have been dashed; I have been thrust into a thousand misfortunes and a thousand barbarian wars.

'But now it is different. I want you to know that, although
I was dead, I have come back to life again; I have escaped your
clutches. In the guise of a dead man I have avoided every eye,
every hand, every plan. And now I live, I move, I breathe the
air, and from this island of Corfu I send to Your Majesty
offensive, hateful news. It will not make very pleasant reading
for you. I have handed over the city of Antioch to my nephew
Tancred, leaving him as a worthy adversary for your generals.
I myself will go to my own country. As far as you and your
friends are concerned, I am a corpse; but to myself and my
friends it is manifest that I am a living man, plotting a diabolical
end for you. In order to throw the Roman world which you
rule into disarray, I who was alive became dead; now I who
died am alive. If I reach the mainland of Italy and cast eyes on
the Lombards and all the Latins and the Germans and our own
Franks, men full of martial valour, then with many a murder
I will make your towns and provinces run with blood, until I
set up my spear in Byzantion itself.' Such was the extreme
arrogance in which the barbarian exulted.

BOOK XII

1. The events that took place during Bohemond's first crossing; his many and obvious plots against the emperor; his attempts to win the sceptre of the Roman Empire for himself; the circumstances of his secret departure from Antioch, carefully prepared and carried out with ease and, one must admit it, with success; his voyage in the role of a corpse and his arrival at Corfu – all these have been described in sufficient detail. Let us now set out what this man got up to next. When the stinking corpse had reached Corfu, as I have explained, he uttered threats against the emperor through the *doux* who was in command there, as I have likewise stated, and having sailed on to Lombardy, set about gathering even more allies than he had before in order to reoccupy the Illyrikon. He entered into negotiations with the king of France for a marriage and took as wife one of his daughters, and dispatched another overseas to Antioch to be wedded to his nephew Tancred.[1] Then, having gathered together enormous forces from every country and town, he summoned the counts with their several contingents and hurried on to cross over to Illyrikon.

The emperor, having received the communications sent to him through Alexios,[2] at once wrote letters to all the countries, to Pisa, to Genoa and to Venice, forewarning them not to be seduced by Bohemond's false words and as a result of these to join his expedition.[3] Bohemond was in fact going round all these towns and provinces, making violent attacks on the emperor, calling him a pagan and an enemy of the Christians.

Now it happened that the Babylonian[4] had taken three hundred counts prisoner, at the time when the endless hordes of

Kelts had crossed from the west into Asia and were striking at
Antioch, Tyre and all the towns and districts in that area. He
was keeping them under guard and in chains; their imprisonment was as terrible as any of ancient times. The news of their
capture and the dreadful things that befell them afterwards
troubled the heart of the emperor, who devoted himself entirely
to their rescue. He sent for Niketas Panoukomites and dispatched him with sums of money to the Babylonian, bearing
letters in which he sought the release of the counts and promised
many favours if they were released from their bonds and set
free. The Babylonian received Panoukomites and listened to the
message which he had been given by the emperor and indeed read
the letter addressed to him, and without further ado, removed
the counts' bonds and released them from prison.[5] However, he
did not grant them complete liberty, instead handing them over
to Panoukomites, and then sending them back to the emperor,
not accepting any of the money which had been provided for him.
Whether he thought it an unsatisfactory ransom for men such as
these, or because he wished to avoid any imputation of bribery
and wanted it to be known that he was not selling them for
money, but doing the emperor a genuine, straightforward
favour, or even because he wanted more, God knows.

When the emperor saw them on their return, he was overjoyed at the barbarian's decision, and surprised too. When he
interrogated them closely about their experiences, he learnt that
they had been kept in prison for a long time, for months in fact,
and had not once seen the sun nor been loosed from their
chains; during all that time they had been denied every kind of
nourishment except bread and water. Their sufferings excited
his pity and he shed tears of sympathy. They were at once
treated with much kindness; money was given to them; all kinds
of fine clothing were provided for them; they were invited to
the baths and in every way attempts were made to ensure their
recovery from such ordeals. They were delighted for their part
with the emperor's friendly attitude. These men, formerly
enemies and opponents, transgressors of the oaths and pledges
made to him, observed well the extraordinary forbearance
which he showed towards them.

After some days he sent for them. 'I am granting you freedom of choice,' he said. 'You can stay as long as you like with us in the city. But if any one of you, mindful of his own family, wishes to go away, he can take his leave of us without impediment and start on his homeward journey, generously provided for with money and all kinds of other necessities for the voyage. I want you to have absolute freedom of choice, to stay here or to leave; I want you to follow your own inclination as free men, and to do as you desire.' For a while the counts, treated with every kind of consideration by the emperor, as I have said, were reluctant to tear themselves away. But the situation changed when Bohemond arrived in Lombardy, which I have already described, eager to recruit greater forces than ever, and on his visits to every town and district often disparaging the emperor, loudly proclaiming in public that he was a pagan and aiding the pagans wholeheartedly. Now when the emperor heard of this, he presented the aforementioned counts with magnificent presents and sent them home, in part because they were now themselves earnestly looking forward to the homeward voyage, and also because they would personally refute Bohemond's calumnies against him.

He then left hurriedly for the main town of Thessaly,[6] to give military training to the new recruits and to check Bohemond and stop him from crossing from Lombardy to our country, as rumours suggested he was about to do. The counts, then, departed from Byzantion and furnished undeniable evidence against Bohemond, branding him a charlatan, incapable of telling the truth; on many occasions they accused him to his face and in every quarter denounced him, bringing forward witnesses worthy of credence – themselves.

2. Everywhere there was talk of Bohemond's invasion. If the emperor was to oppose the Keltic hordes, he would require numerous soldiers and an army of similar proportions. There was no hesitation, no delay. His officers in Koile-Syria, that is to say Kantakouzenos and Monastras, were summoned; the former guarded Laodikeia, the latter Tarsos. At their departure the provinces and towns which they had been in charge of were not neglected. Petzeas was dispatched to Laodikeia with fresh

troops, while Tarsos and all the towns and places which had been held by Monastras were handed to Aspietes.[7] This individual was a member of a noble Armenian family. He had a great reputation for bravery, according to reports from that time, although the present crisis absolutely belied it, at least as far as his leadership was concerned.

Tancred, whom this history had left in Syria, was now governing Antioch. He was constantly spreading stories that he was about to reach Kilikia to lay siege to it and wrest it from the hands of the emperor, because it was his, won from the Turks by his spear. Propaganda of this type was sent out in all directions; nor was that all – he made even worse threats in letters delivered daily to Aspietes. Nor did he confine himself to threats, following through with examples and promising more was to come. Forces of Armenians and Kelts were conscripted from a wide area and these men were being trained daily. His army was thoroughly drilled in battle formations and generally prepared for war. Occasionally it was sent out to forage – the smoke that precedes the flames, so to speak. Siege-engines were made ready and in all kinds of ways Tancred busied himself in organizing the assault.

While he was engaged thus, the Armenian Aspietes was idly taking his ease, devoting himself to heavy drinking bouts by night, as if nobody threatened him, as if there were no cause for alarm, no great peril hanging over him. And yet he was a very courageous man, a fine guardsman of Ares; but when he arrived in Kilikia, far from his master's control and invested with full authority, he completely abandoned himself to a life of luxury. By the time the attack began, this Armenian fellow had become effeminate, spending his time in perpetual debauches, and with no stomach for a fight against the tough, battle-hardened Tancred. The thunderous menace approaching fell on deaf ears, and when Tancred came, armed with the thunderbolt and ravaging Kilikia, Aspietes' eyes never saw the lightning flashes.

Tancred had in fact set out from Antioch suddenly and with a very large army. Splitting it into two, he sent one contingent overland to attack the towns of Mopsos, while the other part

was embarked on triremes and sailed under Tancred's command to the River Saron.[8] This river has its source in the Tauros
Mountains, flows between the two towns of Mopsos, one of
which is in ruins, the other still standing to this day, and then
out into the Syrian Sea. From there, Tancred's fleet sailed as far
as the mouth of the river, up to the two bridges which join the
two towns. In this way Mamistra was encircled and attacked by
Tancred's forces from two sides. From this point, one party was
able to launch an assault from the river without difficulty, while
the other put pressure on the town from dry land.

Aspietes behaved as if nothing unusual was happening; the
noise of soldiers all round his town, like the buzzing of a huge
swarm of bees, left him almost unmoved. What was wrong with
him I do not know, but he was in a condition unworthy of his
normal bravery, which caused him to be heartily detested by
the imperial army. What was likely to happen to the towns of
Kilikia when taken by such a man as Tancred? Apart from
other considerations, Tancred was one of the strongest men of
his time; he was also among those most admired for their
quality and skill as leaders; he was the kind of leader from
whom there was no escape once he had put a siege in place.

At this point, the reader may well wonder how Aspietes'
military ineptitude escaped the emperor's notice. My reply in
defence of my father would be that he was impressed by the
distinction of his family, and that his glorious lineage and the
celebrity of his name contributed much to the appointment of
Aspietes to the command position. After all, he was the head
of the Arsakids,[9] descended from royal stock. For that reason
he was deemed worthy of the position of *stratopedarkhes* of
the whole of the east and promoted to the most exalted ranks
– particularly since the emperor had experience of his personal
courage.

For when the emperor was waging war with Robert Guiscard,
in one of the engagements a certain Kelt, who towered head
and shoulders above the rest, spurred his horse and with levelled
spear fell upon Aspietes like a thunderbolt. The latter took the
violent impact just as he was drawing his sword. He received a
very serious wound, for the spear passing by the lung forced its

way right through him. Far from being thrown into confusion
by the blow or even crashing to the ground, he actually seated
himself more firmly in his saddle and struck at the barbarian's
helmet, splitting both helmet and head in two. They fell then
from their horses, the Kelt dead and Aspietes still breathing.
Those around him took him up, by then completely uncon-
scious, and after tending him, carefully carried him to the
emperor. They showed him the spear and the wound, and told
the story of the Kelt's death. For some reason or other the
emperor recalled his bravery and daring on that occasion, which
together with the man's lineage and the glory of his family,
persuaded him to send Aspietes to Kilikia, as a commander
capable of opposing Tancred. He was, as I have already said,
given the title of *stratopedarkhes*.

3. However, that is enough about that. The officers in the
west received other letters ordering them to march directly to
Sthlanitza.[10] Why? Was the emperor calling on the front-line
fighters while he himself in retirement enjoyed a life of ease and
took pleasure in baths, like some emperors who prefer and
usually follow an animal existence? Not a bit of it. Even the
thought of continuing to live in the palace was repugnant. He
left Byzantion and passing through the centre of the western
provinces arrived at Thessaloniki. It was September, in the
fourteenth indiction and the twentieth year after his seizure of
the reins of empire.[11]

The empress, too, was compelled to leave with him. Her natural inclination[12] would have been to shun public life altogether.
Most of her time was devoted to household duties and her own
pursuits – reading the books of the Saints, I mean, or turning
her mind to good works and acts of charity to mankind, especially to those who from their natural disposition and way of life
she knew were serving God, those who persevered in prayer or
in the singing of hymns. Whenever she had to appear in public
as empress at some important ceremony, she was overcome
with modesty and a blush at once suffused her cheeks.

The philosopher Theano[13] once bared her elbow and someone playfully remarked, 'What a lovely elbow!' 'But not for
public show,' she replied. Well, the empress, my mother, the

image of majesty, the dwelling place of saintliness, so far from being pleased to reveal to the common gaze an elbow or her eyes, was unwilling that even her voice should be heard by strangers. Her modesty was really extraordinary. But since not even gods, as the poet[14] says, fight against necessity, she was forced to accompany the emperor on his frequent expeditions.

Her innate modesty kept her inside the palace; on the other hand, her devotion to him and burning love for him compelled her, however unwillingly, to leave her home, for the following reasons. First, because the disease which attacked his feet necessitated most careful attention, the emperor suffered excruciating pain from his gout, and it was the touch of my mother, the empress, which he appreciated most. She knew exactly how to soothe him, and did so by gentle massage which relieved him of the anguish to some extent. This emperor (in what I am going to say, let no one accuse me of exaggeration, for I do admire the domestic virtues; and let no one suspect that I lie about the emperor, for I am speaking the truth) considered all his own personal affairs and the things that concerned himself as of less consequence than the safety of the towns. Nothing in fact stood between him and his love for the Christians – neither griefs, nor pleasures; neither the ravages of war, nor indeed any other thing, whether great or small; neither the burning heat of the sun, nor the bitter cold of winter, nor the manifold assaults of the barbarians. Against all these he held fast his course, and if he yielded before the confusion of his illnesses, he made up for it by leaping to the defence of his empire.

The second and more important reason why the empress accompanied him was the multitude of conspiracies that were springing up against him, which called for great vigilance, and the capacity of a hundred eyes. For night-time was taken up with plotting against him, as was the middle of the day with each evening spawning some new evil and with worse to follow at first light. God is my witness to this. Was it not right, therefore, that the emperor, assailed by evils so numerous, should also be protected by a thousand eyes, while some fired arrows at him, others sharpened their swords and others, when action became impossible, indulged in calumny and abuse?

Who then had a better right to be at his side than his natural adviser? Who rather than the empress would keep more careful watch over him or pay more stringent attention to the plotters? Who would be quicker to discern what his best interests were, or sharper than she in observing the intrigues of his enemies? It was for these reasons that my mother was everything in every way to my father. By night she was the unsleeping eye, by day his most conspicuous guardian, the good antidote to the perils of the table and the salutary remedy against poisoned food. These were the reasons that thrust aside her natural reserve and gave her courage to face the eyes of men. And yet, even then, she did not forget her customary decorum: a look, a silence and the retinue about her were enough to ensure that to most of them she remained enigmatic. The litter borne by two mules and over it the imperial canopy alone showed that she was accompanying the army; otherwise her royal person was screened from view.

It was only known that some excellent provision was made for the emperor's gout, some sleepless vigil guarded him, an eye wide open and never drowsy watched over his affairs. We, who were loyal to the emperor, shared in this labour with our mistress and mother to protect him, each according to their best ability, with all our heart and soul, never once relaxing our vigil. I have written these words to counter tongues which love to wag and to spite. Blaming that which is blameless (a human characteristic which was after all familiar to Homer's Muse too) only serves to belittle noble deeds, and to subject to reproach those who do not deserve such.

On this particular expedition (the emperor had set off on campaign against Bohemond), the empress went with him willingly and yet with reluctance. It was not necessary for the empress to join in hostilities against the barbarian army. How could she? That might have been enough for Tomyris and Sparethra the Massagetis,[15] but not for my Eirene. Her courage was turned elsewhere and if it was fully armed, it was not with the spear of Athene, nor with the cap of Hades: her spear, shield and sword, with which she nobly ranged herself in battle line against the misfortunes and trials of life which, as the empress knew, the rulers always had to face up to, were hard work, an absolutely relentless fight against the passions, and a sincere faith, in the best traditions of Solomon. Such was the armour of my mother in wars like these, but in all else, as befitted her name, she was a most peaceable woman.[16]

When hostilities against the barbarians were imminent, the emperor made preparations for the struggle, taking care to ensure the security of some strongpoints and fortifying others. He was anxious in general to bring all defences to a state of complete readiness against Bohemond. It was partly for his own sake and for reasons already given that he took the empress with him, but also partly because there was as yet no danger and the moment for battle had not arrived. She took what money she had in gold or in other precious metal and certain other personal possessions and left the capital. Afterwards, on the journey, she gave liberally to all beggars, clad in skins or naked; no one who asked went away empty-handed. And when she arrived at the tent set apart for her and went inside, it was not to lie down at once and rest, but to open it up and all the mendicants were allowed access. To such persons she was very approachable and showed herself ready to be both seen and heard. Nor was it money alone that she gave to the poor; she also dispensed excellent advice. All who were obviously healthy but who preferred a life of indolence were exhorted to work and to action; she urged them to find a way to support themselves, rather than rely, because of their negligence, on going from door to door begging.

No circumstances deterred the empress from such good work. David is depicted mixing his cup with lamentation; but this empress could be seen every day mixing her pity for others with food and drink. There is much that I could say about this particular empress, if it were not that being her daughter I might be suspected of lying to gratify my own mother. However, to those who entertain such thoughts I will use facts to corroborate my argument.

4. When it was known that the emperor had reached Thessaloniki, the men of the western provinces all flocked to him like heavy weights to the centre of gravity. Locusts did not precede

the Kelts as on previous occasions, but a great comet[17] appeared in the sky, greater than any seen in the past. Some likened it to a small beam, others to a javelin. Of course it was natural that the strange events about to take place should in some way be heralded by signs in the heavens. It was visible, shining brightly, for forty whole days and nights. It seemed to rise in the west and make its way eastwards. All who saw it were terrified and asked what meaning this star had.

However, the emperor was absolutely unmoved by all these matters since he considered that they had explanations in nature. Nevertheless, he did question experts on the subject. He therefore summoned Basil, who had been recently appointed *eparkhos* of Byzantion (and whose loyalty to the emperor had been proved in the past), and asked him about the phenomenon. Basil promised an answer on the next day and retired to his lodging place (an ancient monastery dedicated to John the Evangelist), where he assessed the star at sunset. At a loss to understand it and weary from his calculations, he fell asleep and had a vision of the saint, wearing priestly garb. Basil was overjoyed and imagined that he was seeing a real person. Recognizing the saint with fear and trembling he begged him to explain the meaning of the star. 'It indicates an invasion of the Kelts,' came the reply; 'its disappearance will herald their departure.'

Let us leave the comet at that. The emperor reached Thessaloniki, as I have already explained, and prepared for Bohemond's coming. Recruits were trained thoroughly in the use of the bow, in marksmanship and in defending themselves with the shield. He also dispatched letters seeking to recruit foreign troops from different countries, so that when the crisis came they might quickly bring aid. He also took elaborate precautions for Illyrikon; the town of Dyrrakhion was fortified and he named as governor Alexios, the second son of the *Sebastokrator* Isaac. At the same time he gave orders that the Cyclades Islands, the towns of the coast of Asia and of Europe itself make ready a fleet. But this was met with some resistance on the basis that Bohemond was not about to cross yet. The emperor was unimpressed by these arguments, insisting that a commander must be continually on his guard, not preparing merely for the immediate future, but looking far ahead; he should certainly not be caught unawares in the moment of crisis through cutting down expenses – above all when he saw the enemy about to attack.

Once these things had been properly organized, he set off to Stroumpitza and from there went on to Slopimos. News came of the defeat of John,[18] the son of the *sebastokrator*, who had been sent on ahead against the Dalmatians. The emperor sent a considerable force to help him. Bolkan, who was a particularly difficult man, very craftily made inquiries at once about peace negotiations, and provided the hostages which had been demanded from him. For a year and two months the emperor stayed in that area, all the time being fully informed of the whereabouts of Bohemond, who was still in the province of Lombardy. The winter was now coming on[19] and after dismissing his soldiers to their own homes he himself retired to Thessaloniki. While he was on his way to Thessaloniki, the first of the sons of the *Porphyrogennetos* and Emperor John had been born at Balabista with a twin sister.[20] Having attended a ceremony in honour of the great martyr Demetrios,[21] he then went on to the capital city.

The following event then took place. In the centre of Constantine's Forum there was a bronze statue, facing the east and standing on a conspicuous column of porphyry, holding in its right hand a sceptre and in its left a sphere made of bronze. It was said to be a statue of Apollo, but the inhabitants of Constantinople called it, I think, Anthelios. The great Emperor Constantine, father and master of the city, changed this so it had his own name, so it was now called the Statue of the Emperor Constantine. Its ancient and first title continued to be used though, and it was known by everybody as Anelios or Anthelios. South-west winds blowing over a wide area from Africa suddenly blew this statue off its pedestal and hurled it to the ground, at a time when the sun was in the sign of Taurus. To most people this seemed like not a good omen, especially to those not well-disposed to the emperor. They whispered in secret that this accident portended his death. He made light of it: 'I know of one Lord of life and death. And I am absolutely

certain that statues blowing over do not induce death. So when
a Pheidias or one of the stonemasons works at the marble and
turns out a statue, will he really be raising from the dead and
be producing living beings? And suppose he does, what does
that mean for the Creator of all things? "It is I who both take
and give life", as it is said in the Bible.[22] That cannot be said of
the fall or setting up of this or that statue.' In fact, he ascribed
everything to the mighty Providence of God.

5. Fresh troubles had been stirred up against the emperor,
but the agitators were not on this occasion ordinary folk. These
men, proud of their valour and famous lineage, plotted with
murderous intent against the person of the emperor. Now that
I have reached this point in my history, I wonder from where
so great a multitude of troubles came to surround the emperor,
for everything – yes, everything – and from every quarter
assailed him. From his own people[23] there were numerous defec-
tions; from outside, revolts abounded. The emperor had barely
taken a stand against the troubles within, when all burst into
flames outside, as if Fate itself was cajoling barbarians and
revolutionaries at precisely the same time, like some spontaneous generation of Giants. And yet his government and
general administration were in all ways more than usually gentle
and humane, so that there was no one who did not benefit from
his reign.

He rewarded some with honours of distinction and continually enriched them with great liberality. And as for the barbarians, wherever they were, he gave them no pretext for war
and did not provoke them; nevertheless, if they did cause
trouble, he checked them. After all, it is the mark of a bad
general, when all is peaceful, to incite his neighbours to war
intentionally – for peace is the objective of all wars. Invariably
to prefer war instead of peace, to disregard a positive conclusion, is typical of foolish commanders and foolish political
leaders, the mark of men who work for the destruction of
their own state. The Emperor Alexios took just the opposite
approach, cultivating peace sincerely. He cherished its presence
and strove to keep it through every means possible; and he
worried about its absence, often spending sleepless nights

pondering how to make it return. By nature, then, he was a man of peace, but when circumstances forced him he would become most warlike. For my own part I would say confidently of this great man that in him and in him alone the true character of an emperor was seen again in the Roman court – after a long interval; it was as if then, for the first time, the imperial dignity dwelt like some guest in the empire of the Romans.

But, as I said at the beginning of this chapter, I cannot help feeling astonished at the flood of hostile sentiments. Abroad and at home everything was visibly in turmoil. Yet the Emperor Alexios anticipated the furtive designs of his enemies, and by various manoeuvres prevented the mischief from coming too close. In his struggle with traitors at home and barbarians abroad he always outwitted them, frustrated their plans and put a stop to their aims. The facts themselves, it seems to me, give a clue to the destiny of the empire: there was an accumulation of perils from all quarters, the body politic was in confusion, the whole outside world raged against us; it was as if a man were sick, assailed by forces from without and exhausted by physical pain within, but was revived by Providence, finding strength to combat all his troubles. And so, Bohemond, the barbarian whom we have mentioned on many occasions already, was preparing an enormous army against the Roman Empire, at just the same time as the crowd of rebels within was rising up, as has been described above.

There were four ringleaders of this company in all: they were called Anemas (Michael, Leo, ... and ...).[24] They were brothers by birth and on this occasion by intent, for all had the same object in view – to murder the emperor and seize the throne. Other nobles had lent their support: the Antiokhoi, who were of an illustrious family; those known as Exazenos Doukas and Hyaleas – extremely courageous fighters if ever there were; Niketas Kastamonites, a certain Kourtikios and George Basilakios. These men were leading figures in the army, but another conspirator, John Solomon, was a distinguished senator. Because of his great wealth and noble birth, Michael, the foremost of the Anemas tetrarchy, had deceitfully promised to install the latter as emperor. In the senatorial order Solomon might have been a member of the first rank, but in both physical size and character he was exceedingly limited, particularly compared with the other conspirators. He imagined that he had attained the pinnacle of Aristotelian and Platonic studies. In reality, though, his knowledge of philosophy was not far advanced; he had simply been blinded by his own superficiality.[25]

Already he was aiming wholeheartedly at the throne, helped by the Anemas brothers. They were, without question, utter rascals. In fact Michael and his followers did not propose to raise him to imperial power – far from it. They were instead using the man's folly and his wealth to pursue their own intentions. They were regularly helping themselves to that golden stream and, by building up his hopes of empire, subjugated him entirely to their will. Their idea was this: if all went well and Fortune smiled on them rather more, they would edge him out, sending him away on a pleasant sea voyage, while they would lay hands on the sceptre, allot him some minor dignity and wish him good luck. Although they spoke to him of the plot, there was no talk of murdering the emperor, no mention of sword-drawing or battle or wars, lest they should frighten the man. They knew him of old – the very idea of war made him extremely anxious indeed. Anyway, they took this Solomon to their arms, as if he were indeed head of the conspiracy. Others were drawn into it – Skleros and Xeros,[26] who had just completed his term of office as *eparkhos* of Constantinople.

I have already written of Solomon's rather spineless nature; since he knew nothing about the plans being carefully laid by Hyaleas Exazenos and the Anemas brothers, he believed supreme power was already in his grasp, and was holding discussions with certain individuals hoping to win their goodwill by promising gifts and the award of dignities. On one occasion Michael Anemas, the leading actor in the drama, visited him and saw him talking to someone. He asked what the subject of the conversation was. Solomon answered with his customary simplicity: 'He was asking for an honour from us, and once I had given him an undertaking he agreed to join us in the general conspiracy.' Michael despaired of his stupidity, and fearful of the fact that Solomon was unable to bite his own tongue, no longer visited him as before.

6. The soldiers – namely the Anemas brothers, the Antiokhoi and their accomplices – therefore conspired against the emperor's life and waited for a favourable opportunity so that they could carry out the murder of the sovereign without further ado. But when Providence afforded them no chance and time slipped past, the discovery of the plot became an alarming possibility. However, they thought they had found the moment they had been waiting for. When the emperor woke up in the early morning, he liked sometimes to play chess with one of his kinsmen (this was an Assyrian game, which came from them to us); anyway, it sweetened the bitterness of his many worries. The rebels armed themselves for the crime. They intended to pass through the emperor's bedroom, a small room, as if they were looking for him; really, they were hoping to murder him.

Now the imperial bedchamber, where my mother and father happened to be sleeping, lies on the left side of the palace chapel built in honour of the Theometor, although most people said it was dedicated to the great martyr Demetrios. On the right there was a marble atrium in the open air, and the door of the chapel which gave access to it was free to all who wished to go there. It was from that place that they planned to enter the chapel, break down the doors shutting off the imperial bedroom and then, after getting inside in this way, kill the emperor with their swords.

Such were the plans of these wicked men against one who had done them no wrong. But God frustrated their plot. Somebody informed the emperor and they were immediately sent for. First John Solomon and George Basilakios were to be brought to the palace to undergo examination via a small room where the emperor happened to be with his kinsmen, because he knew from experience that they were rather unsophisticated and therefore imagined that he would easily obtain information about their conspiracy. As they repeatedly denied any knowledge of the plot when questioned, the *Sebastokrator* Isaac went out and spoke to Solomon: 'You are well aware, Solomon, of the goodness of my brother the emperor. If you give us all the details of the plot, you will be granted an immediate pardon. If not, you will be subjected to unbearable tortures.' Solomon stared at him. Then, seeing the barbarians who surrounded the *sebastokrator*, with the one-edged swords on their shoulders, he began to tremble and without more ado told him everything. He denounced his fellow conspirators but insisted that he himself knew nothing about the murder. After that they were handed over to the palace guard and imprisoned separately.

The rest were then interrogated about the business. They made a full confession, not even concealing the intention to kill. The details of the soldiers' plot became apparent, notably that Michael Anemas, the ringleader and instigator, had wanted the assassination of the emperor. As a result, they were all banished and their property was confiscated. Solomon's house, a magnificent mansion, was given to the empress, but she characteristically had pity on Solomon's wife and restored it to her, without having removed a single thing from it.

Solomon was imprisoned at Sozopolis. Anemas and the other prominent rebels, after having their heads completely shaved and their beards cut, were paraded through the Agora, before the order was given that their eyes be gouged out. Those in charge of this spectacle grabbed them, clothed them in sackcloth, decorated their heads with ox and sheep entrails to imitate crowns, put them on oxen, not astride the beasts, but riding sideways, and drove them through the courtyard of the palace. In front of them rod-bearers charged, bawling a comic ditty with alternate refrains suited to the occasion. It was a vulgar song in the dialect of the common people and its main theme was as follows: it called on everyone to . . . and see the rebels wearing horns, the rebels who had whetted their swords against the emperor.

People of all ages hurried to see this spectacle; we too, the daughters of the emperor, came out in secret for the same purpose. However, when they saw Michael fixing his gaze on the palace and raising his hands in prayer to heaven, begging through gestures that his arms should be severed from his shoulders, his legs from his body, and that he should be beheaded, every living person was moved to tears and lamentation, not least ourselves, the emperor's daughters. I myself,[27] wishing to save the man from such a fate, called more than once on the empress, my mother, to watch them being subjected to ribald jokes. The truth is, we cared for the men for the emperor's sake: it hurt us to think that he was being deprived of such brave men, especially of Michael, who had the ultimate sentence passed against him.

Seeing how much he was being humiliated by his suffering, I kept putting pressure on my mother, as I have explained, in case there might be some way of rescuing these men and saving them from the danger facing them. Those leading the procession went at a slow pace, in order to win some sympathy for the criminals. My mother hesitated to come (she was seated with the emperor and together they were offering prayers to God before the Theometor). As a result, I went down and stood terrified outside the doors. I did not have the courage to go in, but caught the empress's attention through gesticulation. She understood and came up to watch, and when she saw Michael she wept tears of compassion for him. Back she ran to the emperor and pleaded with him again and again, praying that he spare Michael's eyes.

At once a man was sent to stop the guards. He caught them up, having rushed after them, inside the place called 'The Hands', from which point there can be no rescue from punishment. The emperors, who fixed these bronze hands on a very lofty vantage-point and on a high arch of stone, wanted it to be understood that if any man condemned by law to die was on this side of the bronze hands, and met with clemency from the emperor, he was to be freed from punishment. The hands signified that the emperor took such a man under his protection again, held tight in his hands – he was not yet released from his merciful grasp. If however the condemned passed beyond the hands, it was an outward sign that hereafter even the emperor's power rejected him.

The fate of men under sentence of death therefore depended on Fortune, which I consider to be divine grace, and it is right to call on her for succour. Either the pardon arrives on the near side of the hands, in which case the unfortunate criminals are snatched from danger; or they pass by the hands, and there is no more salvation. For my part, I attribute everything to the Providence of God, which on that occasion rescued the man from blinding. For it was God, it seems to me, who on that day moved us to pity him. The messenger of salvation rushed inside to give the order to Michael's escort before they had left the arch on which the bronze hands were fixed and brought him back. When he reached the tower built near to the palace, he imprisoned him there, according to instructions received beforehand.

7. Michael had not been released from prison before Gregory in his turn was shut up in the same place as Anemas. It was a tower on the ramparts of the city near the Blakhernai Palace and it was named after Anemas. It acquired this name because he was the first person to be incarcerated and spend a long time there. In the course of the twelfth indiction[28] this Gregory, who has appeared in my account before, and who had been promoted *doux* of Trapezous, brought to light a rebellion he had long been planning while still in Trapezous. He had run into Dabatenos, who was on his way back to Constantinople having handed over authority as *doux* to Taronites. He took Dabatenos prisoner on the spot and locked him up in Tebenna – and not only him, in fact, for a considerable number of the leading citizens of Trapezous, including the nephew of Bakkhenos, were also thrown into jail. As they were not freed from their chains, they agreed among themselves to make a concerted attack on the guards who had been posted there by the rebel. They mastered them, led them outside the ramparts and drove them far from the town, and took control of Tebenna.

The emperor wrote frequently to Gregory. Sometimes he tried to recall him, sometimes advised him to give up his wicked enterprise if he wanted a pardon and restoration to his old position; there were times when he actually threatened him if he refused. However, Gregory would not listen. He even sent off a long letter to the emperor in which he abused not only members of the Senate and prominent soldiers, but also close relatives and kinsmen by marriage of the emperor. From the contents of this message Alexios realized that Gregory was rapidly deteriorating, and was on the verge of complete mental breakdown. All hope for him was abandoned, but in the fourteenth indiction,[29] John, the emperor's nephew, son of his eldest sister and a cousin on the paternal side of the rebel, was sent to give him sound advice. That was John's first task, and Alexios thought Gregory might be persuaded by him because of their ties of kinship, both of them being descended from the same ancestors. If the latter refused, John was to launch a major attack on him by sea and by land using the substantial forces he had been sent with.

His arrival was reported to Gregory Taronites, who set out in the direction of Koloneia (a well-fortified place which was impregnable) with the idea of calling on Tanisman[30] for help. John heard about the move as he was about to leave. He detached the Kelts from the rest of his army and sent them after him together with picked Roman soldiers. They overtook him and engaged him in a battle which was bitterly contested. Two noblemen attacked Gregory with their lances, knocked him off his horse and captured him. Later on John carried off the prisoner alive to the emperor. John swore that he would neither see him, under any circumstances, nor speak a word to him on the journey. Nevertheless he defended him vigorously to the emperor, who appeared to want to blind Gregory.

Reluctantly the emperor allowed himself to be persuaded by John's pleading and admitted that the blinding was a mere pretence, but urged him most earnestly not to divulge the verdict. Three days later he ordered Gregory's hair and beard to be shaved to the skin and himself to be led through the middle of the Agora; later, in this condition, he was to be brought to the Anemas Tower. In prison Gregory's stupidity continued; every day he uttered mad prophecies to his guards, but the emperor with great forbearance considered it worthwhile to treat him with much kindness – one day he might mend his ways and show a measure of repentance. It failed, because he remained inexorable, but he did often call for my *kaisar* – in the old days he had been our friend. When that happened, the emperor gave permission to the latter to visit him in an attempt to overcome his terrible depression, and also to give him useful advice. However, Gregory's progress was apparently slow and his period of incarceration was prolonged. After a time he was pardoned and enjoyed more consideration, more honour and gifts than ever before. That was typical of my emperor in cases like his.

8. Having dealt thus with the conspirators and with the rebel Gregory Taronites, the emperor did not forget Bohemond. He sent for Isaac Kontostephanos, appointed him *megas doux* of the fleet and sent him to Dyrrakhion, with the threat that his eyes would be gouged if he failed to arrive there before Bohemond crossed to Illyrikon. He sent regular messages to the *doux* of Dyrrakhion, his nephew Alexios, preparing him for the coming war and warning him to maintain a constant vigil and exhort the coastguards to do likewise so that Bohemond did not cross unobserved. Moreover, he was to be immediately kept informed in writing about any developments.

Such were the precautions taken by the emperor. Kontostephanos had no instructions other than to keep a careful watch over the Straits of Lombardy, to stop Bohemond's convoys, which were sent to Dyrrakhion with all his baggage, and to allow nothing whatever to be transported to him from Lombardy. Unfortunately, when Kontostephanos went off he was ignorant of the natural crossing point for those sailing over to Illyrikon. Nor was that all: he overlooked his orders and sailed to Otranto, a town on the coast of Lombardy. The place was defended by a woman, the mother, so it was said, of Tancred, though whether she was a sister of the notorious Bohemond or not I cannot tell, for I do not really know if Tancred was related to him on his father's or his mother's side.

Having arrived there, Kontostephanos anchored his ships and proceeded to attack the walls, almost taking the place straight off. The highly intelligent and level-headed woman inside the walls had anticipated this when she had seen the ships arrive and had already sent a message to one of her sons asking for assistance quickly. The Roman fleet was full of confidence, as though the place had already fallen to them, and all the sailors had begun acclaiming the emperor. The woman, who was herself in grievous straits, ordered her own people to do likewise. At the

same time she sent ambassadors to Kontostephanos acknowledging the authority of the emperor and promising to negotiate
for peace; she would come to him and together they would
discuss terms, so that full details might be passed on to the
sovereign. She was contriving to keep Kontostephanos in suspense and playing for time, to give her son the chance to reach
her. Then, as they say of the tragic actors, she could throw off
the mask and start the fighting.

The combined acclamations of those within and without
echoed all round the town, while this woman gladiator kept
Kontostephanos' plans up in the air with these cunning words
and her lying promises. Meanwhile the son for whom she was
waiting did arrive, with attendant counts, immediately took on
Kontostephanos and defeated him conclusively. All the sailors,
having no experience of land warfare, threw themselves into
the sea, and the Scythians (of whom quite a number were
serving with the Roman force) rode off in the moment of battle
to plunder, as barbarians are wont to do. By chance six of them
were captured. They were sent to Bohemond and regarded by
him as a great prize; he at once took them with him to Rome.

There he presented himself before the apostolic throne and
in an interview with the pope[31] stirred him to bitter anger
against the Romans. These barbarians had an ancient hatred
for our race and he fostered it. In fact, in order to enrage the
Italian retinue of the pope even more, he exhibited his captured
Scythians, as if providing concrete evidence that the Emperor
Alexios, of all people, was hostile to the Christians because he
set against them barbarian infidels and fearful horse-archers,
brandishing arms and firing arrows. Every time he mentioned
the subject, the Scythians were deliberately exhibited to the
pope, equipped after their fashion and glaring fiercely, as barbarians will. Whenever he could he referred to them as pagans,
in the Latin way, mocking their name and appearance alike.
Not surprisingly, Bohemond's references to the war against the
Christians were designed to convince even a high priest that his
activities were justified, and that it was the Romans who were
hostile. He was at the same time gathering around him a large
force of volunteers made up of many rough and ignorant men.

For what barbarian, from near or far, would not enrol of his own free will in a war against us, if the pontiff approved and the apparent justice of it called to arms every knight, every soldier, every bit of their strength? The pope, cajoled by Bohemond's arguments, gave his support to him and encouraged the crossing to Illyrikon.

We must now return to the battle. The land-based troops fought with great spirit, but the others were swallowed up in the sea waves. After that the Kelts had a glorious chance of victory; however, the braver soldiers and in particular the men of higher rank thwarted them. Most prominent were the famous Nikephoros Exazenos Hyaleas, his cousin Constantine Exazenos, called Doukas, and the bravest of all, Alexander Euphorbenos; there were others, too, of the same rank and fortune. These men, mindful of their furious might, turned, drew their swords and with all their heart and soul did battle with the Kelts. They bore the whole brunt, routed them and won a splendid triumph.

Kontostephanos took advantage of the break in Keltic aggression to weigh anchor and sail with the whole fleet to Avlona. When he first arrived at Dyrrakhion he had dispersed the warships under his command from there as far as Avlona, even to the place known as Khimara – Avlona being a hundred stades from Dyrrakhion and Khimara a further sixty stades on from that. News reached him that Bohemond was speeding up preparations for the landing, and he guessed that the voyage would most probably end at Avlona, since Avlona involved a shorter crossing than Dyrrakhion. Avlona, he decided, must be more strongly defended. Accordingly he left with the other *doukoi* and kept careful watch on the straits at that place. He posted scouts on the summit of the so-called Iason's Hill to observe the sea and keep an eye open for ships.

A certain Kelt who had recently made the crossing confirmed that Bohemond was on the point of sailing. When they heard this, Kontostephanos' men were struck dumb with fear at the thought of a sea battle with Bohemond (the very mention of his name was enough to scare them). So, they pretended to be ill, claiming to need treatment at the baths. Landulph, who led the whole fleet and had vast experience of surprise attacks and of naval warfare over a long period, emphasized his order to be continually on guard and watch closely for Bohemond's coming. Kontostephanos' men sailed for Khimara to the baths, leaving behind the officer called deputy *droungarios* of the fleet with an *exkousaston* monoreme on patrol near Cape Glossa, which is not far from Avlona. As for Landulph, he stayed in the same vicinity with a fair number of ships.

9. Such were the naval dispositions when the men of Kontostephanos went off to take the baths, or rather on the pretext of bathing. Bohemond, meanwhile, arranged about him twelve privateers, all of them biremes with many rowers, so that there was a deafening, echoing noise from the continuous strokes of their oars. Around these ships and on either side he posted transport vessels, forming a circle to protect the battle fleet. Had you seen it from an outpost in the distance, you would have said that this armada under sail was a floating city. Fortune helped Bohemond somewhat, for the sea was calm except for a light breeze from the south which made a ripple on the surface and swelled the sails of the merchantmen. It was enough to make them run with the wind and the rowing ships kept a straight course with them. The noise they made, even in the middle of the Adriatic, could be heard echoing on both mainlands. This barbarian fleet of Bohemond was indeed an astonishing sight and if the men of Kontostephanos shrank from it in dread, I cannot blame them for having done so, nor would I accuse them of cowardice. For even the famous Argonauts would have feared this man with his fleet arranged like this, let alone the men of Kontostephanos, of Landulph and their like.

Landulph, in fact, when he spied Bohemond crossing with his merchantmen of enormous tonnage and in such an awe-inspiring manner, since it was impossible to fight against so many, altered course slightly from Avlona and gave way to Bohemond. The latter had indeed been fortunate. He transported the whole of his army from Bari to Avlona, landed on the opposite shore[32] and promptly set about ravaging all the seaboard with a countless host of Franks and Kelts who had accompanied him, together with the entire contingent of men from the Isle of Thule who normally serve in the Roman army but had through force of circumstances then joined him; not to mention an even stronger force of Germans and Keltiberians. All these men, united in one army, were spread along the whole Adriatic coastline. Everything was systematically plundered. Then he attacked Epidamnos, which we call Dyrrakhion, with the aim of taking this place and then devastating the land beyond it as far as Constantinople.

Bohemond was outstanding as a besieger of cities, surpassing even the famous Demetrios Poliorketes.[33] Concentrating all his attention now on Epidamnos, he brought up every engineering device to capture it. First the army surrounded the town, while other places in the neighbourhood, both close to and some way from Dyrrakhion, were besieged. Sometimes Roman forces opposed him, sometimes there was no resistance at all. After many battles and encounters with much bloodshed, he set about making ready his operations against Dyrrakhion. But before we come to the actions of the tyrant Bohemond, I must comment on the site. The place lies on the coast of the Adriatic Sea: this is itself a vast body of water which is effectively landlocked and separates one coast from that of Italy in width, and in length from the north-east goes from the lands of the barbarian Vetones[34] as far as those of the Apulians. Those are the dimensions of the Adriatic. Dyrrakhion or Epidamnos is itself an ancient Greek settlement, located to the south-west of Elissos which lies to the north-east.

Whether Elissos takes its own name from some river named Elissos which empties into the mighty Drymon or whether it takes this name from some other source, I cannot actually say. But Elissos is a small but absolutely impregnable place on its hill and according to what I have been told, overlooks the plain of Dyrrakhion. Its own invulnerability affords considerable protection to Dyrrakhion both from the mainland and from the sea. The Emperor Alexios took advantage of the position of Elissos to secure Epidamnos on the landward side. The Drymon too, which is a navigable river, allowed him to fortify Dyrrakhion, and to bring in supplies by land and over water for the soldiers and inhabitants there, as well as everything necessary for the soldiers' war equipment.

This river, if I may make some remarks about its course, rises in the highlands of Lake Lykhnis, whose name has now been corrupted by barbarians to Akhris; from Mokros, it flows down through a hundred channels, which we call falls. Separate streams flow from the lake as though from different sources, and all hundred or so continue until they empty into a single river near Deure, which at that point takes the name Drymon. The joining together of all these flows serves to make the river both broad and substantial. It follows the borders of Dalmatia, turns north and then bends south, washing the foothills of Elissos before emptying into the Adriatic Sea.

That will do for the site of Dyrrakhion and Elissos and for the explanation of their dominating position. The emperor was at that time in Constantinople when he learnt from letters from the *doux* of Dyrrakhion that Bohemond had crossed. He hastened his own departure. The *doux* of Dyrrakhion had indeed kept careful watch, denying himself all sleep, when he discovered that Bohemond had made the voyage, disembarked, and pitched his camp on the Illyrian plain. Immediately, he sent for a Scythian, and like the proverbial winged messenger, dispatched him to the emperor with the news of the crossing. The emperor met him on his way back from hunting with dogs. Running in and prostrating himself, with his head to the ground, the man cried in a loud, clear voice that Bohemond had crossed over. All the others who were present stood rooted to the spot, stupefied at the very mention of Bohemond's name. The emperor, however, full of spirit and courage, merely remarked as he unloosed the leather strap of his shoe, 'For the moment let us have lunch. We will attend to Bohemond later.'

BOOK XIII

1. At the time we were all amazed at the emperor's self-control. In fact, although he appeared to belittle the news for the sake of those who were present, he was in fact profoundly disturbed by it. Indeed, he came to the conclusion that he must again leave Byzantion. He knew that once more his cause was going badly at court; nevertheless, having taken steps to ensure what was necessary in the palace and in the Queen of Cities and appointed the eunuch Eustathios Kymineianos as *megas droungarios* of the fleet, and Nikephoros, the son of Dekanos, as governors of the city, he set off with a small group of family members on the first day of November in the first indiction,[1] and reached the imperial tent of purple outside the town of Geranion.

He was unsettled by the fact that the Theometor had not performed the usual miracle[2] at the Church of the Blakhernai when he had departed. He waited therefore four days in that place, and then as the sun was setting went back with the empress. They entered the holy shrine of the Theometor secretly with a few others, and proceeded to sing the usual hymns and to pray with great fervour. When the miracle duly took place after all, he headed off once again, this time bursting with hope.

On the next day he made for Thessaloniki. When he arrived at Khoirovakhoi, he named John Taronites as *eparkhos*. John was a nobleman who from his early childhood had been under the emperor's protection and for a long time served him as an *hypogrammateus*. He was a man of active mind, with a sound knowledge of Roman law, prepared to extol the emperor's ordinances as long as they were written in language worthy of his Imperial Majesty. If he spoke freely, his censures were not devoid of tact: he was the Stagirite's ideal of what a dialectician[3] should be.

After the emperor left Khoirovakhoi, he sent frequent letters to Isaac Kontostephanos, *doux* of the fleet, and to his colleagues, by whom I mean Exazenos Doukas and Hyaleas, with instructions to be constantly on the watch and to stop attempts to join Bohemond from Lombardy. When they arrived at Mestos, the empress wanted to return to the palace, but the emperor compelled her to go further; they both crossed the River Euros and pitched camp at Psyllos.

Alexios, having escaped one assassination, would have fallen victim to a second, had not some divine hand stayed the murderers from their crime. A man who traced his ancestry back to the famous Aronioi[4] on one side, even though he was illegitimate, invited the emperor's opponents to kill him. His secret plan was shared with his brother Theodore. Whether there were others also who were in on the plot, I would prefer not to say. In any case, in return for pieces of silver, they persuaded a Scythian slave called Demetrios to do the killing (the slave's master was Aaron himself). The time agreed for the crime was to be the moment of the empress's departure. The Scythian was then to seize some good opportunity – meeting the emperor in a narrow passage or even catching him unawares in his sleep – and plunge the sword into his side.

Demetrios, who was full of murderous thoughts, sharpened his blade and practised his hand for the bloodshed. At that point, however, Justice brought a new element into the drama. For when the empress did not immediately leave the emperor but continued to accompany him while he from day to day kept her back, the criminals lost heart. They saw the emperor's unsleeping guard, by whom I mean the empress, still lingering on, and they wrote some poison-pen letters which they threw into his tent. (It was not known who had actually been responsible for throwing these in, these *famousa* – a word that means scurrilous writings.) These letters warned the emperor to march on and the empress to take the road to Byzantion. The writers of such missives are dealt with very severely by law: the letters themselves are burnt in the fire, and their perpetrators subjected to the most painful chastisement. The conspirators, having failed in their attempt to kill, had been foolish enough to write this stuff.

One day, after the emperor had lunched and most of his retinue had withdrawn, the only persons remaining with him on this particular occasion were Romanos the Manichaean, the eunuch Basil Psyllos and Theodore, Aaron's brother. Once again a letter was found, thrown under the emperor's couch; it made a violent attack on the empress because she accompanied the emperor and would not go back to the capital. This, of course, was their objective: to have perfect freedom to do what they wanted. The emperor knew the person responsible and was very angry. 'Either you or I,' he said, turning to the empress, 'or someone present right here threw this object.' At the bottom of the note was a postscript: 'I, the monk, write this. For the moment, Emperor, you do not know me, but you will see me in your dreams.'

A certain eunuch called Constantine, who had been a servant of the emperor's father and in charge of his table, but was at this time one of the retinue of the empress, was standing outside his tent about the third watch of the night; he was just finishing the usual hymn when he heard somebody cry out, 'If I don't go to him and tell him everything about your plans – yes, *and* denounce the letters which you keep on throwing at him, then you can count me a dead man.' At once Constantine ordered his own manservant to find out who was speaking. Off he went and recognizing Strategios, Aaron's retainer, took him back to the officer in charge of the emperor's table. Without delay, he revealed everything that he knew. Constantine thereupon took him straight to the emperor.

Their Majesties were asleep. However, he met Basil the eunuch and forced him to tell Alexios what Strategios had admitted. Basil obeyed instantly and took Strategios into the emperor's tent with him. Under interrogation he revealed the whole story of these absurd scribbles, named the ringleader of the attempted assassination and identified the man destined to do the killing. 'My master Aaron,' he said, 'with others not

altogether unknown to Your Majesty plotted against your life.
He retained Demetrios, a servant like me and a Scythian by
birth, to kill you – he is a bloodthirsty fellow, strong in the
arm, ready for any bold deed you like to name, savage and
cruel. They put a two-edged sword in his hand and gave their
brutal order to get close up through steely determination and
then plunge the weapon into the imperial body.'

The emperor was not easily convinced by such stories. 'Make
sure,' he said, 'that you are not inventing this accusation
through some hatred of your masters and fellow slave, but tell
the whole truth and clearly describe what you know. If you are
convicted of lying, these charges will do you no good.' The man
insisted that he was telling the truth and was handed over to
Basil the eunuch; he was to give Basil the ridiculous transcripts.
He took him to Aaron's tent, where they were all asleep, picked
up a soldier's pouch which was full of such scribblings and
handed them over. Day was already breaking when the emperor
examined them. He recognized the man who was planning his
death and instructed the police officials in Constantinople to
exile Aaron's mother to Khoirovakhoi, Aaron himself to . . .
and his brother Theodore to Ankhialos. The emperor's march
had been delayed for five days[5] by these events.

2. While he was on his way to Thessaloniki, contingents
drawn from all parts were concentrating in one area, so he
thought it a good idea to arrange them in battle formation. The
phalanxes at once were halted by companies, the commanders
in front and the officers of the rearguard behind; making up
the middle of the phalanx stood the mass of the soldiers with
their flashing arms, ranged side by side like some city wall (it
was a frightening experience to gaze on that parade). You would
have said they were statues of bronze, metal soldiers, for they
all stood motionless on the plain, only their spears quivering,
as if eager to draw blood. When all was ready he put them in
motion, experimenting with methods of deploying to right or
left. Then the emperor separated the new recruits from the rest
of the army and appointed those whom he had personally
trained and given thorough military education to, as officers.
There were 300 of them in all, young men, tall, in excellent

physical condition, each having just grown their first beard, and all good bowmen and strong, expert javelin-throwers. Despite their different places of origin, they were by now one composite body, the elite of the whole Roman army serving under the emperor as military general. For them, he was emperor, general and instructor. Once more a selection was made: the more talented were promoted battalion commanders and sent to the valleys through which the barbarian army would have to pass. The emperor himself wintered in Thessaloniki.

The tyrant Bohemond, as we have said,[6] had crossed over to our territory with a very powerful fleet, and the entire Frankish army had poured out over our plains. Now he gathered them together and marched against Epidamnos, hoping to take it at the first assault, if he could; if not, he intended to force the whole town to surrender by using siege-engines and rock-throwing catapults. That was his plan. He bivouacked opposite the east gate, over which there is a bronze horseman, and after a reconnaissance he began the siege. For a whole winter he made his preparations and examined every point where Dyrrakhion is vulnerable, but when spring began to smile again, as soon as the crossing was completed, he burnt his cargo ships, and his horse transports – in fact, all the vessels that had brought over his military expedition. He did this both so that his army would not look to the sea, but also because the Roman fleet compelled him to do so. From then on, he devoted himself entirely to the siege.

First he fanned out the barbarian force all round the town. There were skirmishes when detachments of Franks were sent out to fight (the Roman archers shot at them, sometimes from the towers of Dyrrakhion, sometimes from more distant places). Bohemond attacked the enemy and was himself likewise attacked. He gained control of Petroula and the place called Mylos on the far side of the River Diabolis. Other places like them in the neighbourhood of Dyrrakhion all fell into his hands through conquest. These successes were the result of skilful tactics. At the same time he was building machines of war, making movable sheds which carried towers and were equipped with battering rams; others were constructed to protect sappers or men filling up the enemy's ditches. Throughout the winter and summer[7] he was hard at work. By threats and by his actions he terrorized men everywhere.

Nevertheless, he did not manage to overcome true Roman bravery completely. Problems of food supply, too, caused him great difficulty. Everything which had been plundered initially from the area round Dyrrakhion had now been exhausted and other prospective sources had been cut off since the Roman forces had already seized the valleys and the passes, and even the seas for that matter too. Hence came famine that resulted in death for horses, for which there was no fodder, and for men, for whom there was no food. Dysentery also struck and ravaged the barbarian army, apparently caused by some unsuitable diet, by which I of course mean millet; the truth though is that this countless, invincible multitude was visited by the wrath of God, and they dropped dead like flies.[8]

3. But to a man with a tyrannical character like his, someone who threatened to destroy a whole land, this misfortune seemed but a small matter; despite all his troubles he continued to make plans and like a wounded animal gathered himself together, prepared to spring. All his attention was focused on the siege. First of all a tortoise-like contraption was made, carrying a battering ram, an extraordinary, indescribable object. It was pushed up to the eastern side of the town. Its very appearance inspired terror. It had been constructed as follows. A small tortoise-shape was made in a rectangular fashion, with wheels put under it, and ox-hides sewn together at all points covering the top and every side, so that the roof and walls of the machine were indeed, as Homer says, of seven bull's-hides.[9] Then the rams were suspended inside.

When the machine was completed, Bohemond had it brought close to the walls of Dyrrakhion, pushed forward from inside by a great number of men armed with poles. When it was near enough, at just the right distance, they removed the wheels and made it firm on all sides by wooden props in the ground, so that the roof would not sway with the constant pounding. After that men of great strength took up position on either side of the ram and began a violent assault with a regular, rhythmical battering of the wall; each time they pushed with tremendous momentum the ram leapt forward tearing at the wall, then rebounded, only to be thrust at the wall again, trying to make a breach. The action was repeated many times, the ram keeping up its pounding, never ceasing the work of boring into the wall.

Probably the ancient engineers who invented this device near Gadeira[10] called it a ram after the animals, which exercise by butting one another. Anyway, the inhabitants of Dyrrakhion laughed at the barbarians and the men who handled it; this goat-like method of attacking a town wall was in their opinion ridiculous, and the enemy's siege efforts were coming to nothing. They threw open their gates and invited them in, as they mocked the repeated blows of the ram. 'Pounding away at the wall with that,' they said, 'will never make as big a hole as the gate offers.' The bravery of the defenders and the confidence of their commander Alexios, the nephew of the emperor, proved the futility of their tactics at once and the besiegers themselves relaxed their efforts, despairing of taking the town, at least by this method. The defenders' courage and the fact that they had the gall to open the gates right in the faces of the barbarians disheartened them; they abandoned the use of the ram and the contraption stood idle. But idle and immobile though it was, for reasons I have given, fire was hurled on to it from above and it was reduced to ashes.

The Frankish force tried another, more terrifying device. It was moved away towards the northern parts opposite the residence of the *doux*, which is called the *praitorion*. It was set like this: rising ground ended in a hill, not of rock, I would say, but of soil; on this hill the town wall had been built. Opposite it, as we said, Bohemond's men started to dig in a most expert manner. This was another invention of the besiegers for the downfall of cities, and thought up specifically with this place in mind. The sappers dug a mine, advancing like many moles as they bored their underground tunnel. Above ground they were protected by sheds with high roofs against the showers of rocks and arrows; below they made progress with their digging in a straight line, propping up their tunnel roof with wooden posts and making a very broad, long passage. All the time the soil was being carried away in wagons. When the mine had gone far enough, they congratulated themselves as if some great work had been accomplished.

But the defenders had not been negligent. Some way off they dug their own trench, and when it was really large, they sat down along its whole length, listening to find out at what point the besiegers were likely to tunnel. It was not long before they discovered a place where the enemy was striking with spades and digging at the foundations of the wall; they now knew their direction, even more so when they opened up a hole just in front of them and saw the crowd of enemy from their own tunnel. The defenders attacked with fire[11] and torched their adversaries' faces.

Now this fire was chemically prepared in the following manner. From the pine and other similar evergreen trees they gather resin, which burns easily. This is rubbed with sulphur and introduced into reed tubes. A man blows on it with a strong, sustained breath, as though he were playing a pipe, and it then comes in contact with the fire at the end of the tube, bursts into flames and falls like a flash of lightning on the faces in front of it. This was the fire used by the defenders of Dyrrakhion when they came up close to the enemy, burning their beards and faces. Like a swarm of bees pursued with smoke they could be seen fleeing in disorder from their tunnel, which they had entered in such a disciplined way.

So their hard work on this scheme too was in vain and another barbarian idea had come to nothing. Thereupon a third invention was tried – a wooden tower. According to report this siege weapon was not constructed after the failure of the others but had been built a full year earlier. It was the main weapon; the others I have mentioned were merely incidental.

First, however, I must explain briefly the plan of the town of Dyrrakhion. Its wall is interrupted by towers which all round the town rise to a height of eleven feet above the wall. A spiral staircase leads to the top of the towers and they are strengthened by battlements. So much for the town's defensive plan. The walls are of considerable thickness, so wide indeed that more than four horsemen can ride abreast in safety. My passing remarks about the walls have been made in order to clarify to some extent what is going to be said later.

It is hard to explain what the new weapon looked like. Bohemond's barbarians devised it as a kind of tortoise with a tower. According to eyewitnesses its appearance was terrifying, and certainly to those who were directly threatened by it it was a most awe-inspiring sight. It was made in the following manner. A wooden tower was built to a considerable height on a four-sided base. So high was it that it was as much as five or six cubits taller than the town's towers. It was essential to make it so, in order that when the hanging walkways were lowered the enemy ramparts might be easily overrun; the local inhabitants would be continually pushed backwards and would not be able to resist a violent attack launched in this way. It seems likely that the besiegers of Dyrrakhion had an excellent knowledge of optical theory, for without such expertise they would not have judged the height of the walls. If they were ignorant of optical theory, at least they knew how to use a *dioptra*.[12]

The tower was indeed a terrible sight, but it seemed even more terrible in motion. Its base was raised on many rollers and this was done by soldiers inside who jacked it up with levers; as the cause of the movement was invisible, the onlookers were amazed. Like a giant moving above the clouds it was apparently self-propelled. On all sides it had been covered from base to top, and there were many storeys with embrasures of every type all round it from which showers of arrows could be fired. On the topmost floor were brave men, completely armed, sword in hand and well trained for evasive action.

When this dread spectacle drew near the wall, Alexios, the *strategos* of Dyrrakhion, and his soldiers were not caught unprepared. At the same time as Bohemond's structure, like some all-conquering siege-engine, was being put up outside the town, another was being made to oppose it inside. When the defenders saw how tall the enemy's self-moving tower was, and where it had been brought to and set up after its rollers had been removed, they themselves set up opposite it four very long poles like a scaffolding, with a four-sided base, and then they put floors at intervals between the poles; the whole thing was built to a height one cubit above the wooden tower outside the walls. It was completely open, for except at the top where it was covered with a roof, there was no need of protection.

Alexios' men carried up the liquid fire, intending to launch it from the highest storey. But when their plan was put into practice it failed to destroy the tower completely, for the jets of fire barely reached their objective. What were they to do? Well, they filled the gap between the two structures with all kinds of combustible material, on which great streams of oil were poured. The fire was started with brands and torches. For a little time it burned slowly, then caught a slight puff of air and burst into a bright flame as the torrents of liquid fire helped on the work. The whole frightful contraption with its abundance of wood was alight, burning loudly and a terrible sight to behold. It was visible up to thirteen stades away in all directions. The barbarians inside were desperate because of the uproar and great confusion; some were cut off by the conflagration and reduced to ashes, others hurled themselves from the summit to the ground. The tumult was tremendous and there was blind panic as those outside joined in the shouts.

4. So much then for the enormous wooden tower and the barbarians' attempt to take the walls. Now we must continue the story of the emperor. When spring came,[13] the empress returned from Thessaloniki to the capital, while the emperor marched through Pelagonia as far as Diabolis, which is in the foothills and after which the tracks become impassable, as I have mentioned before. As he had been devising a new stratagem to use against the barbarians, Alexios was convinced that there should be a rest from large-scale fighting for a time. He was unwilling to risk a hand-to-hand battle, and so, leaving the impenetrable valleys and the roads that led nowhere as a kind of no-man's-land between the two armies, he posted along the mountain ridges all the officers he could trust with ample forces. The object of this new strategy was to prevent easy access from our side to Bohemond, and also to stop letters reaching our army from the enemy or the sending of friendly greetings. As the Stagirite says, a want of communication has proved the end of many friendships.[14]

Bohemond, the emperor knew, was a man of great cunning and energy, and although he was prepared to meet him face to face in battle, as indeed I have said, he was perpetually seeking ways and means of dealing with him which were entirely different. The emperor, my father, was most impatient for war because of the reasons already mentioned; and so, loving danger and having a long experience of it, he sought to apply the rule of reason and find another way to defeat Bohemond.

The general should not invariably seek victory, in my opinion, by drawing the sword; there are times when he should be prepared to use finesse, if the opportunity appears and events allow it, and so achieve a complete triumph. As we know full well, a general's supreme task is to win, not merely by force of arms, but also by relying on treaties, and there is another way – sometimes, in the right circumstances, an enemy can be beaten by fraud. The emperor seems to have relied on this on this occasion. He wished to stir up discord between the counts and Bohemond, to shake or break their harmony, so this was how he set the stage.

He sent for the *Sebastos* Marinos Neapolites[15] (who was a member of the Maistromilios family); while he had not been entirely faithful to his oath of allegiance and had been led astray by deceitful arguments and promises, the emperor was confident that at least as far as Bohemond was concerned he could tell him his secret plan. Roger[16] (one of the most illustrious Franks) and Peter Aliphas, a man of great renown for his warlike exploits, whose loyalty to the emperor was absolutely dependable, were also summoned. Having called them together, the emperor asked for their advice, to see what steps should he take to defeat Bohemond utterly, to see which of those close to Bohemond were most loyal to him, and how many of them were sympathetic towards his views. When they told him, Alexios impressed on them the necessity of winning over these men by every means. 'If this should happen,' he said, 'the Keltic army will be torn by discord and through these men their common purpose will be smashed.' After telling those we have mentioned of his plan, he required each of them to provide one of his most faithful servants, a man who knew how to hold his tongue.

They readily agreed that they were willing to hand over their finest.

The men arrived, and the emperor set things in motion. He composed letters as though in reply to some of Bohemond's most intimate friends; one would suppose on reading them that these men had written to the emperor, trying to win his friendship and disclosing the private intentions of the tyrant. He then sent out replies thanking them and gladly acknowledging their good wishes. The persons to whom he wrote were Guy, Bohemond's own brother; one of his most distinguished soldiers, a man called Koprisianos; Richard; and a fourth individual, Prigkipatos,[17] a brave man and high-ranking officer in Bohemond's army. There were several others besides. The letters sent to them were fraudulent, for the emperor had received no communication at all of this kind from them. Neither Richard nor any other person like him had expressed good wishes and loyalty in a note. It was he himself who had come up with the idea of the letters and their content.

This play-acting had a purpose: if it came to Bohemond's ears that such men were traitorous, that they had been seduced and had made overtures to the emperor, he would at once be thrown into confusion. His barbaric nature would assert itself, he would maltreat them, and force them to break away; thanks to Alexios' cunning, they would rebel against Bohemond – a thing that had never entered their heads. The general knew, I think, that the opposition is strong when the whole body is welded together and of one mind; but let there be faction, and it splits up into many parts and becomes feebler, an easy prey to its enemies. This was the underlying plan and the secret, treacherous intent of the letters.

This is how Alexios put it into practice. The messengers were instructed to deliver them to the individuals concerned, each letter to the respective addressee. Not only did the missives contain expressions of gratitude, but they also promised donations, gifts from the emperor and extraordinary inducements; he invited them in future to be loyal, to show their loyalty, to conceal nothing of their secret designs. After the messengers he sent one of his own most trustworthy men, who was to follow them undetected and when he saw them getting near to the camp, he was to drive on past them, make his approach ahead of them to Bohemond and pretend that he was a deserter, adding that he was joining the other side because he detested the emperor. He was to feign friendship for Bohemond and even a certain cordiality by openly accusing the persons to whom the letters were addressed, saying that this one and that one (giving their names in detail) had broken their oath of allegiance to him, but had now become friends and allies of the emperor and had become his adherents. Bohemond should beware therefore, lest they planned some sudden attack on himself, an attack that had been a long time coming.

It had to be done in this way, in case Bohemond did something dreadful to the letter carriers. The emperor regarded it as his duty to protect from harm's way these men who had been given orders to follow, but also he sought to reduce Bohemond's affairs to chaos. Nor was this a matter merely of words and counsel – action followed, too. The man I have mentioned approached Bohemond, and after ensuring the safety of the messengers by persuading him to take an oath, told him everything according to the emperor's instructions. When he was asked where he thought they were, he said they had passed through Petroula.

Bohemond sent men to arrest the envoys. He opened the letters and becoming faint, almost collapsed, for he believed they were genuine. He placed the men under close guard, while he himself did not leave his tent for six days, debating what he should do, turning over in his mind numerous possible courses: should the constables appear before him, and should he openly tell his brother Guy of the doubts raised about him? Should they appear before him after the inquiry or without inquiry? Moreover, whom would he appoint as constables in their place? Such men, he knew, were courageous and their withdrawal would consequently cause much harm. He settled the affair as best he could, and although I suspect that he became convinced that the letters were forgeries, he nevertheless treated the men with good humour and confidently allowed them to remain at their posts.

5. The emperor had anticipated the enemy in establishing a considerable force in all the passes, under picked leaders, and every route was denied to the Kelts by means of the so-called *xyloklasiai*. Without delay Michael Kekaumenos became the vigilant defender of Avlona, Hierikho and Kanina; Alexander Kabasilas was put in charge of Petroula, with a mixed corps of infantry – he was a brave soldier who had put many Turks to flight in Asia; Leo Nikerites defended Deure with an adequate garrison; and Eustathios Kamytzes was detailed to guard the passes of Arbanon.

Right from the starter's signal, as they say, Bohemond had sent his brother Guy, a count called Sarakenos, and Kontopaganos to deal with Kabasilas. Some small places in the neighbourhood of Arbanon had previously come over to Bohemond and their inhabitants, who were thoroughly acquainted with the tracks around Arbanon, came to him, explained the exact position of Deure and pointed out the hidden paths. Thereupon Guy divided his army in two: he himself undertook to fight Kamytzes from the front, while Kontopaganos and the Count Sarakenos were ordered to fall upon him from the rear with their local guides from Deure. Both of them approved of this plan, and when Guy launched his frontal attack the others struck at Kamytzes from behind. He suffered terrible casualties, for he could not fight against all of them at once, and when he saw his men in flight he followed them. In this engagement many Romans fell, including Karas, who as a young boy had been accepted and enrolled by the emperor among his nobles, and Skaliarios, the Turk who in the old days had been a famous general in the east but deserted to the emperor and had received holy baptism.

This was what had happened to Kamytzes. Meanwhile Alyates, who was guarding Glabinitza with other picked men, came down to the plain. Whether he did this in order to fight, or to make a reconnaissance of the ground, God knows. By chance some Kelts came across him soon afterwards. They were brave men, in full armour, and at the time divided into two groups: one made a violent onslaught on his front, charging at full gallop (they were fifty in number); the other followed him from the rear silently – as it was marshy terrain. Alyates was unaware of the threat behind him and fought against the others with might and main, not realizing the danger he had exposed himself to. The enemy coming from behind fell upon him with great ferocity. In the battle a count by the name of Kontopaganos hit him with his spear and Alyates, felled to the ground, died instantly. Not a small number of his men fell with him.

When the news reached him, the emperor summoned Kantakouzenos, recognizing his outstanding qualities as a soldier. As I said before, he had been recalled from Laodikeia and had rejoined the emperor. Because an attack on Bohemond could no longer be deferred, he was now sent out with a strong force. The emperor also left camp after him, giving him added encouragement, as it were. He reached a mountain pass called Petra by the natives and near it he halted. He gave Kantakouzenos many strategic tips and explained to him the objectives of the campaign, before sending him to Glabinitza brimming with optimism. He himself returned to Diabolis. On his march Kantakouzenos approached a small place called Mylos. At once he made ready all kinds of seige-engines and besieged it. The Romans moved boldly against the fort, and with some setting fire to the gates and others scaling the walls, with great speed they reached the parapets.

The Kelts, encamped on the far side of the river known as the Bouses, saw what had happened and ran to the castle of Mylos in order to help. Kantakouzenos' scouts (they were barbarians, as has been revealed already) saw this, came back to him in disorder and instead of telling him privately what they had observed, began shouting some way off that the enemy were about to attack. When the soldiers heard of the Kelts' imminent arrival, even though they had climbed the walls, even though they had burnt the gates and more or less had their hands on the place, they were panic-stricken. Every man ran for his horse, but in their mad frenzy and terror they grabbed any horse that came their way.

Kantakouzenos fought hard and made repeated charges into the crowd of frightened men. 'Be men,' he shouted, quoting the poet. 'Recall the spirit and fury of war.'[18] They would not listen.

But he overcame their fear by a clever ruse. 'It would be wrong,' he said, 'to leave the siege-engines to the enemy. They'll be used against ourselves. Set fire to them and then go away in good order.' These words had an immediate effect. With great zeal the instructions were carried out; and not only were the machines burnt, but also the boats on the River Bouses, which made it hard for the Kelts to cross. Kantakouzenos withdrew a short distance until he came to a plain; on the right was the River Kharzanes, on the left a muddy swamp. Taking advantage of this natural protection, he pitched camp on this plain. The Kelts arrived at the riverbank, but their boats had already been destroyed and they went back, disappointed of their hopes and downcast.

Bohemond's brother Guy learnt from them what had happened. He changed direction and picking out his best men sent them to Hierikho and Kanina. They found the valleys guarded by Michael Kekaumenos (who had been given that task by the emperor) and taking advantage of the terrain, which was in their favour, made a confident attack on the Romans and routed them. The Keltic soldier is irresistible when he catches his enemies in a confined space; on flat ground it is easy to deal with him.

6. Encouraged by this success they returned to face Kantakouzenos again. However, when they discovered that the place where he had camped was of no assistance to themselves, they timidly put off the battle. He knew of their advance and throughout the night was busy moving all his army to the other bank of the river. Before the sun had even risen over the horizon, he was himself fully armed and his whole force stood ready for battle. He took up position in front of the line at the centre, with the Turks on his left and the Alan Rosmikes in command of the right wing with his own compatriots. He sent the Scythians on ahead against the Kelts, with instructions to draw the enemy forward by skirmishing; at the same time they were to bombard them continually with arrows, then withdraw again before doubling back against them. The Scythians went off eagerly, but they accomplished nothing, for the Kelts kept their ranks absolutely unbroken and advanced slowly in perfect order. When both armies were close enough for battle, the

Scythians could no longer fire their arrows when faced with the enemy's violent cavalry charges and they fled before them at once. The Turks wanted to offer assistance and launched their own attack, but the Kelts, not in the least worried by their intervention, fought even more fiercely.

When Kantakouzenos saw the rout, he at once brought the *exkousiokrator*, Rosmikes, and his troops into action in order to engage with the Kelts (the Alans had been positioned on the right). Even his effort proved inconclusive, although he roared defiance at them like a lion. At this point, seeing what had happened, Kantakouzenos took fresh courage, as if the battle was just beginning, hurled himself at the Keltic front and split their army into many fragments. The enemy were utterly beaten and were pursued as far as the stronghold of Mylos. Many of the ordinary soldiers were killed, as well as officers, while some of the distinguished counts were taken prisoner: Hugh,[19] his brother who was named Richard, and Kontopaganos. Kantakouzenos then returned victorious. He was keen to impress the emperor as much as possible with his victory, and so he had the heads of many Kelts stuck on the ends of spears and the most illustrious of his captives, Hugh and Kontopaganos, were at once sent to him.

As I write these words, it is nearly time to light the lamps; my pen moves slowly over the paper and I feel myself almost too drowsy to write as the words escape me. I have to use barbaric names and I am compelled to describe in detail a mass of events which occurred in rapid succession; the result is that the main body of the history and the continuous narrative are bound to become disjointed because of interruptions. Let those who are enjoying the text not bear me a grudge for this.[20]

The outstanding warrior Bohemond realized that he was in a really difficult position, under attack from sea and land. Now that his supplies were failing, too, he was in dire straits, so he sent off a strong detachment to all the towns near Avlona, Hierikho and Kanina for plunder. The move did not catch Kantakouzenos off guard: as the poet says, 'nor did sweet slumber hold back the man'.[21] Beroites was rapidly dispatched with a considerable force to oppose the Kelts. He engaged, defeated them and then for good measure set fire to Bohemond's fleet on his way back.

When Bohemond, that most tyrannical of men, heard of this setback, far from being downcast, he became even more bold, as if he had suffered no casualties at all. Another contingent, of 6,000 infantry and cavalry most eager to do battle, was put in the field against Kantakouzenos, with the aim of taking the Roman army and Kantakouzenos himself, for that matter, prisoner. But our general had scouts continually on the watch for the Keltic multitudes, and when he knew they were on the march, he armed himself and his soldiers during the night, impatient for the assault at first light. The Kelts, worn out with marching, lay down for a brief rest by the bank of the River Bouses and there, just as day was breaking, he fell on them, attacking at once. Many prisoners were taken, but more were killed; the rest, swept away by the river currents, were drowned – they escaped the wolf only to meet the lion.

Kantakouzenos sent off all the counts to the emperor and then returned to Timoros, a place which was marshy and almost inaccessible. He remained there for a week, during which time a fair number of scouts, posted in different places, were observing Bohemond's movements, reporting these to him and thereby allowing him to plan accordingly. As it happened, the scouts found a hundred Kelts making rafts on which they intended to cross the river and capture a fort on the far side. The Romans fell upon them unexpectedly and took almost all of them alive, including Bohemond's cousin, a gigantic man ten feet tall and as broad as a second Herakles. It was indeed an extraordinary sight – this huge giant, a really monstrous man, the prisoner of a pygmy of a Scythian. Kantakouzenos sent off the prisoners and gave the order that the tiny Scythian should lead the monster on a chain into the presence of the emperor, probably by way of a joke. When the sovereign heard that they had arrived, he took his seat on the imperial throne and commanded the prisoners to be brought in. In came the Scythian leading this tremendous Kelt on a chain, barely as tall as his waist. Of course there was an instant outburst of laughter from all. The rest of the counts were committed to prison . . .

7. The emperor barely had time to smile at the success of Kantakouzenos, when more news arrived, an ill-starred report that the Roman regiments of Kamytzes and Kabasilas had suffered enormous losses. The emperor did not in any way lose heart, but he was deeply distressed and hurt; he grieved for the dead and for some individuals even shed tears. Nevertheless, Constantine Gabras,[22] a fine soldier and scourge of any enemy, was commissioned to take up position at Petroula. His task was to find out where the Kelts got into the valleys to carry out such a massacre, and then to block their way for the future. Gabras was annoyed, and disappointed by this instruction (he was a conceited fellow, ambitious to undertake only important commands). Without delay the emperor turned to Marianos Maurokatakalon, the husband of the sister of my *kaisar*, a man of great courage, proved by many brave, honest deeds and much liked by the emperor who sent him with a force of 1,000 of the most courageous men. Alongside them was a large number of intimates of the *porphyrogennetoi* as well as my *kaisar*, who were glad of an opportunity to fight. Marianos, however, also had reservations about the expedition; nevertheless, he did retire to his tent to consider the matter.

About the mid-watch of the night, letters arrived from Landulph, who was at the time with Isaac Kontostephanos, the *thalassokrator*. These accused the Kontostephanoi, Isaac, his brother Stephanos and Euphorbenos: they had been neglectful in guarding the Lombardy straits and sometimes had landed for a rest. There was a postscript: 'You, Sir, might be doing all you can in body and in mind to prevent the marauding incursions of the Kelts, but these men have given up and are still sleeping at their post. Because they neglect their duty at sea, the sailors bringing supplies to Bohemond inevitably have time on their side. Those who have recently made the crossing from Lombardy to join Bohemond having waited for a favourable wind (to those sailing from Lombardy to Illyrikon, the strong winds from the south are favourable, those from the north are not) find themselves in a fine position. That being said, a gusting south wind never allows them to anchor in Dyrrakhion; they are forced to coast along from Dyrrakhion and put in at Avlona.

The enemy anchor their transports there, ships of great tonnage bringing over heavy reinforcements of infantry and cavalry, and all the food supplies necessary for Bohemond. After landing they organize a number of markets at which the Kelts can buy plenty of produce for the table.'

The emperor was extremely angry and Isaac was severely censured, and through the threats which he received, was prompted to a more conscientious vigilance in the future. But things did not go according to plan for Kontostephanos. (In spite of trying on more than one occasion to prevent a crossing to Illyrikon, he failed to do so.) The trouble was this: he sailed midway between the two coastlines, but when he spied the Kelts under full sail with a following wind and moving fast in the opposite direction, he could not fight both them and the head-winds at the same time. Even Herakles cannot take on two tasks at once, as they say. He was blown back in due course by the force of the wind. The emperor despaired of all this.

As he knew that Kontostephanos was stationing the Roman fleet in the wrong area, so that the south winds which blew against him were making the voyage easier for the Kelts, he drew him a map of the coasts of Lombardy and Illyrikon, depicting the harbours on either side. He sent this to him, adding written instructions, advising where to moor his ships and from what place to set sail if the wind was favourable, in order to attack the Kelts at sea. Thus he put fresh hope into Kontostephanos and persuaded him to apply himself properly. Isaac, confident again, positioned his vessels where the emperor had told him. There he awaited his chance and when the Lombards were out at sea with a great convoy heading for Illyrikon and the wind was in the right quarter, he intercepted them in mid-straits. Some of their pirate ships were set on fire; more were sent to the bottom of the sea with all hands.

Before news of this reached the emperor, he was much concerned at letters from Landulph and the *doux* of Dyrrakhion and he changed his plans. Marianos Maurokatakalon, whom I mentioned before, was immediately summoned and appointed *doux* of the fleet, while the Petroula mission was entrusted to somebody else. Marianos departed and by some chance at once fell in with the privateers on their way from Lombardy to Bohemond. There were also some cargo vessels. He captured all of them, fully loaded with all kinds of goods. After that the straits between Lombardy and Illyrikon had a tireless guardian, for this individual gave the Kelts no opportunity whatever for further passage to Dyrrakhion.[23]

8. Having set up camp at the foot of the passes near Diabolis, the emperor kept a tight rein on would-be deserters to Bohemond. Messages poured out from his headquarters in a continuous stream to the commanders on the passes: he advised them about the number of men required on the plain of Dyrrakhion to fight Bohemond and the type of battle formation they should adopt as they came down from the hills: they were to make frequent charges on horseback and then withdraw; this manoeuvre was to be repeated often while they fired arrows, but the lancers were to move slowly in their rear, so that if the archers should be swept back too far, they might help and at the same time strike at any Kelt who by chance came within reach. They were issued with a plentiful supply of arrows and told not to hold back in their use; but they were to shoot at the horses rather than the Kelts, for he knew that cuirasses and coats of mail made them almost, if not entirely, invulnerable. Shooting the riders, therefore, would in his opinion be pointless and quite crazy.

Keltic armour consists of a tunic interwoven with iron rings linked one with another; the iron is of good quality, capable of resisting an arrow and giving protection to the soldier's body. This armour is supplemented by a shield, not round but long, broad at the top and tapering to a point; inside it is slightly curved, while the outside is smooth and shiny, and has a flashing bronze boss. Any arrow, whether it be Scythian, Persian or fired by the arms of a Giant, will bounce off that shield and rebound against whoever fired it.

It was for these reasons, I suppose, that the emperor, who had plenty of experience of Keltic armour and our arrows, ordered them not to worry about the men but rather to attack the horses, and to give them wings made of arrows. This way, moreover, the Kelts could be captured easily after dismounting.

For a mounted Kelt is irresistible, able to bore his way through the walls of Babylon, but when he is unsaddled he becomes anyone's prize.

Knowing the perverse nature of those alongside him, the emperor was unwilling to go over the passes, despite his own intense desire to fight it out with Bohemond in a general battle, as has been noted many times by us already. On the battlefield he was more incisive than any sword, a man of fearless disposition, absolutely indomitable; late events though had greatly troubled his spirit, and put him off such an effort.

Bohemond was being cramped by land and sea. (The emperor meanwhile sat like a spectator, watching what was happening on the plains of Illyrikon, although his heart and soul was with his fighting men, sharing in their sweat and toil – there were times when one might say he had more than his share – stimulating the officers posted above the mountain passes to battle and war, and giving advice on methods of attacking the Kelts. Marianos, guarding the sea routes from Lombardy to Illyrikon, categorically stopped all movement eastwards: no three-master, no heavy merchantman, no little two-oared boat was given the slightest chance of reaching Bohemond.) Food supplies brought over by sea, therefore, had failed and so had those extra provisions acquired on the mainland. He realized that the war was being successfully pursued against him with much skill (for example, every time his men left camp for forage or any other necessities, or even led out the horses for drink, the Romans would attack and kill most of them, so that his army was gradually wasting away). Under the circumstances he sent proposals for peace to the *doux* of Dyrrakhion, Alexios.

When one of Bohemond's counts, William Klareles, a man of noble lineage, saw that the whole Keltic force was being wiped out by famine and plague (for some terrible illness had visited them from above), he decided to look to his own safety and deserted to the emperor with fifty horses. He was welcomed by the emperor in turn, who asked how Bohemond was faring; he confirmed the distress caused to the army by the plague and the extreme harshness of their plight. He was thereupon rewarded with the title of *nobellisimos* and showered with gifts and favours.[24] From the letters of Alexios, the emperor also learnt that Bohemond had sued for peace through his envoys; he was aware too that his own entourage was always plotting some new mischief against himself. Each hour saw more developments against him, to the point that he felt more concerned about those close to him than about his foreign enemies. As a result, he concluded that he could not fight against both adversaries with two hands. Making a virtue of necessity, as someone once said, he thought the wiser course was to accept peace with the Kelts and not to reject Bohemond's proposals, not least since he was afraid to advance any further – for the reason I have already mentioned.

He stayed where he was, therefore, facing the enemy on two sides, but his letters to the *doux* of Dyrrakhion instructed him to address Bohemond thus: 'You know perfectly well how many times I have been deceived through trusting your oaths and promises. And if the Holy Gospel did not command Christians in all things to forgive one another, I would not have opened my ears to your proposition. But it is better to be deceived than to offend God and transgress His holy laws. I do not therefore reject your plea. If you do in truth desire peace, if you do indeed abominate the absurd and impossible thing that you have attempted, and if you no longer take pleasure in shedding the blood of Christians, not for the benefit of your own country nor for that of the Christians, but to satisfy the whim of yourself alone and of nobody else, then come in person with as many companions as you like. The distance between us is not great. Whether in the course of negotiations we agree on the same terms, or even disagree, you will in any case return to your camp unharmed according to my promise.'

9. When he heard this, Bohemond demanded that hostages drawn from illustrious figures be surrendered to him; they would be free, but guarded by his counts in his own camp, until he himself returned; otherwise he would not dare to go to the emperor. The emperor chose Marinos Neapolites and the famously courageous Frank Roger, who were both intelligent and well versed in the Latin customs, together with Constantine

Euphorbenos (also an excellent individual in deed and spirit, who had never failed the emperor in anything he had been entrusted with), and finally a certain Adralestos, who understood the Keltic language. These men were sent to Bohemond. They were to cajole him by every argument and persuade him to come of his own free will to the emperor to inform him what he wanted and required from him. If the emperor went along with these requirements, he would get what he wanted; if not, he would return unscathed to his own camp.

Such were the instructions which the emperor gave to the envoys before they were sent off to find Bohemond. When the latter heard of their arrival, he was alarmed that they would notice the collapse of his army and tell the emperor about this; so he rode out far from the camp to meet them. They delivered their message thus: 'The emperor has by no means forgotten the promises and oaths given by you and all the other counts who passed through his realm some time ago. No doubt you see that their transgression has not had any positive effect for you.' At this Bohemond interrupted. 'Enough of that. If the emperor had anything else to tell me, I would like to hear it.'

The envoys went on: 'The emperor, desirous of your safety and the safety of the army under your command, makes this proclamation to you through us as his agents: You know perfectly well that after much suffering, you have proved incapable of taking Dyrrakhion. Moreover you have profited neither yourself nor your men. Nevertheless, if what you desire is not to bring utter destruction on yourself and your people, come to me, the emperor, without fear; thus you may reveal all your own ambitions and listen in turn to my adjudication. If our views coincide, thank God; if not, I will send you back to your own camp unhurt. Furthermore, all those under your command who desire to visit the Holy Sepulchre for worship will be given safe conduct by me; those who prefer to go back to their homes will be free to do so, after receiving liberal gifts from me.'

Bohemond replied to them: 'Now I know that truly eloquent men have been sent to me by the emperor. I ask you then for a full assurance that my reception by the emperor will in no way whatever be dishonourable; that six stades before I reach him

his closest blood relatives will come to meet me; that when I
have approached the imperial tent, at the moment when I enter
its door, the emperor himself will rise from his throne to receive
me with honour; that no reference whatever shall be made to
our past agreements and that I shall in no way be brought to
trial; that I shall have absolute freedom to say whatever I wish,
as I wish. Moreover, I ask that the emperor shall take my hand
and set me at the place of honour; that I, after making my
entrance with two officers, shall be completely excused from
having to bend my knee or bow my head to him as a mark of
respect.'

The envoys listened to these requests. They refused his
demand that the emperor should rise from his throne, saying
that it was presumptuous. Nor was this their only refusal. The
request that he should not kneel or bow to the emperor in
obeisance was also vetoed. On the other hand, they accepted
that some of the emperor's distant relatives should go a reasonable distance to meet and escort him when he was about to
enter the emperor's presence, as a ceremonial mark of respect;
he could, moreover, enter with two officers; nor did they dismiss
the idea that the emperor would take his hand and seat him in
the place of honour.

After these exchanges the ambassadors withdrew to the place
already prepared for them to rest, guarded by a hundred ser-
geants. This was to prevent them going out in the night to
examine the condition of the army, thus becoming more
inclined to treat Bohemond with contempt. On the next day,
with 300 knights and all the counts, Bohemond arrived at the
spot where he had talked with the envoys the day before.
Then, with a retinue of six chosen men, he went to find the
ambassadors, leaving behind the rest who were to await his
return.

The envoys and Bohemond discussed again what had previously been said, and when the latter became over-persistent,
a count named Hugh, who was of impeccable lineage, addressed
Bohemond thus: 'Not one of us who intended to join battle
with the emperor has up till now struck anyone with his lance.
An end, then, to most of this talk. It is peace that we must make

and not war.' A long argument ensued on both sides. Bohemond was angry at having been humiliated by the fact that not all his requests had been granted by the envoys.

Some demands were agreed to while others were not, until finally, making a virtue of necessity, as they say, Bohemond backed down, asking them to swear an oath that he would be received with honour and that if the emperor did not meet his wishes, he would be escorted in safety to his own camp. The Holy Gospels were produced therefore and he formally asked for hostages to be handed over to his brother Guy, to be guarded by him until his return. The ambassadors agreed to this and in turn made counter-demands, asking for the swearing of oaths for the safety of their hostages. When Bohemond agreed to this, oaths were taken on both sides and the hostages, the *Sebastos* Marinos, the man called Adralestos and the Frank Roger, were handed over to Guy, on condition that whether a treaty of peace was concluded with the emperor, or whether their efforts failed, he would send them back to the sovereign unharmed, according to their solemn guarantee.

10. When Bohemond was about to start on his journey to the emperor with Constantine Euphorbenos Katakalon, because the camp was fetid with a most horrible odour – the army had been in the same area for a long time – he wished to move his men and said he was unwilling to do even that without their permission. That is typical of the Kelts: they are inconsistent, changing to opposite extremes in the twinkling of an eye. You can see one and the same man boasting that he will shake the whole world and the very next minute cringing prostrate in the dust – and this is even more likely to happen when they meet stronger characters. The envoys agreed that the camp should be moved, but not more than twelve stades. They added: 'If you wish to do this we will come along with you and see the place ourselves.' Bohemond made no objection to this. They immediately informed the officers who were watching the passes not to make sorties or do them any harm.

Constantine Euphorbenos Katakalon in his turn asked Bohemond to allow him to visit Dyrrakhion. Bohemond granted his request and Katakalon soon arrived there. Having

sought out its commander, Alexios, the son of the *Sebastokrator*
Isaac, he delivered the emperor's message entrusted to him and
also to the picked men who had come down there with him.
The garrison troops were unable to lean over the walls because
of a device invented before by the emperor for use on the
ramparts of Dyrrakhion. Planks of wood were cleverly laid
along the parapets of the citadel. They were not nailed down,
so that if any Latins happened to try clambering up ladders,
they would find no firm foothold if they reached the ramparts;
in fact, they would slip and fall inside the walls, planks and all.
Euphorbenos had a conversation with them, gave them the
emperor's instructions and filled them with confidence. He also
asked questions about conditions in the fort. After being
assured that their affairs were going well, as they had enough
provisions and were in no way worried by Bohemond's
schemes, he set off again. He found Bohemond had set his new
encampment in the agreed place. Together they departed on
the road to the emperor while the rest of the envoys, according
to the promises given beforehand, were left with Guy's men.

Katakalon sent Manuel of Modenos, one of his most trustworthy and faithful servants, ahead to announce Bohemond's
imminent arrival to the emperor. By the time that he drew near
the imperial tent, the arrangements for his reception had been
carried out in the manner settled by the envoys. When
Bohemond went inside, the emperor extended his hand, grasped
that of the former and after the words of welcome as usually
spoken by emperors, seated him near the imperial throne.

The appearance of this man was, to put it briefly, unlike that
of any other man whether Greek or barbarian seen in those
days on Roman soil. The sight of him inspired admiration,
the mention of his name terror. I will describe in detail the
barbarian's characteristics. His stature was such that he
towered almost a full cubit over the tallest men. He was slender
of waist and flanks, with broad shoulders and chest, strong in
the arms; overall he was neither too slender, nor too heavily
built and fleshy, but perfectly proportioned – one might say
that he conformed to the ideal of Polyklitos. His hands were
large, he had a good firm stance, and his neck and back were

compact. If to the astute and meticulous observer he appeared to stoop slightly, that was not caused by any weakness of the vertebrae of the lower spine, but presumably there was some malformation there from birth. The skin all over his body was very pale, except for his face which was pale but with some colour to it too. His hair was light-coloured and did not go down to his shoulders as it does with other barbarians; in fact, the man had no great predilection for long hair, but cut his short, to the ears. Whether his beard was red or of any other colour I cannot say, for the razor had passed over it closely, leaving his chin smoother than any marble. However, it seemed that it would have been red. His eyes were light-blue and gave some hint of the man's spirit and dignity. He breathed freely through nostrils that were broad, worthy of his chest and a fine outlet for the breath that came in gusts from his lungs.

There was a certain charm about him, but it was somewhat dimmed by the alarm his person as a whole inspired. There was a hard, savage quality in his whole aspect, due, I suppose, to his great stature and his eyes; even his laugh sounded like a threat to others. Such was his constitution, mental and physical, that in him both courage and love were armed, both ready for combat. His arrogance was everywhere manifest; he was cunning, too, able to escape from trouble when he had to. His words were carefully chosen and the replies he gave were invariably ambiguous. Only one man, the emperor, could defeat an adversary of such character, and he succeeded in doing so through luck, through eloquence and through the other advantages that Nature had given him.

11. After a brief and somewhat discreet review of what had happened in the past, the emperor turned the conversation in another direction. Bohemond, under the influence of a guilty conscience, studiously avoided any attempt to answer his words and merely remarked, 'I have not come to defend myself against such objections. In fact, I could have said much myself. Now that God has reduced me to this state, I put myself entirely in Your Majesty's hands for the future.' 'Let us forget the past now,' said the emperor. 'But if you want to make peace with us, you must first of all become one of my subjects; then you

must inform your nephew Tancred of this and instruct him to
hand over the city of Antioch to my emissaries in accordance
with our first agreement; moreover you must respect, both now
and in the future, all the other pacts made between us.'

The emperor said more about this, and heard plenty back in
reply; it was clear though that Bohemond had not changed
when he declared: 'It is impossible for me to give such an
undertaking.' When the emperor made certain other demands,
he asked to be allowed to return to his own camp, as he was
allowed to do in accordance with the terms agreed with the
ambassadors. However, the emperor told him, 'I have no one
who can better guarantee your safety than myself.' With these
words he ordered his commanders in a loud voice to make
ready the horses for the road to Dyrrakhion. When Bohemond
heard this, he left the emperor and withdrew to the tent set
apart for him, and he asked to see my *kaisar*, Nikephoros
Bryennios, who had been promoted at that time to the rank of
panhypersebastos.[25] When the latter arrived, he used all his
powers of persuasion – he was unrivalled in public speaking
and in conversation – to convince Bohemond that he should
consent to most of the emperor's terms. Thereupon he took
him by the hand and led him into the imperial tent. On the next
day, under oath and of his own free will, because he considered
it the best course, he accepted the terms in full. They were as
follows:

12. An agreement was made with divinely appointed Your
Majesty when I arrived in the imperial city with my enormous
army of Franks on my way from Europe to Asia to liberate
the Holy Sepulchre. That agreement, in consequence of certain
unexpected events, has since been violated; it must therefore be
in abeyance and of no validity, no longer effective and abro-
gated because of changed circumstances. Your Majesty can
legally have no due claims against me relying on that agreement,
nor can there be any contention about what was stipulated and
committed to writing in it. For when I declared war against
Your Majesty, the divinely appointed emperor, and when I
violated the agreed terms, the charges brought by you against
me likewise became null and void.[26] But now that I have come

to repentance and like some fisherman caught unawares by a storm have learnt my lesson; now that I have regained my senses, helped not least by your spear point to recover my sanity; with the memory of defeat and former wars, I beg to make another agreement with Your Majesty. By the terms of this second pact I shall become the liegeman of Your Highness; if I may speak in more explicit and more definite terms, I shall be your servant and subject, for you have been willing to extend to me your protection and accept me as your liege.

By the terms of this second agreement, which I wish to keep for ever – I swear it by God and all his Saints, since the terms agreed are committed to writing and recited with them as my witnesses – I shall be, from this moment, the loyal man of Your Majesty and of your much-loved son, the Emperor Lord John,[27] the *porphyrogennetos*. I undertake to arm my right hand against all who oppose your power, whether the rebel be a Christian or a stranger to our faith, one of those whom we call pagans. One clause, therefore, contained in the aforementioned accord and accepted by both parties, by Your Majesties and by me, this one clause alone with all the others having been made null and void, I extract and stoutly uphold and cling fast to, namely, that I am the servant and liegeman of both Your Majesties, renewing as it were that which has been rescinded. Whatever happens, I shall not violate this; nor shall there be any reason or method, manifest or obscure, which shall make me appear to be a transgressor of the articles of this present covenant.

But since I am to receive now a region, which will be specified later in this agreement, located in the eastern part of the empire, and confirmed by a chrysobull to which Your Majesty will append his signature in purple ink and a copy of which has been given to me, I accept these lands in the east as a gift from Your Majesties. With the chrysobull as guarantee of the validity of this gift, in return for these lands and towns, I pledge my loyalty to Your Majesties, to you the Great Emperor Lord Alexios Komnenos, and to your thrice-beloved son, the Emperor and Lord John the *porphyrogennetos*. I promise to preserve that loyalty unshaken and immovable as a sure anchor.

Let me repeat what I have said in clearer terms and establish the identity of the signatories. I, Bohemond, the son of Robert Guiscard, make this agreement with Your Highnesses, and I intend to keep this agreement inviolate with Your Majesties; that is to say, with you, the Emperor of the Romans, the Lord Alexios, and with the Emperor, your son the *porphyrogennetos*; and I will be your liegeman, sincere and true, as long as I breathe and am numbered among the living. And I promise to arm against any enemies that may hereafter rise up against the Romans and you, the ever-august Sovereigns of the Roman Empire.

And I commit that when I am commanded by you, with all my army I will be your faithful servant, without evasion, in the hour of need. And if there should be any ill-disposed to your power, unless they are the like of the immortal angels, impervious to wounds inflicted by our weapons or endowed with bodies hard as steel, I will fight them all for Your Majesties. And if I am fit in body and free from wars against barbarian and Turk, I myself with my own hands will fight on your behalf with my army behind me. If I am held fast by some serious illness, as can often happen with mortal men, or if impending war drags me away, then I undertake to send as large a body of reinforcements made up from the brave men surrounding me, and they shall make amends for my absence. For true allegiance, which today I give to Your Majesties, entails the meticulous observance of the terms of agreement, either through my own efforts or, as I have said, through the efforts of others.

I swear to be truly faithful, in general and in particular, to your sovereignty and I pledge my protection for your life – that is, your life here on earth. To guard your life I shall be under arms, like a statue hammered out of iron. But I extend my oath to include your honour and Your Majesties' persons and in the case that some mischief is plotted against you by a criminal enemy, I will destroy and repel them from their evil enterprise. I swear too to defend every land that is yours, towns great and small, the islands themselves – in brief, all land and sea under your jurisdiction from the Adriatic Sea as far as the whole east and the territories of Great Asia included in the Roman boundaries.

Moreover I agree, as God is witness to my agreement and listens to it, never to control and hold any land, any town or any island which either now or in the past is or has been held by the Empire of Constantinople, both in the east and in the west, with the exception of those areas duly given me by Your Highnesses crowned by God, which areas shall be expressly named in the present document.

If I am able to subjugate any land that in the past paid tribute to this empire by driving out its present rulers, then I must refer the question of its government to your decision. If you are willing for me, as your liegeman and loyal servant, to rule over this conquered territory, it shall be so; but if you decide otherwise, I shall hand over the territory to whatever man Your Majesties desire, without any equivocation. I shall accept neither any land betrayed to me by any other person, nor any town, nor any village once subject to imperial authority, as though they were my property; but what is acquired, by siege or without a siege, and has been yours in the past, shall again be yours in the future without me in any way laying claim to them.

I shall neither accept the oath of any other Christian person, nor myself take an oath to another person; nor shall I make any agreement that is likely to hurt you or inflict loss on you and your empire. I shall become the liegeman of no one else, of no other power greater or smaller, without your permission. The one sovereignty to which I pledge my allegiance is that of Your Majesty and of your thrice-beloved son.

If men approach me who have rebelled against the authority of Your Majesty and wish to become my slaves, I shall express my loathing of them and reject them – more than that, I shall take up arms against them. As for the other barbarians who are yet willing to submit to my spear, I shall receive them, but not in my own name; rather, I shall compel them to take oaths on behalf of you and your much-loved son, and I shall take over their lands in the name of Your Majesties. Whatever instructions you give with regard to them, therefore, I undertake to carry out with no evasion.

These promises concern all towns and lands which happen

to be under the jurisdiction of Roman Destiny; with regard to those which have not yet become subject to the Roman Empire, I promise under oath to consider all such lands as I take, whether through battle or not, as having been granted to me by Your Majesties, regardless of if they be Turkish or Armenian, or to use our language, no matter if these lands are pagan or Christian; the people of these nations who come to me and wish to be my slaves I shall receive, on condition that they also become liegemen of Your Majesties. My agreement with the sovereign power shall extend to them also, and so shall the oaths ratified. Of these men those whom you, eternally blessed emperors, wish to be subject to me, shall be so subject; but those whom you desire to add to your domain I shall refer to you, if they acquiesce; and if they do not acquiesce, but reject your overlordship, I shall not even receive them in such circumstances.

With regard to Tancred, my nephew, I shall wage relentless war against him unless he is willing to abandon his hostility to Your Majesties and relax his grip on the towns which belong to you. When these towns are recovered, with his consent or otherwise, it will be I who become their master, holding them on your behalf, as is set out in this chrysobull. Those towns, including Laodikeia in Syria, which are not among this number, will be restored to your realm. Nor shall I on any occasion receive fugitives from your empire, but I shall force them to retrace their steps and return to Your Majesties.

Moreover, in addition to the promises mentioned before, I make further pledges to strengthen the agreement: in order that these terms remain in perpetuity unbroken and inviolate, I accept as guarantors whichever men who will take possession in my name of the land given to me by Your Majesties and the towns and strongpoints you choose to appoint. I will ensure that they swear with the most solemn oaths to keep strict faith with your government, in all respects observing Roman law, and to adhere with punctilious care to all the provisions set down in writing here. I will make them swear by the heavenly powers and the ineluctable wrath of God that if ever I plot against Your Majesties – and may that never come to pass,

never, O Saviour, never, O Justice of God! – they will first for
a period of forty days endeavour by all means to break my
rebellious spirit and restore me to my allegiance to Your Majesties. Such a thing would happen – if indeed it were possible for
it ever to happen – only when sheer madness and lunacy took
hold of me or if I were manifestly driven out of my mind.
However, if I should persist in my folly and remain obdurate
in face of their advice, and if the turbulent blast of lunacy does
seize hold of my soul, then they shall disown me upon oath
and in every way reject me, transferring their own power and
allegiance to your service, while the lands which they control
in my name shall be torn from my hands and given up to your
jurisdiction.

They shall be compelled to do these things under oath and
they shall observe the same loyalty and obedience and goodwill
towards you as I have promised; they will take up arms for
your life and for your temporal honour; they shall always be
ready to do battle for Your Majesties' life and limb lest they
suffer at the hands of some enemy, as long as they are aware of
conspiracies and perils. These things I swear and call to witness
both God and men and the angels of Heaven that I shall indeed
force them by frightful oaths to do and practise them to the
best of their ability. They shall agree to the same terms under
oath as I have about your forts and towns and lands – in brief,
about all the provinces which belong to Your Majesties both in
the east and in the west. And these things they shall do both in
my lifetime and after my death; they shall be subjects of your
empire and serve it faithfully.

All my companions who happen to be here with me will at
once take the oath of allegiance and loyalty to Your August
Majesties, the Lord Alexios, Emperor of the Romans and your
son the Emperor and *Porphyrogennetos*; but all those of my
horsemen and men-at-arms, whom we call knights, who are
not present, will take the same oaths, if Your Majesty sends
me one of your men to Antioch, and he will in turn receive
oaths from them. I, in the meantime, promise to urge them
to pledge allegiance according to precisely the same terms.
Moreover I agree and swear that if it is Your Majesties' wish

that I should take up arms and wage war against those who hold the towns and lands which once were subject to the Empire of Constantinople, I will do this and I will bear arms against them. But if it is not your will that I should declare war, then we will not march against them. For in all things we desire to support your authority and to make every deed dependent on your consent.

All those Saracens and Ishmaelites who congregate in your empire, coming over to your side and surrendering their towns, I will neither prevent nor will I zealously try to win them over to myself, unless indeed when hard-pressed by my forces and driven everywhere into desperate straits they turn under the imminent threat of danger to you for help, thus ensuring their own safety. In the case of all such men, who through fear of the Frankish sword and imminent death turn away to Your Majesties for succour, you will not for this reason lay claim to our prisoners of war, but naturally to those only who of their own free will become your servants, without toil and trouble on our part.

In addition to the other clauses, I also agree to the following: all those soldiers of Lombardy who are willing to cross the Adriatic with me shall also take the oaths and agree to serve Your Majesty; the oaths shall of course be administered to them by an individual of your choice from your empire, whom you yourselves shall send for this very purpose from the other side of the Adriatic. If they reject the oath, they shall in no circumstances be allowed to cross, because of their hostility to our mutual agreement.

As for the lands granted to me[28] in a chrysobull from Your divinely appointed Majesties, it is essential that they should be set out in the present document, as follows; the city of Antioch in Koile-Syria with its fortifications and its dependencies, together with Souetion, which is situated by the sea; Doux with all its dependencies, together with the castles of Kaukas and Loulos, the Wondrous Mountain and Phersia, with all its territory; the military district of St Elias, with its dependent small villages; the military district of Borze and its dependent villages; all the country in the neighbourhood of the military district of Sezer, which the Greeks call Larissa; likewise the military districts of Artakh and Teloukh with their respective fortifications, and with these Germanikeia and the small villages which belong to it; the Black Mountain and all the castles dependent on it, as well as all the plain lying at its feet, except of course the territory of the Roupenioi, Leo and Theodore,[29] the Armenians who have become your liegemen.

In addition to the above-mentioned, the *strategaton* of Pagras, that of Palatza, the theme of Zoume, together with all their dependent castles and small villages, and the country which belongs to each. For all these are included in the chrysobull of Your Majesties as granted to me by the divine power until the end of my life, and as reverting of necessity after my passing from this world to the Empire of New Rome, the Queen of Cities, Constantinople, provided that I keep my faith absolutely unblemished and preserve my loyalty to its sovereignty faultless, in the person of Your ever-august Majesties, and provided that I am the servant and liegeman of its throne and imperial sceptre.

I further agree and swear by the God worshipped in the Church of Antioch that the patriarch of that city will not be of our race, but a man whom Your Majesties will promote, one of the clergy of the Great Church in Constantinople. For in future the throne of Antioch will be occupied by such a man; he will carry out all the duties of an archbishop, the laying on of hands and the other business of the church, according to the privileges of this see.[30]

There were also certain parts cut off from the ducal jurisdiction of Antioch by Your Majesties, since you wished to appropriate them entirely: they are as follows: the theme of Podandon ... the *strategaton* of the town of Tarsos, the town of Adana, the town of Mopsuetsia and Anabarza – in short, the whole territory of Kilikia which is bounded by the Kydnos and the Hermon; likewise the military district of Syrian Laodikeia, similarly the *strategaton* of Gabala, which using barbarian language we call Zebel; the *strategata* of Balaneus, Marakes and Antaras with Antarados, for both the latter are military districts. These are the places which Your Majesties have separated from the general ducal jurisdiction of Antioch and brought under their own sphere of influence.

And I declare that I am content with both what has been conceded to me and what has been kept separate. I will fiercely guard the rights and privileges which I have been granted by you, and that I will not lay claim to those which I have not received. Nor will I cross the frontiers, but will remain within the territories accorded to me, ruling them and enjoying the free use of them as long as I live, according to my previous declaration. After my death, as has already been stipulated, they will revert to their own governments, from which they were transferred to me. I will make sure of this by instructing my governors and my men to hand over all the lands in question to the Roman authorities without fuss, and without equivocation.

These instructions will be given as my last wish. I swear this, and ratify this clause of the treaty: they will carry out the command without delay and without ambiguity. However, let the following addendum be made to the agreement: let it be stated that when your government detached the territories from the jurisdiction of Antioch and from the ducal command of that city, I personally made an urgent request to Your Majesties to grant some compensation, a request which was also endorsed to Your Majesties by pleas of pilgrims; Your Highnesses agreed, and certain themes, lands and towns in the east were granted as compensation.

It is necessary that these should be named here, in order to avoid any ambiguity on the part of Your Majesties and so that my own claims can be justified. They were as follows: the entire theme of Kasiotis, whose capital is Berroia, and known in the barbarian language as Aleppo; the theme of Lapara and its dependent habitations – that is to say, Plasta, the castle of Khonios, Romaina, the castle of Aramisos, the small town of Amira, the castle of Sarbanos, the fort of Telkhampson together with the three Tilia – Sthlabotilin and the other two, the fort of Sgenin and the castle of Kaltzierin; moreover, the following small settlements: Kommermoeri, the district called Kathismatin, Sarsapin and the little village of Mekran. These places are situated in Nearer Syria. The other themes are in Mesopotamia, in the vicinity of the town of Edessa, namely, the theme of Limnia and the theme of Aetos together with their respective fortifications.

There are other points that should not be passed over in silence which concern Edessa and the annual payment of talents in cash to me by Your Majesties; I refer to the 200 pounds stamped with the bust of the Emperor Michael.[31] Apart from that payment, according to the terms of Your Majesties' esteemed chrysobull the dukedom[32] has been granted to me in its entirety, with all its dependent forts and lands, and this authority has not been vested in my person only, for by that same document I am allowed to bequeath it to any person I wish, on the understanding, of course, that he too will bow to the orders and desires of Your Majesties, as liegeman of the same power and authority, subscribing freely to the same agreement as I.[33]

Hereafter, since I have become your liege once for all and have become one of your subjects, it will be my due every year to receive from the imperial treasury the sum of 200 talents, in coin of good quality stamped with the effigy of the Lord Michael, the former emperor, and this payment will be made through some agent of ours, sent from Syria with my letters to you in the imperial city so that he may accept these monies in our name.

And you, eternally revered, august and blessed emperors of the realm of the Romans, will for your part observe the clauses written in the chrysobull of Your Majesties and will keep your promises to the letter. I, then, solemnly confirm the agreements I have made with you by this oath: I swear by the Passion of Christ Our Saviour who suffers no longer, and by His invincible Cross, which for the salvation of all men He endured, and by the All-holy Gospels here before us, which have converted the whole world; with my hand on these Gospels, which I associate with the much honoured Cross of Christ, the Crown of Thorns, the Nails, the Spear that pierced Our Lord's side, giver of life, I swear to you, Lord and Emperor Alexios Komnenos, most powerful and revered, and to your co-Emperor, the thrice-

beloved Lord John *porphyrogennetos*, that all the agreements
made between us and confirmed by me verbally I will observe
and will for ever keep absolutely inviolate. Just as I support
Your Highnesses now, so too will I support you in the future,
with no malicious intent, no treachery, for I will abide by the
undertakings I have given and will in no manner whatsoever
breach my oath to you, nor will I proceed to break my promises,
nor attempt to evade my responsibilities in any way under the
treaty – and this applies not only to myself but also to all those
with me, who are under my jurisdiction and make up the
numbers of my soldiers. Moreover, we shall arm ourselves
against your enemies with breastplate, weapons and spears,
and we shall clasp the right hand of your friends. In thought
and in deed I shall do everything to help and honour the Empire
of the Romans. So may I enjoy the aid of God, of the Cross, of
the Holy Gospels.

These words were committed to writing and the oaths were
administered in the presence of the under-mentioned witnesses
in the month of September of the second indiction, in the year
6617.[34] The names of the witnesses present, who signed beneath
and before whom the treaty was concluded, are as follows:

Mauros of Amalfi and Renard of Taranto, bishops dearly
  beloved of God, together with the clergy who accompanied
  them.
The most reverend abbot of the Holy Monastery of St
  Andrew in Lombardy, on the island of Brindisi, and two
  monks from that monastery.
The leaders of the pilgrims, who made their marks with their
  own hands and whose names have been written beside
  those marks in the handwriting of the bishop of Amalfi,
  dearly beloved of God, who came as papal legate to the
  emperor.

From the imperial court the following signed:
The *Sebastos* Marinos,
Roger, son of Dagobert,
Peter Aliphas,
William of Gant,

Richard of the Principate,
Geoffrey of Mailli,
Humbert, son of Raoul,
Paul the Roman,
the ambassadors who came from the Dacians on behalf of the
   kral, relative of the empress, the župan Peres and Simon,
the ambassadors of Richard Siniskardos,[35] they were the
   Nobellisimos Basil the eunuch and the *Notarios*
   Constantine.

The emperor received this oath, set down in writing, from
Bohemond and in return gave to him the above-mentioned
chrysobull, signed in purple ink according to custom by the
hand of the emperor.

BOOK XIV

1. The emperor had achieved his goal. Bohemond had confirmed the written agreement set out above under oath, swearing by the Holy Gospels put before him and by the spear[1] with
which the impious had pierced the side of Our Saviour. Now,
after handing over all his troops to the emperor to command
and use as he wished, Bohemond asked for permission to return
home. At the same time he requested that his men should be
allowed to winter inside the Roman Empire, that they should
be plentifully supplied with necessities and that when the winter
passed and they had recovered from their many exertions, they
might be granted the privilege of leaving for any destination
they wished. The emperor at once gave his consent. Bohemond
was thereupon honoured with the title of *sebastos*, and provided
with a substantial sum of money, and he retired to his own
camp. Constantine Euphorbenos, surnamed Katakalon, went
with him so as to prevent harm coming to him on the road
from the soldiers of our army, and above all, so as to supervise
the siting of Bohemond's camp in a favourable and safe place,
as well as to satisfy his soldiers' reasonable demands. Having
arrived at his own headquarters, Bohemond handed over his
forces to officers sent for this purpose by the emperor and then,
boarding a monoreme, sailed for Lombardy. Not more than six
months[2] afterwards he paid the price that everyone has to pay
sooner or later.

The emperor was still concerned about the Kelts, however;
so, it was only after settling their affairs properly that he set off
for Byzantion. When he got back, rather than indulging himself
with relaxation and pleasure, he became preoccupied with the

barbarians who had utterly ravaged the coast from Smyrna as far as Attaleia.[3] Not to restore these towns to their former condition, in his opinion, would be a terrible disgrace; their old prosperity must be revived, their inhabitants, scattered in all directions, must be brought back. Far from being insensible to the fate of Attaleia, he did in fact devote much attention to its problems.

Eumathios Philokales (a man of great drive, not only distinguished by birth, but also by his intelligence – he was free-spirited and generous, most faithful to God and to his friends, loyal if ever a man was to his masters even if he was completely ignorant of the ordinary soldier's training, unable to hold a bow, let alone draw it out, or to defend himself with a shield. He was in all other respects, though, extremely proficient, for example in laying ambushes or outwitting the enemy by all kinds of stratagems) came to the emperor and demanded to be put in charge of the defence of Attaleia. The emperor, recognizing his manifold intellectual and practical talents, and knowing that Fortune, whoever she is or is supposed to be, always smiled on him (he had never failed in any task so far), listened to him and decided to give him the necessary forces, not neglecting to pass on much advice as well as the instruction to approach matters with caution.

After arriving at Abydos, Eumathios promptly sailed across the straits to Atramytion. This town had formerly been a very populous place. However, when Tzakhas had ravaged the Smyrna area, he had reduced it to rubble and wiped it out entirely. Eumathios saw the devastation, which was so complete that one would have thought no man had ever lived there, and at once began to restore the town to its former condition, recalling its inhabitants, who had fled, from all over, and also attracting those from elsewhere to settle in the town so that the prosperity it had once known returned. He made inquiries about the Turks and when he discovered that they were at that time in Lampe, he detached some of his forces to attack them. Contact was made with the enemy and in the stern battle which ensued the Romans soon won a victory. They treated the Turks with such abominable cruelty that they even threw their newborn babies into cauldrons of boiling water. Many Turks were massacred, others brought back to Eumathios as prisoners. The Turkish survivors dressed themselves in black, hoping by this sombre garb to demonstrate to their fellow-countrymen their own sufferings. They traversed all the territory occupied by Turks, wailing mournfully and recounting the horrors that had befallen them. Their sad appearance moved all to pity and provoked the desire for revenge.

Eumathios meanwhile arrived at Philadelphia, well pleased with his good progress. An archisatrap called Asan had gained control of Kappadokia, and used the natives as though they were his slaves bought with money; he heard what had happened to the Turks I have already mentioned and mobilized his own forces; to these were added many others called up for service from other areas, so that his army totalled 24,000 men. He set out against Eumathios. As I have said the latter was a clever man, and did not sit idly by in Philadelphia, and rather than relaxing his efforts once he was inside the walls of the town, sent out scouts in all directions; in order that they might not be careless they were supervised by others, who urged them to stay on their guard all through the night, keeping roads and plains alike under close surveillance.

One of these men spotted the Turkish army some way off and ran to tell him. Now Eumathios was quick-witted and swift to appreciate the right course of action and ready to take instantaneous decisions. He realized that his own forces were outnumbered, so at once ordered the gates of the town to be strengthened; nobody, under any circumstances, was to be allowed to climb to the battlements; there was to be no noise at all, no playing of flutes or lyres. In a word, he ensured that passers-by would think the place was absolutely deserted. Asan reached Philadelphia, surrounded the walls with his army and stayed there for three days. As no one appeared to be looking over the walls (the besieged were well protected by the gates, and moreover he had no siege-engines and no catapults), he came to the conclusion that Eumathios' army was insignificant and for that reason lacked the courage to make a sortie, so he turned his attention to another scheme, condemning the enemy's thorough cowardice and treating him with utter contempt. He divided his army, sending off 10,000 men against Kelbianos, others ... to attack Smyrna and Nymphaion, while the rest were to advance on Khliara and Pergamon. All were to engage in plunder. Finally he joined the detachment on its way to attack Smyrna ...

Once Philokales worked out what Asan was up to, he launched all his troops in an attack on the Turks. Pursuing the group which was making for Kelbianos, the Romans caught up with them unawares, launched an offensive at daybreak, mercilessly slaughtered them and liberated all the prisoners who had been held captive. Then they set out in pursuit of the other Turks moving towards Smyrna and Nymphaion; some actually went on ahead of the vanguard and joined battle with them on both flanks, winning a complete victory. Many Turks were killed, and many taken captive; the mere handful who survived fell in flight into the currents of the Maiandros and were promptly drowned. (This river in Phrygia is the most winding of all with its continuous bends and turns.) Gaining confidence from this second triumph, the Romans set off after the remainder. Nothing came of it, though, the Turks having gone too far ahead. They returned, therefore, to Philadelphia, where Eumathios learnt how courageously they had fought and how determined they had been to let no one escape from their clutches. He rewarded them liberally and promised generous favours in future.

2. After Bohemond's death Tancred seized Antioch, dispossessing the emperor and treating the city as his own undisputed property.[4] The emperor thought about the oaths relating to this city which these barbarian Franks were violating, and about the vast sums of money which he had personally spent, and about the many perils he had faced in transporting these enormous armies from the west to Asia; he had always found them a haughty, embittered race. He had sent many Romans to help them against the Turks, for two reasons: first, to save them from massacre at the hands of their enemies (for he was concerned for their welfare as Christians), and secondly, that they, being organized by us, might destroy the towns of the Ishmaelites or

force them to make terms with the emperors of the Romans and thus extend the bounds of Roman territory. In fact, however, his great generosity, his toils and troubles, had won no advantage for the Roman Empire. On the contrary, Antioch was still clung to stubbornly, and other townships too remained out of our hands. The situation was intolerable. Reprisals were absolutely inevitable and they would have to be punished for behaviour so inhuman.

That Tancred should be reaping the benefits of those countless presents and those heaps of gold, as well as of the unstinting support provided by the emperor, including substantial military backing, while the Roman Empire got nothing in return was galling. Furthermore, the Franks looked upon the final victory as theirs, violating their treaties with him and their pledged word, regarding them as worth nothing. To him their conduct was heart-rending, their insolence quite unbearable.

An ambassador was accordingly dispatched to the ruler of Antioch, Tancred, charging him with injustice and perjury; he was told that the emperor would not for ever submit to his scorn, but would repay him for his ingratitude to the Romans. It would be disgraceful if after the expenditure of vast sums of money, after the aid rendered by the elite Roman divisions in order to subdue the whole of Syria and Antioch itself, after his own wholehearted efforts to expand the bounds of Roman power, Tancred was to enjoy luxury – as the result of *his* spending and Alexios' labours.

Such was the emperor's communication through the ambassadors.[5] The barbarian lunatic in his frenzied rage absolutely refused to listen; he could not bear either the truth of these words or the frankness of the envoys, and immediately reacted in the way his race do: glorying in his own boastfulness he babbled that he would set his throne high above the stars and threatened to bore with his spear point through the walls of Babylon; he spoke with emphasis of his might, mouthing out the words like a tragic actor – how he was undaunted, how no one could withstand him; he confidently assured the envoys that whatever happened he would never release his grip on Antioch, even if his adversaries came with hands of fire; he was like the Assyrian,[6] a mighty irresistible giant, with his feet firmly planted on earth like some dead weight, but all Romans were to him nothing more than ants, the feeblest of living things.

When the envoys returned and gave a graphic account of the Kelt's madness, the emperor's anger boiled over and he could no longer be restrained: he wanted to make for Antioch at once. He held a conference of the most distinguished soldiers and all members of the Senate, and asked them for their advice. They unanimously rejected the emperor's plan for an expedition against Tancred for now; first, they said, he must win over the other counts who controlled the places near Antioch, and in particular Baldwin, the king of Jerusalem, and investigate whether they would be prepared to assist him in a campaign against Antioch. If they were found to be hostile to Tancred, then the expedition should be undertaken with confidence; if their attitude was doubtful, the Antioch problem should be solved in some other way.

The emperor concurred with this, and without delay summoned Manuel Boutoumites and another man, who understood the Latin language. They were sent to the counts and the king of Jerusalem, after being fully briefed about the negotiations they would have to conduct with them and with the king of Jerusalem, Baldwin. Inevitably money was required for this mission because of Latin greed; Boutoumites was therefore entrusted with orders for the officer who was then *doux* of Cyprus, Eumathios Philokales, who was to supply them with as many ships as they needed and at the same time great sums of money of all types, of every kind, stamped with any effigy and of all values, to serve as gifts for the counts. The envoys in question and especially Manuel Boutoumites were commanded, after accepting the money from Philokales, to moor their ships at Tripolis. There they were to visit Count Bertrand,[7] the son of St Gilles, who has been mentioned in my history on many occasions. He was to be reminded of his father's loyal service to the emperor and be handed imperial letters before being told: 'It is not right that you should be inferior to your father; your allegiance to us must be as firm and lasting as his. Know that I am on my way to Antioch, where I will exact vengeance for the breaking of fearful oaths made to God and to me. As for you, make sure that you help Tancred in no way, and do your best to win over the counts to our side, so that they also may give him no comfort whatever.'

After their arrival in Cyprus and after they had the money from Philokales and all the ships they required, the envoys sailed directly to Tripolis. They anchored in the harbour, disembarked, found Bertrand and recited the emperor's message to him. They saw that Bertrand was sympathetic and was prepared to satisfy any demand made by the emperor, even if need be to face death gladly on his behalf. He promised solemnly that he would come to pay him homage when he arrived in the Antioch region. With his consent, therefore, they deposited the money they had brought with them in the bishop's residence at Tripolis, as the emperor had suggested. He had feared that if the counts knew who had the money they might seize it, send the envoys away empty-handed and use it for their own and Tancred's pleasure. He judged it wise that they should leave it behind; later, when they had discovered how the others stood, they were to give them the emperor's message, and simultaneously pledge donations and exact oaths – provided of course that the counts were willing to yield to the emperor's demands. Only under those conditions would they be given money. Boutoumites and his companions accordingly left the funds in the bishop's residence at Tripolis.

When Baldwin heard of the arrival of these envoys at Tripolis, however, he lost no time in sending them an invitation through Simon, his brother's son. Of course he was greedy for gold. They left the money behind with Bertrand's consent, and then accompanied Simon, who had come from Jerusalem, and met Baldwin outside Tyre, which he was besieging. He was delighted to welcome them with every sign of friendship. It was the season of Lent and throughout the forty-day period he kept them with him while the siege of Tyre continued,[8] just as I said. The town was protected by impregnable walls, but the fortifications were further strengthened by three defensive features which completely encircled it, with the outer ring enclosing the second, which in turn encompassed the third. They were like three circles, bound together and surrounding the town like a belt.

Baldwin realized he had to destroy these outworks first, and he would only then be able to capture the town itself; they acted as a kind of breastwork, shielding Tyre and averting siege operations. The first and second circles had been demolished by siege-engines; he was now attempting to throw down the third. Its battlements were in fact already in ruins, when he began to relax his efforts; he could have taken it, had he really exerted himself. He thought that later he would climb into the town by ladders; as far as he was concerned, it had already fallen and so he slackened off. This proved to be the salvation of the Saracens: he, with victory at hand, was thoroughly repulsed, while his opponents who had found themselves in the hunter's net, jumped clear of danger. They had used the respite provided by Baldwin's indolence to regroup.

They prevailed thanks to the following stratagem: they pretended to seek a truce and sent ambassadors to Baldwin, but in reality while the peace negotiations were going on they set their minds to their defence; while his hopes were encouraged they were planning methods of attack on him. They had seen much warlike activity, and then the besiegers apparently had lost heart; so one night they filled many earthenware jars with liquid pitch and hurled these at the siege-engines which threatened their walls. The jars of course were shattered and the liquid poured over the timber frames. Lighted torches were then flung on them, together with other jars containing a good supply of naphtha, which caught fire. At once it flared up into a conflagration and their machines were reduced to ashes. As the light of day spread, so the fiery light of flames from the wooden tortoises rose into the town like a tower.

Baldwin's men had due reward then for their carelessness, and when the smoke and flames warned them what had happened they were sorry. Some of the soldiers near the tortoises were taken prisoner, and when the governor of Tyre saw them, six in number, he had them decapitated and their heads slung into Baldwin's camp by catapults. The sight of the fire and the severed heads affected the whole army. They fled on horseback in terror, stricken with panic as if being harassed by the heads, despite all Baldwin's efforts to ride out after them and to recall them and restore their courage. He was, though, singing to deaf men, for once they had abandoned themselves to flight nothing could stop their running – faster, it seemed, than any bird. Eventually they came to a halt, at a garrisoned place known locally as Acre; to these craven runners it was a place of refuge. Naturally Baldwin was discouraged. There was nothing for it but to follow them to that town, although it was against his wishes.

As for Boutoumites, he embarked on Cypriot triremes (there were twelve in all) and sailed along the coast to Acre, where he met Baldwin and delivered the emperor's message in full, according to instructions, adding that the emperor had just reached Seleukeia. In fact this was not true; he was trying to frighten the barbarian into leaving Acre quickly. However, Baldwin was not deceived by this play-acting and charged him roundly with lying. He had already been informed by someone about the emperor's progress; he knew he had advanced a long way down the coast, had taken the pirate vessels which were ravaging the places by the sea and had returned through illness, details of which will be given later in the history. Baldwin told Boutoumites all this and having accused him of fabrication, said, 'You must come with me to the Holy Sepulchre, and from there my envoys will go and inform the emperor of our decisions.'

As soon as he arrived in the Holy City, he asked them for the money sent for him by Alexios, but at this point Boutoumites had something to say: 'If you promise the emperor to help against Tancred, keeping the oath you swore to the emperor when you passed through Constantinople, then you shall have the money.' Baldwin wanted the money, even though it was not the emperor whom he wanted to help, but Tancred; it irked him, nonetheless, to be denied the money. (That is the way of all the barbarians: their mouths gape wide for gifts and money, but they have no intention whatever of doing the things for which the money is offered.) So Baldwin entrusted non-committal letters to Boutoumites and let him go. The envoys

also fell in with Count Joscelin,[9] who had come to worship at
the Holy Sepulchre on the day of the Saviour's resurrection.
They had the usual conversation with him, but as his replies
were like Baldwin's, they returned with nothing accomplished.

Bertrand, they discovered, was no longer alive,[10] and so they
asked for the money deposited in the bishop's residence. However, his son and the bishop of Tripolis again and again put off
the moment of restitution. The envoys used threats: 'If you
don't give back the money to us, you are no true servants of
the emperor. It seems you have not inherited the loyalty of
Bertrand and his father St Gilles. So in future you will have
neither plentiful supplies from Cyprus nor the helping hand of
its *doux*. After that you will die, the victims of famine.' Every
method of persuasion was tried: sometimes they spoke mildly,
sometimes with menaces, but no progress was made. In the end
they thought it necessary to force Bertrand's son to swear a
solemn oath of allegiance to the emperor and then to present
him with the gifts destined originally for his father alone;
namely, coined money of gold and silver and robes of all kinds.
On receipt of these he swore a solemn oath of allegiance to the
emperor and they, having carried off the remainder of the
money to Eumathios, bought with it thoroughbred horses from
Damascus, Edessa and even Arabia. From there they sailed
from the Syrian Sea and the Gulf of Pamphylia, but then begged
to be excused from sailing further, because they considered
crossing by land to be safer. They made for the Kherronesos,
where the emperor was, and after crossing the Hellespont
rejoined him.

3. As thick and fast as snowflakes troubles descended[11] on
the emperor: from the sea the admirals of Pisa, Genoa and
Lombardy were making ready expeditions to ravage all our
coasts, while on the mainland the Emir Saisan[12] had once more
come from the east and was already threatening Philadelphia
and the maritime provinces. The emperor knew that he must
leave the capital and station himself where he could fight on
two fronts. Thus he came to the Kherronesos. From everywhere military forces were gathered by land and sea. A strong
detachment was placed on the far side of the Skamandros at

Atramytion and indeed in the theme of Thrakesion. At that time the *strategos* of Philadelphia was Constantine Gabras, who had enough men to protect the town, while Pergamon, Khliara and the neighbouring locations were under the authority of the half-caste Monastras, who has been mentioned many times above. The other coastal towns, too, were controlled by officers distinguished for their boldness and experience as leaders. They received constant directives from the emperor, who exhorted them to be on their guard, to send out reconnaissance parties in all directions to watch for enemy movements and to report them immediately.

After strengthening the Asian front, he turned his attention to the war on the sea. Some sailors were told to moor their ships in the harbours of Madytos and Koila, to maintain a ceaseless patrol of the straits with light warships and protect the sea routes at all times as they awaited the Frankish navy; others were to sail among the islands and guard them, keeping in range of the Peloponnese and giving it adequate protection. As he wanted to spend some time in the area, he had temporary buildings erected in a suitable place and wintered there.

The fully equipped fleet from Lombardy and other areas weighed anchor and set off; once at sea the admiral in charge detached a squadron of five biremes to take prisoners and gain information about the emperor. They were captured off Abydos with their crews, with only a single vessel managing to rejoin the others. Thanks to this, the admirals of the aforementioned fleet learnt about the emperor's activities, and found out that careful security measures had been taken by land and sea and he was spending the winter in the Kherronesos to encourage his men. Because these dispositions made victory impossible, the enemy changed course and steered their ships elsewhere.

One Kelt in the service of these admirals left the main fleet with his monoreme and sailed off to Baldwin, whom he found besieging Tyre. He had gone off, I believe, with the knowledge of the leaders of the expedition. He gave Baldwin a full account of the emperor's affairs, just as I have described above, and told him how the Romans had captured the warships which had been sent out to reconnoitre. Anyway, he admitted unblushingly that the Keltic commanders, knowing that the emperor was so well prepared, had withdrawn; they had thought it better to sail away with nothing accomplished than to fight and be defeated. As he said this to Baldwin the man still trembled slightly at the dreadful recollection of the Roman fleet.

So much for the Keltic adventures on the sea; by land the emperor was not without his own worries and troubles. A certain Michael from Amastris, who was defending Akrounos, organized a rebellion, seized the town for himself and ravaged the neighbouring lands with a reign of terror. The emperor reacted to the news by sending George Dekanos against him with a strong army. The town was taken after a siege of three months and the traitor was soon on his way to the emperor, who appointed another man in his place. The rebel was stared at angrily by the emperor, who threatened him with numerous punishments before seeming to sentence him to death – something that terrified the individual in question. He soon put the soldier out of his misery though: before the sun had dipped below the horizon, the prisoner was freed, his condemnation to death replaced with countless gifts.

My father the emperor was always like that, even if later he was repaid by everyone with base ingratitude. In the same way long ago Our Lord, Benefactor of the whole world, caused manna to rain down in the desert, fed the multitude on the mountains, led them through the sea dry-footed – yet afterwards He was rejected and insulted and smitten and finally condemned to be crucified by wicked men. But when I reach this point the tears flow before my words; I long to speak of these things and compile a list of these unfeeling men, but I check my tongue, bear with my impatience and over and over again quote to myself the words of the poet: 'Endure, my heart; you have suffered other, worse things before.'[13]

I will say no more about that ingrate soldier. Of the men sent from Khorosan by the Sultan Saisan, some went through the district of Sinaos, while others came through Asia proper. Constantine Gabras, who was in charge of the defence of Philadelphia at the time, heard about it and with his troops made contact with the Turks at Kelbianos. He was the very first to charge at full gallop against them, calling on the rest to follow, and he vanquished the barbarians. When news of this setback reached the sultan, he sent ambassadors to the emperor to sue for peace, stressing that for a long time he had longed to see peace established between the Muslims and the Romans. He had heard accounts of the emperor's exploits against all his enemies from afar, and now that he had personal experience, and recognizing the robe from its hem, the lion from his claws, his mind had turned to thoughts of peace, against his will.

When the envoys from Persia arrived[14] the emperor was seated on his throne, an impressive figure, and the officers in charge of ceremonial arranged in order the soldiers of every nationality, together with those who bear their axes on their shoulders. The envoys were then ushered in and placed before the imperial throne. Alexios asked the usual questions about the sultan and heard their message. He acknowledged that he welcomed and desired peace with all; but the sultan's objectives, he realized, would not all be in the interests of the empire. With much persuasive skill and great cleverness he defended his own position before the envoys and after a long discourse brought them round to his point of view. They were then dismissed to the tent prepared for them and told to consider what had been said; if they wholeheartedly agreed with his proposals, on the next day the treaty would be concluded. They were apparently eager to accept the terms and on the following day a pact was agreed.

The emperor was not concerned merely with his own advantages; he also had in mind the empire itself. He cared more, in fact, for the general welfare than for his own. All the negotiations, therefore, were conducted in the light of Roman sovereignty; that was the criterion for all decisions. His purpose was to ensure that the treaty would last after his death and for a long time. It failed, because when he died affairs took a different course and ended in confusion. However, in the meantime the troubles subsided and there was great harmony. Thereafter we enjoyed peace until the end of his life, but with him all the benefits disappeared and his efforts came to nothing through the stupidity of those who inherited his throne.[15]

4. The commanders of the Frankish fleet were informed about the Roman navy by the survivors of the five warships, as I mentioned, and understanding that the emperor had equipped a fleet[16] and was in the Kherronesos awaiting their arrival, they abandoned their primary objective and decided to avoid Roman territory altogether. The emperor, after wintering in Kalliopolis with the empress who was accompanying him because of his gout, as has been recorded many times above, and after watching carefully for the moment when the Latin fleet typically sailed for home, returned to the capital. Not long after it was announced that the Turks were on the move from all lands of the east, even from Khorosan, to the number of 50,000. Indeed, throughout the whole of his reign the emperor had little opportunity for rest, as enemies one after another sprang up in constant succession. On this occasion the armies were completely mobilized everywhere. Anticipating when these barbarians were likely to launch their attacks on the Christians, he crossed the straits between Byzantion and Damalis.

Not even a painful onset of gout deterred him from this campaign. This malady had afflicted none of his ancestors, so that it was certainly not an inherited disease; nor was it due to indulgence in luxury, as so often happens with the indolent and the pleasure-seekers. I can tell you, though, how it was that the emperor had come to have this condition. One day he was exercising at polo together with Tatikios, whom I have often mentioned. The latter was carried away by his horse and fell on the emperor, whose kneecap was injured by the weight of the impact, with pain affecting the whole of his foot; although he did not show that he was in distress – he was used to pain – he did receive some minor treatment. Little by little the pain wore off, and he resumed his normal routine. That was the prime origin of his gout, for the painful areas attracted rheumatism.

There was a second, more obvious cause of all this illness. Who can claim not to have heard of the time that countless multitudes of Kelts came to the imperial city, setting out from their own countries and invading ours? It was then that the emperor was plunged into a vast ocean of worries. He had long

been aware of their dream of empire; he was aware too of their
overwhelming numbers – more than the grains of sand on the
seashore or all the stars of heaven; the sum total of Roman
forces would equal not one tiny fraction of their number, even
if they were concentrated in one location – much less when they
were dissipated over wide areas, for some were on guard in the
valleys of Serbia and in Dalmatia, others keeping watch near
the Danube against Cuman and Dacian incursions, and many
had been entrusted with the task of preventing Dyrrakhion
from falling to the Kelts once again. Under the circumstances
he devoted his whole attention now to these Kelts and all else
was considered of secondary importance.

The barbarian people who were moving about in secret and
had not yet broken out into open hostility, he kept in check by
granting honours and gifts, while the ambition of the Kelts was
confined by all possible means. The rebellious spirit of his own
subjects caused no less trouble – in fact he suspected them even
more and hastened to protect himself as best he could, dealing
with their plots with skill. But who could possibly describe the
ferment of troubles which descended on him at this period? It
compelled him to become all things to all men, to accommodate
himself as far as he could to circumstances. Like a trained
physician (as the rules of his craft demanded) he had to apply
himself to the most pressing need.

At daybreak, as soon as the sun leapt up over the horizon in
the east, he took his seat on the imperial throne, and every day
on his orders all Kelts were freely admitted to his presence,[17]
both because he liked them to make their own requests, and
also because he enjoyed winning them over to his point of view
with all kinds of different arguments. The Keltic counts are by
nature brazen-faced, violent men, money-grubbers and where
their personal desires are concerned quite unreasonable. They
also surpass all other nations in loquacity. So when they came
to the palace they did so in an undisciplined fashion, every
count bringing with him as many comrades as he wished; after
one came in, then another did, and another after that. Once
there they did not limit the conversation by the water clock,
like the orators of ancient times, but each, whoever he was,

ke for as much time as he wanted with the emperor. Men ... such character, unable to hold their tongue in the slightest, ...d neither respect for the emperor nor thought for the passing of time nor any idea of the bystanders' wrath; instead of giving way to those waiting behind them, they talked on and on with an incessant stream of petitions. Anyone who takes an interest in human nature knows all about their verbosity, their aggression and their finickity manner of speaking. Those who were witnesses to it were familiar with this from experience.

When evening came, after remaining without food all through the day, the emperor would rise from his throne and retire to his private apartment, but even then he was not free from the importunities of the Kelts. They came one after another, not only those who had failed to obtain a hearing during the day, but those who had already been heard returned as well, putting forward this or that excuse for more talk. In the midst of them, calmly enduring their endless chatter, stood the emperor. One could see them there, all asking questions, and him, alone and unchanging, giving them measured replies. But there was no limit to their foolish babbling, and if a court official did try to cut them short, he was himself interrupted by the emperor himself. He knew the traditional pugnacity of the Franks and feared that from some trivial pretext a mighty blaze of trouble might spring up, resulting in serious harm to the prestige of Rome.

It was really a most extraordinary sight. Like a statue wrought by the hammer, made of bronze or cold-forged iron, the emperor would sit through the night, often from evening till midnight, often till third cockcrow, sometimes almost until the sun was shining clearly. His attendants were all worn out, would retire frequently to rest and then come back again – in a bad mood. Thus not one of them would stay upright as long as he did; all kept changing position one way or another: one would sit down, another would turn his head away and rest it on something, and another would prop himself up against a wall. Only one man, the emperor, faced this tremendous task without weakening. Who could possibly describe his stamina? Hundreds of people were talking, each one prattling on at

length, 'brawling away unbridled of tongue',[18] as Homer says.
As one stood aside he passed the conversation on to another,
and he to the next, and so on and on. They stood only in these
intervals but he was on his feet all the time, up to first or even
second cockcrow. After a brief rest, when the sun rose he was
again seated on his throne and once more fresh labours and
renewed troubles succeeded those of the night.

It was for this reason, then, that the emperor was attacked
by the pain in his feet. From that time to the end of his life
the rheumatism came on at regular intervals and caused him
dreadful pain. Despite this he bore it so well that not once did
he murmur in complaint; all he said was, 'I deserve to suffer.
This happens to me justly because of the multitude of my sins.'
And if by chance a cross word did escape his lips he immediately
made the sign of the cross against the assault of the evil demon.
'Flee from me, wicked one,' he would say. 'A curse on you and
your tormenting of Christians!'

I will say no more now about the pain that afflicted him.
Maybe there was someone who contributed to this malady
of his and increased the sufferings he bore. I will give only a
brief outline of the story, not the full details. The empress
smeared the rim of the cup with honey, as it were, and contrived
that he should avoid most of his troubles, for she unceasingly
watched over him. The man I am speaking of must be introduced at this point and considered a third reason for the
emperor's illness, not merely as the immediate cause, but also
the most effective cause, to use words employed by doctors.
He did not attack once and for all and then disappear, but remained with him, a constant companion like the most pernicious humours in the veins. Worse than that, if one reflects
on the man's character, he was not only a cause of the disease,
but he was himself a malady and its most troublesome symp-
tom. But I must bite my tongue and say no more. However
eager I may be to jump on these scoundrels, I must not stray
off my path. I will reserve what I have to say about him to the
appropriate time.

5. Let us return to the Kelts. The emperor was in camp on
the opposite coast, at Damalis (for it is there, in fact, that we

left him). While he was staying there awaiting the arrival of all his retinue and hoping, too, to get relief from his terrible pain, they all crossed, descending on him thick as snowflakes. When the emperor saw the fullness of the moon, he said to the empress, who was with him, tending his feet and lightening his anguish in every way she could, 'If ever the Turks wanted to make a raid, this is a good opportunity for them. I'm sorry I missed the chance.' It was evening when he said this. The next morning at dawn the eunuch in charge of the imperial bedchamber announced that the Turks had attacked Nicaea and showed him a letter from Eustathios Kamytzes, who was in charge of the defence of the town at that time, which gave a full report of their actions.

Without a moment's hesitation or the slightest delay, as if he had completely forgotten the incessant pain, the emperor mounted a war chariot and set out for Nicaea, wielding a whip in his right hand. The soldiers, taking up their spears, went on either side of him, arranged by companies in ordered ranks. Some ran alongside him, others went on ahead, others followed in the rear. All rejoiced at the sight of him marching out against the barbarians, but grieved at the thought of the pain which prevented him from riding on horseback. But he put heart into all of them by his gestures and words, smiling pleasantly and chatting with them. After three days' march he arrived at a place called Aigialoi, from where he intended to sail over to Kibotos. As she saw that he was in a hurry to make the crossing, the empress took her leave of him and set out for the capital.

When the emperor reached Kibotos, a fellow came with the news that the leading satraps commanding the force of 40,000 had divided, with some heading down to Nicaea and the neighbouring districts to plunder, while Monolukos and ... had ravaged the coastal area. Those who had devastated the country near the lake of Nicaea and Prousa, as well as Appollonias, had encamped by the latter town and collected all their booty there. They had then marched on in a body pillaging Lopadion and all the land round it; even Kyzikos, he reported, had been attacked from the sea and had fallen at the first assault, the individual in charge of its defence having put up no resistance at all and then fleeing in disgrace. Kontogmes and the Emir Muhammad,[19] moreover, leading archisatraps, were on their way through Lentiana to Poimanenon, bringing with them much booty and a host of captives, men, women and children who had escaped massacre. After crossing a river called Barenos by the locals, which flows down from a mountain known as Ibis, from which many other rivers flow, such as the Skamandros, the Angelokomites and the Empelos, Monolukos had turned off to Parion and Abydos on the Hellespont; later he passed through Atramytion and Khliara with all his prisoners without shedding a drop of blood or fighting a single battle.

The emperor's reaction to this news was to give Kamytzes, who was *doux* of Nicaea at the time, written instructions to keep in touch with the barbarians and inform him of their activities by letter, but to avoid all combat. He had 500 men for the purpose. Kamytzes left Nicaea and caught up with Kontogmes, the Emir Muhammad and the others at a place called Aorata. Apparently forgetful of the emperor's orders he attacked at once. The enemy were expecting the emperor, and thinking that it was he who was attacking them, fled in terror. They had, though, been able to capture a Scythian and learnt from him that it had been Kamytzes who attacked them. Thereupon they crossed the mountains, took heart and recalled their fellow-countrymen who were scattered all over the countryside through drums and shouting. They all regrouped, recognizing the signal. And so they descended to the plain at the foot of Aorata once again.

Kamytzes, who had seized all their plunder, did not wish to go on to Poimanenon, where he would have been safe (since this is a well-fortified place), but instead marked time round Aorata, unaware that he was doing himself a disservice. The barbarians were now out of danger, and instead of forgetting all about him, were constantly lying in wait. Establishing that he was still in Aorata making arrangements about all the booty and the prisoners, they drew up their forces in companies without delay and soon after midday fell upon him. At the sight of the barbarian multitude the greater part of

Kamytzes' army thought it wise to look to their own safety in flight; he himself, with the Scythians, the Kelts and the more courageous of the Romans fought on bravely. Most of them died there.

Even then Kamytzes still continued the battle with a handful of survivors. He was thrown to the ground when his horse was fatally wounded, but his nephew Katarodon dismounted and offered him his own charger. But Kamytzes, who was a large, heavy man, found it difficult to mount and instead withdrew a little and stood with his back to an oak tree. Having given up all hope of saving his life, he drew his sword and struck at any barbarian who dared to attack him, hitting out at helmets, shoulders or even hands. He would not give in. When the barbarians saw his resistance and that he was killing many and wounding plenty besides, they marvelled at his bravery and were astonished by his resolve. As a result, they decided to spare him. The archisatrap named Muhammad, who knew him of old and recognized him now, stopped his men fighting, who were locked in close combat with him, and dismounted from his horse, with his companions doing the same. He then approached and said, 'Don't prefer death to your own safety. Give me your hand and be spared.' Kamytzes, surrounded as he was by so many barbarians and quite unable to resist any more, gave his hand to Muhammad, who put him on a horse and shackled his feet to prevent an easy escape.

Such were the adventures of Eustathios. The emperor meanwhile, guessing the path by which the enemy would go, chose a different route by Nicaea, Malagina and what is called Basilika (these are valleys and inaccessible ways on the ridges of Mount Olympos). He then came down to Alethina and went on to Akrokos, hurrying to a position from which he could attack the Turks from their front. He hoped to fight a pitched battle with them. The latter, with no thought at all of the Roman army, discovered a part of the valley covered by reeds, and spread out there to rest. When it was announced to the emperor that the barbarians whom he was targeting had occupied the lower parts of the valley, he drew up his battle line a suitable distance away. In front he stationed Constantine Gabras and

Monastras. On the two wings the troops were arranged in squadrons. The rearguard was entrusted to Tzipoureles and Ampelas, officers who had a long and considerable experience of warfare. The centre he led himself, with an overall supervision of the line. In this order he swooped down on the Turks like a thunderbolt and engaged them in battle.

In the stern conflict that followed many of the barbarians died in close combat, many were led away as prisoners. Some took refuge in the reed beds and were safe for a time, but after a notable victory was assured the emperor turned on them too, trying to drive them out of the reeds. His soldiers were unable to do it, however, since the marshy ground and the thickness of the reeds made it impossible to get near them. After surrounding the area with soldiers, the emperor gave the order to start a fire on one side of the reeds, and soon the flames leapt to a great height. In their efforts to escape the fire, those inside fell into the hands of the Roman soldiers. Some were cut down by the sword, others were led off to the emperor.[20]

6. Such was the fate of the barbarians who had come down from Karme. The Emir Muhammad, hearing of the disaster which had befallen the Muslims of Karme, at once joined the Turcomans who dwell in Asia as well as the others in pursuit of the emperor, who therefore found himself both hunter and hunted at the same time. The barbarians with Muhammad were following his tracks from behind while he himself was tracking down those from Karme. He was caught between the two. While he had already defeated one lot, those in pursuit were out of harm's way. Muhammad launched a sudden assault on the emperor's rearguard, when he first came across Ampelas. The latter drew confidence from the fact that he was with the emperor and even though he was otherwise a bold man, charged the Turks without waiting even for the slightest moment for his troops, and threw himself against Muhammad. Tzipoureles followed him.

Before their soldiers could catch up with them, the two men had reached an ancient fortification where Muhammad, an extremely determined man, caught up with them. He shot Ampelas' horse with an arrow, but not the rider who was thrown to the ground. He was promptly surrounded by Turks on foot and killed. Then they spied Tzipoureles charging recklessly on them. His horse they winged, as it were, with their arrows, unseated him and summarily dispatched with their swords. At that point, soldiers posted in the rear, whose duty it was to protect the tired baggage men and the horses, as well as to repel attacks to the best of their ability, caught sight of these Turks, charged them and routed them completely.

Kamytzes was there with them, a prisoner, and when he saw the confusion as the two armies clashed, with some running away and others in pursuit, being a level-headed man he planned his own escape and took to the road. A mounted Kelt met him on the way and gave him his horse, and he then rode on to find the emperor encamped between Philadelphia and Akrokos, on the plain which was large enough to accommodate not one army, but many. When the emperor saw him, he received him warmly and having thanked God for his deliverance, sent him on to the capital. 'Tell them,' he said, 'of your sufferings and of all that you have seen, and inform our relatives that thanks to God we are alive.'

When he learnt of the massacre of Ampelas and Tzipoureles, however, he was deeply grieved. 'We have lost two and gained one,' he remarked. For it was his custom, whenever he had been victorious in war, to inquire whether any of his men had been captured or slain by the enemy, and even if he had routed whole armies in triumph, but had lost one man, however low his rank, he looked upon his victory as nothing; for him it was merely a Cadmean success[21] – not a gain, but a loss. He now personally appointed military governors of the area, George Lebounes and certain others, and left them there with his soldiers while he returned to Constantinople victorious.

Kamytzes reached Damalis and boarded a small boat about the mid-watch of the night. Since he knew that the empress was in the upper part of the palace, he went there and knocked on the gate which faces the sea. The warders asked who he was, but he was unwilling to give his name; he only asked for the gate to be opened to him. After some dispute he revealed his name and was allowed to enter.

The empress, highly delighted, received him outside the door of her bedroom (in the old days they called this the Aristerion). When she saw him dressed like a Turk and limping on both feet because of his wounds in battle, her first inquiry, as she bade him sit down, was about the emperor. Then, after hearing the whole story, learning about the strange and unexpected victory scored by the emperor and seeing the prisoner free, she was quite overcome with joy. Kamytzes was ordered to rest until daybreak and then leave the palace to announce what had happened to the people. So he rose early, still dressed in the clothes in which he had arrived after his extraordinary deliverance from captivity, mounted his horse and rode to the Forum of Constantine. His appearance at once caused general excitement in the city. Everyone was eager to learn of his adventures; everyone longed still more to hear about the emperor. Surrounded by a multitude of men on horseback and on foot, he gave a full account of the war in a clear voice: he spoke of all the misfortunes of the Roman army and, more important, of all the emperor's plans against the barbarians and the full vengeance he had exacted from them by his brilliant victory. Lastly he told them of his own miraculous flight from the barbarians. At these words the whole crowd cheered and the noise of their applause was deafening.

7. With that, Constantinople was alive with stories of the emperor's exploits. Chance had indeed involved him in difficult situations, prejudicial both to himself and the interests of the Romans, so that he was wholly surrounded by a host of troubles. Yet every one of them was thwarted and opposed by his virtues, his vigilance, his energy. Of all the emperors who preceded him, right down to the present day, not one had to grapple with affairs so complicated, with the wickedness of men, at home and abroad, of so many types as we have seen in the lifetime of this sovereign. Maybe it was destined that the Roman people should suffer tribulation with God's permission (for never would I attribute our fate to the movements of the stars), or perhaps Roman power declined to this decadence through the folly of previous rulers. Certain it is that in my

father's reign great disorders and wave on wave of confusion
united to afflict the empire.

For the Scythians from the north, the Kelts from the west
and the Ishmaelites from the east were simultaneously in turmoil; there were perils, too, from the sea, not to mention the
barbarians who ruled the waves, or the countless pirate vessels
launched by wrathful Saracens or by the ambitious Vetones,
who regarded the Roman Empire with jealousy. For all men
look upon it with envy: by nature dominator of other nations,
the Roman Empire is regarded as an enemy by those over
which it lords, and whenever they find an opportunity, all of
them flock from all quarters to attack us by land or by sea. In
the old days, before our time, there was a great buoyancy
about the empire which is lacking today – the burden of government was not so heavy. But in my father's reign, as soon as he
acceded to the throne, a veritable flood of dangers poured in
on him from everywhere: the Kelt was restless and pointed his
spear at him; the Ishmaelite bent his bow; all the nomads and
the whole Scythian nation pressed in on him with their myriad
wagons.

But at this stage of my history the reader perhaps will say
that I am naturally biased. My answer is this: I swear by the
perils the emperor endured for the well-being of the Roman
people, by his sorrows and the travails he suffered on behalf of
the Christians, that I am not favouring him when I say or write
such things. On the contrary, where I perceive that he was
wrong I deliberately transgress the law of nature and stick to
the truth. I regard him as dear, but truth as dearer still. As one
of the philosophers somewhere remarked, 'When two things
are dear, it is best to honour the truth.'[22] I have followed the
actual course of events, without additions of my own, without
suppression, and so I speak and write.

And the proof of this is near to hand. I am not writing the
history of things that happened 10,000 years ago, but there are
men still alive today who knew my father and tell me of his
deeds. They have in fact made a not inconsiderable contribution
to the history, for one reported or recalled to the best of his
ability one fact, while another told me something else – but

there was no discrepancy in their accounts. Most of the time, moreover, we were ourselves present, for we accompanied our father and mother. My life by no means revolved round the home; we did not live a sheltered, pampered existence. From my very cradle – I swear it by God and His Mother – troubles, afflictions, continual misfortunes were my lot, some from without, some from within. As to my physical characteristics, I will not speak of them – the attendants in the women's quarters can describe and talk of them. But if I write of the evils that befell me from without, the troubles I encountered even before I had completed my eighth year and the enemies raised up against me by the wickedness of men, I would need the Siren of Isokrates, the grandiloquence of Pindar, Polemon's vivacity, the Kalliope of Homer, Sappho's lyre[23] or some other power greater still. For no danger, great or small from near or far away, failed to attack us at once. I was truly overwhelmed by the flood and ever since, right up to the present time, even to this moment when I write these words, the sea of misfortunes advances upon me, wave after wave. But I must stop – I have inadvertently drifted away into my own troubles. Now that I have returned to my senses, I will swim against the tide, as it were, and go back to the original subject.

As I was saying, some of my material is the result of my own observations; some I have gathered in various ways from the emperor's comrades-in-arms, who sent us information about the progress of the wars by people who crossed the straits. Above all I have often heard the emperor and George Palaiologos discussing these matters in my presence. Most of the evidence I collected myself, especially in the reign of the third emperor after my father,[24] at a time when all the flattery and lies about his grandfather had disappeared: for all men flatter the current ruler, while no one makes the slightest attempt to over-praise the departed, telling the facts just as they are and describing things just as they happened.

As for myself, apart from the grief caused by my own misfortunes, I mourn now three rulers – my father, the emperor; my mistress and mother, the empress; and to my sorrow, the *kaisar*, my husband. For the most part, therefore, I pass my time in obscurity[25] and devote myself to my books and to the worship of God. Not even the least important people are allowed to visit us, neither those from whom we could have learnt news they had heard from others, nor my father's most intimate friends. For thirty years now, I swear it by the souls of the most blessed emperors, I have not seen, I have not spoken to a friend of my father; many of them of course have passed away, but many too are prevented by fear because of the change in our fortunes. For the powers-that-be have condemned us to this ridiculous position so that we might not be visible, and also so as to be a pitiful spectacle for the masses.

My material[26] – let God and His heavenly Mother and Our Lady be the witnesses of this – has been gathered from insignificant writings, absolutely devoid of literary pretensions, and from old soldiers who were serving in the army at the time that my father seized the Roman sceptre, who fell on hard times and exchanged the turmoil of the outer world for the peaceful life of monks. The documents that came into my possession were written in simple language without embellishment; they adhered closely to the truth, were distinguished by no elegance whatever and were composed in a manner lacking style and free from rhetorical flourish. The accounts given by the old veterans were, in language and thought, similar to those commentaries, and I based the truth of my history on them by examining their narratives and comparing them with what I had written, and what they told me with what I had often heard, from my father in particular and from my uncles both on my father's and on my mother's side. From all these materials the whole fabric of my history – my true history – has been woven.

But I was talking of Kamytzes' escape from the barbarians and his address to the citizens, so we must return to that point. This individual gave an account of what had happened, just as we have described it, and told them of all the devices which the emperor had used against the Ishmaelites. The inhabitants of Constantinople acclaimed the emperor with one mouth and voice, sang his praises, lauded him to the skies, blessed him for his leadership and could not contain themselves for joy because of him. They escorted Kamytzes to his home, filled with happiness and a few days later welcomed the emperor as a victor crowned with laurels, an invincible general, indomitable ruler, *sebastos autokrator*. So much for them. As for the emperor, he entered the palace and after offering thanks to God and His Mother for his safe return, he resumed his usual routine.

For now that the wars abroad had been settled and the rebellions of rebels crushed, he turned his attention to the matter of justice and the laws. He was an outstanding steward in issues to do with peace, just as he was in those relating to war. He was prudent when it came to judging the case of an orphan, and in dispensing justice to the widowed and dealing with every case of wrongdoing with the utmost diligence. Only occasionally did he seek physical relaxation through hunting or other amusements; even then, as in all else, he was the true philosopher, conditioning his body and making it more obedient to his will. For most of the day he laboured hard, but he would relax too, only his relaxation was itself a second labour – the reading of books and their study, the diligent observance of the command to search the Scriptures.[27] Hunting and ball play were of second or even third importance to my father – even when he was still a young man and the wild beast, that is the malady that affected his feet, had not yet entwined itself about him like the coils of some serpent, bruising his heel,[28] as the curse says. But when the affliction first made its appearance and developed to its full strength, then he did devote himself to physical exercises, riding and other games, following medical advice. It was hoped that regular horse riding would disperse some of the fluid that descended to his feet, and therefore he might be relieved of some of the weight that pressed on them. As I have remarked before, my father's malady derived from only one external cause – the labours and fatigue he endured for the glory of the realm of the Romans.

8. Less than a year later he heard a rumour that the Cumans had again crossed the Ister. At the beginning of the eighth indiction, therefore, he left the capital. It was early autumn in the month of November.[29] Recalling all his forces, he then

stationed them at the towns called Philippopolis, Petritzos, Triaditza and in the theme of Nisos, and some as far as Bouranitzova in the Paristrion district. Their instructions were to take particular care of their horses: it was essential that they should be robust enough to carry riders in the event of battle. He himself remained in Philippopolis. This town is situated in the centre of Thrace. On its north side is the River Euros, which flows from the northern tip of Rhodope and after many twists and turns passes Adrianoupolis. With the addition of several tributaries it finally enters the sea near the town of Ainos.

When I mention Philip, I am not referring to the Macedonian, the son of Amyntas, for the present place is more recent than his town, but I mean the Roman Philip,[30] a gigantic man endowed with overpowering physical strength. Before his time it was a small place called Krenides,[31] though some people knew it as Trimous. However, this later Philip, the giant, made it into a large town and surrounded it with walls, at which point it became a celebrated place in Thrace, equipped with an enormous hippodrome and other buildings of note. I myself saw traces of them when I stayed there with the emperor for some reason or other.

The town stands on three hills, each enclosed by a massive high wall. Where it slopes down to the plain and level ground there is a ditch, near the Euros. Once upon a time, it seems, Philippopolis must have been a large and beautiful town, but after the Tauroi and Scythians enslaved the inhabitants in ancient times it was reduced to the condition in which we saw it during my father's reign. Even so we conjectured that it must have been a really great town once upon a time. Among the misfortunes which befell it was the fact that many heretics lived there. Armenians had taken over the place as had the so-called Bogomils, about whom and about whose heresy we will speak at the appropriate time, as well as the Paulicians, an utterly godless sect of the Manichaeans. The latter, as the name implies, were followers of Paul and John, who had drunk at the well of the blasphemy of Manes[32] and had passed it on in unadulterated form to their devotees.

I would have liked to outline the Manichaean doctrine with

a concise explanation and then hasten to refute their atheistic
teachings. However, as I know that everyone regards the heresy
of the Manichaeans as absurd, and at the same time since I am
anxious to press on with the history, the refutation of their
dogma must be omitted. In any case, I am aware that others,
not only men of our own faith, but also Porphyrios,[33] our great
adversary, have already disproved them, demonstrating the
utter foolishness of their belief, in several chapters, when
examining the question of two principles in a most learned
fashion – even though his theory of the unity of God forces
his readers to accept Plato's concept of unity or the One.
We ourselves revere one deity, but not a unity limited to one
person; nor do we accept the One of Plato – that is to say the
Greek 'Ineffable' and the Chaldaean 'Mystery' – on which they
make a great many other principles depend, both mundane and
supernatural.

These disciples of Manes, of Paul and John, the sons of
Kallinike, who were of a savage and unusually cruel disposition
and did not hesitate to cause bloodshed, met defeat at the hands
of that admirable sovereign John Tzimiskes.[34] He removed them
as slaves from Asia, carrying them off from the lands of the
Khalybes and Armenians to Thrace. They were forced to dwell
in the district of Philippopolis, both in order to drive them out
of the heavily fortified towns and strongpoints which they ruled
as tyrants, but also in order to use them as a very efficient
barrier against Scythian incursions, from which the Thracian
area had often suffered because of the barbarians. These had
been in the habit of crossing the mountain passes of Haimos
and overrunning the plains below.

The Haimos is a very long mountain range situated on a line
parallel to Rhodope. It begins at the Black Sea, almost touches
the cataracts and stretches right into the Illyrian regions; the
Adriatic interrupts it, but I think it continues on the opposite
mainland and ends as far away as the forests of Herkynioi.
On either side of its slopes live numerous, extremely wealthy
tribes, Dacians and Thracians to the north, and to the south
Macedonians and Thracians again. In ancient times the nomad
Scythians crossed the Haimos in full force before the time of

Alexios' spear, and his many battles almost annihilated them; up till then, they had ravaged Roman territory, above all the towns which were closest, with the most renowned of these being the previously well-known town of Philippopolis.

John Tzimiskes turned our opponents, these Manichaean heretics, into allies; so far as fighting was concerned they formed a considerable and powerful bulwark against the nomadic Scythians and thereafter the towns, protected now from most of their raids, breathed freely again. The Manichaeans, however, being by nature an independent people, not amenable to discipline, followed their normal customs and reverted to type. Practically all the inhabitants of Philippopolis were in fact Manichaeans, so that they tyrannized the Christians there and plundered their goods, paying little or no attention to the emperor's envoys. Their numbers increased until all the people round the town were heretics. They were joined by another flood of immigrants, Armenians – a brackish stream – as well as by others from the foulest springs of Jacob.[35] It was a meeting place, so to speak, of all polluted waters. And if the immigrants differed from the Manichaeans in doctrine, then they were at least unified in their rebellious activities.

Nevertheless my father, the emperor, pitted his long experience of soldiering against them. Some were taken without a fight; others were enslaved by force of arms. How much work he did there that was valiant and apostolic in nature! Why should he not be praised for this? Was he negligent in military affairs? The east and west resounded with the sound of his military exploits. Did he not treat literature with respect? Once again no, for no man, I am sure, searched the Holy Scriptures more zealously than he, in order to have a ready answer in his debates with the heretics. He alone made use of arms and words alike, for with arms he conquered them and by his arguments he subdued the ungodly. On this occasion it was for an apostolic expedition, rather than a military campaign, that he armed himself against the Manichaeans. And I myself would call him the thirteenth apostle. Some would ascribe that honour to Constantine the Great; however, it seems to me that either Alexios ought to be ranked with the Emperor Constantine, or, if someone quarrelled with that, he should follow immediately after Constantine in both roles – Alexios as emperor and as apostle.[36]

As we were saying, the emperor arrived at Philippopolis, but as the Cumans had not yet appeared, another objective of the expedition became more important: he turned away the Manichaeans from their religion with its bitterness and filled them with the sweet doctrines of our Church. From early morning till afternoon or evening, sometimes till the second or third watch of the night, he invited them to visit him and he instructed them in the orthodox faith, refuting their corrupt heresy. He had with him Eustratios,[37] the bishop of Nicaea, a man with a detailed knowledge of religious and secular texts, more competent when it came to dialectics than the philosophers of the Stoa or the Academy, and also the archbishop of Philippopolis. The emperor's chief assistant at all these interviews, however, was my husband, the *Kaisar* Nikephoros, whom he had trained in the study of the sacred literature. Thus many Manichaeans at this time unhesitatingly sought out the priests in order to confess their sins and receive Holy Baptism. On the other hand, there were many at this same time who clung to their own religion with a passionate devotion surpassing that of the famous Maccabees, quoting from the Holy Scriptures and using them as evidence to support, as they imagined, their contemptible doctrine. Yet the majority even of these fanatics were persuaded by the emperor's untiring arguments and his frequent admonitions, and they too were baptized. The talks went on often from the first appearance of the sun's rays in the east until far into the night, and for him there was no rest, and generally no food, although it was summertime and he was in an open tent.

9. While all this was going on and the battle of words was being fought with the Manichaeans, an individual arrived from the Ister with the news that the Cumans had crossed the river.[38] Without losing a moment the emperor drove towards the Danube with all available men. Reaching Vidyne, he found no barbarians there (they had crossed straight back over when they had heard of the emperor's arrival), and so he immediately

sent a contingent of courageous soldiers to pursue them. Having crossed the Ister they followed the Cumans for three days and nights, but when it became clear that the enemy had made their way to the far side of a tributary of the Danube on rafts, which they carried with them, they returned to the emperor, without having achieved anything.

The emperor was annoyed that the barbarians had not been engaged by his troops, but consoled himself with the reflection that this was after all a kind of victory: they had been repelled by the mere mention of his name; moreover, he had converted many of the disciples of Manes to our faith. So a double trophy was set up: one for a victory over the barbarians by force of arms, the other for the subjection of the heretics through theological debate. He then withdrew to Philippopolis and after a brief rest began his struggles afresh.

Kouleon, Kousinos and Pholos, leaders of the Manichaean heresy and similar in other respects to the Manichaeans, were summoned to meet him every day and engage in a war of words. They were like the rest of their race in other respects, but obstinately persisted in their evil doctrine and, hard as steel, rejected all persuasion; they were also extremely clever at tearing to pieces the Holy Word. They misused their time in distorting its meaning. The contest therefore was twofold, with the emperor on one side, striving with all his might to save them, and these men on the other, arguing stubbornly to the end in order to win a proverbial Cadmean triumph. There they stood, the three of them, sharpening themselves up for the fray, as though they were boar's tusks intent on ripping the emperor's arguments to shreds. If some objection escaped Kousinos, Kouleon seized on it; and if Kouleon was in trouble, Pholos would rise up in opposition; or, one after another, they would rouse themselves to attack the emperor's propositions and refutations, like great waves succeeded by waves greater still. The emperor demolished all their criticism as though it were nothing but a spider's web and quickly stopped their unclean mouths, but as he failed completely to convince them he despaired at last of their foolishness and sent them to the capital. There he allotted them a place to live in, the porticoes round the Great

Palace. Despite them he had not been entirely unsuccessful in his hunting. For the moment, the leaders had not been caught, but every day he led to God a hundred, sometimes more than a hundred, so that the sum total of those who had been caught before and those who were now won over by his words ran into thousands and tens of thousands.

But why should I discuss and spend time on something that the whole world knows, and to which the east like the west bears witness? Whole towns and lands in the grip of all kinds of heresy were in various ways converted to our orthodox beliefs by him. The most prominent of the heretics were rewarded with rich gifts and made officers in the army; the converts of humbler origin, navvies, ploughmen, ox herds and so on, he collected in one place with their wives and children and built a town for them quite near Philippopolis, on the far side of the River Euros. He settled them there. The place was called Alexioupolis, or otherwise Neokastron, a name by which it is better known. To all he gave plough land, vineyards, houses and immovable property. Unlike the gardens of Adonis,[39] which blossom today and fade tomorrow, these gifts of his were not without legal backing. They were secured by chrysobulls. Moreover, instead of confining these privileges to them alone, they could be handed down to their sons and grandsons. And if the male heirs died out, the women could inherit. This is how the emperor magnified the rewards he gave out.

I will say no more on the subject. Much more besides has been omitted. And let no one find fault with the history, as though it were corrupt. There are plenty of people living today who are witnesses to what I have described, and I could not be accused of lying. Having made all necessary arrangements, the emperor left Philippopolis and returned to the capital. The theological struggles were resumed and there were unceasing polemics against Kouleon, Kousinos and their supporters. Kouleon was eventually convinced – he was, I suppose, more intelligent than the others and more capable of understanding the fundamental truth of an argument. He became the gentlest lamb in our fold. Kousinos and Pholos, on the other hand, developed savage tendencies and in spite of the continual hammer-blows of the emperor's arguments, they remained what they were before, men of iron, unheeding and unmalleable. He committed them, therefore, to the prison called Elephantine, for of all the Manichaeans they were the most blasphemous and were bound for deep melancholia. They were provided liberally with all necessities and allowed to die a lonely death in their sins.

BOOK XV

1. Such were the emperor's actions in the matter of Philippopolis and the Manichaeans. Now the barbarians stirred up fresh troubles for him. The Sultan Solymas[1] planned to ravage Asia once more, and so, in order to mount a sturdy opposition to the emperor, forces were summoned from Khorosan and Aleppo. The emperor had already been fully informed of the enemy's plan and decided to march himself as far as Ikonion and launch a full-scale war. This town lay on the borders of the sultanate of Klitziasthlan.[2] Forces from abroad were recruited, together with a strong mercenary contingent, while his own army was called to arms from all quarters. While both generals were getting ready for the war, the emperor was attacked by the old pain in his feet. Forces continued to pour in from all directions, but only in small groups and not all at once because their homelands were so distant from each other, and meanwhile the gout prevented the emperor not merely from putting his plan into operation, but even from walking at all. He was confined to his bed, not so much worried by the anguish he was suffering physically, however, as by the deferment of the campaign against the barbarians. The barbarian Klitziasthlan was not unaware of this: he therefore took advantage of it to ravage the whole of Asia and to make half a dozen or so attacks on the Christians.

The pain was afflicting the emperor as never before: hitherto it had come on only at long intervals; now it was continuous, with severe onsets following one another in quick succession. To Klitziasthlan and those close to him, it seemed that this suffering was a mere pretence: it was not a real illness, but a pretext for lethargy and an excuse for cowardice disguised by the claim of gout. Hence the mockery they indulged in at their drunken orgies. The barbarians, born comedians, made fun of his pains. The gout became a subject for ridicule. They acted the parts of doctor and attendants, introduced 'the emperor' himself and laying him on a bed made fun of him. These childish exhibitions provided much amusement for the barbarians.

The emperor knew what was going on and boiling with anger, was more than ever determined to make war on them. Not long after there was some relief from the gout and he set out for the campaign. After reaching Damalis and sailing across the straits between Kibotos and Aigialoi, he reached Kibotos and from there went on to Lopadion, where he awaited the arrival of his army and the mercenaries he had summoned. When all were gathered together, he moved on with the whole expeditionary force to the fort of St George, near the lake of Nicaea, and from there to Nicaea itself. Three days later he retraced his steps and encamped on this side of the Lopadion bridge not far from the place known as the Fountain of Karykeus. He thought it best that the army cross the bridge first and pitch camp in some suitable spot; then, when all was ready, he himself would cross by the same bridge and have the imperial tent pitched in the centre of the camp.

The resourceful Turks, who were engaged in plundering the plain at the foot of the hills of Lentiana and the place called Kotoiraikia, were terrified at the news of the emperor's advance, and lit numerous fires to give the impression that a great army was there. These beacons shot their flames heavenwards and scared many of the inexperienced. It had no effect whatever, though, on the emperor.

The Turks made off with all the booty and the prisoners. Nevertheless at dawn the emperor hurried to the plain hoping to catch them somewhere in the vicinity, but he had missed the prey. However, he did find many victims still breathing, especially Romans, and many corpses too, which naturally upset him. He wanted to pursue, but as it was impossible for the whole army to overtake the runaways at speed and he was anxious not to lose all the quarry, he quickly detached a force of lightly-armed men, and after telling them what route to follow, sent them off to chase the barbarian scoundrels. He himself set up camp in the neighbourhood of Poimanenon. The Turks were in fact overtaken at a place called Kellia in the native dialect, with all their plunder and captives. The Romans descended on them like a thunderbolt and soon killed most of them, while some were taken alive. They then returned to the emperor with them and with every bit of the plunder in triumph. After commending their action and discovering that the enemy had been totally destroyed, Alexios went back to Lopadion. He remained there for three whole months, partly because his intended path led through waterless tracts (it was the summer season[3] and the heat was unbearable), and partly because he was still awaiting the arrival of the mercenaries. Eventually all met up there and camp was struck. The whole army was then posted on the ridges of Olympos and the Malagina range, while he himself occupied Aer.

At the time the empress was residing on Prinkipos, since news of the emperor's progress after his return to Lopadion would reach her more easily there. As soon as he came to Aer, he sent the imperial galley to fetch her, as he always dreaded the pain in his feet returning, and also as he feared the domestic enemies in his entourage. Her loving care and watchful eye were both required.

2. Less than three days after, about dawn, the attendant in charge of the emperor's bedroom came in and stood by the sovereign's bed. The empress woke up and seeing the man said, 'You have news of a Turkish attack.' When he replied that they were already at the fort of St George, she made a sign to him with her hand not to rouse the emperor. He had in fact heard the report, but kept absolutely still for a time and remained calm. When the sun was rising he attended to his normal tasks, although he was pondering deeply what measures ought to be taken in the circumstances. Before the third hour had passed a second messenger arrived to announce that the barbarians were closer still. The empress had remained with the emperor and although quite understandably frightened, she waited for him to decide what to do. As they made to take a meal a third man

came. Covered in blood, he threw himself at the emperor's feet and swore that danger was now imminent – the barbarians were at hand.

The emperor immediately gave the empress permission to return to Byzantion. Although distraught, she concealed her fear; there was no sign of it in word or manner. She was a brave and resolute woman; like the celebrated figure praised by Solomon in the Book of Proverbs,[4] she displayed no womanly cowardice – the kind of thing we usually see in women when they hear some dreadful news: their very colour proclaims the timidity of their hearts and from their frequent shrieks and wails you would think the danger was closing in on them already. But if the empress was scared, it was for the emperor, lest he should suffer some accident; fear for herself was of secondary importance. In this crisis, indeed, she acted in a manner worthy of her courage and although she parted from him reluctantly and often turned round to look at him, she pulled herself together and with a great effort, much against her will, she parted from the emperor. She went down to the sea and boarded the galley reserved for empresses. It sailed past the coast of Bithynia, but was then held up by a storm and came to anchor off Helenopolis. She stayed there for some time.

So much for the empress. With his soldiers and kinsmen with him, the emperor at once took up arms. They then all rode off towards Nicaea. The barbarians had meanwhile captured an Alan and having learnt of the emperor's advance from him, fled back along the paths by which they had just come. Strabo-basileios and Michael Stypiotes (when the reader sees the name Stypiotes he must not confuse him with the half-barbarian, a slave bought for money and afterwards presented as a gift to the emperor by the Stypiotes I am speaking of here, who was a nobleman) – these two who were fine soldiers with long and honourable records, waited on the ridges of the Germia, closely scanning the roads thereabouts, on the off-chance that the enemy might fall into their trap like some wild beast and so be captured. When they found out that the enemy had arrived, they returned to the ... plains and after taking them on in a fierce encounter, thoroughly defeated them.

The emperor first occupied George's Fort and then the village called Sagoudaous by the locals, not coming across any Turks in the process. However, when he heard what had happened to them at the hands of the brave men whose exploits I have already mentioned – by which I mean those of Stypiotes and Strabobasileios – he commended the daring the Romans had shown from the very outset of the campaign and praised their victory. He then pitched camp close to the walls of the fort. On the next day, having arrived at Helenopolis, he met the empress, who had remained there because of the rough seas. He gave an account of what had happened to the Turks, and how in their desire for victory they had instead met with disaster; how rather than being masters, as they had imagined, they had themselves been mastered and all their plans had gone awry. Thus he relieved her of great anxiety, and set off for Nicaea.

When he got there, he was informed of yet another Turkish invasion, so he went on to Lopadion and stayed there for a short time until news came of large-scale enemy movements in the direction of Nicaea. He collected his forces and turned aside to Kios, but, hearing that they were marching all through the night on the road to Nicaea, he quickly left and passed through that town to Miskoura. Reliable information was received there that the main body of the Turks had not yet arrived; a few men sent by Monolukos were in the Dorylaion area and near Nicaea, watching the emperor's movements and supplying Monolukos with frequent reports about him. He therefore sent Leo Nikerites with the troops under his command to Lopadion. He was instructed to be continually on his guard, to keep the roads under constant surveillance and to report in writing whatever he discovered about the Turks.

The rest of the army meanwhile was stationed at strategic points. At this stage, he decided, it would be wiser to abandon the attack on the sultan, for he guessed that the barbarians who had escaped would spread the news of his offensive among all Turks in Asia; they would be told how contact had been made on various occasions with the Romans and how Turkish assaults had met with stubborn resistance and had finally been defeated with heavy losses, with some taken prisoner, others

killed and only a small number of those who had been wounded
managing to escape. The barbarians hearing these reports
would conclude that he was about to attack and would therefore retreat beyond Ikonion. As a result, all his efforts would be
in vain. He therefore withdrew through Bithynia to Nikomedia,
hoping that his opponents would imagine the danger was past
and return to their old homes; thereafter they would disperse
for plunder with renewed vigour, in the usual Turkish way, and
the sultan himself would resume his previous plan. After his
own men had enjoyed a brief respite and the horses and baggage
animals had built up their strength, the emperor would thus
begin a more vigorous campaign and launch a fierce onslaught.

It was for these reasons that he made for Nikomedia, as I
have mentioned. When he got there, he quartered all the soldiers
he had with him in the villages round about, so that the horses
and pack animals might have sufficient fodder – Bithynia is rich
in grass – and the men could get all the supplies they needed
without difficulty from Byzantion and the neighbourhood by
crossing the bay. He stressed that they should lavish particular
care on their horses, which were not to be used for hunting or
riding at all, so that when the time came they would be fit
enough to carry their riders without distress and ready for
cavalry charges against the enemy.[5]

3. Having taken these precautions he settled down as a kind
of observer some distance away, with guards posted on every
road. As he intended to stay there for several days, he sent for
the empress, for the reason which has been mentioned several
times, so that she would remain with him until he heard of
barbarian incursions and decided to leave. She came to Nikomedia without delay. She realized that some of his enemies were
rejoicing over the emperor's failure to achieve anything. There
were reproaches and whispers[6] everywhere that after such
grand preparations against the Turks and the concentration of
such huge forces he had won no great success, but had retired
to Nikomedia. These things, moreover, were being muttered
not only in dark corners, but quite brazenly in squares, on
highways and at crossroads; she was upset and despondent as
a result. The emperor himself foresaw a happy end to his cam-

paign against his enemies, and being redoubtable in such matters, did not pay the slightest attention to the diatribes of these
individuals or to their indignation; rather, he looked down on
all this as childish games and scoffed at the product of their
immature minds. He cheered the empress with his considered
opinions, and assured her that the very thing for which they
reviled him would be the cause of a greater victory.

For my part, I think that to win a victory by sound planning
requires courage; force of character and energy uninformed by
thought are not enough – they end not in courage, but in
foolhardiness. We are courageous in war against men whom
we can beat; against men too strong for us we are foolhardy.
Thus when danger hangs over us, being unable to make a
frontal assault we change our tactics and seek to conquer the
enemy without resorting to warfare. The prime virtue of a
general is the ability to win a victory without incurring danger
– as Homer says, it is by skill that one charioteer beats another.[7]
Even the famous Cadmean proverb censures a victory fraught
with danger. As far as I am concerned, it has always seemed
best to devise some crafty strategic manoeuvre in the course of
battle, if one's own army cannot match the enemy's strength.
Anyone can find examples of this in the pages of history. There
is no one method of achieving victory, nor one form of it, but
from ancient times up to the present, success has been won in
different ways. Victory means the same thing always, but the
means by which generals attain it are varied and of intricate
patterns. It appears that some of the renowned generals of old
overcame their adversaries by sheer strength, whereas others
prevailed on many occasions by making good use of some
advantage of a different kind.

In the case of my father, the emperor, he sometimes overcame
the enemy through his military powers, and sometimes by a
quick-witted move; indeed, occasionally he even came up with
a cunning plan during a battle itself and because of his decis-
iveness, promptly scored a victory. There were times when he
had recourse to stratagem, at others he entered the battle in
person. Thus many an unexpected victory was won. If ever
there was a man who had an extraordinary love of danger, it

was he; and when dangers continually arose, he faced them in different ways: by marching into them bareheaded and coming to close grips with the barbarians, or on occasions by pretending to avoid conflict and feigning terror. It depended on circumstances and the situation of the moment. To put it briefly I would say this: he would triumph when he fled, and when he was doing the chasing, he would conquer. He landed on his feet when he fell, and would end the right way up, like a three-pointed jack which always sticks up no matter how you throw it.

At this point I must again beg the reader not to rebuke me for being boastful; this is by no means the first time I have defended myself against such an accusation. It is not love for my father which prompts me to these reflections, but the course of events. In any case, is there any good reason why being truthful should prevent the simultaneous love of one's father and of truth itself? I chose to write the truth about a good man, and if that man happens to be the historian's father, it is right that his name should be added as an appendage. But of course the history must by its very nature be founded on truth. There are other ways in which I have demonstrated my love for him, and because of that my enemies have been inspired to sharpen sword and spear against me, which is something anyone who is not ignorant of my life knows well. Besides, I would never betray the truth under the guise of history. There is a time for showing love for one's father, which I did courageously when appropriate, and another for telling the truth, and now that the opportunity has arrived, I will not neglect it. If, as I said, this chance proves that I love my father as well as truth, I do not fear criticism that I have suppressed the facts.

However, we must return to the narrative. As long as the emperor remained camped where he was, there was nothing for him to do but enrol recruits in the main army and put them through a course of intensive training in archery, lance fighting, riding on horseback and practising the various manoeuvres. He also taught them the new battle formation which he himself had invented. Sometimes he rode with them, inspected the ranks and invariably made suggestions for improvement. The summer months were now over and the autumnal equinox was past with shorter days now approaching; it seemed a suitable moment, therefore, for expeditions. Accordingly he drove straight for Ikonion with all his forces, as had been planned from the start.

On his arrival in Nicaea, he detached a contingent of light-armed men under the command of experienced officers from the rest of the army and sent them ahead to make raids on the Turks; they were to work in small groups to forage and skirmish. If they were granted victory by God and routed the enemy, they were forbidden to pursue them far; they must be content with what He had given them and make their way back in good order. They advanced with the emperor to a place known colloquially as Gaita, but after that they went their separate way at once, while he departed with the rest to the bridge near Pithekas. Then, after three days, he arrived on the plain of Dorylaion by way of Armenokastron and a place called Leukai. The plain was clearly large enough for manoeuvres, and as he wished to review the whole army and discover its real potential, he set up camp there. This was an excellent opportunity to try out effectively the battle formation he was again considering, and which he had often described on paper when making his plans (he was not unfamiliar with the *Taktika* of Aelian[8]).

He knew from very long experience that the Turkish battle line differs from that of other peoples. It was not arranged, as Homer says, shield to shield, helmet to helmet, man to man,[9] but their right and left wings and their centre form separate groups with the ranks cut off, as it were, from one another; whenever an attack is made on right or left, the centre springs into action leaving all the rest of the army behind it, in an onslaught that throws the opponent into confusion like a whirl-wind. As for the weapons they use in war, unlike the infamous Kelts they do not fight with lances but completely surround the enemy and shoot at him with arrows; they also defend themselves with arrows at a distance. In hot pursuit the Turk makes prisoners by using his bow; in flight he overwhelms his pursuer with arrows – so that when he shoots an arrow it strikes either the horse or its rider, and having fired it with tremendous force, it passes clean through the body. So skilled are they as archers.

Now the emperor had noticed this since he was exceptionally experienced, so to counteract it he adopted his own battle formation, with the ranks organized in such a way that the Turks would have to shoot from their right at the side protected by the shield, whereas our soldiers would shoot from the left, that is at the side that is unprotected. After careful examination to test the impregnability of this formation he was surprised at its power: it must be, he thought, directly attributable to God – a battle order inspired by angels. Everyone admired it and rejoiced, full of confidence in the emperor's invention. He too, as he contemplated his forces and the plain through which he was about to march, picturing to himself the solidity of his line and calculating that it could never be broken, was full of good hopes and prayed to God that they might be fulfilled.

4. So, having drawn up his men in this formation, he reached Santabaris from where all the leaders were sent on different routes: Kamytzes was detached to march on Polyboton and Kedros (the latter a strongly fortified town held by a satrap called Poukheas), while he ordered Stypiotes to attack the barbarians in Amorion. Two Scythian deserters discovered the plan, went to Poukheas and told him of Kamytzes' advance and also of the emperor's arrival. He was so terrified by this that he fled the place in the middle of the night with his fellow-countrymen. As day was breaking, Kamytzes arrived, but was unable to find Poukheas, nor any other Turk for that matter. Although he found the place full of booty – I am referring to Kedros – he disregarded it; like a hunter who has lost the quarry which was almost in his grasp, Kamytzes was despondent and without a moment's delay turned his horse's head in the direction of Polyboton. He fell on the barbarians suddenly, killing an innumerable number of them, and then, taking all the booty and prisoners with him, set up camp nearby and waited for the emperor. Stypiotes had done much the same when he got to Poimanenon, before he too returned to the emperor.

About sunset the emperor reached Kedros. At once some soldiers approached him with information that an immense group of barbarians was in the small towns of the neighbourhood, which used to owe allegiance to the once famous Bourtzes. The emperor acted quickly. A descendant of this Bourtzes, a certain Bardas,[10] was sent against them with George Lebounes and a Scythian, named Pitikas in his own language, with their respective forces, which were combined to make a substantial unit. Their instructions were to send out foragers when they got there, to ravage all the villages in the area and to remove the inhabitants and bring them to him.

These three men started on their march without delay, but the emperor, sticking to the original plan, was anxious to reach Polyboton and go beyond that as far as Ikonion. While he was making preparations and just about to leave, news came that the Turks and the Sultan Solymas[11] himself, learning of his movements, had set fire to all the crops and plains of Asia, so that there was no food whatever for man or beast. It was reported that another invasion from the more northerly regions[12] was in progress and the rumour spread rapidly throughout Asia. He feared that on the march to Ikonion his army might perish of hunger because food supplies were scarce; he was also worried and suspicious about the barbarians he expected to find there.

He therefore decided to do something which was both prudent and daring – to inquire of God whether he should follow the road to Ikonion, or attack the barbarians in the area of Philomelion. He wrote his questions on two pieces of paper and placed them on the Holy Altar. Then the whole night was spent in singing the hymn of the day and in addressing to God fervent prayers. At dawn the priest went in; taking up one of the papers from the altar he opened it in the presence of all and read aloud that the emperor should choose the road to Philomelion.

So much for the emperor. Bardas Bourtzes, meanwhile, on his march, which has been referred to above, saw a large army hurrying to join Monolukos across the bridge at Zompes. He immediately took up arms, attacked these Turks on the plain of Amorion and won a comprehensive victory. But other Turks, coming from the east and hastening to Monolukos, chanced on Bourtzes' camp before he had returned and carried off the soldiers' baggage and any pack animals they could find. When

Bourtzes came back in triumph loaded with his spoils, he met one of the Turks leaving the camp and learnt from him that the enemy had plundered everything in it, including all his booty, and had already departed. Bourtzes examined the situation carefully: he would have liked to pursue them, but they were moving fast and his own horses were tired; so pursuit was impossible and he abandoned the idea, lest something worse should befall him; instead he continued his march at a slow pace and in good order. By daybreak he had reached the towns that had belonged to his ancestor Bourtzes whom we mentioned earlier and evacuated the whole population. The prisoners were recovered and everything belonging to the barbarians was seized. Then, after a short interval at an appropriate spot to rest himself and his weary horses, he set off back to the emperor at sunrise.

On the way he came across another Turkish force and immediately engaged them in battle and a serious conflict flared up. However, after holding out for a reasonable time the Turks asked for the return of their prisoners and the booty taken from them, promising on their side that if their demands were satisfied they would in future refrain from attacking the Romans and go home. Bourtzes refused to make any concessions and bravely resumed the battle. On the previous day his soldiers had drunk no water at all during the struggle; now, when they reached the bank of a river, they quenched their burning thirst. They did it in relays: while one party carried on fighting, another left the battle and refreshed themselves with a drink.

Bourtzes was a very worried man, for he could see the great courage of the barbarians and that they vastly outnumbered his own men. The position became desperate and a messenger was sent to inform the emperor. The man sent was no ordinary soldier, but George Lebounes, mentioned earlier. As there was no route that was not blocked by masses of Turks, Lebounes hurled himself recklessly into their midst, fought his way through and got safely to the emperor. When the latter learnt what Bourtzes was up against, and furthermore had been briefed more fully on the Turkish masses, he realized that

Bourtzes needed a large number of reinforcements; he therefore straightway armed himself and mobilized his troops. When all were ready in their various military groups, he set out against the barbarians.

The Emperor Michael[13] commanded the vanguard, Bryennios the right wing, Gabras the left and Kekaumenos the rear. As the Turks waited for them in the distance, Nikephoros, the nephew of the empress, who was young and eager for action, rode out in front of the line, taking with him a handful of other devotees of Ares. He fought at close quarters with the first Turk to charge out against him and was wounded in the knee. However, he pierced his assailant's breast with his spear and the man fell from his horse to the ground without a cry. The barbarians behind him, seeing this, turned their backs on the Romans and fled. The emperor, delighted with this young man's bravery, received him on the battlefield and having warmly commended him, continued his march on to Philomelion.

He made it to the lake of the Forty Martyrs and on the next day reached a place called Mesanakta, then moving on to Philomelion and took it by assault. Various detachments under the command of brave officers were sent out subsequently to ravage all the small towns in the vicinity of Ikonion and recover the prisoners. They scattered all over the countryside like herds of wild beasts hunting their prey. All the barbarians' prisoners were recovered and brought back with the baggage to the emperor. The native inhabitants, Romans who were fleeing from barbarian vengeance, followed them of their own free will; there were women with newborn babies, even men and children, all seeking refuge with the emperor, as if he were some kind of sanctuary. The lines were now drawn up in the new formation, and having placed all the prisoners in the centre, as well as the women and children, he retraced his steps. All along the route the march proceeded in perfect safety. Anyone who had seen it would have said that this new arrangement of the force which I have described was a living organism, a moving, fortified town.

5. As they went further, no barbarians appeared. But Mono-lukos was following with a large army and laid ambushes on

either flank, and, when the emperor was going across the plain between Polyboton and the lake I have already mentioned, a detachment from the main barbarian force with no baggage, all lightly-armed and bold fighters lying in wait to left and right, suddenly became visible on the high ground above them. It was the first time that the Archisatrap Monolukos had seen the new formation. He was an old man, with a vast experience of wars and armies, but he was absolutely amazed at the sight of this novel arrangement. He asked who the commanding officer was, and guessed that it must be none other than the Emperor Alexios himself who was the leader of the army and the new formation. He wanted to attack, but did not know how; nevertheless, he ordered his men to shout their war cries. Intending to give the impression to the Romans of a great army, he instructed his men not to run in close order, but in scattered groups and with no set ranks, as outlined above, so as to strike terror into the Romans by the unexpectedness of the sight and the deafening noise of their horses' galloping.

The emperor, though, rode on at the head of the line like a huge tower, or a pillar of fire, or some divine celestial apparition, encouraging his soldiers, telling them to continue in the same formation, building up their confidence. He added, moreover, that it was not for his own safety that he endured such travail, but for the honour and glory of Rome; he was quite ready, he said, to die on behalf of them all. Thus everyone was given fresh courage and each kept his place in the ranks. The march indeed went so smoothly that to the barbarians they seemed not to be moving at all. All through that day the enemy attacked, but made no progress, unable to disrupt the Roman forces in part or as a whole. In the end they ran off again to the hilltops having achieved nothing. There they lit numerous watchfires. Throughout the night they were howling like wolves; occasionally they jeered at the Romans, for there were some half-breeds among them who spoke Greek. When day broke Monolukas told the Turks to do the same again. At this stage the Sultan Klitziasthlan himself arrived. He was astounded at the excellent discipline of the Roman army, but in the way a young man would poked fun at old Monolokos because he had

put off engaging the emperor in battle. 'I have put off coming
to grips with him up till now, because I am old or cowardly,'
said Monolukos, 'but if you have the courage, here's your
chance: try it yourself. The experience will teach you something.' The other made an immediate attack on our rearguard,
while other satraps were instructed to make a frontal assault;
others again were ordered to charge against either flank. The
Kaisar Nikephoros Bryennios, who was in charge of the right
wing, noticed the battle raging in the rear, but for all his eagerness to help checked the anger boiling up inside him towards
the barbarians, being unwilling to expose his inexperience or
youth. So he marched on resolutely with ranks intact and in
perfect order.

As the barbarians fought with determination, the dearest of
my brothers, the *Porphyrogennetos* Andronikos, who was in
command of the left, wheeled round and together with his
troops violently fell on the barbarians. He had just reached the
most wonderful period in his life, a daring soldier in war, but
prudent too, with a quick hand and fine intellect. Here he met
his end, prematurely. In a way that none expected he left us
and disappeared. O, his youth, his physical beauty, those light
vaults into the saddle – where are you now? My grief for him
drives me to tears – but the law of history once more calls me
back. It is extraordinary that nobody nowadays under the stress
of great troubles is turned into stone or a bird or a tree or some
inanimate object; they used to undergo such metamorphoses in
ancient times, though whether that is myth or a true story I do
not know. Maybe it would be better to change one's nature
into something that lacks all feeling, rather than be so sensitive
to evil. Had that been possible, these calamities would in all
probability have turned me to stone.

6. When Nikephoros saw that a hand-to-hand fight had
developed and there was a prospect of defeat, he wheeled about
and hurried with his own men to bring aid. Thereupon the
barbarians fled and with them the Sultan Klitziasthlan. They
galloped off at full speed to the hills. Many were killed in
this battle, but a larger number were captured. The survivors
dispersed. The sultan himself, despairing of his life, escaped

with only one companion, his cup-bearer. They climbed up to a chapel built on a hilltop and surrounded by rows of very tall cypress trees. Hard on their heels came three Scythians and the son of Ouzas in hot pursuit. The sultan changed direction slightly and since he was not recognized by those who were chasing him, saved himself, but the cup-bearer was taken prisoner by the Scythians and brought to the emperor as a great prize of war. He was delighted that the enemy had been beaten in such a convincing manner, but annoyed too because the sultan had not fallen into his hands, escaping by the skin of his teeth, as they say.

At nightfall he set up camp where he was; the barbarian survivors, climbing to the ridges above the Romans, again lit a multitude of watchfires and all night long bayed at them like dogs. Meanwhile a Scythian deserter from the Roman army went off to the sultan. 'Never try to fight the emperor in the daylight,' he said, 'for you will have the worst of it. Since the plain is not large enough, he has pitched his tents very close together. Let your light archers go down, then, and fire volleys of arrows from the foothills at them all through the night. They will do enormous damage to the Romans.'

At this same moment a half-barbarian came from the Turkish camp, slipping out unseen. He told the emperor all about the suggestions made by the renegade Scythian and clearly described the plans being prepared for action against the Romans. Accordingly, the emperor divided his army in two: one group was to remain in camp, vigilant and sober; the rest were to arm, leave camp and anticipate the Turkish advance – they were to engage their attackers in battle. Throughout the hours of darkness the barbarians completely encircled our men, making numerous charges near the foothills and continually firing volleys of arrows at them. But the Romans, obeying the emperor's instructions, protected themselves without breaking rank and when the sun rose the whole column set out again in the same formation, with the booty, all the baggage, the prisoners, of course, and the women and children in the centre. They marched on towards Ampous. A terrible and bitter fight awaited them there. The sultan had drawn together his forces again

and surrounding our army, attacked fiercely from all sides.
Nevertheless he was not strong enough to disrupt the tight
formation of the Romans and after assailing what appeared to
be walls of steel, he was repulsed with nothing achieved. He
spent the whole night in anguish and gloomy thought. At last
in desperation he took counsel with Monolukos and the other
satraps, and with their unanimous approval at dawn he asked
the emperor for terms of peace.

Far from rejecting their request, the emperor received it
favourably, and ordered the call to halt to be sounded at once.
The whole army was instructed to remain where it was, preserv-
ing the same formation, neither dismounting nor removing
baggage from the pack animals; the men were still in full armour
with shield, helmet and spear. The emperor had no other reason
for this except seeking to obviate confusion, and the subsequent
break-up of the column, which would lead to their all being
easily taken prisoner. He was also afraid of the Turks, who
greatly outnumbered his own men and whose attacks were
coming from all quarters. So, in a suitable place, with all his
kinsmen and several picked soldiers on either side of him, the
emperor took up position at the head of his army. On right and
left were those to whom he was related by blood or marriage,
and next to them selected warriors from the various contingents, all in heavy armour. The fiery gleam from their weapons
outshone the rays of the sun.

The sultan then approached[14] with his subordinate satraps,
led by Monolukos, who in age, experience and bravery surpassed all the Turks in Asia. He met the emperor on the plain
between Augoustopolis and Akronios. The satraps, seeing the
emperor some way off, dismounted and made the obeisance
normally reserved for kings, but although the sultan made
several attempts to dismount, the emperor would not let him.
Nevertheless he quickly leapt to the ground and kissed the
emperor's foot. The latter gave him his hand, bidding him
mount one of the nobles' horses. On horseback again he rode
close beside the emperor, when suddenly the latter loosed the
cloak he was wearing and threw it round the sultan's shoulders.
Then, after a brief pause, he made a speech, explaining his

decision in full. 'If you are willing,' he said, 'to yield to the authority of the Empire of the Romans and to put an end to your raids on the Christians, you will enjoy favours and honour, living in freedom for the rest of your lives on lands set aside for you. I refer to the lands where you used to dwell before Romanos Diogenes took power and before he met the sultan in battle – an unfortunate and notorious clash which ended in defeat and capture.[15] It would be wise, therefore, to choose peace rather than war, to refrain from crossing the frontiers of the empire and to be content with your own territories. The advice I give is in your interests and if you listen to it you will never regret it; in fact, you will receive liberal gifts. On the other hand, if you reject it, you can be sure of this: I will exterminate your race.'

The sultan and his satraps readily accepted these terms. 'We would not have come here of our own free will,' they said, 'if we had not chosen to welcome peace with Your Majesty.' When the interview was over, he allowed them to go to the tents assigned to them, promising to ratify the agreements the next day. At the appointed time, then, the treaty was concluded with the sultan whose name was Saisan in the usual way. Huge sums of money were presented to him and the satraps were also rewarded generously. They departed fully satisfied.

Meanwhile news reached the emperor that the sultan's bastard brother Masout,[16] jealous of his power, had plotted to murder Saisan at the instigation of certain satraps – the kind of thing that usually happens. Alexios therefore advised the sultan to wait a little until he had more definite information about the plot; thus he would leave in full possession of the facts and on his guard. But the latter disregarded the emperor's advice; filled with self-confidence he stuck to his original plan. The emperor naturally did not wish to give the impression that he was forcibly detaining the sultan who had come to him voluntarily and thereby incur reproach. He bowed to the Turk's wishes. 'It would be well,' he said, 'to wait a little, but since you have decided to go, you must do the next best thing, as they say, and take with you a reasonable number of Roman cavalry to escort you in safety as far as Ikonion.' The barbarian would not even agree to this; barbarians are arrogant by nature, with their heads almost in the clouds. Anyway he took his leave of the emperor and set out on his homeward path with his great sums of money.

During the night, however, he had a dream. It was no spurious vision, nor a message from Zeus, nor did it incite the barbarian to battle in the guise of the son of Nelelios, as the sweet poem says.[17] It foretold the truth to the barbarian. For he dreamed that while he was breakfasting a multitude of mice surrounded him, eager to snatch the bread from his hands; when he treated them with contempt and tried to drive them away in disgust, they suddenly changed into lions and overpowered him. When he woke up, he told the emperor's soldier who was escorting him on the journey and asked him what the meaning of the dream might be. He solved the problem by saying that mice and lions were his enemies, but the sultan would not believe him, and pushed onwards, without taking precautions. He inevitably sent out men to reconnoitre the road ahead and keep an eye open for enemies on a plundering foray, but these scouts fell in with Masout himself, who was already approaching with a substantial army. They talked with him, joined in the plot against Saisan and then returned to the latter, assuring him they had seen nobody. In no doubt that they were telling the truth, Saisan continued his march in carefree mood when Masout's barbarian forces confronted him.

A certain Gazes, son of the Satrap Asan Katoukh, whom the Sultan Saisan had killed in the past, leapt forward from the ranks and struck him with his spear. He turned in a flash and as he wrenched the spear from Gazes' hands said, 'I didn't know that women, too, are now bearing arms against us.' With these words he fled along the road back to the emperor, but he was stopped by Poukheas, who although he was one of his companions had long ago favoured Masout's party. He pretended to be Saisan's friend and now offered a seemingly better plan; in reality he was laying a trap for him – digging a pit, as it were. He advised him not to return to the emperor, but by making a little detour to enter Tyragion. This is a small place quite near Philomelion. Like a fool, Saisan believed what

Poukheas had told him and went to Tyragion where he received a kindly welcome from the inhabitants, who knew of the emperor's goodwill towards him. But the barbarians arrived, with Masout himself, and after completely encircling the walls settled down to besiege the town. Saisan, leaning over the ramparts, uttered violent threats against his barbarian fellow-countrymen; he went so far as to say that Roman forces under the emperor's command were on their way and unless the Turks stopped their activities, they would suffer this and that punishment. The Romans in the town bravely withstood the Turks with him.

But Poukheas now dropped his mask and revealed his true character. He came down from the walls after promising Saisan that he would encourage the people to even more courageous efforts. In fact, he threatened them and advised them to surrender and throw open the gates to the enemy; otherwise, he said, they would be slain, for huge forces were already on the way from Khorosan itself. Partly because they were frightened by the sheer number of barbarians, partly because Poukheas had convinced them, they allowed the Turks to come in. They arrested Saisan and blinded him. As the instrument normally used for the purpose was lacking, the candelabrum given to Saisan by the emperor was used in its place. The provider of light had become the instrument of darkness and blinding in this instance. However, the sultan could still make out a small ray of light and when he arrived at Ikonion, led by the hand of some guide, he confided this fact to his nurse and she told his wife. In this way the story reached the ears of Masout himself. He was greatly disturbed and extremely angry. Elegmos (one of the most prominent satraps) was sent to strangle the sultan with a bowstring.[18] Thus ended the career of Saisan – the result of his own folly in not heeding the emperor's advice. As for the latter, he continued his march to Constantinople, maintaining the same discipline and good order to the very end.

7. When he hears of things like formation, ranks, prisoners and spoils of war, general and army commanders, the reader will probably imagine that this is the kind of thing mentioned by every historian and poet. But this particular formation really

was unprecedented, causing universal astonishment, such as no one had ever seen before, unrecorded by any historian for the benefit of future generations. On the way to Ikonion he marched in a disciplined way, keeping in step to the sound of the flute, so that an eyewitness would have said the whole army, although it was in motion, was standing immobile and when it was halting, was on the march. In fact, the serried ranks of close-locked shields and marching men gave the impression of immovable mountains; and when they changed direction the whole body moved like one huge beast, animated and directed by one single mind. When the emperor reached Philomelion after rescuing prisoners everywhere from the Turks, the return journey was made slowly, in a leisurely way and at an ant's pace, so to speak, with the captives, women and children, and all the booty in the centre of the column.

Many of the women were pregnant and many men were suffering from disease. When a woman was about to give birth, the emperor ordered a trumpet to sound and everyone halted; the whole army stopped at once wherever it happened to be. After hearing that a child had been born, he gave the general order to advance by another, and unusual, trumpet blast. Again, if someone were on the point of dying, the same thing occurred. The emperor visited the dying man and priests were summoned to sing the appropriate hymns and administer the last sacraments. Thus, when all the customary rites had been performed, and only when the dead had been laid in his tomb and buried, was the column allowed to move on even a short distance. At mealtimes all women and men who were worn out with sickness or old age were invited to the emperor's table; most of his rations were set before them, and he incited his retinue to follow his example in giving. It was a veritable banquet of the gods, with no musical instruments, no flutes, no drums, no music at all to disturb the feasters. By such means Alexios personally supplied the needs of the marchers. On their arrival at Damalis (in the evening) he insisted that there should be no magnificent reception when he reached Constantinople; imperial processions and flamboyant decorations were forbidden. The crossing was postponed to the next day, as indeed it had to be, but he himself immediately embarked on a small boat and reached the palace about dusk.

On the following day he was wholly occupied in tending the prisoners and strangers. All children who had lost their parents and were afflicted by the grievous ills of orphanhood were committed to the care of relatives and to others who, he knew, were respectable people, as well as to the abbots of the holy monasteries, with instructions to treat them not as slaves but as free children, to see that they had a thorough education and to teach them the Sacred Scriptures. Some he introduced into the orphanage which he had personally founded, making it a school rather for those who wanted to learn; they were handed over to the directors there to receive a good general education.

For in the district of the Akropolis, where the entrance to the sea grows wider, he had discovered a site near the enormous church dedicated to the great apostle Paul; here, inside the capital city, he built a second city. The sanctuary itself stood on the highest part like a citadel. This new city was laid out for a few stades in length and width – someone may be able to say how many. All round it in a circle were numerous buildings, houses for the poor and – even better proof of his humanity – dwellings for mutilated persons. One could see them coming there one after another: the blind, the lame, people with some other trouble. Seeing it full of those who were maimed in limb or completely incapacitated, you would have said it was Solomon's Porch.

The main double-aspect circular building was two storeys high, for some of these disabled persons, men and women, live on the upper floor, while others drag themselves along below at street level. So large was this circle that if you wished to visit these folk and started early in the morning, it would be evening before you finished. Such was the city and such its inhabitants. They had no plots of ground, no vineyards, nor any other such possession on which we see men earning their livelihood, but like Job, each of them, man or woman, dwelt in the house built for them and everything, so far as food or clothing are concerned, was provided for them through the emperor's generosity. The most extraordinary thing was that these poor people had as their guardians and administrators of their means of subsistence the emperor himself and his hard-working servants, just as if they were lords with property and all kinds of revenue. For wherever there was an estate lying in a good situation and provided it was easily accessible, he allotted it to these comrades, thus ensuring them wine in abundance and bread and all the other products men eat with bread. The number of persons catered for in this way was incalculable. Rather daringly, perhaps, I would say that the emperor's work could be compared with my Saviour's miracle – that is to say, the feeding of the seven and five thousands.[19] In the latter case, of course, thousands were satisfied by five loaves of bread, for it was God who performed the miracle, whereas here the work of charity was the result of the divine command; moreover, that was a miracle, but we are dealing here with an emperor's liberality in dispensing sustenance to his fellow men.

I myself saw an old woman being assisted by a young girl, a blind person being led by the hand by another man who had his sight, a man without feet making use of the feet of others, a man who had no hands being aided by the hands of his friends, babies being nursed by foster-mothers and the paralysed being waited on by strong, healthy men. In fact, the number of people maintained there was doubled, for some were being cared for, while others looked after them. The emperor could not say to the paralytic: 'Rise up and walk!' – nor bid the blind man see[20] and the man without feet walk. That was the prerogative of the Only-begotten Son, who for our sakes became man and dwelt here on earth for us men. Nevertheless, he did what he could. Servants were allotted to every maimed person and the same care was lavished on the infirm as on the healthy. To describe the nature of this new city which my father built from its foundations, one might say it was four-fold, or rather multi-form, for there were people living on ground level, others on the upper floor, and yet others who cared for both of them.

But who could possibly number those who eat there every day, or estimate the daily expense and the care that was dedicated to each individual's needs? I give credit to Alexios for this, which has outlived him. It was he who set aside the resources of land and sea for them, and it was he who secured for them as much relief from pain as possible. One of the most prominent men acts as *orphanotropheios* of this city with its many thousands of inhabitants. The institution is called 'The Orphanage', because of the emperor's solicitude for orphans and war veterans, but with special emphasis on the orphans. There are tribunals which deal with all these matters and accounts have to be rendered by those who administer the funds of these poor folk. Chrysobulls, moreover, are issued to establish the inalienable rights for those who are maintained there.

A large and impressive body of clergy was appointed to the Church of St Paul, the great herald of our faith, and expensive lighting was provided for it. When you enter this church you would hear antiphonal choirs singing; following Solomon's example, Alexios decreed that there should be male and female choristers in this church dedicated to the Apostle. The work of the deaconesses was also carefully organized. He devoted much thought to Iberian nuns who lived there; in former times it was their custom to beg from door to door whenever they visited Constantinople, but now, thanks to my father's consideration, an enormous convent was built for them and they were provided with food and suitable clothing. The famous Alexander of Macedon might well boast of Alexandria in Egypt, Boukephale in Media and Lysimakhia in Ethiopia, but the Emperor Alexios found more pleasure and pride in this Orphanage than in any of the towns he founded, and which we know were built by him all over the empire.

When you enter, the sanctuaries and monasteries are on your left; on the right of the great church of St Paul stands the grammar school for orphan children drawn from all races, presided over by a master. Boys stand round him, some anxiously puzzling over grammatical questions, others writing out grammatical exercises. You might see a Latin being trained over there; or a Scythian learning Greek; or a Roman handling Greek texts; or an illiterate Greek discovering how to speak his own language correctly – such was Alexios' profound interest in furthering the study of our culture. The technique of grammatical analysis was invented by younger men of our generation.

I am passing over the followers of Stylianos or those of Longibardos and the compilers of catalogues of all kinds, the disciples of Attikos[21] and the members of the clergy of the Great Church, whom I will not mention by name. Today these sublime studies are considered not even of secondary importance; the poets and even the historians, together with the experience to be derived from them, are denied their rightful place. Today it is the game of draughts that is all the rage – and other activities which contravene the law.[22] I say this because it grieves me to see the total neglect of general education. It makes my blood boil, for I myself spent much time on these same exercises. After liberation from the elementary studies I devoted myself to rhetoric, touched on philosophy and in the midst of these sciences eagerly turned to the poets and historians. So the rough edges of my style were smoothed out; thereafter, with the aid of rhetoric, I condemned excessive indulgence in schedography.[23] These personal reminiscences, by the way, are not superfluous: they are intended to reinforce my argument for a general education.

8. Later, in the . . . year of his reign,[24] an extraordinary cloud of heretics appeared, a new, hostile group, hitherto unknown to the Church. For two doctrines, each known to antiquity and representative of what was most evil, most worthless, now merged together: one might say that the impiety of the Manichaeans, which we have also referred to as the Paulician heresy, was united with the blasphemy of the Massalians. The heresy concerned the dogma of the Bogomils,[25] which was an amalgam of those of the Manichaeans and the Massalians. Apparently it was in existence before my father's time, but it went unnoticed, since the Bogomil sect is most adept at feigning virtue. No worldly hair-styles are to be seen among Bogomils: their wickedness is hidden beneath cloak and cowl. The Bogomil wears a sombre look; muffled up to the nose, he walks with a stoop, quietly muttering to himself – but inside he's a ravenous wolf.

This unpleasant race, like a serpent lurking in its hole, was brought to the light and lured out by my father with secret magical incantations. He had recently freed himself of most of his cares in east and west, and was now turning his attention to things more spiritual. In fact, he was in everything superior to all his contemporaries: as a teacher he surpassed the educational experts, as a soldier and a general he excelled the professionals who were most admired.

The infamy of the Bogomils had by now spread far and wide (a certain monk by the name of Basil had been most adept at spreading the heresy of the Bogomils, together with twelve acolytes whom he called apostles and with female followers too – women of loose morals and generally bad character – articulating their evil in every quarter); like some consuming fire, the evil devoured many souls to the point that the emperor could no longer bear it. He instituted a thorough inquiry into the heresy. Some of the Bogomils were brought to the palace; without exception they denounced an individual called Basil as their master, the protagonist of their heresy. One of them, Diblatios, was imprisoned. Since he was unwilling to confess anything, he was subjected to torture. He then admitted that Basil was the leader and he named those who had been chosen as apostles. The emperor therefore entrusted several men with the task of finding him. Basil, archisatrap of Satanael, was brought to light, dressed in monkish garb, austere of face, with a thin beard, very tall.

At once the emperor, wished to discover the man's innermost thoughts through force of persuasion, and summoned him on some religious pretext. He even rose from his seat when Basil came in, made him sit with him and share his own table. The whole line was run out for the catch, with all kinds of tempting bait on the hooks for this voracious monster to swallow; the monk, so practised in villainy, was by every means urged to gulp down the whole treacherous offering. The emperor feigned a desire to become his disciple and maybe he was not alone in this: his brother, the *Sebastokrator* Isaac, also led Basil on. Alexios therefore pretended to regard all his sayings as some divine oracle and gave way to every argument; his one hope, he said, was that the wretched Basil would effect his soul's salvation. 'I, too, most reverend father,' said he (the emperor smeared the cup's rim with honey-sweetness, so that the other in his lunacy might vomit forth his dark beliefs), 'I too admire you for your virtue. I pray you make me understand in some

degree the doctrines that Your Honour teaches, for those of
our Church are all but worthless, in no way conducive to virtue.'
At first Basil was coy; he wrapped the lion's skin tight around
himself – even though he was really an ass – shying away
from these words, yet swelling with conceit at the flattery. The
emperor even had him to his table. At all times the *sebastokrator*
was at his brother the emperor's side, play-acting with him.

Finally Basil did vomit forth the heretical doctrine. In what
way did it happen? A curtain divided the women's quarters
from the room where the imperial brothers were, as this loath-
some creature belched out and plainly declared all his heart's
secrets; meanwhile a *hypogrammateus* behind the curtain
recorded what was said. The fool, to all appearances, was the
teacher, while the emperor played the part of student and
the lesson was committed to writing by the *hypogrammateus*.
The accursed fellow strung everything together, lawful and
unlawful alike; no jot of his blasphemous doctrine was held
back. He went on to denounce our theology, to mock the
entirety of our ecclesiastical administration and as for the
churches, oh my, the sacred churches he called temples of
demons. He considered and condemned as worthless our doctrine of the consecration of the body and blood of our first
High Priest and Victim.

So what next? Well, the emperor threw off his pretence and
drew back the curtain. Then a conference was summoned of all
the Senate, the military establishment and the elders of the
Church. The episcopal throne of Constantinople was at that
time occupied by the Lord Nicholas Grammatikos,[26] most
blessed of patriarchs. The hateful teachings were read aloud,
the proof being incontestable. Indeed, the accused made no
attempt to dispute the charge, but at once proceeded to counter-
attack shamelessly, promising that he was ready to undergo fire
and scourgings, to die a thousand deaths. These misguided
Bogomils are persuaded, you see, that they can endure any
punishment without feeling pain, for angels will pluck them
from the funeral pyre itself. And although all threatened him
and reproached him for his profanity – even those who had
shared in his ruin – he was still the same Basil, inexorable, a

Bogomil through and through. Despite the burning and other tortures held over him, he clung with all his might to his devil, holding fast to his Satanael. He was sent to prison. Many times the emperor sent for him, many times called upon him to renounce his wickedness; but to all the emperor's pleadings he remained unmoved.

I must now relate the extraordinary thing with regards to this. Before the emperor had begun to take sterner measures against him, and after he had confessed his impiety, Basil was taken temporarily to a small house newly built for him quite near the imperial palace. It was evening, the stars above were shining in a cloudless sky and the moon was bright. When about midnight the monk entered his cell, stones were thrown against it in the manner of a hailstorm. Now the stones fell automatically: they were hurled by no hand and no man was to be seen stoning this devilish abbot. Seemingly it was an act of vengeance – Satan's demons were wrathful, outraged no doubt at the betrayal of their secrets to the emperor and the notable persecution of their heresy which followed it. A certain Paraskeuiotes, who had been appointed to guard the diabolical old man and to prevent him talking with others and contaminating them with his own filth, swore with the most frightful oaths that he had heard the clatter of the stones as they were hurled on the ground and on the roof tiles; he had seen them falling in thick showers, one after another; but he had no glimpse anywhere of an individual throwing them. The fall of stones was followed by a sudden earthquake which rocked the ground and the roof tiles had rattled. Nevertheless Paraskeuiotes had not been afraid, or at least that is what he said before he realized that this was devils' work; but when he saw that the stones were raining down, as it were, from heaven and that the wretched old heretic had slunk inside and closed the door behind him, he decided that this was indeed the doing of demons and did not know what to make of it.

9. I will say no more about that omen. It was my intention to expound the whole Bogomilian heresy, but modesty forbids me, as the beautiful Sappho[27] remarks somewhere; although I am a historian, I am also a woman, born in the *porphyra*, most

honoured and firstborn of Alexios' children. As such, common
hearsay is best passed over in silence. Despite my desire to give
a full account, of the heresy of the Bogomils, I cannot – for if I
did my tongue would be sullied. However, those who would
like to learn everything about the Bogomil heresy are referred
to the so-called *Dogmatika Panoplia*,[28] a book compiled on my
father's orders. He sent for a monk named Zygabenos, known
to my mistress, my grandmother on the maternal side, and to
all the clergy. He had a great reputation as a grammarian, was
not unversed in rhetoric and had an unrivalled knowledge of
dogma. The emperor sent for him and commanded him to
compile a list of all heresies, covering each separately and
appending in each case the refutation, using the texts of the
holy fathers. The Bogomilian heresy was included, just as the
impious Basil had interpreted it. The emperor named this book
Dogmatika Panoplia and the volumes are still known by that
name to this day.

But we must return to Basil's downfall. The emperor summoned Basil's disciples and fellow mystics from far and wide,
in particular the so-called twelve apostles; their opinions were
tested and it was found that they truly were followers of Basil.
In fact the evil had deep roots: it had penetrated even the
greatest households and had had an impact on an enormous
number of people. As a result, the emperor condemned the
heretics, with chorus and chorus leader alike to suffer death by
burning. When the Bogomils had been hunted down and
brought together in one place, some clung to their heresy,
but others denied the charges completely, protesting strongly
against their accusers and rejecting the Bogomilian heresy with
scorn. The emperor was not inclined to believe them, and to
prevent possible errors of identification, he devised a novel
scheme to ensure that many a Christian was not confused
for a Bogomil, nor that any Bogomil would be mistaken for a
Christian. This was to reveal who actually was a Christian.

On the next day he took his seat on the imperial throne.
Many members of the Senate were present on this occasion,
together with many of the Holy Synod and certain leading
Naziarioi[29] who were renowned for their learning. All those

being prosecuted for their Bogomil beliefs were made to stand trial before this assembly, and the emperor ordered them to be examined for a second time, one by one. Some admitted that they were Bogomils and vigorously clung to their heresy; others absolutely denied this and called themselves Christians. When they were challenged, they retracted nothing. The emperor glared at them and said, 'Two pyres will have to be lit today. A cross will be planted firmly in the ground next to one of them. Then a choice will be offered to all: those who are prepared to die for their Christian faith will separate themselves from the rest and take up position by the pyre with the cross; the Bogomilian adherents will be thrown on the other. Surely it is better that even Christians should die than live to be hounded down as Bogomils and offend the conscience of the majority. Go away, then, all of you, to whichever pyre you choose.'

With this declaration, the emperor pretended to have brought matters to a close. Accordingly they were seized and led away at once. A huge crowd gathered and stood all about them. Fires were then lit, burning seven times more fiercely than usual, as the hymn writer says, in the place called Tzykanisterin.[30] The flames leapt to the heavens. By one pyre stood the cross. Each of the condemned was given his choice, for all were to be burnt. Now that escape was clearly impossible, the orthodox to a man moved over to the pyre with the cross, truly prepared to suffer martyrdom; the godless adherents of the abominable heresy went off to the other.

Just as they were about to be thrown on the flames, all the bystanders broke into mourning for the Christians; they were filled with indignation against the emperor, unaware of his plan. But an imperial decree was issued just in time to stop the executioners. The emperor had in this way obtained firm evidence of those who were really Bogomils, and so he released the Christians, who had been victims of slander, after giving them many recommendations. The rest were committed once again to prison, keeping Basil's apostles away from them. He then sent for some of these men every day and personally taught them, with frequent exhortations to abandon their abominable cult. Certain church leaders were told to make daily visits to the rest, to instruct them in the orthodox faith and advise them to give up their heretical ideas. And some did change for the better and were freed from prison, but others died in their heresy, still incarcerated, although they were supplied with plentiful food and clothing.

10. As for Basil, since he was the protagonist behind the heresy and showed no sign whatever of remorse, the members of the Holy Synod, the chief Naziarioi, as well as Nicholas, the patriarch of that time, unanimously decided that he must be burnt. The emperor, who had interviewed the man at length on many occasions, cast his vote for the same verdict. He had recognized Basil's perversity and knew that his attachment to the heresy was irrevocable. A huge fire was set, therefore, in the Hippodrome. An enormous trench had been dug and a mass of logs, every one a tall tree, had been piled up to the height of a mountain. Then the pyre was lit and a great multitude of people slowly gathered in the arena and on its steps; everybody waited impatiently to see what would happen. On the other side a cross had been set up and the godless fellow was given an opportunity to recant: if by some chance through dread of the fire he changed his mind and walked over to the cross, he could still escape the burning.

The Bogomils were there in force too, watching their leader Basil. Far from giving way, it was obvious that he despised all punishment and threats, and while he was still some distance from the flames, he laughed at them and boasted that angels would rescue him from the midst of the fire. He quoted David's psalm, softly chanting, 'It shall not come nigh thee; only with thine eyes shalt thou behold.'[31] But when the crowd stood aside and let him see clearly that awe-inspiring sight (for even afar off he could feel the fire and saw the flames rising and shooting out fiery sparks with a noise like thunder, sparks which leapt high in the air to the top of the stone obelisk which stands in the centre of the Hippodrome), then for all his boldness he seemed to flinch before the pyre, and appeared troubled. He darted his eyes now here, now there, struck his hands together and beat his thighs, like a man at his wits' end.

And yet, affected though he was at the mere sight of it, he

was still hard as steel; his iron will was not softened by the fire, nor did the messages sent by the emperor break his resolve. Maybe in this hour of supreme need and misfortune a great madness possessed him, so that he lost his mind and was utterly unable to decide what was best for himself; or perhaps – and this was more likely – the devil that possessed his soul had shed about him a profound darkness. So there stood this Basil, despicable, helpless before every threat, every terror, gaping now at the pyre, now at the spectators. Everyone thought he was quite mad, for he neither rushed to the flames, nor did he altogether turn back, but stayed rooted to the spot where he had first entered the arena, motionless. Now there was much talk going on, as everyone repeated the marvellous prophecies he had made, and the public executioners were afraid lest somehow the demons that protected Basil might perform some extraordinary miracle through the grace of God – the scoundrel might be snatched from the scene of this tremendous fire and then be seen in some public place, where many people met; thus the last error might be worse than the first. So they decided to put him to the test.

While he was talking marvels and boasting that he would be seen unharmed in the midst of the flames, they took his cloak and said, 'Let's see if the fire will catch your clothes!' And straightway they hurled it into the centre of the pyre. So confident was Basil in the demon that was deluding him that he cried, 'Behold my cloak flying up to the sky!' Recognizing the robe from its hem,[32] they seized him and threw him, clothes, shoes and all, into the fire. The flames, as if in rage against him, so thoroughly devoured the wretch that there was no odour and not the slightest change to the smoke with just one thin wispy plume rising from the centre of the flames. For although the elements are stirred against the wicked, they do spare those who are dear to God, just as they once did those young men in Babylon[33] and died down because they were beloved by God, with the fire forming a golden chamber around them. But on this occasion the executioners who lifted the wretched Basil up in their arms had barely placed him on the fire when the flames seemed to leap forward and snatch the charlatan. The crowd

standing by roared in excitement, desperate to throw on the
fire all the rest of Basil's pernicious sect, but the emperor would
not allow this to happen. On his orders they were instead kept
in custody in the porticoes and colonnades of the Great Palace.
The spectators then dispersed. Later these atheists were transferred to a prison of maximum security and after languishing
there for a long time died in their wickedness.

With this act, then, this final triumph, ends the long series of
the emperor's travails and exploits. It had been a reign of
surprising boldness and novelty. I should imagine that men who
were alive then and who associated with him must still be
amazed at what was accomplished in those days. To them it
must seem unreal, like a dream or a vision. Since the accession
of Diogenes, the barbarians had invaded the Roman Empire, at
which point he had taken the first step to deal with them by
launching a disastrous expedition against them. From that time
until the reign of my father, the barbarian terror had gone
unchecked: swords and spears had been sharpened against the
Christians; there had been battles and wars and massacres.
Towns were wiped out, lands ravaged, all the territories of
Rome stained with Christian blood. Some died miserably,
pierced by arrow or lance; others were driven from their homes
and carried off as prisoners of war to the towns of Persia. Dread
seized on all as they hurried to seek refuge from impending
disaster by hiding in caves, forests, mountains and hills. There
they loudly bewailed the fate of their friends in Persia; the few
others who survived in Roman lands mourned the loss of sons
or grieved for their daughters; one wept for a brother, another
for a nephew killed before their time and like women they shed
bitter tears. In those days no walk of life was spared its tears
and lamentation. Apart from a few emperors from that period,
none except Tzimiskes, for example, and Basil even dared to
set foot at all in Asia, until the reign of my father.[34]

11. But why am I writing of these things? I perceive that I
am digressing from the main theme, because the subject of my
history imposes on me a double theme: to relate and to describe
the tragedy of the emperor's life; that is to say, I have to give
an account of his struggles and at the same time to do justice

to all that has caused me heartfelt sorrow. Among the latter I
would count his death and the loss of all that I found worthwhile on earth. Yet I remember certain remarks made by my
father which discouraged me from writing history, inviting me
rather to compose elegies and dirges. For I often heard him
speak thus; I even heard him once reprove the empress when
she was ordering scholars to write a history of his labours, his
many trials and tribulations, so that the record of them might
be handed down to future generations; it would be better, he
said, to grieve for him and deplore his misfortunes.

Less than a year and a half after his return from his campaigning, he was struck down by a second terrible illness. It
threatened his life; in fact it was the cause of his utter collapse
and destruction. Now I dearly loved my father and mother
from when I was in the cradle, and this illness is a subject of
great importance which compels me to transgress the laws of
history, something I really do not want to do; I have to describe
the death of the emperor. There had been a race meeting, and
as a result of the strong wind which was blowing at the time
the humours subsided, as it were, left his extremities and settled
in one of his shoulders. Most of the doctors had no idea at all
of the danger with which we were threatened. But a man named
Nicholas Kallikles[35] predicted fearful troubles; he told us that
he was afraid the humours, having abandoned the extremities,
might move in some other direction and so endanger the
patient's life. We could not believe him – because we did not
want to.

At that time no one, apart from Kallikles, had dreamed of
purifying his system by the use of cathartics. The emperor was
not accustomed to taking purgatives; indeed, he was a total
stranger to drugs. For this reason most of them, and in particular Michael Pantekhnes,[36] who was assisting them, absolutely forbade any recourse to purgatives. Kallikles foresaw
what would happen and told them emphatically, 'For the time
being the matter has left the extremities and attacked the
shoulder and neck, but if we do not get rid of it by purging,
it will move again, to some vital organ, or even to the heart
itself. If that happens, the damage will be irremediable.' On the

orders of the empress I was present myself at this conference, in order to act as arbiter; I heard the doctors' arguments and I personally supported the views of Kallikles; however, the view of the majority proved decisive. Actually on this occasion the humours, having afflicted the emperor's body for the usual number of days, gradually disappeared and the sick man recovered his health.

Before six months had passed,[37] he was assailed by a fatal sickness, probably brought on by anxiety: he was greatly affected by the pressure of daily business and the many cares of government. I often heard him telling the empress about it; in a way he was accusing the disease. 'What on earth is this trouble that affects my breathing? I want to take a deep, full breath and be rid of this anxiety that troubles me, but however often I try I can't lift even once a small fraction of the load that oppresses me. For the rest it's like a deadweight of stone lying on my heart and cutting short my breathing. I can't understand the reason for it, nor why such pain afflicts me. And there's something else I must tell you, darling, for you share my troubles and plans: I often have fits of yawning which interrupt my breathing when I inhale and cause me awful pain. If you have any idea what this new trouble is, please tell me.'

When the empress heard these words and understood what he was suffering, she was very upset; one would think that she participated in the same illness, the same asthmatic condition, so moved was she by the words of the emperor. She frequently summoned the best physicians and made them examine closely the nature of the disease; she begged to be told the immediate and indirect causes of it. They felt his pulse and admitted that they found in every movement evidence of all kinds of irregularities, but they were altogether unable to give a reason for this. They knew that the emperor's diet was not rich; it was indeed extremely moderate and frugal, the sort of food athletes or soldiers have, so that the question of an accumulation of humours from too rich a diet was ruled out; they attributed the difficulty in breathing to some other cause and said the main reason for his illness was overwork and the constant pressure of his worries. His heart, they said, was consequently inflamed and was attracting all the superfluous matter from the rest of his body.

After this, the terrible malady which had gripped the emperor gave him no respite at all: it was throttling him like a noose. Every day it grew worse, attacking him no longer at intervals, but relentlessly, with no interruption, to the point that the emperor was unable to lie on his side, and became so weak that every breath involved great effort. All the doctors were called to discuss the emperor's case, but they were divided in their opinions and argued; each one produced his own diagnosis with its appropriate treatment. Whatever solution was offered, his condition was serious, for he could not for one moment breathe freely. He was forced to sit upright in order to breathe at all; if by chance he did lie on his back or side, the suffocation was awful: to breathe in or exhale even a tiny stream of air became impossible. When sleep pitied and overcame him, there was a danger of asphyxia, so that at all times, asleep or awake, he was at risk of suffocation.

As purgatives were not given to him, the doctors tried blood-letting and made an incision at the elbow; that too proved fruitless. He was just as breathless as before and there was a constant danger that such minimal intake of air would cause him to expire in our arms. However, there was an improvement after a pepper antidote was given. We did not know how to contain ourselves for joy, but we offered up prayers of thanksgiving to God. Nevertheless it was all a delusion, for on the third or fourth day the old breathlessness recurred, the same trouble with his lungs. I wonder if that particular medicine did not in fact make him worse, for it dispersed but could not control the humours; they were driven into the cavities of the arteries and his condition deteriorated.

As a result of that, it was quite beyond our power to find any way of making him lie down comfortably. The disease was now at its peak: all night long, from dusk to dawn, the emperor had no sleep; he was unable to take nourishment properly; it was impossible to give him medicines or other relief. I have often, even constantly, seen my mother spending the whole night with the emperor, seated behind him on his couch, holding him up in her arms, encouraging him somehow to breathe. Tears streamed from her eyes, more than the floods of the Nile. The care she lavished on him through whole days and nights was indescribable; nobody could do justice to the hard work she endured as she nursed him, changing his position again and again, arranging and rearranging the bedcovers to make him comfortable. But nothing whatever gave him even the slightest relief. The malady tightened on the emperor like a noose, or rather it was his constant companion, relentlessly strangling him.

There was no remedy for this disease, so the emperor moved to the part of the palace which faced south; oppressed as he was, the one comfort he enjoyed was derived from movement. The empress made sure that he should have it continually, so she had wooden legs fitted to the head and foot of the imperial couch and gave porters the job of carrying the emperor round on it in relays. Later he was transferred from the Great Palace to the Mangana. Even these precautions made no difference to the emperor's well-being. When the empress saw that the disease was gaining ground, she despaired of all human aid. More fervently than ever she addressed her prayers to God on his behalf, had countless candles lit at every shrine and hymns chanted without pause or intermission. She made gifts to people dwelling in every land, by every sea. All monks living in caves or on mountains or leading their lives in solitude elsewhere were urged to make earnest supplications; and all those who were sick or confined in prisons and worn out with suffering were enriched by her gifts and then called upon to make intercession together for the emperor.

But when his stomach was visibly enlarged to a great size and his feet also swelled up and fever laid him low, some of the doctors, with scant regard for the fever, turned to cauterization. Here again all attempts to cure him were vain and useless; he got no help from the cautery, for his stomach remained in as bad a condition as ever while his breathing was laboured. The humours, as if they emerged from some other source, now made their way to his uvula and seized on what the medical experts[38] call the palate; his gums became swollen, his larynx congested, his tongue inflamed; the oesophagus was constricted and blocked at the end and we were now faced with the terrifying prospect of complete starvation. God knows that I took great trouble over the preparation of his food; every day I brought it to him personally and made certain that it was in a form that was easier for him to take.

Anyway, every attempt to cure the inflamed tumours seemed . . .[39] whatever we and the physicians tried proved to be in vain. Eleven days passed while the disease was in its final stage; it was at its zenith and already threatening his life . . . his condition was dangerous and diarrhoea came on. Thus at this moment one trouble after another rained down on us. Neither the doctors nor we who were tending him knew which way to turn . . . but everything portended disaster. After that our affairs were thrown into confusion and chaos; our normal habits were disturbed; fear and danger hung over our heads. Even in the midst of these immediate perils the courage of the empress never wavered and it was especially at this crisis that she displayed her brave spirit: controlling her own bitter grief she stood firm, like some Olympic victor, wrestling with the cruellest pains. She felt deeply hurt inside and heartbroken as she saw the emperor in this state, but still pulled herself together and endured her sufferings; mortally wounded and pierced to her very soul by the agony, she still refused to give up. And yet the tears flowed freely and the beauty of her face was marred; her soul hung by a thread.

It was the fifteenth day of August[40] (a Thursday), the date when the Dormition of Our Lady, the Immaculate Mother of God, is celebrated; early that morning some of the doctors had anointed the emperor's head, having decided that it was a good idea to do so, before each going home – not doing this rashly, nor because of any urgent need, but rather because they realized the danger the emperor was in. There were three principal doctors, the admirable Nicholas Kallikles, Michael Pantekhnes (who had his family surname) and . . . Michael the eunuch. The whole band of relatives crowded round the empress and forced her to take food . . . she had not slept . . . spent several nights in a row . . . in attendance on the emperor . . . she obeyed.

When the last fainting fit came on, she again . . . having waited anxiously, she perceived the . . . life; she threw herself on the . . . began a continuous wail and beat her breast and lamented the evils that had befallen. She wished to breathe her last there and then, but could not.

Then, although the emperor was on the point of death and was racked by overwhelming pain, as though he was able to dominate death itself . . . was distressed because of the empress and tried with one of his daughters to lessen her anguish. It was the third of his daughters, the *Porphyrogennetos* Eudokia. Maria,[41] behaving like another Mary, even though she was not seated at the feet of My Lord, but rather sat by his head, and so as to refresh him, gave him water to drink from a goblet instead of from a cup which he might find difficult since his palate, and indeed his tongue and larynx too, were all inflamed. Then in a firm, manly voice he gave the empress some advice – his last counsel: 'Why,' he said, 'why do you give yourself up so to grief at my death and force us to anticipate the end that rapidly approaches? Instead of surrendering yourself to the flood of woe that has come upon you, why not consider your own position and the dangers that now threaten you?' Such were his words to her, but they only reopened the wounds of the empress's sorrow.

As for myself, I did all I could; to my friends still living and to men who in the future will read this history I swear by God who knows all things that I was no better than a mad woman, wholly wrapped up in my sorrow. I scorned philosophy and reason then, for I was busy looking after my father, carefully observing his pulse and respiration; then I would turn to my mother and comfort her as best I could. But . . . parts completely incurable . . . the emperor had fainted and we could not bring him round; the empress was on the verge of expiring along with the emperor.

They were in this condition . . . and the words of the psalm[42] that the pains of death encompassed us were so appropriate. I knew then that I had lost my mind . . . for I was mad; I did not know what was to become of me, nor where to turn. I saw the empress plunged into a sea of troubles, and the emperor, lapsing into unconsciousness again and again, was being driven on to his life's end. But when my beloved sister Maria sprinkled cold water and essence of roses on him, he recovered consciousness again and bade her do the same for her mother. Then for the third time he fainted ... it seemed a good idea to move the imperial couch ... those who attended him and ... we moved him to another part of the five-storeyed building, so that he might breathe fresher air and come to again, for that part faced the north and there were no houses ... to the doors.

However, the heir to the throne[43] had already gone away to the house set apart for him in secret when he realized the emperor's ... he hastened his departure and went off quickly to the Great Palace. The city was at the time ... in a state of confusion, but not absolute chaos ... The empress in her wild grief said, 'Let everything be abandoned ... the diadem, empire, authority, all power, and thrones and dominions. Let us begin the funeral incantation.' And I, heedless of all else, wailed with her and joined her in the lament ... they writhed about, wailing desperately. But we brought her back to her senses; the emperor was breathing his last and, as they say, was preparing to give up his soul.

The empress had thrown herself on the ground by his head, still clothed in ... and the purple-dyed slippers ... deeply touched and unable to ... the burning sorrow of her heart. Some of the medical experts returned and after waiting a little felt his pulse ... then the beating of his heart ... nevertheless they spoke in vague terms of the final moment ... and despite appearances held out hopes of recovery. They did this deliberately, knowing that with the emperor's passing the empress too would expire. But the empress, who was an intelligent woman, did not know whether to believe or disbelieve them: she had long regarded them as expert physicians; on the other hand, she saw clearly that the emperor's life hung in the balance. She suspended judgement and kept looking at me, waiting for me to make a contribution, as she had on many other occasions in the past when things were finely balanced, expecting me to make a revelation of some kind. My lady Maria, my most dear sister and the pride of our family, steadfast, paragon of virtue, was standing between the empress and the emperor; the sleeve of her robe from time to time made it impossible for the former to look straight at the emperor.

I again held his wrist in my right hand and took his pulse ... her putting her hands often to her head ... the veil, for under the circumstances she intended to change her dress, but I held her back each time I felt some strength in his pulse. I was deceived ... for apparently it was quite feeble ... but when the great effort of breathing ... the working of artery and lung ceased to function at the same time. I released the emperor's hand and ... to the empress ... I again held his wrist ... asphyxia. She kept nudging me, urging me to tell her about the pulse, but when ... I touched it again and recognized that all his strength was going and the circulation of blood in the arteries had finally stopped, then I turned away, exhausted and cold, my head bowed and both hands covering my eyes. Without a word I stepped back and began to weep. She understood what had happened. Suddenly in the depths of her despair she emitted a loud, piercing wail.

But how can I possibly describe the catastrophe which had overtaken the whole world, and how can I bewail my own troubles? She laid aside her empress's veil and with a razor cut off her lovely hair close to the skin. She threw away the purple-dyed shoes she was wearing and asked for ordinary black sandals. But when she wanted to exchange her purple dress for a black one, no garment of that kind could readily be found. However, my third sister had clothes appropriate to the occasion since she had long before suffered widowhood herself, and the empress accepted these and wore them. She put a simple dark veil on her head. Meanwhile the emperor surrendered to God his holy soul, and my sun went down ... those who were not overcome by their grief let out cries, beat their breasts, raised their voices to heaven in woeful laments ... their benefactor who had ... all for them ... weeping.

Even now I cannot believe that I am still alive and writing this account of the emperor's death. I put my hands to my eyes, wondering if what I am relating here is not all a dream – or maybe not a dream, but perhaps a delusion and I am mad, the victim of some extraordinary and monstrous hallucination. How is it that I am not dead too, and why did I not surrender my soul too and die with him? Why did I not lapse into unconsciousness and perish and if that could not be, then why did I not cast myself down from some high place or throw myself into the waves of the sea? My life with its great misfortunes ... I have recorded, but as the tragic playwright says, there is no suffering, no disaster sent from heaven the burden of which I could not bear.[44] For God has indeed visited me with great calamities: I lost the shining light of the world, the great Alexios; his soul surely triumphed over his poor tortured body.

With that too was extinguished another glorious light, like the moon that brings light to all, the pride, in name and deed, of east and west, the Empress Eirene. And yet we live on, we still breathe the air of life. After that evils multiplied and we were assailed by mighty storms. Finally, the climax of all our woes, we were forced to witness the death of the *kaisar*, and were subjected to such terrible events. After a few days the evil got the upper hand and the doctors' skill failed, and I plunged into an ocean of despair; finally, only one thing irked me – that my soul still lingered on in my body. It seems to me that if I had not been made of steel, or fashioned from some other hard, tough substance ... a stranger to myself, I would have perished at once.

But living I died a thousand deaths. There is a marvellous story told of the famous Niobe[45] ... changed to stone through her sorrow ... Then even after the transformation to a substance which cannot feel, her grief was still immortal. Yet I am more grief-stricken than she: after my misfortunes, great and terrible as they are, I am still alive – to experience yet more. In truth, it would have been better to have been transformed into some unfeeling rock ... with shedding of tears ... I remained ... being so insensitive to disaster ... To endure such suffering and to be treated in an abominable way by people in the palace is more wretched than the troubles of Niobe ... the evil having gone so far ... came to an end.

After the death of both rulers,[46] the loss of the *kaisar* and the grief caused by these events would have sufficed to wear me out, body and soul; but now, like rivers flowing down from high mountains ... the streams of adversity ... united in one torrent flood my house. Let this be the end of my history, then, lest as I write of these sad events I become even more resentful.

Byzantine Rulers

EMPERORS

This list is of names relevant to the *Alexiad*.

Constantine VII	913–59
Romanos II	959–63
Nikephoros II Phokas	963–9
John I Tzimiskes	969–76
Basil II	976–1025
Constantine VIII	1025–8
Romanos III Argyros	1028–34
Michael IV	1034–41
Michael V	1041–2
Theodora and Zoe	1042
Constantine IX Monomakhos	1042–55
Theodora (for a second time)	1055–6
Michael VI	1056–7
Isaac I Komnenos	1057–9
Constantine X Doukas	1059–67
Eudokia	1067, 1071
Romanos IV Diogenes	1067–71
Michael VII Doukas	1071–8
Nikephoros III Botaneiates	1078–81
Alexios I Komnenos	1081–1118
John II Komnenos	1118–43
Manuel I Komnenos	1143–80

POPES OF ROME

The following occupied the throne of St Peter during the period covered by the *Alexiad*:

Gregory VII	1073–85
Victor III	1086–7
Urban II	1088–99
Paschal II	1099–1118

PATRIARCHS OF CONSTANTINOPLE

Kosmas I	1075–81
Eustratios Garidas	1081–4
Nicholas III Grammatikos	1084–1111
John IX Agapetos	1111–34

The House of Doukas

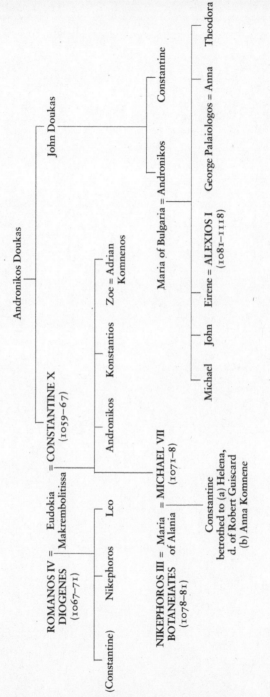

The House of Komnenos

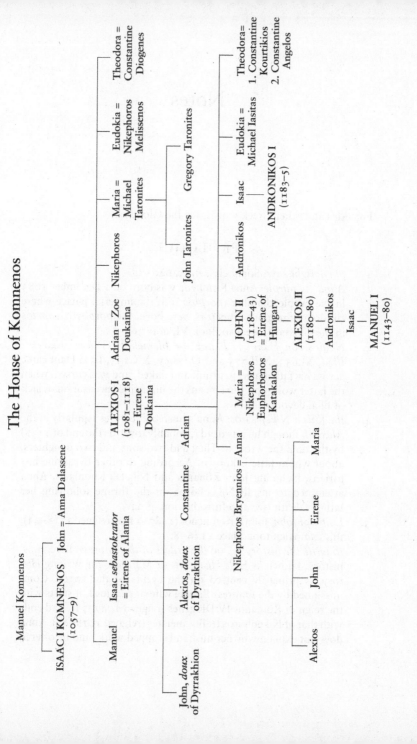

Notes

For titles and other Greek words, see the Glossary.

PROLOGUE

1. *playwright says*: Sophocles, *Ajax*, 646–7.
2. *Anna ... purple*: Anna Komnene was born on 1 December 1083 in the purple chamber (*porphyra*) in the imperial palace where children of reigning emperors were born. See *porphyrogennetos* in the Glossary. See also Book VI, note 36.
3. *Noah's son Ham ... blame the blameless*: Genesis 9:20–27; *Iliad*, XI.653, XIII.775 and *Odyssey*, XX.135, I.32. Ham came across his father asleep, drunk and naked, and was cursed, when the latter woke up. Anna means the unjustified accusation of lack of filial devotion.
4. *the Kaisar Nikephoros*: Anna's husband features regularly in the *Alexiad*, though he was dead (probably towards the end of 1138) by the time she wrote it. They had two sons and two daughters, about whom little is known. According to other Byzantine historians, including John Zonaras and Niketas Khoniates, Anna attempted to install Nikephoros on the throne following her father's death (see also Introduction, p. xiv).
5. *Emperor John*: John II Komnenos (1087–1154, reigned 1118–43); this campaign took place 1136–8.
6. *to write the history ... on the orders of the empress*: Bryennios' history, known as *Hyle Historias*, or *Materials for Writing History*, is primarily centred on the events of the 1070s. Commissioned by the Empress Eirene, wife of Alexios I, it starts with the reign of Romanos IV Diogenes (reigned 1067–71), and ends with that of Nikephoros III Botaneiates (reigned 1078–81). Anna does not explain why her husband stopped work, and he offered

no clues either that his history was not finished or that he was prevented from completing it.

7. *Queen of Cities*: Constantinople. Also referred to by Anna as Byzantion and New Rome (see Book I, note 1), the imperial city and the metropolis.

8. *Timotheos ... for battle*: Orpheus was regarded as the father of singing by Pindar; Timotheos' flute playing was so sweet it provoked Alexander the Great to jump from his seat with excitement.

9. *recalls another*: Euripides, *Hecuba*, 518.

BOOK I

1. *Roman Empire*: The Byzantines called themselves Romans, and referred to their empire and emperor as Roman – with good reason. Although Rome itself had fallen in late antiquity, the eastern half of the Roman Empire had flourished, centred on its eastern capital, 'New Rome'. This city was renamed Constantinople in 330 after the Emperor Constantine I (the Great), but had previously been called Byzantion. Hence the term Byzantine, which Anna Komnene occasionally uses in a general sense, but normally refers to the inhabitants of the metropolis specifically. Wider use of 'Byzantine' to describe the empire, emperor and people of the eastern Roman world only became commonplace in the later Middle Ages.

2. *only fourteen years old ... against the Persians*: Anna often uses archaic terms to refer to the Turks, such as Agarene, Ishmaelite, Saracen and, here, Persian. On Diogenes' fateful campaign, see Book XV, note 15. Anna's comment implies that Alexios was born in 1056; however, it is likely that he was born around 1050.

3. *her eldest son Manuel*: The son of Anna Dalassene (see Book II, note 13), Manuel Komnenos who had been honoured by Romanos IV with the title of *kouropalates* before being given command of the eastern armies. Captured by the Turks in 1070, he was ransomed but was killed in battle the following year.

4. *reign of Michael Doukas*: Michael VII Doukas (reigned 1071–8). See also note 20.

5. *Roussel was a Kelt ... rebel openly*: The terms Kelt, Latin, Frank and Norman are used interchangeably, vaguely and inconsistently by Anna Komnene: Roussel Balliol was a Norman by birth. He was one of a growing number of westerners who had taken

service in the Byzantine army in the second half of the eleventh century. With the collapse of imperial authority in Asia Minor in the mid-1070s, Balliol had brought a swathe of Anatolia under his command, developing what had been a concerted defence against the Turks into a more ambitious attempt to defy the Byzantines themselves. He revolted early in 1074, and was put down *c.* 1076.

6. *his brother*: Isaac Komnenos, Alexios' elder brother, known to have been in charge of the eastern armies only. See also Book II, note 1.

7. *by the Emperor Michael*: In other words, after 1071.

8. *Aemilius . . . second Carthaginian Hannibal*: Three generals from antiquity. Aemilius brought the Third Macedonian War to an end at Pydna in 168 BC; Scipio Africanus conquered Hannibal in 202 BC; Hannibal himself had launched a spectacular invasion of Italy at the start of the Second Punic War (218–202 BC), leading his troops and elephants over the Alps. It is striking that Anna does not choose to compare her father to military leaders from the more recent past.

9. *his second book*: Much of the coverage here is drawn directly from Bryennios' work, on occasion verbatim.

10. *barbarian Toutakh*: Probably Artuk, a commander and supporter of Tutush (Toutouses in the *Alexiad*), who was the son of the Sultan Alp Arslan (1059–72), half-brother of Malik-Shah (see next note), and de facto ruler of Syria, 1078/9–95.

11. *Your sultan*: Malik-Shah, sultan and leader of the Seljuk Turks, 1072–92.

12. *Romans and Turks*: The purported direct speech is designed to show Alexios as an intelligent and resourceful general, but suggests, at least implicitly, that he was not in a strong position, and therefore had to resort to a potent combination of threats, flattery and bribery.

13. *tragic playwright says*: Euripides, fragment 979.

14. *towns of Armeniakon*: The Armeniakon was a *theme* (military province) in north-eastern Asia Minor set up in response to the Arab raids of the seventh century, which had been replaced by a series of smaller districts by the tenth century. Anna uses the term here both to indicate the geographic scale of Turkish gains and also to show her father as a military leader in the old (rather than newer) traditions of Byzantine generalship.

15. *Palamedes himself*: A cunning hero in Greek mythology, Palamedes was able to get the better of that most wily of charac-

ters, Odysseus. See also Book II, chapter 2: hereafter given as II.200.

16. *supposed blinding*: Alexios had a chequered record of blinding and mock-blinding. See for example Nikephoros Diogenes (see Book IX, Chapter 9: hereafter given as IX.9).

17. *grandfather's town*: Kastamon in Paphlagonia, in Asia Minor.

18. *wife of Admetos*: Alkestis was rescued by Herakles from Hades as thanks to her husband who had shown him exemplary hospitality.

19. *Isaac Komnenos*: Isaac I Komnenos (reigned 1057–9) was Alexios' uncle.

20. *deal with Nikephoros Bryennios*: Nikephoros III deposed Michael VII in the spring of 1078, and was crowned on 3 June. Alexios was sent to deal with the uprising in the summer of 1078. Bryennios was either the father or grandfather of Anna Komnene's husband.

21. *married the Empress Maria*: Maria of Alania, daughter of Bagrat IV of Georgia, had been married to Michael VII Doukas, and after Botaneiates seized the throne, she married him. Maria later became close to the Komnenoi, and there were rumours that she would marry Alexios himself (III.1–2).

22. *Turks were in complete control . . . Egyptian Sea*: The extent of Turkish penetration of and control over Asia Minor is repeated at VI. 9 and VI.11.

23. *Immortals*: The *Athanatoi*, an elite *tagma* or military unit revived by Michael VII to fight the Turks. According to Bryennios, the name of 'Immortal' was originally only given to those who had distinguished themselves in battle, but came to apply to the whole battalion.

24. *his brother John*: John Bryennios held the title of *magistros*. He had been aggrieved by the failure of Michael VII to reward him appropriately for his exploits against the Patzinaks.

25. *Maniakes*: George Maniakes had been a successful general, leading several major campaigns in Italy and Sicily before rebelling against the Emperor Constantine IX Monomakhos (reigned 1042–55) in 1042. Bryennios had presumably recruited veterans who had served with Maniakes.

26. *Ares . . . those who saw him*: Anna draws on Greek mythology for her comparisons: Ares was the god of war; the Giants a race of snake-footed beings which were vastly powerful and were defeated finally by Herakles.

27. *Scythian allies*: Anna uses the archaic term Scythian throughout.

This is usually to be understood as meaning Patzinak (or Pecheneg) steppe nomads, a particularly violent and successful tribe who form the centre of Books VII–VIII.

28. *mindful of his furious might*: Homer, *Iliad*, VI.112.

29. *called . . .*: There is a *lacuna* in the text here, presumably reflecting a gap in Anna's information, which she intended to fill in later. Such breaks are not commented on below, unless additional information can be supplied.

30. *as sweet poetry would put it*: Homer, *Iliad*, II.1–2.

31. *my father was blameless*: This account is heavily dependent on that of Nikephoros Bryennios, who also covers it at length. Anna's treatment reflects the desire to highlight the bravery of the Bryennios family, and to accentuate its imperial pretensions. She puts the blame for the blinding on Borilos below.

32. *started from Epidamnos*: The archaic name for Dyrrakhion (III.12). Basilakios rebelled almost immediately after Bryennios had been defeated, and indeed had spoken with John Bryennios about revolting together in 1077. Alexios was sent against Basilakios in the autumn of 1078.

33. *the town of the Thessalians*: Thessaloniki.

34. *a huge Typhon*: A huge and grotesque monster which attempted to replace Zeus as king of the gods.

35. *River Bardarios*: The Vardar river rises in the Pindus mountains and flows down through Thessaly, emptying into the Aegean west of Thessaloniki. It was a primary source of water in the region, offering verdant valleys along its course.

36. *His name was Ioannikios*: Literally, Little John. It is not clear if this is meant as a nickname for Kourtikios. Kourtikios Ioannikios appears frequently in the history of Nikephoros Bryennios, and Anna refers on several occasions to Basil Kourtikios (e.g. V.5), noting that he was known as Ioannikios. These may be the same man.

37. *fumbling about in darkness*: Aristophanes, *Clouds*, 192.

38. *when he fought Alexander*: Homer, *Iliad*, III.361–3.

39. *Erymanthian Boar . . . Herakles*: The capture of this huge and savage wild boar was one of the twelve labours of Herakles, accomplished after an epic struggle.

40. *Robert . . . lust for power*: Robert Guiscard, son of Tancred de Hauteville. In the course of the 1050s and 1060s, Robert had made himself master of almost all of southern Italy, bringing to an end centuries of Byzantine authority in and control of Apulia and Calabria.

41. *on my mother's side*: Anna's mother, the Empress Eirene, was a Doukas by birth and was a cousin of Michael VII.

42. *hostilities which followed*: Following a series of overtures to Robert after his capture of Bari in 1071, an agreement was finally reached in 1074 between Robert and Michael VII, whereby the latter recognized Robert's territorial gains in Italy, granted him the court title of *nobellisimos*, promised a substantial annual payment to him and his followers, and committed to a marriage alliance between his heir, Constantine, and Robert's daughter, Helena. She was duly dispatched to Constantinople in anticipation of the wedding which would take place when both came of age.

43. *multitude in uproar*: Homer, *Iliad*, XVIII.217–29.

44. *he blinded him*: Various elements of this story appear in the narrative histories of Amatus of Montecassino, Geoffrey Malaterra and the Byzantine historian Kekaumenos Katakalon, who name the man treated so shamefully not as Robert's father-in-law, but as Peter of Tyre, the former governor of Bisignano. Anna's (mis)identification shows Robert in the worst possible light.

45. *duke of the whole of Lombardy*: A reference to the Council of Melfi in 1059 which saw Pope Nicholas II (reigned 1059–61) recognize Robert's de facto authority in Lombardy and bestow on him the title of duke.

46. *my own lamentations*: Anna had been engaged to Constantine Doukas from her birth until the mid-1090s. Her anguish is confusing, since she did marry someone else. It is possible that one reason that this marriage did not take place was that Constantine had been implicated in a plot against Alexios – which makes her comments about him here (and indeed elsewhere in the *Alexiad*) all the more difficult to interpret.

47. *the life of a monk*: Michael VII became a monk and later appears to have become metropolitan of Ephesos in Asia Minor, though essentially he remained in Constantinople until his death, *c.* 1090.

48. *Kaisar John, his paternal uncle*: John Doukas, only brother of Constantine X (reigned 1059–67), uncle of Michael VII and grandfather of Eirene Doukaina, wife of Alexios Komnenos. He played an important role during Constantine's reign, holding the title of *kaisar*. In the early 1070s, he was (unsuccessfully) proclaimed emperor in the place of Michael VII by the troops of Roussel Balliol. He withdrew from public life and apparently became a monk in the mid-1070s (see II.6).

49. *call him Rektes*: Anna makes a pun on Raiktor's name, calling him the instigator (*rektes*) of utter chaos.

50. *to get for them from the Roman Empire*: The parading in southern Italy of a man claiming to be Michael VII is well-attested from other sources, as is Robert Guiscard's canvassing to generate support for his proposed attack on Byzantium.

51. *children are scared by Mormo*: A bogey monster popularized by Aristophanes which kept children from misbehaving.

52. *these alliances*: Robert Guiscard's children married into the great noble houses of Barcelona, Narbonne, Roucy and Este. His eldest son, Bohemond, was later to marry the daughter of the king of France, Philip I, while one of his younger sons, Roger Borsa, married the daughter of Robert of Flanders.

53. *the Pope of Rome ... the king of Germany*: Pope Gregory VII (reigned 1073–85); Henry IV, German emperor (reigned 1056–1106). The Investiture Crisis involved the struggle for supremacy over the Church between the papacy and secular leaders in Europe – and specifically with Henry IV. This led to the German emperor being excommunicated on multiple occasions in the 1070s. By 1080 Henry had gone so far as to set up his own pope (or anti-pope) to head up a rival papacy, based in Ravenna. It was not until 1122 that the crisis was finally resolved with the Concordat of Worms.

54. *any crime, any deed of daring*: In her explanation for the quarrel between Henry IV and the pope, Anna strikes at multiple targets, ranging from the corruption of the (Latin) Church to the personal failings of Gregory VII; from the primacy of Constantinople over Rome to the arrogance of foreigners. The intention is to demonize all things western, not least to set up her father as a paragon of goodness in general and as a defender of Byzantium, its institutions and its values in particular.

55. *the Council of Chalcedon*: The Fourth Ecumenical Council in 451 set out among other things that the patriarchate in Constantinople held the ultimate authority in the Christian Church with respect to disputes and appeals by clergy, and as such, was a key point in marking a further shift of power from Old to New Rome.

56. *wherever the pope summoned it*: A formal agreement was indeed made between Robert Guiscard and the pope relating to the expedition against Byzantium, with the latter not only giving his backing to the former, but also providing him with a banner of

St Peter to carry into battle – something which has been widely seen as a key step in the genesis of the Crusades.

57. *Lay hands hastily on no man*: 1 Timothy 5:22.

58. *the prize of his enemies*: At the battle of Elster in 1080, Rudolf and Welf, the Dukes of Swabia and Bavaria respectively, were comprehensively routed by Henry IV after revolting, freeing him to intervene once again in affairs in Italy.

59. *Herod . . . and older men as well*: The unpopularity of the proposed expedition is also noted by William of Apulia. Herod was king of Judaea who according to Matthew 2:16–18 ordered the murder of all male infants in Bethlehem under the age of two, following warnings about the birth of the King of the Jews, and seen as meaning the birth of Jesus Christ.

60. *his brother Boritylas*: Anna probably means Robert Guiscard's nephew, Robert of Loritello.

61. *share in the government*: This means Raoul only returned to Italy from Constantinople after the start of April 1081.

62. *Pege . . . celebrated among Byzantion's churches*: Located just outside Constantinople's Theodosian walls, the Pege complex included a famous church with a monastery attached, a spring with miraculous healing powers and a palace. Dedicated to the Virgin, it was regularly added to by imperial patrons from the sixth century onwards.

63. *the revolt of Alexios*: Spring 1081.

64. *commanders of Dalmatia*: Constantine Bodin and his father Michael were local leaders who had successfully carved out large parts of the northern Balkans in the 1070s, bringing Zeta, Rascia, much of Bosnia and parts of Dalmatia under their own control. Although Anna calls them Dalmatian, they were actually Serbian princes. In 1075, they were granted the title of king by Pope Gregory VII. Anna's reference here is vague in so far as it seems to imply client status. She says they held the title of *exarkhos*, indicating a command position and ultimately one that is subordinate to the emperor.

BOOK II

1. *after being elected by lot*: Isaac Komnenos served as *doux* of Antioch 1074–8, having been *domestikos* of the east beforehand.

2. *her own cousin*: Eirene of Alania, cousin of Maria of Alania, whom Isaac married after 1072. They had at least six children.

3. *were friends*: Orestes and Pylades grew up together as brothers, after Orestes was sent to live with the latter during boyhood by his mother Clytemnestra while she conducted an extramarital affair.

4. *Synadenos ... relative of Nikephoros*: Nikephoros Synadenos was a nephew of the Emperor Nikephoros III Botaneiates. The emperor had no children of his own.

5. *more in store for me*: Empress Maria's anxiety here primarily relates to her desire to secure the succession of her son, Constantine Doukas, but is also an oblique reference to her own disgrace in the mid-1090s.

6. *Kyzikos was captured by the Turks*: At the end of 1080/early 1081.

7. *Euripos*: The body of water separating Euboea and the Greek mainland, famous for its treacherous currents, and where Aristotle supposedly drowned.

8. *The slaves*: Borilos and Germanos.

9. *Agarenes*: The Turks.

10. *Pakourianos ... in Armenia*: An outstanding soldier, he held various important positions in the eastern and western parts of the empire before 1081. That he was placed in charge of the imperial army after Alexios took the throne shows how important his support for the Komnenoi was. Members of the Byzantine aristocracy with origins or property in Armenia had grown in number and importance since the mid-tenth century. The reference is from Homer, *Iliad*, V.801.

11. *Houmpertopoulos*: A Norman who had taken imperial service. He is thought to have been the son of Robert Guiscard's brother Humbert (his name literally means son of Humbert).

12. *Sunday in Cheese week*: The Sunday before Lent, 14 February 1081. Cheese week (*Tyrophagy*) was the week immediately preceding the Lenten fast proper and was so named because dairy products, as well as fish and eggs, were permitted, whereas meat was not.

13. *Anna Dalassene*: Wife of John Komnenos, the brother of the Emperor Isaac I Komnenos. They had eight children – five sons and three daughters, including Manuel, Isaac, Alexios and Adrian.

14. *Palace of Blakhernai ... Hagia Sophia ... Church of the Forty Saints*: The Blakhernai Palace was located in the north-western part of Constantinople and became the residence of the Komnenoi. Hagia Sophia, also referred to by Byzantines and by Anna

as the Great Church and the Church of the Wisdom of God, was completely rebuilt by the Emperor Justinian (reigned 527–65) after the Nika revolts of 532. It was the liturgical centre of Constantinople, of Byzantium and of the orthodox world. The Church of the Forty Saints is better known as that of the Forty Martyrs dedicated to the men who froze to death near Sebasteia in the second century for refusing to denounce their Christian beliefs. Their cult had a wide following in the Byzantine Empire. The church was located between the Forum of Constantine and the Hippodrome.

15. *near the Sidera*: The precise location is not known, but because the convent was near the Sidera gate of the city it was not far from the Blakhernai Palace. It had a history of being a place for the confinement of imperial women, with the Empresses Zoe, Theodora and Maria of Alania – as well as the Komnenoi – spending time there in the eleventh century against their will.

16. *sanctuary . . . Mother of God*: The church and chapel built on a sacred spring by the Empress Pulcheria and the Emperor Marcian (reigned 450–57) and subsequently an important Marian shrine. It was rebuilt after being destroyed by a fire in 1070. Also known as the Church of the Theometor.

17. *The rebels*: I.e. the Komnenoi.

18. *Kosmidion, on the outskirts of the city*: The monastery of Saints Kosmas and Damianos, in the suburbs to the north-west of Constantinople. Built in the fifth century, it was restored and embellished regularly, particularly by the Emperor Michael IV the Paphlagonian (reigned 1034–41), who retired and died there.

19. *George Palaiologos*: Brother-in-law of Alexios Komnenos, and according to Anna, one of her key sources of information (XIV.7).

20. *Aiskhines or Demosthenes*: Famous Athenian orators in the fourth century BC.

21. *Orestias*: An archaic name for Adrianople (Adrianoupolis), the base of the Bryennios family, which provides one reason why the local population opposed Alexios Komnenos.

22. *Michael and John*: Brothers of Alexios' wife, Eirene. Doukas family support was critical in the decision to back Alexios rather than his elder brother as emperor.

23. *purple-dyed sandal*: A key insignia of imperial power in Byzantium, and reserved for the emperor alone.

24. *'Be earnest . . . justice'*: Psalm 45:4.

25. *son of Thunder*: A reference to St John the Divine (Mark 3:17).
26. *army for Alexios*: The heavy religious symbolism and biblical references are intended to place Alexios' acclamation as emperor in a specifically spiritual context.
27. *Melissenos was near Damalis*: Nikephoros Melissenos evidently had well-advanced imperial pretensions, striking both seals and coins bearing the image of his bust and identifying him as emperor. Anna reports in III.4 that he had been rewarded with the title of *kaisar*, promised in 1081 (II.8). There is, however, little evidence that the grant of Thessaloniki also mentioned there was honoured. Melissenos was married to Alexios' sister Eudokia, and while it is usually assumed that this took place before 1081, it is possible that it occurred only after the Komnenoi had seized the throne. Damalis was opposite Constantinople on the eastern side of the Bosphorus.
28. *'Cheater'*: A pun on Manganes' name and the verb *manganein*, to deceive or trick.
29. *Aretai ... overlooking the plain*: The location of the hill and buildings is not precisely known, though a spot 3 km to the west of Constantinople has been suggested.
30. *Varangians from Thule ... Nemitzoi*: The Varangian guard was originally made up of warriors from Scandinavia. By the later tenth century, it included fighters from Kiev and elsewhere by the time of the Komnenian coup. Thule is the generic Byzantine name for the countries of northern Europe, but it is sometimes applied specifically to the British Isles. Although it is known that there was an important contingent of Anglo-Saxon warriors in imperial service in the late eleventh century, it is unclear whether 'Thule' here is intended to refer explicitly to them. Nemitzoi are Germans.
31. *'smiter of walls'*: *Iliad*, V.31.
32. *fourth indiction ... April 6589*: 1 April 1081. It is striking that Anna correlates her father's entry with the religious calendar. Note her disdain in X.9 that the Crusaders should dare attack Constantinople in Holy Week.
33. *following the example of the barbarians*: Anna does little to defend the behaviour of the Komnenian troops in 1081, and her candour is an invaluable corrective to views that the *Alexiad* is a partial history, for she could have watered the coverage down, or omitted it altogether. See also III.5. Zonaras gives a harrowing account of the entry of the Komnenoi into Constantinople (XVIII.20).

34. *'his sweet light'*: Homer, *Odyssey*, XVII.41; also XVI.23.

35. *square of . . . George Sykeotes*: Apparently located between the Kharsian gate and the Church of the Holy Apostles. St George was a sixth-century saint, born in Sykeon in Asia Minor.

36. *The patriarch*: Kosmas became patriarch of Constantinople in August 1075. The kind words about him are perhaps surprising given his effective dismissal only a few months after Alexios was crowned. He did, however, have a reputation for piety during his own lifetime and afterwards.

37. *Botaneiates to abdicate*: Nikephoros abdicated on 4 April 1081, Easter Sunday.

BOOK III

1. *their niece's husband*: Michael's precise identity and relationship with the Komnenoi is not known. He was certainly *logothetes* by 1090, when he oversaw an important compilation of civil law, and still held this position nearly twenty years later, to judge from records relating to Mount Athos. Nothing is known about Rhadenos.

2. *monastery of the Peribleptos*: Monastery in the south-western part of Constantinople dedicated to the Theotokos (Mother of God). It was built by the Emperor Romanos III Argyros (reigned 1028–1034), who was buried there, as was Nikephoros III.

3. *robes of angels*: I.e. he took on a monk's habit.

4. *the words of Homer*: Iliad, X.240.

5. *some evil might befall the child*: The Norman historian Orderic Vitalis, who was writing in the first part of the twelfth century and was well-informed about the court at Constantinople, accuses Alexios of having locked up Constantine Doukas, saying that the boy had been blinded by Nikephoros III. Other sources, from southern Italy to beyond Byzantium's eastern frontier, claim that Alexios' predecessor had castrated Constantine.

6. *I was brought up by the empress*: It is not known why the Empress Maria played such an important role in Anna's upbringing.

7. *upper palace, also called Boukoleon*: Palace in the Boukoleon district of Constantinople, on the shore of the Sea of Marmora, and to the south of the Great Palace.

8. *extremely angry*: Palaiologos was married to Anna Doukaina, the sister of the Empress Eirene, and therefore had a strong vested interest in protecting the Doukas position.

9. *Patroklos-like scheme*: That is, it concealed an ulterior motive. Patroklos had gone into battle with Hector, dressed as Akhilles.

10. *Apelles ... Pheidias ... Gorgon's head*: Renowned artists of classical antiquity, painter and sculptor (including the Parthenon) in the fourth and fifth centuries BC, respectively. Medusa, also known as the Gorgon, turned men into stone just by their looking at her, until she was slain by Perseus.

11. *the Empress Eudokia*: Eudokia Makrembolitissa had been married to Constantine X Doukas and then to his successor, Romanos IV Diogenes. That Alexios was rumoured to be considering abandoning his wife says much about his search for legitimization.

12. *Zoe*: Empress Eudokia's daughter, who was married to Adrian Komnenos, brother of Alexios. The implication here, presumably, is that the empress was seeking to marry Zoe to Botaneiates – so this pre-dates the marriage to Adrian.

13. *Garidas*: Patriarch of Constantinople (May 1081–July 1084), a favourite of Anna Dalassene.

14. *seven days after*: 12 April 1081. The delay in Eirene's coronation is both interesting and significant, showing that jostling for power dominated the first days of Alexios' reign.

15. *Polyklitos*: A famous Hellenistic sculptor from the fifth century BC. This passage on the physical looks of emperor and empress serves as an invaluable template for attitudes to beauty in early medieval Byzantium.

16. *Andronikos and Constantine Doukas*: Presumably references to Eirene's great-grandfather Andronikos Doukas and her great uncle Constantine X.

17. *the eldest of his brothers*: Rather, the eldest of his surviving brothers.

18. *Taronites*: Michael Taronites later revolted against the emperor, even though he was his brother-in-law (IX.8).

19. *in the granting of titles*: Zonaras takes a scathing view of Alexios' various innovations during his reign.

20. *John the Theologian ... Hebdomon*: Church dedicated to the Prodromos (St John the Evangelist), situated in the Hebdomon suburb of Constantinople on the Sea of Marmara. Built by the Emperor Basil II (reigned 976–1025), and where he was buried.

21. *monastery of Kallias*: Named after the Patriarch Antonios II (reigned 893–901), and probably located to the north-west of the Akropolis of Constantinople.

22. *Mangana*: Monastery in the Mangana district of Constantinople,

on the shore to the south-east of the Akropolis of the city. Built
by the Emperor Constantine IX and dedicated to St George, it
soon became one of the principal monasteries of the city.

23. *those set under authority*: Cf. Luke 7:8.

24. *for forty days and nights*: Alexios must have served his penance
in April–May 1081, echoing the time Christ spent in the desert.

25. *the month of August*: Reference to Alexios' departure from the
imperial capital in 1081 to lead the defence against Robert
Guiscard's attack on the empire (see IV.4).

26. *this document*: This remarkable chrysobull is reproduced in full.
It is clearly drawn from the original version of the grant of
executive power to Anna Dalassene or a close copy. Although
the manuscript does not survive, the length, detail and tone of
this passage suggest that this is a faithful version of the command
issued by Alexios. It has been suggested that Anna includes the
complete text as a pointed jibe at her nephew, Manuel I Komnenos (reigned 1143–80), to emphasize how Alexios relied on
senior women within his family group – unlike his grandson, in
other words. Whatever the case, the mandate granted to the
emperor's mother was sweeping and binding – which is in itself
extremely important for our understanding of authority at the
very start of Alexios' reign.

27. *tragic playwright*: Euripides, *Phoenician Women*, 529–30.

28. *Adrianoi ... Kharonoi*: Relatively well-known families in this
period. Bryennios says that Anna Dalassene's father was named
Kharon (after the ferryman at Hades) since whenever he fought
someone, he dispatched them directly to the next life. While the
Kharon name is not unusual, few of its bearers are well-known
or famous in this period.

29. *utter depravity ... the infamous Constantine Monomakhos*:
Michael Psellos alludes to the licentiousness of the court of Constantine IX in his *Chronography*. The contrast is not only with
events before 1081 (as Anna suggests), but those following the
accession of Manuel, where bawdiness and immorality took over
from more ascetic behaviour under Alexios I and John II. See
also Book XIV, note 24.

30. *martyr Thekla ... Emperor Isaac Komnenos*: There were several
churches in Constantinople dedicated to this first-century saint.
It is not known which, if any, were founded by Isaac I Komnenos.
This passage is lifted almost word for word from Psellos'
Chronography.

31. *Dacian ... Mysians*: Anna uses antique names liberally and

inaccurately to identify: here the Patzinaks, Cumans and Oguz, three of the major groupings of steppe-nomad tribes who inhabited the territory stretching from the Danube across the area to the north of the Black Sea. The distinction between the tribes was not always as clear-cut as Anna (and other authors) makes out, since these often could and did incorporate elements of other tribes too. The *De Administrando Imperio* sets out key information on the identities, composition and distinctions of these and other nomadic tribes. Anna's use of classical, Herodotean names is a literary device.

32. *barbarians . . . swords from their shoulders*: The Varangian guard were celebrated for bearing their weapons – typically swords and axes – not round their waists, but over their shoulders.

33. *depths of misery*: Evidently Anna's intention here is to set her father's achievement in context by stressing just how bad the situation was in 1081, but this may be somewhat exaggerated. Nevertheless, there can be no doubt that the prognosis really was bleak for Byzantium at this time.

34. *resisting the Turks*: The references here rather undermine Anna's claims that the Turks controlled all of Asia Minor by 1081: cf. I.1; II.3–4; III.11.

35. *Monomakhatos*: The *doux* of Dyrrakhion (see I.16).

36. *the Latins*: I.e. the Normans.

37. *Hermann . . . Pope of Rome*: Hermann of Lombardy revolted against his uncle Robert Guiscard in 1078 and was an obvious candidate for Alexios to approach for support. As Pope Gregory VII had actively backed Robert's expedition, Anna is either wrong or misguided to say that her father appealed to him for help; alternatively, Alexios was simply desperate. This letter is misplaced for its positioning suggests the emperor made this agreement with Henry IV in the summer of 1081 (and before he had set out against Robert Guiscard). However, it certainly post-dated the fall of Dyrrakhion in the spring of 1082.

38. *the German king*: Henry IV. Anna deliberately refers to him as king rather than emperor.

39. *the old quality . . . bust of Romanos*: Debasement of the Byzantine coinage in the later eleventh century had reached chronic proportions by the time of Alexios' accession, so the commitment to provide coins stamped with the effigy of Romanos IV Diogenes was intended to guarantee the quality of the precious metal in the payment offered to Henry IV.

40. *astropelekin*: An unusual word referring to an ornament of some

kind, perhaps a stone bound with gold, probably worn or carried as a talisman.

41. *Solymas*: Sulayman of Nicaea. Although Anna refers to him as a sultan, his position in the Muslim world was more modest. Nevertheless, he was a prominent and important figure in Asia Minor in the early 1080s, with a crucial power base in Nicaea, which he occupied for Nikephoros Melissenos during the latter's failed attempt on the imperial throne. He was active in south-east Anatolia and eventually managed to secure Antioch before being confronted by allies of the Sultan Malik-Shah.

42. *treaty of peace*: The truce freed Alexios to turn his attention to Robert Guiscard and his attack on Byzantium, so it can be dated to the middle of 1081. The treaty appears to have remained intact for several years, for Alexios complains about its breach at VI.9.

43. *a tremendous storm*: William of Apulia also describes the terrible storm of June 1081 and its catastrophic effect on the invaders and their ships.

44. *an envoy ... from the bishop of Bari*: This man is sometimes presumed to have been a key source for Anna, at least regarding Robert Guiscard's attacks of the 1080s, but his identity is unknown, and it is difficult to specify exactly what information he may have provided or how accurate this may have been. Anna explicitly refers to an oral report, which should perhaps lessen the contribution he may have made.

45. *my digression*: An arcane passage, recording barely relevant notes about Dyrrakhion and the surrounding region from antiquity, much of which relates to the third century BC. Perhaps this is included to show off Anna's knowledge and therefore her skill as a historian.

BOOK IV

1. *17 June*: 1081.

2. *he was the cup-bearer*: The man with the ceremonial responsibility of serving the emperor's wine.

3. *the 'Blues' ... got their name from Venice*: Four chariot-racing teams competed in the Hippodrome in Constantinople: Blues, Greens, Whites and Reds. The rivalry between the first two was particularly intense. The Blues were known as the *Venetoi*; hence Anna's speculation about the origin of their name.

4. *Pallia*: Unidentified location north of Dyrrakhion.

5. *formed a so-called sea harbour*: A classic blockade strategy, recommended by the military manual *Taktika* of Leo VI (reigned 886–912).

6. *put to the sword*: This battle took place in October 1081. The role played by Bohemond here is not recorded in any of the Latin sources, so Anna's mockery is likely poetic licence.

7. *Doge of Venice*: Domenico Silvo (reigned 1071–84). Two sources from southern Italy state that the Venetian victory gave them mastery of the sea.

8. *Maurix*: Probably Michael Maurix (or Mabrikas) who had been *katepano* of Dyrrakhion in the second half of the eleventh century.

9. *the sea*: This chapter is misplaced. The severe drought, and the hardships suffered by Guiscard and the Normans, in fact took place in the winter of 1084–5.

10. *August*: 1081.

11. *Manichaeans*: Manichaeism is an eastern religion based on dualism, that is the belief in separate principles of light and darkness, and the world as the result of conflict between the two. The term was used liberally by Byzantine historians to refer to all forms of dualists (and occasionally, simply as a term of abuse). See also Book VI, note 2 and Book XIV, note 32.

12. *so-called because of his origin*: See Book II, note 11.

13. *Saniskos*: Anna refers to Bohemond here and V.3 by this name, which is not known from any other contemporary writer or document.

14. *Halt! Be Men*: Homer, *Odyssey*, VI.199, and *Iliad*, V.529; VI.112.

15. *Archangel Michael*: The Norman historian Geoffrey Malaterra, who was writing in the early twelfth century, states that the sanctuary was in fact dedicated to St Nicholas, but Anna may have modified this for emphasis, rendering the burning of the holy place not only sacrilege, but an act of sin specifically against St Michael, whose cult had a strong and specifically military following.

16. *the Latins put to flight the Roman army*: The defeat at Dyrrakhion in 1081 ranks as one of the most humiliating and disastrous military defeats suffered by the Byzantine army in the eleventh century, ranking alongside Manzikert in terms of the setback for the empire and its military forces. On this occasion the emperor himself evaded capture – but, as Anna makes clear, only just.

17. *Kake Pleura*: Literally, bad side or flank. In other words, a place with negative connotations.
18. *Sgouritzes*: The horse was named after his colour – Dark Bay.
19. *'No, Agelaos . . . father's woes'*: Homer, *Odyssey*, XX.339.
20. *Komiskortes . . . origin*: There is debate about his name, identity and ethnicity. This name appears to be a contraction of the title *komes tes kortes*, that is, count of the (imperial) stables. Anna's language is vague.

BOOK V

1. *the next spring*: 1082.
2. *submitting to Robert . . . from Amalfi*: Anna implies that Robert Guiscard pressed home his advantage after his heavy defeat of the Byzantine army in October 1081 and that Dyrrakhion fell soon after, but it held out until February 1082. The blame laid on the Amalfitans is misplaced, for a Venetian named Domenico struck a deal with Robert which allowed him to take Dyrrakhion. Anna's error here is likely to be intentional, and a deflection of responsibility from Venice, with whom Alexios had a long and close relationship, to Amalfi, one of the losers in the reconfiguration of the eastern Mediterranean in the late eleventh and early twelfth centuries.
3. *Akhris . . . to Diabolis*: Anna gives no clear indication of how long Alexios stayed in Akhris (modern Ohrid) or in Diabolis before he regrouped in Thessaloniki. Presumably this refers to October/November 1081.
4. *the Synod*: From its position in the text, this synod would seem to date to the first part of 1082, but it is usually dated by modern scholars to the end of 1081, though the basis for this is not clear. It certainly took place before August 1082 when Alexios undertook never to expropriate church treasures again.
5. *doors of the Khalkoprateia*: Literally, Copper Market. Anna is referring to the church of the same name in this central part of Constantinople which was built on the site of an old synagogue around the fifth century. It clearly had elaborate and heavily adorned doors.
6. *hordes of enemies . . . Scythians*: The Patzinak attacks on Byzantium in the mid-1080s.
7. *Leo was condemned . . . his bishopric*: See Book VII, note 10.
8. *the treaty*: Set out at III.10.
9. *Manichaeans . . . Kouleon*: Their participation was previously

noted, when Anna drew attention to their bravery as fighters (IV.4). Zonaras states that Manichaeans were not allowed to fight in the Byzantine army in Alexios' reign.

10. *crossed over to Lombardy*: Early summer 1082.

11. *went back to Rome together with the pope*: Gregory VII was restored to the papal throne in Rome in May 1084.

12. *left Constantinople in . . . May*: 1082. The dating of the sequence of Alexios' initiatives against Bohemond in V.4–5 is confused.

13. *Pounteses . . . deserted to the emperor*: This is not known from elsewhere, and nothing is known about the identity of Pounteses, Reynald and William. However, animosity to Bohemond's leadership evidently did appear during the course of 1082–3 (e.g. V.7).

14. *called on the sultan*: Perhaps Malik-Shah but more likely Suly-man, who had provided Alexios with soldiers after the agreement of a truce in 1081 (IV.2).

15. *arriving . . . day of St George the Martyr*: 23 April 1083. There is little geographic logic to the locations named in this chapter as having been attacked by Bohemond. Nor is it possible to date them more accurately than after spring 1082 and before Bohemond's arrival by Larissa in April 1083.

16. *a letter . . . some frankness*: Anna is either quoting from an original, paraphrasing or using artistic licence, but the inclusion of so bold a letter to and about Alexios is extremely surprising since it pulls no punches about the emperor or his policies. The fact that Larissa had been under siege for six months places the events which follow well into the second half of 1083.

17. *the sanctuary of the great martyr Demetrios*: In Thessaloniki. St Demetrios was a young man from a senatorial family who suffered martyrdom during the persecutions of Diocletian at the start of the fourth century, and in later centuries he became enormously popular in and closely linked with Thessaloniki. Together with St Michael, St George and St Theodore, he had a specifically military resonance in Byzantium and indeed beyond. The encouragement he gave to the emperor therefore carries a deliberate nuance.

18. *Bryennius . . . title of constable*: Bryennius, constable of Apulia, lord of San Mango sul Calore. Anna says he held the title of *phalangarkhes*.

19. *darkness over Egypt long ago*: Cf. Exodus 10:21.

20. *wolf's mouth*: A pun on *Lykostomion*, that is, the mouth of the wolf.

21. *Sarmatians*: Steppe nomads. Anna usually uses this name for Cuman nomads, so presumably Alexios had auxiliaries with them. For 'Homer's words', see *Iliad*, III.23, VII.238–9.

22. *Ouzas*: A member of the Ouzes tribe, another nomad group from the Eurasian steppes.

23. *to right and left*: See *Iliad*, VII.238–9.

24. *Peter Aliphas*: Accompanied Robert Guiscard against Byzantium in 1081 and very nearly killed Alexios in battle (IV.6). He had presumably taken imperial service in the emperor's amnesty of 1083 (VI.1) and became a trusted member of his inner circle, even acting as a witness to the Treaty of Devol on Byzantium's behalf (XIII.12). His descendants, known as the Petraliphai, were prominent in Constantinople in the twelfth century.

25. *returned ... to Constantinople*: Autumn 1083. The occupation of Kastoria is repeated (VI.1).

26. *the reign of Basil ... Monomakhos*: Anna is following Psellos' assessment that scholarship and learning do not appear to have been features of Basil II's court, or his personal interests. This contrasts sharply with the Byzantium of his father, Constantine VII. She also relies on Psellos' account of Constantine IX.

27. *loved philosophical argument*: Anna's claim about her father's love of letters, literature and philosophy is not borne out by other sources, nor indeed by her funeral oration, which makes specific reference to the suspicion with which Alexios and his wife viewed literature in general.

28. *Michael Psellos*: Psellos (1018–c.1078) was one of the most celebrated writers, philosophers and thinkers in Byzantine history. His political career, which spanned the reigns of several emperors, as advisor was one cause of his fame, but his extensive writings were well-known and greatly admired during his lifetime.

29. *image of the Holy Mother of God*: The Theometor, the famous icon of the Mother of God that was kept at the Church of St Cyril in Constantinople.

30. *Psellos withdrew ... Italos was placed in charge*: Psellos was removed from his position during the reign of Michael VII, and withdrew to a monastery. Italos was promoted in 1076, which placed him at the intellectual summit of contemporary Constantinople and of Byzantium as a whole. Anna's portrait of Italos is damning to the point of grotesque (V.9), and is primarily explained by the antagonism between him and Alexios and by the fallout of Italos' disgrace.

31. *Proklos ... Aristotle*: The classic authors who were studied in Constantinople. Proklos (Proclus), Iamblikhos (Iamblichus) and Porphyrios (Porphyry) were Neoplatonist philosophers writing in the fifth, fourth and third centuries AD. After Alexios' death, Anna Komnene commissioned the first commentaries on works by Aristotle, most notably on the *Nicomachean Ethics*. These were written by members of her intellectual circle, but the principal contributors were Eustratios of Nicaea and Michael of Ephesos. See also Introduction, p xiii.

32. *Maximos*: Maximus the Confessor, a hardline theologian of the late sixth–seventh centuries.

33. *close look at other books*: George Tornikes gives a rather different assessment of Eirene's reading habits in the funeral oration he delivered after Anna's death, stating that the empress would only read the New Testament.

34. *repeating the anathema*: March 1082.

BOOK VI

1. *Bryennius occupied Kastoria*: Autumn 1083 (see V.5). Kastoria comes from *kastron*, that is, camp or fortified place.

2. *overcame the Paulicians*: These dualist heretics owed their name to the devotion they showed to St Paul; they believed in separate principles of good and evil. A Paulician community had flourished on the eastern border of the empire from the seventh century and later in the Balkans, following population transfers by Constantine V (reigned 741–75) and John I Tzimiskes (reigned 969–76). Like other Byzantine authors, Anna uses 'Manichaean' as a convenient catch-all for any kind of dualist group, and employs 'Paulician' interchangeably with 'Manichaean'.

3. *One success ... Manichaeans*: This comment linking Alexios' efforts against the Manichaeans with the collapse of Bohemond's attack suggests a date of late 1083/early 1084 for the events that follow. It is possible that the community which Alexios targeted was that of Xantas and Kouleon (IV.4; V.3), and this would mean that he was taking reprisals against an important contingent that had let him down against Robert Guiscard.

4. *He took his seat ... a most impressive figure*: Alexios is presented as a vigorous upholder of orthodox doctrine with heretics, meeting and arguing with them in person, and personally supervising attempts to separate them from their views. Note his dealings

with the Paulicians and with the Bogomils (XIV.8 and XV.8–10).

5. *allowed to go away*: The geographic dispersal was naturally intended to break up the community at Mosynopolis and dissipate their heresy, but had the opposite effect: see VI.4, 14. This incident may have taken place in 1084 (though certainly before 1085).

6. *back to the Queen of Cities*: Presumably late 1083, though note that Alexios' return to Constantinople is therefore given four times (V.7; VI.1; and VI.8).

7. *famous Empress Zoe*: Daughter of Constantine VIII, empress, 1028–50. Three emperors – Romanos III Argyros (reigned 1028–34), Michael IV and Constantine IX – owed their elevation to the throne to their marriages with her.

8. *Antiphonetes . . . the Theometor*: The payments to the individual churches were presumably by way of a financial penance which Alexios either offered to pay, or was encouraged to make by senior clerics. Among the annual payments listed here was a blanket sum to the Antiphonetes, that is, the churches of Khora, Pantepoptes and Pantokrator, all dedicated to Christ the Saviour. On the dating of this synod, see Book V, note 4.

9. *Manichaean called Traulos*: This followed the dispersal of the Manichaeans at Mosynopolis.

10. *Scythians of Paristrion . . . neighbouring area*: Paristrion was a *theme* in the north-eastern Balkans on the southern shore of the lower Danube, centred on the principal garrison town of Dristra. The implication is that the town had been lost by the mid-1080s.

11. *under his control*: This is not strictly true. Alexios spent most of the later 1080s struggling to bring the situation in the north-eastern Balkans under control. Anna is likely referring to Mosynopolis, which takes the narrative back to the end of 1083.

12. *fresh attack . . . Illyrikon*: Guiscard's preparations against Byzantium began in the summer of 1084.

13. *like buzzing swarms of bees*: Iliad, II.87.

14. *Avlona . . . took the town at once*: During the last three months of 1084.

15. *shorter from Otranto*: Anna has previously stated the opposite, namely that the voyage was shorter from Brindisi (I.16). Otranto was indeed closer to the eastern coast of the Adriatic.

16. *Roger and Guy*: Robert Guiscard's sons: Roger Borsa, duke of Apulia and Calabria (1085–1111), and Guy, duke of Amalfi (1073–1108).

17. *he would pay their expenses many times over*: Alexios evidently

did accord some privileges in the latter part of 1084, for it is after this that the doge used the title of imperial *protosebastos* and claimed authority over Dalmatia. It is reasonable to suppose that financial incentives may well have been offered simultaneously. However, these concessions were distinct from the major privileges reported below (see note 21), which were certainly unrelated to the Venetian efforts of 1084.

18. *their crews*: This battle took place at the end of 1084, or perhaps the very start of 1085. Guiscard's cruelty afterwards is not noted by other sources.

19. *Church of St Mark ... Evangelist*: The Cathedral of St Mark in Venice.

20. *all the Amalfitans*: There were communities from many of the Italian maritime states living and trading in Constantinople. Penalizing those from Amalfi was intended to inflate the importance of Venice and its interests in the imperial capital.

21. *completely free of Roman authority*: There has been considerable debate about the date of the concessions awarded to Venice: 1082 or, on the basis of Anna's comments here, in 1084. There can be no doubt that this account is misplaced, its position here suggesting 1085. The earliest copies of the full text of the grant state that it was awarded in 1092, a date which which has much to recommend it.

22. *main thread*: Late 1084/early 1085. Anna misplaces the harsh winter of 1084–5 which had a disastrous effect on Robert Guiscard's forces in 1081 (IV.3).

23. *other son*: Roger Borsa.

24. *seventy years*: Robert Guiscard died on 17 July 1085, on the feast day of St Alexios. He was born around 1015. His tomb stands in the cathedral in Venosa in Apulia.

25. *handed over the town*: Note that Dyrrakhion did not simply surrender to the emperor, and moreover that Alexios apparently had to provide suitable encouragement to its inhabitants.

26. *Seth*: Symeon Seth, a philosopher and writer who was well-known in late-eleventh-century Byzantium, and whose treatise on diet survives, as do works on physics and on heavenly bodies.

27. *Eudoxos ... Manetho*: Eudoxos of Knidios, a student of Plato and author of several texts on astronomy. Manetho, an ancient Egyptian priest who wrote an authoritative history of the pharaohs, and was purported to be the author of an astrological treatise known as the *Book of Sothis*, almost certainly incorrectly.

28. *the famous Egyptian from Alexandria*: Anna may be referring to another astrologer (besides Seth), but her language is unclear.

29. *Eleutherios*: Probably Eleutherios Zebelenos, a contemporary of Symeon Seth – as well as a fellow-countryman.

30. *Katanankes*: Otherwise unknown. Athens was a key centre of Neoplatonist thought in late antiquity.

31. *obscure the main theme ... astrologers*: Ancient scholars who wrote about astrology with no distinction, according to Anna, who is establishing her own authority on this subject. Anna cannot (and does not) conceal her father's ambiguity towards soothsayers, fortune tellers and astrologers. The court of Manuel I saw a great surge in interest in these 'sciences', and it may be that Anna is hedging her bets, billing her father both as critical of astrology and as interested in these 'occult' practices.

32. *Robert ... unswerving loyalty*: This is a flattering portrait of Guiscard, presumably intended to show how valiant and distinguished a foe Alexios had managed to see off.

33. *starting the war ... prematurely*: Refers to the decision to attack Robert Guiscard by Dyrrakhion in 1081.

34. *first of December in the seventh indiction*: 1083. Anna has jumped back to immediately after Bohemond's withdrawal to Italy from Byzantium.

35. *acclaimed after him*: Zonaras states the opposite, namely that Alexios did not allow any share in his power.

36. *a second daughter ... a boy*: Maria Komnene, born 19 September 1085. John II Komnenos, born 13 September 1087. Alexios and Eirene had a further six children – Eudokia, Andronikos, Isaac, Theodora, Manuel and Zoe. Anna barely refers to John and her other siblings. The description of John II is usually taken to be unflattering and ungenerous – perhaps a harsh interpretation of what Anna actually says.

37. *peace treaty with Solymas*: The treaty agreed in mid-1081 (III.11).

38. *Apelkhasem*: Abul-Kasim, emir and governor of Nicaea (reigned 1086–?).

39. *Emir Solymas ... Toutouses*: Emir Solymas: Sulayman, who had taken Nicaea in late 1080/early 1081. Pouzanos is most likely Buzan, a Turkish commander loyal to the Sultan Malik-Shah who was active in eastern Asia Minor in the 1080s and early 1090s. Toutouses is Tutush: see Book I, note 10.

40. *Philaretos ... organized a rebellion*: Philaretos Brakhamios had

been a leading figure in the regime of Romanos IV who had given him the title of *kouropalates*. He revolted against Michael VII, carving out a quasi-independent realm in the east, before capturing Antioch. He was formally named its *doux* by Nikephoros III in 1078. It is likely that he was promoted to the position of *domestikos* only after this date too, and not, as Anna suggests, a decade or so earlier.

41. *attack on the place and captured it . . . great sultan*: The date of this event is uncertain. The sultan is Malik-Shah.

42. *perished wretchedly*: Sulayman took his own life in the second part of 1085.

43. *Siaous . . . doux of Ankhialos*: Siaous means messenger in Arabic. The date of his appointment is unknown; nothing more is known of him, or indeed of any Turkish governor of Ankhialos in this period. There is no other evidence to help date the recovery of Sinope.

44. *Poulkhases*: Abul-Kasim's brother, Buldagi.

45. *Prosoukh . . . new sultan Pargiaroukh*: Anna must mean Bursuk and Barkyaruk (reigned 1092–1105). Bursuk was a high-ranking Seljuk officer, with a strong family connection and loyalty to the sultan. Barkyaruk only became sultan in 1092 (and indeed was not formally proclaimed as such until 1094), so this part of the text is chronologically unreliable.

46. *sebastos*: A very high title indeed, otherwise reserved for the closest intimates of the emperor. Alexios was evidently very concerned to win the support of Abul-Kasim and in the traditional manner, sought to offer him suitable rewards to persuade him of the benefits of co-operation with Byzantium.

47. *recorded about Alkibiades*: The anecdote is about Themistokles in Thucydides, *History of the Peloponnesian War*, I.90–91.

48. *The Paeanian*: Demosthenes, who relates the story about Themistokles in *Contra Leptines*, 73.

49. *Prosoukh arrived . . . to besiege Nicaea*: Anna has returned to the Turkish expedition against Nicaea of the early/mid-1090s.

50. *Pillars of Herakles . . . of Dionysos*: The pillars flanked the Straits of Gibraltar and at an unknown location in India were thought in antiquity to hold up the skies.

51. *Meroë, all the land of the Troglodytes . . . Torrid Zone*: Meroë was a town far up the River Nile, inside modern Ethiopia. The Troglodytes were supposedly a tribe of people living around the southern part of the Red Sea. The Torrid or Tropical Zone refers to lands bounded by the Tropics of Capricorn and Cancer.

Anna paints a rosy picture of the Roman Empire at its notional peak, even if this predates Alexios' reign by many centuries. She does not distinguish between the Roman and Eastern Roman (Byzantine) Empire.

52. *return of Siaous*: Anna now goes back to events of the mid-1080s (VI.9).

53. *sultan's*: Malik-Shah.

54. *strangled him*: The date of Abul-Kasim's death is usually given as the early 1090s. Given the paucity of the sources for Asia Minor in this period and the shortcomings of Anna's chronological framework, it is not possible to establish the date.

55. *the sultan had been murdered*: Malik-Shah (also called Taparas by Anna VI.12) was poisoned (and died) in November 1092, but his vizier, the celebrated Nizam al-Mulk, was murdered in broadly the manner Anna describes, in the autumn of 1092.

56. *Khasioi*: The Assassins. This quasi-religious sect derived their name from the fact that they indulged in hashish and thereby carried out murderous acts after being taken to higher levels.

57. *pride of Nauatos*: A Carthaginian of the third century. The cause of his pride (also X.7) and its exhibition must have been clearer to Anna and her readers than they are now.

58. *the sultan of Khorosan . . . Klitziasthlan*: The dating of the murder is uncertain: presumably it post-dates the accession of Barkyaruk in the early 1090s. Klitziasthlan is Kilidj Arslan, son of Sulayman, who claimed Nicaea for himself some time after the death of Abul-Kasim. The first appearance Kilidj Arslan makes in other sources is dateable only to 1096, so Anna's sequence of events must be handled with caution.

59. *Elkhanes*: A generic term, a contraction of the Arabic word for leader. Anna uses blanket terms for individuals, either because she did not know their real names or as a form of xenophobia and/or snobbery towards these (Muslim) foreigners. Alexios' diplomacy with Elkhanes provides another example of how he sought to stress the benefits of good relations with Byzantium (cf. his approach to heretics within the empire (e.g. IV.4)). Anna is careful nevertheless to underline Alexios' commitment to proselytization and evangelism, stressing this as a personal quality as well as an official policy.

60. *Beliatoba*: Near Philippopolis. Anna is not specific about where this raiding took place, nor does she give any indication either of the scale or the damage caused. The battle is traditionally dated to 1086, but an earlier date of 1085 is more likely.

61. *the Euros*: Antique name for the River Maritza which flows from the Rila through the Rhodope and Balkan ranges into Thrace.

62. *Tatikios ... in pursuit*: He was presumably intending to pick off stragglers, rather than confront the nomad host directly. This is consistent with the use of skirmishing tactics which he had used shortly before this stand-off, and indeed was the correct procedure against a force of this size and disposition. The Lydian chariot evokes Pindar and Plutarch.

BOOK VII

1. *Tzelgou ... Solomon*: This invasion took place in 1087 and is attested in several Latin sources from this period, which also note the involvement of Solomon, who had been deposed as king of Hungary in 1074. However, his motivation and his presence alongside the nomads are not easy to explain. Despite Anna's optimistic figures, this was a very major incursion. The implication is that Alexios' expedition (VII.7), which follows, was an immediate response.

2. *Haimos*: The Balkan mountain range, running from eastern Serbia through modern Bulgaria to the Black Sea.

3. *an eclipse of the sun*: Anna describes a full lunar eclipse of the sun, a key dating marker, which is usually assumed to have been on 1 August 1087.

4. *Atreus' son Agamemnon ... to battle*: Homer, *Iliad*, II.9–91. Zeus sent a dream to Agamemnon inspiring him through a vision of Nestor, the son of Neleus and greatly respected by all the ancient Greeks, to capture Troy.

5. *great town of Peristhlaba*: Great Preslav in north-eastern Bulgaria had been a key settlement, particularly in the reign of the (Bulgar) Emperor Symeon, and in this period, served as the headquarters of the Byzantine civilian and military administration in the region.

6. *36,000 men*: The sudden shift in the numerical strength of the nomads is plausible, even if the figure is not. The intention is to show that the Byzantines were overwhelmed and their defeat owed more to the challenge they faced than to their own shortcomings.

7. *Omophoron of the Mother of the Word*: The *Omophoron* was the cape belonging to the Virgin which was usually kept in the Church of the Theometor in Blakhernai in Constantinople. It

had presumably been brought on campaign by Alexios to solicit Divine Providence for his forces.

8. *Nikephoros ... not bragging*: Anna's praise of the dexterity of Nikephoros Diogenes is surprising, in view of his later attempts to murder the emperor (IX.5–9). These comments also show the militarism of the Komnenian court in the twelfth century, where tales of bravery on the battlefield and of martial exploits formed a key theme.

9. *on to Berroe*: This suggested route is suspect.

10. *Leo ... Palaiologos*: Leo of Chalcedon had been a troublesome critic of the regime of Alexios, and in particular of his decision to expropriate church treasures (V.2). Leo's trenchant criticism in the mid-1080s, when Alexios again looked to the Church to raise funds lay behind his trial and deposition as bishop of Chalcedon in 1085–6. His reputation and indeed Anna's treatment of him here and elsewhere are at odds with his role in saving (or seeming to save) Palaiologos.

11. *bought back the men*: It is not clear how or why the nomads would have made use of monetarized bounty, other than by melting it down. The capture and ransom of so many prisoners, including his brother-in-law, must have been deeply embarrassing and compromising for Alexios in Byzantium.

12. *Tatou reached the Ister with the Cumans*: Although Anna puts the confrontation between the Patzinaks (Scythians here) and the Cumans down to the breaking of a previous agreement, endemic tension and competition between rival individuals and groups of nomads is a more prosaic explanation.

13. *the count of Flanders*: Alexios maintained contact with Robert I, count of Flanders (ruled 1071–93), in the years before the First Crusade. To judge from the position in the text, they met immediately after the expedition against Dristra, but Flemish records indicate the meeting more likely took place at the very end of 1089.

14. *make a truce with the emperor*: The truce is mentioned in a speech given by Theophylaktos of Akhris (Theophylact of Ohrid) in January 1088 – which means that it was agreed by late 1087.

15. *yielded to his wishes*: The date of this second treaty is unclear.

16. *At the beginning of spring*: The start of 1090. Anna tells us little about relations between Alexios and the nomads datable to 1088 or 1089.

17. *Sacred Band of the Spartans*: The soldiers were actually from Thebes.

18. *the elite knights ... arrived*: They reached Byzantium from Flanders around the middle of 1090. The assault on Nikomedia is revealing about the state of play in Asia Minor and on the empire's eastern flank at this time.

19. *Tzakhas*: Çaka, a Turk, established himself in the key town of Smyrna, on the western coast of Asia Minor and set about a stunning series of conquests along the coast and in the eastern Aegean in the late 1080s and early 1090s. The losses outlined by Anna below are essentially the same as those in John the Oxite's speech delivered to the emperor in early 1091. Çaka was married to the daughter of Abul-Kasim (XI.5).

20. *the title of protonobellisimos*: This is not known from other sources. Emperor Nikephoros III, like Alexios, gave high-ranking titles to outsiders in Byzantium, including Turks. However, it is also possible that Anna is seeking to establish that it was her father's predecessor who was ultimately responsible for all the problems posed by Çaka by having brought him into imperial orbit, but the implication is that Alexios compromised this by failing to honour the agreement.

21. *John ... arrives shortly*: This is problematic as Doukas' operations against Çaka are usually dated to 1091 and more often 1092. However, the reference to John spending eleven years in Dyrrakhion means that his recall should be in 1094 at the earliest, given that the town was essentially (though perhaps not fully) recovered in 1083. See also IX.1.

22. *'Night is ... the night'*: Iliad, VII.282.

23. *'the others ... not embrace'*: Iliad, II.1–2.

24. *changed knee for knee*: Homer, Iliad, XI.547.

25. *returned to Byzantion*: Late 1090.

BOOK VIII

1. *Friday of Carnival week*: 16 February 1091. Carnival week (*Apokreos*) preceded Cheese week (see Book II, note 12) in the prelude to Easter. Alexios' instruction was that others join him three days later.

2. *Dekatos ... its name*: Deka means ten in Greek.

3. *Sunday of Carnival week*: 18 February 1091: i.e. Palaiologos must have set out earlier than instructed by the emperor, which should presumably be viewed positively.

4. *'How should ... to flight'*: Deuteronomy 32:30.

5. *Theodore . . . Sunday*: Note that the likely feast of St Theodore referred to here fell on 17 February – so this episode is marginally out of place.

6. *came over*: Anna provides an important clue that Alexios' policies in Asia Minor had been effective: Turks whose support he had secured, one way or another, were now being won over by Çaka.

7. *the spring equinox*: March 1091.

8. *one way or the other*: The Cumans' impatience to fight doubtless owed much to the difficulties of sustaining and provisioning large numbers of men and horses in a set location.

9. *fierce spirit of battle*: See Homer, *Odyssey*, XXIV.319.

10. *twenty-ninth of April*: The Patzinaks were obliterated at Lebounion on 29 April 1091, at least as a military threat. Zonaras says that survivors were settled near Moglena, and doubtless there were other communities, both in Byzantine territory and beyond. (Patzinak escorts accompanied the Crusaders on their way to Constantinople in 1096–7, this time in imperial service.) The significance of the battle though was the scale of Alexios' victory; it did not bring to an end problems posed by nomads (see X.2–4; XIV.8).

11. *near Dristra*: Referring to the disastrous expedition led by Alexios to the Danube region in VII.2–5.

12. *Zygos*: It is not clear where Anna means. It would usually refer to the mountain range, in the north-western Balkans; however, here Anna seems to use it as a specific location. Furthermore, the Cumans were based in the Danube and upper Danube region, rather than in the area suggested here.

13. *act of conspiring*: This incident may be misplaced, as Constantine Houmpertopoulos reappears later (X.2). Although it is often assumed that this means he was rehabilitated by the emperor, it is more likely that the sequence is corrupt.

14. *archbishop of Bulgaria*: Theophylaktos of Akhris, a well-known and well-connected cleric with strong connections to the imperial family.

15. *unpleasant fabrication*: The tension between Isaac and his brother Adrian and his brother-in-law (also Alexios') provides an insight into the discord within the ruling family. The competition for power and position calls into question traditional theories about the solidarity of the family during Alexios' reign. There is little evidence to date this episode. However, if John Doukas can only have been recalled from Dyrrakhion in 1094

(see Book VII, note 21), then the inquiry into John's commitment post-dates Doukas' return. Nevertheless, modern historians follow Anna's sequence of events and date this to 1092.

16. *Theodore Gabras*: A member of an illustrious family which was to have its power base in the important town of Trapezous (Trebizond), on the northern coast of Asia Minor. His heroic exploits, as given here, are the basis for a series of quasi-mythic works on his life, dating to the twelfth century and later, of which several refer to him as a martyr.

17. *to marry Gregory to one of my sisters*: Gregory Gabras did indeed marry Maria Komnene. It is not known if they had any children. Zonaras says that the marriage was annulled on grounds of consanguinity, which is ironic given what Anna says here about why Gregory had not been permitted to marry a daughter of Isaac Komnenos.

18. *Michael ... pinkernes*: Likely the same person who was sent with Manuel Boutoumites to Kilikia at the start of the twelfth century, when he is described as a young man (XI.9). This raises questions about dating, and suggests that the Gabras conspiracy occurred later than Anna implies; it is usually dated in the early 1090s.

19. *the Sacred Nail*: Anna presumably means the Sacred Lance (also in XI.6), which pierced Jesus' side and which had long been held in Constantinople. She may intentionally say 'nail' so as to discredit the Crusader 'discovery' of the same at Antioch in XI.6 – although this is rather oblique (see also Book XIV, note 1).

BOOK IX

1. *summoned from Epidamnos*: Duplicated reference to Doukas' recall from Dyrrakhion: see VII.8 and Book VII, note 21, with the likely date here of 1094 or later.

2. *seized Crete ... taken Cyprus*: Crete and Cyprus had fallen out of imperial control by the start of 1091. Karykes and Rhapsomates are only known from the *Alexiad*. For the latter, it is likely that this is a nickname, rather than a family name, although there were men with this surname in twelfth-century Byzantium; the name refers to someone who has had their eyes torn out (i.e. blinded). It has been argued that Anna conceals the man's identity deliberately, and that it is Nikephoros Diogenes. Again, the involvement of John Doukas here suggests a date of 1094 or later.

3. *Sultan Klitziasthlan*: Kilidj Arslan returned to take over Nicaea
    following the fall from power of Abul-Kasim, reported in VI.12;
    Anna has confused the sequence of events here.

4. *Bolkan ... two solar years*: This should provide a date of 1093
    for Bolkan's incursions, but the language here is arcane. There is
    little to help calculate a time frame for the Byzantine military
    response.

5. *'a trembling ... his cheeks'*: Homer, *Iliad*, III.34–5.

6. *Constantine Doukas*: Born while his father was on the throne
    and therefore in the *porphyra* chamber; this is the last mention of
    Constantine Doukas in the *Alexiad* (or any other contemporary
    source). Presumably he died shortly afterwards, perhaps of com-
    plications arising from the poor health mentioned here. Anna
    takes particular care to stress how well her father had looked
    after Constantine.

7. *Kyperoudes*: According to Bryennios, the Empress Eudokia was
    exiled to an unnamed convent on the shores of the Bosphorus
    which she herself had founded.

8. *governor ... of Crete*: The appointment of Diogenes to Crete is
    curious, as is the comment that he was to enjoy this as his own
    – presumably a reference to the tax revenues. It may have been
    a way for Alexios to park a dangerous rival well out of the way
    of Constantinople, and to buy his silence, if not his support.

9. *'Sparta is ... glorify her'*: Echoes of Euripides and Plutarch.

10. *the Ethiopian ... white man*: Cf. Jeremiah 13:23, i.e. a leopard
    cannot change its spots.

11. *evening on which honour is paid ... Theodore*: There is more
    than one feast dedicated to St Theodore, but the most probable
    date is 8 June 1094.

12. *the day ... of the Great Apostles*: The feast of St Peter and
    St Paul, 29 June 1094.

13. *drove straight for Dalmatia*: The narrative turns again to Alexios'
    efforts to secure the north-western frontier of the empire, taking
    up from IX.5, so the summer of 1094.

14. *Uresis and Stephen Bolkan*: Uros I, župan or prince, of Rascia.
    Stephen must have been a close relative of Bolkan.

15. *Didymos*: Fourth-century cleric and writer who overcame his
    blindness to master the mathematical sciences. Greatly respected
    in his lifetime, his works were declared heretical at church coun-
    cils in the sixth and seventh centuries. Anna is drawing a parallel
    between Didymos' fall from grace and Nikephoros Diogenes'.

16. *was immediately forgiven*: Nothing is known about the rehabili-

tation and second disgrace of Diogenes. The motivations, context and date here are obscure.

BOOK X

1. *Italos ... infamous Neilos*: The condemnation of Italos was in 1082, nearly fifteen years before the events which immediately precede this, while the trial of Neilos was in March 1087. Neilos was condemned at a synod presided over by the emperor himself – which gives some indication of how seriously (and how prominently) religious deviance was dealt with in Alexios' reign.

2. *Arsakes and Tigranes*: Obscure references to men who are otherwise unknown.

3. *Blakhernites was ... condemned*: This is not known from elsewhere, and the date is obscure. By 'Enthusiasts' (below), Anna means Messalian dualist heretics.

4. *Polemo's*: Although a relatively well-known sophist from the first century AD, Polemo is an unusual choice to sit alongside Demosthenes, Homer and Plato as a reference point. Perhaps a device for Anna to show off her own erudition.

5. *Leo ... died of an arrow wound*: This is incorrect (see VII.3), for another Diogenes brother, Constantine, had been killed at Antioch. The mistake is curious, since Constantine Diogenes was married to Theodora, Anna's aunt, and the two families had other links; it may be, therefore, that the error is deliberate, and intended to discredit the impostor.

6. *the year 6592*: August 1084. Nicholas Kyrdiniates, better known as Nicholas III Grammatikos, was patriarch of Constantinople until 1111. He makes only four appearances in the *Alexiad* – in spite of the key roles he played in relations between Constantinople and Rome in the late 1080s and within the Byzantine Church. The lack of coverage of the patriarch and the senior clergy is a distinctive feature of Anna's text.

7. *set out to fight the Cumans*: Most probably spring 1095.

8. *Houmpertopoulos*: He had been implicated in a conspiracy against the emperor (VIII.7), but either he had been rehabilitated or the sequence of events is wrong.

9. *Vlakhs*: A term used by authors to mean different things: from members of the Latinized population of the Byzantine Empire to mountain dwellers, living beyond the reach of the state. This reference captures their ambiguous status, with Poudilos serving

to link the imperial forces with the nomad invaders. Kekaumenos records a Vlakh uprising, led by a Poudilos in 1066.

10. *trick of Zopyros in Cyrus's reign*: Allusion to Herodotus and the story of a Persian satrap who disguised himself in this way to fool the Babylonians, but it took place in the reign of Darius.

11. *the Scythians*: The Cumans.

12. *Maryandenoi*: Antique reference to people from around Claudiopolis in south-western Asia Minor.

13. *Anastasios Dikouros*: Emperor, 491–518. This sets up Alexios as heir and continuer of one of the great Byzantine emperors.

14. *indiction of the ... year*: It might be reasonable to suppose the year is 1096, immediately before the First Crusade, as this follows on. But the *Alexiad* is not always chronologically reliable, and it raises the question of why some gaps were left. Anna is disingenuous, intentionally or otherwise, for Alexios had appealed to Pope Urban II for military aid against the Turks, sending envoys to him at Piacenza in March 1095. Also, as the *Alexiad* makes clear, procedures and provisioning plans were in place once the Crusaders reached Byzantium, which suggests he was not caught by surprise. Perhaps the emperor was stunned not so much by the numbers of armed pilgrims, as by their dubious quality.

15. *Koukoupetros*: Literally, Peter the Cuckoo. Better known from western sources as Peter the Hermit.

16. *Aphrodite ... Khobar*: Not an accurate outline of Muslim beliefs. Anna's purpose is to denigrate and lampoon Islamic practices. Aphrodite, Astarte, Ashtaroth and Khobar were all female goddesses of love.

17. *Godfrey*: Godfrey of Bouillon, duke of Lower Lorraine (ruled 1087–1100) and first king of Jerusalem (reigned 1099–1100). A loyal supporter of Henry IV, fighting with him in Italy and taking his side against the papacy in the Investiture Crisis, he had been rewarded with lands and authority by Henry in the north-western Rhinelands.

18. *cross the Straits of Lombardy*: Anna's geography is shaky. Peter the Hermit made his way overland to Constantinople via Hungary and Bulgaria, and did not cross the Straits of Lombardy (i.e. across the Adriatic) – although other contingents did.

19. *taken prisoner*: 29 September 1096.

20. *Hugh*: Hugh of Vermandois (1053–1101), younger brother of King Philip I of France, and son of Henry I and Anne of Kiev.

21. *John*: His allegiance to the emperor had been tested not long before the First Crusade (VIII.7–8), and his position in

Dyrrakhion was of extreme importance as it gave him responsibility for monitoring and greeting those contingents which passed through Italy.

22. *Count Tzerpenterios*: William of Melun, nicknamed the Carpenter because of his legendary strength.

23. *Count Prebentzas*: His identity has provoked much debate, with some suggesting this refers to Raymond of St Gilles (see note 38), but Richard of the Principate seems more likely.

24. *day . . . memory of Nicholas*: St Nicholas, 6 December 1096.

25. *The tzangra*: This digression is extremely detailed, and on a topic in which it is hard to see Anna having a strong personal interest. Together with the heavy coverage of relations with Byzantium's neighbours and extensive focus on military endeavours, the account of the firing mechanism of a crossbow suggests that either Anna or someone close to her had access to a substantial military archive.

26. *Count Godfrey also made the crossing*: Anna has already implied this in X.5.

27. *won at Larissa*: Alexios' defeat of Bohemond at Larissa in the early summer of 1083 was not quite as glorious as Anna makes out, for the imperial forces did suffer a setback after sacking his camp (V.5–7). Nevertheless, this battle did lead to Bohemond's return to Italy, so in that sense it represented an important achievement for Alexios.

28. *palace . . . Nicholas*: The references are to locations in the Blakhernai area of Constantinople, whose precise locations are unidentified. The Crusaders were evidently focusing their attention on the part of the city most closely associated with the Komnenoi and their followers.

29. *the city had been captured*: 4 April 1081 by the Komnenoi.

30. *the Thursday of Holy Week*: 2 April 1097. The violence of the Crusaders in Holy Week, when fighting was expressly forbidden by the Peace of God, emphasizes the atrocious behaviour of the western knights. But Albert of Aachen, an early-twelfth-century author of an underrated account of the First Crusade, gives 13 January 1097, a date with no explicit or implicit Christian context.

31. *pull the bowstring . . . the bow*: See Iliad, IV.123.

32. *Nor did the dart . . . the ground*: References to Homer's *Iliad* and *Odyssey*, though not accurate.

33. *Count Raoul with, 15,000*: The large contingent led by Raoul marks him out as an important leader, even if the number of his

followers is dubious. No prominent men of this name are known from western sources, so perhaps Anna means Robert of Flanders or Robert of Normandy, both leaders of sizeable forces whom she does not mention.

34. *numerous ... of spring*: Odyssey, IX.51; Iliad, II.468.

35. *how many of them there were*: Estimates of the size vary, but the consolidated Crusader army was extremely large, probably around 60,000 – that is to say huge by contemporary standards. While Latin does not appear to have been widely known in eleventh-century Byzantium, Anna's snobbish comments about the names of the Crusade leaders is faintly amusing given that she has already provided many of them.

36. *Count Baldwin*: Brother of Godfrey of Bouillon, and later king of Jerusalem (reigned 1100–1118).

37. *'out-Cretan the Cretan'*: Or out-fox a fox. Clearly, Cretans had a reputation for cunning.

38. *deep affection for St Gilles*: Raymond IV, count of Toulouse (ruled 1094–1105), also known as Raymond of St Gilles. Considered by many to have been the leader of the First Crusade, and certainly the most experienced and wealthiest of the Crusaders, his family had long contacts with the papacy in the later eleventh century. He makes a belated appearance here but receives a glowing assessment that contrasts with the account by one of his followers, the chronicler Raymond d'Aguilers, who makes plain that there were difficult moments between the count and Alexios in 1096–7 – though they later co-operated. Anna refers to him throughout as Isangeles – i.e. St Gilles.

39. *made the journey ... to Damalion*: April 1097.

BOOK XI

1. *the sultan*: Presumably Kilidj Arslan, who at that time was seeking to establish himself in Asia Minor by taking on the Emir Danishmend and was absent from Nicaea during the siege. The Sultan Barkyaruk paid little attention to the Crusaders until they reached Antioch.

2. *Manuel ... Skleros*: Manuel Komnenos, also known as Manuel Erotikos, father of Isaac I, was entrusted with the defence of Nicaea, a key objective for Skleros, and acquitted himself with distinction. Bardas Skleros was a Byzantine army officer who revolted against the Emperor Basil II in the late 970s.

3. *the lake*: Ascanian Lake, which lies to the west of Nicaea.

4. *enter the town*: Nicaea surrendered to Boutoumites on 19 June
    1097, two days after he had arrived.

5. *Tancred*: A nephew of Bohemond, he later established himself at
    Antioch, following the departure of his uncle for the west. He
    too took the oath to Alexios, albeit reluctantly, in order to
    reinforce the emperor's right to gains the Crusaders made in Asia
    Minor and beyond, including Antioch.

6. *Sultan Tanisman*: Malik Ghazi Gümüshtegin or Danishmend, a
    Turk who had profited from the collapse of the Byzantine provin-
    cial administration and brought a large area of north-eastern Asia
    Minor under his control in the last years of the eleventh century.

7. *like a lion . . . might*: See Homer, *Iliad*, V.299.

8. *three lunar months*: The siege lasted from October 1097 when
    the Crusader army set up around Antioch until taken by assault
    on 3 June 1098. Anna's time frame may be intended to diminish
    the difficulties encountered and the very heavy losses sustained.

9. *the sultan of Khorosan*: This was Barkyaruk's first intervention,
    which suggests that the expedition across Asia Minor, and above
    all its scale, had caught him by surprise.

10. *a certain Armenian*: The western chroniclers ascribe a central
    role to this man (given several names) in allowing Bohemond
    into Antioch and its fall to the Crusaders.

11. *Kourpagan*: A powerful local figure, Kerboga, ruler of Mosul,
    had been entrusted with the task of attacking a very depleted
    Crusader force by Barkyaruk.

12. *Soudi . . . sailed for Cyprus*: Antioch's port, also known as
    St Symeon, located at the mouth of the Orontes river. Tatikios
    set off for Cyprus in early February 1098. The rising hostility
    towards him was marshalled by Bohemond and reflected the
    growing despair of the Crusader force, which by that time was
    experiencing major supply problems while also suffering from
    disease and frustration. Tatikios' departure was perfectly sen-
    sible, as it was necessary to do something to ease the plight of
    the western knights at Antioch.

13. *Tzakhas held Smyrna*: The death of Çaka has already been
    recorded (IX.3). It is usually argued that Anna is mistaken about
    the name of this man or that he was the son of Çaka with the
    same name, but more plausible is that Anna's earlier account is
    misplaced.

14. *He therefore sent for John Doukas*: It is not clear if this is the
    same expedition that Doukas had led against Çaka in VII.8 and
    IX.1–2 and is the third report, or whether this is another, separ-

ate campaign. This expedition took place between the summer of 1097 and the spring of 1098, and its aims were to recover the coastal region, as well as key points in the interior of western Asia Minor. Doukas' route was chosen to take maximum advantage of the pressure created by the Crusader host crossing Anatolia.

15. *arrived at Philomelion . . . from Antioch*: June 1098. This is the climax of Book XI and perhaps of the *Alexiad* as a whole. Anna makes a concerted effort to explain why Alexios did not advance to the aid of the Crusaders at Antioch, and very carefully sets out that his decision was based on: (i) reports he had received, not from Byzantine sources, but from the Crusaders themselves – and important commanders at that; (ii) the imminent arrival of major forces under Kerboga to crush the Crusaders was critical; (iii) the emperor either feared being deposed (like his four predecessors), or was concerned barbarians might capture the imperial capital; and (iv) the fear of mass slaughter of the local population by the Turks. Stephen of Blois had been sent to look for reinforcements at Antioch, only to return home. There is substance to the claims here that the situation in Antioch was presented to Alexios as bleak.

16. *Peter, their bishop*: The hero, as the Latin sources make clear, was not their bishop, Adhemar le Puy, but Peter Bartholomew, a common soldier on the Crusade, who had a vision of St Andrew in which the hiding place of the Holy Lance was revealed.

17. *one named Flanders*: Presumably Robert II, count of Flanders.

18. *after them*: The battle took place on 26 June 1098.

19. *overriding authority of Antioch*: Bohemond remained in Antioch. His failure to complete his pilgrimage to Jerusalem is not commented on by Anna.

20. *it fell*: 15 July 1099.

21. *Amerimnes . . . Ramleh*: Al-Afdal, vizier of the Caliph of Cairo, al-Amir (reigned 1094–1101). Anna uses 'Babylon' and 'Babylonian' to refer to Cairo and Egypt. The response to the Crusaders was contemporaneous with the fall of Jerusalem (15 July 1099) and the battle of Ascalon a month later (12 August), which cemented the Latin conquest of the Holy Land, but Anna chooses to describe the battle at Ramleh which took place in May 1102. She may be confusing the two battles, even though they had dramatically different outcomes.

22. *except Godfrey*: Godfrey had died in 1100 (see also XI.8), however, the general summary provided here is adequate: a major defeat had been inflicted on the Crusaders.

23. *to Edessa*: Baldwin had been in Edessa since 1098, when he had captured it on behalf of, and then from, its Armenian governor Thoros.

24. *to the letter*: Probably the end of 1101/early 1102.

25. *Antarados ... Atapakas of Damascus*: Antarados is Tortosa in the Latin sources. Anna uses the title of atabeg as a first name. She must mean Tugtegin, son of Tutush, who held Damascus at this time. These events also date to 1102.

26. *straining every nerve to capture the place*: 1102. The siege would last for seven years. Anna described above the fortress built by St Gilles with the help of Byzantine engineers, which became known as Mount Pilgrim and as Raymond's Castle.

27. *surrender the town*: Laodikeia in the first months of 1103.

28. *king of Jerusalem*: Baldwin was crowned on 25 December 1100.

29. *two brothers named Flanders*: Albert and Guy of Flanders, who took part in the expedition of 1101.

30. *took Ankyra*: 23 June 1101.

31. *a Monday*: 5 August 1101.

32. *few surviving knights*: The defeat suffered by the second wave of the Crusade resulted in the annihilation of the western force. Only a small handful of knights survived, including St Gilles and Stephen of Blois, who had returned to the east after being goaded by his wife for having come home without reaching Jerusalem.

33. *met with a fatal illness*: The narrative has jumped: St Gilles died on 27 February 1105.

34. *Bohemond read ... missives*: Dates for this correspondence range from 1099 to 1103. On the siege of Antioch, see note 8.

35. *Boutoumites ... with numerous troops*: Most likely 1103.

36. *bishop of Pisa*: Daimbert (Dagobert) of Pisa became patriarch of Jerusalem on his arrival in the Holy Land. He had been archbishop of Pisa since 1085 and was named papal legate by Urban II in 1099 in succession to Adhemar le Puy, who had died shortly after the capture of Antioch. Anna now returns to the dispatch of the Pisan fleet in 1099.

37. *Greek fire*: The naphtha-based viscous liquid (for details, see XIII.3) was a key military resource for the Byzantines, and above all for the imperial navy, which used it as an incendiary weapon in close combat from ship to ship, bringing both tactical advantage and the element of surprise. The Byzantines could project it almost at will at enemy vessels.

38. *sent for Tatikios ... rank of megas doux*: Landulph was a Lom-

bard, probably surnamed Butrumile, who reached high rank in imperial service under Alexios. The entrusting of command positions to him and Tatikios shows that the emperor did not restrict power to members of his family or to the Byzantine aristocracy.

39. *latter half of April*: 1099.

40. *thwarted Bohemond's schemes and restored Kourikos*: Probably 1104. Anna underlines that Bohemond had repeated opportunities to conciliate with the emperor. The stress on his belligerence has an additional poignancy given the abject failure of his military policy towards Byzantium in the early twelfth century.

41. *A year later*: Autumn 1100, although another Genoese fleet was operational in the eastern Mediterranean in 1104.

42. *attacks on the walls*: This assault took place in 1104, while Laodikeia had fallen to Tancred a year earlier.

43. *whole of Kilikia*: Probably in 1104.

44. *came up with a plan*: Bohemond had been captured and imprisoned by Danishmend 1101–3. He was back in Italy by early 1105, so probably left the east towards the end of 1104. The story of the coffin and the faked death is not known from any of the Latin sources, but perhaps was common gossip in Byzantium. The damning portrayal of Bohemond in Corfu sets him up as Alexios' nemesis for Books XII–XIII. Anna's depiction of an aggressive, egotistical figure is intended to contrast with the emperor's meek and modest nature, but also to establish the full extent of Bohemond's humiliation in the Treaty of Devol in XIII.12.

BOOK XII

1. *king of France for a marriage ... nephew Tancred*: Bohemond married Constance, the daughter of Philip I of France in 1106. Tancred was married to Constance's sister Cecilia, thereby further strengthening the links between Antioch and France and between the two families.

2. *Alexios*: Possibly Alexios, *doux* of Corfu, who had met Bohemond shortly beforehand, but more likely Alexios Komnenos, the second son of *Sebastokrator* Isaac (XII.4), nephew of the emperor and *doux* of Dyrrakhion around this time.

3. *join his expedition*: Bohemond canvassed actively and widely for support for a new expedition – either to the Holy Land or against Alexios directly (or both) – in 1105–6. He won crucial backing

from Pope Paschal II (see note 31) and was able to attract substantial forces, above all in France.

4. *the Babylonian*: Al-Afdal, vizier of the caliph of Cairo (see Book XI, note 21).

5. *released them from prison*: This episode appears to duplicate the capture and release of prisoners after the battle of Ramleh in 1102 (XI.7).

6. *main town of Thessaly*: Thessaloniki; 1107.

7. *Aspietes*: Wounded fighting Robert Guiscard in the 1080s (IV.6). His appointment to defend Tarsos dates to 1105/6. He is often thought to be Oshin, lord of Lampron, also known as Ursinus in the Latin sources, which say he made contact with Tancred to betray Mamistra to him. This would explain Anna's ambivalence towards him here.

8. *Mopsos . . . River Saron*: Mopsuetsia (Mamistra) does not stand on the Saron, but on the Jihan; Tarsos is not in Koile-Syria, but in Kilikia (XII.2). This episode is misplaced: Tancred's campaign probably dates to the spring of 1109.

9. *Arsakids*: A Parthian dynasty from classical antiquity which had been prominent in this region. By expropriating their heritage, Anna presumably intended to endorse the claims and status of the Armenians who claimed descent from this ancient family.

10. *Sthlanitza*: An administrative unit in the Balkans with particular responsibility for supplying the army with necessities. Anna has again shifted regional focus.

11. *reins of empire*: September 1105. This was in fact the twenty-fourth year of Alexios' reign.

12. *Her natural inclination*: Anna's portrait of her mother finds an echo in the foundation document of the monastery of the Kekharitomene, which was established by the Empress Eirene and bears witness to her formidable determination, resolve and sharp sense of favouritism.

13. *Theano*: Student, and later supposedly wife, of Pythagoras. The reference is obscure.

14. *the poet*: Simonides of Kea, fragment 4.29–30.

15. *Tomyris and Sparethra the Massagetis*: Classical heroines who fought bravely in battle against Cyrus of Persia in the sixth century BC. Tomyris was queen of the Massagetai, and Sparethra the wife of a Scythian chieftain.

16. *peaceable woman*: Eirene means peace in Greek.

17. *Locusts . . . a great comet*: Locusts preceded the arrival of the First Crusaders in Byzantium (X.5). The comet is recorded by

Fulcher of Chartres and was visible to the naked eye in the spring of 1106.

18. *News came of the defeat*: The dating of the defeat by the Dalmatians (the Serbs) and their subsequent negotiations with the Byzantines is problematic. John Komnenos had been *doux* of Dyrrakhion in the 1090s and had engaged with Byzantium's neighbours to the north without great success. Since he had moved to Larissa, where he was governor by 1101, it is possible this episode is misplaced.

19. *winter was now coming on*: It is not clear if this is 1106 or 1107.

20. *first of the sons . . . twin sister*: Anna's brother John had married Piroska-Eirene of Hungary, *c.* 1104. Their first children were twins, Alexios and Maria, born in February 1106.

21. *in honour of . . . Demetrios*: The feast of St Demetrios falls on 26 October; presumably 1107.

22. *in the Bible*: See Deuteronomy 32:39.

23. *his own people*: Anna might be hinting that it was those who were particularly close to the emperor who were deserting him at this time.

24. *Leo . . . and . . .*: The lack of a full list of conspirators may be revealing, with Anna choosing not to record by name those who conspired against her father. The date of the Anemas conspiracy is uncertain, even though it is also covered by John Zonaras, but since the *sebastokrator* died before November 1104, the plot could not have taken place around 1107 as implied by its position here; *c.* 1102/3 is likely.

25. *superficiality*: Anna takes particular pleasure in belittling Solomon's philosophical limitations. She had her own pretensions in this field (see Introduction), and her interest in philosophy plays a central theme in the elegy written by John Tornikes soon after her death.

26. *Skleros and Xeros*: The identity of these two men is not known, though Xeros may have been an official who is mentioned in a law of 1092, and his position as *eparkhos* means that he was a man of power and influence.

27. *I myself*: One of the principal passages in the *Alexiad* where it is clear that Anna was an eyewitness. Her pleas to prevent the execution of Michael Anemas may not have been as decisive as she thinks, as her father showed remarkable and consistent clemency to would-be rebels.

28. *In the course of the twelfth indiction*: Between September 1103 and August 1104.

29. *fourteenth indiction*: 1105/6. Gregory was the nephew of Michael Taronites, whose disgrace (IX.8) does not seem to have affected the fortunes of Gregory nor of Michael's own son, John Taronites, who was sent by Alexios to reason with his cousin.

30. *calling on Tanisman*: This is fanciful with the aim of discrediting a rebel obvious. Nevertheless, Gregory had proved remarkably effective in Asia Minor, being congratulated by leading figures in Byzantium on more than one occasion for his successes against both Bohemond and Danishmend in the first years of the twelfth century.

31. *the pope*: Although Paschal II (reigned 1099–1118) endorsed Bohemond's expedition, he was pragmatic enough to enter high-level discussions with Alexios about church unity in 1112. This may explain why Anna treats him more leniently than she does Gregory VII (cf. I.13).

32. *landed on the opposite shore*: On 9 or 10 October 1107. According to Fulcher of Chartres, Bohemond commenced his attack on Dyrrakhion on 13 October 1107. The Isle of Thule usually means Britain.

33. *Demetrios Poliorketes*: An unusual choice, for while Demetrios was a successor of Alexander the Great, and did achieve some success, his ambitions had ultimately been thwarted, and his siege of Rhodes had ended in ignominious failure. Perhaps Anna is seeking to draw a parallel between underachievers?

34. *Vetones*: Adriatic pirates who were avowed enemies of the Venetians. Anna's reference seems stylistic, rather than substantive.

BOOK XIII

1. *first indiction*: 1107.

2. *the usual miracle*: Every Friday after sunset, a miracle accompanied the unveiling of the icon of the Virgin, famous for its healing powers. Interruption of the miracle was considered an ill omen. The icon's principal treasure was the *Omophoron* cloak which covered the Virgin's shoulders. Anna reports the emperor as having lost it while fighting the steppe nomads (VII.3), but he must either have only had part of the cloak with him then, or it had been recovered afterwards.

3. *Stagirite's ... dialectician*: Aristotle and his model of the Magnanimous Man, put forward in the *Nicomachean Ethics*.

4. *Aronioi*: A well-known family with connections to the dynasty

that had ruled Bulgaria until the Byzantine reconquest of Basil II.

5. *delayed for five days*: From its position in the text, the conspiracy was uncovered in autumn 1107.

6. *as we have said*: Book XII.9.

7. *winter and summer*: 1107–8.

8. *dropped dead like flies*: Bohemond's predicament must have been worsened by the conditions as supply problems became acute in the winter of 1107/8. As in 1084/5, the Byzantines kept a tight stranglehold on the invading force by land and on sea; coupled with a harsh winter and unforgiving terrain, Bohemond's army rapidly began to suffer the effects of disease and starvation.

9. *seven bull's-hides*: *Iliad*, VII.220.

10. *Gadeira*: Cadiz. Quite why or how this device was traced to southern Spain is not clear.

11. *attacked with fire*: Often known as liquid or Greek fire. Anna's explanation is not entirely accurate. Naphtha was a key chemical which was used to create a liquid which could be shot in ball form and would burn over water. The Emperor Constantine VII urged his son, the future Emperor Romanos II, to keep the formula secret. It was used to great effect by the Byzantine navy (e.g. XI.10) from the later seventh century onwards, and had an application which was as fearsome as it was militarily significant: that the emperor and his forces could control fire and water made an impression on attackers and visitors to Byzantium alike.

12. *dioptra*: A device for measuring angles and distances between celestial objects and in surveying buildings.

13. *When spring came*: 1108.

14. *end of many friendships*: See Aristotle, *Nicomachean Ethics*, VIII.6.

15. *Sebastos Marinos Neapolites*: The Mastromiles family was one of the most important noble families of Naples. Marinos held the title of *sebastos* by the early 1090s when he attended a church synod, although it is not known when or why he had become closely linked to the emperor. Anna's hint that he had not proved entirely loyal shows that even close associates of Alexios had doubts about his leadership. Marinos was nevertheless a valuable enough ally to be forgiven his transgressions, and act as one of the signatories of the final settlement with Bohemond in XIII.12.

16. *Roger*: Little is known about Roger, but his descendants were prominent in Constantinople in the twelfth century.

17. *Prigkipatos*: Anna more likely means Richard of the Principate, rather than a fourth man. He was a cousin of Bohemond.

18. *'Recall the spirit and fury of war'*: Homer, *Iliad*, VI.112.

19. *Hugh*: Presumably Hugh of St Pol, one of Bohemond's officers on the expedition; he had participated in the First Crusade and reached Jerusalem in 1099.

20. *a grudge for this*: Anna's defensiveness may be an indication that she was not entirely confident in her material here.

21. *'nor did . . . the man'*: Homer, *Iliad*, II.2.

22. *Constantine Gabras*: The son of Theodore and brother of Gregory. His apparent intransigence was not punished by Alexios, for he held a command position in Philadelphia and negotiated on behalf of the emperor with the Turks (XIV.3). Anna may be settling a score though, for Constantine proved a problem for the Komnenoi in the 1120s and 1130s, revolting against John II, and only being put down after the emperor led an expedition against him in person in 1139–40.

23. *passage to Dyrrakhion*: Summer 1108.

24. *William Klareles . . . gifts and favours*: William Claret. His defection is mentioned by the historian Albert of Aachen, along with that of Guy, Bohemond's nephew. Some commentators have seen Alexios' efforts to win support among the western knights as a sign that Byzantium lacked effective heavy cavalry, but it is more likely that generous rewards were an effective and trusted way of encouraging would-be deserters to come over to the Byzantines.

25. *rank of panhypersebastos*: According to Zonaras, Bryennios had been promoted to this position at the time of his marriage to Anna.

26. *null and void*: The voiding of the original 1097 agreement is mostly a legal gambit: it was effectively a double indemnity for both sides, and removed from future consideration and discussion the causes and consequences of the breakdown between Byzantium and the Crusaders, and the issue of the oaths taken by the latter in Constantinople in 1096–7.

27. *Emperor Lord John*: Alexios' eldest son had been formally crowned co-emperor in 1092, and his inclusion was an additional security that Bohemond's commitment was extended to Alexios' successor.

28. *the lands granted to me*: The regions listed here give a useful indication of the extent of the geographic area that had been subjected to Antioch by Bohemond and Tancred by 1108. The careful itemization guaranteed that the treaty could be referred to in case of any future dispute.

29. *Roupenioi, Leo and Theodore*: Members of the Roupenid dynasty,

named after the eponymous founder – although he was likely a member of the Caucasian Bagratuni family. He also founded what became the kingdom of Kilikian Armenia. The treaty makes clear that while Alexios held authority over these men and their lands, Bohemond's power locally was such that they had offered him homage.

30. *privileges of this see*: That Alexios was anxious to ensure Antioch had an Orthodox (rather than a Latin) patriarch cast him as defender of the Greek Church, as well as having practical implications in Antioch itself and for the senior hierarchy of the Christian Church as a whole.

31. *bust of the Emperor Michael*: Coinage of Michael VII which had a higher content of gold than the debased coinage of Nikephoros III and that of the first part of the reign of Alexios.

32. *dukedom*: Of Edessa. It is possible that Anna misses this out deliberately, rather than there being a lacuna, since Byzantium retained an interest in Edessa in the mid-twelfth century.

33. *bequeath it to any person ... the same agreement as I*: That Bohemond was being asked to bind his successors to Alexios is curious, in so far as his ability to do so was questionable legally and difficult to enforce in practice.

34. *6617*: 1108. The terms of the treaty seem humiliating for Bohemond, who had to offer homage to Alexios and was compelled to become his liegeman, while renouncing claims on past, current and future conquests. However, Bohemond extracted a substantial annuity from the emperor; carved out a territory (and revenues) of his own in the east; and brokered a face-saving deal that saw him able to refute any accusation that he had broken his 1097 vows to the emperor.

The Treaty of Diabolis (usually called Devol) is an outstandingly important and valuable document, not least since the text is included in full. Among the striking elements is the degree to which it reflects western – rather than Byzantine – customs, terms and legal obligations. Alexios was keen to negotiate in wording that could be understood unequivocally by Bohemond and by westerners in general, and was willing and able to be flexible when negotiating with foreigners. Note that the witnesses were primarily westerners, including those in imperial service, which also tells us something important about its context and intended audience.

35. *Mauros of Amalfi ... Richard Siniskardos*: None of the witnesses was Byzantine, either because they were signatories to a separate

agreement, or because Alexios and his court felt that having western witnesses was appropriate and would provide a more effective way of enforcing the terms in the east as well as in western Europe. *Kral* is a Slavic title, equating to king – and therefore referring to Coloman I of Hungary (reigned 1095–1116) – župan, to princes or governors of *župania* or military districts, presumably also in Hungary.

BOOK XIV

1. *by the spear*: It was no coincidence that Bohemond made his vows on this particular relic: the Crusaders claimed to have found the Holy Lance in Antioch in 1098, and this was a powerful way to refute the discovery as a fraud.

2. *six months*: Bohemond crossed back to Apulia in late 1108 or perhaps early 1109. Although William of Tyre suggests that he died in 1109 (as Anna implies), other Latin chroniclers date his death to early 1111.

3. *as far as Attaleia*: There is no clue as to when the Turks had started their raids on this region.

4. *as his own undisputed property*: Even before Bohemond's death, Tancred had been styling himself as prince of Antioch, and minting his own coinage – both unequivocal statements of independent power. Anna's nuance here is that Antioch belonged to the emperor because of Bohemond's commitment to the Treaty of Devol.

5. *through the ambassadors*: Usually dated to the second half of 1111.

6. *like the Assyrian*: Probably a reference to Ninus the Great, founder and first king of Assyria in the third millennium BC.

7. *Count Bertrand*: Bertrand of St Gilles had journeyed to the east in 1108, three years after the death of his father Raymond. According to Albert of Aachen, when Bertrand had passed through Constantinople he received lavish gifts from the emperor – but Anna only records her father's largess at Tripolis.

8. *siege of Tyre continued*: It started at the end of 1111, and evidently continued well into 1112, as Easter fell on 21 April.

9. *Count Joscelin*: Joscelin de Courtenay, apparently cousin of Baldwin, king of Jerusalem, he later became lord of Edessa, marrying first a Roupenid bride, and then Marie of Antioch. At the time of Anna's writing, Joscelin and his family had become important figures in the Holy Land.

10. *Bertrand ... no longer alive*: He died in January 1112, and was succeeded by his son, Pons.

11. *troubles descended*: This lengthy episode concerning relations with the Crusaders is largely uneventful and even inconsequential from a Byzantine perspective, but presumably it demonstrates that Alexios did what he could to gather support in the Levant, and shows just how difficult it was to deal with individual leaders and their heirs and the constantly changing situation on the ground.

12. *the Emir Saisan*: Probably Malik-Shah, son of Kilidj Arslan and ruler of Ikonion 1107–16. (The sultan of Baghdad at this time was also called Malik-Shah II.) The date is probably *c.* 1112.

13. *'Endure ... things before'*: Homer, *Odyssey*, XX.18.

14. *envoys from Persia arrived*: Ibn al-Atir states that Alexios sent an embassy to the Seljuk sultan in Baghdad around this time seeking conciliation, and even an alliance against the Crusaders.

15. *the stupidity of those who inherited his throne*: A bitter indictment of the policies of John II and Manuel I in Asia Minor, both of whom had more strident dealings with the Turks. Alexios' eastern policy, by contrast, was one of well-judged, limited military action set alongside regular peace initiatives and truces with local rulers and with the sultan.

16. *equipped a fleet*: Summer 1112.

17. *all Kelts were freely admitted to his presence*: Zonaras notes that Alexios was remarkable for his willingness to give time and access to anyone wishing to make requests of him. He does not mention foreigners, noting instead the ready access he gave to Byzantines – not least those of low rank and reduced means.

18. *'brawling ... of tongue'*: *Iliad*, II.212.

19. *Monolukos ... Kontogmes ... Emir Muhammad*: The identities of these Turkish leaders are unknown.

20. *to the emperor*: This episode is not known from elsewhere, and is difficult to date precisely, but spring 1113 has been suggested.

21. *Cadmean success*: Cadmus led an ill-fated life, with successes, such as founding Thebes, mitigated by his unsuccessful search for his sister Europa, who had been carried off by Zeus, and his slaying of a dragon sacred to Ares, for which Cadmus had to endure eight years of penance – with worse to follow. More poignant, then, than a Pyrrhic victory.

22. *'When two ... the truth'*: Aristotle, *Nicomachean Ethics*, I.4.

23. *Siren of Isokrates ... Sappho's lyre*: Classical allusions which allow Anna to demonstrate her learning and reinforce the epic

and Hellenistic theme applied to Alexios, his life and his achievements. The Sirens, half women–half birds, are best known from the *Odyssey*; Isocrates was a celebrated Greek rhetorician of the fourth century BC; Pindar was famed for his lyric poems; Polemon, a follower of Plato from the third century BC, advocated using philosophy to live by, rather than simply study; Kalliope was the Greek muse of epic poetry, Homer her finest exponent; Sappho's lyric poetry was much admired in ancient Greece, and in twelfth-century Constantinople too.

24. *the third emperor after my father*: I.e. Manuel I Komnenos, successor of Alexios' heir, John II. Anna highlights two points of interest: first, that her nephew's reign had spawned ill-warranted and extravagant flattery of him; and secondly, that little attention was paid to the life and times of Alexios I. Manuel took the throne in 1143, which helps date the composition of the *Alexiad*.

25. *I pass my time in obscurity*: Anna appears to have been exiled during or soon after 1118, following a failed attempt to take the throne for herself and her husband, Nikephoros Bryennios. Her seclusion was perhaps not as complete as she implies, to judge from the foundation document of the convent where she is widely thought to have lived. See also Introduction, p. xiv.

26. *My material*: Anna does not mention other sources, but there is little doubt that she had access to a very wide and varied body of material. Her stress on the accounts by simple soldiers is a device aimed at emphasizing both her diligence and her objectivity as a historian.

27. *search the Scriptures*: See John 5:39.

28. *bruising his heel*: Cf. Genesis 3:14–15.

29. *November*: 1114.

30. *the Roman Philip*: Philip, Roman emperor (reigned 244–9), rather than Philip II of Macedon (reigned 359–336 BC), father of Alexander the Great.

31. *Krenides*: Philippi (not Philippopolis) was founded on the site of Krenides. Philippopolis was renamed (after himself) by Philip of Macedon after he conquered the settlement from the Thracians.

32. *Manes*: The spiritual father of Manichaeanism, the eponymous Mani lived in Babylon in the third century, gaining a substantial following during his lifetime.

33. *Porphyrios*: Porphyry, a third-century Neoplatonist, has long been thought to have been the author of an important anti-Christian text. Anna's reference is to the author of a notorious

tract called the *Philosophy of Origins*, which sets out the case for the continuation of pagan beliefs and rituals.

34. *John Tzimiskes*: Emperor, 969–76. Paulicians had also been moved to the Balkans by Constantine V.

35. *Jacob*: Jacob (or James) Baradarios, prelate and bishop of Edessa who preached extensively in the eastern part of Asia Minor in the sixth century. It is not clear which group of his or when they moved to the Balkans.

36. *Constantine the Great … apostle*: Anna adds to her theme of Alexios' orthodoxy: the emperor as an apostle and second in importance only to Constantine I himself makes clear her ambition to establish her father as a devout and specifically Christian ruler.

37. *Eustratios*: Later commissioned to write commentaries on the works of Aristotle by Anna, so the allusion to the Hellenistic scholars is carefully chosen. In 1117, Eustratios was disgraced when he was tried and anathematized by the Church for religious deviance, to which Anna makes no reference.

38. *Cumans had crossed the river*: 1114, although some commentators date the Bzyantine expedition against the nomads and Alexios' efforts to suppress the Paulicians to 1115.

39. *gardens of Adonis*: Ancient Greek women celebrated the festival of Adonis by offering small gardens or pots planted with vegetables and flowers which grew and germinated quickly, but which then died quickly. The emperor's gifts, however, had permanence.

BOOK XV

1. *Sultan Solymas*: Anna presumably means Malik-Shah of Ikonion.

2. *Klitziasthlan*: Kilidj Arslan had died in 1107, having ruled from Nicaea and Ikonion since *c.* 1096.

3. *the summer season*: 1116.

4. *Book of Proverbs*: See Proverbs 31:10–31.

5. *cavalry charges against the enemy*: Alexios knew the effectiveness of heavy cavalry when taking on the Turks, and had learnt from the Latin knights who had fought against and with him since the start of his reign. His instructions about the conditioning of the horses shows the evolution of military tactics in this period.

6. *reproaches and whispers*: The gossip reveals the frustration felt by many in Byzantium with Alexios' policy in Asia Minor.

7. *one charioteer beats another*: Iliad, XXIII.318.

8. *Taktika of Aelian*: Military treatise written in the second century
    AD, which Anna singles out to suggest the depth of her father's
    expertise, rather than refer to his familiarity with more com-
    monly known and recent manuals.

9. *shield to ... to man*: *Iliad*, XIII.131.

10. *Bourtzes, a certain Bardas*: Undoubtedly a descendant of Michael
    Bourtzes, a leading figure in the Byzantine army in the later tenth
    century, achieving much success alongside Nikephoros II Phokas
    and John I Tzimiskes and serving as *doux* of Antioch after its
    recovery in 969.

11. *Sultan Solymas*: Anna means Malik-Shah of Ikonion.

12. *invasion ... more northerly regions*: I.e. an attack by the
    Danishmenids.

13. *Emperor Michael*: An obvious error for Alexios.

14. *The sultan then approached*: Informality with foreigners was one
    of Alexios' hallmarks, and was a dramatic departure from his
    predecessors.

15. *Romanos Diogenes ... defeat and capture*: Romanos IV had
    been heavily defeated and taken prisoner, along with many of
    his soldiers, at Manzikert in August 1071. Although the military
    importance of this battle is played down by modern scholars, the
    symbolic significance of the emperor being captured in battle
    cannot be overstated.

16. *Masout*: Mas'ud, sultan of Ikonion (reigned 1116–55). The
    rivalry between the (half) brothers is only known from the
    Alexiad.

17. *sweet poem says*: Homer, *Iliad*, II.6–34. Anna means Neleus.
    See Book VII, note 4.

18. *strangle the sultan with a bowstring*: Saisan was murdered in
    1117.

19. *feeding of the seven and five thousands*: The feeding of 5,000
    appears in Mark, Luke and John, while Matthew tells of 4,000
    (15:29–39). The 7,000 appears to be wrong.

20. *blind man see*: See Matthew 9:5, 27–30. Other gospel references
    appear below.

21. *Stylianos ... Attikos*: Anna's contemporaries, or at least indi-
    viduals whose names meant something in twelfth-century Byzan-
    tium, but little is known about them and their works.

22. *contravene the law*: Presumably gambling, but certainly games
    and other activities Anna considered a waste of time.

23. *schedography*: Increasingly popular in the later eleventh and
    above all the twelfth centuries, it was effectively reduced and

bite-size learning, and was criticized by serious intellectuals and traditionalists.

24. *Later, in the ... year of his reign*: To judge from its location, the very end of Alexios' reign, in 1117–18; however, the trials of the Bogomils were before the end of 1104, by which time Isaac Komnenos, who was heavily involved in them, had died.

25. *Bogomils*: Literally, beloved of God. Bogomilism centred on a belief of mitigated (rather than absolute) dualism: while followers believed in the principles of good and evil, the latter was ultimately subject to the former. Although this heresy appears to have originated in Bulgaria in the tenth century, it was only in Alexios' reign that it became popular. The impact of Bogomilism on the elite of Constantinople is both striking and surprising. The ascetic mysticism of the heresy's leader, Basil, and his followers was attractive to a wide body of people – and not only to the Balkan peasants as suggested in many (anti)Bogomil texts – for Manuel I Komnenos himself was accused of having Bogomil sympathies. The link between Bogomilism and Manichaeanism and Massalianism was not as clear as Anna states.

26. *Nicholas Grammatikos*: Patriarch, 1084–1111.

27. *Sappho*: Fragment 137.1–2.

28. *Dogmatika Panoplia*: The *Dogmatic Panoply*, written by Euthymios Zigabenos in the first quarter of the twelfth century, provides an outline of a vast range of heresies and religious beliefs (including Judaism and Islam), with detailed refutations. It was presumably intended to be a working compilation for use by the Byzantine clergy. Zigabenos says that he heard Alexios tackle heretics twice in person, which suggests that he was close to senior members of the imperial family, if not to the emperor himself.

29. *Naziarioi*: Monks, from Hebrew *nazir*.

30. *as the hymn writer says ... Tzykanisterin*: See Daniel 3:19. An arena for equestrian games in the Great Palace in Constantinople.

31. *'It shall ... behold'*: Psalm 91:7–8.

32. *Recognizing the robe from its hem*: A Byzantine expression, essentially meaning seeing the wood from the trees.

33. *those young men in Babylon*: Shadrach, Meshach and Abednego, friends of Daniel, who escaped unharmed the fiery furnace set for them by King Nebuchadnezzar for refusing to worship a golden idol (Daniel 3:20–27).

34. *until the reign of my father*: As at the start of the *Alexiad*, Anna highlights her father's preoccupation with Asia Minor and the

east. She devotes little attention to his policies or to his initiatives in Anatolia. John I Tzimiskes and Basil II had been conspicuously successful in the east.

35. *Nicholas Kallikles*: He was written to on several occasions by Theophylaktos of Akhris and was a leading doctor in twelfth-century Byzantium.

36. *Michael Pantekhnes*: Also a recipient of letters from Theophylaktos. He was a poet and has been suggested as a possible candidate as author of the *Timarion*.

37. *Before six months had passed*: 1118.

38. *medical experts*: Anna uses *Asklepiadai*, i.e. followers of Asklepios, son of Apollo and (demi)god of medicine and healing.

39. *tumours seemed . . .*: From here, the text is repeatedly damaged, with the sense often broken.

40. *fifteenth day of August*: 1118, on the feast of the Assumption of the Virgin Mary into heaven.

41. *Eudokia. Maria*: Eudokia, the emperor's third daughter and sixth child, was married to Constantine Iasitas, though she later became a nun. Maria married Nikephoros, the son of Constantine Euphorbenos Katakalon. The list of who did, and who did not, attend the emperor is revealing.

42. *words of the psalm*: See Psalm 18:4.

43. *the heir to the throne*: Zonaras and Khoniates stress that John II Komnenos left his father's side in order to secure power for himself, but not before slipping the imperial ring from the dying emperor's finger, according to the latter. Both suggest John's departure was venal and self-serving.

44. *burden of which I could not bear*: Euripides, *Orestes*, 2.

45. *famous Niobe*: Niobe turned into stone in sorrow after her sons and daughters were killed by Apollo and Artemis, respectively.

46. *After the death of both rulers*: Alexios died in August 1118, Eirene in 1122/3.

Glossary

arkhioinokhoos Chief cup-bearer. Court title given to the man primarily responsible for serving the emperor's wine at banquets.

arkhontopouloi Literally, the sons of leaders. Military unit introduced by Alexios and made up of veterans' sons.

astropelekin Ornament made out of pyrite and gold.

autokrator Title used for the reigning emperor and usually used to distinguish emperor wielding power from co-emperors.

bireme Warship, traditionally with two decks of oars.

brevion, brevia Inventory of reliquaries or other precious church objects.

chrysobull Document bearing the imperial golden *bulla* or seal, signed in purple ink by the emperor.

dioptra Instrument for measuring, commonly used in astrology and surveying to calculate angles and distances between points.

domestikos Originally a general term for a senior position with a range of civil, military and ecclesiastical responsibilities. By this period, primarily a military title denoting command of a battalion. Broadly used by Anna to mean the rank of general.

domestikos of the Schools Primarily the commander of the battalion of the Schools, or *Scholae/Skholai*, one of the most prestigious military units in the empire; by the later eleventh century, the position effectively meant commander-in-chief of the imperial forces as a whole.

domestikos of the West In the tenth century, the office of *domestikos* was divided into two entities, covering the eastern and western halves of the empire. The positions were not uniformly filled nor treated as two parts of a single entity.

doux, doukoi Originally a Latin title (*dux*), given to military commanders, often of a particular district. By Alexios' reign, the responsibilities related to a wider area and had become greater.

Sometimes also used to designate the *domestikos* of the Schools. This title was not hereditary.

doux of the fleet   The commander of the imperial navy. Superseded by the *megas doux* of the fleet around the turn of the twelfth century.

droungarios   High military rank. Anna often uses it with reference to the navy, though by this period, the reduced capabilities of the armed forces meant the responsibilities were limited to the warships protecting Constantinople. Replaced as commander of the imperial fleet by the *megas doux*.

eparkhos   The eparch or prefect in charge of the provisioning and administration of Constantinople. The precise role of the position has been much debated. *The Book of the Eparch* purports to be a detailed guide setting out his duties.

exisotes   Fiscal official, typically verifying, establishing and collecting tax revenues.

exkoussaton   Byzantine naval vessel.

exkouvitoi   Corps originally founded by Leo I as the imperial body-guard. Their role was later diminished by the emergence and reliability of the Varangian guard.

exopolon   Outer ring of defensive fortifications of a citadel.

exousiastes   Master or lord, often used for foreign rulers.

exousiokrator   Literally, one who enjoys releases or exemptions. Anna uses the term with reference to the leader of Alanian allies. It is not clear what benefits were involved.

hetaireia   Unit of the imperial bodyguard, led by a *hetairiarkhes*. According to Bryennios, the unit was made up of aristocratic youths.

hypatos   Consul. The position of *hypatos* of the philosophers was reserved for the senior figure in Byzantine intellectual life, with Michael Psellos the most famous holder of this title.

hyperperilampros   Title meaning 'most illustrious'.

hypertimos   Title meaning 'most honourable'.

hypogrammateus   Under-secretary.

hypostrategos   Subordinate to the *strategos* or general. In other words, deputy commander.

hypostroma   Material holding the seat of a saddle in place.

indiction   Method of dating based on the fiscal cycle instituted by the Emperor Constantine in AD 312. The year is referred to by its position within the fifteen-year cycle.

kaisar   From the Latin title of *Caesar*, and originally applied to the emperor himself, but later to designate his heir apparent. Until the eleventh century, it was the second highest title in the empire, usually reserved for the emperor's sons. Alexios I's reorganization of the hierarchy relegated it to third place, after *sebastokrator*. It was neither a hereditary position, nor was it confined to one or more families.

kanikleios Private secretary of the emperor; this position brought with it the ceremonial responsibility of providing purple ink for the signature of chrysobulls but was also a position of trust and often real influence.

katepano Title given to the governor of certain provinces, roughly equivalent to *doux*.

katepano of Dignities The only known reference to this position is in the *Alexiad*. Perhaps a title for someone whose duties related specifically to foreign affairs and specifically had responsibilities for making payments to non-Byzantines.

kleisoura, kleisourai Mountain pass.

koula Stronghold or fortress.

krites Judge. From the mid-eleventh century, the legal education and duties of lawmakers were greatly expanded.

logothetes High-ranking official and usually head of one of the departments within the bureaucracy.

logothetes of the sekreta Position created by Alexios I early in his reign for the official in charge of the civil administration.

magistros High-ranking dignitary, again based linguistically on a Latin official, but bearing no similarity in terms of position or duty. Diminished in importance as a title during the course of the later tenth and eleventh centuries, mostly through its overuse.

megas domestikos See *domestikos*.

megas doux See *doux of the fleet*.

megas droungarios of the fleet See *droungarios*.

megas hetairiarkhes See *hetaireia*.

megas primikerios Literally, one whose name comes first on a wax tablet. This title referred to the leading official in a given group. Tatikios was the first to hold the title with the prefix of *megas* or great, though the combination was later much used and became one of the highest titles in the Komnenian period. Courtiers with the title of *primikerios* were invariably eunuchs.

monoreme Warship, traditionally with a single deck of oars.

nobellisimos Reserved for members of the imperial family until 1041, and eventually used for the supreme military commanders, one of the first being Alexios Komnenos himself in the 1070s. The title of *protonobellisimos* and elaborate variations eventually also came into use.

nomisma, nomismata   Gold coin(s). The standard unit of high-value currency in Byzantium.

notarios   Notary, who witnessed, verified and codified official and private documents.

omophoron   Cape or stole worn by a bishop.

orphanotropheios   The administrator of the *Orphanotropheion*, the orphanage founded by Alexios I.

panhypersebastos   An intensification of the term *sebastos*. Title conferred by Alexios I on members of leading families, including his son-in-law Nikephoros Bryennios.

patriarch   Incumbent of one of the five leading episcopal sees (Alexandria, Antioch, Constantinople, Jerusalem and Rome – the patriarch of Rome is more commonly known as the pope).

periphanestatos kephale   A title otherwise unfamiliar, but conveying the exalted status of most glorious head or leader.

phalangarkhes   Commander.

pinkernes   Court title held by a eunuch responsible for serving the emperor's wine.

porphyra   Purple chamber in the imperial palace where children were born. Purple was the imperial colour, being used for vestments and footwear.

porphyrogennetos   Literally, born in the purple; either used to designate a child born to a reigning emperor, or one born in the *porphyra* chamber in the palace.

praitorion   An official residence for a high-ranking official.

proedros   Term denoting precedence, used in both civilian and ecclesiastical contexts. As a high civilian rank, used increasingly in the eleventh century, while as an ecclesiastical title, usually used to designate bishops.

protonobellisimos   Literally, the highest holder of the title of *nobellisimos*.

protosebastos   Literally, the first *sebastos*. First came into widespread use with Alexios I as a dignity bestowed upon relatives of the emperor, including his brother Adrian and likely their brother-in-law John Doukas.

protostrator   Literally, chief of the *stratores* or grooms. His primary responsibility was to accompany the emperor on horseback in ceremonies. Clearly however an important title by this time.

protovestiarios/ia   Originally the keeper of the imperial wardrobe, in the male form held by a eunuch. The female form normally refers to the most important of the empress's servants.

sebastokrator   Term created by combining *sebastos* and *autokrator*,

used first by Alexios I as a title for his brother Isaac. During the
Komnenian period, title conferred on emperor's sons and brothers.

sebastos   Originally the equivalent to *augoustus*, meaning venerable
or blessed, but used as the basis of Alexios' reform of the hierarchy
(e.g. *protosebastos*, *panhypersebastos*). The majority of *sebastoi*
were members of the imperial family, though it was also given to a
number of foreigners in this period.

sekreta   A government department. The position of *logothetes of the
sekreta* was introduced by Alexios to oversee internal policy.

sermones   Scouting vessel of some kind.

stade   Unit of measurement, equating to a furlong or 200m or about
600 ft.

strategaton   A military district, and the seat of the *strategos*. Not
often used, and perhaps relates to a temporary command zone.

strategos   See *strategaton*.

stratopedarkhes   Military commander.

tetrakus   Effectively the Latin quadrivium, or the core medieval educational curriculum, made up of geometry, arithmetic, astronomy
and music.

thalassokrator   Literally, ruler of the sea. Admiral or naval commander.

theme   Themes were military districts of the Byzantine Empire set up
in the seventh century which came to have administrative functions
and hierarchies.

theometor   Mary, the Mother of God.

toparkhes   Literally, the governor of a given locality. Could be
applied both to independent governors or rulers, and to Byzantine
governors enjoying relative freedom of action.

topoteretes   Literally, holder of a given locality. Used to designate
the person in charge of a small area or fortress. Sometimes inter-
changeable with *toparkhes*.

trireme   Warship, traditionally with three decks of oars.

tyrophagy   Liturgical term denoting the week before the beginning
of the Lenten fast proper, in which meat is forbidden, but dairy
products, fish and eggs permitted.

tzangra   A crossbow.

vestiarios   Treasurer in charge of the *vestiarion*, or state treasury.

vestiarites   Imperial bodyguard. Seemingly the closest courtiers to
the emperor.

vigla   An army battalion meaning 'The Watch' based in Constantinople. Also the name of an important gate to the imperial capital.

xyloklasiai   Wooden barricades.

Index

Persons are usually entered under their second name (whether or not this is properly a surname), e.g. Komnene, Anna, but a few are under their first name, including Alexios I Komnenos.

A few subentries are alphabetical where this seems to be most useful to the reader, e.g. Constantinople and revolts; the others in the order of the book.

Glossary entries have the page numbers in bold.